GABRIEL MANTZ

THE COMPLETE WORLD CUP

2011-2014

British Library Cataloguing in Publication Data
A catalogue record for this book is available from the British Library

ISBN: 978-1-86223-303-4

72 St. Peter's Avenue, Cleethorpes, N.E. Lincolnshire, DN35 8HU, England
Web site www.soccer-books.co.uk
e-mail info@soccer-books.co.uk

Printed in the UK by 4edge

Dear Readers

The 2014 World Cup was the 20th edition of FIFA's premier competition and the finals tournament was held in Brazil between 12th June and 13th July 2014. No fewer than 203 national teams from the six FIFA Confederations registered for participation so an extensive preliminary round was played in the continental regions to determine which 31 countries were to join the hosts in Brazil. The qualification campaign itself began in June 2011 and, in general, it can be said that there were no great surprises in this preliminary phase. Most of the highly-rated teams earned qualification for the final tournament though some more easily than others. Of some surprise was the weakness of Paraguay who finished bottom of the South American qualification group following a successful World Cup tournament in 2010 and Egypt, the African Champions, again missed the finals tournament after being crushed by Ghana in a decisive play-off. Mexico struggled and finished a surprising 4th place in their qualification group, but this was enough to earn them a play-off against the Oceania winners, New Zealand. In the event, the Mexicans proved much too strong for the Kiwis and gratefully booked their place in Brazil. In Europe, Bosnia-Herzegovina managed to qualify for the finals for the first time in the history of the competition. On the other hand, a number of teams who had previously struggled to reach the final stages of the preliminaries (Iceland, Ethiopia, Burkina Faso and Jordan), did extremely well to reach the play-offs for a place in Brazil but ultimately were unable to overcome stronger opposition and missed out.

The final tournament comprised a total of 64 matches that were played in 12 different cities spread across Brazil's huge land mass. For the first time in a World Championship, the referees were assisted by goal-line technology and FIFA also approved the use of a 'vanishing foam' sprayed by the referees to mark a ten-yard line for the defending team during a free kick and also to draw where the ball is to be placed for a free kick. Both of these new developments proved to be very effective.

2014 was the second time that Brazil had hosted the event, the previous tournament being held back in 1950 and they became the fifth country to have hosted FIFA World Cup for the second time joining Mexico, Italy, France and Germany in this achievement. The final tournament was returning to South America for the first time since the 1978 World Cup held in Argentina and was the fifth generally held in South America. Prior to this edition, all seven tournaments previously held in the Americas (four in South America and three in North and Central America) had been won by teams from South America and this led to the hosts holding great hopes of winning a sixth world title.

All the world champions in the history of the tournament – Argentina, England, Brazil, France, Germany, Italy, Spain and Uruguay – were present in 2014 but surprisingly, the defending champions, Spain, were eliminated in the group stage, as were England and Italy. Uruguay were then eliminated in the second round of 16 teams and France went out at the quarter-final stage. The hosts, Brazil, progressed to the semi-finals but were then absolutely destroyed by the Germans, conceding no less than 5 goals in the first 30 minutes of the game! The final score of 7-1 to the Germans was a fair reflection of the game, with Brazilian manager Felipe Scolari describing the result as the "worst loss by a Brazilian national team ever" and the psychological stress on the players desperate to win at home being blamed as the cause for such a poor performance. To make things even worse for the Brazilian fans, arch-rivals Argentina defeated the Dutch on penalties in the other semi-final to face the Germans for the world title.

The final itself was held at the famous Maracanã Stadium in Rio, and the many Brazilians in the crowd who had bought tickets in advance hoping to see their own team playing were mightily relieved to see Germany defeat Argentina 1-0 through an excellent goal deep into extra-time from Mario Götze. The trophy was thus won for the first time in the Americas by a team not from the American continent. At the same time it should be noted that this was the third consecutive world title won by a European team, proving the supremacy of the old continent over the past decade and taking the overall tally to 11 victories for European countries and 9 victories from South America countries.

In this book you will find complete statistics (with team line-ups including the full names of players) of all matches played in the FIFA World Cup 2014, both in qualifying rounds and the final tournament itself. You will also find a listing of the names of the coaches of the national teams, data about referees who officiated in the final tournament and, of course, all final tournament squads for the 32 teams who qualified.

The Author

FIFA COUNTRY CODES – AFRICA

Algeria	**ALG**
Angola	**ANG**
Benin	**BEN**
Botswana	**BOT**
Burkina Faso	**BFA**
Burundi	**BDI**
Cameroon	**CMR**
Cape Verde Islands	**CPV**
Central African Republic	**CTA**
Chad	**CHA**
Comoros Islands	**COM**
Congo	**CGO**
Congo DR	**COD**
Djibouti	**DJI**
Egypt	**EGY**
Equatorial Guinea	**EQG**
Eritrea	**ERI**
Ethiopia	**ETH**
Gabon	**GAB**
Gambia	**GAM**
Ghana	**GHA**
Guinea	**GUI**
Guinea-Bissau	**GNB**
Ivory Coast	**CIV**
Kenya	**KEN**
Lesotho	**LES**
Liberia	**LBR**
Libya	**LBY**
Madagascar	**MAD**
Malawi	**MWI**
Mali	**MLI**
Mauritania	**MTN**
Mauritius	**MRI**
Morocco	**MAR**
Mozambique	**MOZ**
Namibia	**NAM**
Niger	**NIG**
Nigeria	**NGA**
Rwanda	**RWA**
São Tome e Principe	**STP**
Senegal	**SEN**
Seychelles	**SEY**
Sierra Leone	**SLE**
Somalia	**SOM**
South Africa	**RSA**
Sudan	**SUD**
Swaziland	**SWZ**
Tanzania	**TAN**
Togo	**TOG**
Tunisia	**TUN**
Uganda	**UGA**
Zambia	**ZAM**
Zimbabwe	**ZIM**

FIFA COUNTRY CODES – ASIA

Afghanistan	**AFG**
Australia	**AUS**
Bahrain	**BHR**
Bangladesh	**BAN**
Bhutan	**BHU**
Brunei	**BRU**
Cambodia	**CAM**
China P.R.	**CHN**
Chinese Taipei	**TPE**
Guam	**GUM**
Hong Kong	**HKG**
India	**IND**
Indonesia	**IDN**
Iran	**IRN**
Iraq	**IRQ**
Japan	**JPN**
Jordan	**JOR**
Kuwait	**KUW**
Kyrgyzstan	**KGZ**
Laos	**LAO**
Lebanon	**LIB**
Macau	**MAC**
Malaysia	**MAS**
Maldives	**MDV**
Mongolia	**MGL**
Myanmar	**MYA**
Nepal	**NEP**
Korea D.P.R.	**PRK**
Oman	**OMA**
Pakistan	**PAK**
Palestine	**PAL**
Philippines	**PHI**
Qatar	**QAT**
Saudi Arabia	**KSA**
Singapore	**SIN**
Korea Republic	**KOR**
Sri Lanka	**SRI**
Syria	**SYR**
Tajikistan	**TJK**
Thailand	**THA**
Timor-Leste	**TLS**
Turkmenistan	**TKM**
United Arab Emirates	**UAE**
Uzbekistan	**UZB**
Vietnam	**VIE**
Yemen	**YEM**

FIFA COUNTRY CODES – EUROPE

Albania	**ALB**	Latvia	**LVA**
Andorra	**AND**	Liechtenstein	**LIE**
Armenia	**ARM**	Lithuania	**LTU**
Austria	**AUT**	Luxembourg	**LUX**
Azerbaijan	**AZE**	Macedonia	**MKD**
Belarus	**BLR**	Malta	**MLT**
Belgium	**BEL**	Moldova	**MDA**
Bosnia-Herzegovina	**BIH**	Montenegro	**MNE**
Bulgaria	**BUL**	Northern Ireland	**NIR**
Croatia	**CRO**	Norway	**NOR**
Cyprus	**CYP**	Poland	**POL**
Czech Republic	**CZE**	Portugal	**POR**
Denmark	**DEN**	Republic of Ireland	**IRL**
England	**ENG**	Romania	**ROU**
Estonia	**EST**	Russia	**RUS**
Faroe Islands	**FRO**	San Marino	**SMR**
Finland	**FIN**	Scotland	**SCO**
France	**FRA**	Serbia	**SRB**
Georgia	**GEO**	Slovakia	**SVK**
Germany	**GER**	Slovenia	**SVN**
Greece	**GRE**	Spain	**ESP**
Holland	**NED**	Sweden	**SWE**
Hungary	**HUN**	Switzerland	**SUI**
Iceland	**ISL**	Turkey	**TUR**
Israel	**ISR**	Ukraine	**UKR**
Italy	**ITA**	Wales	**WAL**
Kazakhstan	**KAZ**		

FIFA COUNTRY CODES – NORTH & CENTRAL AMERICA

Anguilla	**AIA**	Haiti	**HAI**
Antigua & Barbuda	**ATG**	Honduras	**HON**
Aruba	**ARU**	Jamaica	**JAM**
Bahamas	**BAH**	Martinique	**MTQ**
Barbados	**BRB**	Mexico	**MEX**
Belize	**BLZ**	Montserrat	**MSR**
Bermuda	**BER**	Netherlands Antilles	**ANT**
British Virgin Islands	**VGB**	Nicaragua	**NIC**
Canada	**CAN**	Panama	**PAN**
Cayman Islands	**CAY**	Puerto Rico	**PUR**
Costa Rica	**CRC**	Saint Lucia	**LCA**
Cuba	**CUB**	Saint Kitts and Nevis	**SKN**
Dominica	**DMA**	Saint Martin	**SMT**
Dominican Republic	**DOM**	St. Vincent and the Grenadines	**VIN**
El Salvador	**SLV**	Sint Maarten	**SXM**
French Guiana	**GYF**	Suriname	**SUR**
Grenada	**GRN**	Trinidad & Tobago	**TRI**
Guadeloupe	**GPE**	Turks and Caicos Islands	**TCA**
Guatemala	**GUA**	United States of America	**USA**
Guyana	**GUI**	US Virgin Islands	**VIR**

FIFA COUNTRY CODES – SOUTH AMERICA

Argentina	**ARG**	Ecuador	**ECU**
Bolivia	**BOL**	Paraguay	**PAR**
Brazil	**BRA**	Peru	**PER**
Chile	**CHI**	Uruguay	**URU**
Colombia	**COL**	Venezuela	**VEN**

FIFA COUNTRY CODES – OCEANIA

American Samoa	**ASA**	Samoa	**SAM**
Cook Islands	**COK**	Solomon Islands	**SOL**
Fiji	**FIJ**	Tahiti	**TAH**
New Caledonia	**NCL**	Tonga	**TGA**
New Zealand	**NZL**	Vanuatu	**VAN**
Papua New Guinea	**PNG**		

SUMMARY

WORLD CUP PRELIMINARIES

A total of 203 teams entered the preliminaries competition, with Brazil, as the host, being qualified automatically for the World Cup Final Tournament. Overall, 820 matches were played, the first preliminary matches were played on 15 June 2011 and qualification concluded on 20 November 2013. Above a table with the Continental Confederations, the number of participating teams and the number of places allocated for the final tournament:

Confederation	Number of starting teams	Number of places for the final tournament
UEFA (Europe)	53	13
CONMEBOL (South America)	9	5**
CONCACAF (North, Central American and Caribbean)	35	3***
CAF (Africa)	52	5
AFC (Asia)	43	4**
OCF (Oceania)	11	0***
Intercontinental Play-Off** South America – Asia	-	1
Intercontinental Play-Off*** North & Central America - Oceania	-	1
TOTAL	**203**	**32**

EUROPE

The draw for the qualifying groups was held in Rio de Janeiro (Brazil) on 30 July 2011. The July 2011 FIFA World Rankings were used to seed the teams. Before drawing, the 53 European teams were seeded into 6 pots:

Pot 1: Spain, Holland, Germany, England, Portugal, Italy, Croatia, Norway, Greece.
Pot 2: France, Montenegro, Russia, Sweden, Denmark, Slovenia, Turkey, Serbia, Slovakia.
Pot 3: Switzerland, Israel, Republic of Ireland, Belgium, Czech Republic, Bosnia-Herzegovina, Belarus, Ukraine, Hungary.
Pot 4: Bulgaria, Romania, Georgia, Lithuania, Albania, Scotland, Northern Ireland, Austria, Poland.
Pot 5: Armenia, Finland, Estonia, Cyprus, Latvia, Moldova, Macedonia, Azerbaijan, Faroe Islands.
Pot 6: Wales, Liechtenstein, Iceland, Kazakhstan, Luxembourg, Malta, Andorra, San Marino.

The 53 teams were drawn into nine groups of six teams and one group of five teams. The nine group-winners were qualified directly, while the eight best second-placed teams contested home and away play-off matches for the remaining four places. In determining the best eight second-placed teams, the results against teams finishing last in the six-team groups were not counted for consistency between the five- and six-team groups.

The 9 qualifying groups were as following:

GROUP A
Croatia, Serbia, Belgium, Scotland, Macedonia, Wales.

GROUP B
Italy, Denmark, Czech Republic, Bulgaria, Armenia, Malta.

GROUP C
Germany, Sweden, Republic of Ireland, Austria, Faroe Islands, Kazakhstan.

GROUP D
Holland, Turkey, Hungary, Romania, Estonia, Andorra.

GROUP E
Norway, Slovenia, Switzerland, Albania, Cyprus, Iceland.

GROUP F
Portugal, Russia, Israel, Northern Ireland, Azerbaijan, Luxembourg.

GROUP G
Greece, Slovakia, Bosnia-Herzegovina, Lithuania, Latvia, Liechtenstein.

GROUP H
England, Montenegro, Ukraine, Poland, Moldova, San Marino.

GROUP I
Spain, France, Belarus, Georgia, Finland.

GROUP A

07.09.2012	Cardiff	Wales - Belgium	0-2(0-1)
07.09.2012	Zagreb	Croatia - FYR Macedonia	1-0(0-0)
08.09.2012	Glasgow	Scotland - Serbia	0-0
11.09.2012	Glasgow	Scotland - FYR Macedonia	1-1(1-1)
11.09.2012	Novi Sad	Serbia - Wales	6-1(3-1)
11.09.2012	Brussels	Belgium - Croatia	1-1(1-1)
12.10.2012	Cardiff	Wales - Scotland	2-1(0-1)
12.10.2012	Belgrade	Serbia - Belgium	0-3(0-1)
12.10.2012	Skopje	FYR Macedonia - Croatia	1-2(1-1)
16.10.2012	Osijek	Croatia - Wales	2-0(1-0)
16.10.2012	Skopje	FYR Macedonia - Serbia	1-0(0-0)
16.10.2012	Brussels	Belgium - Scotland	2-0(0-0)
22.03.2013	Zagreb	Croatia - Serbia	2-0(2-0)
22.03.2013	Glasgow	Scotland - Wales	1-2(1-0)
22.03.2013	Skopje	FYR Macedonia - Belgium	0-2(0-1)
26.03.2013	Swansea	Wales - Croatia	1-2(1-0)
26.03.2013	Novi Sad	Serbia - Scotland	2-0(0-0)
26.03.2013	Brussels	Belgium - FYR Macedonia	1-0(0-0)
07.06.2013	Zagreb	Croatia - Scotland	0-1(0-1)
07.06.2013	Brussels	Belgium - Serbia	2-1(1-0)
06.09.2013	Skopje	FYR Macedonia - Wales	2-1(1-1)
06.09.2013	Glasgow	Scotland - Belgium	0-2(0-1)
06.09.2013	Belgrade	Serbia - Croatia	1-1(0-0)
10.09.2013	Cardiff	Wales - Serbia	0-3(0-2)
10.09.2013	Skopje	FYR Macedonia - Scotland	1-2(0-0)
11.10.2013	Zagreb	Croatia - Belgium	1-2(0-2)
11.10.2013	Cardiff	Wales - FYR Macedonia	1-0(0-0)
15.10.2013	Glasgow	Scotland - Croatia	2-0(1-0)
15.10.2013	Jagodina	Serbia - FYR Macedonia	5-1(3-0)
15.10.2013	Brussels	Belgium - Wales	1-1(0-0)

FINAL STANDINGS

1.	**BELGIUM**	10	8	2	0	18 - 4	26
2.	**Croatia**	10	5	2	3	12 - 9	17
3.	Serbia	10	4	2	4	18 - 11	14
4.	Scotland	10	3	2	5	8 - 12	11
5.	Wales	10	3	1	6	9 - 20	10
6.	Macedonia	10	2	1	7	7 - 16	7

Belgium qualified for the Final Tournament; Croatia qualified for the Play-Offs.

07.09.2012, Cardiff City Stadium, Cardiff; Attendance: 20,156
Referee: Stefan Johannesson (Sweden)

WALES - BELGIUM 0-2(0-1)

WAL: Glyn Oliver Myhill, Christopher Ross Gunter, Adam James Matthews, Darcy James Blake, James Michael Collins, Ashley Errol Williams, David Alexander Edwards (80.Andrew Philip King), Simon Richard Church (72.Thomas Henry Alex Robson-Kanu), Steven William Morison (72.Samuel Michael Vokes), Aaron James Ramsey, Gareth Frank Bale. Trainer: Christopher Patrick Coleman.

BEL: Thibaut Nicolas Marc Courtois, Vincent Jean Mpoy Kompany, Thomas Vermaelen, Jan Bert Lieve Vertonghen, Mousa Sidi Yaya Dembélé (64.Kevin De Bruyne), Guillaume Gillet, Marouane Abdellatif Fellaini-Bakkioui, Axel Laurent Angel Lambert Witsel, Eden Michael Hazard, Kevin Antonio Joel Gislain Mirallas y Castillo (46.Romelu Menama Lukaku), Dries Mertens. Trainer: Marc Robert Wilmots.

Goals: 0-1 Vincent Jean Mpoy Kompany (42), 0-2 Jan Bert Lieve Vertonghen (83).

Cautions: Samuel Michael Vokes, Ashley Errol Williams / Guillaume Gillet, Jan Bert Lieve Vertonghen.

Sent off: James Michael Collins (26).

07.09.2012, Stadion Maksimir, Zagreb; Attendance: 13,883
Referee: Alon Yefet (Israel)

CROATIA - MACEDONIA 1-0(0-0)

CRO: Stipe Pletikosa, Ivan Strinić, Josip Šimunić, Vedran Ćorluka (81.Domagoj Vida), Darijo Srna, Ivan Rakitić (46.Niko Kranjčar), Ognjen Vukojević, Luka Modrić, Ivan Perišić, Mario Mandžukić, Eduardo Alves Da Silva (62.Nikica Jelavić). Trainer: Igor Štimac.

MKD: Martin Bogatinov, Daniel Georgievski, Goran Popov, Nikolče Novevski, Vanče Šikov, Ivan Tričkovski (73.Dragan Gjorgiev), Stevica Ristić (80.Mirko Ivanovski), Goran Pandev, Nikola Gligorov (82.Darko Tasevski), Muhamed Demiri, Agim Ibraimi. Trainer: Čedomir Janevski.

Goal: 1-0 Nikica Jelavić (69).

Cautions: Josip Šimunić, Niko Kranjčar, Ognjen Vukojević, Nikica Jelavić / Muhamed Demiri, Daniel Georgievski.

08.09.2012, Hampden Park, Glasgow; Attendance: 47,369
Referee: Jonas Eriksson (Sweden)

SCOTLAND - SERBIA 0-0

SCO: Allan James McGregor, Alan Hutton, Paul Andrew Dixon, Christophe Didier Berra, Gary Robert Caldwell, Charles Graham Adam, James Clark Morrison (81.James Charles Mackie), Andrew Neil Webster, Kenneth Miller (81.Jordan Luke Rhodes), Robert Snodgrass (69.James Forrest), Steven John Naismith. Trainer: Craig William Levein.

SRB: Vladimir Stojković, Milan Biševac, Matija Nastasić, Branislav Ivanović, Zoran Tošić, Aleksandar Kolarov, Srđan Mijailović (46.Ljubomir Fejsa), Aleksandar Ignjovski, Miloš Ninković, Filip Đuričić (84.Dejan Lekić), Darko Lazović (58.Dušan Tadić). Trainer: Siniša Mihajlović.

Cautions: Robert Snodgrass / Matija Nastasić, Miloš Ninković, Milan Biševac.

11.09.2012, Hampden Park, Glasgow; Attendance: 32,430
Referee: Sergei Karasev (Russia)

SCOTLAND - MACEDONIA 1-1(1-1)

SCO: Allan James McGregor, Alan Hutton, Paul Andrew Dixon, Christophe Didier Berra, Gary Robert Caldwell, James Clark Morrison (66.Jordan Luke Rhodes), Andrew Neil Webster, Kenneth Miller (58.Charles Graham Adam), James Charles Mackie (77.Steven John Naismith), Shaun Richard Maloney, James Forrest. Trainer: Craig William Levein.

MKD: Martin Bogatinov, Daniel Georgievski, Goran Popov, Nikolče Novevski, Vanče Šikov, Ivan Tričkovski (38.Ferhan Hasani), Goran Pandev, Nikola Gligorov (70.Veliče Šumulikoski), Muhamed Demiri, Agim Ibraimi (89.Darko Tasevski), Mirko Ivanovski. Trainer: Čedomir Janevski.

Goals: 0-1 Nikolče Novevski (11), 1-1 Kenneth Miller (43).

Cautions: Charles Graham Adam / Agim Ibraimi, Ferhan Hasani, Nikola Gligorov, Goran Pandev, Veliče Šumulikoski.

11.09.2012, Referee: Duarte Nuno Pereira Gomes (Portugal)
Stadion Karađorđe, Novi Sad; Attendance: 10,660

SERBIA - WALES 6-1(3-1)

SRB: Vladimir Stojković, Ljubomir Fejsa, Milan Biševac, Matija Nastasić, Branislav Ivanović, Zoran Tošić (70.Miralem Sulejmani), Dušan Tadić, Aleksandar Kolarov, Aleksandar Ignjovski (85.Srđan Mijailović), Filip Đuričić (81.Dejan Lekić), Lazar Marković. Trainer: Siniša Mihajlović.
WAL: Glyn Oliver Myhill, Christopher Ross Gunter, Adam James Matthews (46.Samuel Derek Ricketts), David Alexander Edwards (46.David Owen Vaughan), Darcy James Blake, Ashley Errol Williams, Joseph Michael Allen (71.Andrew Philip King), Simon Richard Church, Steven William Morison, Aaron James Ramsey, Gareth Frank Bale. Trainer: Christopher Patrick Coleman.
Goals: 1-0 Aleksandar Kolarov (16), 2-0 Zoran Tošić (24), 2-1 Gareth Frank Bale (31), 3-1 Filip Đuričić (37), 4-1 Dušan Tadić (55), 5-1 Branislav Ivanović (80), 6-1 Miralem Sulejmani (90).
Cautions: Darcy James Blake, Aaron James Ramsey.

11.09.2012, Stade „Roi Baudouin", Bruxelles; Attendance: 39,987
Referee: Alberto Undiano Mallenco (Spain)

BELGIUM - CROATIA 1-1(1-1)

BEL: Thibaut Nicolas Marc Courtois, Vincent Jean Mpoy Kompany, Thomas Vermaelen, Jan Bert Lieve Vertonghen, Mousa Sidi Yaya Dembélé (72.Kevin De Bruyne), Guillaume Gillet, Steven Arnold Defour (67.Marouane Abdellatif Fellaini-Bakkioui), Axel Laurent Angel Lambert Witsel, Eden Michael Hazard, Dries Mertens (81.Kevin Antonio Joel Gislain Mirallas y Castillo), Christian Benteke Liolo. Trainer: Marc Robert Wilmots.
CRO: Stipe Pletikosa, Ivan Strinić, Gordon Schildenfeld, Josip Šimunić, Josip Radošević (78.Ognjen Vukojević), Darijo Srna, Luka Modrić, Ivan Perišić, Domagoj Vida, Mario Mandžukić (88.Nikola Kalinić), Nikica Jelavić (59.Ivica Olić). Trainer: Igor Štimac.
Goals: 0-1 Ivan Perišić (6), 1-1 Guillaume Gillet (45+1).
Cautions: Mousa Sidi Yaya Dembélé, Guillaume Gillet / Darijo Srna, Gordon Schildenfeld.

12.10.2012, Cardiff City Stadium, Cardiff; Attendance: 23,249
Referee: Florian Meyer (Germany)

WALES - SCOTLAND 2-1(0-1)

WAL: Lewis Peter Price, Christopher Ross Gunter, Benjamin Thomas Davies, David Owen Vaughan, Darcy James Blake, Ashley Errol Williams, Joseph Michael Allen, Joseph Christopher Ledley (72.Thomas Henry Alex Robson-Kanu), Steven William Morison (66.Craig Martin Davies), Aaron James Ramsey, Gareth Frank Bale. Trainer: Christopher Patrick Coleman.
SCO: Allan James McGregor, Alan Hutton, Christophe Didier Berra, Gary Robert Caldwell, Shaun Richard Maloney, Darren Barr Fletcher, Scott Brown (46.Charles Graham Adam), Steven Kenneth Fletcher, James Clark Morrison (87.Kenneth Miller), Kristian Arran Commons (87.James Charles Mackie), Daniel Fox. Trainer: Craig William Levein.
Goals: 0-1 James Clark Morrison (27), 1-1 Gareth Frank Bale (80), 2-1 Gareth Frank Bale (87 penalty).
Cautions: Gareth Frank Bale, Aaron James Ramsey, Joseph Michael Allen / Gary Robert Caldwell.

12.10.2012, Stadion Crvena Zvezda, Beograd; Attendance: 21,650
Referee: Pavel Královec (Czech Republic)

SERBIA - BELGIUM 0-3(0-1)

SRB: Željko Brkić, Milan Biševac, Matija Nastasić, Branislav Ivanović, Zoran Tošić (67.Alen Stevanović), Dušan Tadić (81.Dejan Lekić), Aleksandar Kolarov, Srđan Mijailović, Aleksandar Ignjovski, Filip Đuričić (56.Marko Šćepović), Lazar Marković. Trainer: Siniša Mihajlović.
BEL: Thibaut Nicolas Marc Courtois, Vincent Jean Mpoy Kompany, Thomas Vermaelen, Jan Bert Lieve Vertonghen, Tobias Albertine Maurits Alderweireld, Mousa Sidi Yaya Dembélé, Axel Laurent Angel Lambert Witsel, Eden Michael Hazard (55.Dries Mertens), Nacer Chadli, Kevin De Bruyne (87.Kevin Antonio Joel Gislain Mirallas y Castillo), Christian Benteke Liolo. Trainer: Marc Robert Wilmots.
Goals: 0-1 Christian Benteke Liolo (34), 0-2 Kevin De Bruyne (68), 0-3 Kevin Antonio Joel Gislain

Mirallas y Castillo (90+1).
Cautions: Aleksandar Kolarov / Christian Benteke Liolo, Axel Laurent Angel Lambert Witsel.

12.10.2012, „Philip II“ Arena, Skopje; Attendance: 25,230
Referee: Peter Rasmussen (Denmark)
MACEDONIA - CROATIA **1-2(1-1)**
MKD: Martin Bogatinov, Daniel Georgievski, Goran Popov (82.Ferhan Hasani), Nikolče Novevski, Vanče Šikov (75.Boban Grnčarov), Ivan Tričkovski, Veliče Šumulikoski (54.Nikola Gligorov), Stevica Ristić, Goran Pandev, Muhamed Demiri, Agim Ibraimi. Trainer: Čedomir Janevski.
CRO: Stipe Pletikosa, Ivan Strinić, Josip Šimunić, Vedran Ćorluka, Darijo Srna, Ivan Rakitić, Ognjen Vukojević, Luka Modrić (84.Milan Badelj), Ivan Perišić, Mario Mandžukić (72.Nikola Kalinić), Nikica Jelavić (64.Jorge Sammir Cruz Campos). Trainer: Igor Štimac.
Goals: 1-0 Agim Ibraimi (16), 1-1 Vedran Ćorluka (33), 1-2 Ivan Rakitić (60).
Cautions: Stevica Ristić, Goran Pandev / Vedran Ćorluka, Ognjen Vukojević, Luka Modrić.

16.10.2012, Stadion Gradski vrt, Osijek; Attendance: 17,500
Referee: Alexandru Tudor (Romania)
CROATIA - WALES **2-0(1-0)**
CRO: Stipe Pletikosa, Ivan Strinić, Josip Šimunić, Dejan Lovren (46.Gordon Schildenfeld), Darijo Srna, Ivan Rakitić, Luka Modrić, Ivan Perišić (85.Domagoj Vida), Milan Badelj, Mario Mandžukić, Eduardo Alves Da Silva (77.Niko Kranjčar). Trainer: Igor Štimac.
WAL: Lewis Peter Price, Christopher Ross Gunter, Benjamin Thomas Davies, David Owen Vaughan, Darcy James Blake, Ashley Errol Williams, Joseph Michael Allen, Steven William Morison (61.Simon Richard Church), Andrew Philip King (72.Samuel Michael Vokes), Gareth Frank Bale, Joseph Christopher Ledley (82.Thomas Henry Alex Robson-Kanu). Trainer: Christopher Patrick Coleman.
Goals: 1-0 Mario Mandžukić (27), 2-0 Eduardo Alves Da Silva (57).
Cautions: Dejan Lovren, Ivan Strinić / Christopher Ross Gunter.

16.10.2012, „Philip II“ Arena, Skopje; Attendance: 26,181
Referee: Hendrikus Sebastiaan Hermanus Nijhuis (Holland)
MACEDONIA - SERBIA **1-0(0-0)**
MKD: Tome Pačovski, Daniel Georgievski, Nikolče Novevski, Boban Grnčarov, Ferhan Hasani, Muhamed Demiri (86.Veliče Šumulikoski), Nikola Gligorov, Darko Tasevski (73.Ivan Tričkovski), Aleksandar Lazevski, Agim Ibraimi, Mirko Ivanovski (90+1.Stefan Ristovski). Trainer: Čedomir Janevski.
SRB: Željko Brkić, Nenad Tomović, Aleksandar Kolarov, Milan Biševac, Matija Nastasić, Zoran Tošić, Dušan Tadić (68.Branislav Ivanović), Ljubomir Fejsa, Aleksandar Ignjovski, Filip Đuričić (61.Dejan Lekić), Lazar Marković (74.Miralem Sulejmani). Trainer: Siniša Mihajlović.
Goal: 1-0 Agim Ibraimi (59 penalty).
Cautions: Nikola Gligorov, Nikolče Novevski, Daniel Georgievski, Boban Grnčarov / Milan Biševac, Lazar Marković.
Sent off: Nenad Tomović (59).

16.10.2012, Stade „Roi Baudouin“, Bruxelles; Attendance: 44,132
Referee: Tom Harald Hagen (Norway)
BELGIUM - SCOTLAND **2-0(0-0)**
BEL: Thibaut Nicolas Marc Courtois, Vincent Jean Mpoy Kompany, Thomas Vermaelen, Jan Bert Lieve Vertonghen, Tobias Albertine Maurits Alderweireld, Mousa Sidi Yaya Dembélé (46.Eden Michael Hazard), Axel Laurent Angel Lambert Witsel, Nacer Chadli, Kevin De Bruyne, Dries Mertens (46.Kevin Antonio Joel Gislain Mirallas y Castillo), Christian Benteke Liolo (87.Petit-Pelé M'Boyo Ilombé). Trainer: Marc Robert Wilmots.
SCO: Allan James McGregor, Alan Hutton, Christophe Didier Berra, Gary Robert Caldwell, Shaun Richard Maloney, Darren Barr Fletcher, Steven Kenneth Fletcher (76.Kenneth Miller), James Clark Morrison (80.Matthew Phillips), James McArthur, Kristian Arran Commons (46.James Charles Mackie), Daniel Fox. Trainer: Craig William Levein.
Goals: 1-0 Christian Benteke Liolo (68), 2-0 Vincent Jean Mpoy Kompany (71).
Cautions: Nacer Chadli / Allan James McGregor.

22.03.2013, Stadion Maksimir, Zagreb; Attendance: 35,722
Referee: Cüneyt Çakır (Turkey)
CROATIA - SERBIA **2-0(2-0)**
CRO: Stipe Pletikosa, Ivan Strinić (82.Dejan Lovren), Josip Šimunić, Vedran Ćorluka, Mateo Kovačić, Darijo Srna, Ivan Rakitić, Luka Modrić, Ivica Olić (83.Ognjen Vukojević), Niko Kranjčar (63.Domagoj Vida), Mario Mandžukić. Trainer: Igor Štimac.
SRB: Željko Brkić, Alen Stevanović (57.Dušan Tadić), Matija Nastasić, Neven Subotić, Branislav Ivanović, Zoran Tošić, Marko Šćepović (9.Filip Đorđević), Aleksandar Kolarov, Ivan Radovanović, Aleksandar Ignjovski (75.Raća Petrović), Filip Đuričić. Trainer: Siniša Mihajlović.
Goals: 1-0 Mario Mandžukić (23), 2-0 Ivica Olić (37).
Cautions: Aleksandar Kolarov, Neven Subotić, Raća Petrović.

22.03.2013, Hampden Park, Glasgow; Attendance: 39,365
Referee: Antony Gautier (France)
SCOTLAND - WALES **1-2(1-0)**
SCO: Allan James McGregor, Alan Hutton, Charles Patrick Mulgrew, Grant Hanley, Gary Robert Caldwell, Graham Dorrans (64.Charles Graham Adam), Robert Snodgrass, James McArthur, Steven Kenneth Fletcher (5.Kenneth Miller), Shaun Richard Maloney, Christopher Robert Burke (86.Jordan Luke Rhodes). Trainer: Gordon David Strachan.
WAL: Glyn Oliver Myhill, Christopher Ross Gunter, Benjamin Thomas Davies, Joseph Christopher Ledley (89.Simon Richard Church), Samuel Derek Ricketts, Ashley Errol Williams, Jack David Collison (58.Andrew Philip King), Craig Douglas Bellamy, Thomas Henry Alex Robson-Kanu, Aaron James Ramsey, Gareth Frank Bale (46.Jonathan Peter Williams). Trainer: Christopher Patrick Coleman.
Goals: 1-0 Grant Hanley (45+2), 1-1 Aaron James Ramsey (72 penalty), 1-2 Thomas Henry Alex Robson-Kanu (74).
Cautions: Robert Snodgrass, Kenneth Miller, Grant Hanley / Thomas Henry Alex Robson-Kanu, Aaron James Ramsey.
Sent off: Robert Snodgrass (71), Aaron James Ramsey (90+5).

22.03.2013, „Philip II“ Arena, Skopje; Attendance: 15,947
Referee: Deniz Aytekin (Germany)
MACEDONIA - BELGIUM **0-2(0-1)**
MKD: Tome Pačovski, Aleksandar Todorovski, Nikolče Novevski, Boban Grnčarov, Adis Jahović (58.Mirko Ivanovski), Goran Pandev, Ferhan Hasani (82.Darko Tasevski), Muhamed Demiri, Aleksandar Lazevski, Agim Ibraimi, Ivan Tričkovski (82.Aleksandar Trajkovski). Trainer: Čedomir Janevski.
BEL: Thibaut Nicolas Marc Courtois, Daniel Van Buyten, Thomas Vermaelen, Jan Bert Lieve Vertonghen, Tobias Albertine Maurits Alderweireld, Mousa Sidi Yaya Dembélé, Marouane Abdellatif Fellaini-Bakkioui, Axel Laurent Angel Lambert Witsel, Kevin De Bruyne, Kevin De Bruyne, Christian Benteke Liolo (85.Nacer Chadli). Trainer: Marc Robert Wilmots.
Goals: 0-1 Kevin De Bruyne (26), 0-2 Kevin De Bruyne (62 penalty).
Cautions: Muhamed Demiri, Aleksandar Lazevski, Boban Grnčarov, Mirko Ivanovski / Thomas Vermaelen.

26.03.2013, Liberty Stadium, Swansea; Attendance: 12,534
Referee: Luca Banti (Italy)
WALES - CROATIA **1-2(1-0)**
WAL: Glyn Oliver Myhill, Christopher Ross Gunter, Benjamin Thomas Davies, Joseph Christopher Ledley, James Michael Collins, Ashley Errol Williams, Jonathan Peter Williams, Craig Douglas Bellamy, Thomas Henry Alex Robson-Kanu (64.Ashley Darel Jazz Richards), Andrew Philip King (84.Simon Richard Church), Gareth Frank Bale. Trainer: Christopher Patrick Coleman.
CRO: Stipe Pletikosa, Ivan Strinić (73.Ivica Olić), Vedran Ćorluka, Dejan Lovren, Darijo Srna, Ivan Rakitić, Luka Modrić, Jorge Sammir Cruz Campos (61.Mateo Kovačić), Milan Badelj (46.Gordon Schildenfeld), Mario Mandžukić, Eduardo Alves Da Silva. Trainer: Igor Štimac.
Goals: 1-0 Gareth Frank Bale (21 penalty), 1-1 Dejan Lovren (77), 1-2 Eduardo Alves Da Silva (87).
Cautions: Thomas Henry Alex Robson-Kanu / Vedran Ćorluka, Dejan Lovren, Luka Modrić, Mateo Kovačić.

26.03.2013, Stadion Karađorđe, Novi Sad; Attendance: 6,500
Referee: István Vad (Hungary)
SERBIA - SCOTLAND **2-0(0-0)**
SRB: Vladimir Stojković, Matija Nastasić, Neven Subotić, Branislav Ivanović, Dušan Tadić (69.Filip Đorđević), Ljubomir Fejsa (85.Rača Petrović), Luka Milivojević, Nenad Tomović, Dušan Basta, Filip Đuričić, Zoran Tošić (90+3.Alen Stevanović). Trainer: Siniša Mihajlović.
SCO: David James Marshall, Alan Hutton, Grant Hanley, Steven Gordon Whittaker, Gary Robert Caldwell, Steven John Naismith, James McArthur (46.Charles Graham Adam), Jordan Luke Rhodes (80.Kenneth Miller), Shaun Richard Maloney (80.Christopher Robert Burke), George Jan Boyd, Liam Robert Bridcutt. Trainer: Gordon David Strachan.
Goals: 1-0 Filip Đuričić (60), 2-0 Filip Đuričić (66).
Cautions: Zoran Tošić, Matija Nastasić, Vladimir Stojković / Charles Graham Adam, Jordan Luke Rhodes, Liam Robert Bridcutt.

26.03.2013, Stade „Roi Baudouin", Bruxelles; Attendance: 44,230
Referee: Olegário Manuel Bártolo Faustino Benquerença (Portugal)
BELGIUM - MACEDONIA 1-0(0-0)
BEL: Thibaut Nicolas Marc Courtois, Vincent Jean Mpoy Kompany, Thomas Vermaelen, Jan Bert Lieve Vertonghen, Tobias Albertine Maurits Alderweireld, Mousa Sidi Yaya Dembélé (54.Nacer Chadli), Axel Laurent Angel Lambert Witsel, Eden Michael Hazard (90+2.Marouane Abdellatif Fellaini-Bakkioui), Kevin De Bruyne, Dries Mertens (46.Kevin Antonio Joel Gislain Mirallas y Castillo), Christian Benteke Liolo. Trainer: Marc Robert Wilmots.
MKD: Tome Pačovski, Daniel Georgievski, Nikolče Novevski, Vanče Šikov, Ivan Tričkovski (65.Aleksandar Trajkovski), Goran Pandev, Stefan Ristovski (70.Aleksandar Todorovski), Nikola Gligorov, Agim Ibraimi, Mirko Ivanovski, Darko Tasevski (46.Ferhan Hasani). Trainer: Čedomir Janevski.
Goal: 1-0 Eden Michael Hazard (62).
Cautions: Kevin Antonio Joel Gislain Mirallas y Castillo / Ferhan Hasani.

07.06.2013, Stadion Maksimir, Zagreb; Attendance: 25,016
Referee: David Fernández Borbalán (Spain)
CROATIA - SCOTLAND 0-1(0-1)
CRO: Stipe Pletikosa, Ivan Strinić (70.Nikola Kalinić), Josip Šimunić, Gordon Schildenfeld, Darijo Srna, Ivan Perišić (56.Eduardo Alves Da Silva), Ivan Rakitić, Mateo Kovačić, Jorge Sammir Cruz Campos, Mario Mandžukić (88.Niko Kranjčar), Ivica Olić. Trainer: Igor Štimac.
SCO: Allan James McGregor, Russell Kenneth Alexander Martin, Alan Hutton, Steven Gordon Whittaker, Grant Hanley, Shaun Richard Maloney (75.Craig Ian Conway), James Clark Morrison, James McArthur, Barry Bannan (63.Steven John Naismith), Leigh Griffiths (64.Jordan Luke Rhodes), Robert Snodgrass. Trainer: Gordon David Strachan.
Goal: 0-1 Robert Snodgrass (26).
Cautions: Ivan Rakitić / Allan James McGregor, James McArthur, Steven Gordon Whittaker.

07.06.2013, Stade „Roi Baudouin", Bruxelles; Attendance: 45,844
Referee: Stéphane Lannoy (France)
BELGIUM - SERBIA 2-1(1-0)
BEL: Thibaut Nicolas Marc Courtois, Vincent Jean Mpoy Kompany, Daniel Van Buyten, Jan Bert Lieve Vertonghen, Tobias Albertine Maurits Alderweireld, Marouane Abdellatif Fellaini-Bakkioui (71.Mousa Sidi Yaya Dembélé), Axel Laurent Angel Lambert Witsel, Nacer Chadli, Kevin De Bruyne (82.Romelu Menama Lukaku), Kevin Antonio Joel Gislain Mirallas y Castillo (64.Eden Michael Hazard), Christian Benteke Liolo. Trainer: Marc Robert Wilmots.
SRB: Vladimir Stojković, Milan Biševac, Neven Subotić, Branislav Ivanović, Aleksandar Kolarov, Dušan Basta, Ljubomir Fejsa, Lazar Marković, Aleksandar Mitrović (69.Marko Šćepović), Dušan Tadić, Luka Milivojević (69.Raća Petrović). Trainer: Siniša Mihajlović.
Goals: 1-0 Kevin De Bruyne (13), 2-0 Marouane Abdellatif Fellaini-Bakkioui (60), 2-1 Aleksandar Kolarov (87).
Cautions: Aleksandar Mitrović, Milan Biševac.

06.09.2013, „Philip II“ Arena, Skopje; Attendance: 18,000
Referee: Sascha Kever (Switzerland)
MACEDONIA - WALES 2-1(1-1)
MKD: Tome Pačovski, Daniel Georgievski (77.Aleksandar Lazevski), Nikolče Novevski, Vanče Šikov, Ivan Tričkovski, Goran Pandev, Stefan Ristovski, Nikola Gligorov, Jovan Kostovski (86.Daniel Mojsov), Agim Ibraimi (61.Aleksandar Trajkovski), Darko Tasevski. Trainer: Čedomir Janevski.
WAL: Glyn Oliver Myhill, Christopher Ross Gunter, Benjamin Thomas Davies, Joseph Christopher Ledley, Samuel Derek Ricketts, Craig Douglas Bellamy, Ashley Errol Williams, David Owen Vaughan (85.Samuel Michael Vokes), Jack David Collison (79.Adam James Matthews), Aaron James Ramsey, Jonathan Peter Williams (62.Andrew Lawrence Crofts). Trainer: Christopher Patrick Coleman.
Goals: 1-0 Ivan Tričkovski (20), 1-1 Aaron James Ramsey (39 penalty), 2-1 Aleksandar Trajkovski (80).
Cautions: Stefan Ristovski, Goran Pandev, Jovan Kostovski, Agim Ibraimi / David Owen Vaughan, Craig Douglas Bellamy, Ashley Errol Williams, Andrew Lawrence Crofts.

06.09.2013, Hampden Park, Glasgow; Attendance: 40,284
Referee: Paolo Tagliavento (Italy)
SCOTLAND - BELGIUM 0-2(0-1)
SCO: David James Marshall, Alan Hutton, Steven Gordon Whittaker, Russell Kenneth Alexander Martin, Grant Hanley, Shaun Richard Maloney, Charles Patrick Mulgrew, Scott Brown, Leigh Griffiths (68.Jordan Luke Rhodes), Robert Snodgrass (59.Ikechi Anya), James Forrest (86.Ross McCormack). Trainer: Gordon David Strachan.
BEL: Thibaut Nicolas Marc Courtois, Daniel Van Buyten, Jan Bert Lieve Vertonghen, Nicolas Robert Christian Lombaerts (77.Sébastien Pocognoli), Tobias Albertine Maurits Alderweireld, Marouane Abdellatif Fellaini-Bakkioui (68.Kevin Antonio Joel Gislain Mirallas y Castillo), Steven Arnold Defour (87.Mousa Sidi Yaya Dembélé), Axel Laurent Angel Lambert Witsel, Nacer Chadli, Kevin De Bruyne, Christian Benteke Liolo. Trainer: Marc Robert Wilmots.
Goals: 0-1 Steven Arnold Defour (34), 0-2 Kevin Antonio Joel Gislain Mirallas y Castillo (89).
Cautions: Robert Snodgrass / Marouane Abdellatif Fellaini-Bakkioui, Nicolas Robert Christian Lombaerts.

06.09.2013, Stadion Crvena Zvezda, Beograd; Attendance: 30,000
Referee: Dr. Felix Brych (Germany)
SERBIA - CROATIA 1-1(0-0)
SRB: Vladimir Stojković, Matija Nastasić, Branislav Ivanović, Neven Subotić, Zoran Tošić (56.Miralem Sulejmani), Aleksandar Mitrović, Aleksandar Kolarov, Nemanja Matić, Ljubomir Fejsa, Filip Đuričić (56.Dušan Tadić), Lazar Marković (79.Rađa Petrović). Trainer: Siniša Mihajlović.
CRO: Stipe Pletikosa, Vedran Ćorluka, Josip Šimunić, Dejan Lovren, Darijo Srna, Ivan Rakitić (77.Nikica Jelavić), Ognjen Vukojević, Ivica Olić (57.Ivan Perišić), Luka Modrić, Mario Mandžukić, Eduardo Alves Da Silva (64.Mateo Kovačić). Trainer: Igor Štimac.
Goals: 0-1 Mario Mandžukić (53), 1-1 Aleksandar Mitrović (66).
Cautions: Aleksandar Mitrović, Zoran Tošić, Ljubomir Fejsa, Nemanja Matić / Eduardo Alves Da Silva, Ognjen Vukojević, Darijo Srna.
Sent off: Nemanja Matić (75), Josip Šimunić (81).

10.09.2013, Cardiff City Stadium, Cardiff; Attendance: 10,923
Referee: Szymon Marciniak (Poland)

WALES - SERBIA **0-3(0-2)**

WAL: Glyn Oliver Myhill, Christopher Ross Gunter, Adam James Matthews, Joseph Christopher Ledley (75.Thomas Henry Alex Robson-Kanu), Daniel Leon Gabbidon, Benjamin Thomas Davies, Andrew Philip King (58.Gareth Frank Bale), Craig Douglas Bellamy, Samuel Michael Vokes, Aaron James Ramsey, Andrew Lawrence Crofts (58.David Owen Vaughan). Trainer: Christopher Patrick Coleman.

SRB: Vladimir Stojković, Milan Biševac, Matija Nastasić, Branislav Ivanović, Aleksandar Kolarov, Ivan Radovanović (67.Luka Milivojević), Ljubomir Fejsa (90+2.Rađa Petrović), Filip Đorđević, Filip Đuričić, Lazar Marković, Dušan Tadić (88.Nenad Krstičić). Trainer: Siniša Mihajlović.

Goals: 0-1 Filip Đorđević (8), 0-2 Aleksandar Kolarov (38), 0-3 Lazar Marković (55).

Cautions: Andrew Lawrence Crofts / Ljubomir Fejsa.

10.09.2013, „Philip II" Arena, Skopje; Attendance: 14,093
Referee: Fredy Fautrel (France)

MACEDONIA - SCOTLAND **1-2(0-0)**

MKD: Tome Pačovski, Daniel Georgievski, Nikolče Novevski, Vanče Šikov, Ivan Tričkovski, David Babunski (42.Darko Tasevski), Goran Pandev, Aleksandar Trajkovski (57.Mirko Ivanovski), Stefan Ristovski, Ostoja Stjepanović, Adis Jahović (83.Jovan Kostovski). Trainer: Čedomir Janevski.

SCO: David James Marshall (46.Matthew Gilks), Steven Gordon Whittaker (80.Lee Wallace), Russell Kenneth Alexander Martin, Grant Hanley, Shaun Richard Maloney, Alan Hutton, Charles Patrick Mulgrew, Scott Brown, Steven John Naismith, Barry Bannan (78.James McArthur), Ikechi Anya. Trainer: Gordon David Strachan.

Goals: 0-1 Ikechi Anya (60), 1-1 Jovan Kostovski (85), 1-2 Shaun Richard Maloney (89).

Cautions: Ostoja Stjepanović, Vanče Šikov / Charles Patrick Mulgrew, Steven Gordon Whittaker, Ikechi Anya.

11.10.2013, Stadion Maksimir, Zagreb; Attendance: 13,000
Referee: Howard Melton Webb (England)

CROATIA - BELGIUM **1-2(0-2)**

CRO: Stipe Pletikosa, Ivan Strinić, Vedran Ćorluka, Ivan Perišić (46.Nikola Kalinić), Dejan Lovren, Ivan Rakitić (76.Niko Kranjčar), Mateo Kovačić (65.Ognjen Vukojević), Domagoj Vida, Luka Modrić, Šime Vrsaljko, Mario Mandžukić. Trainer: Igor Štimac.

BEL: Thibaut Nicolas Marc Courtois, Daniel Van Buyten, Jan Bert Lieve Vertonghen, Nicolas Robert Christian Lombaerts, Tobias Albertine Maurits Alderweireld, Marouane Abdellatif Fellaini-Bakkioui, Steven Arnold Defour (84.Mousa Sidi Yaya Dembélé), Axel Laurent Angel Lambert Witsel, Eden Michael Hazard, Kevin De Bruyne (65.Kevin Antonio Joel Gislain Mirallas y Castillo), Romelu Menama Lukaku (69.Nacer Chadli). Trainer: Marc Robert Wilmots.

Goals: 0-1 Romelu Menama Lukaku (16), 0-2 Romelu Menama Lukaku (38), 1-2 Niko Kranjčar (84).

Cautions: Mario Mandžukić, Šime Vrsaljko, Vedran Ćorluka, Luka Modrić / Marouane Abdellatif Fellaini-Bakkioui.

11.10.2013, Cardiff City Stadium, Cardiff; Attendance: 11,257
Referee: Suren Baliyan (Armenia)

WALES - MACEDONIA **1-0(0-0)**

WAL: Wayne Robert Hennessey, Neil John Taylor, Declan Christopher John, David Owen Vaughan, Christopher Ross Gunter, James Michael Collins, Andrew Philip King, Craig Douglas Bellamy, Simon Richard Church (90+1.Jermaine Maurice Easter), Aaron James Ramsey, Thomas Henry Alex Robson-Kanu. Trainer: Christopher Patrick Coleman.

MKD: Tome Pačovski, Ezgjan Alioski, Nikolče Novevski, Vanče Šikov, Muhamed Demiri (85.Jovan Kostovski), Goran Pandev, Stefan Ristovski, Predrag Ranđelović, Ostoja Stjepanović (75.Darko Tasevski), Agim Ibraimi, Mirko Ivanovski (80.Aleksandar Trajkovski). Trainer: Zoran Stratev.

Goal: 1-0 Simon Richard Church (67).

Cautions: Declan Christopher John, Neil John Taylor, Wayne Robert Hennessey / Vanče Šikov.

15.10.2013, Hampden Park, Glasgow; Attendance: 30,172
Referee: Ovidiu Haţegan (Romania)
SCOTLAND - CROATIA **2-0(1-0)**
SCO: Allan James McGregor, Alan Hutton, Charles Patrick Mulgrew, Russell Kenneth Alexander Martin, Grant Hanley, Barry Bannan (89.Christopher Robert Burke), Scott Brown, James Clark Morrison, Steven John Naismith, Robert Snodgrass (82.James McArthur), Ikechi Anya (77.Graham Dorrans). Trainer: Gordon David Strachan.
CRO: Stipe Pletikosa, Ivan Strinić, Vedran Ćorluka, Dejan Lovren, Darijo Srna, Ognjen Vukojević, Luka Modrić, Domagoj Vida, Niko Kranjčar (68.Ivan Perišić), Mario Mandžukić (80.Nikica Jelavić), Nikola Kalinić (59.Eduardo Alves Da Silva). Trainer: Igor Štimac.
Goals: 1-0 Robert Snodgrass (28), 2-0 Steven John Naismith (73).
Cautions: James Clark Morrison / Ognjen Vukojević.

15.10.2013, Stadion Jagodina, Jagodina; Attendance: 8,294
Referee: Richard Trutz (Slovakia)
SERBIA - MACEDONIA **5-1(3-0)**
SRB: Vladimir Stojković, Antonio Rukavina (83.Branislav Trajković), Matija Nastasić, Branislav Ivanović, Zoran Tošić, Dušan Tadić, Aleksandar Kolarov, Nemanja Matić, Luka Milivojević (76.Rađa Petrović), Dušan Basta, Filip Đorđević (62.Stefan Šćepović). Trainer: Siniša Mihajlović.
MKD: Tome Pačovski, Ezgjan Alioski, Nikolče Novevski, Boban Grnčarov, Muhamed Demiri (56.David Babunski), Stefan Ristovski, Predrag Ranđelović, Ostoja Stjepanović, Agim Ibraimi (46.Aleksandar Trajkovski), Jovan Kostovski, Mirko Ivanovski (81.Adis Jahović). Trainer: Zoran Stratev.
Goals: 1-0 Stefan Ristovski (16 own goal), 2-0 Dušan Basta (29), 3-0 Aleksandar Kolarov (38 penalty), 4-0 Dušan Tadić (54), 5-0 Stefan Šćepović (74), 5-1 Adis Jahović (83).
Cautions: Stefan Ristovski, Predrag Ranđelović, Jovan Kostovski, Boban Grnčarov.

15.10.2013, Referee: Sergei Karasev (Russia)
Stade „Roi Baudouin", Bruxelles; Attendance: 45,401
BELGIUM - WALES **1-1(0-0)**
BEL: Thibaut Nicolas Marc Courtois, Daniel Van Buyten (72.Jan Bert Lieve Vertonghen), Thomas Vermaelen, Sébastien Pocognoli, Tobias Albertine Maurits Alderweireld, Mousa Sidi Yaya Dembélé, Axel Laurent Angel Lambert Witsel, Nacer Chadli (58.Eden Michael Hazard), Kevin De Bruyne, Kevin Antonio Joel Gislain Mirallas y Castillo (78.Zakaria Bakkali), Romelu Menama Lukaku. Trainer: Marc Robert Wilmots.
WAL: Wayne Robert Hennessey, Ashley Darel Jazz Richards, Neil John Taylor, David Owen Vaughan, Christopher Ross Gunter, James Michael Collins (57.James Steven Wilson), Andrew Philip King, Craig Douglas Bellamy, Simon Richard Church (70.Samuel Michael Vokes), Aaron James Ramsey, Thomas Henry Alex Robson-Kanu (87.Harry Wilson). Trainer: Christopher Patrick Coleman.
Goals: 1-0 Kevin De Bruyne (64), 1-1 Aaron James Ramsey (88).
Cautions: James Michael Collins, Craig Douglas Bellamy.

GROUP B

07.09.2012	Ta'Qali	Malta - Armenia	0-1(0-0)
07.09.2012	Sofia	Bulgaria - Italy	2-2(1-2)
08.09.2012	København	Denmark - Czech Republic	0-0
11.09.2012	Modena	Italy - Malta	2-0(1-0)
11.09.2012	Sofia	Bulgaria - Armenia	1-0(1-0)
12.10.2012	Plzen	Czech Republic - Malta	3-1(1-1)
12.10.2012	Yerevan	Armenia - Italy	1-3(1-1)
12.10.2012	Sofia	Bulgaria - Denmark	1-1(1-1)
16.10.2012	Praha	Czech Republic - Bulgaria	0-0
16.10.2012	Milano	Italy - Denmark	3-1(2-1)
22.03.2013	Sofia	Bulgaria - Malta	6-0(2-0)
22.03.2013	Olomouc	Czech Republic - Denmark	0-3(0-0)
26.03.2013	Yerevan	Armenia - Czech Republic	0-3(0-0)
26.03.2013	København	Denmark - Bulgaria	1-1(0-0)
26.03.2013	Ta'Qali	Malta - Italy	0-2(0-2)
07.06.2013	Yerevan	Armenia - Malta	0-1(0-1)
07.06.2013	Praha	Czech Republic - Italy	0-0
11.06.2013	København	Denmark - Armenia	0-4(0-2)
06.09.2013	Praha	Czech Republic - Armenia	1-2(0-1)
06.09.2013	Ta'Qali	Malta - Denmark	1-2(1-1)
06.09.2013	Palermo	Italy - Bulgaria	1-0(1-0)
10.09.2013	Yerevan	Armenia - Denmark	0-1(0-0)
10.09.2013	Ta'Qali	Malta - Bulgaria	1-2(0-1)
10.09.2013	Torino	Italy - Czech Republic	2-1(0-1)
11.10.2013	Yerevan	Armenia - Bulgaria	2-1(1-0)
11.10.2013	Ta'Qali	Malta - Czech Republic	1-4(0-2)
11.10.2013	København	Denmark - Italy	2-2(1-1)
15.10.2013	København	Denmark - Malta	6-0(4-0)
15.10.2013	Napoli	Italy - Armenia	2-2(1-1)
15.10.2013	Sofia	Bulgaria - Czech Republic	0-1(0-0)

FINAL STANDINGS

1.	**ITALY**	10	6	4	0	19	-	9	22
2.	Denmark	10	4	4	2	17	-	12	16
3.	Czech Republic	10	4	3	3	13	-	9	15
4.	Bulgaria	10	3	4	3	14	-	9	13
5.	Armenia	10	4	1	5	12	-	13	13
6.	Malta	10	1	0	9	5	-	28	3

Italy qualified for the Final Tournament.

07.09.2012, National Stadium, Ta) Qali; Attendance: 3,517
Referee: Rene Eisner (Austria)

MALTA - ARMENIA 0-1(0-0)

MLT: Andrew Hogg, Luke Dimech, Alexander Muscat, Andrei Agius, Steve Borg, Gareth Sciberras, Roderick Briffa (85.Shaun Bajada), Andrew Cohen (74.Jonathan Caruana), Daniel Bogdanović, Michael Mifsud, André Schembri. Trainer: Pietro Ghedin (Italy).

ARM: Gevorg Kasparov, Robert Arzumanyan (79.Valeri Vazgen Aleksanyan), Sargis Hovsepyan, Hrayr Mkoyan, Henrikh Mkhitaryan, Karlen Mkrtchyan, Marcos Piñeiro Pizelli (64.Artur Sarkisov), Levon Hayrapetyan, Artak Yedigaryan (52.David Manoyan), Aras Özbiliz, Yura Movsisyan. Trainer: Vardan Minasyan.

Goal: 0-1 Artur Sarkisov (70).

Cautions: Gareth Sciberras, Luke Dimech / Hrayr Mkoyan, Sargis Hovsepyan.

07.09.2012, Nationalen stadion "Vasil Levski", Sofia; Attendance: 12,993
Referee: Martin Atkinson (England)

BULGARIA - ITALY 2-2(1-2)

BUL: Nikolai Mihailov, Stanislav Manolev, Nikolay Bodurov, Veselin Minev, Ivelin Popov (82.Aleksandar Tonev), Yordan Minev, Ivan Ivanov, Georgi Milanov, Vladimir Gadzhev (80.Sarmov Zdravkov), Svetoslav Dyakov, Emil Gargorov (62.Iliyan Mitsanski). Trainer: Lyuboslav Penev.

ITA: Gianluigi Buffon, Andrea Barzagli, Leonardo Bonucci, Angelo Ogbonna (69.Federico Peluso), Daniele De Rossi, Andrea Pirlo, Christian Maggio, Claudio Marchisio, Emanuele Giaccherini (64.Alessandro Diamanti), Pablo Daniel Osvaldo, Sebastian Giovinco (73.Mattia Destro). Trainer: Cesare Claudio Prandelli.

Goals: 1-0 Stanislav Manolev (30), 1-1 Pablo Daniel Osvaldo (36), 1-2 Pablo Daniel Osvaldo (40), 2-2 Georgi Milanov (66).

Cautions: Vladimir Gadzhev, Ivelin Popov, Svetoslav Dyakov / Daniele De Rossi, Angelo Ogbonna, Alessandro Diamanti.

08.09.2012, Parken Stadion, København; Attendance: 24,004
Referee: Wolfgang Stark (Germany)

DENMARK - CZECH REPUBLIC 0-0

DEN: Stephan Maigaard Andersen, Daniel Agger, Simon Kjær, Lars Christian Jacobsen, Daniel Wass, Michael Krohn-Dehli, William Kvist Jørgensen, Thomas Fauerskov Kristensen (58.Leon Hougaard Andreasen), Christian Dannemann Eriksen, Dennis Rommedahl (80.Tobias Pilegaard Mikkelsen), Nicolai Jørgensen (71.Andreas Evald Cornelius). Trainer: Morten Per Olsen.

CZE: Petr Čech, Tomáš Sivok, Marek Suchý, Michal Kadlec, Theodor Gebre Selassie, Jaroslav Plašil (75.Vladimír Darida), Tomáš Hübschman, Petr Jiráček, Tomáš Pekhart, Jan Rezek (89.Josef Hušbauer), Matěj Vydra (73.František Rajtoral). Trainer: Michal Bílek.

Cautions: William Kvist Jørgensen, Tobias Pilegaard Mikkelsen, Andreas Evald Cornelius.

11.09.2012, Stadio "Alberto Braglia", Modena; Attendance: 18,000
Referee: Antti Munukka (Finland)

ITALY - MALTA 2-0(1-0)

ITA: Gianluigi Buffon, Andrea Barzagli, Leonardo Bonucci, Mattia Cassani, Federico Peluso, Andrea Pirlo, Antonio Nocerino, Claudio Marchisio, Alessandro Diamanti (46.Lorenzo Insigne), Pablo Daniel Osvaldo (69.Giampaolo Pazzini), Mattia Destro (82.Sebastian Giovinco). Trainer: Cesare Claudio Prandelli.

MLT: Andrew Hogg, Alexander Muscat (86.Ryan Camilleri), Gareth Sciberras, Edward Herrera, Steve Borg, Andrei Agius, Luke Dimech, Roderick Briffa, Daniel Bogdanović (69.Andrew Cohen), Michael Mifsud, André Schembri. Trainer: Pietro Ghedin (Italy).

Goals: 1-0 Mattia Destro (5), 2-0 Federico Peluso (90+2).

Cautions: Alexander Muscat, André Schembri, Andrew Cohen, Andrew Hogg.

11.09.2012, Nationalen stadion "Vasil Levski", Sofia; Attendance: 17,883
Referee: Stephan Studer (Switzerland)
BULGARIA - ARMENIA 1-0(1-0)
BUL: Nikolai Mihailov, Stanislav Manolev, Nikolay Bodurov, Yordan Minev, Ivelin Popov (79.Emil Gargorov), Veselin Minev, Ivan Ivanov, Georgi Milanov, Vladimir Gadzhev (60.Sarmov Zdravkov), Iliyan Mitsanski (66.Dimitar Rangelov), Svetoslav Dyakov. Trainer: Lyuboslav Penev.
ARM: Roman Anatoliy Berezovsky, Robert Arzumanyan, Sargis Hovsepyan, Hrayr Mkoyan, Artur Yedigaryan (76.Artur Sarkisov), Gevorg Ghazaryan, Henrikh Mkhitaryan, Karlen Mkrtchyan, Levon Hayrapetyan (43.Artak Yedigaryan), Aras Özbiliz (54.Marcos Piñeiro Pizelli), Yura Movsisyan. Trainer: Vardan Minasyan.
Goal: 1-0 Stanislav Manolev (43).
Cautions: Georgi Milanov, Svetoslav Dyakov, Nikolai Mihailov, Emil Gargorov / Artak Yedigaryan, Karlen Mkrtchyan, Gevorg Ghazaryan, Artur Yedigaryan, Sargis Hovsepyan.
Sent off: Svetoslav Dyakov (73), Marcos Piñeiro Pizelli (73), Gevorg Ghazaryan (77).

12.10.2012, Stadion města Plzně, Plzeň; Attendance: 10,358
Referee: Anar Salmanov (Azerbaijan)
CZECH REPUBLIC - MALTA 3-1(1-1)
CZE: Petr Čech, Tomáš Sivok, František Rajtoral (61.Milan Petržela), Michal Kadlec, David Limberský, Theodor Gebre Selassie, Jaroslav Plašil, Tomáš Hübschman, Petr Jiráček (73.Vladimír Darida), Tomáš Pekhart (81.David Lafata), Jan Rezek. Trainer: Michal Bílek.
MLT: Andrew Hogg, Luke Dimech, Edward Herrera, Steve Borg, Alexander Muscat, Andrei Agius, Gareth Sciberras, Shaun Bajada (89.Ayrton Azzopardi), Roderick Briffa, Michael Mifsud, André Schembri (87.Paul Fenech). Trainer: Pietro Ghedin (Italy).
Goals: 1-0 Theodor Gebre Selassie (34), 1-1 Roderick Briffa (38), 2-1 Tomáš Pekhart (52), 3-1 Jan Rezek (67).

12.10.2012, Hrazdan Stadium, Yerevan; Attendance: 32,000
Referee: Marijo Strahonja (Croatia)
ARMENIA - ITALY 1-3(1-1)
ARM: Roman Anatoliy Berezovsky, Robert Arzumanyan, Valeri Vazgen Aleksanyan, Hrayr Mkoyan, Artur Yedigaryan (65.Edgar Manucharyan), Henrikh Mkhitaryan, Karlen Mkrtchyan, Artak Yedigaryan, David Manoyan (77.Artur Sarkisov), Aras Özbiliz, Yura Movsisyan. Trainer: Vardan Minasyan.
ITA: Gianluigi Buffon, Andrea Barzagli, Leonardo Bonucci, Domenico Criscito, Daniele De Rossi, Andrea Pirlo (74.Emanuele Giaccherini), Riccardo Montolivo (88.Antonio Candreva), Christian Maggio, Claudio Marchisio, Pablo Daniel Osvaldo, Sebastian Giovinco (60.Stephan Kareem El Shaarawy). Trainer: Cesare Claudio Prandelli.
Goals: 0-1 Andrea Pirlo (11 penalty), 1-1 Henrikh Mkhitaryan (27), 1-2 Daniele De Rossi (64), 1-3 Pablo Daniel Osvaldo (82).
Cautions: Hrayr Mkoyan, Artur Yedigaryan, Karlen Mkrtchyan, Edgar Manucharyan, Valeri Vazgen Aleksanyan / Leonardo Bonucci, Sebastian Giovinco.

12.10.2012, Nationalen stadion "Vasil Levski", Sofia; Attendance: 20,780
Referee: Tony Chapron (France)
BULGARIA - DENMARK 1-1(1-1)
BUL: Nikolai Mihailov, Stanislav Manolev, Nikolay Bodurov, Yordan Minev, Dimitar Rangelov (61.Aleksandar Tonev), Ivelin Popov (85.Valeri Bojinov), Ivan Bandalovski, Ivan Ivanov, Georgi Milanov, Vladimir Gadzhev, Georgi Iliev (35.Iliya Milanov). Trainer: Lyuboslav Penev.
DEN: Stephan Maigaard Andersen, Daniel Agger, Simon Kjær, Lars Christian Jacobsen, Daniel Wass (54.Patrick Jan Mtiliga), Michael Krohn-Dehli, William Kvist Jørgensen, Thomas Fauerskov Kristensen (36.Andreas Evald Cornelius), Christian Dannemann Eriksen (90+2.Jakob Poulsen), Dennis Rommedahl, Nicklas Bendtner. Trainer: Morten Per Olsen.
Goals: 1-0 Dimitar Rangelov (7), 1-1 Nicklas Bendtner (40).

Cautions: Patrick Jan Mtiliga, Andreas Evald Cornelius.
Sent off: Ivan Bandalovski (27).

16.10.2012, Generali Arena, Praha; Attendance: 16,163
Referee: Vladislav Bezborodov (Russia)
CZECH REPUBLIC - BULGARIA 0-0
CZE: Petr Čech, Tomáš Sivok, František Rajtoral (58.Vladimír Darida), Michal Kadlec, David Limberský, Theodor Gebre Selassie, Jaroslav Plašil, Tomáš Hübschman, Petr Jiráček, Tomáš Pekhart (58.Matěj Vydra), Jan Rezek (80.David Lafata). Trainer: Michal Bílek.
BUL: Nikolai Mihailov, Stanislav Manolev, Petar Zanev (42.Iliya Milanov), Nikolay Bodurov, Yordan Minev, Ivelin Popov (75.Aleksandar Tonev), Ivan Ivanov, Georgi Milanov, Vladimir Gadzhev (61.Valeri Bojinov), Svetoslav Dyakov, Georgi Iliev. Trainer: Lyuboslav Penev.
Cautions: Theodor Gebre Selassie / Svetoslav Dyakov, Georgi Iliev, Ivan Ivanov, Yordan Minev.

16.10.2012, Stadio "Giuseppe Meazza", Milano; Attendance: 37,027
Referee: Damir Skomina (Slovenia)
ITALY - DENMARK 3-1(2-1)
ITA: Morgan De Sanctis, Andrea Barzagli, Giorgio Chiellini, Federico Balzaretti, Ignazio Abate, Daniele De Rossi, Andrea Pirlo, Riccardo Montolivo (86.Emanuele Giaccherini), Claudio Marchisio (74.Antonio Candreva), Pablo Daniel Osvaldo, Mario Balotelli (89.Mattia Destro). Trainer: Cesare Claudio Prandelli.
DEN: Stephan Maigaard Andersen, Daniel Agger, Simon Kjær, Lars Christian Jacobsen, Michael Krohn-Dehli (83.Jakob Poulsen), Michael Silberbauer (72.Kasper Wellemberg Lorentzen), Nicolai Stokholm, William Kvist Jørgensen (60.Thomas Kahlenberg), Christian Dannemann Eriksen, Dennis Rommedahl, Nicklas Bendtner. Trainer: Morten Per Olsen.
Goals: 1-0 Riccardo Montolivo (34), 2- Daniele De Rossi 0 (37), William Kvist Jørgensen (45+1), 3-1 Mario Balotelli (54).
Cautions: Daniele De Rossi, Morgan De Sanctis / William Kvist Jørgensen, Nicolai Stokholm, Nicklas Bendtner.
Sent off: Pablo Daniel Osvaldo (46).

22.03.2013, Nationalen stadion "Vasil Levski", Sofia; Attendance: *played behind closed doors*
Referee: Eitan Shemeulevitch (Israel)
BULGARIA - MALTA 6-0(2-0)
BUL: Nikolai Mihailov, Nikolay Bodurov, Yordan Minev (63.Radoslav Dimitrov), Ivelin Popov, Veselin Minev, Ivan Ivanov, Georgi Milanov, Vladimir Gadzhev (70.Sarmov Zdravkov), Aleksandar Tonev, Georgi Iliev, Emil Gargorov (56.Valeri Bojinov). Trainer: Lyuboslav Penev.
MLT: Andrew Hogg, Jonathan Caruana, Andrei Agius (56.Ryan Camilleri), Luke Dimech, Roderick Briffa, Michael Mifsud, Clayton Failla, Paul Fenech (70.Rowen Muscat), Edward Herrera, Ryan Fenech, André Schembri. Trainer: Pietro Ghedin (Italy).
Goals: 1-0 Aleksandar Tonev (6), 2-0 Aleksandar Tonev (38), 3-0 Ivelin Popov (47), 4-0 Emil Gargorov (55), 5-0 Aleksandar Tonev (68), 6-0 Ivan Ivanov (78).
Cautions: Yordan Minev.

22.03.2013, Andrův stadion, Olomouc; Attendance: 12,288
Referee: Manuel Jorge Neves Moreira de Sousa (Portugal)
CZECH REPUBLIC - DENMARK 0-3(0-0)
CZE: Petr Čech, Tomáš Sivok, Michal Kadlec, David Limberský, Theodor Gebre Selassie, Jaroslav Plašil (74.Libor Kozák), Petr Jiráček (61.Tomáš Rosický), Ladislav Krejčí (64.Bořek Dočkal), Vladimír Darida, David Lafata, Matěj Vydra. Trainer: Michal Bílek.
DEN: Stephan Maigaard Andersen, Daniel Agger, Simon Kjær, Simon Busk Poulsen, Lars Christian Jacobsen, Michael Krohn-Dehli, Nicolai Stokholm, Niki Dige Zimling, Christian Dannemann Eriksen, Nicolai Jørgensen (66.Dennis Rommedahl), Andreas Evald Cornelius (83.Simon Makienok Christoffersen). Trainer: Morten Per Olsen.
Goals: 0-1 Andreas Evald Cornelius (57), 0-2 Simon Kjær (67), 0-3 Niki Dige Zimling (82).

Cautions: Vladimír Darida, Tomáš Sivok, Libor Kozák / Nicolai Stokholm, Niki Dige Zimling.

26.03.2013, Republican Stadium, Yerevan; Attendance: 14,403
Referee: Cristian Balaj (Romania)
ARMENIA - CZECH REPUBLIC 0-3(0-0)
ARM: Roman Anatoliy Berezovsky, Robert Arzumanyan, Valeri Vazgen Aleksanyan, Gevorg Ghazaryan (60.Artur Sarkisov), Henrikh Mkhitaryan, Marcos Piñeiro Pizelli, Kamo Hovhannisyan, Taron Voskanyan, Karen Muradyan (78.David Manoyan), Edgar Manucharyan (50.Aras Özbiliz), Yura Movsisyan. Trainer: Vardan Minasyan.
CZE: Petr Čech, Tomáš Sivok (43.Marek Suchý), Michal Kadlec, David Limberský, Theodor Gebre Selassie, Jaroslav Plašil, Tomáš Rosický, Tomáš Hübschman, Vladimír Darida (85.Petr Jiráček), David Lafata (74.Daniel Kolář), Matěj Vydra. Trainer: Michal Bílek.
Goals: 0-1 Matěj Vydra (47), 0-2 Matěj Vydra (81), 0-3 Daniel Kolář (90+4).
Cautions: Gevorg Ghazaryan, Yura Movsisyan.

26.03.2013, Parken Stadion, København; Attendance: 22,357
Referee: Fırat Aydınus (Turkey)
DENMARK - BULGARIA 1-1(0-0)
DEN: Stephan Maigaard Andersen, Daniel Agger, Simon Kjær, Simon Busk Poulsen, Lars Christian Jacobsen, Michael Krohn-Dehli (69.Lasse Schöne), Nicolai Stokholm, Niki Dige Zimling (86.Simon Makienok Christoffersen), Christian Dannemann Eriksen, Dennis Rommedahl (54.Nicolai Jørgensen), Andreas Evald Cornelius. Trainer: Morten Per Olsen.
BUL: Nikolai Mihailov, Veselin Minev, Nikolay Bodurov (23.Radoslav Dimitrov) , Ivelin Popov (70.Georgi Iliev), Stanislav Manolev (87.Emil Gargorov), Ivan Ivanov, Iliya Milanov, Georgi Milanov, Vladimir Gadzhev, Aleksandar Tonev, Svetoslav Dyakov. Trainer: Lyuboslav Penev.
Goals: 0-1 Stanislav Manolev (51), 1-1 Daniel Agger (63 penalty).
Cautions: Nicolai Jørgensen / Radoslav Dimitrov, Georgi Milanov.

26.03.2013, National Stadium, Ta) Qali; Attendance: 17,011
Referee: Serdar Gözübüyük (Holland)
MALTA - ITALY 0-2(0-2)
MLT: Justin Haber, Jonathan Caruana, Alexander Muscat, Edward Herrera, Gareth Sciberras, Luke Dimech, Clayton Failla (82.Andrew Cohen), Roderick Briffa, Ryan Camilleri, Michael Mifsud (88.Terence Vella), André Schembri. Trainer: Pietro Ghedin (Italy).
ITA: Gianluigi Buffon, Andrea Barzagli, Leonardo Bonucci, Ignazio Abate, Mattia De Sciglio, Andrea Pirlo, Riccardo Montolivo, Claudio Marchisio, Emanuele Giaccherini (61.Antonio Candreva), Mario Balotelli (86.Alberto Gilardino), Stephan Kareem El Shaarawy (75.Alessio Cerci). Trainer: Cesare Claudio Prandelli.
Goals: 0-1 Mario Balotelli (8 penalty), 0-2 Mario Balotelli (45).
Cautions: Gianluigi Buffon.

07.06.2013, Republican Stadium, Yerevan; Attendance: 8,500
Referee: Arnold Hunter (Northern Ireland)
ARMENIA - MALTA 0-1(0-1)
ARM: Roman Anatoliy Berezovsky, Robert Arzumanyan, Valeri Vazgen Aleksanyan, Henrikh Mkhitaryan, Karlen Mkrtchyan, Marcos Piñeiro Pizelli, David Manoyan (66.Artur Sarkisov), Kamo Hovhannisyan, Taron Voskanyan, Aras Özbiliz, Edgar Manucharyan (46.Yura Movsisyan). Trainer: Vardan Minasyan.
MLT: Justin Haber, Jonathan Caruana, Luke Dimech, Alexander Muscat, Ryan Camilleri, Clayton Failla, Roderick Briffa (84.Rowen Muscat), Edward Herrera, Gareth Sciberras (57.Paul Fenech), Michael Mifsud (90+2.Terence Vella), André Schembri. Trainer: Pietro Ghedin (Italy).
Goal: 0-1 Michael Mifsud (8).
Cautions: Roderick Briffa, Alexander Muscat, Jonathan Caruana, Luke Dimech.

07.06.2013, Generali Arena, Praha; Attendance: 18,235
Referee: Svein Oddvar Moen (Norway)

CZECH REPUBLIC - ITALY 0-0

CZE: Petr Čech, Tomáš Sivok, Michal Kadlec, David Limberský (20.Marek Suchý), Theodor Gebre Selassie, Jaroslav Plašil, Tomáš Rosický, Tomáš Hübschman, Petr Jiráček (86.Daniel Kolář), Vladimír Darida (75.Václav Kadlec), Libor Kozák. Trainer: Michal Bílek.

ITA: Gianluigi Buffon, Andrea Barzagli, Leonardo Bonucci, Giorgio Chiellini, Ignazio Abate, Daniele De Rossi, Andrea Pirlo (77.Alberto Aquilani), Riccardo Montolivo, Claudio Marchisio, Mario Balotelli, Stephan Kareem El Shaarawy (46.Sebastian Giovinco). Trainer: Cesare Claudio Prandelli.

Cautions: Vladimír Darida / Mario Balotelli, Riccardo Montolivo.

Sent off: Mario Balotelli (72).

11.06.2013, Parken Stadion, København; Attendance: 14,284
Referee: Aleksei Nikolaev (Russia)

DENMARK - ARMENIA 0-4(0-2)

DEN: Stephan Maigaard Andersen, Simon Kjær, Simon Busk Poulsen, Andreas Bjelland (46.Tetchi Jores Charlemagne Ulrich Okore), Lars Christian Jacobsen, Michael Krohn-Dehli, Niki Dige Zimling (28.Nicklas Pedersen; 53.Simon Makienok Christoffersen), William Kvist Jørgensen, Christian Dannemann Eriksen, Dennis Rommedahl, Andreas Evald Cornelius. Trainer: Morten Per Olsen.

ARM: Roman Anatoliy Berezovsky, Robert Arzumanyan, Valeri Vazgen Aleksanyan, Varazdat Haroyan, Artur Yedigaryan (86.Marcos Piñeiro Pizelli), Gevorg Ghazaryan, Henrikh Mkhitaryan, Karlen Mkrtchyan, Kamo Hovhannisyan, Aras Özbiliz (90+1.Norair Aslanyan-Mamedov), Yura Movsisyan (84.Artur Sarkisov). Trainer: Vardan Minasyan.

Goals: 0-1 Yura Movsisyan (1), 0-2 Aras Özbiliz (19), 0-3 Yura Movsisyan (59), 0-4 Henrikh Mkhitaryan (82).

Cautions: Michael Krohn-Dehli / Varazdat Haroyan, Robert Arzumanyan.

06.09.2013, Eden Arena, Praha; Attendance: 17,628
Referee: Antony Gautier (France)

CZECH REPUBLIC - ARMENIA 1-2(0-1)

CZE: Petr Čech, Tomáš Sivok, Michal Kadlec, David Limberský (65.Marek Suchý), Theodor Gebre Selassie, Jaroslav Plašil, Tomáš Rosický, Josef Hušbauer, Petr Jiráček (62.Ondřej Vaněk), Michael Rabušic (55.Václav Kadlec), Libor Kozák Trainer: Michal Bílek.

ARM: Roman Anatoliy Berezovsky (69.Gevorg Kasparov), Robert Arzumanyan, Hrayr Mkoyan, Varazdat Haroyan, Artur Yedigaryan, Gevorg Ghazaryan, Henrikh Mkhitaryan, Karlen Mkrtchyan, Kamo Hovhannisyan (76.Marcos Piñeiro Pizelli), Aras Özbiliz (28.Levon Hayrapetyan), Yura Movsisyan. Trainer: Vardan Minasyan.

Goals: 0-1 Karlen Mkrtchyan (31), 1-1 Tomáš Rosický (70), 1-2 Gevorg Ghazaryan (90+2).

Cautions: David Limberský, Josef Hušbauer, Tomáš Rosický / Aras Özbiliz, Robert Arzumanyan, Yura Movsisyan, Artur Yedigaryan.

06.09.2013, National Stadium, Ta) Qali; Attendance: 5,576
Referee: Anastasios Sidiropoulos (Greece)

MALTA - DENMARK 1-2(1-1)

MLT: Justin Haber, Gareth Sciberras, Andrei Agius, Clayton Failla, Roderick Briffa, Edward Herrera (89.Andrew Cohen), John Mintoff (75.Ryan Fenech), Rowen Muscat, Ryan Camilleri, Michael Mifsud (81.Terence Vella), André Schembri. Trainer: Pietro Ghedin (Italy).

DEN: Stephan Maigaard Andersen, Daniel Agger, Simon Kjær, Lars Christian Jacobsen, Nicolai Møller Boilesen, Leon Hougaard Andreasen (72.Casper Sloth), William Kvist Jørgensen, Christian Dannemann Eriksen, Nicklas Pedersen, Martin Braithwaite Christensen (84.Viktor Gorridsen Fischer), Rasmus Falk Jensen (46.Michael Krohn-Dehli). Trainer: Morten Per Olsen.

Goals: 0-1 Leon Hougaard Andreasen (2), 1-1 Clayton Failla (38), 1-2 Ryan Camilleri (52 own goal).

Cautions: Andrei Agius, Roderick Briffa, John Mintoff, Terence Vella.

06.09.2013, Stadio "Renzo Barbera", Palermo; Attendance: 28,662
Referee: Carlos Velasco Carballo (Spain)

ITALY - BULGARIA **1-0(1-0)**

ITA: Gianluigi Buffon, Leonardo Bonucci, Giorgio Chiellini, Ignazio Abate (80.Christian Maggio), Luca Antonelli (63.Davide Astori), Daniele De Rossi, Andrea Pirlo, Thiago Motta, Antonio Candreva, Alberto Gilardino, Lorenzo Insigne (64.Emanuele Giaccherini). Trainer: Cesare Claudio Prandelli.
BUL: Nikolai Mihailov, Stanislav Manolev (55.Georgi Iliev), Nikolay Bodurov, Yordan Minev, Ivelin Popov, Aleksandar Tonev (61.Dimitar Rangelov), Veselin Minev, Ivan Ivanov, Todor Nedelev, Vladimir Gadzhev, Svetoslav Dyakov (76.Spas Delev). Trainer: Lyuboslav Penev.
Goal: 1-0 Alberto Gilardino (38).
Cautions: Emanuele Giaccherini.

10.09.2013, Hrazdan Stadium, Yerevan; Attendance: 23,000
Referee: Hendrikus Sebastiaan Hermanus Nijhuis (Holland)

ARMENIA - DENMARK **0-1(0-0)**

ARM: Gevorg Kasparov, Hrayr Mkoyan, Varazdat Haroyan, Artur Yedigaryan, Gevorg Ghazaryan, Henrikh Mkhitaryan, Karlen Mkrtchyan (27.Artur Sarkisov; 46.Sargis Adamyan), Marcos Piñeiro Pizelli (70.David Manoyan), Levon Hayrapetyan, Kamo Hovhannisyan, Aras Özbiliz. Trainer: Vardan Minasyan.
DEN: Stephan Maigaard Andersen, Daniel Agger, Andreas Bjelland, Peter Ankersen, Nicolai Møller Boilesen, Michael Krohn-Dehli, Niki Dige Zimling (45+2.Casper Sloth), William Kvist Jørgensen, Christian Dannemann Eriksen, Nicki Niels Bille Nielsen (83.Simon Makienok Christoffersen), Martin Braithwaite Christensen (66.Viktor Gorridsen Fischer). Trainer: Morten Per Olsen.
Goal: 0-1 Daniel Agger (73 penalty).
Cautions: Varazdat Haroyan, Artur Yedigaryan / Peter Ankersen, William Kvist Jørgensen, Nicolai Møller Boilesen.
Sent off: Varazdat Haroyan (73).

10.09.2013, National Stadium, Ta. Qali; Attendance: 4,884
Referee: Alexandru Tudor (Romania)

MALTA - BULGARIA **1-2(0-1)**

MLT: Justin Haber, Gareth Sciberras, Andrei Agius, Edward Herrera, Luke Dimech, Clayton Failla (66.Ryan Fenech), Rowen Muscat, Ryan Camilleri (8.Jonathan Caruana), Alexander Muscat, Michael Mifsud (77.Terence Vella), André Schembri. Trainer: Pietro Ghedin (Italy).
BUL: Nikolai Mihailov, Nikolay Bodurov, Ivelin Popov, Radoslav Dimitrov, Todor Nedelev (67.Spas Delev), Veselin Minev, Ivan Ivanov, Georgi Milanov (81.Hristo Zlatinski), Vladimir Gadzhev, Svetoslav Dyakov, Emil Gargorov (61.Dimitar Rangelov). Trainer: Lyuboslav Penev.
Goals: 0-1 Radoslav Dimitrov (9), 0-2 Emil Gargorov (59), 1-2 Edward Herrera (77).
Cautions: André Schembri, Ryan Fenech / Dimitar Rangelov, Nikolay Bodurov, Svetoslav Dyakov.

10.09.2013, Juventus Stadium, Torino; Attendance: 35,299
Referee: Jonas Eriksson (Sweden)

ITALY - CZECH REPUBLIC **2-1(0-1)**

ITA: Gianluigi Buffon, Leonardo Bonucci, Manuel Pasqual (78.Angelo Ogbonna), Giorgio Chiellini, Daniele De Rossi, Andrea Pirlo, Riccardo Montolivo (86.Thiago Motta), Christian Maggio, Antonio Candreva, Emanuele Giaccherini (46.Pablo Daniel Osvaldo), Mario Balotelli. Trainer: Cesare Claudio Prandelli.
CZE: Petr Čech, Tomáš Sivok, Václav Procházka, Marek Suchý, David Limberský, Theodor Gebre Selassie (77.Michael Rabušic), Jaroslav Plašil, Tomáš Rosický (38.Daniel Kolář), Petr Jiráček, Vladimír Darida (56.Ondřej Vaněk), Libor Kozák. Trainer: Michal Bílek.
Goals: 0-1 Libor Kozák (19), 1-1 Giorgio Chiellini (51), 2-1 Mario Balotelli (54 penalty).
Cautions: Mario Balotelli / Theodor Gebre Selassie, Daniel Kolář, Libor Kozák.
Sent off: Daniel Kolář (89).

11.10.2013, Republican Stadium, Yerevan; Attendance: 11,000
Referee: Dr. Felix Brych (Germany)
ARMENIA - BULGARIA **2-1(1-0)**
ARM: Roman Anatoliy Berezovsky, Robert Arzumanyan (12.Valeri Vazgen Aleksanyan), Hrayr Mkoyan, Gevorg Ghazaryan, Henrikh Mkhitaryan, Karlen Mkrtchyan, Levon Hayrapetyan, Kamo Hovhannisyan, Aras Özbiliz (54.Marcos Piñeiro Pizelli), Yura Movsisyan, Artur Sarkisov (90+4.David Manoyan). Trainer: Vardan Minasyan.
BUL: Vladislav Stoyanov, Stanislav Manolev (59.Aleksandar Tonev), Petar Zanev, Nikolay Bodurov, Yordan Minev, Ivelin Popov, Georgi Milanov (69.Ventsislav Hristov), Vladimir Gadzhev, Ivan Ivanov, Svetoslav Dyakov, Emil Gargorov (69.Hristo Zlatinski). Trainer: Lyuboslav Penev.
Goals: 1-0 Aras Özbiliz (45+1), 1-1 Ivelin Popov (61), 2-1 Yura Movsisyan (87).
Cautions: Robert Arzumanyan, Yura Movsisyan / Svetoslav Dyakov, Yordan Minev.
Sent off: Nikolay Bodurov (44), Svetoslav Dyakov (63).

11.10.2013, National Stadium, Ta'Qali; Attendance: 4,530
Referee: Matej Jug (Slovenia)
MALTA - CZECH REPUBLIC **1-4(0-2)**
MLT: Justin Haber, Jonathan Caruana (57.Andrei Agius), Luke Dimech, Alexander Muscat, Clayton Failla (87.Ryan Fenech), Roderick Briffa, Andrew Cohen, John Mintoff, Rowen Muscat, Ryan Camilleri (80.Paul Fenech), Michael Mifsud. Trainer: Pietro Ghedin (Italy).
CZE: Petr Čech, Tomáš Sivok, František Rajtoral, Marek Suchý, Michal Kadlec, Jaroslav Plašil, Tomáš Hübschman, Bořek Dočkal, Josef Hušbauer, David Lafata (85.Petr Jiráček), Václav Kadlec (74.Tomáš Pekhart; 90+3.Ondřej Vaněk). Trainer: Josef Pešice.
Goals: 0-1 Tomáš Hübschman (3), 0-2 David Lafata (33), 1-2 Michael Mifsud (47), 1-3 Václav Kadlec (51), 1-4 Tomáš Pekhart (90).
Cautions: Michael Mifsud / Tomáš Sivok.

11.10.2013, Parken Stadion, København; Attendance: 35,305
Referee: Stéphane Lannoy (France)
DENMARK - ITALY **2-2(1-1)**
DEN: Stephan Maigaard Andersen, Daniel Agger, Andreas Bjelland, Lars Christian Jacobsen, Nicolai Møller Boilesen, Michael Krohn-Dehli, Niki Dige Zimling (82.Leon Hougaard Andreasen), William Kvist Jørgensen, Christian Dannemann Eriksen, Nicklas Bendtner (84.Simon Makienok Christoffersen), Martin Braithwaite Christensen (46.Emil Larsen). Trainer: Morten Per Olsen.
ITA: Gianluigi Buffon, Lorenzo De Silvestri, Giorgio Chiellini, Federico Balzaretti, Andrea Ranocchia, Thiago Motta, Riccardo Montolivo (82.Alberto Gilardino), Claudio Marchisio (68.Alberto Aquilani), Antonio Candreva, Alessandro Diamanti (77.Alessio Cerci), Pablo Daniel Osvaldo. Trainer: Cesare Claudio Prandelli.
Goals: 0-1 Pablo Daniel Osvaldo (28), 1-1 Nicklas Bendtner (45+1), 2-1 Nicklas Bendtner (79), 2-2 Alberto Aquilani (90+1).
Cautions: Andreas Bjelland, Niki Dige Zimling, Nicklas Bendtner, Nicolai Møller Boilesen.

15.10.2013, Parken Stadion, København; Attendance: 11,479
Referee: Aleksandar Stavrev (Macedonia)
DENMARK - MALTA **6-0(4-0)**
DEN: Kasper Peter Schmeichel, Daniel Agger, Andreas Bjelland, Peter Ankersen, Michael Krohn-Dehli, William Kvist Jørgensen, Thomas Joseph Delaney, Emil Larsen, Christian Dannemann Eriksen (53.Kasper Kusk Vangsgaard), Casper Sloth (65.Leon Hougaard Andreasen), Morten Nicolas Rasmussen (75.Nicki Niels Bille Nielsen). Trainer: Morten Per Olsen.
MLT: Justin Haber, Alexander Muscat, Andrei Agius, Clayton Failla, Roderick Briffa, Edward Herrera (82.Ryan Fenech), John Mintoff, Rowen Muscat, Ryan Camilleri, Michael Mifsud, André Schembri. Trainer: Pietro Ghedin (Italy).
Goals: 1-0 Morten Nicolas Rasmussen (9), 2-0 Daniel Agger (11 penalty), 3-0 Andreas Bjelland (28), 4-0 Daniel Agger (39 penalty), 5-0 Morten Nicolas Rasmussen (74), 6-0 Nicki Niels Bille Nielsen (84).
Cautions: Daniel Agger / John Mintoff, Andrei Agius.

15.10.2013, Stadio "San Paolo", Napoli; Attendance: 22,000
Referee: Michael Oliver (England)

ITALY - ARMENIA 2-2(1-1)

ITA: Federico Marchetti, Leonardo Bonucci, Manuel Pasqual, Ignazio Abate, Davide Astori, Andrea Pirlo, Alberto Aquilani (73.Giuseppe Rossi), Riccardo Montolivo, Alessandro Florenzi (60.Antonio Candreva), Pablo Daniel Osvaldo (46.Mario Balotelli), Lorenzo Insigne. Trainer: Cesare Claudio Prandelli.

ARM: Roman Anatoliy Berezovsky, Robert Arzumanyan, Hrayr Mkoyan, Varazdat Haroyan, Artur Yedigaryan (90.Marcos Piñeiro Pizelli), Gevorg Ghazaryan, Henrikh Mkhitaryan, Karlen Mkrtchyan, Levon Hayrapetyan (63.Kamo Hovhannisyan), Aras Özbiliz (78.Artur Sarkisov), Yura Movsisyan. Trainer: Vardan Minasyan.

Goals: 0-1 Yura Movsisyan (5), 1-1 Alessandro Florenzi (24), 1-2 Henrikh Mkhitaryan (70), 2-2 Mario Balotelli (76).

Cautions: Manuel Pasqual / Varazdat Haroyan, Robert Arzumanyan.

15.10.2013, Nationalen stadion "Vasil Levski", Sofia; Attendance: 25,464
Referee: Viktor Kassai (Hungary)

BULGARIA - CZECH REPUBLIC 0-1(0-0)

BUL: Vladislav Stoyanov, Stanislav Manolev, Petar Zanev, Yordan Minev, Ivelin Popov, Ivan Ivanov, Vladimir Gadzhev, Iliya Milanov, Georgi Milanov (46.Dimitar Rangelov), Ventsislav Hristov (73.Simeon Slavchev), Emil Gargorov (56.Marcos Antônio Malachias Júnior „Marquinhos"). Trainer: Lyuboslav Penev.

CZE: Petr Čech, František Rajtoral, Marek Suchý, Michal Kadlec, Ondřej Mazuch, Jaroslav Plašil, Tomáš Hübschman, Bořek Dočkal (84.Ondřej Vaněk), Petr Jiráček (90+1.Josef Hušbauer), Libor Kozák, Václav Kadlec (90.David Lafata). Trainer: Josef Pešice.

Goal: 0-1 Bořek Dočkal (52).

Cautions: Georgi Milanov, Petar Zanev, Iliya Milanov, Stanislav Manolev / Michal Kadlec, František Rajtoral.

Sent off: Petar Zanev (75).

GROUP C

07.09.2012	Hannover	Germany - Faroe Islands	3-0(1-0)
07.09.2012	Astana	Kazakhstan - Republic of Ireland	1-2(1-0)
11.09.2012	Malmö	Sweden - Kazakhstan	2-0(1-0)
11.09.2012	Wien	Austria - Germany	1-2(0-1)
12.10.2012	Tórshavn	Faroe Islands - Sweden	1-2(0-0)
12.10.2012	Dublin	Republic of Ireland - Germany	1-6(0-2)
12.10.2012	Astana	Kazakhstan - Austria	0-0
16.10.2012	Tórshavn	Faroe Islands - Republic of Ireland	1-4(0-0)
16.10.2012	Wien	Austria - Kazakhstan	4-0(1-0)
16.10.2012	Berlin	Germany - Sweden	4-4(3-0)
22.03.2013	Wien	Austria - Faroe Islands	6-0(3-0)
22.03.2013	Stockholm	Sweden - Republic of Ireland	0-0
23.03.2013	Astana	Kazakhstan - Germany	0-3(0-2)
26.03.2013	Dublin	Republic of Ireland - Austria	2-2(2-1)
26.03.2013	Nürnberg	Germany - Kazakhstan	4-1(3-0)
07.06.2013	Dublin	Republic of Ireland - Faroe Islands	3-0(1-0)
07.06.2013	Wien	Austria - Sweden	2-1(2-0)
11.06.2013	Stockholm	Sweden - Faroe Islands	2-0(1-0)
06.09.2013	Dublin	Republic of Ireland - Sweden	1-2(1-1)
06.09.2013	München	Germany - Austria	3-0(1-0)
06.09.2013	Astana	Kazakhstan - Faroe Islands	2-1(0-1)
10.09.2013	Tórshavn	Faroe Islands - Germany	0-3(0-1)
10.09.2013	Wien	Austria - Republic of Ireland	1-0(0-0)
10.09.2013	Astana	Kazakhstan - Sweden	0-1(0-1)
11.10.2013	Tórshavn	Faroe Islands - Kazakhstan	1-1(1-0)
11.10.2013	Stockholm	Sweden - Austria	2-1(0-1)
11.10.2013	Köln	Germany - Republic of Ireland	3-0(1-0)
15.10.2013	Tórshavn	Faroe Islands - Austria	0-3(0-1)
15.10.2013	Dublin	Republic of Ireland - Kazakhstan	3-1(2-1)
15.10.2013	Stockholm	Sweden - Germany	3-5(2-1)

FINAL STANDINGS

1.	**GERMANY**	10	9	1	0	36	-	10	28
2.	**Sweden**	10	6	2	2	19	-	14	20
3.	Austria	10	5	2	3	20	-	10	17
4.	Republic of Ireland	10	4	2	4	16	-	17	14
5.	Kazakhstan	10	1	2	7	6	-	21	5
6.	Faroe Islands	10	0	1	9	4	-	29	1

Germany qualified for the Final Tournament; Sweden qualified for the Play-Offs.

07.09.2012, AWD-Arena, Hannover; Attendance: 32,769
Referee: Robert Madden (Scotland)

GERMANY - FAROE ISLANDS 3-0(1-0)

GER: Manuel Peter Neuer, Philipp Lahm, Per Mertesacker, Mats Julian Hummels, Holger Felix Badstuber, Mesut Özil, Sami Khedira, Marco Reus, Mario Götze (87.Julian Draxler), Miroslav Josef Klose (75.Lukas Josef Podolski), Thomas Müller (68.André Horst Schürrle). Trainer: Joachim Löw.
FRO: Gunnar Nielsen, Odmar Færø, Pól Jóhannus Justinussen, Rógvi Baldvinsson, Jónas Þór Næs, Símun Samuelsen (65.Hjalgrím Elttør), Fróði Benjaminsen, Daniel Udsen (46.Súni Olsen), Hallur Hansson, Christian Lamhauge Holst, Jóan Símun Edmundsson (84.Klæmint Andrasson Olsen). Trainer: Lars Christian Olsen (Denmark).
Goals: 1-0 Mario Götze (28), 2-0 Mesut Özil (54), 3-0 Mesut Özil (72).
Cautions: Philipp Lahm / Rógvi Baldvinsson.

07.09.2012, Astana Arena, Astana; Attendance: 12,384
Referee: Ionuţ Avram (Romania)

KAZAKHSTAN - REPUBLIC OF IRELAND 1-2(1-0)

KAZ: Andrei Sidelnikov, Heinrich Schmidtgal, Mikhail Rozhkov, Kairat Nurdauletov, Aleksandr Kislitsyn, Aleksandr Kirov, Mukhtar Mukhtarov, Tanat Nuserbaev (69.Bauyrzhan Dzholchiev), Ulan Konysbayev (85.Sergey Gridin), Anatoliy Bogdanov, Sergey Ostapenko. Trainer: Miroslav Beránek (Czech Republic).
IRL: Keiren Westwood, Darren O'Dea, John Francis O'Shea, Stephen Robert Ward, Sean Patrick St. Ledger-Hall, Aiden John McGeady, Glenn David Whelan, James McCarthy, Simon Richard Cox (58.Kevin Edward Doyle), Robert David Keane, Jonathan Ronald Walters (71.Shane Patrick Long). Trainer: Giovanni Luciano Giuseppe Trapattoni (Italy).
Goals: 1-0 Kayrat Nurdauletov (37), 1-1 Robbie Keane (88 penalty), 1-2 Kevin Doyle (90).
Cautions: Tanat Nuserbaev, Sergey Ostapenko, Mikhail Rozhkov.

11.09.2012, Swedbank Stadion, Malmö; Attendance: 20,414
Referee: Serhiy Boiko (Ukraine)

SWEDEN - KAZAKHSTAN 2-0(1-0)

SWE: Andreas Isaksson, Jonas Olsson, Andreas Granqvist, Behrang Safari, Carl Mikael Lustig, Pontus Anders Mikael Wernbloom, Rasmus Cristoffer Elm (63.Anders Gunnar Svensson), Sebastian Bengt Ulf Larsson, Zlatan Ibrahimović, Johan Erik Calvin Elmander (85.Marcus Berg), Nils Ola Toivonen (56.Emir Bajrami). Trainer: Erik Anders Hamrén.
KAZ: Andrei Sidelnikov, Heinrich Schmidtgal, Mikhail Rozhkov, Viktor Dmitrenko, Kairat Nurdauletov, Aleksandr Kislitsyn, Aleksandr Kirov, Tanat Nuserbaev (68.Sergey Gridin), Anatoliy Bogdanov, Sergey Ostapenko (46.Marat Shakhmetov), Pavel Shabalin (84.Bauyrzhan Islamkhan). Trainer: Miroslav Beránek (Czech Republic).
Goals: 1-0 Rasmus Cristoffer Elm (37), 2-0 Marcus Berg (90+4).
Cautions: Johan Erik Calvin Elmander, Zlatan Ibrahimović / Marat Shakhmetov.

11.09.2012, „Ernst Happel" Stadion, Wien; Attendance: 47,000
Referee: Björn Kuipers (Holland)

AUSTRIA - GERMANY 1-2(0-1)

AUT: Robert Almer, György Garics, Sebastian Prödl, Emanuel Pogatetz, Christian Fuchs, Julian Baumgartlinger (85.Marc Janko), Veli Kavlak, Marko Arnautovic, Zlatko Junuzovic, Andreas Ivanschitz (75.Jakob Jantscher), Martin Harnik (55.Guido Burgstaller). Trainer: Marcel Koller (Switzerland).
GER: Manuel Peter Neuer, Philipp Lahm, Mats Julian Hummels, Holger Felix Badstuber, Marcel Schmelzer, Mesut Özil, Sami Khedira, Toni Kroos, Marco Reus (46.Mario Götze), Miroslav Josef Klose (75.Lukas Josef Podolski), Thomas Müller. Trainer: Joachim Löw.
Goals: 0-1 Marco Reus (44), 0-2 Mesut Özil (52 penalty), 1-2 Zlatko Junuzovic (57).
Cautions: Sebastian Prödl, Christian Fuchs, Julian Baumgartlinger / Philipp Lahm.

12.10.2012, Tórsvøllur Stadium, Tórshavn; Attendance: 5,079
Referee: Anastasios Sidiropoulos (Greece)

FAROE ISLANDS - SWEDEN 1-2(0-0)

FRO: Gunnar Nielsen, Odmar Færø, Pól Jóhannus Justinussen, Rógvi Baldvinsson, Jónas Þór Næs, Símun Samuelsen, Fróði Benjaminsen, Daniel Udsen (85.Hjalgrím Elttør), Hallur Hansson (83.Súni Olsen), Christian Lamhauge Holst (71.Arnbjørn Theodor Hansen), Jóan Símun Edmundsson. Trainer: Lars Christian Olsen (Denmark).

SWE: Andreas Isaksson, Jonas Olsson, Martin Olsson, Andreas Granqvist, Carl Mikael Lustig, Kim Mikael Källström (62.Anders Gunnar Svensson), Christian Ulf Wilhelmsson (62.Alexander Kačaniklić), Pontus Anders Mikael Wernbloom, Sebastian Bengt Ulf Larsson, Zlatan Ibrahimović, Mathias Ranégie (77.Marcus Berg). Trainer: Erik Anders Hamrén.

Goals: 1-0 Rógvi Baldvinsson (57), 1-1 Alexander Kačaniklić (65), 1-2 Zlatan Ibrahimović (75).

Cautions: Fróði Benjaminsen, Daniel Udsen, Hallur Hansson / Pontus Anders Mikael Wernbloom.

12.10.2012, Referee: Nicola Rizzoli (Italy)
Aviva Stadium, Dublin; Attendance: 49,850

REPUBLIC OF IRELAND - GERMANY 1-6(0-2)

IRL: Keiren Westwood, Darren O'Dea, John Francis O'Shea, Séamus Coleman, Stephen Robert Ward, Aiden John McGeady (69.Andrew Declan Keogh), Keith Declan Fahey (52.Shane Patrick Long), James McCarthy, Keith Joseph Andrews, Simon Richard Cox (84.Robert Brady), Jonathan Ronald Walters. Trainer: Giovanni Luciano Giuseppe Trapattoni (Italy).

GER: Manuel Peter Neuer, Per Mertesacker, Jérôme Agyenim Boateng, Holger Felix Badstuber, Marcel Schmelzer, Bastian Schweinsteiger, Mesut Özil, Sami Khedira (46.Toni Kroos), Marco Reus (66.Lukas Josef Podolski), Miroslav Josef Klose (72.André Horst Schürrle), Thomas Müller. Trainer: Joachim Löw.

Goals: 0-1 Marco Reus (32), 0-2 Marco Reus (40), 0-3 Mesut Özil (55 penalty), 0-4 Miroslav Josef Klose (58), 0-5 Toni Kroos (61), 0-6 Toni Kroos (83), 1-6 Andrew Declan Keogh (90+2).

Cautions: Darren O'Dea, Shane Patrick Long / Marco Reus, Holger Felix Badstuber.

12.10.2012, Astana Arena, Astana; Attendance: 12,900
Referee: Tamás Bognár (Hungary)

KAZAKHSTAN - AUSTRIA 0-0

KAZ: Andrei Sidelnikov, Mikhail Rozhkov, Viktor Dmitrenko, Kairat Nurdauletov, Aleksandr Kirov, Valeriy Korobkin, Marat Khayrullin (90+1.Mukhtar Mukhtarov), Tanat Nuserbaev (86.Azat Nurgaliyev), Ulan Konysbayev (90+3.Sergey Gridin), Anatoliy Bogdanov, Sergey Ostapenko. Trainer: Miroslav Beránek (Czech Republic).

AUT: Robert Almer, György Garics, Sebastian Prödl, Emanuel Pogatetz, Christian Fuchs, Julian Baumgartlinger (63.Marc Janko), Veli Kavlak, Marko Arnautovic, Zlatko Junuzovic, Andreas Ivanschitz (73.Jakob Jantscher), Martin Harnik (84.Andreas Weimann). Trainer: Marcel Koller (Switzerland).

Cautions: Tanat Nuserbaev, Sergey Ostapenko, Mikhail Rozhkov / Marc Janko.

16.10.2012, Tórsvøllur Stadium, Tórshavn; Attendance: 4,300
Referee: Lorenc Jemini (Albania)

FAROE ISLANDS - REPUBLIC OF IRELAND 1-4(0-0)

FRO: Gunnar Nielsen, Odmar Færø (61.Erling Dávidsson Jacobsen), Pól Jóhannus Justinussen, Rógvi Baldvinsson, Jónas Þór Næs, Símun Samuelsen, Fróði Benjaminsen, Daniel Udsen (61.Arnbjørn Theodor Hansen), Hallur Hansson, Christian Lamhauge Holst, Jóan Símun Edmundsson (80.Hjalgrím Elttør). Trainer: Lars Christian Olsen (Denmark).

IRL: Keiren Westwood, Darren O'Dea, John Francis O'Shea, Séamus Coleman, Marc David Wilson, Aiden John McGeady, James McCarthy, Keith Joseph Andrews (90.David John Meyler), Robert David Keane (79.Shane Patrick Long), Jonathan Ronald Walters, Robert Brady (46.Simon Richard Cox). Trainer: Giovanni Luciano Giuseppe Trapattoni (Italy).

Goals: 0-1 Marc David Wilson (46), 0-2 Jonathan Ronald Walters (53), 1-2 Arnbjørn Theodor Hansen (69), 1-3 Pól Jóhannus Justinussen (73 own goal), 1-4 Darren O'Dea (88).

Cautions: Arnbjørn Theodor Hansen / Aiden John McGeady.

16.10.2012, „Ernst Happel“ Stadion, Wien; Attendance: 43,000
Referee: Jakob Kehlet (Denmark)
AUSTRIA - KAZAKHSTAN 4-0(1-0)
AUT: Robert Almer, Florian Klein, Sebastian Prödl (59.Aleksandar Dragovic), Emanuel Pogatetz, Christian Fuchs, Veli Kavlak, David Alaba (80.Christoph Leitgeb), Martin Harnik, Zlatko Junuzovic, Marko Arnautovic, Marc Janko (80.Jakob Jantscher). Trainer: Marcel Koller (Switzerland).
KAZ: Andrei Sidelnikov, Viktor Dmitrenko (74.Mark Gorman), Kairat Nurdauletov, Aleksandr Kirov, Mukhtar Mukhtarov, Valeriy Korobkin, Azat Nurgaliyev (83.Marat Khayrullin), Ulan Konysbayev, Anatoliy Bogdanov, Marat Shakhmetov (70.Bauyrzhan Islamkhan), Sergey Gridin. Trainer: Miroslav Beránek (Czech Republic).
Goals: 1-0 Marc Janko (24), 2-0 Marc Janko (63), 3-0 David Alaba (71), 4-0 Martin Harnik (90+3).
Cautions: Martin Harnik, Veli Kavlak / Anatoliy Bogdanov, Azat Nurgaliyev.

16.10.2012, Olympiastadion, Berlin; Attendance: 72,369
Referee: Pedro Proença Oliveira Alves Garcia (Portugal)
GERMANY - SWEDEN 4-4(3-0)
GER: Manuel Peter Neuer, Philipp Lahm, Per Mertesacker, Jérôme Agyenim Boateng, Holger Felix Badstuber, Bastian Schweinsteiger, Mesut Özil, Toni Kroos, Marco Reus (88.Lukas Josef Podolski), Miroslav Josef Klose, Thomas Müller (67.Mario Götze). Trainer: Joachim Löw.
SWE: Andreas Isaksson, Jonas Olsson, Andreas Granqvist, Behrang Safari, Carl Mikael Lustig, Samuel Tobias Holmén (46.Alexander Kačaniklić), Pontus Anders Mikael Wernbloom (46.Kim Mikael Källström), Rasmus Cristoffer Elm, Sebastian Bengt Ulf Larsson (78.Tobias Sana), Zlatan Ibrahimović, Johan Erik Calvin Elmander. Trainer: Erik Anders Hamrén.
Goals: 1-0 Miroslav Josef Klose (8), 2-0 Miroslav Josef Klose (15), 3-0 Per Mertesacker (39), 4-0 Mesut Özil (55), 4-1 Zlatan Ibrahimović (62), 4-2 Carl Mikael Lustig (64), 4-3 Johan Erik Calvin Elmander (76), 4-4 Rasmus Cristoffer Elm (90+3).
Cautions: Marco Reus, Philipp Lahm, Bastian Schweinsteiger / Andreas Isaksson.

22.03.2013, „Ernst Happel“ Stadion, Wien; Attendance: 24,200
Referee: Oleksandr Derdo (Ukraine)
AUSTRIA - FAROE ISLANDS 6-0(3-0)
AUT: Heinz Lindner, György Garics, Aleksandar Dragovic, Emanuel Pogatetz, Christian Fuchs (72.Markus Suttner), Veli Kavlak (56.Christoph Leitgeb), David Alaba, Marko Arnautovic, Andreas Ivanschitz (63.Andreas Weimann), Zlatko Junuzovic, Philipp Hosiner. Trainer: Marcel Koller (Switzerland).
FRO: Gunnar Nielsen, Odmar Færø, Pól Jóhannus Justinussen, Rógvi Baldvinsson, Jónas Þór Næs, Símun Samuelsen (72.Pætur Dam Jacobsen), Fróði Benjaminsen, Hallur Hansson, Christian Lamhauge Holst, Jóan Símun Edmundsson (78.Arnbjørn Theodor Hansen), Hjalgrím Elttør (87.Atli Gregersen). Trainer: Lars Christian Olsen (Denmark).
Goals: 1-0 Philipp Hosiner (8), 2-0 Philipp Hosiner (20), 3-0 Andreas Ivanschitz (28), 4-0 Zlatko Junuzovic (77), 5-0 David Alaba (78), 6-0 György Garics (82).
Cautions: Philipp Hosiner / Hallur Hansson, Jónas Þór Næs, Fróði Benjaminsen.

22.03.2013, Friends Arena, Stockholm; Attendance: 49,436
Referee: Alberto Undiano Mallenco (Spain)
SWEDEN - REPUBLIC OF IRELAND 0-0
SWE: Andreas Isaksson, Jonas Olsson, Andreas Granqvist, Behrang Safari, Carl Mikael Lustig (46.Mikael Antonsson), Kim Mikael Källström, Rasmus Cristoffer Elm, Sebastian Bengt Ulf Larsson (87.Jakup Jimmy Durmaz), Alexander Kačaniklić, Zlatan Ibrahimović, Glenn Tobias Hysén (73.Nils Ola Toivonen). Trainer: Erik Anders Hamrén.
IRL: David Forde, John Francis O'Shea, Séamus Coleman, Marc David Wilson, Ciaran Clark, Paul Jason Green, James McCarthy, James McClean (83.Andrew Declan Keogh), Shane Patrick Long (87.Conor Sammon), Robert David Keane (76.Wesley Hoolahan), Jonathan Ronald Walters. Trainer:

Giovanni Luciano Giuseppe Trapattoni (Italy).
Cautions: Paul Jason Green, James McCarthy, Séamus Coleman.

23.03.2013, Astana Arena, Astana; Attendance: 29,300
Referee: Anastassios Kakos (Greece)
KAZAKHSTAN - GERMANY **0-3(0-2)**
KAZ: Andrei Sidelnikov, Heinrich Schmidtgal, Viktor Dmitrenko, Kairat Nurdauletov, Aleksandr Kirov, Mark Gorman, Marat Khayrullin (65.Ulan Konysbayev), Yuriy Logvinenko, Maksat Bayzhanov (36.Valeriy Korobkin), Sergey Ostapenko (82.Kazbek Geteriyev), Bauyrzhan Dzholchiev. Trainer: Miroslav Beránek (Czech Republic).
GER: Manuel Peter Neuer, Philipp Lahm, Per Mertesacker, Benedikt Höwedes, Marcel Schmelzer, Bastian Schweinsteiger, Mesut Özil, Sami Khedira (82.İlkay Gündoğan), Mario Götze, Julian Draxler (19.Lukas Josef Podolski), Thomas Müller (82.André Horst Schürrle). Trainer: Joachim Löw.
Goals: 0-1 Thomas Müller (20), 0-2 Mario Götze (22), 0-3 Thomas Müller (73).
Cautions: Yuriy Logvinenko, Valeriy Korobkin, Viktor Dmitrenko / Bastian Schweinsteiger, Benedikt Höwedes.

26.03.2013, Aviva Stadium, Dublin; Attendance: 35,100
Referee: Marijo Strahonja (Croatia)
REPUBLIC OF IRELAND - AUSTRIA **2-2(2-1)**
IRL: David Forde, John Francis O'Shea, Séamus Coleman, Marc David Wilson, Ciaran Clark (72.Sean Patrick St. Ledger-Hall), Glenn David Whelan, James McCarthy, James McClean, Shane Patrick Long (83.Paul Jason Green), Conor Sammon, Jonathan Ronald Walters. Trainer: Giovanni Luciano Giuseppe Trapattoni (Italy).
AUT: Heinz Lindner, György Garics, Aleksandar Dragovic, Emanuel Pogatetz, Christian Fuchs, Veli Kavlak (69.Andreas Weimann), David Alaba, Martin Harnik, Zlatko Junuzovic (27.Julian Baumgartlinger), Marko Arnautovic, Philipp Hosiner (62.Marc Janko). Trainer: Marcel Koller (Switzerland).
Goals: 0-1 Martin Harnik (11), 1-1 Jonathan Ronald Walters (25 penalty), 2-1 Jonathan Ronald Walters (45+1), 2-2 David Alaba (90+3).
Cautions: James McCarthy, John Francis O'Shea, , Shane Patrick Long / Veli Kavlak, David Alaba.

26.03.2013, Frankenstadion, Nürnberg; Attendance: 43,520
Referee: Halis Özkahya (Turkey)
GERMANY - KAZAKHSTAN **4-1(3-0)**
GER: Manuel Peter Neuer, Philipp Lahm, Per Mertesacker, Jérôme Agyenim Boateng, Marcel Schmelzer, Mesut Özil, Sami Khedira, Marco Reus (90.Marcell Jansen), İlkay Gündoğan, Mario Götze, Thomas Müller. Trainer: Joachim Löw.
KAZ: Andrei Sidelnikov, Heinrich Schmidtgal, Viktor Dmitrenko, Kairat Nurdauletov (46.Bauyrzhan Dzholchiev), Konstantin Engel, Aleksandr Kirov, Mark Gorman, Mukhtar Mukhtarov, Valeriy Korobkin, Ulan Konysbayev (78.Dmitriy Shomko), Sergey Ostapenko (64.Zhambyl Kukeyev). Trainer: Miroslav Beránek (Czech Republic).
Goals: 1-0 Marco Reus (23), 2-0 Mario Götze (27), 3-0 İlkay Gündoğan (31), 3-1 Heinrich Schmidtgal (46), 4-1 Marco Reus (90).

07.06.2013, Aviva Stadium, Dublin; Attendance: 30,805
Referee: Mattias Gestranius (Finland)
REPUBLIC OF IRELAND - FAROE ISLANDS 3-0(1-0)
IRL: David Forde, John Francis O'Shea, Séamus Coleman, Sean Patrick St. Ledger-Hall, Marc David Wilson (82.Stephen Michael David Kelly), Aiden John McGeady (77.James McClean), Glenn David Whelan, Wesley Hoolahan, Simon Richard Cox, Robert David Keane, Jonathan Ronald Walters (74.Conor Sammon). Trainer: Giovanni Luciano Giuseppe Trapattoni (Italy).
FRO: Gunnar Nielsen, Pól Jóhannus Justinussen, Jónhard Frederiksberg, Atli Gregersen, Heini Vatnsdal, Rógvi Baldvinsson, Símun Samuelsen, Súni Olsen, Christian Lamhauge Holst (84.Hans Pauli Samuelsen), Páll Andrasson Klettskarð (64.Jóan Símun Edmundsson), Ári Mohr Jónsson. Trainer: Lars Christian Olsen (Denmark).
Goals: 1-0 Robert David Keane (5), 2-0 Robert David Keane (55), 3-0 Robert David Keane (81).
Cautions: Wesley Hoolahan / Heini Vatnsdal, Pól Jóhannus Justinussen, Rógvi Baldvinsson.

07.06.2013, „Ernst Happel" Stadion, Wien; Attendance: 48,500
Referee: Gianluca Rocchi (Italy)
AUSTRIA - SWEDEN 2-1(2-0)
AUT: Robert Almer, György Garics, Aleksandar Dragovic, Emanuel Pogatetz (28.Sebastian Prödl), Christian Fuchs, David Alaba, Julian Baumgartlinger, Martin Harnik, Zlatko Junuzovic (75.Franz Schiemer), Marko Arnautovic, Marc Janko (46.Andreas Weimann). Trainer: Marcel Koller (Switzerland).
SWE: Andreas Isaksson, Jonas Olsson, Oscar Wendt, Andreas Granqvist, Carl Mikael Lustig, Kim Mikael Källström (70.Nils Ola Toivonen), Rasmus Cristoffer Elm (61.Anders Gunnar Svensson), Sebastian Bengt Ulf Larsson, Alexander Kačaniklić, Zlatan Ibrahimović, Johan Erik Calvin Elmander (84.Jakup Jimmy Durmaz). Trainer: Erik Anders Hamrén.
Goals: 1-0 David Alaba (26 penalty), 2-0 Marc Janko (32), 2-1 Johan Erik Calvin Elmander (82).
Cautions: Julian Baumgartlinger, Aleksandar Dragovic / Andreas Isaksson, Johan Erik Calvin Elmander.

11.06.2013, Friends Arena, Stockholm; Attendance: 32,858
Referee: Nikolay Yordanov (Bulgaria)
SWEDEN - FAROE ISLANDS 2-0(1-0)
SWE: Pär Johan Åke Hansson, Andreas Granqvist, Pierre Thomas Robin Bengtsson, Per Jörgen Nilsson, Carl Mikael Lustig, Kim Mikael Källström (58.Anders Gunnar Svensson), Sebastian Bengt Ulf Larsson (63.Jakup Jimmy Durmaz), Albin Ekdal, Alexander Kačaniklić, Zlatan Ibrahimović, Nils Ola Toivonen (83.Jonas Olsson). Trainer: Erik Anders Hamrén.
FRO: Gunnar Nielsen, Pól Jóhannus Justinussen, Atli Gregersen, Johan Troest Davidsen, Viljormur í Heiðunum Davidsen, Jónas Þór Næs, Súni Olsen (41.Heini Vatnsdal), Fróði Benjaminsen, Hallur Hansson (87.Páll Andrasson Klettskarð), Christian Lamhauge Holst (59.Símun Samuelsen), Jóan Símun Edmundsson. Trainer: Lars Christian Olsen (Denmark).
Goals: 1-0 Zlatan Ibrahimović (35), 2-0 Zlatan Ibrahimović (82 penalty).
Cautions: Pól Jóhannus Justinussen, Símun Samuelsen, Christian Lamhauge Holst, Fróði Benjaminsen.
Sent off: Andreas Granqvist (79).

06.09.2013, Aviva Stadium, Dublin; Attendance: 50,000
Referee: Damir Skomina (Slovenia)

REPUBLIC OF IRELAND - SWEDEN 1-2(1-1)

IRL: David Forde, Richard Patrick Dunne, John Francis O'Shea, Séamus Coleman, Marc David Wilson, Glenn David Whelan, James McCarthy, James McClean (74.Anthony Neil James Pilkington), Shane Patrick Long, Robert David Keane, Jonathan Ronald Walters (68.Simon Richard Cox). Trainer: Giovanni Luciano Giuseppe Trapattoni (Italy).

SWE: Andreas Isaksson, Martin Olsson, Per Jörgen Nilsson, Mikael Antonsson, Carl Mikael Lustig (64.Adam Johansson), Anders Gunnar Svensson (68.Pontus Anders Mikael Wernbloom), Sebastian Bengt Ulf Larsson, Albin Ekdal, Alexander Kačaniklić, Zlatan Ibrahimović, Johan Erik Calvin Elmander (90+2.Jonas Olsson). Trainer: Erik Anders Hamrén.

Goals: 1-0 Robert David Keane (22), 1-1 Johan Erik Calvin Elmander (33), 1-2 Anders Gunnar Svensson (57).

Cautions: Richard Patrick Dunne, Glenn David Whelan / Albin Ekdal.

06.09.2013, Allianz Arena, München; Attendance: 68,000
Referee: Milorad Mažić (Serbia)

GERMANY - AUSTRIA 3-0(1-0)

GER: Manuel Peter Neuer, Philipp Lahm, Per Mertesacker, Jérôme Agyenim Boateng, Marcel Schmelzer (46.Benedikt Höwedes), Mesut Özil, Sami Khedira, Toni Kroos, Marco Reus (90+2.Julian Draxler), Miroslav Josef Klose (82.Sven Bender), Thomas Müller. Trainer: Joachim Löw.

AUT: Robert Almer, György Garics (78.Florian Klein), Aleksandar Dragovic, Emanuel Pogatetz, Christian Fuchs, Veli Kavlak, David Alaba, Martin Harnik, Andreas Ivanschitz (67.Guido Burgstaller), Marko Arnautovic (67.Marcel Sabitzer), Andreas Weimann. Trainer: Marcel Koller (Switzerland).

Goals: 1-0 Miroslav Josef Klose (33), 2-0 Toni Kroos (51), 3-0 Thomas Müller (88).

Cautions: Marco Reus, Sami Khedira, Miroslav Josef Klose / Andreas Weimann, Veli Kavlak, Emanuel Pogatetz, Florian Klein.

06.09.2013, Astana Arena, Astana; Attendance: 9,000
Referee: Johnny Casanova (San Marino)

KAZAKHSTAN - FAROE ISLANDS 2-1(0-1)

KAZ: Andrei Sidelnikov, Viktor Dmitrenko, Kairat Nurdauletov, Aleksandr Kislitsyn (85.Sergey Ostapenko), Valeriy Korobkin, Yuriy Logvinenko, Nurbol Zhumaskaliyev (90+2.Marat Khayrullin), Dmitriy Shomko, Anatoliy Bogdanov, Sergey Khizhnichenko, Aleksey Shchetkin (46.Andrey Finonchenko). Trainer: Miroslav Beránek (Czech Republic).

FRO: Gunnar Nielsen, Johan Troest Davidsen, Viljormur í Heiðunum Davidsen, Rógvi Baldvinsson, Jónas Þór Næs, Súni Olsen, Fróði Benjaminsen, Hallur Hansson (81.Heini Vatnsdal), Christian Lamhauge Holst, Jóan Símun Edmundsson (81.Páll Andrasson Klettskarð), Christian Restorff Mouritsen. Trainer: Lars Christian Olsen (Denmark).

Goals: 0-1 Fróði Benjaminsen (23), 1-1 Nurbol Zhumaskaliyev (49 penalty), 2-1 Andrey Finonchenko (63).

Cautions: Jónas Þór Næs, Hallur Hansson.

10.09.2013, Tórsvøllur Stadium, Tórshavn; Attendance: 4,118
Referee: Gediminas Mažeika (Lithuania)

FAROE ISLANDS - GERMANY 0-3(0-1)

FRO: Gunnar Nielsen, Pól Jóhannus Justinussen, Atli Gregersen, Johan Troest Davidsen, Viljormur í Heiðunum Davidsen, Rógvi Baldvinsson, Súni Olsen, Fróði Benjaminsen, Daniel Udsen (68.Christian Restorff Mouritsen), Christian Lamhauge Holst (76.Hallur Hansson), Jóan Símun Edmundsson (68.Páll Andrasson Klettskarð). Trainer: Lars Christian Olsen (Denmark).

GER: Manuel Peter Neuer, Philipp Lahm, Per Mertesacker, Jérôme Agyenim Boateng, Marcel Schmelzer, Mesut Özil, Sami Khedira, Toni Kroos, Julian Draxler (75.André Horst Schürrle), Miroslav Josef Klose (79.Maximilian Kruse), Thomas Müller (84.Sidney Sam). Trainer: Joachim Löw.

Goals: 0-1 Per Mertesacker (22), 0-2 Mesut Özil (74 penalty), 0-3 Thomas Müller (84).

Cautions: Pól Jóhannus Justinussen.
Sent off: Atli Gregersen (73).

10.09.2013, „Ernst Happel" Stadion, Wien; Attendance: 48,500
Referee: Olegário Manuel Bártolo Faustino Benquerença (Portugal)
AUSTRIA - REPUBLIC OF IRELAND 1-0(0-0)
AUT: Robert Almer, György Garics, Aleksandar Dragovic, Sebastian Prödl, Christian Fuchs, Julian Baumgartlinger, Veli Kavlak (46.Christoph Leitgeb), Martin Harnik, David Alaba, Guido Burgstaller (61.Marko Arnautovic), Andreas Weimann (73.Marc Janko). Trainer: Marcel Koller (Switzerland).
IRL: David Forde, Richard Patrick Dunne, John Francis O'Shea (49.Ciaran Clark), Séamus Coleman, Marc David Wilson, Paul Jason Green, James McCarthy, Anthony Neil James Pilkington (73.James McClean), Shane Patrick Long (81.Conor Sammon), Robert David Keane, Jonathan Ronald Walters. Trainer: Giovanni Luciano Giuseppe Trapattoni (Italy).
Goal: 1-0 David Alaba (84).
Cautions: John Francis O'Shea, Robert David Keane, Richard Patrick Dunne.

10.09.2013, Astana Arena, Astana; Attendance: 24,000
Referee: Miroslav Zelinka (Czech Republic)
KAZAKHSTAN - SWEDEN 0-1(0-1)
KAZ: Andrei Sidelnikov, Viktor Dmitrenko, Kairat Nurdauletov, Aleksandr Kislitsyn, Mark Gorman, Valeriy Korobkin, Maksat Bayzhanov (77.Marat Khayrullin), Dmitriy Shomko, Anatoliy Bogdanov, Sergey Khizhnichenko (90+2.Aleksey Shchetkin), Andrey Finonchenko. Trainer: Miroslav Beránek (Czech Republic).
SWE: Andreas Isaksson, Martin Olsson, Adam Johansson, Per Jörgen Nilsson, Mikael Antonsson, Anders Gunnar Svensson (87.Kim Mikael Källström), Sebastian Bengt Ulf Larsson (70.Jakup Jimmy Durmaz), Albin Ekdal, Alexander Kačaniklić, Zlatan Ibrahimović, Johan Erik Calvin Elmander (81.Glenn Tobias Hysén). Trainer: Erik Anders Hamrén.
Goal: 0-1 Zlatan Ibrahimović (1).
Cautions: Sergey Khizhnichenko, Viktor Dmitrenko / Albin Ekdal.

11.10.2013, Tórsvøllur Stadium, Tórshavn; Attendance: 1,870
Referee: Dumitru Muntean (Moldova)
FAROE ISLANDS - KAZAKHSTAN 1-1(1-0)
FRO: Gunnar Nielsen, Pól Jóhannus Justinussen, Johan Troest Davidsen, Viljormur í Heiðunum Davidsen, Rógvi Baldvinsson, Jónas Þór Næs, Fróði Benjaminsen, Daniel Udsen (77.Súni Olsen), Hallur Hansson, Christian Lamhauge Holst, Jóan Símun Edmundsson (77.Páll Andrasson Klettskarð). Trainer: Lars Christian Olsen (Denmark).
KAZ: Andrei Sidelnikov, Aleksandr Kislitsyn, Konstantin Engel, Mark Gorman, Aleksey Muldarov (80.Yuriy Logvinenko), Valeriy Korobkin, Nurbol Zhumaskaliyev (71.Maksat Bayzhanov), Dmitriy Shomko, Anatoliy Bogdanov, Sergey Khizhnichenko, Andrey Finonchenko (90+2.Aleksey Shchetkin). Trainer: Miroslav Beránek (Czech Republic).
Goals: 1-0 Hallur Hansson (41), 1-1 Andrey Finonchenko (55).
Cautions: Dmitriy Shomko.

11.10.2013, Friends Arena, Stockholm; Attendance: 49,416
Referee: Cüneyt Çakır (Turkey)
SWEDEN - AUSTRIA **2-1(0-1)**
SWE: Andreas Isaksson, Martin Olsson, Per Jörgen Nilsson, Mikael Antonsson, Carl Mikael Lustig (65.Jakup Jimmy Durmaz), Anders Gunnar Svensson (81.Pontus Anders Mikael Wernbloom), Rasmus Cristoffer Elm (73.Kim Mikael Källström), Sebastian Bengt Ulf Larsson, Alexander Kačaniklić, Zlatan Ibrahimović, Johan Erik Calvin Elmander. Trainer: Erik Anders Hamrén.
AUT: Robert Almer, György Garics, Sebastian Prödl, Emanuel Pogatetz, Christian Fuchs, Aleksandar Dragovic, Martin Harnik (74.Andreas Weimann), Zlatko Junuzovic (64.Christoph Leitgeb), David Alaba, Marko Arnautovic, Marc Janko (80.Andreas Ivanschitz). Trainer: Marcel Koller (Switzerland).
Goals: 0-1 Martin Harnik (29), 1-1 Martin Olsson (56), 2-1 Zlatan Ibrahimović (86).
Cautions: Zlatan Ibrahimović / Marc Janko.
Sent off: Marko Arnautovic (90).

11.10.2013, RheinEnergieStadion, Köln; Attendance: 46,237
Referee: Serge Gumienny (Belgium)
GERMANY - REPUBLIC OF IRELAND **3-0(1-0)**
GER: Manuel Peter Neuer, Marcell Jansen, Philipp Lahm, Per Mertesacker, Jérôme Agyenim Boateng, Bastian Schweinsteiger, Mesut Özil, Sami Khedira (82.Maximilian Kruse), Toni Kroos, Thomas Müller (88.Sidney Sam), André Horst Schürrle (86.Mario Götze). Trainer: Joachim Löw.
IRL: David Forde, Séamus Coleman, Damien Finbarr Delaney, Stephen Michael David Kelly, Marc David Wilson, Ciaran Clark, Glenn David Whelan, Darron Thomas Daniel Gibson, James McCarthy, Kevin Edward Doyle, Anthony Stokes. Trainer: Noel King.
Goals: 1-0 Sami Khedira (11), 2-0 André Horst Schürrle (58), 3-0 Mesut Özil (90+1).
Cautions: Sami Khedira / Anthony Stokes.

15.10.2013, Tórsvøllur Stadium, Tórshavn; Attendance: 3,100
Referee: Liran Liany (Israel)
FAROE ISLANDS - AUSTRIA **0-3(0-1)**
FRO: Gunnar Nielsen, Pól Jóhannus Justinussen, Johan Troest Davidsen, Viljormur í Heiðunum Davidsen, Rógvi Baldvinsson, Jónas Þór Næs, Súni Olsen (82.Jóan Símun Edmundsson), Fróði Benjaminsen, Hallur Hansson, Christian Lamhauge Holst (71.Christian Restorff Mouritsen), Páll Andrasson Klettskarð (74.Klæmint Andrasson Olsen). Trainer: Lars Christian Olsen (Denmark).
AUT: Heinz Lindner, Florian Klein, Sebastian Prödl (80.Manuel Ortlechner), Emanuel Pogatetz, Christian Fuchs (71.Markus Suttner), Aleksandar Dragovic, Martin Harnik (70.Marcel Sabitzer), Veli Kavlak, David Alaba, Andreas Ivanschitz, Philipp Hosiner. Trainer: Marcel Koller (Switzerland).
Goals: 0-1 Andreas Ivanschitz (16), 0-2 Sebastian Prödl (64), 0-3 David Alaba (67 penalty).
Cautions: Johan Troest Davidsen, Hallur Hansson, Jóan Símun Edmundsson / Aleksandar Dragovic, Emanuel Pogatetz.

15.10.2013, Aviva Stadium, Dublin; Attendance: 21,700
Referee: Vadims Direktorenko (Latvia)
REPUBLIC OF IRELAND - KAZAKHSTAN **3-1(2-1)**
IRL: David Forde, Richard Patrick Dunne, John Francis O'Shea, Séamus Coleman, Marc David Wilson, Andrew Matthew Reid (75.Aiden John McGeady), Darron Thomas Daniel Gibson (37.Glenn David Whelan), James McCarthy, Kevin Edward Doyle, Robert David Keane, Anthony Stokes (87.Wesley Hoolahan). Trainer: Noel King.
KAZ: Andrei Sidelnikov, Viktor Dmitrenko, Aleksandr Kislitsyn (32.Andrey Finonchenko), Konstantin Engel, Mark Gorman, Andrey Karpovich (84.Pavel Shabalin), Valeriy Korobkin, Maksat Bayzhanov, Dmitriy Shomko, Sergey Khizhnichenko, Aleksey Shchetkin (61.Igor Yurin). Trainer: Miroslav Beránek (Czech Republic).
Goals: 0-1 Dmitriy Shomko (13), 1-1 Robert David Keane (17 penalty), 2-1 John Francis O'Shea (26), 3-1 Dmitriy Shomko (77 own goal).
Cautions: Aleksandr Kislitsyn.

15.10.2013, Friends Arena, Stockholm; Attendance: 49,251
Referee: William Collum (Scotland)

SWEDEN - GERMANY **3-5(2-1)**

SWE: Johan Wiland, Martin Olsson, Pierre Thomas Robin Bengtsson, Per Jörgen Nilsson, Mikael Antonsson, Kim Mikael Källström, Rasmus Cristoffer Elm (58.Anders Gunnar Svensson), Sebastian Bengt Ulf Larsson, Alexander Kačaniklić (73.Jakup Jimmy Durmaz), Nils Ola Toivonen (84.Pontus Anders Mikael Wernbloom), Glenn Tobias Hysén. Trainer: Erik Anders Hamrén.

GER: Manuel Peter Neuer, Marcell Jansen, Philipp Lahm, Jérôme Agyenim Boateng, Mats Julian Hummels, Bastian Schweinsteiger, Mesut Özil (82.Julian Draxler), Toni Kroos, Thomas Müller (46.Mario Götze), Maximilian Kruse (75.Benedikt Höwedes), André Horst Schürrle. Trainer: Joachim Löw.

Goals: 1-0 Glenn Tobias Hysén (6), 2-0 Alexander Kačaniklić (42), 2-1 Mesut Özil (45), 2-2 Mario Götze (52), 2-3 André Horst Schürrle (57), 2-4 André Horst Schürrle (66), 3-4 Glenn Tobias Hysén (69), 3-5 André Horst Schürrle (76).

Cautions: Martin Olsson / André Horst Schürrle, Mats Julian Hummels, Benedikt Höwedes.

GROUP D

07.09.2012	Amsterdam	Holland - Turkey	2-0(1-0)
07.09.2012	Andorra La Vella	Andorra - Hungary	0-5(0-2)
07.09.2012	Tallinn	Estonia - Romania	0-2(0-0)
11.09.2012	Budapest	Hungary - Holland	1-4(1-2)
11.09.2012	Bucureşti	Romania - Andorra	4-0(2-0)
11.09.2012	Istanbul	Turkey - Estonia	3-0(1-0)
12.10.2012	Rotterdam	Holland - Andorra	3-0(2-0)
12.10.2012	Istanbul	Turkey - Romania	0-1(0-1)
12.10.2012	Tallinn	Estonia - Hungary	0-1(0-0)
16.10.2012	Andorra La Vella	Andorra - Estonia	0-1(0-0)
16.10.2012	Budapest	Hungary - Turkey	3-1(1-1)
16.10.2012	Bucureşti	Romania - Holland	1-4(1-3)
22.03.2013	Andorra La Vella	Andorra - Turkey	0-2(0-2)
22.03.2013	Budapest	Hungary - Romania	2-2(1-0)
22.03.2013	Amsterdam	Holland - Estonia	3-0(0-0)
26.03.2013	Tallinn	Estonia - Andorra	2-0(1-0)
26.03.2013	Istanbul	Turkey - Hungary	1-1(0-0)
26.03.2013	Amsterdam	Holland - Romania	4-0(1-0)
06.09.2013	Kayseri	Turkey - Andorra	5-0(2-0)
06.09.2013	Bucureşti	Romania - Hungary	3-0(2-0)
06.09.2013	Tallinn	Estonia - Holland	2-2(1-1)
10.09.2013	Budapest	Hungary - Estonia	5-1(3-0)
10.09.2013	Andorra La Vella	Andorra - Holland	0-2(0-0)
10.09.2013	Bucureşti	Romania - Turkey	0-2(0-1)
11.10.2013	Amsterdam	Holland - Hungary	8-1(4-0)
11.10.2013	Andorra La Vella	Andorra - Romania	0-4(0-1)
11.10.2013	Tallinn	Estonia - Turkey	0-2(0-1)
15.10.2013	Budapest	Hungary - Andorra	2-0(0-0)
15.10.2013	Bucureşti	Romania - Estonia	2-0(1-0)
15.10.2013	Istanbul	Turkey - Holland	0-2(0-1)

FINAL STANDINGS

1.	**HOLLAND**	10	9	1	0	34	-	5	28
2.	**Romania**	10	6	1	3	19	-	12	19
3.	Hungary	10	5	2	3	21	-	20	17
4.	Turkey	10	5	1	4	16	-	9	16
5.	Estonia	10	2	1	7	6	-	20	7
6.	Andorra	10	0	0	10	0	-	30	0

Holland qualified for the Final Tournament; Romania qualified for the Play-Offs.

07.09.2012, Amsterdam Arena, Amsterdam; Attendance: 49,500
Referee: Carlos Velasco Carballo (Spain)
HOLLAND - TURKEY 2-0(1-0)
NED: Timothy Michael Krul, John Gijsbert Alan Heitinga (86.Ron Peter Vlaar), Daryl Janmaat (46.Ricardo van Rhijn), Rolando Maximiliano Martins Indi, Jetro Willems, Arjen Robben, Wesley Sneijder, Kevin Strootman, Jordy Clasie (50.Leroy Johan Fer), Robin van Persie, Luciano Narsingh. Trainer: Aloysius Paulus Maria van Gaal.
TUR: Tolga Zengin, Hasan Ali Kaldırım, Ömer Toprak, Semih Kaya, Hamit Altıntop, Emre Belözoğlu (60.Nuri Şahin), Arda Turan, Mehmet Topal, Tunay Torun (82.Mevlüt Erdinç), Sercan Sararer-Osuna (70.Burak Yılmaz), Umut Bulut. Trainer: Abdullah Avcı.
Goals: 1-0 Robin van Persie (17), 2-0 Luciano Narsingh (90+3).
Cautions: Jetro Willems / Hasan Ali Kaldırım, Tunay Torun, Hamit Altıntop.

07.09.2012, Estadi Comunal de Aixovall, Andorra La Vella; Attendance: 815
Referee: Emir Alecković (Bosnia-Herzegovina)
ANDORRA - HUNGARY 0-5(0-2)
AND: Josep Antonio Gómes Moreira, Ildefons Lima Solà, Emili Josep García Miramontes, Marc Vales González, Adrián Rodrígues Gonçalves, Marc García Renom (80.David Maneiro Ton), Márcio Vieira de Vasconcelos, Sergio Moreno Marín (69.Sebastià Gomez Pérez), Marc Pujol Pons, Fernando José Silva García, Ludovic Clemente Garcés (72.Iván Lorenzo Roncero). Trainer: Jesús Luis Álvarez de Eulate "Koldo".
HUN: Ádám Bogdán, Roland Juhász, Vilmos Vanczák, Zsolt Korcsmár, Zoltán Lipták, Tamás Hajnal (75.Ákos Elek), Zoltán Gera (46.Tamás Priskin), Vladimir Koman, Zsolt Laczkó, Balázs Dzsudzsák, Ádám Csaba Szalai (82.Krisztián Németh). Trainer: Sándor Egervári.
Goals: 0-1 Roland Juhász (12), 0-2 Zoltán Gera (32 penalty), 0-3 Ádám Csaba Szalai (54), 0-4 Tamás Priskin (68), 0-5 Vladimir Koman (82).
Cautions: Ludovic Clemente Garcés, Marc García Renom, Sergio Moreno Marín, Marc Vales González, Marc Pujol Pons / Vladimir Koman.
Sent off: Marc Vales González (67).

07.09.2012, A. Le Coq Arena, Tallinn; Attendance: 7,936
Referee: Milorad Mažić (Serbia)
ESTONIA - ROMANIA 0-2(0-0)
EST: Sergei Pareiko, Enar Jääger, Igor Morozov, Ragnar Klavan, Aleksandr Dmitrijev, Sander Puri (76.Tarmo Kink), Konstantin Vassiljev, Martin Vunk (61.Vladimir Voskoboinikov), Andres Oper, Henrik Ojamaa (46.Joel Lindpere), Taijo Teniste. Trainer: Tarmo Rüütli.
ROU: Bogdan Ionuţ Lobonţ, Dorin Nicolae Goian (90+2.Marius Valeriu Gǎman), Rǎzvan Dincǎ Raţ, Alexandru Mǎţel, Vlad Iulian Chiricheş, Costin Lazǎr (66.Mihai Doru Pintilii), Gabriel Andrei Torje, Cristian Tǎnase, Alexandru Bourceanu, Ciprian Andrei Marica (85.Marius Constantin Niculae), Gheorghe Teodor Grozav. Trainer: Victor Piţurcǎ.
Goals: 0-1 Gabriel Andrei Torje (55), 0-2 Ciprian Andrei Marica (75).
Cautions: Aleksandr Dmitrijev / Gheorghe Teodor Grozav, Ciprian Andrei Marica.

11.09.2012, „Ferenc Puskás" Stadion, Budapest; Attendance: 22,700
Referee: Pedro Proença Oliveira Alves Garcia (Portugal)
HUNGARY - HOLLAND 1-4(1-2)
HUN: Ádám Bogdán, Roland Juhász, Vilmos Vanczák, Zsolt Korcsmár, Zoltán Lipták, Zoltán Gera (80.Krisztián Németh), Ákos Elek (61.Ádám Gyurcsó), Vladimir Koman (46.Tamás Hajnal), Balázs Dzsudzsák, József Varga, Tamás Priskin. Trainer: Sándor Egervári.
NED: Maarten Stekelenburg, Ron Peter Vlaar, Rolando Maximiliano Martins Indi (64.Joris Mathijsen), Ricardo van Rhijn, Jetro Willems, Wesley Sneijder, Kevin Strootman (78.Adam Maher), Jordy Clasie, Robin van Persie (46.Dirk Jan Klaas Huntelaar), Jeremain Marciano Lens, Luciano Narsingh. Trainer: Aloysius Paulus Maria van Gaal.
Goals: 0-1 Jeremain Marciano Lens (3), 1-1 Balázs Dzsudzsák (7 penalty), 1-2 Rolando Maximiliano Martins Indi (19), 1-3 Jeremain Marciano Lens (53), 1-4 Dirk Jan Klaas Huntelaar (75).

Cautions: Zsolt Korcsmár, Roland Juhász, Balázs Dzsudzsák / Jordy Clasie, Adam Maher.

11.09.2012, Arena Naţională, Bucureşti; Attendance: 24,630
Referee: Pavle Radovanović (Montenegro)
ROMANIA - ANDORRA **4-0(2-0)**
ROU: Bogdan Ionuţ Lobonţ (46.Anton Ciprian Tătăruşanu), Alexandru Măţel, Vlad Iulian Chiricheş, Marius Valeriu Găman, Răzvan Dincă Raţ, Costin Lazăr, Gabriel Andrei Torje, Cristian Tănase (80.Alexandru Iulian Maxim), Alexandru Bourceanu, Ciprian Andrei Marica (54.Raul Andrei Rusescu), Gheorghe Teodor Grozav. Trainer: Victor Piţurcă.
AND: Josep Antonio Gómes Moreira, Ildefons Lima Solà, Emili Josep García Miramontes, Adrián Rodrígues Gonçalves, Marc García Renom, Josep Manuel Ayala Díaz, Márcio Vieira de Vasconcelos, Iván Lorenzo Roncero, Marc Pujol Pons (79.Carlos Eduardo Peppe Britos), Ludovic Clemente Garcés (86.Sergio Moreno Marín), Sebastià Gomez Pérez (69.Fernando José Silva García). Trainer: Jesús Luis Álvarez de Eulate "Koldo".
Goals: 1-0 Gabriel Andrei Torje (29), 2-0 Costin Lazăr (44), 3-0 Marius Valeriu Găman (90+1), 4-0 Alexandru Iulian Maxim (90+3).
Cautions: Ildefons Lima Solà.

11.09.2012, „Şükrü Saracoğlu" Stadyumu, Istanbul; Attendance: 44,168
Referee: Marcin Borski (Poland)
TURKEY - ESTONIA **3-0(1-0)**
TUR: Tolga Zengin, Gökhan Gönül, Hasan Ali Kaldırım, Ömer Toprak, Semih Kaya, Emre Belözoğlu (82.Nuri Şahin), Arda Turan, Mehmet Topal, Sercan Sararer-Osuna (68.Tunay Torun), Burak Yılmaz, Umut Bulut (68.Selçuk İnan). Trainer: Abdullah Avcı.
EST: Sergei Pareiko, Dmitri Kruglov, Enar Jääger, Ragnar Klavan, Andres Oper (56.Ats Purje), Tarmo Kink (77.Kaimar Saag), Joel Lindpere (56.Sander Puri), Konstantin Vassiljev, Martin Vunk, Taijo Teniste, Taavi Rähn. Trainer: Tarmo Rüütli.
Goals: 1-0 Emre Belözoğlu (44), 2-0 Umut Bulut (60), 3-0 Selçuk İnan (75).
Cautions: Ats Purje.
Sent off: Enar Jääger (19).

12.10.2012, Stadion Feijenoord, Rotterdam; Attendance: 43,000
Referee: Aleksei Kulbakov (Belarus)
HOLLAND - ANDORRA **3-0(2-0)**
NED: Maarten Stekelenburg, John Gijsbert Alan Heitinga, Ron Peter Vlaar, Daryl Janmaat, Rolando Maximiliano Martins Indi, Rafael Ferdinand van der Vaart (70.Ibrahim Afellay), Nigel de Jong, Kevin Strootman (74.Urby Emanuelson), Dirk Jan Klaas Huntelaar, Jeremain Marciano Lens (70.Dirk Kuijt), Ruben Schaken. Trainer: Aloysius Paulus Maria van Gaal.
AND: Josep Antonio Gómes Moreira, Ildefons Lima Solà, Marc Vales González, Adrián Rodrígues Gonçalves (52.Moisés San Nicolás Schellens), Marc García Renom, Josep Manuel Ayala Díaz, Márcio Vieira de Vasconcelos, Víctor Hugo Moreira Teixeira (82.Marc Bernaus Cano), Iván Lorenzo Roncero, Marc Pujol Pons, Sebastià Gomez Pérez (75.Sergio Moreno Marín). Trainer: Jesús Luis Álvarez de Eulate "Koldo".
Goals: 1-0 Rafael Ferdinand van der Vaart (7), 2-0 Dirk Jan Klaas Huntelaar (15), 3-0 Ruben Schaken (50).
Cautions: Daryl Janmaat / Víctor Hugo Moreira Teixeira.

12.10.2012, „Şükrü Saracoğlu“ Stadyumu, Istanbul; Attendance: 46,203
Referee: Howard Melton Webb (England)
TURKEY - ROMANIA **0-1(0-1)**
TUR: Volkan Demirel, Gökhan Gönül, Hasan Ali Kaldırım, Ömer Toprak, Semih Kaya, Hamit Altıntop (61.Mevlüt Erdinç), Emre Belözoğlu (80.Nuri Şahin), Arda Turan, Mehmet Topal, Sercan Sararer-Osuna (69.Emre Çolak), Umut Bulut. Trainer: Abdullah Avcı.
ROU: Anton Ciprian Tătăruşanu, Dorin Nicolae Goian, Gabriel Sebastian Tamaş, Răzvan Dincă Raţ, Vlad Iulian Chiricheş, Gabriel Andrei Torje, Alexandru Bourceanu, Mihai Doru Pintilii, Ciprian Andrei Marica (79.Alexandru Mihăiţă Chipciu), Bogdan Sorin Stancu (82.Adrian Mutu), Gheorghe Teodor Grozav (50.Răzvan Vasile Cociş). Trainer: Victor Piţurcă.
Goal: 0-1 Gheorghe Teodor Grozav (45).
Cautions: Dorin Nicolae Goian.

12.10.2012, A. Le Coq Arena, Tallinn; Attendance: 5,661
Referee: Liran Liany (Israel)
ESTONIA - HUNGARY **0-1(0-0)**
EST: Sergei Pareiko, Tihhon Šišov, Taavi Rähn, Igor Morozov, Dmitri Kruglov, Sander Puri (69.Sergei Mošnikov), Andres Oper, Tarmo Kink (86.Martin Vunk), Joel Lindpere, Henrik Ojamaa (52.Ats Purje), Konstantin Vassiljev. Trainer: Tarmo Rüütli.
HUN: Ádám Bogdán, Roland Juhász, Norbert Mészáros, Zsolt Korcsmár (62.Ákos Elek), Tamás Kádár, Tamás Hajnal, Zoltán Gera (80.Imre Szabics), Balázs Dzsudzsák, József Varga, Tamás Koltai (84.Ádám Gyurcsó), Ádám Csaba Szalai. Trainer: Sándor Egervári.
Goal: 0-1 Tamás Hajnal (46).
Cautions: Taavi Rähn, Konstantin Vassiljev / Balázs Dzsudzsák, Ádám Csaba Szalai, Roland Juhász.

16.10.2012, Estadi Comunal de Aixovall, Andorra La Vella; Attendance: 723
Referee: Dimitar Meckarovski (Macedonia)
ANDORRA - ESTONIA **0-1(0-0)**
AND: Josep Antonio Gómes Moreira, Ildefons Lima Solà, Marc Vales González, Marc García Renom, Moisés San Nicolás Schellens, Josep Manuel Ayala Díaz (77.Gabriel Riera Lancha), Márcio Vieira de Vasconcelos, Víctor Hugo Moreira Teixeira (69.Ludovic Clemente Garcés), Iván Lorenzo Roncero, Marc Pujol Pons, Fernando José Silva García (80.Emili Josep García Miramontes). Trainer: Jesús Luis Álvarez de Eulate “Koldo”.
EST: Sergei Pareiko, Tihhon Šišov, Taavi Rähn, Ragnar Klavan, Dmitri Kruglov, Ats Purje, Konstantin Vassiljev, Joel Lindpere (70.Sander Puri), Tarmo Kink (83.Henrik Ojamaa), Andres Oper, Tarmo Neemelo (46.Martin Vunk). Trainer: Tarmo Rüütli.
Goal: 0-1 Andres Oper (57).
Cautions: Fernando José Silva García, Josep Manuel Ayala Díaz / Andres Oper.

16.10.2012, „Ferenc Puskás“ Stadion, Budapest; Attendance: 21,563
Referee: Daniele Orsato (Italy)
HUNGARY - TURKEY **3-1(1-1)**
HUN: Ádám Bogdán, Vilmos Vanczák, Norbert Mészáros, Zsolt Korcsmár, Tamás Kádár, Tamás Hajnal (78.Ádám Pintér), Ákos Elek (46.Máté Pátkai), Zoltán Gera, Vladimir Koman (73.Tamás Koltai), József Varga, Ádám Csaba Szalai. Trainer: Sándor Egervári.
TUR: Volkan Demirel, Egemen Korkmaz, Hasan Ali Kaldırım, Ömer Toprak, Nuri Şahin, Hamit Altıntop, Emre Belözoğlu, Caner Erkin (75.Umut Bulut), Mehmet Ekici (64.Sercan Sararer-Osuna), Tunay Torun (46.Aydın Yılmaz), Mevlüt Erdinç. Trainer: Abdullah Avcı.
Goals: 0-1 Mevlüt Erdinç (22), 1-1 Vladimir Koman (31), 2-1 Ádám Csaba Szalai (50), 3-1 Zoltán Gera (57 penalty).
Cautions: Ákos Elek, Máté Pátkai, Zoltán Gera / Caner Erkin, Hamit Altıntop, Egemen Korkmaz, Ömer Toprak.

16.10.2012, Arena Naţională, Bucureşti; Attendance: 53,329
Referee: Craig Thomson (Scotland)
ROMANIA - HOLLAND **1-4(1-3)**
ROU: Anton Ciprian Tătăruşanu, Dorin Nicolae Goian, Gabriel Sebastian Tamaş, Răzvan Dincă Raţ, Vlad Iulian Chiricheş, Gabriel Andrei Torje (66.Adrian Dumitru Popa), Alexandru Bourceanu (61.Costin Lazăr), Mihai Doru Pintilii, Ciprian Andrei Marica, Bogdan Sorin Stancu, Gheorghe Teodor Grozav (75.Adrian Mutu). Trainer: Victor Piţurcă.
NED: Maarten Stekelenburg, John Gijsbert Alan Heitinga, Ron Peter Vlaar, Rolando Maximiliano Martins Indi, Ricardo van Rhijn, Rafael Ferdinand van der Vaart (77.Ibrahim Afellay), Nigel de Jong, Kevin Strootman, Robin van Persie, Jeremain Marciano Lens (89.Eljero George Rinaldo Elia), Luciano Narsingh. Trainer: Aloysius Paulus Maria van Gaal.
Goals: 0-1 Jeremain Marciano Lens (9), 0-2 Rolando Maximiliano Martins Indi (29), 1-2 Ciprian Andrei Marica (40), 1-3 Rafael Ferdinand van der Vaart (45+1 penalty), 1-4 Robin van Persie (86).
Cautions: Alexandru Bourceanu, Gabriel Sebastian Tamaş, Răzvan Dincă Raţ / Kevin Strootman, Jeremain Marciano Lens, Nigel de Jong.

22.03.2013, Estadi Comunal de Aixovall, Andorra La Vella; Attendance: 910
Referee: Nerijus Dunauskas (Lithuania)
ANDORRA - TURKEY **0-2(0-2)**
AND: Josep Antonio Gómes Moreira, Ildefons Lima Solà, Marc Vales González, Cristian Martínez Alejo (69.Ludovic Clemente Garcés), Marc García Renom, Moisés San Nicolás Schellens, Josep Manuel Ayala Díaz (78.Xavier Andorrà Julià), Carlos Eduardo Peppe Britos (83.Emili Josep García Miramontes), Márcio Vieira de Vasconcelos, Víctor Hugo Moreira Teixeira, Sebastià Gomez Pérez. Trainer: Jesús Luis Álvarez de Eulate "Koldo".
TUR: Onur Recep Kıvrak, Gökhan Gönül, Hasan Ali Kaldırım, Semih Kaya, Bekir İrtegün, Nuri Şahin (90+1.Kerim Frei Koyunlu), Arda Turan, Selçuk İnan, Sercan Sararer-Osuna (58.Alper Potuk), Burak Yılmaz, Umut Bulut (81.Olcay Şahan). Trainer: Abdullah Avcı.
Goals: 0-1 Selçuk İnan (30), 0-2 Burak Yılmaz (45+1).
Cautions: Carlos Eduardo Peppe Britos, Xavier Andorrà Julià / Bekir İrtegün.

22.03.2013, „Ferenc Puskás" Stadion, Budapest; Attendance: *behind closed doors*
Referee: Wolfgang Stark (Germany)
HUNGARY - ROMANIA **2-2(1-0)**
HUN: Gábor Király, Vilmos Vanczák, Norbert Mészáros, Zsolt Korcsmár, Tamás Kádár, Tamás Hajnal (80.István Kovács), Vladimir Koman, Balázs Dzsudzsák (90.Péter Halmosi), Ádám Pintér, Imre Szabics (58.József Varga), Ádám Csaba Szalai. Trainer: Sándor Egervári.
ROU: Anton Ciprian Tătăruşanu, Dorin Nicolae Goian, Gabriel Sebastian Tamaş, Ştefan Daniel Radu, Vlad Iulian Chiricheş, Gabriel Andrei Torje (66.Alexandru Iulian Maxim), Alexandru Bourceanu, Mihai Doru Pintilii (86.Alexandru Mihăiţă Chipciu), Adrian Mutu, Bogdan Sorin Stancu, Gheorghe Teodor Grozav (71.Raul Andrei Rusescu). Trainer: Victor Piţurcă.
Goals: 1-0 Vilmos Vanczák (16), 1-1 Adrian Mutu (68 penalty), 2-1 Balázs Dzsudzsák (71 penalty), 2-2 Alexandru Mihăiţă Chipciu (90+2).
Cautions: Dorin Nicolae Goian, Adrian Mutu, Vlad Iulian Chiricheş.

22.03.2013, Amsterdam Arena, Amsterdam; Attendance: 48,675
Referee: Vitaly Meshkov (Russia)
HOLLAND - ESTONIA 3-0(0-0)
NED: Kenneth Harold Vermeer, Daryl Janmaat, Stefan de Vrij, Rolando Maximiliano Martins Indi, Wesley Sneijder (36.Rafael Ferdinand van der Vaart), Jonathan Alexander de Guzmán (86.Jordy Clasie), Kevin Strootman, Daley Blind, Arjen Robben, Robin van Persie, Jeremain Marciano Lens (73.Ruben Schaken). Trainer: Aloysius Paulus Maria van Gaal.
EST: Sergei Pareiko, Enar Jääger, Igor Morozov, Ragnar Klavan, Taijo Teniste, Sander Puri, Martin Vunk, Konstantin Vassiljev, Dmitri Kruglov (62.Tarmo Kink), Henrik Ojamaa (77.Joel Lindpere), Andres Oper (46.Sergei Zenjov). Trainer: Tarmo Rüütli.
Goals: 1-0 Rafael Ferdinand van der Vaart (47), 2-0 Robin van Persie (72), 3-0 Ruben Schaken (84).
Cautions: Arjen Robben.

26.03.2013, A. Le Coq Arena, Tallinn; Attendance: 5,237
Referee: Ján Valášek (Slovakia)
ESTONIA - ANDORRA 2-0(1-0)
EST: Sergei Pareiko, Enar Jääger, Igor Morozov, Raio Piiroja, Taijo Teniste, Henri Anier (55.Joel Lindpere), Konstantin Vassiljev, Sergei Mošnikov, Ats Purje (76.Sergei Zenjov), Tarmo Kink, Jarmo Ahjupera (55.Andres Oper). Trainer: Tarmo Rüütli.
AND: Josep Antonio Gómes Moreira, Ildefons Lima Solà, Marc Vales González, Cristian Martínez Alejo, Marc García Renom, Moisés San Nicolás Schellens, Josep Manuel Ayala Díaz, Carlos Eduardo Peppe Britos (66.Emili Josep García Miramontes), Márcio Vieira de Vasconcelos, Víctor Hugo Moreira Teixeira (79.Marc Bernaus Cano), Sebastià Gomez Pérez (85.Fernando José Silva García). Trainer: Jesús Luis Álvarez de Eulate "Koldo".
Goals: 1-0 Henri Anier (45), 2-0 Joel Lindpere (61).
Cautions: Víctor Hugo Moreira Teixeira.

26.03.2013, „Şükrü Saracoğlu" Stadyumu, Istanbul; Attendance: 37,904
Referee: Milorad Mažić (Serbia)
TURKEY - HUNGARY 1-1(0-0)
TUR: Onur Recep Kıvrak, Gökhan Gönül, Hasan Ali Kaldırım, Semih Kaya, Bekir İrtegün, Nuri Şahin (90.Kerim Frei Koyunlu), Arda Turan, Selçuk İnan, Alper Potuk (70.Hamit Altıntop), Burak Yılmaz, Umut Bulut (80.Mevlüt Erdinç). Trainer: Abdullah Avcı.
HUN: Gábor Király, Vilmos Vanczák, Norbert Mészáros, Zsolt Korcsmár (46.Richárd Guzmics), Tamás Kádár, Tamás Hajnal (68.Dániel Böde), Vladimir Koman, Balázs Dzsudzsák, Ádám Pintér, József Varga, Ádám Csaba Szalai (78.Ákos Elek). Trainer: Sándor Egervári.
Goals: 1-0 Burak Yılmaz (64), 1-1 Dániel Böde (71).
Cautions: Bekir İrtegün, Burak Yılmaz / József Varga, Balázs Dzsudzsák, Dániel Böde, Gábor Király.

26.03.2013, Amsterdam Arena, Amsterdam; Attendance: 47,496
Referee: Mark Clattenburg (England)
HOLLAND - ROMANIA 4-0(1-0)
NED: Kenneth Harold Vermeer, Daryl Janmaat, Stefan de Vrij, Rolando Maximiliano Martins Indi, Arjen Robben, Rafael Ferdinand van der Vaart (80.Jordy Clasie), Jonathan Alexander de Guzmán (74.Adam Maher), Kevin Strootman, Daley Blind, Robin van Persie (86.Siem de Jong), Jeremain Marciano Lens. Trainer: Aloysius Paulus Maria van Gaal.
ROU: Costel Fane Pantilimon, Gabriel Sebastian Tamaş, Răzvan Dincă Raţ, Vlad Iulian Chiricheş, Florin Gardoş, Cristian Tănase (60.Alexandru Mihăiţă Chipciu), Alexandru Bourceanu, Mihai Doru Pintilii, Adrian Dumitru Popa (63.Gabriel Andrei Torje), Bogdan Sorin Stancu, Gheorghe Teodor Grozav (69.Adrian Mutu). Trainer: Victor Piţurcă.
Goals: 1-0 Rafael Ferdinand van der Vaart (12), 2-0 Robin van Persie (56), 3-0 Robin van Persie (65 penalty), 4-0 Jeremain Marciano Lens (90).
Cautions: Rolando Maximiliano Martins Indi, Daley Blind / Alexandru Mihăiţă Chipciu.

06.09.2013, Kadir Has Stadyumu, Kayseri; Attendance: 21,923
Referee: Sven Bindels (Luxembourg)
TURKEY - ANDORRA **5-0(2-0)**
TUR: Volkan Demirel, Gökhan Gönül, Ömer Toprak, Semih Kaya, Nuri Şahin (65.Olcay Şahan), Arda Turan, Mehmet Topal, Caner Erkin, Gökhan Töre (82.Hakan Çalhanoğlu), Burak Yılmaz (78.Alper Potuk), Umut Bulut. Trainer: Fatih Terim.
AND: Ferran Pol Pérez, Ildefons Lima Solà, Emili Josep García Miramontes, Marc Vales González, Cristian Martínez Alejo, Marc García Renom, Moisés San Nicolás Schellens, Josep Manuel Ayala Díaz (80.Carlos Eduardo Peppe Britos), Iván Lorenzo Roncero (61.Márcio Vieira de Vasconcelos), Marc Pujol Pons, Sebastià Gomez Pérez (69.Gabriel Riera Lancha). Trainer: Jesús Luis Álvarez de Eulate "Koldo".
Goals: 1-0 Umut Bulut (35), 2-0 Umut Bulut (39), 3-0 Burak Yılmaz (64), 4-0 Umut Bulut (67), 5-0 Arda Turan (90+3).
Cautions: Moisés San Nicolás Schellens, Ferran Pol Pérez, Emili Josep García Miramontes.

06.09.2013, Arena Naţională, Bucureşti; Attendance: 41,405
Referee: Alberto Undiano Mallenco (Spain)
ROMANIA - HUNGARY **3-0(2-0)**
ROU: Anton Ciprian Tătăruşanu, Dorin Nicolae Goian, Răzvan Dincă Raţ, Alexandru Măţel, Vlad Iulian Chiricheş, Gabriel Andrei Torje (58.Cristian Tănase), Alexandru Bourceanu, Mihai Doru Pintilii, Alexandru Iulian Maxim (64.Adrian Dumitru Popa), Ciprian Andrei Marica (79.Ovidiu Ştefan Hoban), Bogdan Sorin Stancu. Trainer: Victor Piţurcă.
HUN: Ádám Bogdán, Vilmos Vanczák, Zsolt Korcsmár (34.Tamás Hajnal), Richárd Guzmics, Zoltán Lipták, Tamás Kádár, Vladimir Koman (85.Imre Szabics), Balázs Dzsudzsák, József Varga (68.Gergő Lovrencsics), Dániel Böde, Ádám Csaba Szalai. Trainer: Sándor Egervári.
Goals: 1-0 Ciprian Andrei Marica (2), 2-0 Mihai Doru Pintilii (31), 3-0 Cristian Tănase (88).
Cautions: Alexandru Bourceanu / Zsolt Korcsmár, Zoltán Lipták, Vilmos Vanczák.

06.09.2013, A. Le Coq Arena, Tallinn; Attendance: 10,210
Referee: Serhiy Boyko (Ukraine)
ESTONIA - HOLLAND **2-2(1-1)**
EST: Sergei Pareiko, Enar Jääger, Raio Piiroja, Ragnar Klavan, Dmitri Kruglov, Henrik Ojamaa (90+6.Mikk Reintam), Aleksandr Dmitrijev, Martin Vunk, Joel Lindpere (85.Gert Kams), Konstantin Vassiljev, Henri Anier (56.Sergei Zenjov). Trainer: Tarmo Rüütli.
NED: Michel Armand Vorm, Daryl Janmaat, Stefan de Vrij (67.Jeffrey Kevin van Homoet Bruma), Rolando Maximiliano Martins Indi, Jetro Willems (75.Jonathan Alexander de Guzmán), Arjen Robben, Wesley Sneijder, Stefanus Johannes Schaars, Kevin Strootman, Robin van Persie, Jeremain Marciano Lens (67.Dirk Kuijt). Trainer: Aloysius Paulus Maria van Gaal.
Goals: 0-1 Arjen Robben (2), 1-1 Konstantin Vassiljev (14), 2-1 Konstantin Vassiljev (57), 2-2 Robin van Persie (90+4 penalty).
Cautions: Raio Piiroja, Enar Jääger, Aleksandr Dmitrijev, Konstantin Vassiljev, Sergei Pareiko / Rolando Maximiliano Martins Indi, Arjen Robben, Dirk Kuijt.
Sent off: Raio Piiroja (90+3).

10.09.2013, „Ferenc Puskás" Stadion, Budapest; Attendance: 7,741
Referee: Aleksei Kulbakov (Belarus)
HUNGARY - ESTONIA **5-1(3-0)**
HUN: Ádám Bogdán, Vilmos Vanczák, Richárd Guzmics, Tamás Kádár, Tamás Hajnal, Vladimir Koman, Zsolt Laczkó (62.Szilárd Devecseri), Balázs Dzsudzsák, Ákos Elek (76.Gábor Gyömbér), Dániel Böde, Krisztián Németh (86.Péter Szakály). Trainer: Sándor Egervári.
EST: Sergei Pareiko, Enar Jääger, Mikk Reintam, Ragnar Klavan, Taijo Teniste, Ats Purje (46.Henrik Ojamaa), Martin Vunk, Sergei Mošnikov, Tarmo Kink (76.Gert Kams), Jarmo Ahjupera (46.Sergei Zenjov), Henri Anier. Trainer: Tarmo Rüütli.
Goals: 1-0 Ragnar Klavan (11 own goal), 2-0 Tamás Hajnal (21), 3-0 Dániel Böde (41), 3-1 Tarmo Kink (48), 4-1 Krisztián Németh (69), 5-1 Balázs Dzsudzsák (85).

Cautions: Zsolt Laczkó, Richárd Guzmics / Ats Purje, Enar Jääger, Martin Vunk, Tarmo Kink, Mikk Reintam.

10.09.2013, Estadi Comunal de Aixovall, Andorra La Vella; Attendance: 1,100
Referee: Ante Vučemilović-Šimunović Jr. (Croatia)

ANDORRA - HOLLAND 0-2(0-0)

AND: Ferran Pol Pérez, Ildefons Lima Solà, Emili Josep García Miramontes, Marc Vales González, Cristian Martínez Alejo, Marc García Renom, Moisés San Nicolás Schellens, Márcio Vieira de Vasconcelos, Gabriel Riera Lancha (72.Víctor Hugo Moreira Teixeira), Iván Lorenzo Roncero (59.Sergio Moreno Marín), Marc Pujol Pons (85.Josep Manuel Ayala Díaz). Trainer: Jesús Luis Álvarez de Eulate "Koldo".
NED: Michel Armand Vorm, Ron Peter Vlaar, Daryl Janmaat, Stefan de Vrij, Jetro Willems (46.Adam Maher), Wesley Sneijder (78.Dirk Kuijt), Stefanus Johannes Schaars, Kevin Strootman, Robin van Persie, Jeremain Marciano Lens, Ruben Schaken. Trainer: Aloysius Paulus Maria van Gaal.
Goals: 0-1 Robin van Persie (50), 0-2 Robin van Persie (54).
Cautions: Moisés San Nicolás Schellens, Ildefons Lima Solà, Iván Lorenzo Roncero, Márcio Vieira de Vasconcelos / Ron Peter Vlaar.

10.09.2013, Arena Naţională, Bucureşti; Attendance: 44,537
Referee: Svein Oddvar Moen (Norway)

ROMANIA - TURKEY 0-2(0-1)

ROU: Anton Ciprian Tătăruşanu, Dorin Nicolae Goian, Răzvan Dincă Raţ, Alexandru Măţel, Vlad Iulian Chiricheş, Gabriel Andrei Torje (46.Adrian Dumitru Popa), Cristian Tănase (78.Gheorghe Bucur), Ovidiu Ştefan Hoban, Mihai Doru Pintilii, Ciprian Andrei Marica (46.Alexandru Iulian Maxim), Bogdan Sorin Stancu. Trainer: Victor Piţurcă.
TUR: Volkan Demirel, Gökhan Gönül, Ömer Toprak, Semih Kaya, Arda Turan, Mehmet Topal, Selçuk İnan, Caner Erkin, Gökhan Töre (84.Mevlüt Erdinç), Burak Yılmaz (72.Olcay Şahan), Umut Bulut (90.Ersan Adem Gülüm). Trainer: Fatih Terim.
Goals: 0-1 Burak Yılmaz (22), 0-2 Mevlüt Erdinç (90+4).
Cautions: Răzvan Dincă Raţ / Semih Kaya, Volkan Demirel, Arda Turan.

11.10.2013, Amsterdam Arena, Amsterdam; Attendance: 52,027
Referee: Martin Atkinson (England)

HOLLAND - HUNGARY 8-1(4-0)

NED: Michel Armand Vorm, Ron Peter Vlaar, Daryl Janmaat, Jeffrey Kevin van Homoet Bruma, Arjen Robben, Rafael Ferdinand van der Vaart, Nigel de Jong, Kevin Strootman (81.Leroy Johan Fer), Daley Blind, Robin van Persie (61.Dirk Kuijt), Jeremain Marciano Lens. Trainer: Aloysius Paulus Maria van Gaal.
HUN: Ádám Bogdán, Vilmos Vanczák, Zsolt Korcsmár, Richárd Guzmics, Tamás Kádár (46.Szilárd Devecseri), Tamás Hajnal (46.Ákos Elek), Vladimir Koman, Balázs Dzsudzsák, József Varga, Dániel Böde, Krisztián Németh (79.Nemanja Nikolić). Trainer: Sándor Egervári.
Goals: 1-0 Robin van Persie (16), 2-0 Kevin Strootman (25), 3-0 Jeremain Marciano Lens (38), 4-0 Robin van Persie (44), 4-1 Balázs Dzsudzsák (47 penalty), 5-1 Robin van Persie (53), 6-1 Szilárd Devecseri (65 own goal), 7-1 Rafael Ferdinand van der Vaart (86), 8-1 Arjen Robben (90).
Cautions: Nigel de Jong / Szilárd Devecseri, Krisztián Németh, Richárd Guzmics.

11.10.2013, Estadi Comunal de Aixovall, Andorra La Vella; Attendance: 1,100
Referee: Stephan Klossner (Switzerland)

ANDORRA - ROMANIA **0-4(0-1)**

AND: Ferran Pol Pérez, Emili Josep García Miramontes, Marc Vales González (63.Óscar Sonejee Masand), Cristian Martínez Alejo, Adrián Rodrígues Gonçalves (79.Iván Lorenzo Roncero), Marc García Renom, Josep Manuel Ayala Díaz, Márcio Vieira de Vasconcelos, Gabriel Riera Lancha, Sergio Moreno Marín, Marc Pujol Pons (47.Carlos Eduardo Peppe Britos). Trainer: Jesús Luis Álvarez de Eulate "Koldo".

ROU: Bogdan Ionuţ Lobonţ, Dorin Nicolae Goian, Iasmin Latovlevici, Alexandru Măţel, Vlad Iulian Chiricheş, Costin Lazăr, Gabriel Andrei Torje, Alexandru Bourceanu, Alexandru Iulian Maxim (69.Cristian Tănase), Claudiu Andrei Keşerü (59.Ciprian Andrei Marica), Bogdan Sorin Stancu (82.Gheorghe Teodor Grozav). Trainer: Victor Piţurcă.

Goals: 0-1 Claudiu Andrei Keşerü (43), 0-2 Bogdan Sorin Stancu (53), 0-3 Gabriel Andrei Torje (63 penalty), 0-4 Costin Lazăr (85).

Cautions: Josep Manuel Ayala Díaz, Marc Pujol Pons, Adrián Rodrígues Gonçalves, Gabriel Riera Lancha, Cristian Martínez Alejo / Vlad Iulian Chiricheş.

11.10.2013, A. Le Coq Arena, Tallinn; Attendance: 8,572
Referee: Nicola Rizzoli (Italy)

ESTONIA - TURKEY **0-2(0-1)**

EST: Sergei Pareiko, Gert Kams (66.Tarmo Kink), Raio Piiroja (34.Mikk Reintam), Ragnar Klavan, Taijo Teniste, Henrik Ojamaa (75.Sander Puri), Aleksandr Dmitrijev, Martin Vunk, Dmitri Kruglov, Konstantin Vassiljev, Sergei Zenjov. Trainer: Tarmo Rüütli.

TUR: Volkan Demirel, Gökhan Gönül, Ömer Toprak, Semih Kaya, Arda Turan (87.Olcan Adın), Mehmet Topal, Selçuk İnan, Caner Erkin, Gökhan Töre (83.Alper Potuk), Burak Yılmaz (80.Olcay Şahan), Umut Bulut. Trainer: Fatih Terim.

Goals: 0-1 Umut Bulut (22), 0-2 Burak Yılmaz (47).

Cautions: Caner Erkin.

15.10.2013, „Ferenc Puskás" Stadion, Budapest; Attendance: 5,200
Referee: Daniel Stefanski (Poland)

HUNGARY - ANDORRA **2-0(0-0)**

HUN: Gábor Király, Vilmos Vanczák, Norbert Mészáros, Zoltán Lipták (46.Zsolt Korcsmár), Szilárd Devecseri (46.József Varga), Vladimir Koman, Balázs Dzsudzsák, Ákos Elek, Zoltán Stieber, Nemanja Nikolić, Ádám Csaba Szalai (75.Krisztián Németh). Trainer: József Csábi.

AND: Ferran Pol Pérez, Ildefons Lima Solà, Óscar Sonejee Masand, Emili Josep García Miramontes, Cristian Martínez Alejo, Marc García Renom, Moisés San Nicolás Schellens, Carlos Eduardo Peppe Britos (80.Xavier Vieira de Vasconcelos), Márcio Vieira de Vasconcelos, Gabriel Riera Lancha (63.Víctor Hugo Moreira Teixeira), Iván Lorenzo Roncero (87.Ludovic Clemente Garcés). Trainer: Jesús Luis Álvarez de Eulate "Koldo".

Goals: 1-0 Nemanja Nikolić (51), 2-0 Ildefons Lima Solà (76 own goal).

Cautions: Szilárd Devecseri, Norbert Mészáros, Vladimir Koman / Iván Lorenzo Roncero, Moisés San Nicolás Schellens, Márcio Vieira de Vasconcelos, Víctor Hugo Moreira Teixeira, Óscar Sonejee Masand.

Sent off: Moisés San Nicolás Schellens (38).

15.10.2013, Arena Naţională, Bucureşti; Attendance: 18,852
Referee: Marijo Strahonja (Croatia)
ROMANIA - ESTONIA **2-0(1-0)**
ROU: Anton Ciprian Tătăruşanu, Alexandru Măţel, Dorin Nicolae Goian, Florin Gardoş, Răzvan Dincă Raţ, Costin Lazăr (79.Ovidiu Ştefan Hoban), Cristian Tănase, Alexandru Bourceanu, Ciprian Andrei Marica, Gheorghe Bucur (57.Gabriel Andrei Torje), Bogdan Sorin Stancu (46.Gheorghe Teodor Grozav). Trainer: Victor Piţurcă.
EST: Sergei Pareiko, Enar Jääger, Mikk Reintam, Ragnar Klavan, Sander Puri (58.Henrik Ojamaa), Aleksandr Dmitrijev, Konstantin Vassiljev, Joel Lindpere (75.Dmitri Kruglov), Tarmo Kink, Sergei Zenjov (46.Henri Anier), Taijo Teniste. Trainer: Tarmo Rüütli.
Goals: 1-0 Ciprian Andrei Marica (30 penalty), 2-0 Ciprian Andrei Marica (81).
Cautions: Florin Gardoş, Alexandru Bourceanu / Sergei Pareiko, Ragnar Klavan, Aleksandr Dmitrijev.

15.10.2013, „Şükrü Saracoğlu" Stadyumu, Istanbul; Attendance: 41,814
Referee: Olegário Manuel Bártolo Faustino Benquerença (Portugal)
TURKEY - HOLLAND **0-2(0-1)**
TUR: Volkan Demirel, Gökhan Gönül, Hasan Ali Kaldırım, Ömer Toprak, Semih Kaya, Arda Turan, Olcan Adın (56.Olcay Şahan), Mehmet Topal, Selçuk İnan (74.Cenk Tosun), Burak Yılmaz (56.Gökhan Töre), Umut Bulut. Trainer: Fatih Terim.
NED: Jasper Cillessen, Ron Peter Vlaar, Daryl Janmaat, Rolando Maximiliano Martins Indi (46.Jeffrey Kevin van Homoet Bruma), Arjen Robben, Wesley Sneijder, Leroy Johan Fer, Daley Blind, Jordy Clasie, Robin van Persie (46.Dirk Kuijt), Jeremain Marciano Lens (89.Memphis Depay). Trainer: Aloysius Paulus Maria van Gaal.
Goals: 0-1 Arjen Robben (8), 0-2 Wesley Sneijder (47).
Cautions: Hasan Ali Kaldırım / Rolando Maximiliano Martins Indi, Daley Blind, Daryl Janmaat.

GROUP E

07.09.2012	Reykjavík	Iceland - Norway	2-0(1-0)
07.09.2012	Tiranë	Albania - Cyprus	3-1(1-1)
07.09.2012	Ljubljana	Slovenia - Switzerland	0-2(0-1)
11.09.2012	Lárnaka	Cyprus - Iceland	1-0(0-0)
11.09.2012	Oslo	Norway - Slovenia	2-1(1-1)
11.09.2012	Luzern	Switzerland - Albania	2-0(1-0)
12.10.2012	Tiranë	Albania - Iceland	1-2(1-1)
12.10.2012	Bern	Switzerland - Norway	1-1(0-0)
12.10.2012	Maribor	Slovenia - Cyprus	2-1(1-0)
16.10.2012	Reykjavík	Iceland - Switzerland	0-2(0-0)
16.10.2012	Lárnaka	Cyprus - Norway	1-3(1-1)
16.10.2012	Tiranë	Albania - Slovenia	1-0(1-0)
22.03.2013	Ljubljana	Slovenia - Iceland	1-2(1-0)
22.03.2013	Oslo	Norway - Albania	0-1(0-0)
23.03.2013	Nicosia	Cyprus - Switzerland	0-0
07.06.2013	Reykjavík	Iceland - Slovenia	2-4(2-2)
07.06.2013	Tiranë	Albania - Norway	1-1(1-0)
08.06.2013	Genève	Switzerland - Cyprus	1-0(0-0)
06.09.2013	Oslo	Norway - Cyprus	2-0(1-0)
06.09.2013	Bern	Switzerland - Iceland	4-4(3-1)
06.09.2013	Ljubljana	Slovenia - Albania	1-0(1-0)
10.09.2013	Oslo	Norway - Switzerland	0-2(0-1)
10.09.2013	Reykjavík	Iceland - Albania	2-1(1-1)
10.09.2013	Nicosia	Cyprus - Slovenia	0-2(0-1)
11.10.2013	Reykjavík	Iceland - Cyprus	2-0(0-0)
11.10.2013	Tiranë	Albania - Switzerland	1-2(0-0)
11.10.2013	Maribor	Slovenia - Norway	3-0(2-0)
15.10.2013	Nicosia	Cyprus - Albania	0-0
15.10.2013	Oslo	Norway - Iceland	1-1(1-1)
15.10.2013	Bern	Switzerland - Slovenia	1-0(0-0)

FINAL STANDINGS

1.	**SWITZERLAND**	10	7	3	0	17	-	6	24
2.	**Iceland**	10	5	2	3	17	-	15	17
3.	Slovenia	10	5	0	5	14	-	11	15
4.	Norway	10	3	3	4	10	-	13	12
5.	Albania	10	3	2	5	9	-	11	11
6.	Cyprus	10	1	2	7	4	-	15	5

Switzerland qualified for the Final Tournament; Iceland qualified for the Play-Offs.

07.09.2012, Laugardalsvöllur, Reykjavík; Attendance: 8,352
Referee: Anthony Gautier (France)
ICELAND - NORWAY **2-0(1-0)**
ISL: Hannes Þór Halldórsson, Grétar Rafn Steinsson, Ragnar Sigurðsson, Bjarni Ólafur Eiríksson, Birkir Bjarnason, Kári Árnason (50.Sölvi Geir Ottesen Jónsson), Emil Hallfreðsson (90+1.Eggert Gunnþór Jónsson), Aron Einar Malmquist Gunnarsson, Helgi Valur Daníelsson, Gylfi Þór Sigurðsson, Rúrik Gíslason (72.Alfreð Finnbogason). Trainer: Lars Edvin Lagerbäck (Sweden).
NOR: Espen Bugge Pettersen, John Arne Semundseth Riise, Brede Paulsen Hangeland, Espen Ruud, Kjetil Wæhler, Bjørn Helge Semundseth Riise (90.Markus Henriksen), Håvard Nordtveit, Magnus Wolff Eikrem, Tarik Elyounoussi, Daniel Omoya Braaten (66.Alexander Toft Søderlund), Mohammed Abdellaoue (66.Joshua Christian Kojo King). Trainer: Egil Roger Olsen.
Goals: 1-0 Kári Árnason (22), 2-0 Alfreð Finnbogason (81).
Cautions: Aron Einar Malmquist Gunnarsson / Bjørn Helge Semundseth Riise.

07.09.2012, Stadiumi „Qemal Stafa", Tiranë; Attendance: 9,400
Referee: Artyom Kuchin (Kazakhstan)
ALBANIA - CYPRUS **3-1(1-1)**
ALB: Samir Ujkani, Mërgim Mavraj, Andi Lila, Armend Ropqir Rrackar Dallku, Lorik Agim Cana, Burim Nue Kukeli, Ervin Bulku, Alban Syla Meha, Emiljano Vila (72.Erjon Bogdani), Hamdi Salihi (81.Edgar Çani), Armando Sadiku (58.Jahmir Hyka). Trainer: Giovanni De Biasi (Italy).
CYP: Antonis Georgallides (46.Christos Mastrou), Elias Charalambous, Georgios Merkis, Dossa Momad Omar Hassamo Júnior, Efstathios Panayotis Aloneftis, Marios Nicolaou, Constantinos Charalambides (56.Demetris Christofi), Constantinos Makrides, Vincent Laban, Jason Demetriou, Michalis Konstantinou (76.Andreas Avraam). Trainer: Nikolaos Nioplias (Greece).
Goals: 1-0 Armando Sadiku (36), 1-1 Vincent Laban (45+5), 2-1 Edgar Çani (84), 3-1 Erjon Bogdani (87).
Cautions: Lorik Agim Cana, Alban Syla Meha, Armando Sadiku, Erjon Bogdani / Vincent Laban, Constantinos Makrides.

07.09.2012, Stadion Stožice, Ljubljana; Attendance: 13,213
Referee: Paolo Tagliavento (Italy)
SLOVENIA - SWITZERLAND **0-2(0-1)**
SLO: Jasmin Handanović, Boštjan Cesar, Bojan Jokić, Mišo Brečko, Marko Šuler, Valter Birsa (61.Josip Iličić), Armin Bačinović, Aleksander Radosavljevič (80.Jasmin Kurtič), Zlatko Dedić (55.Zlatan Ljubijankić), Andraž Kirm, Tim Matavž. Trainer: Slaviša Stojanović.
SUI: Diego Orlando Benaglio, Johan Danon Djourou-Gbadjere, Stephan Lichtsteiner, Steve von Bergen, Ricardo Iván Rodríguez Araya, Tranquillo Barnetta, Valon Behrami, Gökhan Inler, Xherdan Shaqiri (74.Blerim Džemaili), Granit Xhaka (85.Gelson da Conceição Tavares Fernandes), Eren Derdiyok. Trainer: Ottmar Hitzfeld (Germany).
Goals: 0-1 Granit Xhaka (20), 0-2 Gökhan Inler (51).
Cautions: Andraž Kirm, Josip Iličić / Tranquillo Barnetta, Ricardo Iván Rodríguez Araya.
Sent off: Tranquillo Barnetta (75).

11.09.2012, Stádio „Antonis Papadopoulos", Lárnaka; Attendance: 1,600
Referee: Sébastien Delferiere (Belgium)
CYPRUS - ICELAND **1-0(0-0)**
CYP: Anastasios Kissas, Elias Charalambous, Georgios Merkis, Dossa Momad Omar Hassamo Júnior, Marios Nicolaou, Constantinos Makrides (90+2.Jason Demetriou), Vincent Laban, Siniša Dobrašinović (77.Valentinos Sielis), Demetris Christofi, Athos Solomou, Michalis Konstantinou (66.Efstathios Panayotis Aloneftis). Trainer: Nikolaos Nioplias (Greece).
ISL: Hannes Þór Halldórsson, Sölvi Geir Ottesen Jónsson, Ragnar Sigurðsson, Birkir Már Sævarsson, Bjarni Ólafur Eiríksson (63.Ari Freyr Skúlason), Birkir Bjarnason, Emil Hallfreðsson (46.Alfreð Finnbogason), Aron Einar Malmquist Gunnarsson, Helgi Valur Daníelsson (77.Jóhann Berg Guðmundsson), Gylfi Þór Sigurðsson, Rúrik Gíslason. Trainer: Lars Edvin Lagerbäck (Sweden).
Goal: 1-0 Constantinos Makrides (57).

Cautions: Anastasios Kissas, Valentinos Sielis, Vincent Laban / Rúrik Gíslason, Jóhann Berg Guðmundsson.
Sent off: Sölvi Geir Ottesen Jónsson (87).

11.09.2012, Ullevaal Stadion, Oslo; Attendance: 11,168
Referee: Fırat Aydınus (Turkey)
NORWAY - SLOVENIA **2-1(1-1)**
NOR: Rune Almenning Jarstein, John Arne Semundseth Riise, Brede Paulsen Hangeland, Espen Ruud, Kjetil Wæhler, Ruben Yttergård Jenssen, Håvard Nordtveit (53.Bjørn Helge Semundseth Riise), Markus Henriksen, Tarik Elyounoussi (89.Alexander Toft Søderlund), Daniel Omoya Braaten, Mohammed Abdellaoue (46.Joshua Christian Kojo King). Trainer: Egil Roger Olsen.
SLO: Jan Oblak, Boštjan Cesar, Bojan Jokić, Mišo Brečko, Marko Šuler, Valter Birsa (7.Nejc Pečnik), Armin Bačinović (61.Darijan Matič), Josip Iličić, Jasmin Kurtič, Zlatan Ljubijankić (90.Dejan Kelhar), Tim Matavž. Trainer: Slaviša Stojanović.
Goals: 0-1 Kjetil Wæhler (16 own goal), 1-1 Markus Henriksen (26), John Arne Semundseth Riise (90+3 penalty).
Cautions: Håvard Nordtveit, Espen Ruud / Bojan Jokić, Boštjan Cesar, Dejan Kelhar.

11.09.2012, Swissporarena, Luzern; Attendance: 16,500
Referee: Ovidiu Alin Haţegan (Romania)
SWITZERLAND - ALBANIA **2-0(1-0)**
SUI: Diego Orlando Benaglio, Johan Danon Djourou-Gbadjere, Stephan Lichtsteiner, Steve von Bergen, Ricardo Iván Rodríguez Araya, Valon Behrami (72.Blerim Džemaili), Gökhan Inler, Valentin Stocker (79.Admir Mehmedi), Xherdan Shaqiri, Granit Xhaka (90+1.Josip Drmić), Eren Derdiyok. Trainer: Ottmar Hitzfeld (Germany).
ALB: Samir Ujkani, Mërgim Mavraj, Andi Lila, Armend Ropqir Rrackar Dallku, Lorik Agim Cana, Ansi Agolli, Burim Nue Kukeli (72.Jahmir Hyka), Ervin Bulku, Alban Syla Meha, Emiljano Vila (55.Odise Roshi), Erjon Bogdani (55.Edgar Çani). Trainer: Giovanni De Biasi (Italy).
Goals: 1-0 Xherdan Shaqiri (23), 2-0 Gökhan Inler (68 penalty).
Cautions: Valon Behrami, Eren Derdiyok, Valentin Stocker, Gökhan Inler / Armend Ropqir Rrackar Dallku.

12.10.2012, Stadiumi „Qemal Stafa", Tiranë; Attendance: 8,200
Referee: Tony Asumaa (Finland)
ALBANIA - ICELAND **1-2(1-1)**
ALB: Samir Ujkani, Mërgim Mavraj, Andi Lila, Armend Ropqir Rrackar Dallku, Lorik Agim Cana, Burim Nue Kukeli, Ervin Bulku, Gilman Lika (75.Hamdi Salihi), Alban Syla Meha (46.Odise Roshi), Edgar Çani (85.Erjon Bogdani), Armando Sadiku. Trainer: Giovanni De Biasi (Italy).
ISL: Hannes Þór Halldórsson, Grétar Rafn Steinsson, Ragnar Sigurðsson, Ari Freyr Skúlason, Birkir Bjarnason (85.Jóhann Berg Guðmundsson), Kári Árnason, Emil Hallfreðsson, Aron Einar Malmquist Gunnarsson, Gylfi Þór Sigurðsson, Rúrik Gíslason (68.Birkir Már Sævarsson), Alfreð Finnbogason (90+2.Eggert Gunnþór Jónsson). Trainer: Lars Edvin Lagerbäck (Sweden).
Goals: 0-1 Birkir Bjarnason (19), 1-1 Edgar Çani (28), 1-2 Gylfi Þór Sigurðsson (81).
Cautions: Burim Nue Kukeli, Edgar Çani, Mërgim Mavraj / Kári Árnason, Aron Einar Malmquist Gunnarsson, Alfreð Finnbogason, Grétar Rafn Steinsson, Gylfi Þór Sigurðsson.

12.10.2012, Stade de Suisse, Bern; Attendance: 30,712
Referee: David Fernández Borbalán (Spain)
SWITZERLAND - NORWAY 1-1(0-0)
SUI: Diego Orlando Benaglio, Stephan Lichtsteiner, Johan Danon Djourou-Gbadjere, Steve von Bergen, Ricardo Iván Rodríguez Araya, Tranquillo Barnetta (71.Mario Gavranović), Valon Behrami (90+2.Blerim Džemaili), Gökhan Inler, Xherdan Shaqiri, Granit Xhaka, Eren Derdiyok. Trainer: Ottmar Hitzfeld (Germany).
NOR: Rune Almenning Jarstein, John Arne Semundseth Riise, Brede Paulsen Hangeland, Espen Ruud, Vegard Forren, Ruben Yttergård Jenssen (80.Magnus Wolff Eikrem), Håvard Nordtveit, Markus Henriksen, Tarik Elyounoussi (90+2.Jonathan Parr), Daniel Omoya Braaten, Alexander Toft Søderlund (64.Joshua Christian Kojo King). Trainer: Egil Roger Olsen.
Goals: 1-0 Mario Gavranović (79), 1-1 Brede Paulsen Hangeland (81).
Cautions: Eren Derdiyok, Stephan Lichtsteiner, Diego Orlando Benaglio / Håvard Nordtveit, Ruben Yttergård Jenssen, Daniel Omoya Braaten.

12.10.2012, Stadion Ljudski vrt, Maribor; Attendance: 7,988
Referee: Ivan Kružliak (Slovakia)
SLOVENIA - CYPRUS 2-1(1-0)
SLO: Samir Handanović, Boštjan Cesar, Bojan Jokić, Mišo Brečko, Marko Šuler, Aleksander Radosavljevič (90+1.Dominic Maroh), Josip Iličić (84.Goran Cvijanovič), Jasmin Kurtič, Zlatko Dedić (68.Kevin Kampl), Andraž Kirm, Tim Matavž. Trainer: Slaviša Stojanović.
CYP: Anastasios Kissas, Elias Charalambous, Paraskevas Christou, Valentinos Sielis, Angelis Charalambous, Constantinos Charalambides (79.Efstathios Panayotis Aloneftis), Siniša Dobrašinović, Demetris Christofi, Jason Demetriou, Christos Marangos (46.Kostakis Artymatas), Michalis Konstantinou (64.Georgios Efrem). Trainer: Nikolaos Nioplias (Greece).
Goals: 1-0 Tim Matavž (38), 2-0 Tim Matavž (61), 2-1 Efstathios Panayotis Aloneftis (83).
Cautions: Boštjan Cesar, Jasmin Kurtič / Valentinos Sielis, Christos Marangos, Jason Demetriou.
Sent off: Boštjan Cesar (89).

16.10.2012, Laugardalsvöllur, Reykjavík; Attendance: 8,369
Referee: Alan Kelly (Republic of Ireland)
ICELAND - SWITZERLAND 0-2(0-0)
ISL: Hannes Þór Halldórsson, Grétar Rafn Steinsson, Ragnar Sigurðsson, Ari Freyr Skúlason, Birkir Bjarnason, Kári Árnason, Eggert Gunnþór Jónsson (82.Guðjón Baldvinsson), Emil Hallfreðsson, Gylfi Þór Sigurðsson, Rúrik Gíslason (70.Jóhann Berg Guðmundsson), Alfreð Finnbogason. Trainer: Lars Edvin Lagerbäck (Sweden).
SUI: Diego Orlando Benaglio, Johan Danon Djourou-Gbadjere, Stephan Lichtsteiner, Steve von Bergen, Ricardo Iván Rodríguez Araya, Tranquillo Barnetta (90+1.Timm Klose), Valon Behrami, Gökhan Inler, Xherdan Shaqiri (79.Blerim Džemaili), Granit Xhaka, Mario Gavranović (83.Admir Mehmedi). Trainer: Ottmar Hitzfeld (Germany).
Goals: 0-1 Tranquillo Barnetta (66), 0-2 Mario Gavranović (79).
Cautions: Eggert Gunnþór Jónsson, Rúrik Gíslason, Grétar Rafn Steinsson, Kári Árnason, Emil Hallfreðsson / Diego Orlando Benaglio.

16.10.2012, Stádio „Antonis Papadopoulos", Lárnaka; Attendance: 2,493
Referee: Paweł Gil (Poland)

CYPRUS - NORWAY 1-3(1-1)

CYP: Anastasios Kissas (55.Antonis Georgallides), Elias Charalambous, Dossa Momad Omar Hassamo Júnior, Angelis Charalambous (46.Jason Demetriou), Efstathios Panayotis Aloneftis (88.Nestoras Mitidis), Marios Nicolaou, Vincent Laban, Siniša Dobrašinović, Demetris Christofi, Georgios Efrem, Athos Solomou. Trainer: Nikolaos Nioplias (Greece).

NOR: Rune Almenning Jarstein, John Arne Semundseth Riise, Brede Paulsen Hangeland, Espen Ruud, Vegard Forren, Ruben Yttergård Jenssen (75.Valon Berisha), Markus Henriksen, Magnus Wolff Eikrem (90+2.Ardian Gashi), Tarik Elyounoussi, Daniel Omoya Braaten, Alexander Toft Søderlund (46.Joshua Christian Kojo King). Trainer: Egil Roger Olsen.

Goals: 1-0 Efstathios Panayotis Aloneftis (42), 1-1 Brede Paulsen Hangeland (45), 1-2 Tarik Elyounoussi (81 penalty), 1-2 Joshua Christian Kojo King (83).

Cautions: Jason Demetriou, Siniša Dobrašinović, Efstathios Panayotis Aloneftis, Elias Charalambous / Espen Ruud, Daniel Omoya Braaten, John Arne Semundseth Riise.

16.10.2012, Stadiumi „Qemal Stafa", Tiranë; Attendance: 9,000
Referee: Martin Hansson (Sweden)

ALBANIA - SLOVENIA 1-0(1-0)

ALB: Etrit Berisha, Mërgim Mavraj, Andi Lila, Lorik Agim Cana, Ansi Agolli, Burim Nue Kukeli, Ervin Bulku, Odise Roshi, Emiljano Vila (84.Armend Ropqir Rrackar Dallku), Edgar Çani (75.Debatik Curri), Armando Sadiku (46.Hamdi Salihi). Trainer: Giovanni De Biasi (Italy).

SLO: Samir Handanović, Bojan Jokić, Mišo Brečko, Marko Šuler, Dominic Maroh, Aleš Mertelj, Aleksander Radosavljevič (77.Kevin Kampl), Josip Iličić (73.Mirnes Sead Šišić), Zlatko Dedić (59.Džengis Čavušević), Andraž Kirm, Tim Matavž. Trainer: Slaviša Stojanović.

Goal: 1-0 Odise Roshi (37).

Cautions: Odise Roshi, Emiljano Vila, Andi Lila / Aleš Mertelj, Josip Iličić, Andraž Kirm, Marko Šuler.

22.03.2013, Referee: Stavros Tritsonis (Greece)
Stadion Stožice, Ljubljana; Attendance: 6,500

SLOVENIA - ICELAND 1-2(1-0)

SLO: Samir Handanović, Boštjan Cesar, Bojan Jokić, Mišo Brečko, Valter Birsa (52.Dejan Lazarević), Aleksander Radosavljevič, Josip Iličić, Rene Krhin (79.Zlatko Dedić), Jasmin Kurtič, Milivoje Novakovič, Zlatan Ljubijankić (65.Tim Matavž). Trainer: Srečko Katanec.

ISL: Hannes Þór Halldórsson, Sölvi Geir Ottesen Jónsson, Ragnar Sigurðsson, Birkir Már Sævarsson, Ari Freyr Skúlason, Birkir Bjarnason, Emil Hallfreðsson (76.Eiður Smári Guðjohnsen), Aron Einar Malmquist Gunnarsson, Gylfi Þór Sigurðsson, Kolbeinn Sigþórsson (90+2.Helgi Valur Daníelsson), Alfreð Finnbogason (46.Jóhann Berg Guðmundsson). Trainer: Lars Edvin Lagerbäck (Sweden).

Goals: 1-0 Milivoje Novakovič (34), 1-1 Gylfi Þór Sigurðsson (55), 1-2 Gylfi Þór Sigurðsson (78).

Cautions: Milivoje Novakovič / Sölvi Geir Ottesen Jónsson, Jóhann Berg Guðmundsson, Gylfi Þór Sigurðsson.

22.03.2013, Ullevaal Stadion, Oslo; Attendance: 11,207
Referee: Bernie Raymond „Kevin" Blom (Holland)

NORWAY - ALBANIA 0-1(0-0)

NOR: Rune Almenning Jarstein, John Arne Semundseth Riise, Brede Paulsen Hangeland, Tom Høgli, Vegard Forren, Ruben Yttergård Jenssen, Håvard Nordtveit, Markus Henriksen, Tarik Elyounoussi (62.Joshua Christian Kojo King), Mohammed Abdellaoue, Alexander Toft Søderlund (75.Valon Berisha). Trainer: Egil Roger Olsen.

ALB: Etrit Berisha, Mërgim Mavraj, Andi Lila, Armend Ropqir Rrackar Dallku (80.Elseid Hysaj), Lorik Agim Cana, Ansi Agolli, Ervin Bulku, Odise Roshi, Migjen Xhevat Basha, Hamdi Salihi (90.Debatik Curri), Edgar Çani (75.Erjon Bogdani). Trainer: Giovanni De Biasi (Italy).

Goal: 0-1 Hamdi Salihi (66).

Cautions: Vegard Forren / Odise Roshi, Lorik Agim Cana, Andi Lila, Ansi Agolli.
Sent off: Andi Lila (89).

23.03.2013, Neo Stádio GPS, Nicosia; Attendance: 2,045
Referee: Manuel Gräfe (Germany)
CYPRUS - SWITZERLAND 0-0
CYP: Antonis Georgallides, Elias Charalambous, Christos Theofilou, Dossa Momad Omar Hassamo Júnior, Marios Nicolaou, Constantinos Charalambides (75.Nektarios Alexandrou), Constantinos Makrides, Vincent Laban, Siniša Dobrašinović, Demetris Christofi (90+5.Pieros Soteriou), Athos Solomou (54.Georgios Efrem). Trainer: Nikolaos Nioplias (Greece).
SUI: Yann Sommer, Stephan Lichtsteiner, Johan Danon Djourou-Gbadjere (52.Philippe Sylvain Senderos), Steve von Bergen, Ricardo Iván Rodríguez Araya, Valon Behrami (76.Eren Derdiyok), Gökhan Inler, Valentin Stocker, Xherdan Shaqiri, Haris Seferović, Innocent Nkasiobi Emeghara (46.Granit Xhaka). Trainer: Ottmar Hitzfeld (Germany).
Cautions: Athos Solomou, Christos Theofilou / Haris Seferović, Steve von Bergen, Philippe Sylvain Senderos.

07.06.2013, Laugardalsvöllur, Reykjavík; Attendance: 9,202
Referee: Felix Zwayer (Germany)
ICELAND - SLOVENIA 2-4(2-2)
ISL: Hannes Þór Halldórsson, Ragnar Sigurðsson, Birkir Már Sævarsson (84.Gunnar Heiðar Þorvaldsson), Ari Freyr Skúlason, Birkir Bjarnason, Kári Árnason, Emil Hallfreðsson (64.Rúrik Gíslason), Aron Einar Malmquist Gunnarsson (53.Eiður Smári Guðjohnsen), Helgi Valur Daníelsson, Kolbeinn Sigþórsson, Alfreð Finnbogason. Trainer: Lars Edvin Lagerbäck (Sweden).
SLO: Samir Handanović, Boštjan Cesar, Branko Ilič, Bojan Jokić, Mišo Brečko, Valter Birsa (90+1.Andraž Struna), Kevin Kampl (73.Aleksander Radosavljevič), Rene Krhin, Jasmin Kurtič, Milivoje Novakovič (87.Tim Matavž), Andraž Kirm. Trainer: Srečko Katanec.
Goals: 0-1 Andraž Kirm (11), 1-1 Birkir Bjarnason (22), 2-1 Alfreð Finnbogason (26 penalty), 2-2 Valter Birsa (31 penalty), 2-3 Boštjan Cesar (61), 2-4 Rene Krhin (86).
Cautions: Birkir Már Sævarsson, Kolbeinn Sigþórsson / Branko Ilič, Boštjan Cesar, Rene Krhin.

07.06.2013, Stadiumi „Qemal Stafa“, Tiranë; Attendance: 15,600
Referee: William Collum (Scotland)
ALBANIA - NORWAY 1-1(1-0)
ALB: Etrit Berisha, Mërgim Mavraj, Armend Ropqir Rrackar Dallku, Admir Teli, Valdet Rama, Ansi Agolli, Ervin Bulku (90+1.Elseid Hysaj), Emiljano Vila (85.Ergys Kaçe), Migjen Xhevat Basha, Hamdi Salihi (78.Tefik Osmani), Edgar Çani. Trainer: Giovanni De Biasi (Italy).
NOR: Rune Almenning Jarstein, Brede Paulsen Hangeland, Espen Ruud, Tore Reginiussen, Tom Høgli, Ruben Yttergård Jenssen (86.Per Ciljan Skjelbred), Håvard Nordtveit, Markus Henriksen, Tarik Elyounoussi (46.Valon Berisha), Daniel Omoya Braaten, Joshua Christian Kojo King (71.Alexander Toft Søderlund). Trainer: Egil Roger Olsen.
Goals: 1-0 Valdet Rama (40), 1-1 Tom Høgli (87).
Cautions: Armend Ropqir Rrackar Dallku, Migjen Xhevat Basha / Espen Ruud, Tore Reginiussen.

08.06.2013, Stade de Genève, Genève; Attendance: 16,900
Referee: Paolo Mazzoleni (Italy)
SWITZERLAND - CYPRUS 1-0(0-0)
SUI: Diego Orlando Benaglio, Johan Danon Djourou-Gbadjere, Stephan Lichtsteiner, Steve von Bergen, Ricardo Iván Rodríguez Araya, Valon Behrami (67.Blerim Džemaili), Gökhan Inler, Valentin Stocker (77.Tranquillo Barnetta), Xherdan Shaqiri, Mario Gavranović, Josip Drmić (74.Haris Seferović). Trainer: Ottmar Hitzfeld (Germany).
CYP: Antonis Georgallides, Elias Charalambous, Christos Theofilou (90+4.Siniša Dobrašinović), Georgios Merkis, Angelis Charalambous, Efstathios Panayotis Aloneftis (62.Charalambos Kyriakou), Marios Nicolaou, Constantinos Makrides, Vincent Laban, Nektarios Alexandrou, Pieros Soteriou. Trainer: Nikolaos Nioplias (Greece).
Goal: 1-0 Haris Seferović (90).
Cautions: Gökhan Inler / Angelis Charalambous, Pieros Soteriou, Constantinos Makrides, Elias Charalambous.

06.09.2013, Ullevaal Stadion, Oslo; Attendance: 11,295
Referee: Kenn Hansen (Denmark)
NORWAY - CYPRUS 2-0(1-0)
NOR: Rune Almenning Jarstein, Brede Paulsen Hangeland, Espen Ruud, Tom Høgli, Johan Lædre Bjørdal, Ardian Gashi, Magnus Wolff Eikrem, Tarik Elyounoussi (64.Joshua Christian Kojo King), Daniel Omoya Braaten (81.Alexander Toft Søderlund), Mohammed Abdellaoue, Stefan Marius Johansen (75.Ruben Yttergård Jenssen). Trainer: Egil Roger Olsen.
CYP: Antonis Georgallides, Christos Theofilou, Georgios Merkis, Dossa Momad Omar Hassamo Júnior, Efstathios Panayotis Aloneftis, Marios Nicolaou (52.Pieros Soteriou), Constantinos Charalambides (54.Jason Demetriou), Vincent Laban, Siniša Dobrašinović (73.Kostakis Artymatas), Nektarios Alexandrou, Nestoras Mitidis. Trainer: Nikolaos Nioplias (Greece).
Goals: 1-0 Tarik Elyounoussi (43), 2-0 Joshua Christian Kojo King (66).
Cautions: Efstathios Panayotis Aloneftis.

06.09.2013, Stade de Suisse, Bern; Attendance: 26,000
Referee: Sergei Karasev (Russia)
SWITZERLAND - ICELAND 4-4(3-1)
SUI: Diego Orlando Benaglio, Stephan Lichtsteiner, Steve von Bergen, Ricardo Iván Rodríguez Araya, Fabian Lukas Schär, Valon Behrami, Blerim Džemaili, Valentin Stocker (79.Tranquillo Barnetta), Xherdan Shaqiri (89.Timm Klose), Granit Xhaka (76.Josip Drmić), Haris Seferović. Trainer: Ottmar Hitzfeld (Germany).
ISL: Hannes Þór Halldórsson, Ragnar Sigurðsson, Birkir Már Sævarsson (82.Ólafur Ingi Skúlason), Ari Freyr Skúlason, Birkir Bjarnason, Kári Árnason, Aron Einar Malmquist Gunnarsson, Helgi Valur Daníelsson (46.Eiður Smári Guðjohnsen), Jóhann Berg Guðmundsson, Gylfi Þór Sigurðsson, Kolbeinn Sigþórsson. Trainer: Lars Edvin Lagerbäck (Sweden).
Goals: 0-1 Stephan Lichtsteiner (3), 1-1 Jóhann Berg Guðmundsson (15), 2-1 Fabian Lukas Schär (27), 3-1 Stephan Lichtsteiner (30), 4-1 Blerim Džemaili (54 penalty), 4-2 Kolbeinn Sigþórsson (68), 4-3 Jóhann Berg Guðmundsson (56), 4-4 Jóhann Berg Guðmundsson (90+1).
Cautions: Blerim Džemaili, Josip Drmić / Aron Einar Malmquist Gunnarsson, Kári Árnason.

06.09.2013, Stadion Stožice, Ljubljana; Attendance: 13,843
Referee: István Vad (Hungary)

SLOVENIA - ALBANIA **1-0(1-0)**

SLO: Samir Handanović, Branko Ilič, Bojan Jokić, Mišo Brečko, Dejan Kelhar, Valter Birsa (74.Aleš Mertelj), Kevin Kampl (90+1.Zlatan Ljubijankić), Rene Krhin, Jasmin Kurtič, Milivoje Novakovič (83.Tim Matavž), Andraž Kirm. Trainer: Srečko Katanec.
ALB: Etrit Berisha, Andi Lila, Admir Teli, Lorik Agim Cana, Valdet Rama, Ansi Agolli, Ervin Bulku (53.Hamdi Salihi), Odise Roshi, Migjen Xhevat Basha (80.Amir Abrashi), Ergys Kaçe, Edgar Çani (71.Agon Mehmeti). Trainer: Giovanni De Biasi (Italy).
Goal: 1-0 Kevin Kampl (19).
Cautions: Jasmin Kurtič, Samir Handanović / Ansi Agolli.

10.09.2013, Ullevaal Stadion, Oslo; Attendance: 16,631
Referee: Howard Melton Webb (England)

NORWAY - SWITZERLAND **0-2(0-1)**

NOR: Rune Almenning Jarstein, Brede Paulsen Hangeland, Espen Ruud, Tom Høgli (70.Omar Elabdellaoui), Johan Lædre Bjørdal, Håvard Nordtveit, Magnus Wolff Eikrem (64.Ruben Yttergård Jenssen), Tarik Elyounoussi, Daniel Omoya Braaten, Stefan Marius Johansen, Marcus Pedersen (22.Joshua Christian Kojo King). Trainer: Egil Roger Olsen.
SUI: Diego Orlando Benaglio, Stephan Lichtsteiner, Steve von Bergen, Ricardo Iván Rodríguez Araya, Fabian Lukas Schär, Valon Behrami, Gökhan Inler, Valentin Stocker (74.Gelson da Conceição Tavares Fernandes), Xherdan Shaqiri (90.Blerim Džemaili), Granit Xhaka (90+5.Philippe Sylvain Senderos), Haris Seferović. Trainer: Ottmar Hitzfeld (Germany).
Goals: 0-1 Fabian Lukas Schär (12), 0-2 Fabian Lukas Schär (51).
Cautions: Espen Ruud.

10.09.2013, Laugardalsvöllur, Reykjavík; Attendance: 9,768
Referee: Andre Marriner (England)

ICELAND - ALBANIA **2-1(1-1)**

ISL: Hannes Þór Halldórsson, Ragnar Sigurðsson, Birkir Már Sævarsson (90+2.Hallgrímur Jónasson), Ari Freyr Skúlason, Birkir Bjarnason, Kári Árnason, Aron Einar Malmquist Gunnarsson, Jóhann Berg Guðmundsson, Gylfi Þór Sigurðsson, Eiður Smári Guðjohnsen (79.Ólafur Ingi Skúlason), Kolbeinn Sigþórsson. Trainer: Lars Edvin Lagerbäck (Sweden).
ALB: Etrit Berisha, Andi Lila, Armend Ropqir Rrackar Dallku (82.Jürgen Gjasula), Admir Teli, Lorik Agim Cana, Valdet Rama, Odise Roshi, Migjen Xhevat Basha (64.Ervin Bulku), Ergys Kaçe, Hamdi Salihi, Edgar Çani (64.Ahmed Januzi). Trainer: Giovanni De Biasi (Italy).
Goals: 0-1 Valdet Rama (9), 1-1 Birkir Bjarnason (13), 2-1 Kolbeinn Sigþórsson (47).
Cautions: Gylfi Þór Sigurðsson / Ergys Kaçe, Armend Ropqir Rrackar Dallku, Admir Teli, Ahmed Januzi.

10.09.2013, Neo Stádio GPS, Nicosia; Attendance: 714
Referee: Ruddy Buquet (France)

CYPRUS - SLOVENIA **0-2(0-1)**

CYP: Antonis Georgallides, Elias Charalambous, Christos Theofilou (46.Jason Demetriou), Georgios Merkis, Dossa Momad Omar Hassamo Júnior, Constantinos Makrides, Vincent Laban, Siniša Dobrašinović (68.Marios Nicolaou), Georgios Eleftheriou (33.Constantinos Charalambides), Nektarios Alexandrou, Pieros Soteriou. Trainer: Nikolaos Nioplias (Greece).
SLO: Samir Handanović, Boštjan Cesar, Branko Ilič, Mišo Brečko, Andraž Struna, Valter Birsa (59.Josip Iličić), Aleš Mertelj, Kevin Kampl, Milivoje Novakovič (90+3.Željko Filipović), Zlatan Ljubijankić (89.Tim Matavž), Andraž Kirm. Trainer: Srečko Katanec.
Goals: 0-1 Milivoje Novakovič (12), 0-2 Josip Iličić (80).
Cautions: Georgios Merkis, Dossa Momad Omar Hassamo Júnior / Mišo Brečko, Andraž Struna, Andraž Kirm.

11.10.2013, Laugardalsvöllur, Reykjavík; Attendance: 9,767
Referee: István Vad (Hungary)

ICELAND - CYPRUS 2-0(0-0)

ISL: Hannes Þór Halldórsson, Ragnar Sigurðsson, Birkir Már Sævarsson, Ari Freyr Skúlason, Birkir Bjarnason, Kári Árnason, Aron Einar Malmquist Gunnarsson (77.Helgi Valur Daníelsson), Jóhann Berg Guðmundsson, Gylfi Þór Sigurðsson (82.Rúrik Gíslason), Eiður Smári Guðjohnsen (66.Alfreð Finnbogason), Kolbeinn Sigþórsson. Trainer: Lars Edvin Lagerbäck (Sweden).
CYP: Antonis Georgallides, Georgios Merkis, Lefteris Mertakkas, Angelis Charalambous, Efstathios Panayotis Aloneftis, Constantinos Charalambides (67.Georgios Efrem), Vincent Laban, Jason Demetriou, Georgios Vasiliou, Nektarios Alexandrou (84.Kyriakos Pavlou), Nestoras Mitidis (75.Pieros Soteriou). Trainer: Nikolaos Nioplias (Greece).
Goals: 1-0 Kolbeinn Sigþórsson (60), 2-0 Gylfi Þór Sigurðsson (76).
Cautions: Constantinos Charalambides, Georgios Merkis, Efstathios Panayotis Aloneftis.

11.10.2013, Stadiumi „Qemal Stafa", Tiranë; Attendance: 14,000
Referee: Pedro Proença Oliveira Alves Garcia (Portugal)

ALBANIA - SWITZERLAND 1-2(0-0)

ALB: Etrit Berisha, Mërgim Mavraj, Andi Lila, Lorik Agim Cana, Valdet Rama (85.Agon Mehmeti), Ansi Agolli, Shkëlzen Gashi (55.Odise Roshi), Ervin Bulku, Amir Abrashi (64.Jahmir Hyka), Ergys Kaçe, Hamdi Salihi. Trainer: Giovanni De Biasi (Italy).
SUI: Diego Orlando Benaglio, Steve von Bergen, Michael Rico Lang, Ricardo Iván Rodríguez Araya, Fabian Lukas Schär, Valon Behrami, Gökhan Inler, Valentin Stocker (68.Gelson da Conceição Tavares Fernandes), Xherdan Shaqiri (53.Admir Mehmedi), Granit Xhaka, Haris Seferović (89.Blerim Džemaili). Trainer: Ottmar Hitzfeld (Germany).
Goals: 0-1 Xherdan Shaqiri (47), 0-2 Michael Rico Lang (77), 1-2 Hamdi Salihi (89 penalty).
Cautions: Shkëlzen Gashi, Lorik Agim Cana / Steve von Bergen, Fabian Lukas Schär, Diego Orlando Benaglio.

11.10.2013, Stadion Ljudski vrt, Maribor; Attendance: 10,890
Referee: Carlos Velasco Carballo (Spain)

SLOVENIA - NORWAY 3-0(2-0)

SLO: Samir Handanović, Boštjan Cesar, Branko Ilič, Mišo Brečko, Andraž Struna, Nejc Pečnik (70.Zlatan Ljubijankić), Aleš Mertelj, Kevin Kampl (81.Rene Krhin), Jasmin Kurtič, Milivoje Novakovič (90+2.Roman Bezjak), Andraž Kirm. Trainer: Srečko Katanec.
NOR: Rune Almenning Jarstein, Brede Paulsen Hangeland, Tom Høgli, Johan Lædre Bjørdal, Per Ciljan Skjelbred, Magnus Wolff Eikrem (73.Øyvind Storflor), Omar Elabdellaoui, Tarik Elyounoussi, Daniel Omoya Braaten (61.Ola Williams Kamara), Mohammed Abdellaoue (80.Frode Johnsen), Stefan Marius Johansen. Trainer: Per-Mathias Høgmo.
Goals: 1-0 Milivoje Novakovič (13), 2-0 Milivoje Novakovič (14),3-0 Milivoje Novakovič (49).
Cautions: Brede Paulsen Hangeland.

15.10.2013, Neo Stádio GPS, Nicosia; Attendance: 341
Referee: Ivan Bebek (Croatia)

CYPRUS - ALBANIA 0-0

CYP: Antonis Georgallides, Dossa Momad Omar Hassamo Júnior, Angelis Charalambous, Marios Nicolaou, Vincent Laban, Georgios Efrem, Jason Demetriou, Georgios Vasiliou, Nektarios Alexandrou (46.Efstathios Panayotis Aloneftis), Nestoras Mitidis (65.Kyriakos Pavlou), Pieros Soteriou (86.Andreas Avraam). Trainer: Nikolaos Nioplias (Greece).
ALB: Etrit Berisha, Mërgim Mavraj, Andi Lila, Lorik Agim Cana, Valdet Rama, Ansi Agolli, Ervin Bulku (72.Amir Abrashi), Jahmir Hyka (72.Agon Mehmeti), Odise Roshi, Ergys Kaçe, Hamdi Salihi (87.Bekim Balaj). Trainer: Giovanni De Biasi (Italy).
Cautions: Vincent Laban / Lorik Agim Cana, Ergys Kaçe, Amir Abrashi, Mërgim Mavraj.

15.10.2013, Ullevaal Stadion, Oslo; Attendance: 6,796
Referee: Paolo Tagliavento (Italy)

NORWAY - ICELAND 1-1(1-1)

NOR: Rune Almenning Jarstein, Brede Paulsen Hangeland, Tore Reginiussen, Tom Høgli, Alexander Banor Tettey, Per Ciljan Skjelbred (86.Frode Johnsen), Omar Elabdellaoui, Ola Williams Kamara (55.Valon Berisha), Tarik Elyounoussi, Daniel Omoya Braaten (74.Mohammed Abdellaoue), Stefan Marius Johansen. Trainer: Per-Mathias Høgmo.
ISL: Hannes Þór Halldórsson, Ragnar Sigurðsson, Birkir Már Sævarsson, Ari Freyr Skúlason, Birkir Bjarnason, Kári Árnason, Aron Einar Malmquist Gunnarsson, Jóhann Berg Guðmundsson (90+2.Rúrik Gíslason), Gylfi Þór Sigurðsson, Eiður Smári Guðjohnsen (59.Alfreð Finnbogason), Kolbeinn Sigþórsson. Trainer: Lars Edvin Lagerbäck (Sweden).
Goals: 0-1 Kolbeinn Sigþórsson (12), 1-1 Daniel Omoya Braaten (30).
Cautions: Birkir Már Sævarsson.

15.10.2013, Stade de Suisse, Bern; Attendance: 22,014
Referee: Björn Kuipers (Holland)

SWITZERLAND - SLOVENIA 1-0(0-0)

SUI: Yann Sommer, Johan Danon Djourou-Gbadjere, Philippe Sylvain Senderos, Reto Pirmin Ziegler, Michael Rico Lang, Tranquillo Barnetta (71.Pajtim Kasami), Blerim Džemaili, Gökhan Inler, Granit Xhaka, Admir Mehmedi (87.Gelson da Conceição Tavares Fernandes), Haris Seferović (70.Eren Derdiyok). Trainer: Ottmar Hitzfeld (Germany).
SLO: Samir Handanović, Boštjan Cesar, Branko Ilič, Mišo Brečko, Andraž Struna, Nejc Pečnik (42.Tim Matavž), Aleš Mertelj (79.Zlatan Ljubijankić), Kevin Kampl (86.Dejan Lazarević), Jasmin Kurtič, Milivoje Novakovič, Andraž Kirm. Trainer: Srečko Katanec.
Goal: 1-0 Granit Xhaka (74).
Cautions: Granit Xhaka / Branko Ilič, Nejc Pečnik, Andraž Struna, Aleš Mertelj, Boštjan Cesar.

GROUP F

07.09.2012	Moskva	Russia - Northern Ireland	2-0(1-0)
07.09.2012	Luxembourg	Luxembourg - Portugal	1-2(1-1)
07.09.2012	Bakı	Azerbaijan - Israel	1-1(0-0)
11.09.2012	Belfast	Northern Ireland - Luxembourg	1-1(1-0)
11.09.2012	Tel Aviv	Israel - Russia	0-4(0-2)
11.09.2012	Braga	Portugal - Azerbaijan	3-0(0-0)
12.10.2012	Moskva	Russia - Portugal	1-0(1-0)
12.10.2012	Luxembourg	Luxembourg - Israel	0-6(0-3)
16.10.2012	Tel Aviv	Israel - Luxembourg	3-0(2-0)
16.10.2012	Moskva	Russia - Azerbaijan	1-0(0-0)
16.10.2012	Porto	Portugal - Northern Ireland	1-1(0-1)
14.11.2012	Belfast	Northern Ireland - Azerbaijan	1-1(0-1)
22.03.2013	Tel Aviv	Israel - Portugal	3-3(2-1)
22.03.2013	Luxembourg	Luxembourg - Azerbaijan	0-0
26.03.2013	Belfast	Northern Ireland - Israel	0-2(0-0)
26.03.2013	Bakı	Azerbaijan - Portugal	0-2(0-0)
07.06.2013	Lisboa	Portugal - Russia	1-0(1-0)
07.06.2013	Bakı	Azerbaijan - Luxembourg	1-1(0-0)
14.08.2013	Belfast	Northern Ireland - Russia	1-0(1-0)
06.09.2013	Kazan	Russia - Luxembourg	4-1(2-0)
06.09.2013	Belfast	Northern Ireland - Portugal	2-4(1-1)
07.09.2013	Tel Aviv	Israel - Azerbaijan	1-1(0-0)
10.09.2013	St. Petersburg	Russia - Israel	3-1(0-0)
10.09.2013	Luxembourg	Luxembourg - Northern Ireland	3-2(1-1)
11.10.2013	Luxembourg	Luxembourg - Russia	0-4(0-3)
11.10.2013	Lisboa	Portugal - Israel	1-1(1-0)
11.10.2013	Bakı	Azerbaijan - Northern Ireland	2-0(0-0)
15.10.2013	Coimbra	Portugal - Luxembourg	3-0(2-0)
15.10.2013	Tel Aviv	Israel - Northern Ireland	1-1(1-0)
15.10.2013	Bakı	Azerbaijan - Russia	1-1(0-1)

FINAL STANDINGS

1.	**RUSSIA**	10	7	1	2	20	-	5	22
2.	**Portugal**	10	6	3	1	20	-	9	21
3.	Israel	10	3	5	2	19	-	14	14
4.	Azerbaijan	10	1	6	3	7	-	11	9
5.	Northern Ireland	10	1	4	5	9	-	17	7
6.	Luxembourg	10	1	3	6	7	-	26	6

Russia qualified for the Final Tournament; Portugal qualified for the Play-Offs.

07.09.2012, Lokomotiv Stadium, Moskva; Attendance: 14,300
Referee: Antonio Mateu Lahoz (Spain)
RUSSIA - NORTHERN IRELAND **2-0(1-0)**
RUS: Igor Akinfeev, Vasili Berezutski, Sergei Ignashevich, Aleksandr Anyukov, Vladimir Bystrov, Dmitri Kombarov, Roman Shirokov, Viktor Fayzulin (85.Denis Glushakov), Igor Denisov, Alan Dzagoev (58.Aleksandr Kokorin), Aleksandr Kerzhakov. Trainer: Fabio Capello (Italy).
NIR: Roy Eric Carroll, Aaron William Hughes, Christopher Patrick Baird, Gareth Gerald McAuley, Jonathan Grant Evans, Craig George Cathcart, Steven Davis, Christopher Brunt, Corry John Evans (84.Dean Andrew Shiels), Kyle Lafferty, Jamie John Ward (76.Andrew Little). Trainer: Michael Andrew Martin O'Neill.
Goals: 1-0 Viktor Fayzulin (30), 2-0 Roman Shirokov (78 penalty).
Cautions: Aleksandr Anyukov / Christopher Patrick Baird, Craig George Cathcart, Gareth Gerald McAuley.

07.09.2012, Stade „Josy Barthel“, Luxembourg; Attendance: 8,125
Referee: Kristo Tohver (Estonia)
LUXEMBOURG - PORTUGAL **1-2(1-1)**
LUX: Jonathan Joubert, Mario Mutsch, Tom Schnell, Ante Bukvić, Guy Blaise, Lars Christian Krogh Gerson, Ben Payal, Mathias Jänisch, Gilles Bettmer, Daniel Alves Da Mota (79.Maurice John Deville), Aurélien Joachim. Trainer: Luc Holtz.
POR: Rui Pedro dos Santos Patrício, Képler Laveran Lima Ferreira „Pepe“, Bruno Eduardo Regufe Alves, Fábio Alexandre da Silva Coentrão, João Pedro da Silva Pereira, Raul José Trindade Meireles (67.Custódio Miguel Dias de Castro), Luís Carlos Almeida da Cunha „Nani“ (81.Rúben Micael Freitas da Ressureição), Miguel Luís Pinto Veloso (46.Silvestre Manuel Gonçalves Varela), João Filipe Iria Santos Moutinho, Cristiano Ronaldo dos Santos Aveiro, Hélder Manuel Marques Postiga. Trainer: Paulo Jorge Gomes Bento.
Goals: 1-0 Daniel Alves Da Mota (13), 1-1 Cristiano Ronaldo dos Santos Aveiro (28), 1-2 Hélder Manuel Marques Postiga (54).
Cautions: Bruno Eduardo Regufe Alves, Silvestre Manuel Gonçalves Varela.

07.09.2012, „Tofiq Bahramov“ Stadium, Bakı; Attendance: 22,211
Referee: Matej Jug (Slovenia)
AZERBAIJAN - ISRAEL **1-1(0-0)**
AZE: Kamran Ağayev, Rəşad Ferhad Sadıqov, Elnur Fazahir Allahverdiyev, Ruslan Ibrahim Abışov, Mahir Ağateyyub Şükürov, Maksim Medvedev, Ali Gökdemir (59.Əfran Amit İsmayılov), Aleksandr Çertoqanov (76.Rahid Alakbar Əmirquliyev), Branimir Subašić, Vaqif Füzuli Cavadov, Rauf Sahraman Əliyev (58.Cihan Özkara). Trainer: Hans-Hubert Vogts (Germany).
ISR: David Aouate, Yoav Ziv, Dan Mori, Eitan Tibi, Yuval Spungin, Gil Vermouth, Bibras Natkho, Gal Alberman, Maor Melikson (71.Hen Ezra), Tomer Hemed (67.Omer Damari), Itay Menachem Shechter (74.Yosef Shai Benayoun). Trainer: Eli Guttman.
Goals: 0-1 Bibras Natkho (50), 1-1 Ruslan Ibrahim Abışov (65).
Cautions: Ruslan Ibrahim Abışov / Tomer Hemed, Dan Mori, Hen Ezra.

11.09.2012, Windsor Park, Belfast; Attendance: 10,674
Referee: Vlado Glodjović (Serbia)
NORTHERN IRELAND - LUXEMBOURG **1-1(1-0)**
NIR: Roy Eric Carroll, Aaron William Hughes, Christopher Patrick Baird, Gareth Gerald McAuley, Jonathan Grant Evans, Ryan McGivern, Shane Kevin Ferguson (74.Jamie John Ward), Steven Davis, Christopher Brunt, Dean Andrew Shiels (83.Oliver James Norwood), Kyle Lafferty. Trainer: Michael Andrew Martin O'Neill.
LUX: Jonathan Joubert, Mario Mutsch, Tom Schnell, Ante Bukvić, Guy Blaise, Lars Christian Krogh Gerson (50.Chris Philipps), Ben Payal, Mathias Jänisch, Gilles Bettmer (90+3.Eric Hoffmann), Daniel Alves Da Mota, Aurélien Joachim (46.Maurice John Deville). Trainer: Luc Holtz.
Goals: 1-0 Dean Andrew Shiels (14), 1-1 Daniel Alves Da Mota (86).
Cautions: Gareth Gerald McAuley, Kyle Lafferty, Christopher Brunt / Gilles Bettmer, Maurice John

Deville.

11.09.2012, National Stadium, Ramat Gan, Tel Aviv; Attendance: 28,131
Referee: Mark Clattenburg (England)
ISRAEL - RUSSIA **0-4(0-2)**
ISR: David Aouate, Tal Ben Haim, Yoav Ziv, Eitan Tibi, Yuval Spungin, Yosef Shai Benayoun (74.Gil Vermouth), Bibras Natkho, Almog Cohen (46.Eden Ben Basat), Hen Ezra, Maharan Radi, Itay Menachem Shechter (46.Ben Sahar). Trainer: Eli Guttman.
RUS: Igor Akinfeev, Vasili Berezutski, Sergei Ignashevich, Aleksandr Anyukov (50.Andrey Yeshchenko), Vladimir Bystrov (23.Aleksandr Samedov), Dmitri Kombarov, Roman Shirokov, Igor Denisov, Denis Glushakov, Aleksandr Kerzhakov, Aleksandr Kokorin (34.Viktor Fayzulin). Trainer: Fabio Capello (Italy).
Goals: 0-1 Aleksandr Kerzhakov (7), 0-2 Aleksandr Kokorin (18), 0-3 Aleksandr Kerzhakov (64), 0-4 Viktor Fayzulin (78).
Cautions: Eitan Tibi, Yoav Ziv / Denis Glushakov, Sergei Ignashevich.

11.09.2012, Estádio Municipal, Braga; Attendance: 29,971
Referee: Szymon Marciniak (Poland)
PORTUGAL - AZERBAIJAN **3-0(0-0)**
POR: Rui Pedro dos Santos Patrício, Képler Laveran Lima Ferreira „Pepe“, Bruno Eduardo Regufe Alves, Fábio Alexandre da Silva Coentrão, João Pedro da Silva Pereira, Raul José Trindade Meireles, Luís Carlos Almeida da Cunha „Nani“ (77.Rúben Filipe Marques Amorim), Miguel Luís Pinto Veloso (63.Silvestre Manuel Gonçalves Varela), João Filipe Iria Santos Moutinho, Cristiano Ronaldo dos Santos Aveiro, Hélder Manuel Marques Postiga (87.Éderzito António Macedo Lopes „Éder“). Trainer: Paulo Jorge Gomes Bento.
AZE: Kamran Ağayev, Rəşad Ferhad Sadıqov, Elnur Fazahir Allahverdiyev, Ruslan Ibrahim Abışov, Volodimir Levin, Mahir Ağateyyub Şükürov, Maksim Medvedev, Ali Gökdemir (89.Aleksandr Çertoqanov), Cavid Shakir Hüseynov (59.Əfran Amit İsmayılov), Rahid Alakbar Əmirquliyev, Cihan Özkara (72.Branimir Subašić). Trainer: Hans-Hubert Vogts (Germany).
Goals: 1-0 Silvestre Manuel Gonçalves Varela (63), 2-0 Hélder Manuel Marques Postiga (85), 3-0 Bruno Eduardo Regufe Alves (88).
Cautions: Cristiano Ronaldo dos Santos Aveiro / Kamran Ağayev.

12.10.2012, Luzhniki Stadium, Moskva; Attendance: 54,212
Referee: Viktor Kassai (Hungary)
RUSSIA - PORTUGAL **1-0(1-0)**
RUS: Igor Akinfeev, Vasili Berezutski, Sergei Ignashevich, Aleksandr Anyukov, Vladimir Bystrov (83.Aleksandr Samedov), Dmitri Kombarov, Roman Shirokov, Viktor Fayzulin (46.Denis Glushakov), Igor Denisov, Aleksandr Kerzhakov (65.Andrey Yeshchenko), Aleksandr Kokorin. Trainer: Fabio Capello (Italy).
POR: Rui Pedro dos Santos Patrício, Képler Laveran Lima Ferreira „Pepe“, Bruno Eduardo Regufe Alves, Fábio Alexandre da Silva Coentrão (20.Hugo Miguel Almeida Costa Lopes), João Pedro da Silva Pereira, Luís Carlos Almeida da Cunha „Nani“, Miguel Luís Pinto Veloso, João Filipe Iria Santos Moutinho, Rúben Micael Freitas da Ressureição (67.Silvestre Manuel Gonçalves Varela), Cristiano Ronaldo dos Santos Aveiro, Hélder Manuel Marques Postiga (75.Éderzito António Macedo Lopes „Éder“). Trainer: Paulo Jorge Gomes Bento.
Goal: 1-0 Aleksandr Kerzhakov (6).
Cautions: Roman Shirokov, Aleksandr Kokorin / Miguel Luís Pinto Veloso.

12.10.2012, Stade „Josy Barthel“, Luxembourg; Attendance: 2,631
Referee: Leontios Trattou (Cyprus)
LUXEMBOURG - ISRAEL 0-6(0-3)
LUX: Jonathan Joubert, Mario Mutsch, Tom Schnell (18.Charles Leweck), Ante Bukvić, Chris Philipps, Lars Christian Krogh Gerson, Ben Payal (78.Eric Hoffmann), Mathias Jänisch, Gilles Bettmer, Daniel Alves Da Mota, Aurélien Joachim (61.Maurice John Deville). Trainer: Luc Holtz.
ISR: David Aouate, Dan Mori, Eitan Tibi (55.Dekel Keinan), Yuval Spungin, Gal Shish (57.Yoav Ziv), Bibras Natkho (77.Nir Bitton), Gal Alberman, Maharan Radi, Maor Melikson, Tomer Hemed, Eden Ben Basat. Trainer: Eli Guttman.
Goals: 0-1 Maharan Radi (4), 0-2 Eden Ben Basat (12), 0-3 Tomer Hemed (27), 0-4 Maor Melikson (61), 0-5 Tomer Hemed (74), 0-6 Tomer Hemed (90+1).
Cautions: Mathias Jänisch.

16.10.2012, National Stadium, Ramat Gan, Tel Aviv; Attendance: 20,400
Referee: Harald Lechner (Austria)
ISRAEL - LUXEMBOURG 3-0(2-0)
ISR: David Aouate, Yoav Ziv, Dekel Keinan, Dan Mori, E. Gabai, Bibras Natkho, Gal Alberman, Maharan Radi (56.Gil Vermouth; 71.Hen Ezra), Maor Melikson (81.Shimon Abuhatzira), Tomer Hemed, Eden Ben Basat. Trainer: Eli Guttman.
LUX: Jonathan Joubert, Mario Mutsch, Eric Hoffmann, Guy Blaise, Charles Leweck, Ben Payal, René Peters (80.Chris Philipps), Gilles Bettmer, Laurent Jans, Daniel Alves Da Mota (86.Tom Laterza), Aurélien Joachim (46.Maurice John Deville). Trainer: Luc Holtz.
Goals: 1-0 Tomer Hemed (13), 2-0 Eden Ben Basat (35), 3-0 Tomer Hemed (48).
Cautions: Eden Ben Basat / Mario Mutsch, Ben Payal, Eric Hoffmann.

16.10.2012, Luzhniki Stadium, Moskva; Attendance: 15,033
Referee: Aleksandar Stavrev (Macedonia)
RUSSIA - AZERBAIJAN 1-0(0-0)
RUS: Igor Akinfeev, Vasili Berezutski, Sergei Ignashevich, Andrey Yeshchenko, Dmitri Kombarov, Aleksandr Samedov (62.Vladimir Bystrov), Roman Shirokov, Viktor Fayzulin (46.Denis Glushakov), Igor Denisov, Aleksandr Kerzhakov (79.Alan Dzagoev), Aleksandr Kokorin. Trainer: Fabio Capello (Italy).
AZE: Kamran Ağayev, Ruslan Ibrahim Abışov, Volodimir Levin, Mahir Ağateyyub Şükürov, Maksim Medvedev, Ali Gökdemir, Aleksandr Çertoqanov (84.Rauf Sahraman Əliyev), Branimir Subašić (63.Rahid Alakbar Əmirquliyev), Vügar Nadirov (46.Cavid Shakir Hüseynov), Vaqif Füzuli Cavadov, Cihan Özkara. Trainer: Hans-Hubert Vogts (Germany).
Goal: 1-0 Roman Shirokov (84 penalty).
Cautions: Vasili Berezutski / Maksim Medvedev, Vaqif Füzuli Cavadov, Vügar Nadirov, Kamran Ağayev.

16.10.2012, Estádio do Dragão, Porto; Attendance: 48,711
Referee: Thorsten Kinhöfer (Germany)
PORTUGAL - NORTHERN IRELAND 1-1(0-1)
POR: Rui Pedro dos Santos Patrício,Képler Laveran Lima Ferreira „Pepe“, Bruno Eduardo Regufe Alves, João Pedro da Silva Pereira (74.Éderzito António Macedo Lopes „Éder“), Hugo Miguel Almeida Costa Lopes (46.Rúben Filipe Marques Amorim), Luís Carlos Almeida da Cunha „Nani“, Miguel Luís Pinto Veloso, João Filipe Iria Santos Moutinho, Rúben Micael Freitas da Ressureição (61.Silvestre Manuel Gonçalves Varela), Cristiano Ronaldo dos Santos Aveiro, Hélder Manuel Marques Postiga. Trainer: Paulo Jorge Gomes Bento.
NIR: Roy Eric Carroll, Aaron William Hughes, Christopher Patrick Baird, Jonathan Grant Evans, Craig George Cathcart, Ryan McGivern, Steven Davis, Niall McGinn, Corry John Evans, Oliver James Norwood, Kyle Lafferty. Trainer: Michael Andrew Martin O'Neill.
Goals: 0-1 Niall McGinn (30), 1-1 Hélder Manuel Marques Postiga (79).
Cautions: Képler Laveran Lima Ferreira „Pepe“ / Aaron William Hughes.

14.11.2012, Windsor Park, Belfast; Attendance: 12,372
Referee: Viktor Shvetsov (Ukraine)

NORTHERN IRELAND - AZERBAIJAN 1-1(0-1)

NIR: Roy Eric Carroll, Aaron William Hughes, Christopher Patrick Baird, Gareth Gerald McAuley, Craig George Cathcart (82.David Healy), Shane Kevin Ferguson, Daniel Patrick Lafferty, Steven Davis, Niall McGinn (67.Christopher Brunt), Dean Andrew Shiels (55.Patrick James McCourt), Kyle Lafferty. Trainer: Michael Andrew Martin O'Neill.

AZE: Salahat Ağayev, Ruslan Ibrahim Abışov, Volodimir Levin, Rasim Ramaldanov (71.Elhad Nəziri), Maksim Medvedev, Ali Gökdemir (63.Badavi Hüseynov), Cavid Shakir Hüseynov, Rahid Alakbar Əmirquliyev, Vügar Nadirov, Rauf Sahraman Əliyev, Cihan Özkara (79.Vaqif Füzuli Cavadov). Trainer: Hans-Hubert Vogts (Germany).

Goals: 0-1 Rauf Sahraman Əliyev (5), 1-1 David Healy (90+6).

Cautions: Dean Andrew Shiels, Kyle Lafferty, Christopher Patrick Baird, David Healy / Volodimir Levin, Rauf Sahraman Əliyev, Cavid Shakir Hüseynov, Salahat Ağayev.

22.03.2013, National Stadium, Ramat Gan, Tel Aviv; Attendance: 38,600
Referee: Stéphane Lannoy (France)

ISRAEL - PORTUGAL 3-3(2-1)

ISR: David Aouate, Tal Ben Haim, Eitan Tibi, Rami Gershon, Yuval Spungin, Bibras Natkho, Sheran Yeini, Beram Kayal, Maor Melikson (73.Lior Refaelov), Tomer Hemed (64.Eliran Atar), Eden Ben Basat (81.Yosef Shai Benayoun). Trainer: Eli Guttman.

POR: Rui Pedro dos Santos Patrício, Képler Laveran Lima Ferreira „Pepe", Bruno Eduardo Regufe Alves (74.Hugo Miguel Pereira de Almeida), Fábio Alexandre da Silva Coentrão, João Pedro da Silva Pereira, Raul José Trindade Meireles, Miguel Luís Pinto Veloso (60.Carlos Jorge Neto Martins), João Filipe Iria Santos Moutinho, Cristiano Ronaldo dos Santos Aveiro, Hélder Manuel Marques Postiga, Silvestre Manuel Gonçalves Varela (60.Adelino André Vieira de Freitas „Vieirinha"). Trainer: Paulo Jorge Gomes Bento.

Goals: 0-1 Bruno Eduardo Regufe Alves (2), 1-1 Tomer Hemed (24), 2-1 Eden Ben Basat (40), 3-1 Rami Gershon (70), 3-2 Hélder Manuel Marques Postiga (72), 3-3 Fábio Alexandre da Silva Coentrão (90+3).

Cautions: Beram Kayal, Tomer Hemed, Maor Melikson / Fábio Alexandre da Silva Coentrão, Carlos Jorge Neto Martins, Cristiano Ronaldo dos Santos Aveiro.

22.03.2013, Stade „Josy Barthel", Luxembourg; Attendance: 1,324
Referee: Padraigh Sutton (Republic of Ireland)

LUXEMBOURG - AZERBAIJAN 0-0

LUX: Jonathan Joubert, Mario Mutsch (90+4.Gilles Bettmer), Eric Hoffmann, Tom Schnell, Chris Philipps, Lars Christian Krogh Gerson, Mathias Jänisch, Stefano Bensi, Laurent Jans, Daniel Alves Da Mota (67.Tom Laterza), Aurélien Joachim (90+3.Maurice John Deville). Trainer: Luc Holtz.

AZE: Kamran Ağayev, Rəşad Ferhad Sadıqov, Ruslan Ibrahim Abışov, Mahir Ağateyyub Şükürov, Rasim Ramaldanov, Maksim Medvedev, Rəşad Äbulfaz Sadiqov (87.Cavid Shakir Hüseynov), Əfran Amit İsmayılov, Vaqif Füzuli Cavadov (59.Vügar Nadirov), Rauf Sahraman Əliyev, Pardis Fardjad-Azad (71.Cihan Özkara). Trainer: Hans-Hubert Vogts (Germany).

Cautions: Aurélien Joachim, Mathias Jänisch / Pardis Fardjad-Azad.

26.03.2013, Windsor Park, Belfast; Attendance: 11,200
Referee: Hannes Kaasik (Estonia)
NORTHERN IRELAND - ISRAEL 0-2(0-0)
NIR: Roy Eric Carroll, Aaron William Hughes, Gareth Gerald McAuley, Jonathan Grant Evans, Shane Kevin Ferguson (73.Joshua Brendan David Magennis), Daniel Patrick Lafferty, Steven Davis, Christopher Brunt, Samuel Gary Clingan (79.Patrick James McCourt), Niall McGinn, Martin Andrew Paterson (83.David Healy). Trainer: Michael Andrew Martin O'Neill.
ISR: David Aouate, Tal Ben Haim, Eitan Tibi, Rami Gershon, Yuval Spungin, Bibras Natkho, Sheran Yeini, Maharan Radi (60.Eran Zahavy), Maor Melikson (70.Lior Refaelov), Itay Menachem Shechter (86.Yosef Shai Benayoun), Eden Ben Basat. Trainer: Eli Guttman.
Goals: 0-1 Lior Refaelov (77), 0-2 Eden Ben Basat (84).
Cautions: Jonathan Grant Evans, Christopher Brunt.

26.03.2013, „Tofiq Bahramov" Stadium, Bakı; Attendance: 24,558
Referee: Andre Marriner (England)
AZERBAIJAN - PORTUGAL 0-2(0-0)
AZE: Kamran Ağayev, Rəşad Ferhad Sadıqov, Ruslan Ibrahim Abışov, Mahir Ağateyyub Şükürov, Rasim Ramaldanov, Maksim Medvedev, Elvin Nasradin Məmmədov (69.Pardis Fardjad-Azad), Cavid Shakir Hüseynov, Əfran Amit İsmayılov, Vügar Nadirov (62.Volodimir Levin), Rauf Sahraman Əliyev. Trainer: Hans-Hubert Vogts (Germany).
POR: Rui Pedro dos Santos Patrício, Képler Laveran Lima Ferreira „Pepe", Bruno Eduardo Regufe Alves, Fábio Alexandre da Silva Coentrão, João Pedro da Silva Pereira, Raul José Trindade Meireles (58.Hugo Miguel Pereira de Almeida), Daniel Miguel Alves Gomes „Danny" (73.Silvestre Manuel Gonçalves Varela), Miguel Luís Pinto Veloso, João Filipe Iria Santos Moutinho, Adelino André Vieira de Freitas „Vieirinha", Hélder Manuel Marques Postiga (82.Custódio Miguel Dias de Castro). Trainer: Paulo Jorge Gomes Bento.
Goals: 0-1 Bruno Eduardo Regufe Alves (63), 0-2 Hugo Miguel Pereira de Almeida (79).
Cautions: Rəşad Ferhad Sadıqov, Mahir Ağateyyub Şükürov, Vügar Nadirov, Rauf Sahraman Əliyev / Képler Laveran Lima Ferreira „Pepe".
Sent off: Rauf Sahraman Əliyev (55).

07.06.2013, Estádio da Luz, Lisboa; Attendance: 54,697
Referee: Damir Skomina (Slovenia)
PORTUGAL - RUSSIA 1-0(1-0)
POR: Rui Pedro dos Santos Patrício, Bruno Eduardo Regufe Alves, Fábio Alexandre da Silva Coentrão, João Pedro da Silva Pereira, Luís Carlos Novo Neto, Raul José Trindade Meireles (73.Rúben Filipe Marques Amorim), Miguel Luís Pinto Veloso, João Filipe Iria Santos Moutinho, Adelino André Vieira de Freitas „Vieirinha" (90+2.Custódio Miguel Dias de Castro), Cristiano Ronaldo dos Santos Aveiro, Hélder Manuel Marques Postiga (66.Luís Carlos Almeida da Cunha „Nani"). Trainer: Paulo Jorge Gomes Bento.
RUS: Igor Akinfeev, Vasili Berezutski, Sergei Ignashevich, Aleksandr Anyukov (31.Aleksei Kozlov), Yuri Zhirkov, Vladimir Bystrov, Dmitri Kombarov, Roman Shirokov, Viktor Fayzulin (21.Denis Glushakov), Igor Denisov, Aleksandr Kerzhakov (68.Fyodor Smolov). Trainer: Fabio Capello (Italy).
Goal: 1-0 Hélder Manuel Marques Postiga (9).
Cautions: Luís Carlos Novo Neto.

07.06.2013, Bakcell Arena, Bakı; Attendance: 9,258
Referee: Mihály Fábián (Hungary)
AZERBAIJAN - LUXEMBOURG 1-1(0-0)
AZE: Kamran Ağayev, Rəşad Ferhad Sadıqov, Elnur Fazahir Allahverdiyev, Ruslan Ibrahim Abışov, Mahir Ağateyyub Şükürov, Rasim Ramaldanov, Rəşad Äbulfaz Sadiqov, Rahid Alakbar Əmirquliyev (62.Branimir Subašić), Araz Abdulla Abdullayev (84.Elvin Nasradin Məmmədov), Vaqif Füzuli Cavadov, Rüfət Dadaşov. Trainer: Hans-Hubert Vogts (Germany).
LUX: Jonathan Joubert, Mario Mutsch, Eric Hoffmann, Massimo Martino, Maxime Chanot, Chris Philipps (46.Ben Payal), Lars Christian Krogh Gerson, Stefano Bensi, Laurent Jans, Aurélien Joachim, Maurice John Deville (27.Tom Laterza; 48.Daniel Alves Da Mota). Trainer: Luc Holtz.
Goals: 1-0 Ruslan Ibrahim Abışov (71), 1-1 Stefano Bensi (80).
Cautions: Vaqif Füzuli Cavadov, Rəşad Ferhad Sadıqov / Mario Mutsch, Stefano Bensi, Eric Hoffmann, Tom Laterza.
Sent off: Branimir Subašić (85).

14.08.2013, Windsor Park, Belfast; Attendance: 11,178
Referee: Tom Harald Hagen (Norway)
NORTHERN IRELAND - RUSSIA 1-0(1-0)
NIR: Roy Eric Carroll, Aaron William Hughes, Gareth Gerald McAuley, Craig George Cathcart, Shane Kevin Ferguson, Daniel Patrick Lafferty, Steven Davis, Niall McGinn (82.Corry John Evans), Oliver James Norwood, Martin Andrew Paterson (86.William Donald Grigg), Jamie John Ward. Trainer: Michael Andrew Martin O'Neill.
RUS: Igor Akinfeev, Vasili Berezutski, Sergei Ignashevich, Aleksandr Anyukov, Vladimir Bystrov, Dmitri Kombarov, Roman Shirokov, Viktor Fayzulin, Igor Denisov, Alan Dzagoev (46.Denis Cheryshev; 52.Aleksandr Samedov), Aleksandr Kerzhakov (46.Artyom Dzyuba). Trainer: Fabio Capello (Italy).
Goal: 1-0 Martin Andrew Paterson (43).
Cautions: Daniel Patrick Lafferty, Martin Andrew Paterson / Vasili Berezutski.

06.09.2013, Centralny Stadium, Kazan; Attendance: 18,525
Referee: Robert Madden (Scotland)
RUSSIA - LUXEMBOURG 4-1(2-0)
RUS: Igor Akinfeev, Sergei Ignashevich, Vladimir Granat, Aleksei Kozlov, Vladimir Bystrov (68.Aleksandr Samedov), Dmitri Kombarov, Roman Shirokov (82.Aleksandr Ryazantsev), Viktor Fayzulin, Igor Denisov, Aleksandr Kerzhakov, Aleksandr Kokorin (46.Aleksei Ionov). Trainer: Fabio Capello (Italy).
LUX: Jonathan Joubert, Chris Philipps, Lars Christian Krogh Gerson (66.René Peters), Ben Payal, Mathias Jänisch, Stefano Bensi (77.Antonio Luisi), Tom Laterza, Laurent Jans, Daniel Alves Da Mota, Aurélien Joachim, David Turpel (60.Yannick Bastos). Trainer: Luc Holtz.
Goals: 1-0 Aleksandr Kokorin (1), 2-0 Aleksandr Kokorin (36), 3-0 Aleksandr Kerzhakov (59), 3-1 Aurélien Joachim (90), 4-1 Aleksandr Samedov (90+3).
Cautions: Ben Payal.

06.09.2013, Windsor Park, Belfast; Attendance: 13,629
Referee: Daniel Miguel Alves Gomes „Danny“ Desmond Makkelie (Holland)

NORTHERN IRELAND - PORTUGAL 2-4(1-1)

NIR: Roy Eric Carroll, Gareth Gerald McAuley, Jonathan Grant Evans, Lee James Stephen Hodson, Shane Kevin Ferguson (76.Christopher Patrick Baird), Steven Davis, Christopher Brunt, Niall McGinn (67.Kyle Lafferty), Oliver James Norwood, Martin Andrew Paterson, Jamie John Ward (71.Corry John Evans). Trainer: Michael Andrew Martin O'Neill.

POR: Rui Pedro dos Santos Patrício, Képler Laveran Lima Ferreira „Pepe“, Bruno Eduardo Regufe Alves, Fábio Alexandre da Silva Coentrão, João Pedro da Silva Pereira, Raul José Trindade Meireles (55.Luís Carlos Almeida da Cunha „Nani“), Miguel Luís Pinto Veloso, João Filipe Iria Santos Moutinho, Adelino André Vieira de Freitas „Vieirinha“ (65.Nélson Miguel Castro Oliveira), Cristiano Ronaldo dos Santos Aveiro (90.Rúben Filipe Marques Amorim), Hélder Manuel Marques Postiga. Trainer: Paulo Jorge Gomes Bento.

Goals: 0-1 Bruno Eduardo Regufe Alves (21), 1-1 Gareth Gerald McAuley (36), 2-1 Jamie John Ward (52), 2-2 Cristiano Ronaldo dos Santos Aveiro (68), 2-3 Cristiano Ronaldo dos Santos Aveiro (77), 2-4 Cristiano Ronaldo dos Santos Aveiro (83).

Cautions: Steven Davis, Christopher Brunt, Roy Eric Carroll, Oliver James Norwood / Képler Laveran Lima Ferreira „Pepe“,Cristiano Ronaldo dos Santos Aveiro, Fábio Alexandre da Silva Coentrão.

Sent off: Hélder Manuel Marques Postiga (43), Christopher Brunt (61), Kyle Lafferty (80).

07.09.2013, National Stadium, Ramat Gan, Tel Aviv; Attendance: 21,250
Referee: Stefan Johannesson (Sweden)

ISRAEL - AZERBAIJAN 1-1(0-0)

ISR: David Aouate, Tal Ben Haim, Eitan Tibi, Ofir Davidzada, Bibras Natkho, Gal Alberman (72.Maharan Radi), Eran Zahavy (62.Elyaniv Felix Barda), Hen Ezra (62.Lior Refaelov), Sheran Yeini, Maor Melikson, Itay Menachem Shechter. Trainer: Eli Guttman.

AZE: Kamran Ağayev, Rəşad Ferhad Sadıqov, Elnur Fazahir Allahverdiyev (46.Qara Elxan Qarayev), Ruslan Ibrahim Abışov (78.Cavid Shakir Hüseynov), Mahir Ağateyyub Şükürov, Rasim Ramaldanov (71.Volodimir Levin), Rahid Alakbar Əmirquliyev, Araz Abdulla Abdullayev, Rauf Sahraman Əliyev, Cihan Özkara, Rüfət Dadaşov. Trainer: Hans-Hubert Vogts (Germany).

Goals: 0-1 Rahid Alakbar Əmirquliyev (61), 1-1 Itay Menachem Shechter (73).

Cautions: Eitan Tibi / Ruslan Ibrahim Abışov, Rasim Ramaldanov, Elnur Fazahir Allahverdiyev.

10.09.2013, Petrovsky Stadium, St. Petersburg; Attendance: 21,107
Referee: Manuel Gräfe (Germany)

RUSSIA - ISRAEL 3-1(0-0)

RUS: Igor Akinfeev, Vasili Berezutski, Sergei Ignashevich, Aleksei Kozlov, Dmitri Kombarov, Aleksandr Samedov, Roman Shirokov, Viktor Fayzulin (46.Alan Dzagoev), Igor Denisov (46.Denis Glushakov), Aleksandr Kerzhakov, Aleksandr Kokorin (77.Vladimir Bystrov). Trainer: Fabio Capello (Italy).

ISR: David Aouate, Tal Ben Haim, Dekel Keinan, Ofir Davidzada, Bibras Natkho, Gal Alberman (71.Maharan Radi), Eran Zahavy, Lior Refaelov, Sheran Yeini, Maor Melikson (46.Hen Ezra), Elyaniv Felix Barda (65.Itay Menachem Shechter). Trainer: Eli Guttman.

Goals: 1-0 Vasili Berezutski (49), 2-0 Aleksandr Kokorin (52), 3-0 Denis Glushakov (74), 3-1 Eran Zahavy (90+3).

Cautions: Dmitri Kombarov, Sergei Ignashevich / David Aouate, Ofir Davidzada.

10.09.2013, Stade „Josy Barthel“, Luxembourg; Attendance: 4,114
Referee: Robert Malek (Poland)

LUXEMBOURG - NORTHERN IRELAND 3-2(1-1)

LUX: Jonathan Joubert, Mario Mutsch, Chris Philipps, Lars Christian Krogh Gerson, Mathias Jänisch, Stefano Bensi, Tom Laterza, Laurent Jans, Daniel Alves Da Mota (89.Ante Bukvić), Aurélien Joachim, David Turpel (68.Antonio Luisi). Trainer: Luc Holtz.

NIR: Roy Eric Carroll, Gareth Gerald McAuley, Jonathan Grant Evans, Lee James Stephen Hodson, Shane Kevin Ferguson (60.William Robert McKay), Daniel Patrick Lafferty (80.William Donald Grigg), Steven Davis, Niall McGinn (35.Michael Joseph O'Connor), Oliver James Norwood, Martin Andrew Paterson, Jamie John Ward. Trainer: Michael Andrew Martin O'Neill.

Goals: 0-1 Martin Andrew Paterson (14), 1-1 Aurélien Joachim (45+1), 2-1 Stefano Bensi (78), 2-2 Gareth Gerald McAuley (82), 3-2 Mathias Jänisch (87).

Cautions: Aurélien Joachim / Gareth Gerald McAuley.

11.10.2013, Stade „Josy Barthel“, Luxembourg; Attendance: 5,354
Referee: Stephan Studer (Switzerland)

LUXEMBOURG - RUSSIA 0-4(0-3)

LUX: Jonathan Joubert, Mario Mutsch, Chris Philipps, Lars Christian Krogh Gerson, Mathias Jänisch, Stefano Bensi, Tom Laterza, Laurent Jans, Daniel Alves Da Mota (62.Yannick Bastos), Antonio Luisi (76.Massimo Martino), David Turpel (31.Ben Payal). Trainer: Luc Holtz.

RUS: Igor Akinfeev, Vasili Berezutski, Vladimir Granat, Aleksei Kozlov, Dmitri Kombarov (85.Georgi Shchennikov), Aleksandr Samedov, Roman Shirokov, Viktor Fayzulin, Denis Glushakov, Aleksandr Kerzhakov, Aleksandr Kokorin (46.Yuri Zhirkov; 65.Vladimir Bystrov). Trainer: Fabio Capello (Italy).

Goals: 0-1 Aleksandr Samedov (9), 0-2 Viktor Fayzulin (39), 0-3 Denis Glushakov (45+2), 0-4 Aleksandr Kerzhakov (73).

Cautions: Daniel Alves Da Mota.

11.10.2013, Estádio "José Alvalade", Lisboa; Attendance: 48,317
Referee: Tom Harald Hagen (Norway)

PORTUGAL - ISRAEL 1-1(1-0)

POR: Rui Pedro dos Santos Patrício, Ricardo Miguel Moreira da Costa, Képler Laveran Lima Ferreira „Pepe“, Vitorino Gabriel Pacheco Antunes, Luís Carlos Almeida da Cunha „Nani“, Miguel Luís Pinto Veloso (87.Éderzito António Macedo Lopes „Éder“), João Filipe Iria Santos Moutinho, Rúben Micael Freitas da Ressureição (69.Josué Filipe Soares Pesqueira), André Gomes Magalhães de Almeida, Cristiano Ronaldo dos Santos Aveiro, Hugo Miguel Pereira de Almeida (70.Nélson Miguel Castro Oliveira). Trainer: Paulo Jorge Gomes Bento.

ISR: David Aouate, Tal Ben Haim, Eyal Meshumar, Omri Ben Harush, Eitan Tibi, Bibras Natkho, Eran Zahavy (83.Omer Damari), Sheran Yeini, Maharan Radi (67.Lior Refaelov), Elyaniv Felix Barda (60.Tal Ben Haim), Eden Ben Basat. Trainer: Eli Guttman.

Goals: 1-0 Ricardo Miguel Moreira da Costa (28), 1-1 Eden Ben Basat (85).

Cautions: Képler Laveran Lima Ferreira „Pepe“,Cristiano Ronaldo dos Santos Aveiro / Lior Refaelov.

11.10.2013, Bakcell Arena, Bakı; Attendance: 10,100
Referee: Andrea De Marco (Italy)

AZERBAIJAN - NORTHERN IRELAND 2-0(0-0)

AZE: Kamran Ağayev, Rəşad Ferhad Sadıqov, Elnur Fazahir Allahverdiyev, Mahir Ağateyyub Şükürov, Rasim Ramaldanov, Qara Elxan Qarayev, Rahid Alakbar Əmirquliyev, Araz Abdulla Abdullayev (82.Cihan Özkara), Vügar Nadirov (46.Cavid Shakir Hüseynov), Rauf Sahraman Əliyev, Rüfət Dadaşov (90+3.Badavi Hüseynov). Trainer: Hans-Hubert Vogts (Germany).
NIR: Roy Eric Carroll, Gareth Gerald McAuley, Jonathan Grant Evans, Craig George Cathcart, Lee James Stephen Hodson (66.Niall McGinn), Shane Kevin Ferguson, Steven Davis, Christopher Brunt (73.William Robert McKay), Oliver James Norwood, Martin Andrew Paterson, Jamie John Ward (84.William Donald Grigg). Trainer: Michael Andrew Martin O'Neill.
Goals: 1-0 Rüfət Dadaşov (58), 2-0 Mahir Ağateyyub Şükürov (90+4).
Cautions: Rasim Ramaldanov / Oliver James Norwood, Gareth Gerald McAuley.
Sent off: Jonathan Grant Evans (90+4).

15.10.2013, Estádio Cidade de Coimbra, Coimbra; Attendance: 18,955
Referee: Bülent Yıldırım (Turkey)

PORTUGAL - LUXEMBOURG 3-0(2-0)

POR: Rui Pedro dos Santos Patrício, Ricardo Miguel Moreira da Costa (59.Henrique Sereno Fonseca), Fábio Alexandre da Silva Coentrão (76.Vitorino Gabriel Pacheco Antunes), Luís Carlos Novo Neto, Luís Carlos Almeida da Cunha „Nani", Miguel Luís Pinto Veloso (58.Hugo Miguel Pereira de Almeida), João Filipe Iria Santos Moutinho, André Gomes Magalhães de Almeida, Josué Filipe Soares Pesqueira, Hélder Manuel Marques Postiga, Silvestre Manuel Gonçalves Varela. Trainer: Paulo Jorge Gomes Bento.
LUX: Jonathan Joubert, Mario Mutsch, Chris Philipps, Lars Christian Krogh Gerson, Ben Payal (61.René Peters), Mathias Jänisch, Stefano Bensi (46.Antonio Luisi), Tom Laterza, Laurent Jans, Daniel Alves Da Mota (82.Massimo Martino), Aurélien Joachim. Trainer: Luc Holtz.
Goals: 1-0 Silvestre Manuel Gonçalves Varela (30), 2-0 Luís Carlos Almeida da Cunha „Nani" (36), 3-0 Hélder Manuel Marques Postiga (78).
Cautions: Josué Filipe Soares Pesqueira, Fábio Alexandre da Silva Coentrão / Chris Philipps, Lars Christian Krogh Gerson, Daniel Alves Da Mota.
Sent off: Aurélien Joachim (28).

15.10.2013, National Stadium, Ramat Gan, Tel Aviv; Attendance: 12,785
Referee: Laurent Duhamel (France)

ISRAEL - NORTHERN IRELAND 1-1(1-0)

ISR: David Aouate, Tal Ben Haim (46.Dekel Keinan), Eyal Meshumar, Eitan Tibi, Ofir Davidzada, Bibras Natkho, Eran Zahavy (71.Tal Ben Haim), Lior Refaelov (79.Itay Menachem Shechter), Sheran Yeini, Maor Melikson, Eden Ben Basat. Trainer: Eli Guttman.
NIR: Roy Eric Carroll, Christopher Patrick Baird, Rory Alexander McArdle, Craig George Cathcart, Lee James Stephen Hodson, Daniel Patrick Lafferty (78.Shane Kevin Ferguson), Steven Davis, Samuel Gary Clingan, Niall McGinn (65.Jamie John Ward), Corry John Evans (24.Christopher Brunt), Martin Andrew Paterson. Trainer: Michael Andrew Martin O'Neill.
Goals: 1-0 Eden Ben Basat (43), 1-1 Steven Davis (72).
Cautions: Sheran Yeini / Craig George Cathcart.

15.10.2013, Bakcell Arena, Bakı; Attendance: 11,000
Referee: Milorad Mažić (Serbia)

AZERBAIJAN - RUSSIA **1-1(0-1)**

AZE: Kamran Ağayev, Rəşad Ferhad Sadıqov, Elnur Fazahir Allahverdiyev, Ruslan Ibrahim Abışov, Volodimir Levin, Mahir Ağateyyub Şükürov, Maksim Medvedev, Araz Abdulla Abdullayev (79.Rahid Alakbar Əmirquliyev), Əfran Amit İsmayılov (46.Qara Elxan Qarayev), Rauf Sahraman Əliyev, Rüfət Dadaşov (83.Vaqif Füzuli Cavadov). Trainer: Hans-Hubert Vogts (Germany).
RUS: Igor Akinfeev, Vasili Berezutski, Sergei Ignashevich, Aleksei Kozlov, Dmitri Kombarov, Aleksandr Samedov (82.Pavel Mamaev), Roman Shirokov, Viktor Fayzulin (46.Oleg Shatov), Denis Glushakov, Aleksandr Kerzhakov, Aleksandr Kokorin. Trainer: Fabio Capello (Italy).
Goals: 0-1 Roman Shirokov (16), 1-1 Vaqif Füzuli Cavadov (90).
Cautions: Aleksandr Samedov, Denis Glushakov.
Sent off: Maksim Medvedev (73).

GROUP G

07.09.2012	Vaduz	Liechtenstein - Bosnia-Herzegovina	1-8(0-4)
07.09.2012	Vilnius	Lithuania - Slovakia	1-1(1-1)
07.09.2012	Riga	Latvia - Greece	1-2(1-0)
11.09.2012	Zenica	Bosnia-Herzegovina - Latvia	4-1(2-1)
11.09.2012	Bratislava	Slovakia - Liechtenstein	2-0(1-0)
11.09.2012	Peiraiás	Greece - Lithuania	2-0(0-0)
12.10.2012	Vaduz	Liechtenstein - Lithuania	0-2(0-0)
12.10.2012	Bratislava	Slovakia - Latvia	2-1(2-0)
12.10.2012	Peiraiás	Greece - Bosnia-Herzegovina	0-0
16.10.2012	Zenica	Bosnia-Herzegovina - Lithuania	3-0(3-0)
16.10.2012	Riga	Latvia - Liechtenstein	2-0(1-0)
16.10.2012	Bratislava	Slovakia - Greece	0-1(0-0)
22.03.2013	Vaduz	Liechtenstein - Latvia	1-1(1-1)
22.03.2013	Žilina	Slovakia - Lithuania	1-1(1-1)
22.03.2013	Zenica	Bosnia-Herzegovina - Greece	3-1(2-0)
07.06.2013	Riga	Latvia - Bosnia-Herzegovina	0-5(0-0)
07.06.2013	Vilnius	Lithuania - Greece	0-1(0-0)
07.06.2013	Vaduz	Liechtenstein - Slovakia	1-1(1-0)
06.09.2013	Riga	Latvia - Lithuania	2-1(2-1)
06.09.2013	Vaduz	Liechtenstein - Greece	0-1(0-0)
06.09.2013	Zenica	Bosnia-Herzegovina - Slovakia	0-1(0-0)
10.09.2013	Marijampole	Lithuania - Liechtenstein	2-0(2-0)
10.09.2013	Žilina	Slovakia - Bosnia-Herzegovina	1-2(1-0)
10.09.2013	Peiraiás	Greece - Latvia	1-0(0-0)
11.10.2013	Vilnius	Lithuania - Latvia	2-0(1-0)
11.10.2013	Zenica	Bosnia-Herzegovina - Liechtenstein	4-1(4-0)
11.10.2013	Peiraiás	Greece - Slovakia	1-0(1-0)
15.10.2013	Peiraiás	Greece - Liechtenstein	2-0(1-0)
15.10.2013	Kaunas	Lithuania - Bosnia-Herzegovina	0-1(0-0)
15.10.2013	Riga	Latvia - Slovakia	2-2(0-2)

FINAL STANDINGS

1.	**BOSNIA-HERZEGOVINA**	10	8	1	1	30	-	6	25
2.	**Greece**	10	8	1	1	12	-	4	25
3.	Slovakia	10	3	4	3	11	-	10	13
4.	Lithuania	10	3	2	5	9	-	11	11
5.	Latvia	10	2	2	6	10	-	20	8
6.	Liechtenstein	10	0	2	8	4	-	25	2

Bosnia-Herzegovina qualified for the Final Tournament; Greece qualified for the Play-Offs.

07.09.2012, Rheinpark Stadion, Vaduz; Attendance: 5,900
Referee: Marco Borg (Malta)
LIECHTENSTEIN - BOSNIA-HERZEGOVINA 1-8(0-4)
LIE: Peter Karl Jehle, Franz Burgmeier, Martin Stocklasa, Yves Oehri, Daniel Kaufmann, Ivan Quintans, Michele Polverino, Nicolas Hasler (89.Fabian Eberle), Vinzenz Flatz (46.Mathias Christen), Philippe Erne (71.Thomas Beck), David Hasler. Trainer: Hans-Peter Zaugg (Switzerland).
BIH: Asmir Begović, Emir Spahić, Avdija Vršajević, Toni Šunjić, Ognjen Vranješ, Zvezdjan Misimović (79.Muamer Svraka), Sejad Salihović, Miralem Pjanić (79.Damir Vrančić), Adnan Zahirović (78.Senijad Ibričić), Vedad Ibišević, Edin Džeko. Trainer: Safet Sušić.
Goals: 0-1 Zvezdjan Misimović (26), 0-2 Zvezdjan Misimović (31), 0-3 Vedad Ibišević (33), 0-4 Vedad Ibišević (40), 0-5 Edin Džeko (46), 1-5 Mathias Christen (60), 1-6 Edin Džeko (65), 1-7 Edin Džeko (81), 1-8 Edin Džeko (83).
Cautions: Mathias Christen, Thomas Beck.

07.09.2012, LFF stadionas, Vilnius; Attendance: 4,000
Referee: Carlos Clos Gómez (Spain)
LITHUANIA - SLOVAKIA 1-1(1-1)
LTU: Žydrūnas Karčemarskas, Marius Žaliūkas, Arūnas Klimavičius, Vytautas Andriuškevičius, Valdemar Borovskij, Saulius Mikoliūnas (75.Tadas Labukas), Deividas Šemberas, Edgaras Česnauskis (59.Arvydas Novikovas), Ramūnas Radavičius, Gediminas Vičius (67.Deividas Česnauskis), Darvydas Šernas. Trainer: Csaba László (Hungary).
SVK: Ján Mucha, Martin Škrtel, Radoslav Zabavník, Tomáš Hubočan, Peter Pekarík, Marek Sapara, Marek Hamšík (86.Juraj Kucka), Viktor Pečovský, Miroslav Stoch (61.Michal Breznaník), Marek Bakoš (79.Martin Jakubko), Michal Ďuriš. Trainer: Stanislav Griga & Michal Hipp.
Goals: 1-0 Marius Žaliūkas (18), 1-1 Marek Sapara (41).
Cautions: Gediminas Vičius, Tadas Labukas / Martin Škrtel, Marek Bakoš.
Sent off: Viktor Pečovský (55), Tadas Labukas (90+6).

07.09.2012, Skonto stadions, Riga; Attendance: 7,956
Referee: Ivan Bebek (Croatia)
LATVIA - GREECE 1-2(1-0)
LVA: Andris Vaņins, Kaspars Gorkšs, Ritus Krjauklis, Deniss Ivanovs, Oskars Kļava, Ivans Lukjanovs, Aleksandrs Cauņa, Oļegs Laizāns (80.Edgars Gauračs), Aleksandrs Fertovs (76.Ritvars Rugins), Artjoms Rudņevs, Aleksejs Višņakovs (75.Māris Verpakovskis). Trainer: Aleksandrs Starkovs.
GRE: Orestis-Spyridon Karnezis, Vasileios Torosidis, Kyriakos Papadopoulos, Sokratis Papastathopoulos, Nikolaos Spyropoulos, Konstantinos Katsouranis, Alexandros Tziolis, Giánnis Maniatis, Konstantinos Fortounis (80.José LIoyd Holebas), Theofanis Gekas, Konstantinos Mitroglou (46.Giórgos Samaras; 69.Sotiris Ninis). Trainer: Fernando Manuel Costa Santos (Portugal).
Goals: 1-0 Aleksandrs Cauņa (41 penalty), 1-1 Nikolaos Spyropoulos (57), 1-2 Theofanis Gekas (69).
Cautions: Kaspars Gorkšs, Ivans Lukjanovs, Oskars Kļava / Giánnis Maniatis, Alexandros Tziolis.

11.09.2012, Stadion Bilino Polje, Zenica; Attendance: 11,900
Referee: Deniz Aytekin (Germany)
BOSNIA-HERZEGOVINA - LATVIA 4-1(2-1)
BIH: Asmir Begović, Emir Spahić, Mensur Mujdža, Ognjen Vranješ, Zvezdjan Misimović, Sejad Salihović (90+1.Toni Šunjić), Miralem Pjanić, Senad Lulić (30.Avdija Vršajević), Adnan Zahirović, Vedad Ibišević (87.Haris Medunjanin), Edin Džeko. Trainer: Safet Sušić.
LVA: Andris Vaņins, Kaspars Gorkšs, Ritus Krjauklis, Deniss Ivanovs, Oskars Kļava, Ivans Lukjanovs (80.Artūrs Zjuzins), Aleksandrs Cauņa, Oļegs Laizāns, Ritvars Rugins, Artjoms Rudņevs (61.Māris Verpakovskis), Aleksejs Višņakovs (61.Vladimirs Kamešs). Trainer: Aleksandrs Starkovs.
Goals: 0-1 Kaspars Gorkšs (5), 1-1 Zvezdjan Misimović (12 penalty), 2-1 Miralem Pjanić (44), 3-1 Zvezdjan Misimović (54), 4-1 Edin Džeko (90+2).
Cautions: Ritus Krjauklis, Artjoms Rudņevs.

11.09.2012, Štadión Pasienky, Bratislava; Attendance: 4,326
Referee: Simon Lee Evans (Wales)
SLOVAKIA - LIECHTENSTEIN 2-0(1-0)
SVK: Dušan Kuciak, Martin Škrtel, Ľubomír Guldan, Radoslav Zabavník, Peter Pekarík, Kornel Saláta, Marek Sapara, Marek Hamšík (82.Juraj Kucka), Miroslav Stoch, Vladimír Weiss (63.Michal Breznaník), Marek Bakoš (60.Martin Jakubko). Trainer: Stanislav Griga & Michal Hipp.
LIE: Peter Karl Jehle, Franz Burgmeier, Martin Stocklasa, Yves Oehri, Daniel Kaufmann, Michele Polverino, Mathias Christen (84.Vinzenz Flatz), Nicolas Hasler, Thomas Beck (70.Fabian Eberle), Philippe Erne, David Hasler. Trainer: Hans-Peter Zaugg (Switzerland).
Goals: 1-0 Marek Sapara (37), 2-0 Martin Jakubko (79).
Cautions: Radoslav Zabavník, Vladimír Weiss, Martin Jakubko / Michele Polverino, Franz Burgmeier, Mathias Christen, David Hasler.

11.09.2012, Stádio „Yeorgios Karaïskákis“, Peiraiás; Attendance: 21,466
Referee: Mark Courtney (Northern Ireland)
GREECE - LITHUANIA 2-0(0-0)
GRE: Orestis-Spyridon Karnezis, Vasileios Torosidis, Kyriakos Papadopoulos, Sokratis Papastathopoulos, Nikolaos Spyropoulos, Konstantinos Katsouranis, Alexandros Tziolis, Sotiris Ninis, Giánnis Maniatis (46.Konstantinos Mitroglou), Konstantinos Fortounis (69.José Lloyd Holebas), Theofanis Gekas (80.Charalampos Mavrias). Trainer: Fernando Manuel Costa Santos (Portugal).
LTU: Žydrūnas Karčemarskas, Marius Žaliūkas, Arūnas Klimavičius, Egidijus Vaitkūnas, Valdemar Borovskij (46.Deividas Česnauskis), Saulius Mikoliūnas, Deividas Šemberas, Edgaras Česnauskis, Gediminas Vičius, Andrius Velička (76.Arvydas Novikovas), Darvydas Šernas (57.Artūras Rimkevičius). Trainer: Csaba László (Hungary).
Goals: 1-0 Sotiris Ninis (55), 2-0 Konstantinos Mitroglou (72).
Cautions: Kyriakos Papadopoulos / Edgaras Česnauskis, Gediminas Vičius, Darvydas Šernas, Artūras Rimkevičius, Saulius Mikoliūnas.

12.10.2012, Rheinpark Stadion, Vaduz; Attendance: 1,112
Referee: Slavko Vinčić (Slovenia)
LIECHTENSTEIN - LITHUANIA 0-2(0-0)
LIE: Benjamin Büchel, Franz Burgmeier, Martin Stocklasa, Yves Oehri, Daniel Kaufmann, Ivan Quintans, Michele Polverino, Nicolas Hasler (73.Niklas Kieber), Sandro Wieser (84.Lucas Eberle), Thomas Beck, Philippe Erne (87.Philipp Ospelt). Trainer: Hans-Peter Zaugg (Switzerland).
LTU: Žydrūnas Karčemarskas, Marius Žaliūkas, Arūnas Klimavičius, Tadas Kijanskas, Deividas Česnauskis (58.Darvydas Šernas), Saulius Mikoliūnas, Deividas Šemberas, Edgaras Česnauskis, Ramūnas Radavičius (90+1.Marius Stankevičius), Arvydas Novikovas, Tomas Danilevičius (87.Artūras Rimkevičius). Trainer: Csaba László (Hungary).
Goals: 0-1 Edgaras Česnauskis (50), 0-2 Edgaras Česnauskis (74).
Cautions: Thomas Beck, Philippe Erne, Ivan Quintans / Deividas Šemberas, Saulius Mikoliūnas, Edgaras Česnauskis, Marius Stankevičius.

12.10.2012, Štadión Pasienky, Bratislava; Attendance: 4,012
Referee: Daniel Miguel Alves Gomes „Danny“ Desmond Makkelie (Holland)
SLOVAKIA - LATVIA 2-1(2-0)
SVK: Dušan Kuciak, Martin Škrtel (90.Ján Ďurica), Peter Pekarík, Kornel Saláta, Marek Sapara, Marek Hamšík, Viktor Pečovský, Michal Breznaník, Miroslav Stoch, Vladimír Weiss (43.Michal Ďuriš), Marek Bakoš (60.Filip Hološko). Trainer: Stanislav Griga & Michal Hipp.
LVA: Andris Vaņins, Kaspars Gorkšs, Ritus Krjauklis, Deniss Ivanovs, Oskars Kļava, Ivans Lukjanovs (53.Edgars Gauračs), Aleksandrs Cauņa (77.Māris Verpakovskis), Oļegs Laizāns (70.Ritvars Rugins), Aleksandrs Fertovs, Artjoms Rudņevs, Aleksejs Višņakovs. Trainer: Aleksandrs Starkovs.
Goals: 1-0 Marek Hamšík (5 penalty), 2-0 Marek Sapara (9), 2-1 Māris Verpakovskis (84 penalty).
Cautions: Michal Breznaník, Miroslav Stoch / Andris Vaņins, Oskars Kļava, Ritus Krjauklis, Edgars Gauračs.

12.10.2012, Stádio „Yeorgios Karaïskákis", Peiraiás; Attendance: 26,211
Referee: Antonio Damato (Italy)
GREECE - BOSNIA-HERZEGOVINA 0-0
GRE: Orestis-Spyridon Karnezis, Stylianos Malezas (67.Giórgos Karagounis), Vasileios Torosidis, Sokratis Papastathopoulos, Nikolaos Spyropoulos, Konstantinos Katsouranis, Alexandros Tziolis, Giánnis Maniatis (80.Konstantinos Mitroglou), Konstantinos Fortounis, Giórgos Samaras, Theofanis Gekas (57.Dimitrios Salpingidis). Trainer: Fernando Manuel Costa Santos (Portugal).
BIH: Asmir Begović, Emir Spahić, Mensur Mujdža, Ognjen Vranješ, Zvezdjan Misimović, Haris Medunjanin (74.Senijad Ibričić), Sejad Salihović, Senad Lulić (75.Miroslav Stevanović), Adnan Zahirović, Vedad Ibišević, Edin Džeko. Trainer: Safet Sušić.
Cautions: Giórgos Samaras, Konstantinos Fortounis / Edin Džeko, Ognjen Vranješ.

16.10.2012, Referee: Miroslav Zelinka (Czech Republic)
Stadion Bilino Polje, Zenica; Attendance: 11,920
BOSNIA-HERZEGOVINA - LITHUANIA 3-0(3-0)
BIH: Asmir Begović, Emir Spahić, Mensur Mujdža (58.Avdija Vršajević), Ognjen Vranješ, Zvezdjan Misimović, Sejad Salihović, Miralem Pjanić (66.Miroslav Stevanović), Senad Lulić (74.Ervin Zukanović), Adnan Zahirović, Vedad Ibišević, Edin Džeko. Trainer: Safet Sušić.
LTU: Žydrūnas Karčemarskas, Marius Žaliūkas, Marius Stankevičius, Arūnas Klimavičius, Tadas Kijanskas, Valdemar Borovskij, Deividas Šemberas, Mindaugas Panka (85.Linas Pilibaitis), Ramūnas Radavičius (46.Darvydas Šernas), Arvydas Novikovas, Tadas Labukas (66.Artūras Rimkevičius). Trainer: Csaba László (Hungary).
Goals: 1-0 Vedad Ibišević (28), 2-0 Edin Džeko (34), 3-0 Miralem Pjanić (40).
Cautions: Miroslav Stevanović / Arūnas Klimavičius, Valdemar Borovskij, Marius Žaliūkas.

16.10.2012, Skonto stadions, Riga; Attendance: 3,500
Referee: István Kovács (Hungary)
LATVIA - LIECHTENSTEIN 2-0(1-0)
LVA: Andris Vaņins, Kaspars Gorkšs, Nauris Bulvītis, Deniss Ivanovs, Aleksandrs Cauņa, Oļegs Laizāns (65.Edgars Gauračs), Aleksandrs Fertovs, Ritvars Rugins, Māris Verpakovskis (85.Artūrs Zjuzins), Artjoms Rudņevs, Vladimirs Kamešs (74.Aleksejs Višņakovs). Trainer: Aleksandrs Starkovs.
LIE: Cengiz Biçer, Franz Burgmeier, Martin Stocklasa, Yves Oehri, Daniel Kaufmann, Ivan Quintans, Michele Polverino, Mathias Christen, Nicolas Hasler (85.Lucas Eberle), Sandro Wieser, Philippe Erne (80.Niklas Kieber). Trainer: Hans-Peter Zaugg (Switzerland).
Goals: 1-0 Vladimirs Kamešs (29), 2-0 Edgars Gauračs (77).
Cautions: Ritvars Rugins, Deniss Ivanovs / Daniel Kaufmann, Sandro Wieser, Martin Stocklasa.
Sent off: Daniel Kaufmann (60).

16.10.2012, Referee: William Collum (Scotland)
Štadión Pasienky, Bratislava; Attendance: 7,494
SLOVAKIA - GREECE 0-1(0-0)
SVK: Dušan Kuciak, Martin Škrtel, Radoslav Zabavník, Kornel Saláta, Marek Sapara, Marek Hamšík, Juraj Kucka (82.Karim Abdul-Jabbar Guédé), Viktor Pečovský, Michal Breznaník, Miroslav Stoch (69.Vladimír Weiss), Michal Ďuriš (72.Filip Hološko). Trainer: Stanislav Griga & Michal Hipp.
GRE: Orestis-Spyridon Karnezis, Dimitrios Siovas (76.Giórgos Fotakis), Vasileios Torosidis, Sokratis Papastathopoulos, Nikolaos Spyropoulos, Konstantinos Katsouranis, Alexandros Tziolis, Sotiris Ninis (66.Giórgos Karagounis), Giórgos Samaras, Theofanis Gekas (59.Konstantinos Mitroglou), Dimitrios Salpingidis. Trainer: Fernando Manuel Costa Santos (Portugal).
Goal: 0-1 Dimitrios Salpingidis (63).
Cautions: Marek Sapara, Filip Hološko, Michal Breznaník / Orestis-Spyridon Karnezis, Dimitrios Salpingidis.

22.03.2013, Rheinpark Stadion, Vaduz; Attendance: 1,150
Referee: Kevin Clancy (Scotland)
LIECHTENSTEIN - LATVIA 1-1(1-1)
LIE: Peter Karl Jehle, Franz Burgmeier, Martin Stocklasa, Yves Oehri (46.Ivan Quintans), Michele Polverino, Mathias Christen (72.Thomas Beck), Nicolas Hasler, Sandro Wieser, Mario Frick, Philippe Erne (90+4.Olcay Gür), David Hasler. Trainer: Rene Pauritsch (Austria).
LVA: Andris Vaņins, Kaspars Gorkšs, Deniss Ivanovs, Oskars Kļava, Artis Lazdiņš, Aleksandrs Cauņa, Oļegs Laizāns (46.Aleksejs Višņakovs), Ritvars Rugins, Māris Verpakovskis (66.Edgars Gauračs), Artjoms Rudņevs, Vladimirs Kamešs (56.Jurijs Žigajevs). Trainer: Aleksandrs Starkovs.
Goals: 1-0 Michele Polverino (17), 1-1 Aleksandrs Cauņa (30).
Cautions: Martin Stocklasa, Franz Burgmeier, Michele Polverino, Nicolas Hasler / Ritvars Rugins, Artis Lazdiņš.

22.03.2013, Štadión pod Dubňom, Žilina; Attendance: 4,560
Referee: Michael Oliver (England)
SLOVAKIA - LITHUANIA 1-1(1-1)
SVK: Dušan Kuciak, Martin Škrtel, Tomáš Hubočan, Ján Ďurica, Marek Sapara, Dušan Švento, Marek Hamšík, Juraj Kucka, Viktor Pečovský (70.Marek Bakoš), Róbert Mak (64.Michal Ďuriš), Martin Jakubko. Trainer: Stanislav Griga & Michal Hipp.
LTU: Žydrūnas Karčemarskas (46.Giedrius Arlauskis), Tomas Mikuckis, Tadas Kijanskas, Saulius Mikoliūnas, Deividas Šemberas, Edgaras Česnauskis, Kęstutis Ivaškevičius, Mindaugas Panka, Mindaugas Kalonas (69.Arvydas Novikovas), Darvydas Šernas (90.Vytautas Lukša), Deivydas Matulevičius. Trainer: Csaba László (Hungary).
Goals: 0-1 Darvydas Šernas (19), 1-1 Martin Jakubko (40).
Cautions: Martin Škrtel, Martin Jakubko / Mindaugas Panka, Deividas Šemberas, Darvydas Šernas, Tadas Kijanskas.

22.03.2013, Stadion Bilino Polje, Zenica; Attendance: 11,100
Referee: Björn Kuipers (Holland)
BOSNIA-HERZEGOVINA - GREECE 3-1(2-0)
BIH: Asmir Begović, Emir Spahić, Mensur Mujdža (84.Avdija Vršajević), Ervin Zukanović, Ognjen Vranješ, Zvezdjan Misimović, Haris Medunjanin (79.Elvir Rahimić), Senad Lulić, Adnan Zahirović, Vedad Ibišević (84.Miroslav Stevanović), Edin Džeko. Trainer: Safet Sušić.
GRE: Orestis-Spyridon Karnezis, José Lloyd Holebas, Avraam Papadopoulos, Vasileios Torosidis, Sokratis Papastathopoulos, Giórgos Tzavellas (46.Theofanis Gekas), Giórgos Karagounis, Konstantinos Katsouranis, Alexandros Tziolis (58.Giánnis Maniatis), Giórgos Samaras, Dimitrios Salpingidis (73.Lazaros Christodoulopoulos). Trainer: Fernando Manuel Costa Santos (Portugal).
Goals: 1-0 Edin Džeko (29), 2-0 Vedad Ibišević (36), 3-0 Edin Džeko (53), 3-1 Theofanis Gekas (90+3).
Cautions: Senad Lulić / Giórgos Tzavellas, Konstantinos Katsouranis.

07.06.2013, Skonto stadions, Riga; Attendance: 7,700
Referee: Michael Leslie Dean (England)
LATVIA - BOSNIA-HERZEGOVINA 0-5(0-0)
LVA: Andris Vaņins, Kaspars Gorkšs, Nauris Bulvītis, Pāvels Mihadjuks, Deniss Ivanovs, Oskars Kļava, Aleksandrs Fertovs, Alans Siņeļņikovs, Edgars Gauračs (64.Valērijs Šabala), Māris Verpakovskis (15.Artis Lazdiņš), Vladimirs Kamešs (59.Vladislavs Gabovs). Trainer: Aleksandrs Starkovs.
BIH: Asmir Begović, Emir Spahić, Mensur Mujdža, Ervin Zukanović, Haris Medunjanin (70.Miroslav Stevanović), Elvir Rahimić (70.Edin Višća), Sejad Salihović (79.Senijad Ibričić), Miralem Pjanić, Senad Lulić, Vedad Ibišević, Edin Džeko. Trainer: Safet Sušić.
Goals: 0-1 Senad Lulić (48), 0-2 Vedad Ibišević (53), 0-3 Haris Medunjanin (63), 0-4 Miralem Pjanić (80), 0-5 Edin Džeko (82).
Cautions: Alans Siņeļņikovs, Valērijs Šabala.

Sent off: Aleksandrs Fertovs (11).

07.06.2013, LFF stadionas, Vilnius; Attendance: 4,500
Referee: Olegário Manuel Bártolo Faustino Benquerença (Portugal)
LITHUANIA - GREECE 0-1(0-0)
LTU: Emilijus Zubas, Marius Stankevičius, Tomas Mikuckis, Tadas Kijanskas, Valdemar Borovskij, Saulius Mikoliūnas (73.Artūras Žulpa), Edgaras Česnauskis, Kęstutis Ivaškevičius (86.Tadas Eliošius), Mindaugas Panka, Mindaugas Kalonas, Deivydas Matulevičius (86.Deividas Česnauskis). Trainer: Csaba László (Hungary).
GRE: Orestis-Spyridon Karnezis, José Lloyd Holebas (46.Giórgos Tzavellas), Vasileios Torosidis, Sokratis Papastathopoulos, Konstantinos Manolas, Giórgos Karagounis, Konstantinos Katsouranis (85.Alexandros Tziolis), Lazaros Christodoulopoulos, Giánnis Maniatis, Giórgos Samaras, Theofanis Gekas (65.Dimitrios Salpingidis). Trainer: Fernando Manuel Costa Santos (Portugal).
Goal: 0-1 Lazaros Christodoulopoulos (20).
Cautions: Edgaras Česnauskis, Kęstutis Ivaškevičius / Giórgos Karagounis, Giórgos Samaras, Dimitrios Salpingidis.

07.06.2013, Rheinpark Stadion, Vaduz; Attendance: 1,623
Referee: Martin Strömbergsson (Sweden)
LIECHTENSTEIN - SLOVAKIA 1-1(1-0)
LIE: Peter Karl Jehle, Yves Oehri, Daniel Kaufmann, Andreas Christen, Ivan Quintans, Martin Büchel, Mathias Christen (90.Thomas Beck), Nicolas Hasler, Sandro Wieser (90+5.Robin Gubser), Mario Frick (24.Franz Josef Vogt), David Hasler. Trainer: Rene Pauritsch (Austria).
SVK: Dušan Kuciak, Tomáš Hubočan (46.Lukáš Pauschek), Marián Čišovský, Ján Ďurica, Marek Sapara, Dušan Švento, Marek Hamšík, Miroslav Stoch, Róbert Mak, Richard Lásik (24.Tomáš Ďubek), Filip Hološko (70.Marek Bakoš). Trainer: Stanislav Griga & Michal Hipp.
Goals: 1-0 Martin Büchel (13), 1-1 Ján Ďurica (73).
Cautions: Mathias Christen / Lukáš Pauschek.

06.09.2013, Skonto stadions, Riga; Attendance: 7,306
Referee: Sébastien Delferiere (Belgium)
LATVIA - LITHUANIA 2-1(2-1)
LVA: Andris Vaņins, Kaspars Gorkšs, Vladislavs Gabovs, Nauris Bulvītis, Vitālijs Maksimenko, Juris Laizāns, Alans Siņeļņikovs, Ritvars Rugins (74.Artis Lazdiņš), Artūrs Zjuzins (64.Aleksandrs Cauņa), Artjoms Rudņevs (90+3.Renārs Rode), Valērijs Šabala. Trainer: Marians Pahars.
LTU: Žydrūnas Karčemarskas, Marius Stankevičius, Tomas Mikuckis, Tadas Kijanskas, Saulius Mikoliūnas (73.Evaldas Razulis), Mindaugas Panka, Mindaugas Kalonas (86.Edgaras Česnauskis), Gediminas Vičius, Arvydas Novikovas (50.Deividas Česnauskis), Darvydas Šernas, Deivydas Matulevičius. Trainer: Csaba László (Hungary).
Goals: 1-0 Nauris Bulvītis (20), 2-0 Artūrs Zjuzins (42), 2-1 Deivydas Matulevičius (44).
Cautions: Artjoms Rudņevs, Valērijs Šabala / Mindaugas Panka, Deivydas Matulevičius, Tomas Mikuckis.

06.09.2013, Rheinpark Stadion, Vaduz; Attendance: 2,680
Referee: Stanislav Todorov (Bulgaria)
LIECHTENSTEIN - GREECE 0-1(0-0)
LIE: Peter Karl Jehle, Franz Burgmeier, Martin Stocklasa, Yves Oehri, Ivan Quintans, Michele Polverino, Mathias Christen (90+2.Robin Gubser), Nicolas Hasler, Sandro Wieser (86.Seyhan Yildiz), Mario Frick (28.Andreas Christen), David Hasler. Trainer: Rene Pauritsch (Austria).
GRE: Orestis-Spyridon Karnezis, José Lloyd Holebas, Dimitrios Siovas, Vasileios Torosidis, Sokratis Papastathopoulos, Konstantinos Katsouranis, Lazaros Christodoulopoulos (84.Dimitrios Papadopoulos), Panagiotis Giórgos Kone (46.Sotiris Ninis), Giánnis Maniatis, Panagiotis Tachtsidis (67.Giórgos Karagounis), Konstantinos Mitroglou. Trainer: Fernando Manuel Costa Santos (Portugal).
Goal: 0-1 Konstantinos Mitroglou (72).
Cautions: Franz Burgmeier, Mario Frick, David Hasler, Mathias Christen, Nicolas Hasler, Michele

Polverino / Panagiotis Giórgos Kone, Vasileios Torosidis, José Lloyd Holebas.
Sent off: José Lloyd Holebas (59), David Hasler (66).

06.09.2013, Stadion Bilino Polje, Zenica; Attendance: 11,620
Referee: Nicola Rizzoli (Italy)
BOSNIA-HERZEGOVINA - SLOVAKIA 0-1(0-0)
BIH: Asmir Begović, Emir Spahić, Avdija Vršajević (65.Edin Višća), Ermin Bičakčić, Zvezdjan Misimović (78.Miroslav Stevanović), Haris Medunjanin (82.Izet Hajrović), Sejad Salihović, Miralem Pjanić, Senad Lulić, Vedad Ibišević, Edin Džeko. Trainer: Safet Sušić.
SVK: Ján Mucha, Martin Škrtel, Tomáš Hubočan, Peter Pekarík, Ján Ďurica, Stanislav Šesták (61.Erik Jendrišek), Marek Hamšík (72.Karim Abdul-Jabbar Guédé), Juraj Kucka, Viktor Pečovský, Vladimír Weiss, Adam Nemec (86.Martin Jakubko). Trainer: Ján Kozák.
Goal: 0-1 Viktor Pečovský (77).
Cautions: Stanislav Šesták.

10.09.2013, ARVI futbolo arena, Marijampolė; Attendance: 1,955
Referee: Lasha Silagava (Georgia)
LITHUANIA - LIECHTENSTEIN 2-0(2-0)
LTU: Žydrūnas Karčemarskas, Tomas Mikuckis, Tadas Kijanskas, Vytautas Andriuškevičius, Deividas Česnauskis, Saulius Mikoliūnas, Edgaras Česnauskis (78.Darvydas Šernas), Kęstutis Ivaškevičius, Mindaugas Kalonas (72.Mantas Kuklys), Gediminas Vičius, Deivydas Matulevičius (90+3.Gratas Sirgėdas). Trainer: Csaba László (Hungary).
LIE: Peter Karl Jehle, Franz Burgmeier, Martin Stocklasa, Yves Oehri, Daniel Kaufmann, Andreas Christen, Ivan Quintans, Michele Polverino, Mathias Christen, Sandro Wieser, Robin Gubser (75.Philippe Erne). Trainer: Rene Pauritsch (Austria).
Goals: 1-0 Deivydas Matulevičius (18), 2-0 Tadas Kijanskas (40).
Cautions: Vytautas Andriuškevičius, Gediminas Vičius, Edgaras Česnauskis / Robin Gubser, Franz Burgmeier, Sandro Wieser, Yves Oehri.

10.09.2013, Štadión pod Dubňom, Žilina; Attendance: 9,438
Referee: David Fernández Borbalán (Spain)
SLOVAKIA - BOSNIA-HERZEGOVINA 1-2(1-0)
SVK: Ján Mucha, Martin Škrtel, Tomáš Hubočan, Peter Pekarík, Ján Ďurica, Stanislav Šesták (62.Erik Jendrišek), Marek Hamšík, Juraj Kucka, Viktor Pečovský, Vladimír Weiss (82.Martin Jakubko), Adam Nemec (82.Róbert Mak). Trainer: Ján Kozák.
BIH: Asmir Begović, Emir Spahić, Mensur Mujdža (47.Adnan Zahirović), Ermin Bičakčić, Zvezdjan Misimović (77.Izet Hajrović), Haris Medunjanin, Sejad Salihović (69.Edin Višća), Miralem Pjanić, Senad Lulić, Vedad Ibišević, Edin Džeko. Trainer: Safet Sušić.
Goals: 1-0 Marek Hamšík (43), 1-1 Ermin Bičakčić (70), 1-2 Izet Hajrović (78).
Cautions: Tomáš Hubočan / Miralem Pjanić, Vedad Ibišević, Haris Medunjanin, Asmir Begović.

10.09.2013, Stádio „Yeorgios Karaïskákis", Peiraiás; Attendance: 18,983
Referee: Kristinn Jakobsson (Iceland)
GREECE - LATVIA 1-0(0-0)
GRE: Orestis-Spyridon Karnezis, Dimitrios Siovas, Vasileios Torosidis, Sokratis Papastathopoulos, Giórgos Tzavellas (74.Giórgos Karagounis), Konstantinos Katsouranis, Sotiris Ninis, Giánnis Maniatis, Giórgos Samaras (88.Giánnis Fetfatzidis), Konstantinos Mitroglou, Dimitrios Salpingidis (64.Lazaros Christodoulopoulos). Trainer: Fernando Manuel Costa Santos (Portugal).
LVA: Aleksandrs Koļinko, Kaspars Gorkšs, Vladislavs Gabovs, Nauris Bulvītis, Vitālijs Maksimenko, Juris Laizāns, Artis Lazdiņš (62.Alans Siņeļņikovs), Aleksandrs Cauņa, Ritvars Rugins, Artūrs Zjuzins (68.Artūrs Karašausks), Māris Verpakovskis (79.Deniss Rakels). Trainer: Marians Pahars.
Goal: 1-0 Dimitrios Salpingidis (58).
Cautions: Konstantinos Katsouranis / Māris Verpakovskis.
Sent off: Ritvars Rugins (86), Konstantinos Katsouranis (90+3).

11.10.2013, LFF stadionas, Vilnius; Attendance: 2,900
Referee: Petur Reinert (Faroe Islands)

LITHUANIA - LATVIA 2-0(1-0)

LTU: Giedrius Arlauskis, Marius Žaliūkas, Egidijus Vaitkūnas, Tadas Kijanskas, Valdemar Borovskij, Saulius Mikoliūnas (76.Gratas Sirgėdas), Kęstutis Ivaškevičius, Mindaugas Panka, Mindaugas Kalonas, Deivydas Matulevičius (58.Evaldas Razulis), Fiodor Černych (72.Nerijus Valskis). Trainer: Igoris Pankratjevas.

LVA: Andris Vaņins, Kaspars Gorkšs, Vladislavs Gabovs (73.Andrejs Kovaļovs), Nauris Bulvītis, Vitālijs Maksimenko, Juris Laizāns, Aleksandrs Fertovs, Artūrs Zjuzins, Māris Verpakovskis (77.Eduards Višņakovs), Deniss Rakels (66.Ivans Lukjanovs), Valērijs Šabala. Trainer: Marians Pahars.

Goals: 1-0 Fiodor Černych (7), 2-0 Saulius Mikoliūnas (68).

Cautions: Mindaugas Panka, Mindaugas Kalonas, Kęstutis Ivaškevičius.

11.10.2013, Stadion Bilino Polje, Zenica; Attendance: 11,200
Referee: Richard Liesveld (Holland)

BOSNIA-HERZEGOVINA - LIECHTENSTEIN 4-1(4-0)

BIH: Asmir Begović, Emir Spahić, Avdija Vršajević, Ermin Bičakčić, Zvezdjan Misimović, Haris Medunjanin (62.Senijad Ibričić), Sejad Salihović, Miralem Pjanić (62.Izet Hajrović), Senad Lulić (62.Zoran Kvržić), Vedad Ibišević, Edin Džeko. Trainer: Safet Sušić.

LIE: Peter Karl Jehle, Martin Stocklasa, Yves Oehri, Daniel Kaufmann, Andreas Christen, Ivan Quintans (57.Philippe Erne), Michele Polverino, Mathias Christen (64.Seyhan Yildiz), Nicolas Hasler, Robin Gubser, David Hasler (80.Burak Eris). Trainer: Rene Pauritsch (Austria).

Goals: 1-0 Edin Džeko (27), 2-0 Zvezdjan Misimović (34), 3-0 Vedad Ibišević (38), 4-0 Edin Džeko (39), 4-1 Nicolas Hasler (61).

11.10.2013, Stádio „Yeorgios Karaïskákis", Peiraiás; Attendance: 21,067
Referee: Deniz Aytekin (Germany)

GREECE - SLOVAKIA 1-0(1-0)

GRE: Orestis-Spyridon Karnezis, José Lloyd Holebas, Vasileios Torosidis, Sokratis Papastathopoulos, Konstantinos Manolas, Lazaros Christodoulopoulos (58.Sotiris Ninis), Alexandros Tziolis, Giánnis Maniatis, Giórgos Samaras, Konstantinos Mitroglou (90.Giánnis Fetfatzidis), Dimitrios Salpingidis (76.Giórgos Karagounis). Trainer: Fernando Manuel Costa Santos (Portugal).

SVK: Ján Mucha, Martin Škrtel, Tomáš Hubočan, Peter Pekarík, Ján Ďurica, Stanislav Šesták (63.Martin Jakubko), Juraj Kucka, Viktor Pečovský (64.Karim Abdul-Jabbar Guédé), Miroslav Stoch, Vladimír Weiss, Adam Nemec (77.Michal Ďuriš). Trainer: Ján Kozák.

Goal: 1-0 Martin Škrtel (44 own goal).

Cautions: José Lloyd Holebas, Giánnis Maniatis / Peter Pekarík, Vladimír Weiss, Miroslav Stoch, Martin Jakubko, Tomáš Hubočan.

Sent off: Martin Škrtel (90).

15.10.2013, Stádio „Yeorgios Karaïskákis", Peiraiás; Attendance: 18,676
Referee: Libor Kovařík (Czech Republic)

GREECE - LIECHTENSTEIN 2-0(1-0)

GRE: Orestis-Spyridon Karnezis, José Lloyd Holebas, Dimitrios Siovas, Loukas Vyntra, Giórgos Karagounis, Konstantinos Katsouranis, Alexandros Tziolis, Panagiotis Giórgos Kone (46.Andreas Samaris), Giórgos Samaras (70.Lazaros Christodoulopoulos), Konstantinos Mitroglou (86.Stefanos Klaus Athanasiadis), Dimitrios Salpingidis. Trainer: Fernando Manuel Costa Santos (Portugal).

LIE: Peter Karl Jehle, Franz Burgmeier, Martin Stocklasa, Yves Oehri, Daniel Kaufmann, Andreas Christen, Michele Polverino, Mathias Christen (82.Philippe Erne), Nicolas Hasler, Sandro Wieser, David Hasler (90+1.Seyhan Yildiz). Trainer: Rene Pauritsch (Austria).

Goals: 1-0 Dimitrios Salpingidis (7), 2-0 Giórgos Karagounis (81).

Cautions: Panagiotis Giórgos Kone, Dimitrios Salpingidis / Franz Burgmeier, Yves Oehri, Martin Stocklasa.

15.10.2013, "S. Dariaus ir S. Girėno“ stadionas, Kaunas; Attendance: 6,239
Referee: Felix Zwayer (Germany)

LITHUANIA - BOSNIA-HERZEGOVINA 0-1(0-0)

LTU: Giedrius Arlauskis, Marius Žaliūkas, Egidijus Vaitkūnas, Tadas Kijanskas, Valdemar Borovskij, Saulius Mikoliūnas (69.Nerijus Valskis), Mindaugas Panka, Mindaugas Kalonas, Gediminas Vičius, Deivydas Matulevičius (78.Evaldas Razulis), Fiodor Černych (85.Gratas Sirgėdas). Trainer: Igoris Pankratjevas.
BIH: Asmir Begović, Emir Spahić, Avdija Vršajević (70.Adnan Zahirović), Ermin Bičakčić, Zvezdjan Misimović, Haris Medunjanin, Sejad Salihović, Miralem Pjanić, Senad Lulić, Vedad Ibišević, Edin Džeko. Trainer: Safet Sušić.
Goal: 0-1 Vedad Ibišević (68).
Cautions: Egidijus Vaitkūnas, Deivydas Matulevičius, Gediminas Vičius, Nerijus Valskis, Valdemar Borovskij / Senijad Ibričić (on the bench).

15.10.2013, Skonto stadions, Riga; Attendance: 3,813
Referee: Yevhen Aranovskiy (Ukraine)

LATVIA - SLOVAKIA 2-2(0-2)

LVA: Aleksandrs Koļinko, Kaspars Gorkšs, Nauris Bulvītis, Renārs Rode, Vitālijs Maksimenko, Juris Laizāns (53.Artūrs Zjuzins), Artis Lazdiņš, Aleksandrs Fertovs, Andrejs Kovaļovs, Eduards Višņakovs (85.Māris Verpakovskis), Valērijs Šabala. Trainer: Marians Pahars.
SVK: Matúš Kozáčik, Peter Pekarík, Kornel Saláta, Ján Ďurica, Dušan Švento, Tomáš Kóňa, Stanislav Šesták (62.Karim Abdul-Jabbar Guédé), Juraj Kucka (86.Viktor Pečovský), Erik Jendrišek, Martin Jakubko (56.Marek Bakoš), Michal Ďuriš. Trainer: Ján Kozák.
Goals: 0-1 Martin Jakubko (9), 0-2 Kornel Saláta (16), 1-2 Valērijs Šabala (47), 2-2 Renārs Rode (90+2).
Cautions: Valērijs Šabala, Eduards Višņakovs, Artis Lazdiņš / Juraj Kucka.

GROUP H

07.09.2012	Podgorica	Montenegro - Poland	2-2(2-1)
07.09.2012	Chişinău	Moldova - England	0-5(0-3)
11.09.2012	London	England - Ukraine	1-1(0-1)
11.09.2012	Serravalle	San Marino - Montenegro	0-6(0-2)
11.09.2012	Wrocław	Poland - Moldova	2-0(1-0)
12.10.2012	London	England - San Marino	5-0(2-0)
12.10.2012	Chişinău	Moldova - Ukraine	0-0
16.10.2012	Serravalle	San Marino - Moldova	0-2(0-0)
16.10.2012	Kyiv	Ukraine - Montenegro	0-1(0-1)
17.10.2012	Warszawa	Poland - England	1-1(0-1)
14.11.2012	Podgorica	Montenegro - San Marino	3-0(2-0)
22.03.2013	Warszawa	Poland - Ukraine	1-3(1-3)
22.03.2013	Serravalle	San Marino - England	0-8(0-5)
22.03.2013	Chişinău	Moldova - Montenegro	0-1(0-0)
26.03.2013	Warszawa	Poland - San Marino	5-0(2-0)
26.03.2013	Odessa	Ukraine - Moldova	2-1(0-0)
26.03.2013	Podgorica	Montenegro - England	1-1(0-1)
07.06.2013	Chişinău	Moldova - Poland	1-1(1-1)
07.06.2013	Podgorica	Montenegro - Ukraine	0-4(0-0)
06.09.2013	London	England - Moldova	4-0(3-0)
06.09.2013	Warszawa	Poland - Montenegro	1-1(1-1)
06.09.2013	Lviv	Ukraine - San Marino	9-0(4-0)
10.09.2013	Serravalle	San Marino - Poland	1-5(1-3)
10.09.2013	Kyiv	Ukraine - England	0-0
11.10.2013	Chişinău	Moldova - San Marino	3-0(0-0)
11.10.2013	London	England - Montenegro	4-1(0-0)
11.10.2013	Kharkiv	Ukraine - Poland	1-0(0-0)
15.10.2013	London	England - Poland	2-0(1-0)
15.10.2013	Serravalle	San Marino - Ukraine	0-8(0-3)
15.10.2013	Podgorica	Montenegro - Moldova	2-5(0-1)

FINAL STANDINGS

1.	**ENGLAND**	10	6	4	0	31	-	4	22
2.	**Ukraine**	10	6	3	1	28	-	4	21
3.	Montenegro	10	4	3	3	18	-	17	15
4.	Poland	10	3	4	3	18	-	12	13
5.	Moldova	10	3	2	5	12	-	17	11
6.	San Marino	10	0	0	10	1	-	54	0

England qualified for the Final Tournament; Ukraine qualified for the Play-Offs.

07.09.2012, Stadion pod Goricom, Podgorica; Attendance: 11,420
Referee: Kristinn Jakobsson (Iceland)

MONTENEGRO - POLAND **2-2(2-1)**

MNE: Mladen Božović, Marko Baša, Milan Jovanović (65.Filip Kasalica), Elsad Zverotić, Savo Pavićević, Vladimir Volkov, Stefan Savić, Nikola Drinčić (84.Miodrag Džudović), Simon Vukčević (71.Milorad Peković), Mirko Vučinić, Stevan Jovetić. Trainer: Branislav Brnović.
POL: Przemysław Tytoń, Marcin Wasilewski, Jakub Wawrzyniak, Łukasz Piszczek, Kamil Glik, Eugen Polanski, Ludovic Obraniak, Kamil Grosicki (46.Adrian Mierzejewski), Jakub Błaszczykowski, Ariel Borysiuk (69.Rafał Murawski), Robert Lewandowski (90+2.Marek Saganowski). Trainer: Waldemar Fornalik.
Goals: 0-1 Jakub Błaszczykowski (6 penalty), 1-1 Nikola Drinčić (27), 2-1 Mirko Vučinić (45+2), 2-2 Adrian Mierzejewski (55).
Cautions: Mirko Vučinić, Savo Pavićević, Miodrag Džudović / Eugen Polanski.
Sent off: Savo Pavićević (69), Ludovic Obraniak (73).

07.09.2012, Arena Zimbru, Chişinău; Attendance: 10,500
Referee: Paulus Hendrikus Martinus „Pol" van Boekel (Holland)

MOLDOVA - ENGLAND **0-5(0-3)**

MDA: Stanislav Namaşco, Alexandru Epureanu, Victor Golovatenco, Simeon Bulgaru, Igor Armaş, Serghei Covalciuc, Alexandru Suvorov (46.Alexandru Dedov), Alexandru Onică, Alexandru Gaţcan, Artur Pătraş, Igor Picuşceac (77.Eugen Sidorenco; 85.Gheorghe Ovsianicov). Trainer: Ion Caras.
ENG: Charles Joseph John Hart, Glen McLeod Johnson, Joleon Patrick Lescott, John George Terry, Leighton John Baines, Steven George Gerrard (46.Michael Carrick), Frank James Lampard, James Philip Milner, Thomas William Cleverley, Alexander Mark David Oxlade-Chamberlain (58.Theo James Walcott), Jermain Colin Defoe (68.Daniel Nii Tackie Mensah Welbeck). Trainer: Roy Hodgson.
Goals: 0-1 Frank James Lampard (4 penalty), 0-2 Frank James Lampard (29), 0-3 Jermain Colin Defoe (32), 0-4 James Philip Milner (74), 0-5 Leighton John Baines (83).
Cautions: Simeon Bulgaru / Glen McLeod Johnson.

11.09.2012, The National Stadium, Wembley, London; Attendance: 68,102
Referee: Cüneyt Çakır (Turkey)

ENGLAND - UKRAINE **1-1(0-1)**

ENG: Charles Joseph John Hart, Glen McLeod Johnson, Philip Nikodem Jagielka, Joleon Patrick Lescott, Leighton John Baines (73.Ryan Dominic Bertrand), Steven George Gerrard, James Philip Milner, Frank James Lampard, Thomas William Cleverley (62.Daniel Nii Tackie Mensah Welbeck), Alexander Mark David Oxlade-Chamberlain (69.Daniel Andre Sturridge), Jermain Colin Defoe. Trainer: Roy Hodgson.
UKR: Andriy Pyatov, Yevhen Selin (75.Vyacheslav Shevchuk), Yaroslav Rakytskiy, Yevhen Khacheridi, Oleh Husyev, Ruslan Rotan (90+2.Serhiy Nazarenko), Anatoliy Tymoshchuk, Yevhen Konoplyanka, Denys Harmash, Andriy Yarmolenko, Roman Zozulya (89.Marko Dević). Trainer: Oleh Blokhin.
Goals: 0-1 Yevhen Konoplyanka (39), 1-1 Frank James Lampard (87 penalty).
Cautions: Jermain Colin Defoe, Steven George Gerrard, Joleon Patrick Lescott, James Philip Milner, Glen McLeod Johnson / Yevhen Selin, Denys Harmash, Yevhen Khacheridi.
Sent off: Steven George Gerrard (88).

11.09.2012, Stadio Olimpico, Serravalle; Attendance: 1,947
Referee: Neil Louis Kilcoyne Doyle (Republic of Ireland)
SAN MARINO - MONTENEGRO 0-6(0-2)
SMR: Aldo Junior Simoncini, Fabio Vitaioli, Alessandro Della Valle, Davide Simoncini, Michele Cervellini, Cristian Brolli (84.Damiano Vannucci), Alex Gasperoni, Matteo Coppini, Manuel Marani (64.Enrico Cibelli), Matteo Giampaolo Vitaioli (80.Pier Filippo Mazza), Danilo Ezequiel Rinaldi. Trainer: Giampaolo Mazza.
MNE: Mladen Božović, Marko Baša, Miodrag Džudović, Vladimir Volkov, Stefan Savić, Milorad Peković, Simon Vukčević (66.Elsad Zverotić), Dejan Damjanović, Fatos Bećiraj (75.Filip Kasalica), Stevan Jovetić, Luka Đorđević (66.Andrija Delibašić). Trainer: Branislav Brnović.
Goals: 0-1 Luka Đorđević (24), 0-2 Fatos Bećiraj (26), 0-3 Fatos Bećiraj (51), 0-4 Elsad Zverotić (69), 0-5 Andrija Delibašić (78), 0-6 Andrija Delibašić (82).
Cautions: Fabio Vitaioli, Davide Simoncini, Enrico Cibelli, Michele Cervellini / Luka Đorđević.

11.09.2012, Stadion Miejski, Wrocław; Attendance: 26,145
Referee: Ilias Spathas (Greece)
POLAND - MOLDOVA 2-0(1-0)
POL: Przemysław Tytoń, Marcin Wasilewski, Jakub Wawrzyniak, Łukasz Piszczek, Kamil Glik, Eugen Polanski, Jakub Błaszczykowski, Ariel Borysiuk (75.Grzegorz Krychowiak), Adrian Mierzejewski (71.Artur Sobiech), Marek Saganowski (46.Waldemar Sobota), Robert Lewandowski. Trainer: Waldemar Fornalik.
MDA: Stanislav Namaşco, Alexandru Epureanu, Victor Golovatenco, Petru Racu, Igor Armaş, Serghei Covalciuc, Stanislav Ivanov (73.Alexandru Onică), Alexandru Suvorov (81.Serghei Alexeev), Alexandru Gaţcan, Artur Pătraş (46.Gheorghe Ovsianicov), Igor Picuşceac. Trainer: Ion Caras.
Goals: 1-0 Jakub Błaszczykowski (33 penalty), 2-0 Jakub Wawrzyniak (81).
Cautions: Marcin Wasilewski / Alexandru Gaţcan.

12.10.2012, The National Stadium, Wembley, London; Attendance: 86,645
Referee: Gediminas Mažeika (Lithuania)
ENGLAND - SAN MARINO 5-0(2-0)
ENG: Charles Joseph John Hart, Kyle Andrew Walker, Philip Nikodem Jagielka, Gary James Cahill, Leighton John Baines, Michael Carrick (66.Jonjo Shelvey), Theo James Walcott (10.Aaron Justin Lennon), Thomas William Cleverley, Alexander Mark David Oxlade-Chamberlain, Daniel Nii Tackie Mensah Welbeck, Wayne Mark Rooney (73.Andrew Thomas Carroll). Trainer: Roy Hodgson.
SMR: Aldo Junior Simoncini, Fabio Vitaioli (84.Simone Bacciocchi), Alessandro Della Valle, Davide Simoncini, Michele Cervellini, Mirko Palazzi, Cristian Brolli, Alex Gasperoni, Matteo Coppini (76.Lorenzo Buscarini), Enrico Cibelli, Danilo Ezequiel Rinaldi (79.Andy Selva). Trainer: Giampaolo Mazza.
Goals: 1-0 Wayne Mark Rooney (35 penalty), 2-0 Daniel Nii Tackie Mensah Welbeck (37), 3-0 Wayne Mark Rooney (70), 4-0 Daniel Nii Tackie Mensah Welbeck (72), 5-0 Alexander Mark David Oxlade-Chamberlain (77).
Cautions: Aldo Junior Simoncini, Danilo Ezequiel Rinaldi.

12.10.2012, Arena Zimbru, Chişinău; Attendance: 12,500
Referee: Clément Turpin (France)
MOLDOVA - UKRAINE 0-0
MDA: Stanislav Namaşco, Alexandru Epureanu, Victor Golovatenco, Petru Racu, Simeon Bulgaru, Serghei Covalciuc (61.Alexandru Paşcenco), Alexandru Suvorov (79.Gheorghe Ovsianicov), Alexandru Onică, Alexandru Dedov, Alexandru Gaţcan, Igor Picuşceac (84.Anatolie Doroş). Trainer: Ion Caras.
UKR: Andriy Pyatov, Taras Mychalyk, Yevhen Selin, Yevhen Khacheridi, Bohdan Butko, Oleh Husyev (79.Marko Dević), Ruslan Rotan, Anatoliy Tymoshchuk, Denys Harmash (60.Yevhen Seleznyov), Andriy Yarmolenko, Roman Zozulya (74.Artem Milevskiy). Trainer: Andriy Bal.
Cautions: Alexandru Onică / Ruslan Rotan, Yevhen Khacheridi.

16.10.2012, Stadio Olimpico, Serravalle; Attendance: 736
Referee: Marios Panayi (Cyprus)
SAN MARINO - MOLDOVA 0-2(0-0)
SMR: Aldo Junior Simoncini, Fabio Vitaioli, Gianluca Bollini, Alessandro Della Valle, Davide Simoncini, Michele Cervellini, Mirko Palazzi (46.Damiano Vannucci), Pier Filippo Mazza (61.Enrico Cibelli), Lorenzo Buscarini, Manuel Marani (67.Andy Selva), Matteo Giampaolo Vitaioli. Trainer: Giampaolo Mazza.
MDA: Stanislav Namaşco, Alexandru Epureanu, Victor Golovatenco, Simeon Bulgaru, Vitalie Bordian, Alexandru Suvorov (59.Artur Pătraş), Alexandru Onică, Alexandru Dedov (71.Serghei Dadu), Alexandru Gaţcan, Serghei Alexeev, Igor Picuşceac (81.Eugeniu Cebotaru). Trainer: Ion Caras.
Goals: 0-1 Serghei Dadu (72 penalty), 0-2 Alexandru Epureanu (78).
Cautions: Matteo Giampaolo Vitaioli, Davide Simoncini, Fabio Vitaioli, Lorenzo Buscarini / Vitalie Bordian.

16.10.2012, Olympiyskiy Stadium, Kyiv; Attendance: 50,597
Referee: Michael Koukoulakis (Greece)
UKRAINE - MONTENEGRO 0-1(0-1)
UKR: Andriy Pyatov, Oleksandr Kucher, Taras Mychalyk, Yevhen Selin, Bohdan Butko (62.Andriy Yarmolenko), Oleh Husyev, Ruslan Rotan, Anatoliy Tymoshchuk, Yevhen Konoplyanka, Marko Dević (52.Roman Zozulya), Yevhen Seleznyov (82.Serhiy Nazarenko). Trainer: Andriy Bal.
MNE: Mladen Božović, Marko Baša, Miodrag Džudović, Milan Jovanović, Elsad Zverotić (88.Mitar Novaković), Vladimir Volkov, Stefan Savić, Milorad Peković, Nikola Drinčić, Dejan Damjanović (72.Simon Vukčević), Stevan Jovetić (86.Mirko Vučinić). Trainer: Branislav Brnović.
Goal: 0-1 Dejan Damjanović (45).
Cautions: Oleksandr Kucher, Oleh Husyev, Yevhen Selin / Milorad Peković, Elsad Zverotić, Nikola Drinčić, Mladen Božović, Stefan Savić, Mirko Vučinić.

17.10.2012, Stadion Narodowy, Warszawa; Attendance: 47,000
Referee: Gianluca Rocchi (Italy)
POLAND - ENGLAND 1-1(0-1)
POL: Przemysław Tytoń, Marcin Wasilewski, Jakub Wawrzyniak, Łukasz Piszczek, Kamil Glik, Eugen Polanski, Ludovic Obraniak (90.Ariel Borysiuk), Kamil Grosicki (83.Arkadiusz Milik), Grzegorz Krychowiak, Paweł Wszołek (63.Adrian Mierzejewski), Robert Lewandowski. Trainer: Waldemar Fornalik.
ENG: Charles Joseph John Hart, Glen McLeod Johnson, Ashley Cole, Philip Nikodem Jagielka, Joleon Patrick Lescott, James Philip Milner, Steven George Gerrard, Michael Carrick, Thomas William Cleverley, Jermain Colin Defoe (67.Daniel Nii Tackie Mensah Welbeck), Wayne Mark Rooney (73.Alexander Mark David Oxlade-Chamberlain). Trainer: Roy Hodgson.
Goals: 0-1 Wayne Mark Rooney (31), 1-1 Kamil Glik (70).
Cautions: Eugen Polanski, Kamil Glik / Ashley Cole.

14.11.2012, Stadion pod Goricom, Podgorica; Attendance: 7,158
Referee: Sándor Szabó (Hungary)
MONTENEGRO - SAN MARINO 3-0(2-0)
MNE: Mladen Božović, Marko Baša (71.Ivan Kecojević), Elsad Zverotić, Savo Pavićević, Vladimir Volkov, Stefan Savić (46.Luka Đorđević), Simon Vukčević, Mitar Novaković, Fatos Bećiraj, Filip Kasalica (77.Blažo Igumanović), Andrija Delibašić. Trainer: Branislav Brnović.
SMR: Aldo Junior Simoncini, Gianluca Bollini, Alessandro Della Valle, Giacomo Benedettini (84.Alex Della Valle), Michele Cervellini, Mirko Palazzi, Damiano Vannucci, Matteo Coppini, Enrico Cibelli (89.Alex Gasperoni), Matteo Giampaolo Vitaioli (73.Lorenzo Buscarini), Danilo Ezequiel Rinaldi. Trainer: Giampaolo Mazza.
Goals: 1-0 Andrija Delibašić (14), 2-0 Andrija Delibašić (31), 3-0 Elsad Zverotić (68).
Cautions: Mitar Novaković / Gianluca Bollini, Giacomo Benedettini, Alessandro Della Valle.

22.03.2013, Stadion Narodowy, Warszawa; Attendance: 55,565
Referee: Pavel Královec (Czech Republic)

POLAND - UKRAINE **1-3(1-3)**

POL: Artur Boruc, Sebastian Boenisch, Marcin Wasilewski, Łukasz Piszczek, Kamil Glik, Radosław Majewski (76.Łukasz Teodorczyk), Jakub Błaszczykowski, Maciej Rybus (46.Jakub Kosecki), Grzegorz Krychowiak, Daniel Łukasik (59.Ludovic Obraniak), Robert Lewandowski. Trainer: Waldemar Fornalik.

UKR: Andriy Pyatov, Oleksandr Kucher, Vyacheslav Shevchuk, Artem Fedetskiy, Yevhen Khacheridi, Oleh Husyev (90+3.Mykola Morozyuk), Ruslan Rotan, Taras Stepanenko (60.Anatoliy Tymoshchuk), Denys Harmash (90+2.Roman Bezus), Andriy Yarmolenko, Roman Zozulya. Trainer: Mykhaylo Fomenko.

Goals: 0-1 Andriy Yarmolenko (2), 0-2 Oleh Husyev (7), 1-2 Łukasz Piszczek (18), 1-3 Roman Zozulya (45).

Cautions: Daniel Łukasik / Ruslan Rotan, Denys Harmash, Taras Stepanenko, Anatoliy Tymoshchuk, Mykola Morozyuk.

22.03.2013, Stadio Olimpico, Serravalle; Attendance: 4,952
Referee: Alain Bieri (Switzerland)

SAN MARINO - ENGLAND **0-8(0-5)**

SMR: Aldo Junior Simoncini, Fabio Vitaioli, Alessandro Della Valle, Davide Simoncini, Michele Cervellini, Mirko Palazzi, Fabio Bollini (81.Carlo Valentini), Alex Gasperoni, Enrico Cibelli (65.Lorenzo Buscarini), Andy Selva (75.Danilo Ezequiel Rinaldi), Matteo Giampaolo Vitaioli. Trainer: Giampaolo Mazza.

ENG: Charles Joseph John Hart, Kyle Andrew Walker, Joleon Patrick Lescott, Christopher Lloyd Smalling, Leighton John Baines, Thomas William Cleverley (56.Leon Osman), Alexander Mark David Oxlade-Chamberlain, Frank James Lampard (67.Scott Matthew Parker), Ashley Simon Young, Jermain Colin Defoe, Wayne Mark Rooney (56.Daniel Andre Sturridge). Trainer: Roy Hodgson.

Goals: 0-1 Alessandro Della Vella (12 own goal), 0-2 Alexander Mark David Oxlade-Chamberlain (28), 0-3 Jermain Colin Defoe (35), 0-4 Ashley Simon Young (39), 0-5 Frank James Lampard (42), 0-6 Wayne Mark Rooney (54), 0-7 Daniel Andre Sturridge (70), 0-8 Jermain Colin Defoe (77).

Cautions: Davide Simoncini, Michele Cervellini.

22.03.2013, Arena Zimbru, Chişinău; Attendance: 5,400
Referee: Daniele Orsato (Italy)

MOLDOVA - MONTENEGRO **0-1(0-0)**

MDA: Serghei Paşcenco, Alexandru Epureanu, Victor Golovatenco, Simeon Bulgaru, Vitalie Bordian, Artur Ioniţă, Eugen Sidorenco, Alexandru Paşcenco, Alexandru Dedov, Alexandru Gaţcan, Serghei Gheorghiev (77.Nicolae Josan). Trainer: Ion Caras.

MNE: Mladen Božović, Marko Baša, Vladimir Božović (65.Simon Vukčević), Elsad Zverotić, Savo Pavićević, Vladimir Volkov, Stefan Savić, Milorad Peković, Mirko Vučinić (80.Mitar Novaković), Stevan Jovetić, Filip Kasalica (46.Dejan Damjanović). Trainer: Branislav Brnović.

Goal: 0-1 Mirko Vučinić (78).

Cautions: Serghei Gheorghiev, Alexandru Gaţcan / Milorad Peković, Savo Pavićević.

Sent off: Milorad Peković (61), Alexandru Gaţcan (90+1).

26.03.2013, Stadion Narodowy, Warszawa; Attendance: 43,008
Referee: Ken Henry Johnsen (Norway)
POLAND - SAN MARINO 5-0(2-0)
POL: Artur Boruc, Jakub Wawrzyniak, Łukasz Piszczek, Kamil Glik (46.Jakub Kosecki), Bartosz Salamon (87.Marcin Wasilewski), Eugen Polanski, Kamil Grosicki, Adrian Mierzejewski, Grzegorz Krychowiak, Robert Lewandowski, Arkadiusz Milik (59.Łukasz Teodorczyk). Trainer: Waldemar Fornalik.
SMR: Aldo Junior Simoncini, Fabio Vitaioli, Gianluca Bollini (57.Simone Bacciocchi), Alessandro Della Valle, Mirko Palazzi, Alex Della Valle (80.Lorenzo Buscarini), Fabio Bollini, Alex Gasperoni, Matteo Coppini, Andy Selva (51.Danilo Ezequiel Rinaldi), Matteo Giampaolo Vitaioli. Trainer: Giampaolo Mazza.
Goals: 1-0 Robert Lewandowski (21 penalty), 2-0 Łukasz Piszczek (28), 3-0 Robert Lewandowski (50 penalty), 4-0 Łukasz Teodorczyk (60), 5-0 Jakub Kosecki (90+2).
Cautions: Eugen Polanski, Grzegorz Krychowiak, Arkadiusz Milik / Alessandro Della Valle, Alex Della Valle, Fabio Vitaioli, Alex Gasperoni, Simone Bacciocchi.

26.03.2013, Chornomorets Stadium, Odessa; Attendance: 31,948
Referee: Kenn Hansen (Denmark)
UKRAINE - MOLDOVA 2-1(0-0)
UKR: Andriy Pyatov, Oleksandr Kucher, Vyacheslav Shevchuk, Artem Fedetskiy, Yevhen Khacheridi, Oleh Husyev (90.Dmytro Grechyshkin), Anatoliy Tymoshchuk, Taras Stepanenko, Yevhen Seleznyov (62.Roman Bezus), Andriy Yarmolenko, Roman Zozulya. Trainer: Mykhaylo Fomenko.
MDA: Stanislav Namaşco, Alexandru Epureanu, Victor Golovatenco, Simeon Bulgaru, Vitalie Bordian, Artur Ioniţă, Eugen Sidorenco, Alexandru Paşcenco (67.Alexandru Onică), Alexandru Dedov (78.Alexandru Suvorov), Serghei Gheorghiev, Igor Bugaiov (69.Anatolie Doroş). Trainer: Ion Caras.
Goals: 1-0 Andriy Yarmolenko (61), 2-0 Yevhen Khacheridi (70), 2-1 Alexandru Suvorov (80).
Cautions: Yevhen Seleznyov / Serghei Gheorghiev.
Sent off: Taras Stepanenko (90+2).

26.03.2013, Stadion pod Goricom, Podgorica; Attendance: 11,300
Referee: Jonas Eriksson (Sweden)
MONTENEGRO - ENGLAND 1-1(0-1)
MNE: Mladen Božović, Marko Baša, Miodrag Džudović, Vladimir Božović (75.Andrija Delibašić), Elsad Zverotić, Vladimir Volkov, Stefan Savić, Simon Vukčević (63.Miloš Krkotić), Mitar Novaković (46.Dejan Damjanović), Mirko Vučinić, Stevan Jovetić. Trainer: Branislav Brnović.
ENG: Charles Joseph John Hart, Glen McLeod Johnson, Joleon Patrick Lescott, Christopher Lloyd Smalling, Ashley Cole, James Philip Milner, Steven George Gerrard, Michael Carrick, Thomas William Cleverley (77.Ashley Simon Young), Daniel Nii Tackie Mensah Welbeck, Wayne Mark Rooney. Trainer: Roy Hodgson.
Goals: 0-1 Wayne Mark Rooney (6), 1-1 Dejan Damjanović (76).
Cautions: Mitar Novaković, Vladimir Volkov, Miodrag Džudović, Miloš Krkotić / Glen McLeod Johnson, Daniel Nii Tackie Mensah Welbeck.

07.06.2013, Arena Zimbru, Chişinău; Attendance: 8,726
Referee: Fernando Teixeira Vitienes (Spain)
MOLDOVA - POLAND 1-1(1-1)
MDA: Stanislav Namaşco, Alexandru Epureanu, Victor Golovatenco, Vitalie Bordian (71.Eugeniu Cebotaru), Igor Armaş, Alexandru Suvorov (74.Alexandru Paşcenco), Artur Ioniţă, Alexandru Antoniuc (82.Gheorghe Ovsianicov), Eugen Sidorenco, Alexandru Dedov, Alexandru Gaţcan. Trainer: Ion Caras.
POL: Artur Boruc, Artur Jędrzejczyk, Jakub Wawrzyniak, Marcin Komorowski, Bartosz Salamon, Eugen Polanski (79.Artur Sobiech), Jakub Błaszczykowski, Maciej Rybus (64.Jakub Kosecki), Adrian Mierzejewski (62.Piotr Sebastian Zieliński), Grzegorz Krychowiak, Robert Lewandowski. Trainer: Waldemar Fornalik.

Goals: 0-1 Jakub Błaszczykowski (6), 1-1 Eugen Sidorenco (36).
Cautions: Alexandru Antoniuc, Alexandru Gaţcan.

07.06.2013, Stadion pod Goricom, Podgorica; Attendance: 11,996
Referee: Manuel Gräfe (Germany)
MONTENEGRO - UKRAINE **0-4(0-0)**
MNE: Mladen Božović, Marko Baša, Vladimir Božović (63.Andrija Delibašić), Elsad Zverotić, Savo Pavićević, Vladimir Volkov, Ivan Kecojević, Milorad Peković, Mirko Vučinić, Stevan Jovetić (43.Dejan Damjanović), Filip Kasalica (75.Fatos Bećiraj). Trainer: Branislav Brnović.
UKR: Andriy Pyatov, Artem Fedetskiy, Yaroslav Rakytskiy, Oleh Husyev, Ruslan Rotan (90+1.Roman Bezus), Anatoliy Tymoshchuk, Edmar Halovskyi de Lacerda, Yevhen Konoplyanka, Denys Harmash (69.Serhiy Kravchenko), Andriy Yarmolenko (90+2.Aleksandr Kovpak), Roman Zozulya. Trainer: Mykhaylo Fomenko.
Goals: 0-1 Denys Harmash (51), 0-2 Yevhen Konoplyanka (77), 0-3 Artem Fedetskiy (84), 0-4 Roman Bezus (90+3).
Cautions: Vladimir Volkov, Savo Pavićević, Vladimir Božović, Dejan Damjanović / Ruslan Rotan, Artem Fedetskiy.
Sent off: Roman Zozulya (45+1), Vladimir Volkov (66), Savo Pavićević (79).

06.09.2013, The National Stadium, Wembley, London; Attendance: 61,607
Referee: Ivan Kružliak (Slovakia)
ENGLAND - MOLDOVA **4-0(3-0)**
ENG: Charles Joseph John Hart, Kyle Andrew Walker, Gary James Cahill, Philip Nikodem Jagielka, Ashley Cole (46.Leighton John Baines), Steven George Gerrard, Jack Andrew Garry Wilshere (60.Ross Barkley), Frank James Lampard, Theo James Walcott, Rickie Lee Lambert (71.James Philip Milner), Daniel Nii Tackie Mensah Welbeck. Trainer: Roy Hodgson.
MDA: Stanislav Namaşco, Alexandru Epureanu, Victor Golovatenco, Simeon Bulgaru (58.Alexandru Suvorov), Vitalie Bordian, Igor Armaş, Artur Ioniţă (19.Alexandru Onică), Alexandru Antoniuc, Eugen Sidorenco, Alexandru Dedov, Serghei Gheorghiev (85.Alexandru Paşcenco). Trainer: Ion Caras.
Goals: 1-0 Steven George Gerrard (12), 2-0 Rickie Lee Lambert (26), 3-0 Daniel Nii Tackie Mensah Welbeck (45+1), 4-0 Daniel Nii Tackie Mensah Welbeck (50).
Cautions: Daniel Nii Tackie Mensah Welbeck / Victor Golovatenco.

06.09.2013, Stadion Narodowy, Warszawa; Attendance: 45,652
Referee: Björn Kuipers (Holland)
POLAND - MONTENEGRO **1-1(1-1)**
POL: Artur Boruc, Artur Jędrzejczyk, Jakub Wawrzyniak (27.Sebastian Boenisch), Łukasz Szukała, Kamil Glik, Jakub Błaszczykowski, Mateusz Klich, Waldemar Sobota (62.Paweł Wszołek), Grzegorz Krychowiak, Piotr Sebastian Zieliński (75.Adrian Mierzejewski), Robert Lewandowski. Trainer: Waldemar Fornalik.
MNE: Mladen Božović, Marko Baša, Miodrag Džudović, Vladimir Božović, Elsad Zverotić, Stefan Savić, Branko Bošković, Nikola Drinčić, Miloš Krkotić (46.Simon Vukčević), Mirko Vučinić (36.Filip Kasalica), Dejan Damjanović (85.Fatos Bećiraj). Trainer: Branislav Brnović.
Goals: 0-1 Dejan Damjanović (11), 1-1 Robert Lewandowski (16).
Cautions: Łukasz Szukała, Kamil Glik / Vladimir Božović, Mirko Vučinić, Filip Kasalica, Miodrag Džudović.

06.09.2013, Arena Lviv, Lviv; Attendance: 34,190
Referee: Neil Louis Kilcoyne Doyle (Republic of Ireland)
UKRAINE - SAN MARINO 9-0(4-0)
UKR: Andriy Pyatov, Vyacheslav Shevchuk (60.Oleh Husyev), Artem Fedetskiy, Yaroslav Rakytskiy, Yevhen Khacheridi, Anatoliy Tymoshchuk (60.Roman Bezus), Edmar Halovskyi de Lacerda, Yevhen Konoplyanka, Marko Dević, Yevhen Seleznyov, Andriy Yarmolenko (75.Dmytro Khomchenovskyi). Trainer: Mykhaylo Fomenko.
SMR: Federico Valentini, Fabio Vitaioli, Carlo Valentini (57.Gianluca Bollini), Davide Simoncini, Michele Cervellini, Mirko Palazzi, Gabriele Genghini, Alex Gasperoni (88.Danilo Ezequiel Rinaldi), Matteo Coppini (69.Lorenzo Buscarini), Andy Selva, Matteo Giampaolo Vitaioli. Trainer: Giampaolo Mazza.
Goals: 1-0 Marko Dević (11), 2-0 Yevhen Seleznyov (26), 3-0 Edmar Halovskyi de Lacerda (32), 4-0 Yevhen Khacheridi (45), 5-0 Yevhen Konoplyanka (50), 6-0 Yevhen Khacheridi (54), 7-0 Roman Bezus (63), 8-0 Artem Fedetskiy (74), 9-0 Yaroslav Rakytskiy (90+3).
Cautions: Marko Dević, Yevhen Khacheridi / Davide Simoncini, Matteo Coppini, Carlo Valentini, Fabio Vitaioli.

10.09.2013, Stadio Olimpico, Serravalle; Attendance: 1,597
Referee: Marco Borg (Malta)
SAN MARINO - POLAND 1-5(1-3)
SMR: Aldo Junior Simoncini, Fabio Vitaioli, Gianluca Bollini, Alessandro Della Valle, Mirko Palazzi (69.Enrico Cibelli), Alex Gasperoni (42.Michele Cervellini), Lorenzo Buscarini, Pietro Calzolari, Andy Selva, Matteo Giampaolo Vitaioli, Danilo Ezequiel Rinaldi (80.Alessandro Bianchi). Trainer: Giampaolo Mazza.
POL: Artur Boruc, Sebastian Boenisch, Piotr Celeban, Artur Jędrzejczyk, Bartosz Salamon, Jakub Błaszczykowski (72.Adrian Mierzejewski), Mateusz Klich, Waldemar Sobota, Grzegorz Krychowiak (79.Paweł Wszołek), Piotr Sebastian Zieliński, Paweł Brożek (55.Marcin Robak). Trainer: Waldemar Fornalik.
Goals: 0-1 Piotr Sebastian Zieliński (10), 1-1 Alessandro Della Valle (22), 1-2 Jakub Błaszczykowski (23), 1-3 Waldemar Sobota (34), 1-4 Piotr Sebastian Zieliński (66), 1-5 Adrian Mierzejewski (75).
Cautions: Gianluca Bollini, Matteo Giampaolo Vitaioli, Lorenzo Buscarini, Pietro Calzolari / Mateusz Klich, Marcin Robak.

10.09.2013, Olympiyskiy Stadium, Kyiv; Attendance: 69,890
Referee: Pedro Proença Oliveira Alves Garcia (Portugal)
UKRAINE - ENGLAND 0-0
UKR: Andriy Pyatov, Oleksandr Kucher, Vyacheslav Shevchuk, Artem Fedetskiy, Yevhen Khacheridi, Oleh Husyev (68.Roman Bezus), Edmar Halovskyi de Lacerda, Taras Stepanenko, Yevhen Konoplyanka, Andriy Yarmolenko (90+3.Dmytro Khomchenovskyi), Roman Zozulya (90.Yevhen Seleznyov). Trainer: Mykhaylo Fomenko.
ENG: Charles Joseph John Hart, Kyle Andrew Walker, Gary James Cahill, Philip Nikodem Jagielka, Ashley Cole, Steven George Gerrard, Frank James Lampard, Jack Andrew Garry Wilshere (68.Ashley Simon Young), James Philip Milner, Rickie Lee Lambert, Theo James Walcott (88.Thomas William Cleverley). Trainer: Roy Hodgson.
Cautions: Oleksandr Kucher / Kyle Andrew Walker.

11.10.2013, Arena Zimbru, Chişinău; Attendance: 7,348
Referee: Ignasi Villamayor Rozados (Andorra)

MOLDOVA - SAN MARINO 3-0(0-0)

MDA: Ilie Cebanu, Victor Golovatenco, Vitalie Bordian, Igor Armaş, Artur Ioniţă, Eugen Sidorenco, Alexandru Dedov, Alexandru Gaţcan (86.Andrei Cojocari), Gheorghe Andronic (68.Alexandru Suvorov), Viorel Frunză, Anatolie Doroş (46.Alexandru Antoniuc). Trainer: Ion Caras.
SMR: Aldo Junior Simoncini, Fabio Vitaioli, Carlo Valentini (80.Lorenzo Gasperoni), Maicol Berretti (63.Manuel Battistini), Alessandro Della Valle, Davide Simoncini, Michele Cervellini, Mirko Palazzi, Alex Gasperoni, Enrico Cibelli, Danilo Ezequiel Rinaldi (81.Alessandro Bianchi). Trainer: Giampaolo Mazza.
Goals: 1-0 Viorel Frunză (55), 2-0 Eugen Sidorenco (59), 3-0 Eugen Sidorenco (89).
Cautions: Alexandru Gaţcan, Artur Ioniţă / Mirko Palazzi, Michele Cervellini, Enrico Cibelli, Alex Gasperoni.

11.10.2013, The National Stadium, Wembley, London; Attendance: 83,807
Referee: Alberto Undiano Mallenco (Spain)

ENGLAND - MONTENEGRO 4-1(0-0)

ENG: Charles Joseph John Hart, Kyle Andrew Walker, Gary James Cahill, Philip Nikodem Jagielka, Leighton John Baines, Steven George Gerrard (87.James Philip Milner), Andros Darryl Townsend (80.Jack Andrew Garry Wilshere), Frank James Lampard (65.Michael Carrick), Daniel Andre Sturridge, Wayne Mark Rooney, Daniel Nii Tackie Mensah Welbeck.Trainer: Roy Hodgson.
MNE: Vukašin Poleksić, Milan Jovanović, Elsad Zverotić, Savo Pavićević (57.Fatos Bećiraj), Vladimir Volkov (72.Simon Vukčević), Stefan Savić, Ivan Kecojević, Branko Bošković, Nikola Drinčić, Dejan Damjanović, Stevan Jovetić (81.Filip Kasalica). Trainer: Branislav Brnović.
Goals: 1-0 Wayne Mark Rooney (48), 2-0 Branko Bošković (62 own goal), 2-1 Dejan Damjanović (71), 3-1 Andros Darryl Townsend (78), 4-1 Daniel Andre Sturridge (90+3).
Cautions: Kyle Andrew Walker / Savo Pavićević, Vladimir Volkov.

11.10.2013, Metalist Stadium, Kharkiv; Attendance: 39,136
Referee: Jonas Eriksson (Sweden)

UKRAINE - POLAND 1-0(0-0)

UKR: Andriy Pyatov, Vyacheslav Shevchuk, Artem Fedetskiy, Yaroslav Rakytskiy, Yevhen Khacheridi, Ruslan Rotan, Edmar Halovskyi de Lacerda (90+2.Roman Bezus), Taras Stepanenko, Yevhen Konoplyanka, Andriy Yarmolenko (90.Oleh Husyev), Roman Zozulya (61.Marko Dević). Trainer: Mykhaylo Fomenko.
POL: Artur Boruc, Grzegorz Wojtkowiak, Artur Jędrzejczyk, Łukasz Szukała, Kamil Glik, Mariusz Lewandowski (76.Piotr Sebastian Zieliński), Jakub Błaszczykowski, Mateusz Klich (66.Adrian Mierzejewski), Waldemar Sobota (61.Sławomir Peszko), Grzegorz Krychowiak, Robert Lewandowski. Trainer: Waldemar Fornalik.
Goal: 1-0 Andriy Yarmolenko (64).
Cautions: Taras Stepanenko, Edmar Halovskyi de Lacerda, Yaroslav Rakytskiy, Yevhen Khacheridi / Sławomir Peszko, Łukasz Szukała.

15.10.2013, The National Stadium, Wembley, London; Attendance: 85,186
Referee: Damir Skomina (Slovenia)
ENGLAND - POLAND **2-0(1-0)**
ENG: Charles Joseph John Hart, Christopher Lloyd Smalling, Gary James Cahill, Philip Nikodem Jagielka, Leighton John Baines, Steven George Gerrard, Andros Darryl Townsend (86.James Philip Milner), Michael Carrick (71.Frank James Lampard), Daniel Andre Sturridge, Wayne Mark Rooney, Daniel Nii Tackie Mensah Welbeck (82.Jack Andrew Garry Wilshere). Trainer: Roy Hodgson.
POL: Wojciech Szczęsny, Piotr Celeban, Grzegorz Wojtkowiak, Artur Jędrzejczyk, Kamil Glik, Mariusz Lewandowski (46.Mateusz Klich), Jakub Błaszczykowski, Adrian Mierzejewski (76.Piotr Sebastian Zieliński), Waldemar Sobota (65.Sławomir Peszko), Grzegorz Krychowiak, Robert Lewandowski. Trainer: Waldemar Fornalik.
Goals: 1-0 Wayne Mark Rooney (41), 2-0 Steven George Gerrard (88).
Cautions: Frank James Lampard, Wayne Mark Rooney / Artur Jędrzejczyk.

15.10.2013, Stadio Olimpico, Serravalle; Attendance: 1,268
Referee: Harald Lechner (Austria)
SAN MARINO - UKRAINE **0-8(0-3)**
SMR: Aldo Junior Simoncini, Fabio Vitaioli (84.Gabriele Genghini), Carlo Valentini (74.Giacomo Benedettini), Maicol Berretti (60.Alex Della Valle), Alessandro Della Valle, Davide Simoncini, Michele Cervellini, Mirko Palazzi, Manuel Battistini, Matteo Giampaolo Vitaioli, Danilo Ezequiel Rinaldi. Trainer: Giampaolo Mazza.
UKR: Andriy Pyatov, Oleksandr Kucher, Vyacheslav Shevchuk, Vitaliy Mandzyuk, Oleh Husyev, Ruslan Rotan, Anatoliy Tymoshchuk, Yevhen Konoplyanka (77.Mykola Morozyuk), Marko Dević, Yevhen Seleznyov (64.Roman Bezus), Andriy Yarmolenko (66.Artem Fedetskiy). Trainer: Mykhaylo Fomenko.
Goals: 0-1 Yevhen Seleznyov (13 penalty), 0-2 Marko Dević (15), 0-3 Yevhen Seleznyov (19), 0-4 Marko Dević (51), 0-5 Andriy Yarmolenko (55), 0-6 Marko Dević (58 penalty), 0-7 Roman Bezus (66), 0-8 Vitaliy Mandzyuk (90).
Cautions: Alessandro Della Valle, Matteo Giampaolo Vitaioli, Davide Simoncini, Fabio Vitaioli, Michele Cervellini / Yevhen Konoplyanka.
Sent off: Mirko Palazzi (56), Alessandro Della Valle (90).

15.10.2013, Stadion pod Goricom, Podgorica; Attendance: 5,770
Referee: Robert Schörgenhofer (Austria)
MONTENEGRO - MOLDOVA **2-5(0-1)**
MNE: Vukašin Poleksić, Vladimir Božović, Milan Jovanović (4.Miloš Krkotić), Elsad Zverotić, Savo Pavićević, Ivan Kecojević, Branko Bošković (46.Filip Kasalica), Nikola Drinčić, Dejan Damjanović, Fatos Bećiraj (77.Marko Vešović), Stevan Jovetić. Trainer: Branislav Brnović.
MDA: Ilie Cebanu, Victor Golovatenco, Petru Racu, Vitalie Bordian, Igor Armaş, Artur Ioniţă, Alexandru Antoniuc, Eugen Sidorenco (85.Viorel Frunză), Alexandru Dedov, Alexandru Gaţcan, Serghei Gheorghiev. Trainer: Ion Caras
Goals: 0-1 Alexandru Antoniuc (28), 1-1 Stevan Jovetić (55 penalty), 1-2 Igor Armaş (62), 1-3 Eugen Sidorenco (64), 1-4 Artur Ioniţă (73), 1-5 Alexandru Antoniuc (89), 2-5 Stevan Jovetić (90+1).
Cautions: Stevan Jovetić, Nikola Drinčić, Miloš Krkotić, Marko Vešović / Serghei Gheorghiev, Alexandru Gaţcan, Alexandru Dedov, Victor Golovatenco.

GROUP I

07.09.2012	Tbilisi	Georgia - Belarus	1-0(0-0)
07.09.2012	Helsinki	Finland - France	0-1(0-1)
11.09.2012	Paris	France - Belarus	3-1(0-0)
11.09.2012	Tbilisi	Georgia - Spain	0-1(0-0)
12.10.2012	Helsinki	Finland - Georgia	1-1(0-0)
12.10.2012	Minsk	Belarus - Spain	0-4(0-2)
16.10.2012	Minsk	Belarus - Georgia	2-0(2-0)
16.10.2012	Madrid	Spain - France	1-1(1-0)
22.03.2013	Gijón	Spain - Finland	1-1(0-0)
22.03.2013	Paris	France - Georgia	3-1(1-0)
26.03.2013	Paris	France - Spain	0-1(0-0)
07.06.2013	Helsinki	Finland - Belarus	1-0(0-0)
11.06.2013	Gomel	Belarus - Finland	1-1(0-1)
06.09.2013	Helsinki	Finland - Spain	0-2(0-1)
06.09.2013	Tbilisi	Georgia - France	0-0
10.09.2013	Tbilisi	Georgia - Finland	0-1(0-0)
10.09.2013	Gomel	Belarus - France	2-4(1-0)
11.10.2013	Palma de Mallorca	Spain - Belarus	2-1(0-0)
15.10.2013	Paris	France - Finland	3-0(1-0)
15.10.2013	Albacete	Spain - Georgia	2-0(1-0)

FINAL STANDINGS

1.	**SPAIN**	8	6	2	0	14	-	3	20
2.	**France**	8	5	2	1	15	-	6	17
3.	Finland	8	2	3	3	5	-	9	9
4.	Georgia	8	1	2	5	3	-	10	5
5.	Belarus	8	1	1	6	7	-	16	4

Spain qualified for the Final Tournament; France qualified for the Play-Offs.

07.09.2012, Dinamo Arena, Tbilisi; Attendance: 20,000
Referee: Stanislav Todorov (Bulgaria)

GEORGIA - BELARUS 1-0(0-0)

GEO: Giorgi Loria, Zurab Khizanishvili, Aleksandre Amisulashvili, Gia Grigalava, Guram Kashia, Jaba Kankava, Murtaz Daushvili, David Targamadze, Jano Ananidze (74.Tornike Gorgiashvili), Tornike Okriashvili (83.Irakli Sirbiladze), Levan Mchedlidze (56.Davit Kvirkvelia). Trainer: Temuri Ketsbaia.
BLR: Syarhey Vyeramko, Dzyanis Palyakow, Dmitry Verkhovtsov, Aleksandr Martynovich, Alyaksandr Kulchiy, Anton Putsila, Yan Tsiharaw (62.Stanislaw Drahun), Maksim Zhavnerchik (34.Syarhey Balanovich), Pavel Nyakhaychyk (30.Maksim Bardachov), Renan Bardini Bressan, Syarhey Kornilenko. Trainer: Heorhiy Kandratsyew.
Goal: 1-0 Tornike Okriashvili (52).
Cautions: Jaba Kankava, Giorgi Loria / Aleksandr Martynovich.

07.09.2012, Olympiastadion, Helsinki; Attendance: 35,111
Referee: Craig Thomson (Scotland)

FINLAND - FRANCE 0-1(0-1)

FIN: Lukáš Hrádecký, Kari Arkivuo, Niklas Moisander, Joona Toivio, Roman Eremenko, Tim Sparv, Markus Olof Halsti, Kasper Woldemar Hämäläinen (78.Njazi Kuqi), Përparim Hetemaj (65.Alexei Eremenko jr.), Alexander Michael Ring, Teemu Pukki. Trainer: Mika-Matti Petteri Paatelainen.
FRA: Hugo Lloris, Anthony Réveillère, Patrice Latyr Evra, Mamadou Sakho, Mapou Yanga-Mbiwa, Franck Henry Pierre Ribéry (89.Bafétimbi Gomis), Rio Antonio Zoba Mavuba, Jérémy Ménez (62.Mathieu Valbuena), Yohan Cabaye (72.Blaise Matuidi), Vassiriki Abou Diaby, Karim Mostafa Benzema. Trainer: Didier Claude Deschamps.
Goal: 0-1 Vassiriki Abou Diaby (20).
Cautions: Markus Olof Halsti, Tim Sparv, Niklas Moisander / Yohan Cabaye, Mapou Yanga-Mbiwa, Blaise Matuidi.

11.09.2012, Stade de France, Saint-Denis, Paris; Attendance: 52,552
Referee: Hüseyin Göçek (Turkey)

FRANCE - BELARUS 3-1(0-0)

FRA: Hugo Lloris, Christophe Jallet, Patrice Latyr Evra, Mamadou Sakho, Mapou Yanga-Mbiwa, Franck Henry Pierre Ribéry (90+1.Jérémy Ménez), Rio Antonio Zoba Mavuba, Yohan Cabaye (75.Blaise Matuidi), Étienne Capoue, Karim Mostafa Benzema, Olivier Giroud (61.Mathieu Valbuena). Trainer: Didier Claude Deschamps.
BLR: Syarhey Vyeramko, Artsyom Radzkow, Dzyanis Palyakow, Maksim Bardachov, Dmitry Verkhovtsov (70.Syarhey Balanovich), Aleksandr Martynovich, Anton Putsila, Renan Bardini Bressan (46.Alyaksandr Kulchiy), Syarhey Kislyak, Stanislaw Drahun, Vitaliy Rodionov (62.Syarhey Kornilenko). Trainer: Heorhiy Kandratsyew.
Goals: 1-0 Étienne Capoue (49), 2-0 Christophe Jallet (68), 2-1 Anton Putsila (72), 3-1 Franck Henry Pierre Ribéry (80).
Cautions: Mapou Yanga-Mbiwa / Dmitry Verkhovtsov.

11.09.2012, Dinamo Arena, Tbilisi; Attendance: 54,598
Referee: Svein Oddvar Moen (Norway)

GEORGIA - SPAIN 0-1(0-0)

GEO: Giorgi Loria (73.Roin Kvaskhvadze), Zurab Khizanishvili, Aleksandre Amisulashvili, Davit Kvirkvelia, Guram Kashia, Ucha Lobjanidze, Jaba Kankava, Murtaz Daushvili, David Targamadze (64.Nika Dzalamidze), Tornike Okriashvili, Levan Mchedlidze (79.Irakli Sirbiladze). Trainer: Temuri Ketsbaia.
ESP: Iker Casillas Fernández, Sergio Ramos García, Álvaro Arbeloa Coca (80.Francesc Fàbregas Soler „Cesc Fàbregas“), Gerard Piqué i Bernabeu, Jordi Alba Ramos, Andrés Iniesta Luján, Xabier Alonso Olano „Xabi Alonso“, Xavier Hernández i Creus „Xavi“, David Josué Jiménez Silva (64.Santiago Cazorla González), Sergio Busquets Burgos (57.Pedro Eliezer Rodríguez Ledesma), Roberto Soldado

Rillo. Trainer: Vicente del Bosque González.
Goal: 0-1 Roberto Soldado Rillo (86).

12.10.2012, Olympiastadion, Helsinki; Attendance: 12,607
Referee: Yevhen Aranovskiy (Ukraine)
FINLAND - GEORGIA **1-1(0-0)**
FIN: Niki Mäenpää, Jukka Raitala, Niklas Moisander, Juhani Ojala, Jere Juhani Uronen, Roman Eremenko, Tim Sparv, Alexei Eremenko jr., Kasper Woldemar Hämäläinen, Alexander Michael Ring, Teemu Pukki (62.Përparim Hetemaj). Trainer: Mika-Matti Petteri Paatelainen.
GEO: Nukri Revishvili, Zurab Khizanishvili, Aleksandre Amisulashvili, Gia Grigalava, Guram Kashia, Aleksandre Kobakhidze, Jaba Kankava, Murtaz Daushvili, David Targamadze (81.Levan Kenia), Tornike Okriashvili (67.Jano Ananidze), Levan Mchedlidze (59.Davit Devdariani). Trainer: Temuri Ketsbaia.
Goals: 0-1 Guram Kashia (56), 1-1 Kasper Woldemar Hämäläinen (62).
Cautions: Alexei Eremenko jr., Përparim Hetemaj / Tornike Okriashvili.
Sent off: Alexei Eremenko jr. (59).

12.10.2012, Dynama Stadium, Minsk; Attendance: 28,800
Referee: Serge Gumienny (Belgium)
BELARUS - SPAIN **0-4(0-2)**
BLR: Syarhey Vyeramko, Yahor Filipenka, Pavel Plaskonny, Maksim Bardachov, Igor Shitov, Aleksandr Martynovich, Alyaksandr Hleb, Yan Tsiharaw, Alyaksandr Valadzko (46.Syarhey Kislyak), Stanislaw Drahun (79.Andrey Chukhley), Vitaliy Rodionov (65.Renan Bardini Bressan). Trainer: Heorhiy Kandratsyew.
ESP: Iker Casillas Fernández, Sergio Ramos García (70.Raúl Albiol Tortajada), Álvaro Arbeloa Coca, Jordi Alba Ramos, Francesc Fàbregas Soler „Cesc Fàbregas", Xabier Alonso Olano „Xabi Alonso", Xavier Hernández i Creus „Xavi" (76.David Villa Sánchez), David Josué Jiménez Silva (56.Andrés Iniesta Luján), Santiago Cazorla González, Sergio Busquets Burgos, Pedro Eliezer Rodríguez Ledesma. Trainer: Vicente del Bosque González.
Goals: 0-1 Jordi Alba Ramos (12), 0-2 Pedro Eliezer Rodríguez Ledesma (21), 0-3 Pedro Eliezer Rodríguez Ledesma (69), 0-4 Pedro Eliezer Rodríguez Ledesma (79).
Cautions: Stanislaw Drahun, Igor Shitov / David Josué Jiménez Silva.

16.10.2012, Dynama Stadium, Minsk; Attendance: 15,300
Referee: Robert Schörgenhofer (Austria)
BELARUS - GEORGIA **2-0(2-0)**
BLR: Syarhey Vyeramko, Yahor Filipenka, Dzyanis Palyakow, Maksim Bardachov, Dmitry Verkhovtsov, Alyaksandr Hleb, Yan Tsiharaw, Renan Bardini Bressan (85.Alyaksandr Valadzko), Alyaksandr Pawlaw (83.Syarhey Kislyak), Stanislaw Drahun, Vitaliy Rodionov (90+1.Andrey Chukhley). Trainer: Heorhiy Kandratsyew.
GEO: Nukri Revishvili, Zurab Khizanishvili, Aleksandre Amisulashvili, Gia Grigalava, Guram Kashia, Aleksandre Kobakhidze, Jaba Kankava, Murtaz Daushvili, Davit Devdariani (46.Levan Mchedlidze), David Targamadze (75.Levan Kenia), Tornike Okriashvili (49.Jano Ananidze). Trainer: Temuri Ketsbaia.
Goals: 1-0 Renan Bardini Bressan (6), 2-0 Stanislaw Drahun (28).
Cautions: Yan Tsiharaw, Dzyanis Palyakow, Maksim Bardachov, Alyaksandr Hleb / David Targamadze, Tornike Okriashvili, Zurab Khizanishvili, Jaba Kankava, Gia Grigalava, Levan Mchedlidze.

16.10.2012, Estadio "Vicente Calderón", Madrid; Attendance: 46,825
Referee: Dr. Felix Brych (Germany)
SPAIN - FRANCE **1-1(1-0)**
ESP: Iker Casillas Fernández, Sergio Ramos García, Álvaro Arbeloa Coca (50.Juan Francisco Torres Belén „Juanfran"), Jordi Alba Ramos, Francesc Fàbregas Soler „Cesc Fàbregas", Andrés Iniesta Luján (75.Fernando José Torres Sanz), Xabier Alonso Olano „Xabi Alonso", Xavier Hernández i Creus „Xavi", David Josué Jiménez Silva (13.Santiago Cazorla González), Sergio Busquets Burgos, Pedro Eliezer Rodríguez Ledesma. Trainer: Vicente del Bosque González.
FRA: Hugo Lloris, Mathieu Debuchy, Patrice Latyr Evra, Mamadou Sakho, Laurent Koscielny, Franck Henry Pierre Ribéry, Blaise Matuidi, Jérémy Ménez (68.Moussa Sissoko), Yohan Cabaye, Maxime Gonalons (57.Mathieu Valbuena), Karim Mostafa Benzema (88.Olivier Giroud). Trainer: Didier Claude Deschamps.
Goals: 1-0 Sergio Ramos García (25), 1-1 Olivier Giroud (90+4).
Cautions: Juan Francisco Torres Belén „Juanfran" / Laurent Koscielny, Maxime Gonalons.

22.03.2013, Estadio El Molinón, Gijón; Attendance: 27,637
Referee: Ovidiu Haţegan (Romania)
SPAIN - FINLAND **1-1(0-0)**
ESP: Víctor Valdés i Arribas, Sergio Ramos García, Álvaro Arbeloa Coca, Gerard Piqué i Bernabeu, Jordi Alba Ramos, Francesc Fàbregas Soler „Cesc Fàbregas" (76.Juan Manuel Mata García „Juan Mata"), Andrés Iniesta Luján, David Josué Jiménez Silva, Santiago Cazorla González (46.Pedro Eliezer Rodríguez Ledesma), Sergio Busquets Burgos, David Villa Sánchez (65.Álvaro Negredo Sánchez). Trainer: Vicente del Bosque González.
FIN: Niki Mäenpää, Kari Arkivuo, Jukka Raitala, Niklas Moisander, Joona Toivio, Teemu Tainio (69.Tim Sparv), Roman Eremenko, Kasper Woldemar Hämäläinen, Përparim Hetemaj, Alexander Michael Ring, Teemu Pukki (90+4.Markus Olof Halsti). Trainer: Mika-Matti Petteri Paatelainen.
Goals: 1-0 Sergio Ramos García (49), 1-1 Teemu Pukki (79).
Cautions: David Josué Jiménez Silva / Niki Mäenpää, Niklas Moisander.

22.03.2013, Stade de France, Saint-Denis, Paris; Attendance: 71,147
Referee: Ivan Bebek (Croatia)
FRANCE - GEORGIA **3-1(1-0)**
FRA: Hugo Lloris, Christophe Jallet, Gaël Clichy, Mamadou Sakho, Raphaël Varane, Franck Henry Pierre Ribéry (78.Jérémy Ménez), Blaise Matuidi (81.Moussa Sissoko), Mathieu Valbuena (66.Loïc Rémy), Paul Labile Pogba, Karim Mostafa Benzema, Olivier Giroud. Trainer: Didier Claude Deschamps.
GEO: Giorgi Loria, Zurab Khizanishvili, Aleksandre Amisulashvili, Davit Kvirkvelia, Guram Kashia, Ucha Lobjanidze, Aleksandre Kobakhidze, Murtaz Daushvili, David Targamadze (84.Nikoloz Gelashvili), Jano Ananidze (46.Levan Kenia), Mate Vatsadze (73.Vladimer Dvalishvili). Trainer: Temuri Ketsbaia.
Goals: 1-0 Olivier Giroud (45+1), 2-0 Mathieu Valbuena (47), 3-0 Franck Henry Pierre Ribéry (61), 3-1 Aleksandre Kobakhidze (71).
Cautions: Aleksandre Amisulashvili.

26.03.2013, Stade de France, Saint-Denis, Paris; Attendance: 78,329
Referee: Viktor Kassai (Hungary)
FRANCE - SPAIN **0-1(0-0)**
FRA: Hugo Lloris, Christophe Jallet (90+2.Olivier Giroud), Patrice Latyr Evra, Laurent Koscielny, Raphaël Varane, Franck Henry Pierre Ribéry, Blaise Matuidi, Mathieu Valbuena, Yohan Cabaye (70.Jérémy Ménez), Paul Labile Pogba, Karim Mostafa Benzema (82.Moussa Sissoko). Trainer: Didier Claude Deschamps.
ESP: Víctor Valdés i Arribas, Sergio Ramos García, Ignacio Monreal Eraso „Nacho Monreal", Álvaro Arbeloa Coca, Gerard Piqué i Bernabeu, Andrés Iniesta Luján (90+3.Juan Manuel Mata García „Juan Mata"), Xabier Alonso Olano „Xabi Alonso", Xavier Hernández i Creus „Xavi", Sergio Busquets Burgos, David Villa Sánchez (61.Jesús Navas González), Pedro Eliezer Rodríguez Ledesma (76.Francesc Fàbregas Soler „Cesc Fàbregas"). Trainer: Vicente del Bosque González.
Goal: 0-1 Pedro Eliezer Rodríguez Ledesma (58).
Cautions: Yohan Cabaye, Blaise Matuidi, Paul Labile Pogba / Xavier Hernández i Creus „Xavi",Francesc Fàbregas Soler „Cesc Fàbregas",Álvaro Arbeloa Coca.
Sent off: Paul Labile Pogba (78).

07.06.2013, Olympiastadion, Helsinki; Attendance: 24,916
Referee: Eli Hacmon (Israel)
FINLAND - BELARUS **1-0(0-0)**
FIN: Niki Mäenpää, Petri Pasanen, Kari Arkivuo (53.Jarkko Erkki Hurme), Jukka Raitala, Teemu Tainio (68.Tim Sparv), Roman Eremenko, Markus Olof Halsti, Kasper Woldemar Hämäläinen, Përparim Hetemaj, Alexander Michael Ring, Teemu Pukki (77.Mikael Kaj Forssell). Trainer: Mika-Matti Petteri Paatelainen.
BLR: Syarhey Vyeramko, Yahor Filipenka, Maksim Bardachov, Igor Shitov (78.Tsimafey Kalachyov), Aleksandr Martynovich, Alyaksandr Hleb, Anton Putsila, Syarhey Balanovich (17.Pavel Nyakhaychyk), Syarhey Kislyak, Stanislaw Drahun (66.Alyaksandr Pawlaw), Vitaliy Rodionov. Trainer: Heorhiy Kandratsyew.
Goal: 1-0 Igor Shitov (57 own goal).
Cautions: Markus Olof Halsti, Petri Pasanen / Pavel Nyakhaychyk.
Sent off: Pavel Nyakhaychyk (90+1).

11.06.2013, Central Stadium, Gomel; Referee:; Attendance: 10,100
Libor Kovařík (Czech Republic)
BELARUS - FINLAND **1-1(0-1)**
BLR: Syarhey Vyeramko, Vitaliy Trubila, Dmitry Verkhovtsov, Aleh Veratsila (46.Syarhey Kislyak), Aleksandr Martynovich (79.Pavel Sitko), Alyaksandr Hleb, Anton Putsila (64.Renan Bardini Bressan), Tsimafey Kalachyov, Stanislaw Drahun, Edhar Alyakhnovich, Vitaliy Rodionov. Trainer: Heorhiy Kandratsyew.
FIN: Niki Mäenpää, Petri Pasanen, Jukka Raitala, Niklas Moisander, Jarkko Erkki Hurme, Roman Eremenko, Tim Sparv, Kasper Woldemar Hämäläinen (83.Paulus Arajuuri), Përparim Hetemaj, Alexander Michael Ring, Teemu Pukki (76.Timo Furuholm). Trainer: Mika-Matti Petteri Paatelainen.
Goals: 0-1 Teemu Pukki (24), 1-1 Dmitry Verkhovtsov (85).
Cautions: Vitaliy Rodionov, Aleh Veratsila, Syarhey Kislyak / Përparim Hetemaj, Roman Eremenko, Jarkko Erkki Hurme, Paulus Arajuuri.

06.09.2013, Olympiastadion, Helsinki; Attendance: 37,492
Referee: Ivan Bebek (Croatia)

FINLAND - SPAIN 0-2(0-1)

FIN: Niki Mäenpää, Petri Pasanen, Kari Arkivuo, Niklas Moisander, Joona Toivio, Teemu Tainio (69.Riku Riski), Roman Eremenko, Markus Olof Halsti, Rasmus Schüller, Alexander Michael Ring (69.Kasper Woldemar Hämäläinen), Teemu Pukki (81.Erfan Zeneli). Trainer: Mika-Matti Petteri Paatelainen.

ESP: Iker Casillas Fernández, Sergio Ramos García, Raúl Albiol Tortajada, Jordi Alba Ramos, Francesc Fàbregas Soler „Cesc Fàbregas" (71.Álvaro Negredo Sánchez), Andrés Iniesta Luján, Xavier Hernández i Creus „Xavi", Mario Suárez Mata, Jorge Resurrección Merodio „Koke", David Villa Sánchez (55.Jesús Navas González), Pedro Eliezer Rodríguez Ledesma (81.Santiago Cazorla González). Trainer: Vicente del Bosque González.

Goals: 0-1 Jordi Alba Ramos (19), 0-2 Álvaro Negredo Sánchez (86).

Cautions: Mario Suárez Mata.

06.09.2013, Dinamo Arena, Tbilisi; Attendance: 26,360
Referee: Fırat Aydınus (Turkey)

GEORGIA - FRANCE 0-0

GEO: Giorgi Loria, Aleksandre Amisulashvili, Gia Grigalava, Akaki Khubutia, Guram Kashia, Ucha Lobjanidze, Aleksandre Kobakhidze (60.Elguja Grigalashvili), Jaba Kankava, Jano Ananidze (69.David Targamadze), Tornike Okriashvili, Nikoloz Gelashvili (79.Vladimer Dvalishvili). Trainer: Temuri Ketsbaia.

FRA: Hugo Lloris, Éric Sylvain Abidal, Bacary Sagna, Patrice Latyr Evra, Laurent Koscielny, Franck Henry Pierre Ribéry, Mathieu Valbuena, Moussa Sissoko, Josuha Guilavogui (78.Samir Nasri), Karim Mostafa Benzema (62.André-Pierre Gignac), Olivier Giroud. Trainer: Didier Claude Deschamps.

Cautions: Tornike Okriashvili, Giorgi Loria.

10.09.2013, "Mikheil Meskhi" Stadium, Tbilisi; Attendance: 25,321
Referee: Leontios Trattou (Cyprus)

GEORGIA - FINLAND 0-1(0-0)

GEO: Nukri Revishvili, Aleksandre Amisulashvili, Gia Grigalava, Akaki Khubutia, Guram Kashia, Ucha Lobjanidze, Aleksandre Kobakhidze (46.David Targamadze), Jaba Kankava, Jano Ananidze (83.Vladimer Dvalishvili), Tornike Okriashvili, Nikoloz Gelashvili (57.Elguja Grigalashvili). Trainer: Temuri Ketsbaia.

FIN: Niki Mäenpää, Kari Arkivuo, Veli Lampi, Niklas Moisander, Juhani Ojala, Teemu Tainio, Roman Eremenko, Kasper Woldemar Hämäläinen (89.Riku Riski), Përparim Hetemaj, Alexander Michael Ring (71.Tim Sparv), Teemu Pukki (90+2.Rasmus Schüller). Trainer: Mika-Matti Petteri Paatelainen.

Goal: 0-1 Roman Eremenko (74 penalty).

Cautions: Akaki Khubutia, Jaba Kankava, David Targamadze, Gia Grigalava / Përparim Hetemaj, Veli Lampi, Juhani Ojala, Tim Sparv.

Sent off: Jaba Kankava (75).

10.09.2013, Central Stadium, Gomel; Attendance: 12,203
Referee: Daniele Orsato (Italy)

BELARUS - FRANCE 2-4(1-0)

BLR: Syarhey Vyeramko, Yahor Filipenka, Maksim Bardachov, Dmitry Verkhovtsov (77.Vitaliy Rodionov), Aleksandr Martynovich, Alyaksandr Hleb, Anton Putsila, Syarhey Balanovich, Yan Tsiharaw (83.Renan Bardini Bressan), Tsimafey Kalachyov, Stanislaw Drahun (71.Edhar Alyakhnovich). Trainer: Heorhiy Kandratsyew.

FRA: Hugo Lloris, Éric Sylvain Abidal, Bacary Sagna, Gaël Clichy, Laurent Koscielny, Franck Henry Pierre Ribéry (80.Moussa Sissoko), Blaise Matuidi, Mathieu Valbuena (90+3.Josuha Guilavogui), Paul Labile Pogba, Florent Dimitri Payet (61.Samir Nasri), Olivier Giroud. Trainer: Didier Claude Deschamps.

Goals: 1-0 Yahor Filipenka (32), 1-1 Franck Henry Pierre Ribéry (47 penalty), 2-1 Tsimafey

Kalachyov (57), 2-2 Franck Henry Pierre Ribéry (64), 2-3 Samir Nasri (71), 2-4 Paul Labile Pogba (73).
Cautions: Yahor Filipenka, Syarhey Vyeramko, Alyaksandr Hleb / Gaël Clichy.

11.10.2013, Estadio Iberostar, Palma de Mallorca; Attendance: 22,900
Referee: Hendrikus Sebastiaan Hermanus Nijhuis (Holland)
SPAIN - BELARUS 2-1(0-0)
ESP: Víctor Valdés i Arribas, Sergio Ramos García, Ignacio Monreal Eraso „Nacho Monreal“ (46.Andrés Iniesta Luján), Álvaro Arbeloa Coca, Gerard Piqué i Bernabeu, Francesc Fàbregas Soler „Cesc Fàbregas“ (84.Jorge Resurrección Merodio „Koke“), Xavier Hernández i Creus „Xavi“, David Josué Jiménez Silva, Sergio Busquets Burgos, Miguel Pérez Cuesta „Michu“ (57.Álvaro Negredo Sánchez), Pedro Eliezer Rodríguez Ledesma. Trainer: Vicente del Bosque González.
BLR: Alyaksandr Hutar, Yahor Filipenka, Maksim Bardachov, Dmitry Verkhovtsov, Aleksandr Martynovich (80.Syarhey Kislyak), Anton Putsila (77.Syarhey Kornilenko), Syarhey Balanovich, Yan Tsiharaw, Tsimafey Kalachyov, Stanislaw Drahun, Vitaliy Rodionov (55.Syarhey Krivets). Trainer: Trainer: Heorhiy Kandratsyew.
Goals: 1-0 Xavier Hernández i Creus „Xavi“ (61), 2-0 Álvaro Negredo Sánchez (78), 2-1 Syarhey Kornilenko (89).
Cautions: Gerard Piqué i Bernabeu / Aleksandr Martynovich, Maksim Bardachov, Tsimafey Kalachyov, Stanislaw Drahun, Dmitry Verkhovtsov.

15.10.2013, Stade de France, Saint-Denis, Paris; Attendance: 70,156
Referee: Michael Koukoulakis (Greece)
FRANCE - FINLAND 3-0(1-0)
FRA: Hugo Lloris, Éric Sylvain Abidal, Mathieu Debuchy, Patrice Latyr Evra, Laurent Koscielny, Blaise Matuidi (70.Yohan Cabaye), Mathieu Valbuena, Samir Nasri (71.Loïc Rémy), Paul Labile Pogba, Franck Henry Pierre Ribéry, Olivier Giroud (81.Karim Mostafa Benzema). Trainer: Didier Claude Deschamps.
FIN: Niki Mäenpää, Petri Pasanen, Kari Arkivuo, Veli Lampi, Teemu Tainio (64.Joona Toivio), Roman Eremenko, Markus Olof Halsti, Kasper Woldemar Hämäläinen (79.Riku Riski), Përparim Hetemaj, Alexander Michael Ring, Teemu Pukki (86.Timo Furuholm). Trainer: Mika-Matti Petteri Paatelainen.
Goals: 1-0 Franck Henry Pierre Ribéry (8), 2-0 Joona Toivio (75 own goal), 3-0 Karim Mostafa Benzema (87).
Cautions: Mathieu Debuchy, Patrice Latyr Evra / Alexander Michael Ring.

15.10.2013, Estadio "Carlos Belmonte", Albacete; Attendance: 16,133
Referee: Florian Meyer (Germany)
SPAIN - GEORGIA 2-0(1-0)
ESP: Iker Casillas Fernández, Sergio Ramos García, Juan Francisco Torres Belén „Juanfran“, Gerard Piqué i Bernabeu, Alberto Moreno Pérez, Andrés Iniesta Luján (82.Francisco Román Alarcón Suárez „Isco“), Xavier Hernández i Creus „Xavi“ (66.Jorge Resurrección Merodio „Koke“), Jesús Navas González, Sergio Busquets Burgos, Álvaro Negredo Sánchez, Pedro Eliezer Rodríguez Ledesma (58.Juan Manuel Mata García „Juan Mata“). Trainer: Vicente del Bosque González.
GEO: Giorgi Loria, Davit Kvirkvelia, Akaki Khubutia, Guram Kashia, Giorgi Khidesheli, Ucha Lobjanidze, Aleksandre Kobakhidze, Irakli Dzaria, Shota Grigalashvili (70.Avtandil Ebralidze), Elguja Grigalashvili (75.Levan Khmaladze), Nikoloz Gelashvili (87.Irakli Modebadze). Trainer: Temuri Ketsbaia.
Goals: 1-0 Álvaro Negredo Sánchez (26), 2-0 Juan Manuel Mata García „Juan Mata“ (61).
Cautions: Akaki Khubutia.

PLAY-OFFS

RANKING OF SECOND-PLACED TEAMS
(matches against the sixth-placed team in each group are not included)

1.	Greece	8	6	1	1	9	-	4	19
2.	France	8	5	2	1	15	-	6	17
3.	Portugal	8	4	3	1	15	-	8	15
4.	Ukraine	8	4	3	1	11	-	4	15
5.	Sweden	8	4	2	2	15	-	13	14
6.	Iceland	8	4	2	2	15	-	14	14
7.	Romania	8	4	1	3	11	-	12	13
8.	Croatia	8	3	2	3	9	-	8	11
9.	Denmark	8	2	4	2	9	-	11	10

For the draw for the ties, helded in Zürich on 21 October 2013, the eight teams being seeded according to the October 2013 FIFA World Rankings:

Pot A: Portugal, Greece, Croatia, Ukraine.
Pot B: France, Sweden, Romania, Iceland.

15.11.2013	Reykjavík	Iceland - Croatia	0-0
15.11.2013	Lisboa	Portugal - Sweden	1-0(0-0)
15.11.2013	Kyiv	Ukraine - France	2-0(0-0)
15.11.2013	Peiraiás	Greece - Romania	3-1(2-1)
19.11.2013	Zagreb	Croatia - Iceland	2-0(1-0)
19.11.2013	Stockholm	Sweden - Portugal	2-3(0-0)
19.11.2013	Paris	France - Ukraine	3-0(2-0)
19.11.2013	Bucureşti	Romania - Greece	1-1(0-1)

CROATIA, **PORTUGAL**, **FRANCE** and **GREECE** qualified for the 2014 World Cup Final Tournament.

FIRST LEGS

15.11.2013, Laugardalsvöllur, Reykjavík; Attendance: 9,767
Referee: Alberto Undiano Mallenco (Spain)
ICELAND - CROATIA 0-0
ISL: Hannes Þór Halldórsson, Ragnar Sigurðsson, Ari Freyr Skúlason, Ólafur Ingi Skúlason, Birkir Bjarnason, Kári Árnason, Aron Einar Malmquist Gunnarsson, Jóhann Berg Guðmundsson, Gylfi Þór Sigurðsson, Kolbeinn Sigþórsson (46.Eiður Smári Guðjohnsen), Alfreð Finnbogason (63.Rúrik Gíslason). Trainer: Lars Edvin Lagerbäck (Sweden).
CRO: Stipe Pletikosa, Josip Šimunić, Vedran Ćorluka, Danijel Pranjić, Darijo Srna, Ivan Rakitić, Luka Modrić, Ivan Perišić, Ivo Iličević (47.Ivica Olić), Mario Mandžukić (87.Leon Benko), Eduardo Alves Da Silva (72.Ante Rebić). Trainer: Niko Kovač.
Sent off: Ólafur Ingi Skúlason (50).

15.11.2013, Estádio da Luz, Lisboa; Attendance: 61,467
Referee: Nicola Rizzoli (Italy)
PORTUGAL - SWEDEN 1-0(0-0)
POR: Rui Pedro dos Santos Patrício, Képler Laveran Lima Ferreira „Pepe", Bruno Eduardo Regufe Alves, Fábio Alexandre da Silva Coentrão, João Pedro da Silva Pereira, Raul José Trindade Meireles (79.Josué Filipe Soares Pesqueira), Luís Carlos Almeida da Cunha „Nani", Miguel Luís Pinto Veloso, João Filipe Iria Santos Moutinho, Cristiano Ronaldo dos Santos Aveiro, Hélder Manuel Marques Postiga (66.Hugo Miguel Pereira de Almeida). Trainer: Paulo Jorge Gomes Bento.
SWE: Andreas Isaksson, Martin Olsson, Per Jörgen Nilsson, Mikael Antonsson, Carl Mikael Lustig, Kim Mikael Källström (78.Anders Gunnar Svensson), Rasmus Cristoffer Elm (72.Pontus Anders Mikael Wernbloom), Sebastian Bengt Ulf Larsson, Alexander Kačaniklić, Zlatan Ibrahimović, Johan Erik Calvin Elmander (88.Alexander Clas Robin Gerndt). Trainer: Erik Anders Hamrén.
Goal: 1-0 Cristiano Ronaldo dos Santos Aveiro (82).
Cautions: João Pedro da Silva Pereira, Cristiano Ronaldo dos Santos Aveiro / Sebastian Bengt Ulf Larsson, Johan Erik Calvin Elmander.

15.11.2013, Olympiyskiy Stadium, Kyiv; Attendance: 67,732
Referee: Cüneyt Çakır (Turkey)
UKRAINE - FRANCE 2-0(0-0)
UKR: Andriy Pyatov, Oleksandr Kucher, Vyacheslav Shevchuk, Artem Fedetskiy, Yevhen Khacheridi, Ruslan Rotan, Edmar Halovskyi de Lacerda (76.Roman Bezus), Taras Stepanenko, Yevhen Konoplyanka (90+2.Oleh Husyev), Andriy Yarmolenko, Roman Zozulya (86.Yevhen Seleznyov). Trainer: Mykhaylo Fomenko.
FRA: Hugo Lloris, Éric Sylvain Abidal, Mathieu Debuchy, Patrice Latyr Evra, Laurent Koscielny, Blaise Matuidi, Samir Nasri (80.Mathieu Valbuena), Paul Labile Pogba, Franck Henry Pierre Ribéry, Loïc Rémy (62.Moussa Sissoko), Olivier Giroud (70.Karim Mostafa Benzema). Trainer: Didier Claude Deschamps.
Goals: 1-0 Roman Zozulya (62), 2-0 Andriy Yarmolenko (82 penalty).
Cautions: Vyacheslav Shevchuk, Artem Fedetskiy, Oleksandr Kucher / Olivier Giroud, Moussa Sissoko.
Sent off: Laurent Koscielny (90+1), Oleksandr Kucher (90+5).

15.11.2013, Stádio „Yeorgios Karaïskákis“, Peiraiás; Attendance: 26,200
Referee: Pedro Proença Oliveira Alves Garcia (Portugal)

GREECE - ROMANIA 3-1(2-1)

GRE: Orestis-Spyridon Karnezis, José Lloyd Holebas, Dimitrios Siovas, Vasileios Torosidis, Sokratis Papastathopoulos, Konstantinos Katsouranis (86.Andreas Samaris), Alexandros Tziolis, Giánnis Maniatis (77.Giórgos Karagounis), Giórgos Samaras, Konstantinos Mitroglou (80.Theofanis Gekas), Dimitrios Salpingidis. Trainer: Fernando Manuel Costa Santos (Portugal).
ROU: Bogdan Ionuţ Lobonţ, Alexandru Măţel, Dorin Nicolae Goian, Florin Gardoş, Răzvan Dincă Raţ, Alexandru Bourceanu (74.Costin Lazăr), Răzvan Vasile Cociş, Gabriel Andrei Torje (75.Gheorghe Teodor Grozav), Cristian Tănase (87.Alexandru Iulian Maxim), Ciprian Andrei Marica, Bogdan Sorin Stancu. Trainer: Victor Piţurcă.
Goals: 1-0 Konstantinos Mitroglou (14), 1-1 Bogdan Sorin Stancu (19), 2-1 Dimitrios Salpingidis (21), 3-1 Konstantinos Mitroglou (67).
Cautions: Dimitrios Siovas, Konstantinos Katsouranis / Alexandru Bourceanu, Răzvan Vasile Cociş, Dorin Nicolae Goian, Costin Lazăr, Răzvan Dincă Raţ.
Sent off: Costin Lazăr (90+2).

SECOND LEGS

19.11.2013, Stadion Maksimir, Zagreb; Attendance: 22,612
Referee: Björn Kuipers (Holland)

CROATIA - ICELAND 2-0(1-0)

CRO: Stipe Pletikosa, Darijo Srna, Vedran Ćorluka, Josip Šimunić, Danijel Pranjić, Mateo Kovačić (75.Ante Rebić), Ivan Perišić, Ivan Rakitić, Luka Modrić (90.Dejan Lovren), Mario Mandžukić, Ivica Olić (81.Nikica Jelavić). Trainer: Niko Kovač.
ISL: Hannes Þór Halldórsson, Ragnar Sigurðsson, Birkir Már Sævarsson, Ari Freyr Skúlason, Birkir Bjarnason, Kári Árnason, Aron Einar Malmquist Gunnarsson (73.Emil Hallfreðsson), Jóhann Berg Guðmundsson, Gylfi Þór Sigurðsson, Eiður Smári Guðjohnsen (65.Rúrik Gíslason), Alfreð Finnbogason. Trainer: Lars Edvin Lagerbäck (Sweden).
Goals: 1-0 Mario Mandžukić (27), 2-0 Darijo Srna (47).
Cautions: Ivica Olić, Josip Šimunić / Ragnar Sigurðsson, Emil Hallfreðsson.
Sent off: Mario Mandžukić (38).

19.11.2013, Friends Arena, Stockholm; Attendance: 49,766
Referee: Howard Melton Webb (England)

SWEDEN - PORTUGAL 2-3(0-0)

SWE: Andreas Isaksson, Martin Olsson, Per Jörgen Nilsson, Mikael Antonsson, Carl Mikael Lustig, Kim Mikael Källström, Rasmus Cristoffer Elm (46. Anders Gunnar Svensson), Sebastian Bengt Ulf Larsson (90.Alexander Clas Robin Gerndt), Alexander Kačaniklić (82.Jakup Jimmy Durmaz), Zlatan Ibrahimović, Johan Erik Calvin Elmander. Trainer: Erik Anders Hamrén.
POR: Rui Pedro dos Santos Patrício, Képler Laveran Lima Ferreira „Pepe“, Bruno Eduardo Regufe Alves, Fábio Alexandre da Silva Coentrão (52.Vitorino Gabriel Pacheco Antunes), João Pedro da Silva Pereira, Raul José Trindade Meireles (73.William Silva de Carvalho), Luís Carlos Almeida da Cunha „Nani“, Miguel Luís Pinto Veloso, João Filipe Iria Santos Moutinho, Cristiano Ronaldo dos Santos Aveiro, Hugo Miguel Pereira de Almeida (82.Ricardo Miguel Moreira da Costa). Trainer: Paulo Jorge Gomes Bento.
Goals: 0-1 Cristiano Ronaldo dos Santos Aveiro (50), 1-1 Zlatan Ibrahimović (50), 2-1 Zlatan Ibrahimović (72), 2-2 Cristiano Ronaldo dos Santos Aveiro (77), 2-3 Cristiano Ronaldo dos Santos Aveiro (79).
Cautions: Martin Olsson, Anders Gunnar Svensson, Kim Mikael Källström, Jakup Jimmy Durmaz / Luís Carlos Almeida da Cunha „Nani“.

19.11.2013, Stade de France, Saint-Denis, Paris; Attendance: 77,098
Referee: Damir Skomina (Slovenia)
FRANCE - UKRAINE **3-0(2-0)**
FRA: Hugo Lloris, Mathieu Debuchy (78.Bacary Sagna), Patrice Latyr Evra, Mamadou Sakho, Raphaël Varane, Blaise Matuidi, Mathieu Valbuena, Yohan Cabaye, Franck Henry Pierre Ribéry, Paul Labile Pogba, Karim Mostafa Benzema (82.Olivier Giroud). Trainer: Didier Claude Deschamps.
UKR: Andriy Pyatov, Vyacheslav Shevchuk, Vitaliy Mandzyuk, Yaroslav Rakytskiy, Yevhen Khacheridi, Ruslan Rotan, Edmar Halovskyi de Lacerda, Yevhen Konoplyanka, Roman Bezus (64.Oleh Husyev), Andriy Yarmolenko, Roman Zozulya (76.Yevhen Seleznyov). Trainer: Mykhaylo Fomenko.
Goals: 1-0 Mamadou Sakho (22), 2-0 Karim Mostafa Benzema (34), 3-0 Mamadou Sakho (72).
Cautions: Mamadou Sakho, Patrice Latyr Evra, Mathieu Debuchy / Ruslan Rotan, Yevhen Khacheridi, Vitaliy Mandzyuk.
Sent off: Yevhen Khacheridi (47).

19.11.2013, Arena Naţională, Bucureşti; Attendance: 49,793
Referee: Milorad Mažić (Serbia)
ROMANIA - GREECE **1-1(0-1)**
ROU: Anton Ciprian Tătăruşanu, Alexandru Măţel, Vlad Iulian Chiricheş, Dorin Nicolae Goian, Răzvan Dincă Raţ (26.Iasmin Latovlevici), Gabriel Andrei Torje (56.Marius Constantin Niculae), Cristian Tănase, Ovidiu Ştefan Hoban, Alexandru Iulian Maxim, Ciprian Andrei Marica, Bogdan Sorin Stancu (87.Gheorghe Teodor Grozav). Trainer: Victor Piţurcă.
GRE: Orestis-Spyridon Karnezis, José Lloyd Holebas, Dimitrios Siovas (80.Konstantinos Manolas), Vasileios Torosidis (72.Loukas Vyntra), Sokratis Papastathopoulos, Giórgos Karagounis (73.Andreas Samaris), Alexandros Tziolis, Giánnis Maniatis, Giórgos Samaras, Konstantinos Mitroglou, Dimitrios Salpingidis. Trainer: Fernando Manuel Costa Santos (Portugal).
Goals: 0-1 Konstantinos Mitroglou (23), 1-1 Vasileios Torosidis (55 own goal).
Cautions: Konstantinos Mitroglou, José Lloyd Holebas, Alexandros Tziolis.

SOUTH AMERICA

All 9 FIFA-affiliated CONMEBOL national associations have entered the World Cup qualifiers, Brazil as hosts of the Final Tournament being qualified automatically. The format of the qualifying tournament is identical to the previous four editions., all national teams played a home and away match against each other competing team. The top-4 national teams were qualified automatically for the Final Tournament. The 5th placed South American team will play against the 5th placed team from the Asian Football Confederation Qualifiers.

QUALIFYING MATCHES RESULTS

Round 1			
07.10.2011	Montevideo	Uruguay - Bolivia	4-2(3-1)
07.10.2011	Quito	Ecuador - Venezuela	2-0(2-0)
07.10.2011	Buenos Aires	Argentina - Chile	4-1(2-0)
07.10.2011	Lima	Peru - Paraguay	2-0(0-0)
Round 2			
11.10.2011	La Paz	Bolivia - Colombia	1-2(0-0)
11.10.2011	Santiago	Chile - Peru	4-2(2-0)
11.10.2011	Asunción	Paraguay - Uruguay	1-1(0-0)
11.10.2011	Puerto la Cruz	Venezuela - Argentina	1-0(0-0)
Round 3			
11.11.2011	Buenos Aires	Argentina - Bolivia	1-1(0-0)
11.11.2011	Montevideo	Uruguay - Chile	4-0(0-0)
11.11.2011	Barranquilla	Colombia - Venezuela	1-1(1-0)
11.11.2011	Asunción	Paraguay - Ecuador	2-1(0-0)
Round 4			
15.11.2011	Barranquilla	Colombia - Argentina	1-2(0-0)
15.11.2011	Quito	Ecuador - Peru	2-0(0-0)
15.11.2011	Santiago	Chile - Paraguay	2-0(1-0)
15.11.2011	San Cristóbal	Venezuela - Bolivia	1-0(1-0)
Round 5			
02.06.2012	Buenos Aires	Argentina - Ecuador	4-0(3-0)
02.06.2012	La Paz	Bolivia - Chile	0-2(0-0)
02.06.2012	Montevideo	Uruguay - Venezuela	1-1(1-0)
03.06.2012	Lima	Peru - Colombia	0-1(0-0)
Round 6			
09.06.2012	La Paz	Bolivia - Paraguay	3-1(1-0)
09.06.2012	Puerto la Cruz	Venezuela - Chile	0-2(0-0)
10.06.2012	Quito	Ecuador - Colombia	1-0(0-0)
10.06.2012	Montevideo	Uruguay - Peru	4-2(2-1)
Round 7			
07.09.2012	Barranquilla	Colombia - Uruguay	4-0(1-0)
07.09.2012	Quito	Ecuador - Bolivia	1-0(0-0)
07.09.2012	Córdoba	Argentina - Paraguay	3-1(2-1)
07.09.2012	Lima	Peru - Venezuela	2-1(0-1)
Round 8			
11.09.2012	Santiago	Chile - Colombia	1-3(1-0)
11.09.2012	Montevideo	Uruguay - Ecuador	1-1(0-1)
11.09.2012	Lima	Peru - Argentina	1-1(1-1)
11.09.2012	Asunción	Paraguay - Venezuela	0-2(0-1)
Round 9			
12.10.2012	Mendoza	Argentina - Uruguay	3-0(0-0)

12.10.2012	Barranquilla	Colombia - Paraguay	2-0(0-0)
12.10.2012	Quito	Ecuador - Chile	3-1(1-1)
12.10.2012	La Paz	Bolivia - Peru	1-1(0-1)
Round 10			
16.10.2012	La Paz	Bolivia - Uruguay	4-1(2-0)
16.10.2012	Asunción	Paraguay - Peru	1-0(0-0)
16.10.2012	Santiago	Chile - Argentina	1-2(0-2)
16.10.2012	Puerto La Cruz	Venezuela - Ecuador	1-1(1-1)
Round 11			
22.03.2013	Buenos Aires	Argentina - Venezuela	3-0(2-0)
22.03.2013	Montevideo	Uruguay - Paraguay	1-1(0-0)
22.03.2013	Lima	Peru - Chile	1-0(0-0)
22.03.2013	Barranquilla	Colombia - Bolivia	5-0(1-0)
Round 12			
26.03.2013	La Paz	Bolivia - Argentina	1-1(1-1)
26.03.2013	Quito	Ecuador - Paraguay	4-1(1-1)
26.03.2013	Santiago	Chile - Uruguay	2-0(1-0)
26.03.2013	Ciudad Guayana	Venezuela - Colombia	1-0(1-0)
Round 13			
07.06.2013	Buenos Aires	Argentina - Colombia	0-0
07.06.2013	La Paz	Bolivia - Venezuela	1-1(0-0)
07.06.2013	Asunción	Paraguay - Chile	1-2(0-1)
07.06.2013	Lima	Peru - Ecuador	1-0(1-0)
Round 14			
11.06.2013	Barranquilla	Ecuador - Argentina	1-1(1-1)
11.06.2013	Santiago	Chile - Bolivia	3-1(2-1)
11.06.2013	Quito	Colombia - Peru	2-0(2-0)
11.06.2013	Ciudad Guayana	Venezuela - Uruguay	0-1(0-1)
Round 15			
06.09.2013	Barranquilla	Colombia - Ecuador	1-0(1-0)
06.09.2013	Asunción	Paraguay - Bolivia	4-0(1-0)
06.09.2013	Santiago	Chile - Venezuela	3-0(2-0)
06.09.2013	Lima	Peru - Uruguay	1-2(0-1)
Round 16			
10.09.2013	La Paz	Bolivia - Ecuador	1-1(0-0)
10.09.2013	Montevideo	Uruguay - Colombia	2-0(0-0)
10.09.2013	Puerto La Cruz	Venezuela - Peru	3-2(1-1)
10.09.2013	Asunción	Paraguay - Argentina	2-5(1-2)
Round 17			
11.10.2013	Barranquilla	Colombia - Chile	3-3(0-3)
11.10.2013	Quito	Ecuador - Uruguay	1-0(1-0)
11.10.2013	San Cristóbal	Venezuela - Paraguay	1-1(0-1)
11.10.2013	Buenos Aires	Argentina - Peru	3-1(2-1)
Round 18			
15.10.2013	Asunción	Paraguay - Colombia	1-2(1-1)
15.10.2013	Santiago	Chile - Ecuador	2-1(2-0)
15.10.2013	Montevideo	Uruguay - Argentina	3-2(2-2)
15.10.2013	Lima	Peru - Bolivia	1-1(1-1)

FINAL STANDINGS

1.	**ARGENTINA**	16	9	5	2	35 - 15	32
2.	**COLOMBIA**	16	9	3	4	27 - 13	30
3.	**CHILE**	16	9	1	6	29 - 25	28
4.	**ECUADOR**	16	7	4	5	20 - 16	25
5.	**Uruguay**	16	7	4	5	25 - 25	25
6.	Venezuela	16	5	5	6	14 - 20	20
7.	Peru	16	4	3	9	17 - 26	15
8.	Bolivia	16	2	6	8	17 - 30	12
9.	Paraguay	16	3	3	10	17 - 31	12

Argentina, Colombia, Chile and Ecuador qualified for the FIFA World Cup final tournament.
Uruguay qualified for the Intercontinental play-offs against an Asian team (Jordan).

07.10.2011, Estadio Centenario, Montevideo; Attendance: 25,500
Referee: Víctor Hugo Carrillo Casanova (Peru)
URUGUAY - BOLIVIA 4-2(3-1)
URU: Néstor Fernando Muslera Micol, José Martín Cáceres Silva, Diego Alfredo Lugano Morena, Diego Roberto Godín Leal, Victorio Maximiliano Pereira Páez, Diego Fernando Pérez Aguado, Egidio Raúl Arévalo Ríos, Álvaro Daniel Pereira Barragán (56.Jorge Ciro Fucile Perdomo), Luis Alberto Suárez Díaz, Edinson Roberto Cavani Gómez (70.Cristian Gabriel Rodríguez Barotti), Diego Martín Forlán Corazzo. Trainer: Óscar Wáshington Tabárez Silva.
BOL: Carlos Erwin Arias Égüez, Ronald Raldes Balcázar, Ronald Taylor Rivero Khun, Luis Alberto Gutiérrez Herrera, Christian Israel Vargas Claros, Rudy Alejandro Cardozo Fernández, Wálter Alberto Flores Condarco (81.José Luis Chávez Sánchez), Jaime Robles Céspedes, Mauricio Saucedo Guardia (46.Alcides Peña Jiménez), Edivaldo Rojas Hermoza (60.Joselito Vaca Velasco), Marcelo Moreno Martins. Trainer: Gustavo Domingo Quinteros Desabato.
Goals: 1-0 Luis Alberto Suárez Díaz (3), 1-1 Rudy Alejandro Cardozo Fernández (18), 2-1 Diego Alfredo Lugano Morena (25), 3-1 Edinson Roberto Cavani Gómez (34), 4-1 Diego Alfredo Lugano Morena (71), 4-2 Marcelo Moreno Martins (86).
Cautions: Egidio Raúl Arévalo Ríos, Álvaro Daniel Pereira Barragán, Victorio Maximiliano Pereira Páez, Luis Alberto Suárez Díaz / Edivaldo Rojas Hermoza, Luis Alberto Gutiérrez Herrera, Ronald Raldes Balcázar, Ronald Taylor Rivero Khun.

07.10.2011, Estadio Olimpico "Atahualpa", Quito; Attendance: 32,278
Referee: Enrique Roberto Osses Zencovich (Chile)
ECUADOR - VENEZUELA 2-0(2-0)
ECU: Máximo Orlando Banguera Valdivieso, Jairo Rolando Campos León, Frickson Rafael Erazo Vivero, Christian Andrés Suárez Valencia (69.Alex Leonardo Bolaños Reascos), Walter Orlando Ayoví Corozo, Christian Fernando Noboa Tello (77.Michael Antonio Arroyo Mina), Luis Fernando Saritama Padilla, Luis Antonio Valencia Mosquera, Jaime Javier Ayoví Corozo, Christian Rogelio Benítez Betancourt (83.Édison Vicente Méndez Méndez), Juan Carlos Paredes Reasco. Trainer: Reinaldo Rueda Rivera (Colombia).
VEN: Renny Vicente Vega Hernández, Franklin José Lucena Peña, José Manuel Rey Cortegoso, José Manuel Velázquez Rodríguez, José Luis Granados Asprilla, Giácomo Di Giorgi Zerillo, Francisco Javier Flores Sequera (58.Ágnel José Flores Hernández), Luis Manuel Seijas Gunther, Jesús Manuel Meza Moreno, Fernando Luis Aristeguieta de Luca (46.Alejandro Enrique Moreno Riera), Giancarlo Gregorio Maldonado Marrero (72.Frank Feltscher Martínez). Trainer: César Alejandro Farías Acosta.
Goals: 1-0 Jaime Javier Ayoví Corozo (15), 2-0 Christian Rogelio Benítez Betancourt (28).
Cautions: Christian Fernando Noboa Tello, Michael Antonio Arroyo Mina / Luis Manuel Seijas Gunther, José Manuel Rey Cortegoso.
Sent off: José Manuel Rey Cortegoso (78).

07.10.2011, Estadio Monumental „Antonio Vespucio Liberti“, Buenos Aires; Attendance: 26,161
Referee: Wilmar Alexander Roldán Pérez (Colombia)

ARGENTINA - CHILE 4-1(2-0)

ARG: Mariano Gonzalo Andújar, Nicolás Andrés Burdisso, Nicolás Hernán Gonzalo Otamendi, Faustino Marcos Alberto Rojo, Pablo Javier Zabaleta Girod, Éver Maximiliano David Banega (72.Fabián Andrés Rinaudo), Rodrigo Braña, José Ernesto Sosa (80.Eduardo Antonio Salvio), Ángel Fabián di María Hernández (85.Jonás Manuel Gutiérrez), Lionel Andrés Messi, Gonzalo Gerardo Higuaín. Trainer: Alejandro Sabella.

CHI: Claudio Andrés Bravo Muñoz, Waldo Alonso Ponce Carrizo, Mauricio Aníbal Isla Isla, Gonzalo Alejandro Jara Reyes, Carlos Emilio Carmona Tello, Arturo Erasmo Vidal Pardo, Matías Ariel Fernández Fernández (81.Cristóbal Andrés Jorquera Torres), Jorge Luis Valdivia Toro, Jean André Emanuel Beausejour Coliqueo (55.Marcos Andrés González Salazar), Mauricio Ricardo Pinilla Ferrera (55.Eduardo Jesús Vargas Rojas), Humberto Andrés Suazo Pontivo. Trainer: Claudio Daniel Borghi Bidos (Argentina).

Goals: 1-0 Gonzalo Gerardo Higuaín (7), 2-0 Lionel Andrés Messi (25), 3-0 Gonzalo Gerardo Higuaín (51), 3-1 Matías Ariel Fernández Fernández (59), 4-1 Gonzalo Gerardo Higuaín (62).

Cautions: Éver Maximiliano David Banega, Faustino Marcos Alberto Rojo / Jean André Emanuel Beausejour Coliqueo, Gonzalo Alejandro Jara Reyes.

07.10.2011, Estadio Nacional „José Díaz“, Lima; Attendance: 39,600
Referee: Sergio Fabián Pezzotta (Argentina)

PERU - PARAGUAY 2-0(0-0)

PER: Raúl Omar Fernández Valverde, Wilmer Santiago Acasiete Ariadela, Alberto Junior Rodríguez Valdelomar, Roberto Carlos Guizasola La Rosa, Juan Manuel Vargas Risco, Víctor Yoshimar Yotún Flores, Adan Adolfo Balbín Silva, Paulo Rinaldo Cruzado Durand (90.Carlos Augusto Lobatón Espejo), Jefferson Agustín Farfán Guadalupe, José Paolo Guerrero Gonzales (91.Luis Jan Piers Advíncula Castrillón), Claudio Miguel Pizarro Bosio. Trainer: Sergio Apraham Markarián Abrahamian (Uruguay).

PAR: Diego Daniel Barreto Cáceres, Paulo César da Silva Barrios, Elvis Israel Marecos (28.Miguel Ángel Ramón Samudio), Iván Rodrigo Piris Leguizamón, Darío Anastacio Verón Maldonado, Édgar Osvaldo Barreto Cáceres, Cristián Miguel Riveros Núñez, Marcelo Alejandro Estigarribia Balmori, Hernán Arsenio Pérez González (65.Óscar René Cardozo Marín), Robin Ariel Ramírez González (54.Wilson Omar Pittoni Rodríguez), Roque Luis Santa Cruz Cantero. Trainer: Francisco Javier Arce Rolón.

Goals: 1-0 José Paolo Guerrero Gonzales (47), 2-0 José Paolo Guerrero Gonzales (73).

Cautions: Iván Rodrigo Piris Leguizamón, Óscar René Cardozo Marín.

11.10.2011, Estadio „Hernándo Siles Zuazo“, La Paz; Attendance: 33,155
Referee: Carlos Arecio Amarilla Demarqui (Paraguay)

BOLIVIA - COLOMBIA 1-2(0-0)

BOL: Daniel Vaca Tasca, Ronald Raldes Balcázar, Ronald Taylor Rivero Khun, Lorgio Álvarez Roca (76.José Luis Chávez Sánchez), Luis Alberto Gutiérrez Herrera (71.Jhasmani Campos Dávalos), Rudy Alejandro Cardozo Fernández, Wálter Alberto Flores Condarco, Jaime Robles Céspedes, Pablo Daniel Escobar Olivetti, Juan Carlos Arce Justiniano, Marcelo Moreno Martins (71.Augusto Andaveris Iriondo). Trainer: Gustavo Domingo Quinteros Desabato.

COL: David Ospina Ramírez, Aquivaldo Mosquera Romaña, Luis Amaranto Perea Mosquera, Pablo Estifer Armero, Juan Camilo Zúñiga Mosquera, Carlos Alberto Sánchez Moreno, Abel Enrique Aguilar Tapias, Freddy Alejandro Guarín Vásquez (69.Diego Ferney Chará Zamora), James David Rodríguez Rubio, Dorlan Mauricio Pabón Ríos (60.Dayro Mauricio Moreno Galindo), Teófilo Antonio Gutiérrez Roncancio (78.Radamel Falcao García Zárate). Trainer: Leonel de Jesús Álvarez Zuleta.

Goals: 0-1 Dorlan Mauricio Pabón Ríos (48), 1-1 Wálter Alberto Flores Condarco (85), 1-2 Radamel Falcao García Zárate (90+3).

Cautions: Pablo Daniel Escobar Olivetti, Ronald Raldes Balcázar, José Luis Chávez Sánchez / Luis Amaranto Perea Mosquera.

11.10.2011, Estadio Monumental „David Arellano", Santiago; Attendance: 39,000
Referee: Raúl Orosco Delgadillo (Bolivia)

CHILE - PERU 4-2(2-0)

CHI: Claudio Andrés Bravo Muñoz, Marcos Andrés González Salazar, Waldo Alonso Ponce Carrizo, Mauricio Aníbal Isla Isla, Gonzalo Alejandro Jara Reyes, Gary Alexis Medel Soto, Arturo Erasmo Vidal Pardo, Jorge Luis Valdivia Toro (90.Carlos Emilio Carmona Tello), Jean André Emanuel Beausejour Coliqueo, Humberto Andrés Suazo Pontivo (72.Esteban Efraín Paredes Quintanilla), Eduardo Jesús Vargas Rojas (84.Matías Ariel Fernández Fernández). Trainer: Claudio Daniel Borghi Bidos (Argentina).

PER: Raúl Omar Fernández Valverde, Wilmer Santiago Acasiete Ariadela (87.William Medardo Chiroque Távara), Alberto Junior Rodríguez Valdelomar, Renzo Revoredo Zuazo, Juan Manuel Vargas Risco, Víctor Yoshimar Yotún Flores (46.Roberto Carlos Guizasola La Rosa), Adan Adolfo Balbín Silva (46.Carlos Augusto Lobatón Espejo), Paulo Rinaldo Cruzado Durand, Jefferson Agustín Farfán Guadalupe, José Paolo Guerrero Gonzales, Claudio Miguel Pizarro Bosio. Trainer: Sergio Apraham Markarián Abrahamian (Uruguay).

Goals: 1-0 Waldo Alonso Ponce Carrizo (2), 2-0 Eduardo Jesús Vargas Rojas (18), 3-0 Gary Alexis Medel Soto (47), 3-1 Claudio Miguel Pizarro Bosio (49), 3-2 Jefferson Agustín Farfán Guadalupe (59), 4-2 Humberto Andrés Suazo Pontivo (63 penalty).

Cautions: Humberto Andrés Suazo Pontivo, Gonzalo Alejandro Jara Reyes, Jean André Emanuel Beausejour Coliqueo / Paulo Rinaldo Cruzado Durand, Raúl Omar Fernández Valverde.

11.10.2011, Estadio Defensores del Chaco, Asunción; Attendance: 12,922
Referee: Wilson Luiz Seneme (Brazil)

PARAGUAY - URUGUAY 1-1(0-0)

PAR: Diego Daniel Barreto Cáceres, Paulo César da Silva Barrios, Darío Anastacio Verón Maldonado, Carlos Bonet Cáceres (79.Hernán Arsenio Pérez González), Víctor Javier Cáceres Centurión (77.Roque Luis Santa Cruz Cantero), Édgar Osvaldo Barreto Cáceres, Richard Ortíz Busto, Cristián Miguel Riveros Núñez, Marcelo Alejandro Estigarribia Balmori, Óscar René Cardozo Marín (67.Luis Nery Caballero Chamorro), Nelson Antonio Haedo Valdéz. Trainer: Francisco Javier Arce Rolón.

URU: Néstor Fernando Muslera Micol, Victorio Maximiliano Pereira Páez, Diego Alfredo Lugano Morena, Diego Roberto Godín Leal, José Martín Cáceres Silva, Diego Fernando Pérez Aguado (58.Sebastián Eguren Ledesma), Egidio Raúl Arévalo Ríos, Edinson Roberto Cavani Gómez, Álvaro Daniel Pereira Barragán (65.Álvaro Rafael González Luengo), Luis Alberto Suárez Díaz, Diego Martín Forlán Corazzo (83.Cristian Gabriel Rodríguez Barotti). Trainer: Óscar Wáshington Tabárez Silva.

Goals: 0-1 Diego Martín Forlán Corazzo (68), 1-1 Richard Ortíz Busto (90+2).

Cautions: Óscar René Cardozo Marín / Diego Roberto Godín Leal, Victorio Maximiliano Pereira Páez, Diego Alfredo Lugano Morena.

11.10.2011, Estadio „José Antonio Anzoátegui", Puerto La Cruz; Attendance: 35,600
Referee: Roberto Carlos Silvera Calcerrada (Uruguay)

VENEZUELA - ARGENTINA 1-0(0-0)

VEN: Renny Vicente Vega Hernández, Fernando Gabriel Amorebieta Mardaras, Gabriel Alejandro Cichero Konarek, Franklin José Lucena Peña, Oswaldo Augusto Vizcarrondo Araujo, Roberto José Rosales Altuve, Tomás Eduardo Rincón Hernández, Juan Fernando Arango Sáenz, César Eduardo González Amais (83.Julio Álvarez Mosquera), Nicolás Ladislao Fedor Flores (89.Alejandro Enrique Moreno Riera), José Salomón Rondón Giménez (76.Frank Feltscher Martínez). Trainer: César Alejandro Farías Acosta.

ARG: Mariano Gonzalo Andújar, Nicolás Andrés Burdisso, Nicolás Hernán Gonzalo Otamendi, Faustino Marcos Alberto Rojo, Pablo Javier Zabaleta Girod (66.Éver Maximiliano David Banega), Martín Gastón Demichelis, Javier Alejandro Mascherano, José Ernesto Sosa (74.Rodrigo Sebastián Palacio), Ángel Fabián di María Hernández (84.Javier Matías Pastore), Lionel Andrés Messi, Gonzalo Gerardo Higuaín. Trainer: Alejandro Sabella.

Goal: 1-0 Fernando Gabriel Amorebieta Mardaras (61).

Cautions: Javier Alejandro Mascherano, Faustino Marcos Alberto Rojo.

11.11.2011, Estadio Monumental „Antonio Vespucio Liberti", Buenos Aires; Attendance: 27,592
Referee: Carlos Alfredo Vera Rodríguez (Ecuador)

ARGENTINA - BOLIVIA 1-1(0-0)

ARG: Sergio Germán Romero, Nicolás Andrés Burdisso, Clemente Juan Rodríguez, Pablo Javier Zabaleta Girod, Martín Gastón Demichelis, Javier Alejandro Mascherano (82.José Ernesto Sosa), Fernando Rubén Gago, Ricardo Gabriel Álvarez (59.Ezequiel Iván Lavezzi), Javier Matías Pastore, Lionel Andrés Messi, Gonzalo Gerardo Higuaín. Trainer: Alejandro Sabella.

BOL: Carlos Erwin Arias Égüez, Luis Javier Méndez Moza, Ronald Taylor Rivero Khun, Luis Alberto Gutiérrez Herrera, Rudy Alejandro Cardozo Fernández, Christian Israel Vargas Claros, Wálter Alberto Flores Condarco, Jaime Robles Céspedes, Pablo Daniel Escobar Olivetti (84.José Luis Chávez Sánchez), Edivaldo Rojas Hermoza (54.Ronald Segovia Calzadilla), Marcelo Moreno Martins (77.Augusto Andaveris Iriondo). Trainer: Gustavo Domingo Quinteros Desabato.

Goals: 0-1 Marcelo Moreno Martins (56), 1-1 Ezequiel Iván Lavezzi (60).

Cautions: Clemente Juan Rodríguez / Marcelo Moreno Martins, Jaime Robles Céspedes.

11.11.2011, Estadio Centenario, Montevideo; Attendance: 40,500
Referee: Héctor Walter Baldassi (Argentina)

URUGUAY - CHILE 4-0(0-0)

URU: Néstor Fernando Muslera Micol, José Martín Cáceres Silva, Diego Alfredo Lugano Morena, Diego Roberto Godín Leal, Álvaro Daniel Pereira Barragán, Álvaro Rafael González Luengo (69.Sebastián Eguren Ledesma), Diego Fernando Pérez Aguado, Egidio Raúl Arévalo Ríos, Gastón Ezequiel Ramírez Pereyra (57.Washington Sebastián Abreu Gallo), Luis Alberto Suárez Díaz (76.Cristian Gabriel Rodríguez Barotti), Edinson Roberto Cavani Gómez. Trainer: Óscar Wáshington Tabárez Silva.

CHI: Claudio Andrés Bravo Muñoz, Pablo Andrés Contreras Fica, Marcos Andrés González Salazar, Waldo Alonso Ponce Carrizo, Matías Daniel Campos Toro, Marcelo Alfonso Díaz Rojas (61.Esteban Efraín Paredes Quintanilla), Mauricio Aníbal Isla Isla, Gary Alexis Medel Soto, Matías Ariel Fernández Fernández, Humberto Andrés Suazo Pontivo (61.Milovan Petar Mirošević Albornoz), Eduardo Jesús Vargas Rojas (73.Gustavo Javier Canales). Trainer: Claudio Daniel Borghi Bidos (Argentina).

Goals: 1-0 Luis Alberto Suárez Díaz (42), 2-0 Luis Alberto Suárez Díaz (45), 3-0 Luis Alberto Suárez Díaz (68), 4-0 Luis Alberto Suárez Díaz (73).

Cautions: José Martín Cáceres Silva, Cristian Gabriel Rodríguez Barotti / Pablo Andrés Contreras Fica, Gary Alexis Medel Soto.

11.11.2011, Estadio Metropolitano "Roberto Meléndez", Barranquilla; Attendance: 49,612
Referee: Omar Andrés Ponce Manzo (Ecuador)

COLOMBIA - VENEZUELA 1-1(1-0)

COL: David Ospina Ramírez, Luis Amaranto Perea Mosquera, Mario Alberto Yepes Díaz, Pablo Estifer Armero, Gerardo Enrique Vallejo Matute, Gustavo Adolfo Bolívar Zapata, Freddy Alejandro Guarín Vásquez, James David Rodríguez Rubio (90+1.Dayro Mauricio Moreno Galindo), Dorlan Mauricio Pabón Ríos (77.Cristian Camilo Marrugo Rodríguez), Teófilo Antonio Gutiérrez Roncancio (85.Carlos Darwin Quintero Villalba), Jackson Arley Martínez Valencia. Trainer: Leonel de Jesús Álvarez Zuleta.

VEN: Renny Vicente Vega Hernández, Fernando Gabriel Amorebieta Mardaras, Gabriel Alejandro Cichero Konarek, Oswaldo Augusto Vizcarrondo Araujo, Roberto José Rosales Altuve, Tomás Eduardo Rincón Hernández (64.Juan Francisco Guerra), Ágnel José Flores Hernández, Juan Fernando Arango Sáenz, César Eduardo González Amais, Nicolás Ladislao Fedor Flores (58.José Salomón Rondón Giménez), Alejandro Enrique Moreno Riera (71.Frank Feltscher Martínez). Trainer: César Alejandro Farías Acosta.

Goals: 1-0 Freddy Alejandro Guarín Vásquez (11), 1-1 Frank Feltscher Martínez (79).

Cautions: Luis Amaranto Perea Mosquera / Tomás Eduardo Rinçón Hernández.

11.11.2011, Estadio Defensores del Chaco, Asunción; Attendance: 11,173
Referee: José Hernando Buitrago Arango (Colombia)

PARAGUAY - ECUADOR 2-1(0-0)

PAR: Diego Daniel Barreto Cáceres, Paulo César da Silva Barrios, Darío Anastacio Verón Maldonado, Carlos Bonet Cáceres, Víctor Javier Cáceres Centurión, Víctor Hugo Ayala Núñez, Richard Ortíz Busto, Cristián Miguel Riveros Núñez, Marcelo Alejandro Estigarribia Balmori (79.Miguel Ángel Ramón Samudio), Lucas Ramón Barrios Cáceres (63.Julio Daniel dos Santos Rodríguez), Nelson Antonio Haedo Valdéz (74.Luis Nery Caballero Chamorro). Trainer: Francisco Javier Arce Rolón.
ECU: Máximo Orlando Banguera Valdivieso, Frickson Rafael Erazo Vivero, Gabriel Eduardo Achilier Zurita, Eduardo Javier Morante Rosas, Christian Andrés Suárez Valencia (60.Jefferson Antonio Montero Vite), Walter Orlando Ayoví Corozo, Christian Fernando Noboa Tello, Luis Fernando Saritama Padilla (78.Joao Robin Rojas Mendoza), Luis Antonio Valencia Mosquera, Jaime Javier Ayoví Corozo, Félix Alexander Borja Valencia (70.Édison Vicente Méndez Méndez). Trainer: Reinaldo Rueda Rivera (Colombia).
Goals: 1-0 Cristián Miguel Riveros Núñez (47), 2-0 Darío Anastacio Verón Maldonado (58), 2-1 Joao Robin Rojas Mendoza (90+2).
Cautions: Eduardo Javier Morante Rosas, Jaime Javier Ayoví Corozo, Félix, Luis Fernando Saritama Padilla, Gabriel Eduardo Achilier Zurita, Christian Fernando Noboa Tello.

15.11.2011, Estadio Metropolitano "Roberto Meléndez", Barranquilla; Attendance: 49,600
Referee: Sálvio Spínola Fagundes Filho (Brazil)

COLOMBIA - ARGENTINA 1-2(0-0)

COL: David Ospina Ramírez, Aquivaldo Mosquera Romaña, Mario Alberto Yepes Díaz, Pablo Estifer Armero, Juan Camilo Zúñiga Mosquera, Gustavo Adolfo Bolívar Zapata, Abel Enrique Aguilar Tapias (75.Diego Alejandro Arias Hincapie), James David Rodríguez Rubio, Dorlan Mauricio Pabón Ríos (60.Dayro Mauricio Moreno Galindo), Jackson Arley Martínez Valencia (75.Carlos Darwin Quintero Villalba), Gustavo Adrián Ramos Vásquez. Trainer: Leonel de Jesús Álvarez Zuleta.
ARG: Sergio Germán Romero, Nicolás Andrés Burdisso (37.Leandro Desábato), Federico Fernández, Clemente Juan Rodríguez, Pablo Javier Zabaleta Girod, Javier Alejandro Mascherano, Rodrigo Braña, Pablo Horacio Guiñazú (46.Sergio Leonel Agüero del Castillo), José Ernesto Sosa, Lionel Andrés Messi, Gonzalo Gerardo Higuaín (86.Fernando Rubén Gago). Trainer: Alejandro Sabella.
Goals: 1-0 Dorlan Mauricio Pabón Ríos (44), 1-1 Lionel Andrés Messi (61), 1-2 Sergio Leonel Agüero del Castillo (84).
Cautions: Pablo Estifer Armero / Nicolás Andrés Burdisso, Rodrigo Braña, Sergio Leonel Agüero del Castillo.

15.11.2011, Estadio Olimpico "Atahualpa", Quito; Attendance: 34,481
Referee: Jorge Luis Larrionda Pietrafesa (Uruguay)

ECUADOR - PERU 2-0(0-0)

ECU: Máximo Orlando Banguera Valdivieso, Jairo Rolando Campos León, Frickson Rafael Erazo Vivero (37.Eduardo Javier Morante Rosas), Segundo Alejandro Castillo Nazareno, Walter Orlando Ayoví Corozo, Luis Fernando Saritama Padilla (81.Tilson Oswaldo Minda Suscal), Luis Antonio Valencia Mosquera, Jaime Javier Ayoví Corozo, Christian Rogelio Benítez Betancourt, Juan Carlos Paredes Reasco, Joao Robin Rojas Mendoza (46.Édison Vicente Méndez Méndez). Trainer: Reinaldo Rueda Rivera (Colombia).
PER: Raúl Omar Fernández Valverde, Wilmer Santiago Acasiete Ariadela, Christian Guillermo Martín Ramos Garagay, Walter Ricardo Vílchez Soto, Renzo Revoredo Zuazo, Juan Manuel Vargas Risco, Edwin Retamoso Palomino, Carlos Augusto Lobatón Espejo (46.Michael Fidel Guevara Legua), Jefferson Agustín Farfán Guadalupe (66.Luis Jan Piers Advíncula Castrillón), José Paolo Guerrero Gonzales, Claudio Miguel Pizarro Bosio (63.William Medardo Chiroque Távara). Trainer: Sergio Apraham Markarián Abrahamian (Uruguay).
Goals: 1-0 Édison Vicente Méndez Méndez (69), 2-0 Christian Rogelio Benítez Betancourt (88).
Cautions: Segundo Alejandro Castillo Nazareno, Christian Rogelio Benítez Betancourt / Carlos Augusto Lobatón Espejo, Renzo Revoredo Zuazo.

15.11.2011, Estadio Nacional „Julio Martínez Prádanos", Santiago; Attendance: 44,726
Referee: Héber Roberto Lopes (Brazil)

CHILE - PARAGUAY 2-0(1-0)

CHI: Claudio Andrés Bravo Muñoz, Pablo Andrés Contreras Fica, Marcos Andrés González Salazar, Waldo Alonso Ponce Carrizo, Mauricio Aníbal Isla Isla, Gary Alexis Medel Soto, Charles Mariano Aránguiz Sandoval, Matías Ariel Fernández Fernández (86.Milovan Petar Mirošević Albornoz), Alexis Alejandro Sánchez Sánchez, Humberto Andrés Suazo Pontivo (70.Matías Daniel Campos Toro), Eduardo Jesús Vargas Rojas (78.Esteban Efraín Paredes Quintanilla). Trainer: Claudio Daniel Borghi Bidos (Argentina).

PAR: Diego Daniel Barreto Cáceres, Julio César Manzur Caffarena, Darío Anastacio Verón Maldonado, Carlos Bonet Cáceres (46.Hernán Arsenio Pérez González), Sergio Daniel Aquino, Víctor Hugo Ayala Núñez, Cristián Miguel Riveros Núñez, Miguel Ángel Ramón Samudio, Julio Daniel dos Santos Rodríguez (61.Édgar Milciades Benítez Santander), Marcelo Alejandro Estigarribia Balmori (74.Óscar René Cardozo Marín), Nelson Antonio Haedo Valdéz. Trainer: Francisco Javier Arce Rolón.

Goals: 1-0 Pablo Andrés Contreras Fica (28), 2-0 Matías Daniel Campos Toro (86).

Cautions: Mauricio Aníbal Isla Isla, Alexis Alejandro Sánchez Sánchez / Julio Daniel dos Santos Rodríguez, Miguel Ángel Ramón Samudio, Darío Anastacio Verón Maldonado, Sergio Daniel Aquino.

15.11.2011, Estadio Pueblo Nuevo, San Cristóbal; Attendance: 33,351
Referee: Georges Buckley De Maritens (Peru)

VENEZUELA - BOLIVIA 1-0(1-0)

VEN: Renny Vicente Vega Hernández, Fernando Gabriel Amorebieta Mardaras, Gabriel Alejandro Cichero Konarek, Oswaldo Augusto Vizcarrondo Araujo, Roberto José Rosales Altuve, Tomás Eduardo Rincón Hernández, Julio Álvarez Mosquera (71.Franklin José Lucena Peña), Juan Fernando Arango Sáenz, César Eduardo González Amais (64.Frank Feltscher Martínez), Giancarlo Gregorio Maldonado Marrero (77.Rolf Günther Feltscher Martínez), José Salomón Rondón Giménez. Trainer: César Alejandro Farías Acosta.

BOL: Carlos Erwin Arias Égüez, Ronald Raldes Balcázar, Ronald Taylor Rivero Khun, Luis Alberto Gutiérrez Herrera, Christian Israel Vargas Claros, Rudy Alejandro Cardozo Fernández (77.Augusto Andaveris Iriondo), José Luis Chávez Sánchez, Jaime Robles Céspedes, Ronald Segovia Calzadilla (58.Jhasmani Campos Dávalos), Pablo Daniel Escobar Olivetti (58.Juan Carlos Arce Justiniano), Marcelo Moreno Martins. Trainer: Gustavo Domingo Quinteros Desabato.

Goal: 1-0 Oswaldo Augusto Vizcarrondo Araujo (24).

Cautions: José Salomón Rondón Giménez, César Eduardo González Amais / Jhasmani Campos Dávalos, Jaime Robles Céspedes, Marcelo Moreno Martins.

02.06.2012, Estadio Monumental „Antonio Vespucio Liberti", Buenos Aires; Attendance: 50,000
Referee: Víctor Hugo Rivera Chávez (Peru)

ARGENTINA - ECUADOR 4-0(3-0)

ARG: Sergio Germán Romero, Pablo Javier Zabaleta Girod, Federico Fernández, Ezequiel Marcelo Garay González, Clemente Juan Rodríguez, Fernando Rubén Gago, Javier Alejandro Mascherano, Ángel Fabián di María Hernández (83.Maximiliano Rubén Rodríguez), Lionel Andrés Messi, Sergio Leonel Agüero del Castillo (63.José Ernesto Sosa), Gonzalo Gerardo Higuaín (74.Ezequiel Iván Lavezzi). Trainer: Alejandro Sabella.

ECU: Alexander Domínguez Carabalí, Jorge Daniel Guagua Tamayo, Jairo Rolando Campos León, Gabriel Eduardo Achilier Zurita, Luis Fernando Saritama Padilla (40.Jaime Javier Ayoví Corozo), Luis Antonio Valencia Mosquera, Christian Fernando Noboa Tello, Pedro Ángel Quiñónez Rodríguez, Walter Orlando Ayoví Corozo, Christian Rogelio Benítez Betancourt (84.Alex Renato Ibarra Mina), Cristian Andrés Suárez Valencia (46.Jefferson Antonio Montero Vite). Trainer: Reinaldo Rueda Rivera (Colombia).

Goals: 1-0 Sergio Leonel Agüero del Castillo (19), 2-0 Gonzalo Gerardo Higuaín (29), 3-0 Lionel Andrés Messi (31), 4-0 Ángel Fabián di María Hernández (76).

Cautions: Federico Fernández, Sergio Leonel Agüero del Castillo, Gonzalo Gerardo Higuaín, Javier Alejandro Mascherano / Jaime Javier Ayoví Corozo.

02.06.2012, Estadio „Hernándo Siles Zuazo", La Paz; Attendance: 34,389
Referee: Alfredo Stalin Intriago Ortega (Ecuador)

BOLIVIA - CHILE 0-2(0-0)

BOL: Daniel Vaca Tasca, Luis Alberto Gutiérrez Herrera, Luis Javier Méndez Moza, Christian Israel Vargas Claros, Ronald Taylor Rivero Khun, Jhasmani Campos Dávalos (57.Rudy Alejandro Cardozo Fernández), Alejandro Saúl Chumacero Bracamonte, Pablo Daniel Escobar Olivetti (73.Alcides Peña Jiménez), Wálter Alberto Flores Condarco, Juan Carlos Arce Justiniano, Ricardo Pedriel Suárez (70.Augusto Andaveris Iriondo). Trainer: Gustavo Domingo Quinteros Desabato.

CHI: Claudio Andrés Bravo Muñoz, Pablo Andrés Contreras Fica, Osvaldo Alexis González Sepúlveda, José Manuel Rojas Bahamondes, Marcelo Alfonso Díaz Rojas, Eugenio Esteban Mena Reveco, Matías Ariel Fernández Fernández (74.Luis Pedro Figueroa Sepúlveda), Arturo Erasmo Vidal Pardo, Charles Mariano Aránguiz Sandoval (88.Braulio Antonio Leal Salvo), Alexis Alejandro Sánchez Sánchez, Humberto Andrés Suazo Pontivo (78.Eduardo Jesús Vargas Rojas). Trainer: Claudio Daniel Borghi Bidos (Argentina).

Goals: 0-1 Charles Mariano Aránguiz Sandoval (45+3), 0-2 Arturo Erasmo Vidal Pardo (83).

Cautions: Jhasmani Campos Dávalos, Luis Javier Méndez Moza, Ronald Taylor Rivero Khun, Wálter Alberto Flores Condarco, Augusto Andaveris Iriondo / Eugenio Esteban Mena Reveco.

Sent off: Luis Alberto Gutiérrez Herrera (54).

02.06.2012, Estadio Centenario, Montevideo; Attendance: 57,000
Referee: Antonio Javier Arias Alvarenga (Paraguay)

URUGUAY - VENEZUELA 1-1(1-0)

URU: Néstor Fernando Muslera Micol, Victorio Maximiliano Pereira Páez, Diego Alfredo Lugano Morena (78.Sebastián Coates Nión), José Martín Cáceres Silva, Diego Roberto Godín Leal, Álvaro Daniel Pereira Barragán, Diego Fernando Pérez Aguado (75.Álvaro Rafael González Luengo), Egidio Raúl Arévalo Ríos, Luis Alberto Suárez Díaz, Diego Martín Forlán Corazzo (88.Washington Sebastián Abreu Gallo), Edinson Roberto Cavani Gómez. Trainer: Óscar Wáshington Tabárez Silva.

VEN: Renny Vicente Vega Hernández, Roberto José Rosales Altu, Oswaldo Augusto Vizcarrondo Araujo, Fernando Gabriel Amorebieta Mardaras, Gabriel Alejandro Cichero Konarek, Juan Fernando Arango Sáenz, Tomás Eduardo Rincón Hernández, Giácomo Di Giorgi Zerillo (75.Yohandry José Orozco Cujía), Frank Feltscher Martínez (55.Nicolás Ladislao Fedor Flores), Luis Manuel Seijas Gunther (88.Grenddy Adrián Perozo Rincón), José Salomón Rondón Giménez. Trainer: César Alejandro Farías Acosta.

Goals: 1-0 Diego Martín Forlán Corazzo (39), 1-1 José Salomón Rondón Giménez (84).

Cautions: Diego Fernando Pérez Aguado, Diego Alfredo Lugano Morena / Tomás Eduardo Rincón Hernández, Fernando Gabriel Amorebieta Mardaras, Giácomo Di Giorgi Zerillo.

03.06.2012, Estadio Nacional, Lima; Attendance: 35,724
Referee: Néstor Fabián Pitana (Argentina)

PERU - COLOMBIA 0-1(0-0)

PER: Diego Alonso Penny Valdez, John Christian Galliquio Castro, Jesús Martín Álvarez Hurtado, Renzo Revoredo Zuazo (69.Raúl Mario Ruidíaz Misitich), Víctor Yoshimar Yotún Flores, Christian Guillermo Martín Ramos Garagay, Paulo Rinaldo Cruzado Durand, Luis Alberto Ramírez Lucay, Carlos Augusto Lobatón Espejo (58.William Medardo Chiroque Távara), José Paolo Guerrero Gonzales, André Martín Carrillo Díaz (85.Jefferson Agustín Farfán Guadalupe). Trainer: Sergio Apraham Markarián Abrahamian (Uruguay).

COL: David Ospina Ramírez, Mario Alberto Yepes Díaz, Luis Amaranto Perea Mosquera, Aquivaldo Mosquera Romaña, Pablo Estifer Armero, Carlos Alberto Sánchez Moreno, Freddy Alejandro Guarín Vásquez (87.Alexander Mejía Sabalsa), Juan Guillermo Cuadrado Bello (72.Aldo Leão Ramírez), James David Rodríguez Rubio (90+1.Jackson Arley Martínez Valencia), Radamel Falcao García Zárate, Dorlan Mauricio Pabón Ríos. Trainer: José Néstor Pékerman (Argentina).

Goal: 0-1 James David Rodríguez Rubio (51).

Cautions: Jesús Martín Álvarez Hurtado, Christian Guillermo Martín Ramos Garagay / Aquivaldo Mosquera Romaña, Luis Amaranto Perea Mosquera, Mario Alberto Yepes Díaz, Aldo Leão Ramírez.

09.06.2012, Estadio „Hernándo Siles Zuazo“, La Paz; Attendance: 17,320
Referee: Roberto Carlos Silvera Calcerrada (Uruguay)

BOLIVIA - PARAGUAY **3-1(1-0)**

BOL: Sergio Daniel Galarza Solíz, Christian Israel Vargas Claros, Ronny Jiménez Mendonza, Juan Gabriel Valverde Rivera, José Carlos Barba Paz, Gualberto Mojica Olmos (73.José Luis Chávez Sánchez), Alejandro Saúl Chumacero Bracamonte, Pablo Daniel Escobar Olivetti (85.Rudy Alejandro Cardozo Fernández), Wálter Alberto Flores Condarco, Marcelo Moreno Martins (84.Augusto Andaveris Iriondo), Alcides Peña Jiménez. Trainer: Gustavo Domingo Quinteros Desabato.

PAR: Justo Wilmar Villar Viveros, Paulo César da Silva Barrios, Aureliano Torres Román, Adalberto Román Benítez, Ricardo Mazacotte, Cristián Miguel Riveros Núñez, Osvaldo David Martínez Arce, Eric Fabián Ramos Jara (58.Édgar Milciades Benítez Santander), Lorenzo Eduardo Aranda (74.Hernán Arsenio Pérez González), Nelson Antonio Haedo Valdéz, Pablo Daniel Zeballos Ocampos (69.Luis Nery Caballero Chamorro). Trainer: Francisco Javier Arce Rolón.

Goals: 1-0 Alcides Peña Jiménez (9), 2-0 Pablo Daniel Escobar Olivetti (69), 3-0 Pablo Daniel Escobar Olivetti (80), 3-1 Cristián Miguel Riveros Núñez (83).

Cautions: Gualberto Mojica Olmos, Alcides Peña Jiménez, Christian Israel Vargas Claros, Wálter Alberto Flores Condarco, José Carlos Barba Paz / Adalberto Román Benítez, Paulo César da Silva Barrios, Ricardo Mazacotte.

09.06.2012, Estadio „José Antonio Anzoátegui“, Puerto La Cruz; Attendance: 35,000
Referee: José Hernando Buitrago Arango (Colombia)

VENEZUELA - CHILE **0-2(0-0)**

VEN: Renny Vicente Vega Hernández, Roberto José Rosales Altu, Oswaldo Augusto Vizcarrondo Araujo, Grenddy Adrián Perozo Rincón, Gabriel Alejandro Cichero Konarek, Juan Fernando Arango Sáenz, Giácomo Di Giorgi Zerillo, Luis Manuel Seijas Gunther (82.Yohandry José Orozco Cujía), Julio Álvarez Mosquera (64.Juan Francisco Guerra), José Salomón Rondón Giménez, Nicolás Ladislao Fedor Flores (64.Yonathan Alexander Del Valle Rodríguez). Trainer: César Alejandro Farías Acosta.

CHI: Claudio Andrés Bravo Muñoz, Pablo Andrés Contreras Fica (65.Luis Pedro Figueroa Sepúlveda), Osvaldo Alexis González Sepúlveda, José Manuel Rojas Bahamondes (30.Marcos Andrés González Salazar), Marcelo Alfonso Díaz Rojas, Eugenio Esteban Mena Reveco, Matías Ariel Fernández Fernández, Arturo Erasmo Vidal Pardo, Charles Mariano Aránguiz Sandoval, Alexis Alejandro Sánchez Sánchez, Humberto Andrés Suazo Pontivo (79.Sebastián Andrés Pinto Perurena). Trainer: Claudio Daniel Borghi Bidos (Argentina).

Goals: 0-1 Matías Ariel Fernández Fernández (85), 0-2 Charles Mariano Aránguiz Sandoval (90+1).

Cautions: Gabriel Alejandro Cichero Konarek, Oswaldo Augusto Vizcarrondo Araujo, Juan Francisco Guerra, Grenddy Adrián Perozo Rincón / Pablo Andrés Contreras Fica, Miguel Ángel Pinto Jerez (on the bench).

10.06.2012, Estadio Olimpico "Atahualpa", Quito; Attendance: 37,352
Referee: Wilson Luiz Seneme (Brazil)
ECUADOR - COLOMBIA 1-0(0-0)
ECU: Alexander Domínguez Carabalí, Jairo Rolando Campos León, Frickson Rafael Erazo Vivero, Segundo Alejandro Castillo Nazareno, Luis Antonio Valencia Mosquera, Christian Fernando Noboa Tello, Joao Robin Rojas Mendoza (72.Édison Vicente Méndez Méndez), Walter Orlando Ayoví Corozo, Juan Carlos Paredes Reasco, Jefferson Antonio Montero Vite (78.Luis Fernando Saritama Padilla), Christian Rogelio Benítez Betancourt (90+4.Tilson Oswaldo Minda Suscal). Trainer: Reinaldo Rueda Rivera (Colombia).
COL: David Ospina Ramírez, Mario Alberto Yepes Díaz, Luis Amaranto Perea Mosquera (35.Juan Camilo Zúñiga Mosquera), Aquivaldo Mosquera Romaña, Pablo Estifer Armero, Elkin Soto Jaramillo (73.Luis Fernando Muriel Fruto), Carlos Alberto Sánchez Moreno, Freddy Alejandro Guarín Vásquez (66.Juan Guillermo Cuadrado Bello), James David Rodríguez Rubio, Radamel Falcao García Zárate, Dorlan Mauricio Pabón Ríos. Trainer: José Néstor Pékerman (Argentina).
Goal: 1-0 Christian Rogelio Benítez Betancourt (54).
Cautions: Christian Rogelio Benítez Betancourt / Aquivaldo Mosquera Romaña, Mario Alberto Yepes Díaz.
Sent off: Christian Fernando Noboa Tello (86).

10.06.2012, Estadio Centenario, Montevideo; Attendance: 55,000
Referee: Leandro Pedro Vuaden (Brazil)
URUGUAY - PERU 4-2(2-1)
URU: Néstor Fernando Muslera Micol, Victorio Maximiliano Pereira Páez, José Martín Cáceres Silva, Sebastián Coates Nión, Diego Roberto Godín Leal, Álvaro Daniel Pereira Barragán (60.Cristian Gabriel Rodríguez Barotti), Diego Fernando Pérez Aguado, Egidio Raúl Arévalo Ríos, Luis Alberto Suárez Díaz (90.Sebastián Eguren Ledesma), Diego Martín Forlán Corazzo (61.Gastón Ezequiel Ramírez Pereyra), Edinson Roberto Cavani Gómez. Trainer: Óscar Wáshington Tabárez Silva.
PER: Diego Alonso Penny Valdez, John Christian Galliquio Castro, Jesús Martín Álvarez Hurtado, Christian Guillermo Martín Ramos Garagay, Víctor Yoshimar Yotún Flores, Paulo Rinaldo Cruzado Durand, Luis Alberto Ramírez Lucay, Antonio Emiliano Gonzáles Canchari (46.Carlos Augusto Lobatón Espejo), Luis Jan Piers Advíncula Castrillón (69.Christian Alberto Cueva Bravo), José Paolo Guerrero Gonzales, José Carlos Fernández Piedra (77.André Martín Carrillo Díaz). Trainer: Sergio Apraham Markarián Abrahamian (Uruguay).
Goals: 1-0 Sebastián Coates Nión (15), 2-0 Victorio Maximiliano Pereira Páez (30), 2-1 Diego Roberto Godín Leal (40 own goal), 2-2 José Paolo Guerrero Gonzales (48), 3-2 Cristian Gabriel Rodríguez Barotti (63), 4-2 Sebastián Eguren Ledesma (90+4).
Cautions: Luis Alberto Suárez Díaz / Luis Alberto Ramírez Lucay, Christian Guillermo Martín Ramos Garagay, José Paolo Guerrero Gonzales, John Christian Galliquio Castro.

07.09.2012, Estadio Metropolitano "Roberto Meléndez", Barranquilla; Attendance: 45,000
Referee: Héber Roberto Lopes (Brazil)
COLOMBIA - URUGUAY 4-0(1-0)
COL: David Ospina Ramírez, Luis Amaranto Perea Mosquera, Carlos Enrique Valdés Parra, Abel Enrique Aguilar Tapias (78.Aldo Leão Ramírez), Juan Camilo Zúñiga Mosquera, Macnelly Torres Berrío, Edwin Armando Valencia Rodríguez, Pablo Estifer Armero, Radamel Falcao García Zárate, Teófilo Antonio Gutiérrez Roncancio (80.Carlos Darwin Quintero Villalba), James David Rodríguez Rubio (83.Carlos Alberto Sánchez Moreno). Trainer: José Néstor Pékerman (Argentina).
URU: Néstor Fernando Muslera Micol, Diego Alfredo Lugano Morena, Victorio Maximiliano Pereira Páez (55.Gastón Ezequiel Ramírez Pereyra), Diego Roberto Godín Leal, Mauricio Bernardo Victorino Dansilio (46.Álvaro Rafael González Luengo), Álvaro Daniel Pereira Barragán, Diego Fernando Pérez Aguado, Cristian Gabriel Rodríguez Barotti, Egidio Raúl Arévalo Ríos (73.Walter Alejandro Gargano Guevara), Diego Martín Forlán Corazzo, Edinson Roberto Cavani Gómez. Trainer: Óscar Wáshington Tabárez Silva.
Goals: 1-0 Radamel Falcao García Zárate (2), 2-0 Teófilo Antonio Gutiérrez Roncancio (48), 3-0

Teófilo Antonio Gutiérrez Roncancio (52), 4-0 Juan Camilo Zúñiga Mosquera (90+1).
Cautions: Walter Alejandro Gargano Guevara.

07.09.2012, Estadio Olímpico Atahualpa, Quito; Attendance: 32,213
Referee: Juan Ernesto Soto Arevalo (Venezuela)
ECUADOR - BOLIVIA 1-0(0-0)
ECU: Alexander Domínguez Carabalí, Jayro Rolando Campos León, Frickson Rafael Erazo Vivero, Segundo Alejandro Castillo Nazareno, Luis Fernando Saritama Padilla, Luis Antonio Valencia Mosquera, Walter Orlando Ayoví Corozo, Juan Carlos Paredes Reasco, Jefferson Antonio Montero Vite (46.Michael Antonio Arroyo Mina), Jaime Javier Ayoví Corozo (57.Felipe Salvador Caicedo Corozo), Arrinton Narciso Mina Villalba (87.Dennys Andrés Quiñonez Espinoza). Trainer: Reinaldo Rueda Rivera (Colombia).
BOL: Hugo Suárez Vaca, Ronald Raldes Balcázar, Luis Alberto Gutiérrez Herrera, Luis Javier Méndez Moza, Christian Israel Vargas Claros, José Carlos Barba Paz, Gualberto Mojica Olmos (84.Diego Aroldo Cabrera Flores), Mauricio Saucedo Guardia (46.Alcides Peña Jiménez), José Luis Chávez Sánchez (77.Alejandro Saúl Chumacero Bracamonte), Marcelo Moreno Martins, Pedro Jesús Azogue Rojas. Trainer: Francisco Xabier Azcargorta Uriarte (Spain).
Goal: 1-0 Felipe Salvador Caicedo Corozo (73 penalty).
Cautions: Felipe Salvador Caicedo Corozo / José Luis Chávez Sánchez, Ronald Raldes Balcázar, Gualberto Mojica Olmos.

07.09.2012, Estadio "Mario Alberto Kempes", Córdoba; Attendance: 57,000
Referee: Wilson Luiz Seneme (Brazil)
ARGENTINA - PARAGUAY 3-1(2-1)
ARG: Sergio Germán Romero, Hugo Armando Campagnaro, Federico Fernández, Ezequiel Marcelo Garay González, Faustino Marcos Alberto Rojo, Fernando Rubén Gago, Rodrigo Braña (87.Lucas Rodrigo Biglia), Ezequiel Iván Lavezzi (65.Rodrigo Sebastián Palacio), Lionel Andrés Messi, Ángel Fabián di María Hernández (79.Pablo Horacio Guiñazú), Gonzalo Gerardo Higuaín. Trainer: Alejandro Sabella.
PAR: Justo Wilmar Villar Viveros, Paulo César da Silva Barrios, Antolín Alcaraz Viveros, Iván Rodrigo Piris Leguizamón, Cristian Miguel Riveros Núñez, Jonathan Fabbro (59.Óscar René Cardozo Marín), Víctor Javier Cáceres Centurión, Víctor Hugo Ayala Núñez, Richard Ortíz Busto, Roque Luis Santa Cruz Cantero (59.Nelson Antonio Haedo Valdéz), Marcelo Alejandro Estigarribia Balmori (73.Édgar Milciades Benítez Santander). Trainer: Gerardo Cono Pelusso Boyrie (Uruguay).
Goals: 1-0 Ángel Fabián di María Hernández (2), 1-1 Jonathan Fabbro (18 penalty), 2-1 Gonzalo Gerardo Higuaín (31), 3-1 Lionel Andrés Messi (63).
Cautions: Rodrigo Sebastián Palacio, Rodrigo Braña / Richard Ortíz Busto, Iván Rodrigo Piris Leguizamón, Víctor Javier Cáceres Centurión, Nelson Antonio Haedo Valdéz.

07.09.2012, Estadio Nacional, Lima; Attendance: 34,703
Referee: Martín Emilio Vázquez Broquetas (Uruguay)

PERU - VENEZUELA 2-1(0-1)

PER: Raúl Omar Fernández Valverde, Alberto Junior Rodríguez Valdelomar, Renzo Revoredo Zuazo (73.Roberto Carlos Guizasola La Rosa), Carlos Augusto Zambrano Ochandarte, Paulo Rinaldo Cruzado Durand, Luis Alberto Ramírez Lucay, Víctor Yoshimar Yotún Flores, Juan Manuel Vargas Risco, José Paolo Guerrero Gonzáles (49.André Martín Carrillo Díaz), Claudio Miguel Pizarro Bosio, Jefferson Agustín Farfán Guadalupe (79.Carlos Augusto Lobatón Espejo). Trainer: Sergio Apraham Markarián Abrahamian (Uruguay).

VEN: Renny Vicente Vega Hernández, Oswaldo Augusto Vizcarrondo Araujo, Roberto José Rosales Altuve, Rolf Günther Feltscher Martínez, Gabriel Alejandro Cichero Konarek, Andrés José Túñez Arceo, Juan Fernando Arango Sáenz, Ágnel José Flores Hernández, Francisco Javier Flores Sequera (63.César Eduardo González Amais), Luis Manuel Seijas Gunther (74.Frank Feltscher Martínez), Nicolás Ladislao Fedor Flores (69.José Salomón Rondón Giménez). Trainer: César Alejandro Farías Acosta.

Goals: 0-1 Juan Fernando Arango Sáenz (43), 1-1 Jefferson Agustín Farfán Guadalupe (47), 2-1 Jefferson Agustín Farfán Guadalupe (59).

Cautions: Claudio Miguel Pizarro Bosio, Jefferson Agustín Farfán Guadalupe / Gabriel Alejandro Cichero Konarek, Rolf Günther Feltscher Martínez.

Sent off: Gabriel Alejandro Cichero Konarek (67).

11.09.2012, Estadio Monumental "David Arellano", Santiago; Attendance: 38,000
Referee: Víctor Hugo Carrillo (Peru)

CHILE - COLOMBIA 1-3(1-0)

CHI: Claudio Andrés Bravo Muñoz, Marcos Andrés González Salazar, Eugenio Esteban Mena Reveco, Gonzalo Alejandro Jara Reyes, Mauricio Aníbal Isla Isla (67.Antenor Junior Fernándes da Silva Vitoria), Matías Ariel Fernández Fernández, Arturo Erasmo Vidal Pardo, Marcelo Alfonso Díaz Rojas, Gary Alexis Medel Soto, Alexis Alejandro Sánchez Sánchez (82.Mauricio Ricardo Pinilla Ferrera), Humberto Andrés Suazo Pontivo (71.Sebastián Andrés Pinto Perurena). Trainer: Claudio Daniel Borghi Bidos (Argentina).

COL: David Ospina Ramírez, Mario Alberto Yepes Díaz (46.Juan Guillermo Cuadrado Bello), Luis Amaranto Perea Mosquera, Abel Enrique Aguilar Tapias, Juan Camilo Zúñiga Mosquera, Macnelly Torres Berrío (69.Aldo Leão Ramírez), Edwin Armando Valencia Rodríguez, Pablo Estifer Armero, Radamel Falcao García Zárate, Teófilo Antonio Gutiérrez Roncancio, James David Rodríguez Rubio (75.Carlos Alberto Sánchez Moreno). Trainer: José Néstor Pékerman (Argentina).

Goals: 1-0 Matías Ariel Fernández Fernández (41), 1-1 James David Rodríguez Rubio (59), 1-2 Radamel Falcao García Zárate (74), 1-3 Teófilo Antonio Gutiérrez Roncancio (77).

Cautions: Arturo Erasmo Vidal Pardo, Humberto Andrés Suazo Pontivo, Marcelo Alfonso Díaz Rojas, Eugenio Esteban Mena Reveco, Mauricio Ricardo Pinilla Ferrera / Mario Alberto Yepes Díaz, Luis Amaranto Perea Mosquera, Abel Enrique Aguilar Tapias.

Sent off: Gary Alexis Medel Soto (34), Abel Enrique Aguilar Tapias (84).

11.09.2012, Estadio Centenario, Montevideo; Attendance: 38,000
Referee: Carlos Arecio Amarilla Demarqui (Paraguay)
URUGUAY - ECUADOR 1-1(0-1)
URU: Néstor Fernando Muslera Micol, Diego Alfredo Lugano Morena, Victorio Maximiliano Pereira Páez, Diego Roberto Godín Leal, Álvaro Daniel Pereira Barragán (46.Álvaro Rafael González Luengo), Diego Fernando Pérez Aguado (59.Cristian Gabriel Rodríguez Barotti), Egidio Raúl Arévalo Ríos (46.Walter Alejandro Gargano Guevara), Gastón Ezequiel Ramírez Pereyra, Luis Alberto Suárez Díaz, Diego Martín Forlán Corazzo, Edinson Roberto Cavani Gómez. Trainer: Óscar Wáshington Tabárez Silva.
ECU: Alexander Domínguez Carabalí, Jayro Rolando Campos León, Frickson Rafael Erazo Vivero, Segundo Alejandro Castillo Nazareno, Luis Fernando Saritama Padilla (84.Alex Renato Ibarra Mina), Luis Antonio Valencia Mosquera, Walter Orlando Ayoví Corozo, Tilson Oswaldo Minda Suscal, Juan Carlos Paredes Reasco, Christian Rogelio Benítez Betancourt (90+2.Gabriel Eduardo Achilier Zurita), Felipe Salvador Caicedo Corozo (58.Jaime Javier Ayoví Corozo). Trainer: Reinaldo Rueda Rivera (Colombia).
Goals: 0-1 Felipe Salvador Caicedo Corozo (7 penalty), 1-1 Edinson Roberto Cavani Gómez (67).
Cautions: Diego Alfredo Lugano Morena, Álvaro Daniel Pereira Barragán, Luis Alberto Suárez Díaz, Gastón Ezequiel Ramírez Pereyra / Tilson Oswaldo Minda Suscal, Jayro Rolando Campos León, Alexander Domínguez Carabalí, Christian Rogelio Benítez Betancourt, Luis Antonio Valencia Mosquera.
Sent off: Luis Antonio Valencia Mosquera (90+4).

11.09.2012, Estadio Nacional, Lima; Attendance: 34,111
Referee: Wilmar Alexander Roldán Pérez (Colombia)
PERU - ARGENTINA 1-1(1-1)
PER: Raúl Omar Fernández Valverde, Alberto Junior Rodríguez Valdelomar, Carlos Augusto Zambrano Ochandarte, Luis Jan Piers Advíncula Castrillón, Paulo Rinaldo Cruzado Durand, Luis Alberto Ramírez Lucay (87.José Paolo Guerrero Gonzáles), Carlos Augusto Lobatón Espejo (46.Josepmir Aarón Ballón Villacorta), Víctor Yoshimar Yotún Flores, Claudio Miguel Pizarro Bosio, Jefferson Agustín Farfán Guadalupe, André Martín Carrillo Díaz (77.Cristopher Paolo César Hurtado Huertas). Trainer: Sergio Apraham Markarián Abrahamian (Uruguay).
ARG: Sergio Germán Romero, Hugo Armando Campagnaro, Federico Fernández, Ezequiel Marcelo Garay González, Faustino Marcos Alberto Rojo, Fernando Rubén Gago (61.Pablo Horacio Guiñazú), Javier Alejandro Mascherano, Ezequiel Iván Lavezzi (74.Enzo Nicolás Pérez), Ángel Fabián di María Hernández (89.Maximiliano Rubén Rodríguez), Lionel Andrés Messi, Gonzalo Gerardo Higuaín. Trainer: Alejandro Sabella.
Goals: 1-0 Carlos Augusto Zambrano Ochandarte (22), 1-1 Gonzalo Gerardo Higuaín (37).
Cautions: Luis Jan Piers Advíncula Castrillón, Carlos Augusto Lobatón Espejo, Claudio Miguel Pizarro Bosio, Luis Alberto Ramírez Lucay / Hugo Armando Campagnaro, Ángel Fabián di María Hernández.

11.09.2012, Estadio Defensores del Chaco, Asunción; Attendance: 13,680
Referee: Enrique Roberto Osses Zencovich (Chile)
PARAGUAY - VENEZUELA 0-2(0-1)
PAR: Justo Wilmar Villar Viveros, Paulo César da Silva Barrios, Darío Anastacio Verón Maldonado, Antolín Alcaraz Viveros (70.Víctor Hugo Ayala Núñez), Carlos Bonet Cáceres, Miguel Ángel Ramón Samudio (41.Marcelo Alejandro Estigarribia Balmori), Cristian Miguel Riveros Núñez, Jonathan Fabbro, Víctor Javier Cáceres Centurión (65.Julio Daniel dos Santos Rodríguez), Nelson Antonio Haedo Valdéz, Óscar René Cardozo Marín. Trainer: Gerardo Cono Pelusso Boyrie (Uruguay).
VEN: Daniel Hernández Santos, Oswaldo Augusto Vizcarrondo Araujo, Roberto José Rosales Altuve, Andrés José Túñez Arceo, Alexander David González Sibulo, Juan Fernando Arango Sáenz, César Eduardo González Amais (80.Edgar Fernando Pérez Greco), Franklin José Lucena Peña, Luis Manuel Seijas Gunther (87.Ágnel José Flores Hernández), José Salomón Rondón Giménez, Josef Alexander Martínez (73.Richard José Blanco Delgado). Trainer: César Alejandro Farías Acosta.

Goals: 0-1 José Salomón Rondón Giménez (45), 0-2 José Salomón Rondón Giménez (68).
Cautions: Antolín Alcaraz Viveros, Darío Anastacio Verón Maldonado, Julio Daniel dos Santos Rodríguez, Marcelo Alejandro Estigarribia Balmori / César Eduardo González Amais, Oswaldo Augusto Vizcarrondo Araujo, Luis Manuel Seijas Gunther.

12.10.2012, Estadio Malvinas Argentinas, Mendoza; Attendance: 31,997
Referee: Leandro Pedro Vuaden (Brazil)
ARGENTINA - URUGUAY 3-0(0-0)
ARG: Sergio Germán Romero, Pablo Javier Zabaleta Girod, Federico Fernández, Ezequiel Marcelo Garay González, Faustino Marcos Alberto Rojo (67.Hugo Armando Campagnaro), Fernando Rubén Gago, Javier Alejandro Mascherano, Ángel Fabián di María Hernández, Lionel Andrés Messi, Sergio Leonel Agüero del Castillo (79.Pablo Horacio Guiñazú), Gonzalo Gerardo Higuaín (83.Hernán Barcos). Lionel Andrés Messi (66), Sergio Leonel Agüero del Castillo (75), Lionel Andrés Messi (80). Trainer: Alejandro Sabella.
URU: Néstor Fernando Muslera Micol, Diego Alfredo Lugano Morena (64.Andrés Scotti Ponce de León), Victorio Maximiliano Pereira Páez, José Martín Cáceres Silva, Diego Roberto Godín Leal, Walter Alejandro Gargano Guevara, Álvaro Rafael González Luengo (68.Cristian Gabriel Rodríguez Barotti), Egidio Raúl Arévalo Ríos, Luis Alberto Suárez Díaz, Diego Martín Forlán Corazzo, Edinson Roberto Cavani Gómez. Trainer: Óscar Wáshington Tabárez Silva.
Goals: 1-0 Lionel Andrés Messi (66), 2-0 Sergio Leonel Agüero del Castillo (75), 3-0 Lionel Andrés Messi (80).
Cautions: José Martín Cáceres Silva, Diego Alfredo Lugano Morena, Diego Roberto Godín Leal, Victorio Maximiliano Pereira Páez.

12.10.2012, Estadio Metropolitano "Roberto Meléndez", Barranquilla; Attendance: 45,000
Referee: Sergio Fabián Pezzotta (Argentina)
COLOMBIA - PARAGUAY 2-0(0-0)
COL: David Ospina Ramírez, Mario Alberto Yepes Díaz, Carlos Enrique Valdés Parra, Juan Camilo Zúñiga Mosquera, Macnelly Torres Berrío (74.Carlos Alberto Sánchez Moreno), Edwin Armando Valencia Rodríguez (84.Elkin Soto Jaramillo), Aldo Leão Ramírez (46.Juan Guillermo Cuadrado Bello), Pablo Estifer Armero, Radamel Falcao García Zárate, Teófilo Antonio Gutiérrez Roncancio, James David Rodríguez Rubio. Trainer: José Néstor Pékerman (Argentina).
PAR: Diego Daniel Barreto Cáceres, Paulo César da Silva Barrios, Pablo César Aguilar Benítez, Iván Rodrigo Piris Leguizamón, Cristian Miguel Riveros Núñez, Víctor Javier Cáceres Centurión, Víctor Hugo Ayala Núñez, Richard Ortíz Busto, Nelson Antonio Haedo Valdéz (62.Luis Nery Caballero Chamorro), Marcelo Alejandro Estigarribia Balmori (66.Édgar Milciades Benítez Santander), José Ariel Núñez Portelli (79.Jonathan Fabbro). Trainer: Gerardo Cono Pelusso Boyrie (Uruguay).
Goals: 1-0, Radamel Falcao García Zárate (52), 2-0 Radamel Falcao García Zárate (89).
Cautions: Edwin Armando Valencia Rodríguez, Teófilo Antonio Gutiérrez Roncancio / Cristian Miguel Riveros Núñez, Marcelo Alejandro Estigarribia Balmori, Richard Ortíz Busto.

12.10.2012, Estadio Olímpico Atahualpa, Quito; Attendance: 32,600
Referee: Héber Roberto Lopes (Brazil)
ECUADOR - CHILE **3-1(1-1)**
ECU: Alexander Domínguez Carabalí, Gabriel Eduardo Achilier Zurita, Frickson Rafael Erazo Vivero, Segundo Alejandro Castillo Nazareno, Luis Fernando Saritama Padilla, Walter Orlando Ayoví Corozo, Juan Carlos Paredes Reasco, Alex Renato Ibarra Mina (78.Jefferson Antonio Montero Vite), Christian Rogelio Benítez Betancourt, Joao Robin Rojas Mendoza (74.Christian Fernando Noboa Tello), Felipe Salvador Caicedo Corozo (68.Jaime Javier Ayoví Corozo). Trainer: Reinaldo Rueda Rivera (Colombia).
CHI: Miguel Ángel Pinto Jérez, Gonzalo Alejandro Jara Reyes, Pablo Andrés Contreras Fica, Mauricio Aníbal Isla Isla, Osvaldo Alexis González Sepúlveda, Matías Ariel Fernández Fernández (60.Antenor Junior Fernándes da Silva Vitoria), Arturo Erasmo Vidal Pardo, Marcelo Alfonso Díaz Rojas, Felipe Ignacio Seymour Dobud (68.Mark Dennis González Hoffmann), Jean André Emanuel Beausejour Coliqueo (78.Eduardo Jesús Vargas Rojas), Alexis Alejandro Sánchez Sánchez. Trainer: Claudio Daniel Borghi Bidos (Argentina).
Goals: 0-1 Juan Carlos Paredes Reasco (25 own goal), 1-1 Felipe Salvador Caicedo Corozo (33), 2-1 Felipe Salvador Caicedo Corozo (57 penalty), 3-1 Segundo Alejandro Castillo Nazareno (90+3).
Cautions: Felipe Salvador Caicedo Corozo, Luis Fernando Saritama Padilla / Pablo Andrés Contreras Fica, Osvaldo Alexis González Sepúlveda.
Sent off: Pablo Andrés Contreras Fica (54), Arturo Erasmo Vidal Pardo (86).

12.10.2012, Estadio "Hernando Siles Zuazo", La Paz; Attendance: 36,500
Referee: Carlos Alfredo Vera Rodríguez (Ecuador)
BOLIVIA - PERU **1-1(0-1)**
BOL: Hugo Suárez Vaca, Ronald Raldes Balcázar, Luis Javier Méndez Moza, Christian Israel Vargas Claros (46.Marcelo Moreno Martins), Juan Gabriel Valverde Rivera, Jhasmani Campos Dávalos, Alejandro Saúl Chumacero Bracamonte, Wálter Alberto Flores Condarco, Rudy Alejandro Cardozo Fernández, Juan Carlos Arce Justiniano (75.Miguel Gerardo Suárez Savino), Alcides Peña Jiménez (46.Ronald Segovia Calzadilla). Trainer: Francisco Xabier Azcargorta Uriarte (Spain).
PER: José Aurelio Carvallo Alonso, Wilmer Santiago Acasiete Ariadela, Jhoel Alexander Herrera Zegarra, Rafael Nicanor Farfán Quispe, Christian Guillermo Martín Ramos Garagay, Juan Carlos Mariño Márquez (79.Christian Alberto Cueva Bravo), Juan Elías Cominges Mayorga (60.Álvaro Francisco Ampuero García-Rossell), William Medardo Chiroque Távara, Edwin Retamoso Palomino, Joel Melchor Sánchez Alegría, Irven Beybe Ávila Acero (61.Wilmer Alexander Aguirre Vásquez). Trainer: Sergio Apraham Markarián Abrahamian.
Goals: 0-1 Juan Carlos Mariño Márquez (22), 1-1 Alejandro Saúl Chumacero Bracamonte (51).
Cautions: Rudy Alejandro Cardozo Fernández, Wálter Alberto Flores Condarco, Juan Gabriel Valverde Rivera, Marcelo Moreno Martins / Rafael Nicanor Farfán Quispe, Wilmer Santiago Acasiete Ariadela, Joel Melchor Sánchez Alegría.

16.10.2012, Estadio "Hernando Siles Zuazo", La Paz; Attendance: 25,402
Referee: Víctor Hugo Rivera Chávez (Peru)
BOLIVIA - URUGUAY **4-1(2-0)**
BOL: Sergio Daniel Galarza Solíz, Ronald Raldes Balcázar, Edward Mauro Zenteno Álvarez, Luis Alberto Gutiérrez Herrera, Marvin Orlando Bejarano Jiménez, Gualberto Mojica Olmos (69.Jhasmani Campos Dávalos), Alejandro Saúl Chumacero Bracamonte, Rudy Alejandro Cardozo Fernández, Marcelo Moreno Martins (58.Juan Carlos Arce Justiniano), Carlos Enrique Saucedo Urgel, Pedro Jesús Azogue Rojas (73.Alejandro Meleán Villarroel). Trainer: Francisco Xabier Azcargorta Uriarte (Spain).
URU: Néstor Fernando Muslera Micol, Andrés Scotti Ponce de León, Victorio Maximiliano Pereira Páez (36.Edinson Roberto Cavani Gómez), Mauricio Bernardo Victorino Dansilio, Álvaro Daniel Pereira Barragán, Cristian Gabriel Rodríguez Barotti, Walter Alejandro Gargano Guevara (36.Marcelo Nicolás Lodeiro Benítez), Álvaro Rafael González Luengo, Egidio Raúl Arévalo Ríos, Luis Alberto Suárez Díaz, Diego Martín Forlán Corazzo (66.Álvaro Fernández Gay). Trainer: Óscar Wáshington Tabárez Silva.

Goals: 1-0 Carlos Enrique Saucedo Urgel (6), 2-0 Gualberto Mojica Olmos (27), 3-0 Carlos Enrique Saucedo Urgel (51), 4-0 Carlos Enrique Saucedo Urgel (55), 4-1 Luis Alberto Suárez Díaz (81).
Cautions: Ronald Raldes Balcázar, Alejandro Saúl Chumacero Bracamonte / Álvaro Daniel Pereira Barragán.

16.10.2012, Estadio Defensores del Chaco, Asunción; Attendance: 10,114
Referee: Pablo Alejandro Lunati (Argentina)
PARAGUAY - PERU **1-0(0-0)**
PAR: Diego Daniel Barreto Cáceres, Paulo César da Silva Barrios, Pablo César Aguilar Benítez, Miguel Ángel Ramón Samudio, Iván Rodrigo Piris Leguizamón, Julio Daniel dos Santos Rodríguez, Cristian Miguel Riveros Núñez, Fidencio Oviedo Domínguez, Nelson Antonio Haedo Valdéz (46.Luis Nery Caballero Chamorro), Édgar Milciades Benítez Santander (83.Jonathan Fabbro), José Ariel Núñez Portelli (75.Víctor Javier Cáceres Centurión). Trainer: Gerardo Cono Pelusso Boyrie (Uruguay).
PER: Raúl Omar Fernández Valverde, Alberto Junior Rodríguez Valdelomar (16.Christian Guillermo Martín Ramos Garagay), Carlos Augusto Zambrano Ochandarte, Luis Jan Piers Advíncula Castrillón, Paulo Rinaldo Cruzado Durand, Luis Alberto Ramírez Lucay, Víctor Yoshimar Yotún Flores (81.Raúl Mario Ruidíaz Misitich), Juan Manuel Vargas Risco, José Paolo Guerrero Gonzáles (66.André Martín Carrillo Díaz), Claudio Miguel Pizarro Bosio, Jefferson Agustín Farfán Guadalupe. Trainer: Sergio Apraham Markarián Abrahamian (Uruguay).
Goal: 1-0 Pablo César Aguilar Benítez (53).
Cautions:), Édgar Milciades Benítez Santander, José Ariel Núñez Portelli, Víctor Javier Cáceres Centurión / Christian Guillermo Martín Ramos Garagay, Luis Jan Piers Advíncula Castrillón, José Paolo Guerrero Gonzáles.

16.10.2012, Estadio Nacional, Santiago; Attendance: 45,000
Referee: Antonio Arias Alvarenga (Paraguay)
CHILE - ARGENTINA **1-2(0-2)**
CHI: Miguel Ángel Pinto Jérez, Marcos Andrés González Salazar, Gonzalo Alejandro Jara Reyes, Mauricio Aníbal Isla Isla, Mark Dennis González Hoffmann (75.Felipe Alejandro Gutiérrez Leiva), Matías Ariel Fernández Fernández, Marcelo Alfonso Díaz Rojas, Gary Alexis Medel Soto, Jean André Emanuel Beausejour Coliqueo, Alexis Alejandro Sánchez Sánchez, Sebastián Andrés Pinto Perurena (55.Eduardo Jesús Vargas Rojas). Trainer: Claudio Daniel Borghi Bidos (Argentina).
ARG: Sergio Germán Romero, Hugo Armando Campagnaro, Federico Fernández, Ezequiel Marcelo Garay González, Pablo Javier Zabaleta Girod, Fernando Rubén Gago, Javier Alejandro Mascherano, Lionel Andrés Messi, Ángel Fabián di María Hernández (77.José Ernesto Sosa), Gonzalo Gerardo Higuaín (61.Pablo Horacio Guiñazú), Sergio Leonel Agüero del Castillo (82.Hernán Barcos). Trainer: Alejandro Sabella.
Goals: 0-1 Lionel Andrés Messi (28), 0-2 Gonzalo Gerardo Higuaín (31), 1-2 Felipe Alejandro Gutiérrez Leiva (90+1).
Cautions: Jean André Emanuel Beausejour Coliqueo, Marcelo Alfonso Díaz Rojas, Eduardo Jesús Vargas Rojas / Ángel Fabián di María Hernández.

16.10.2012, Estadio "José Antonio Anzoátegui", Puerto La Cruz; Attendance: 35,076
Referee: Néstor Fabián Pitana (Argentina)
VENEZUELA - ECUADOR 1-1(1-1)
VEN: Daniel Hernández Santos, Fernando Gabriel Amorebieta Mardaras, Roberto José Rosales Altuve, Grenddy Adrián Perozo Rincón, Alexander David González Sibulo (82.Gabriel Alejandro Cichero Konarek), Juan Fernando Arango Sáenz, Franklin José Lucena Peña, Evelio de Jesús Hernández Guedez, Edgar Fernando Pérez Greco (57.Ronald Alejandro Vargas Aranguren), José Salomón Rondón Giménez, Josef Alexander Martínez (68.Nicolás Ladislao Fedor Flores). Trainer: César Alejandro Farías Acosta.
ECU: Alexander Domínguez Carabalí, Gabriel Eduardo Achilier Zurita, Frickson Rafael Erazo Vivero, Segundo Alejandro Castillo Nazareno, Luis Antonio Valencia Mosquera, Christian Fernando Noboa Tello (80.Jefferson Antonio Montero Vite), Walter Orlando Ayoví Corozo, Michael Antonio Arroyo Mina (88.Joao Robin Rojas Mendoza), Juan Carlos Paredes Reasco, Christian Rogelio Benítez Betancourt, Jaime Javier Ayoví Corozo (71.Tilson Oswaldo Minda Suscal). Trainer: Reinaldo Rueda Rivera (Colombia).
Goals: 1-0 Juan Fernando Arango Sáenz (6), 1-1 Segundo Alejandro Castillo Nazareno (23).
Cautions: Ronald Alejandro Vargas Aranguren, Evelio de Jesús Hernández Guedez / Christian Fernando Noboa Tello, Michael Antonio Arroyo Mina, Segundo Alejandro Castillo Nazareno.

22.03.2013, Estadio Monumental "Antonio Vespucio Liberti", Buenos Aires; Attendance: 40,000
Referee: Víctor Hugo Carrillo (Peru)
ARGENTINA - VENEZUELA 3-0(2-0)
ARG: Sergio Germán Romero, Pablo Javier Zabaleta Girod, Federico Fernández, Ezequiel Marcelo Garay González, Faustino Marcos Alberto Rojo, Fernando Rubén Gago (62.Éver Maximiliano David Banega), Javier Alejandro Mascherano, Walter Damián Montillo, Lionel Andrés Messi, Ezequiel Iván Lavezzi (83.Maximiliano Rubén Rodríguez), Gonzalo Gerardo Higuaín (80.Rodrigo Sebastián Palacio). Trainer: Alejandro Sabella.
VEN: Daniel Hernández Santos, Oswaldo Augusto Vizcarrondo Araujo, Gabriel Alejandro Cichero Konarek, Andrés José Túñez Arceo, Alexander David González Sibulo, Juan Fernando Arango Sáenz (75.César Eduardo González Amais), Franklin José Lucena Peña, Tomás Eduardo Rincón Hernández, Luis Manuel Seijas Gunther (57.Rómulo Otero Vásquez), Frank Feltscher Martínez, José Salomón Rondón Giménez (82.Nicolás Ladislao Fedor Flores). Trainer: César Alejandro Farías Acosta.
Goals: 1-0 Gonzalo Gerardo Higuaín (29), 2-0 Lionel Andrés Messi (43 penalty), 3-0 Gonzalo Gerardo Higuaín (59).
Cautions: Gonzalo Gerardo Higuaín, Pablo Javier Zabaleta Girod / Alexander David González Sibulo, Tomás Eduardo Rincón Hernández, Franklin José Lucena Peña, Nicolás Ladislao Fedor Flores.

22.03.2013, Estadio Centenario, Montevideo; Attendance: 32,000
Referee: Wilmar Alexander Roldán Pérez (Colombia)
URUGUAY - PARAGUAY 1-1(0-0)
URU: Néstor Fernando Muslera Micol, Diego Alfredo Lugano Morena, Victorio Maximiliano Pereira Páez (68.Gastón Ezequiel Ramírez Pereyra), Diego Roberto Godín Leal, Álvaro Daniel Pereira Barragán, Diego Fernando Pérez Aguado (46.Egidio Raúl Arévalo Ríos), Cristian Gabriel Rodríguez Barotti (46.Edinson Roberto Cavani Gómez), Álvaro Rafael González Luengo, Marcelo Nicolás Lodeiro Benítez, Luis Alberto Suárez Díaz, Diego Martín Forlán Corazzo. Trainer: Óscar Wáshington Tabárez Silva.
PAR: Diego Daniel Barreto Cáceres, Paulo César da Silva Barrios, Pablo César Aguilar Benítez, Miguel Ángel Ramón Samudio, Iván Rodrigo Piris Leguizamón, Cristian Miguel Riveros Núñez, Fidencio Oviedo Domínguez, Víctor Hugo Ayala Núñez, Richard Ortíz Busto (66.Édgar Milciades Benítez Santander), Nelson Antonio Haedo Valdéz (80.Jonathan Fabbro), Óscar René Cardozo Marín (66.Luis Nery Caballero Chamorro). Trainer: Gerardo Cono Pelusso Boyrie (Uruguay).
Goals: 1-0 Luis Alberto Suárez Díaz (82), 1-1 Édgar Milciades Benítez Santander (86).
Cautions: Diego Roberto Godín Leal, Diego Fernando Pérez Aguado, Victorio Maximiliano Pereira Páez, Álvaro Rafael González Luengo / Óscar René Cardozo Marín, Fidencio Oviedo Domínguez,

Pablo César Aguilar Benítez, Luis Nery Caballero Chamorro.

22.03.2013, Estadio Nacional, Lima; Attendance: 43,000
Referee: Diego Hernán Abal (Argentina)
PERU - CHILE 1-0(0-0)
PER: Raúl Omar Fernández Valverde, Alberto Junior Rodríguez Valdelomar, Jhoel Alexander Herrera Zegarra, Christian Guillermo Martín Ramos Garagay (23.Jesús Martín Álvarez Hurtado), Paulo Rinaldo Cruzado Durand, Luis Alberto Ramírez Lucay, Cristopher Paolo César Hurtado Huertas, Carlos Augusto Lobatón Espejo (46.Juan Carlos Mariño Márquez), Víctor Yoshimar Yotún Flores, Claudio Miguel Pizarro Bosio (79.José Yordy Reyna Serna), Jefferson Agustín Farfán Guadalupe. Trainer: Sergio Apraham Markarián Abrahamian (Uruguay).
CHI: Claudio Andrés Bravo Muñoz, Marcos Andrés González Salazar, Eugenio Esteban Mena Reveco, Mauricio Aníbal Isla Isla, José Manuel Rojas Bahamondes, Gary Alexis Medel Soto, Charles Mariano Aránguiz Sandoval (54.Francisco Andrés Silva Gajardo), Jean André Emanuel Beausejour Coliqueo (70.Nicolás Ignacio Castillo Mora), Carlos Emilio Carmona Tello, Alexis Alejandro Sánchez Sánchez, Eduardo Jesús Vargas Rojas (75.Antenor Junior Fernándes da Silva Vitoria). Trainer: Jorge Luis Sampaoli Moya(Argentina).
Goal: 1-0 Jefferson Agustín Farfán Guadalupe (87).
Cautions: Carlos Augusto Lobatón Espejo, Juan Carlos Mariño Márquez, Luis Alberto Ramírez Lucay / Alexis Alejandro Sánchez Sánchez.

22.03.2013, Estadio Metropolitano "Roberto Meléndez", Barranquilla; Attendance: 40,478
Referee: Carlos Alfredo Vera Rodríguez (Ecuador)
COLOMBIA - BOLIVIA 5-0(1-0)
COL: David Ospina Ramírez, Mario Alberto Yepes Díaz, Carlos Enrique Valdés Parra, Abel Enrique Aguilar Tapias, Juan Camilo Zúñiga Mosquera, Macnelly Torres Berrío (86.Aldo Leão Ramírez), Edwin Armando Valencia Rodríguez, Juan Guillermo Cuadrado Bello (79.Pablo Estifer Armero), Radamel Falcao García Zárate, Teófilo Antonio Gutiérrez Roncancio, James David Rodríguez Rubio (83.Fredy Alejandro Guarín Vásquez). Trainer: José Néstor Pékerman (Argentina).
BOL: Carlos Erwin Arias Égüez (46.Sergio Daniel Galarza Solíz), Edward Mauro Zenteno Álvarez, Luis Alberto Gutiérrez Herrera, Marvin Orlando Bejarano Jiménez, Ronny Jiménez Mendonza, Ronald Lázaro García Justiniano (57.Juan Carlos Arce Justiniano), Gualberto Mojica Olmos, Alejandro Saúl Chumacero Bracamonte, Marcelo Moreno Martins, Carlos Enrique Saucedo Urgel (46.Rudy Alejandro Cardozo Fernández), Wálter Veizaga Argote. Trainer: Francisco Xabier Azcargorta Uriarte (Spain).
Goals: 1-0 Macnelly Torres Berrío (21), 2-0 Carlos Enrique Valdés Parra (50), 3-0 Teófilo Antonio Gutiérrez Roncancio (62), 4-0 Radamel Falcao García Zárate (87), 5-0 Pablo Estifer Armero (90+3).
Cautions: Mario Alberto Yepes Díaz / Marvin Orlando Bejarano Jiménez.

26.03.2013, Estadio "Hernando Siles Zuazo", La Paz; Attendance: 35,000
Referee: Enrique Roberto Osses Zencovich (Chile)
BOLIVIA - ARGENTINA 1-1(1-1)
BOL: Sergio Daniel Galarza Solíz, Ronald Raldes Balcázar, Edward Mauro Zenteno Álvarez, Luis Alberto Gutiérrez Herrera, Jair Torrico Camacho (46.Marvin Orlando Bejarano Jiménez), Alejandro Saúl Chumacero Bracamonte, Rudy Alejandro Cardozo Fernández (73.Gualberto Mojica Olmos), Diego Bejarano Ibañez (65.Juan Carlos Arce Justiniano), Marcelo Moreno Martins, Carlos Enrique Saucedo Urgel, Wálter Veizaga Argote. Trainer: Francisco Xabier Azcargorta Uriarte (Spain).
ARG: Sergio Germán Romero, José María Basanta Pavone, Hugo Armando Campagnaro, Sebastián Enrique Domínguez, Gino Peruzzi Lucchetti, Clemente Juan Rodríguez, Javier Alejandro Mascherano, Éver Maximiliano David Banega (62.Leonardo Daniel Ponzio), Ángel Fabián di María Hernández (90.Pablo Horacio Guiñazú), Lionel Andrés Messi, Rodrigo Sebastián Palacio (86.Franco Matías Di Santo). Trainer: Alejandro Sabella.
Goals: 1-0 Marcelo Moreno Martins (25), 1-1 Éver Maximiliano David Banega (44).
Cautions: Luis Alberto Gutiérrez Herrera, Ronald Raldes Balcázar / Éver Maximiliano David Banega, Javier Alejandro Mascherano.

26.03.2013, Estadio Olímpico Atahualpa, Quito; Attendance: 33,048
Referee: Sandro Meira Ricci (Brazil)

ECUADOR - PARAGUAY 4-1(1-1)

ECU: Alexander Domínguez Carabalí, Gabriel Eduardo Achilier Zurita, Frickson Rafael Erazo Vivero, Luis Antonio Valencia Mosquera, Christian Fernando Noboa Tello, Pedro Ángel Quiñónez Rodríguez (70.Luis Fernando Saritama Padilla), Walter Orlando Ayoví Corozo, Juan Carlos Paredes Reasco, Jefferson Antonio Montero Vite (84.Alex Renato Ibarra Mina), Christian Rogelio Benítez Betancourt, Felipe Salvador Caicedo Corozo (80.Joao Robin Rojas Mendoza). Trainer: Reinaldo Rueda Rivera (Colombia).

PAR: Diego Daniel Barreto Cáceres, Paulo César da Silva Barrios, Pablo César Aguilar Benítez, Miguel Ángel Ramón Samudio, Iván Rodrigo Piris Leguizamón (60.Nelson Antonio Haedo Valdéz), Cristian Miguel Riveros Núñez, Fidencio Oviedo Domínguez, Víctor Hugo Ayala Núñez, Richard Ortíz Busto (46.Víctor Javier Cáceres Centurión), Édgar Milciades Benítez Santander, Luis Nery Caballero Chamorro (78.Pablo César Leonardo Velázquez Centurión). Trainer: Gerardo Cono Pelusso Boyrie (Uruguay).

Goals: 0-1 Luis Nery Caballero Chamorro (15), 1-1 Felipe Salvador Caicedo Corozo (38), 2-1 Jefferson Antonio Montero Vite (50), 3-1 Christian Rogelio Benítez Betancourt (54), 4-1 Jefferson Antonio Montero Vite (75).

Cautions: Felipe Salvador Caicedo Corozo, Frickson Rafael Erazo Vivero / Iván Rodrigo Piris Leguizamón, Pablo César Aguilar Benítez, Víctor Hugo Ayala Núñez.

26.03.2013, Estadio Nacional „Julio Martínez Prádanos“, Santiago; Attendance: 43,816
Referee: Néstor Fabián Pitana (Argentina)

CHILE - URUGUAY 2-0(1-0)

CHI: Claudio Andrés Bravo Muñoz, Gonzalo Alejandro Jara Reyes, Eugenio Esteban Mena Reveco, Mauricio Aníbal Isla Isla (85.Marcos Andrés González Salazar), José Manuel Rojas Bahamondes, Marcelo Alfonso Díaz Rojas, Gary Alexis Medel Soto, Charles Mariano Aránguiz Sandoval (59.Matías Ariel Fernández Fernández), Jean André Emanuel Beausejour Coliqueo (70.Carlos Emilio Carmona Tello), Esteban Efraín Paredes Quintanilla, Eduardo Jesús Vargas Rojas. Trainer: Jorge Luis Sampaoli Moya (Argentina).

URU: Néstor Fernando Muslera Micol, Diego Alfredo Lugano Morena, Diego Roberto Godín Leal, Álvaro Daniel Pereira Barragán, Matías Aguirregaray Guruceaga (46.Alejandro Daniel Silva González), Álvaro Rafael González Luengo, Egidio Raúl Arévalo Ríos, Marcelo Nicolás Lodeiro Benítez (82.Cristian Gabriel Rodríguez Barotti), Gastón Ezequiel Ramírez Pereyra (70.Diego Martín Forlán Corazzo), Luis Alberto Suárez Díaz, Edinson Roberto Cavani Gómez. Trainer: Óscar Wáshington Tabárez Silva.

Goals: 1-0 Esteban Efraín Paredes Quintanilla (10), 2-0 Eduardo Jesús Vargas Rojas (77).

Cautions: Gonzalo Alejandro Jara Reyes, Charles Mariano Aránguiz Sandoval, Marcelo Alfonso Díaz Rojas / atías Aguirregaray Guruceaga, Alejandro Daniel Silva González, Luis Alberto Suárez Díaz, Egidio Raúl Arévalo Ríos.

26.03.2013, Estadio Polideportivo Cachamay, Ciudad Guayana; Attendance: 41,250
Referee: Antonio Javier Arias Alvarenga (Paraguay)

VENEZUELA - COLOMBIA 1-0(1-0)

VEN: Daniel Hernández Santos, Oswaldo Augusto Vizcarrondo Araujo, Gabriel Alejandro Cichero Konarek (84.Rolf Günther Feltscher Martínez), Andrés José Túñez Arceo (61.Ágnel José Flores Hernández), Alexander David González Sibulo, Juan Fernando Arango Sáenz, César Eduardo González Amais, Franklin José Lucena Peña, Tomás Eduardo Rincón Hernández, José Salomón Rondón Giménez, Fernando Luis Aristeguieta de Luca (68.Nicolás Ladislao Fedor Flores). Trainer: César Alejandro Farías Acosta.

COL: David Ospina Ramírez, Luis Amaranto Perea Mosquera (83.Aldo Leão Ramírez), Carlos Enrique Valdés Parra, Abel Enrique Aguilar Tapias, Juan Camilo Zúñiga Mosquera, Macnelly Torres Berrío (75.Carlos Arturo Bacca Ahumada), Edwin Armando Valencia Rodríguez, Pablo Estifer Armero, Juan Guillermo Cuadrado Bello (65.Teófilo Antonio Gutiérrez Roncancio), Radamel Falcao García Zárate, James David Rodríguez Rubio. Trainer: José Néstor Pékerman (Argentina).

Goal: 1-0 José Salomón Rondón Giménez (13).
Cautions: Franklin José Lucena Peña, José Salomón Rondón Giménez, Nicolás Ladislao Fedor Flores / Edwin Armando Valencia Rodríguez.

07.06.2013, Estadio Monumental "Antonio Vespucio Liberti", Buenos Aires; Attendance: 44,807
Referee: Marlon Escalante Álvarez (Venezuela)
ARGENTINA - COLOMBIA 0-0
ARG: Sergio Germán Romero, Pablo Javier Zabaleta Girod, Ezequiel Marcelo Garay González, Federico Fernández, Faustino Marcos Alberto Rojo, Javier Alejandro Mascherano, Lucas Rodrigo Biglia, Ángel Fabián di María Hernández, Walter Damián Montillo (58.Lionel Andrés Messi), Sergio Leonel Agüero del Castillo (81.Ezequiel Iván Lavezzi), Gonzalo Gerardo Higuaín. Trainer: Alejandro Sabella.
COL: David Ospina Ramírez, Mario Alberto Yepes Díaz, Cristián Eduardo Zapata Valencia, Abel Enrique Aguilar Tapias (60.Alexander Mejía Sabalsa), Juan Camilo Zúñiga Mosquera, Carlos Alberto Sánchez Moreno, Aldo Leão Ramírez, Pablo Estifer Armero, Radamel Falcao García Zárate, Jackson Arley Martínez Valencia (46.Luis Amaranto Perea Mosquera), James David Rodríguez Rubio (34.Juan Guillermo Cuadrado Bello). Trainer: José Néstor Pékerman (Argentina).
Cautions: Lucas Rodrigo Biglia, Ezequiel Marcelo Garay González, Pablo Javier Zabaleta Girod / Abel Enrique Aguilar Tapias, Juan Guillermo Cuadrado Bello, Mario Alberto Yepes Díaz, Aldo Leão Ramírez, Juan Camilo Zúñiga Mosquera.
Sent off: Gonzalo Gerardo Higuaín (26), Jackson Arley Martínez Valencia (26).

07.06.2013, Estadio "Hernando Siles Zuazo", La Paz; Attendance: 10,155
Referee: Patricio Loustau (Argentina)
BOLIVIA - VENEZUELA 1-1(0-0)
BOL: Sergio Daniel Galarza Solíz, Ronald Raldes Balcázar (74.Jhasmani Campos Dávalos), Ronald Eguino Segovia, Edward Mauro Zenteno Álvarez, Alejandro Saúl Chumacero Bracamonte, Rudy Alejandro Cardozo Fernández, Wálter Veizaga Argote, Daniel Andrés Chávez Betancourt (46.Gualberto Mojica Olmos), Juan Carlos Arce Justiniano, Carlos Enrique Saucedo Urgel, Marcelo Moreno Martins (64.Juan Eduardo Fierro Ribera). Trainer: Francisco Xabier Azcargorta Uriarte (Spain)
VEN: Renny Vicente Vega Hernández, Roberto José Rosales Altuve, Grenddy Adrián Perozo Rincón, Gabriel Alejandro Cichero Konarek, Juan Fernando Arango Sáenz (81.Rolf Günther Feltscher Martínez), César Eduardo González Amais (71.Alexander David González Sibulo), Ágnel José Flores Hernández, Tomás Eduardo Rincón Hernández, Luis Manuel Seijas Gunther, Richard José Blanco Delgado (65.Evelio de Jesús Hernández Guedez), Josef Alexander Martínez. Trainer: César Alejandro Farías Acosta.
Goals: 0-1 Juan Fernando Arango Sáenz (58), 1-1 Jhasmani Campos Dávalos (86).
Cautions: Juan Carlos Arce Justiniano.
Sent off: Ronald Eguino Segovia (90+3).

07.06.2013, Estadio Defensores del Chaco, Asunción; Attendance: 30,000
Referee: Leandro Pedro Vuaden (Brazil)
PARAGUAY - CHILE 1-2(0-1)
PAR: Justo Wilmar Villar Viveros, Paulo César da Silva Barrios, Salustiano Antonio Candia Galeano, Marcos Antonio Cáceres Centurión, Miguel Ángel Ramón Samudio, Julio Daniel dos Santos Rodríguez (80.Luis Nery Caballero Chamorro), Cristian Miguel Riveros Núñez (58.Richard Ortíz Busto), Fidencio Oviedo Domínguez, Óscar René Cardozo Marín, Dante Rafael López Fariña (59.Roque Luis Santa Cruz Cantero), Édgar Milciades Benítez Santander. Trainer: Gerardo Cono Pelusso Boyrie (Uruguay).
CHI: Claudio Andrés Bravo Muñoz, Marcos Andrés González Salazar, Eugenio Esteban Mena Reveco, Mauricio Aníbal Isla Isla, José Manuel Rojas Bahamondes, Arturo Erasmo Vidal Pardo, Marcelo Alfonso Díaz Rojas, Gary Alexis Medel Soto, Esteban Efraín Paredes Quintanilla (59.Matías Ariel Fernández Fernández), Alexis Alejandro Sánchez Sánchez (90+3.Sebastián Andrés Pinto Perurena), Eduardo Jesús Vargas Rojas (85.Felipe Alejandro Gutiérrez Leiva). Trainer: Jorge Luis Sampaoli Moya (Argentina).
Goals: 0-1 Eduardo Jesús Vargas Rojas (41), 0-2 Arturo Erasmo Vidal Pardo (56), 1-2 Roque Luis

Santa Cruz Cantero (88).
Cautions: Cristian Miguel Riveros Núñez, Richard Ortíz Busto, Salustiano Antonio Candia Galeano / Felipe Alejandro Gutiérrez Leiva, Mauricio Aníbal Isla Isla.

07.06.2013, Estadio Nacional, Lima; Attendance: 37,000
Referee: Marcelo de Lima Henrique (Brazil)
PERU - ECUADOR 1-0(1-0)
PER: Raúl Omar Fernández Valverde, Alberto Junior Rodríguez Valdelomar, Jhoel Alexander Herrera Zegarra, Carlos Augusto Zambrano Ochandarte, Luis Alberto Ramírez Lucay, Edwin Retamoso Palomino, Víctor Yoshimar Yotún Flores, Juan Manuel Vargas Risco (81.Álvaro Francisco Ampuero García-Rossell), José Paolo Guerrero Gonzáles, Claudio Miguel Pizarro Bosio (90+2.Christian Guillermo Martín Ramos Garagay), Jefferson Agustín Farfán Guadalupe (89.Luis Jan Piers Advíncula Castrillón). Trainer: Sergio Apraham Markarián Abrahamian (Uruguay).
ECU: Alexander Domínguez Carabalí, Jorge Daniel Guagua Tamayo, Frickson Rafael Erazo Vivero, Segundo Alejandro Castillo Nazareno, Luis Antonio Valencia Mosquera, Christian Fernando Noboa Tello, Walter Orlando Ayoví Corozo, Juan Carlos Paredes Reasco (75.Alex Renato Ibarra Mina), Jefferson Antonio Montero Vite, Christian Rogelio Benítez Betancourt (87.Marlon Jonathan de Jesús Pavón), Joao Robin Rojas Mendoza (64.Felipe Salvador Caicedo Corozo). Trainer: Reinaldo Rueda Rivera (Colombia).
Goal: 1-0 Claudio Miguel Pizarro Bosio (11).
Cautions: Carlos Augusto Zambrano Ochandarte, José Paolo Guerrero Gonzáles, Luis Alberto Ramírez Lucay / Joao Robin Rojas Mendoza, Christian Rogelio Benítez Betancourt, Jorge Daniel Guagua Tamayo, Luis Antonio Valencia Mosquera.

11.06.2013, Estadio Olímpico Atahualpa, Quito; Attendance: 35,000
Referee: Enrique Cáceres Villafante (Paraguay)
ECUADOR - ARGENTINA 1-1(1-1)
ECU: Alexander Domínguez Carabalí, Jorge Daniel Guagua Tamayo, Frickson Rafael Erazo Vivero, Segundo Alejandro Castillo Nazareno, Luis Antonio Valencia Mosquera, Christian Fernando Noboa Tello (69.Luis Fernando Saritama Padilla), Walter Orlando Ayoví Corozo, Juan Carlos Paredes Reasco (70.Alex Renato Ibarra Mina), Jefferson Antonio Montero Vite, Joao Robin Rojas Mendoza (88.Juan Luis Anangonó León), Felipe Salvador Caicedo Corozo. Trainer: Reinaldo Rueda Rivera (Colombia).
ARG: Sergio Germán Romero, Ezequiel Marcelo Garay González, José María Basanta Pavone, Federico Fernández, Faustino Marcos Alberto Rojo, Gino Peruzzi Lucchetti, Javier Alejandro Mascherano, Ángel Fabián di María Hernández, Éver Maximiliano David Banega (76.Lucas Rodrigo Biglia), Rodrigo Sebastián Palacio (90+1.Rodrigo Braña), Sergio Leonel Agüero del Castillo (61.Lionel Andrés Messi). Trainer: Alejandro Sabella.
Goals: 0-1 Sergio Leonel Agüero del Castillo (4 penalty), 1-1 Segundo Alejandro Castillo Nazareno (17).
Cautions: Alexander Domínguez Carabalí, Felipe Salvador Caicedo Corozo, Luis Fernando Saritama Padilla / Ángel Fabián di María Hernández, Federico Fernández, Ezequiel Marcelo Garay González, José María Basanta Pavone.
Sent off: Javier Alejandro Mascherano (86).

11.06.2013, Estadio Nacional, Santiago; Attendance: 45,000
Referee: Darío Agustín Ubriaco (Uruguay)

CHILE - BOLIVIA 3-1(2-1)

CHI: Claudio Andrés Bravo Muñoz, Marcos Andrés González Salazar, José Manuel Rojas Bahamondes, Gary Alexis Medel Soto, David Marcelo Pizarro Cortés, Arturo Erasmo Vidal Pardo, Marcelo Alfonso Díaz Rojas, Eugenio Esteban Mena Reveco (75.Jean André Emanuel Beausejour Coliqueo), Esteban Efraín Paredes Quintanilla (54.Gonzalo Alejandro Jara Reyes), Alexis Alejandro Sánchez Sánchez, Eduardo Jesús Vargas Rojas. Trainer: Jorge Luis Sampaoli Moya (Argentina).
BOL: Sergio Daniel Galarza Solíz, Ronald Raldes Balcázar, Edward Mauro Zenteno Álvarez, Luis Alberto Gutiérrez Herrera, Gualberto Mojica Olmos, Alejandro Saúl Chumacero Bracamonte (46.Rudy Alejandro Cardozo Fernández), Vicente Arze Camacho (70.Jhasmani Campos Dávalos), Diego Bejarano Ibáñez, Wálter Veizaga Argote, Daniel Andrés Chávez Betancourt (46.Edivaldo Rojas Hermoza), Marcelo Moreno Martins. Trainer: Francisco Xabier Azcargorta Uriarte (Spain).
Goals: 1-0 Eduardo Jesús Vargas Rojas (16), 2-0 Alexis Alejandro Sánchez Sánchez (18), 2-1 Marcelo Moreno Martins (32), 3-1 Arturo Erasmo Vidal Pardo (90+3).
Cautions: Wálter Veizaga Argote, Vicente Arze Camacho, Luis Alberto Gutiérrez Herrera.

11.06.2013, Estadio Metropolitano "Roberto Meléndez", Barranquilla; Attendance: 42,265
Referee: Sandro Meira Ricci (Brazil)

COLOMBIA - PERU 2-0(2-0)

COL: David Ospina Ramírez, Mario Alberto Yepes Díaz, Luis Amaranto Perea Mosquera, Abel Enrique Aguilar Tapias (83.Alexander Mejía Sabalsa), Juan Camilo Zúñiga Mosquera, Macnelly Torres Berrío, Carlos Alberto Sánchez Moreno, Pablo Estifer Armero, Juan Guillermo Cuadrado Bello (77.Fredy Alejandro Guarín Vásquez), Radamel Falcao García Zárate, Teófilo Antonio Gutiérrez Roncancio (81.Luis Fernando Muriel Fruto). Trainer: José Néstor Pékerman (Argentina).
PER: Raúl Omar Fernández Valverde, Alberto Junior Rodríguez Valdelomar, Jhoel Alexander Herrera Zegarra (32.Jefferson Agustín Farfán Guadalupe), Carlos Augusto Zambrano Ochandarte, Luis Jan Piers Advíncula Castrillón, Josepmir Aarón Ballón Villacorta, Edwin Retamoso Palomino (64.Carlos Augusto Lobatón Espejo), Víctor Yoshimar Yotún Flores (31.André Martín Carrillo Díaz), Juan Manuel Vargas Risco, José Paolo Guerrero Gonzáles, Claudio Miguel Pizarro Bosio. Trainer: Sergio Apraham Markarián Abrahamian (Uruguay).
Goals: 1-0 Radamel Falcao García Zárate (13 penalty), 2-0 Teófilo Antonio Gutiérrez Roncancio (45).
Cautions: Radamel Falcao García Zárate, Luis Amaranto Perea Mosquera, Carlos Augusto Zambrano Ochandarte, Mario Alberto Yepes Díaz / Víctor Yoshimar Yotún Flores, Jhoel Alexander Herrera Zegarra, Juan Manuel Vargas Risco.
Sent off: Carlos Augusto Zambrano Ochandarte (70).

11.06.2013, Estadio Polideportivo Cachamay, Ciudad Guayana; Attendance: 36,297
Referee: Paulo César de Oliveira (Brazil)

VENEZUELA - URUGUAY 0-1(0-1)

VEN: Daniel Hernández Santos, Oswaldo Augusto Vizcarrondo Araujo, Roberto José Rosales Altuve, Gabriel Alejandro Cichero Konarek (58.Luis Manuel Seijas Gunther), Andrés José Túñez Arceo, Juan Fernando Arango Sáenz, César Eduardo González Amais (74.Richard José Blanco Delgado), Franklin José Lucena Peña, Tomás Eduardo Rincón Hernández, Frank Feltscher Martínez (56.Fernando Luis Aristeguieta de Luca), José Salomón Rondón Giménez. Trainer: César Alejandro Farías Acosta.
URU: Néstor Fernando Muslera Micol, Diego Alfredo Lugano Morena, Victorio Maximiliano Pereira Páez, José Martín Cáceres Silva, Diego Roberto Godín Leal, Diego Fernando Pérez Aguado (76.Sebastián Eguren Ledesma), Cristian Gabriel Rodríguez Barotti (85.Álvaro Daniel Pereira Barragán), Walter Alejandro Gargano Guevara, Gastón Ezequiel Ramírez Pereyra (60.Álvaro Rafael González Luengo), Diego Martín Forlán Corazzo, Edinson Roberto Cavani Gómez. Trainer: Óscar Wáshington Tabárez Silva.
Goal: 0-1 Edinson Roberto Cavani Gómez (28).
Cautions: Franklin José Lucena Peña, Tomás Eduardo Rincón Hernández, Fernando Luis Aristeguieta de Luca / José Martín Cáceres Silva, Diego Alfredo Lugano Morena, Diego Fernando Pérez Aguado,

Sebastián Eguren Ledesma.
Sent off: Tomás Eduardo Rincón Hernández (84).

06.09.2013, Estadio Metropolitano "Roberto Meléndez", Barranquilla; Attendance: 46,000
Referee: Héber Roberto Lopes (Brazil)
COLOMBIA - ECUADOR 1-0(1-0)
COL: David Ospina Ramírez, Luis Amaranto Perea Mosquera, Carlos Enrique Valdés Parra, Abel Enrique Aguilar Tapias (46.Juan Guillermo Cuadrado Bello), Juan Camilo Zúñiga Mosquera, Macnelly Torres Berrío (75.Alexander Mejía Sabalsa), Carlos Alberto Sánchez Moreno, Pablo Estifer Armero, James David Rodríguez Rubio, Radamel Falcao García Zárate, Teófilo Antonio Gutiérrez Roncancio (82.Jackson Arley Martínez Valencia). Trainer: José Néstor Pékerman (Argentina).
ECU: Máximo Orlando Banguera Valdivieso, Gabriel Eduardo Achilier Zurita, Walter Orlando Ayoví Corozo, Juan Carlos Paredes Reasco, Frickson Rafael Erazo Vivero, Segundo Alejandro Castillo Nazareno, Édison Vicente Méndez Méndez (46.Jorge Daniel Guagua Tamayo), Luis Antonio Valencia Mosquera, Christian Fernando Noboa Tello, Enner Remberto Valencia Lastra (69.Joao Robin Rojas Mendoza), Jefferson Antonio Montero Vite (77.Alex Renato Ibarra Mina). Trainer: Reinaldo Rueda Rivera (Colombia).
Goal: 1-0 James David Rodríguez Rubio (30).
Cautions: Carlos Enrique Valdés Parra, Carlos Alberto Sánchez Moreno, Pablo Estifer Armero / Joao Robin Rojas Mendoza.
Sent off: Gabriel Eduardo Achilier Zurita (28).

06.09.2013, Estadio Defensores del Chaco, Asunción; Attendance: 20,000
Referee: Víctor Hugo Carrillo (Peru)
PARAGUAY - BOLIVIA 4-0(1-0)
PAR: Antony Domingo Silva Cano, Paulo César da Silva Barrios, Salustiano Antonio Candia Galeano, Miguel Ángel Ramón Samudio, Gustavo Raúl Gómez Portillo, Jonathan Fabbro (66.Arnaldo Antonio Sanabria Ayala), Wilson Omar Pittoni Rodríguez (71.Sergio Daniel Aquino), Víctor Hugo Ayala Núñez, Richard Ortíz Busto, Roque Luis Santa Cruz Cantero, Ángel Rodrigo Romero Villamayor (65.Óscar David Romero Villamayor). Trainer: Víctor Genés.
BOL: Sergio Daniel Galarza Solíz, Ronald Raldes Balcázar, Edemir Rodríguez Mercado, Edward Mauro Zenteno Álvarez (46.Rudy Alejandro Cardozo Fernández), Luis Alberto Gutiérrez Herrera, Abraham Cabrera Scarpin, José Luis Chávez Sánchez (68.Leandro Marcelo Maygua Ríos), Vicente Arze Camacho (46.Juan Carlos Arce Justiniano), Danny Brayhan Bejarano Yañez, Marcelo Moreno Martins, Pedro Jesús Azogue Rojas. Trainer: Francisco Xabier Azcargorta Uriarte (Spain).
Goals: 1-0 Jonathan Fabbro (16), 2-0 Roque Luis Santa Cruz Cantero (47), 3-0 Richard Ortíz Busto (80), 4-0 Gustavo Raúl Gómez Portillo (83).
Cautions: Luis Alberto Gutiérrez Herrera, Danny Brayhan Bejarano Yañez.

06.09.2013, Estadio Nacional „Julio Martínez Prádanos", Santiago; Attendance: 46,500
Referee: Sandro Meira Ricci (Brazil)
CHILE - VENEZUELA 3-0(2-0)
CHI: Claudio Andrés Bravo Muñoz, Marcos Andrés González Salazar, Eugenio Esteban Mena Reveco, Jorge Luis Valdivia Toro (73.Jean André Emanuel Beausejour Coliqueo), Arturo Erasmo Vidal Pardo, Mauricio Aníbal Isla Isla, Marcelo Alfonso Díaz Rojas, Gary Alexis Medel Soto, Charles Mariano Aránguiz Sandoval (58.David Marcelo Pizarro Cortés), Alexis Alejandro Sánchez Sánchez, Eduardo Jesús Vargas Rojas (84.Ángelo José Henríquez Iturra). Trainer: Jorge Luis Sampaoli Moya (Argentina).
VEN: Daniel Hernández Santos, Oswaldo Augusto Vizcarrondo Araujo, Roberto José Rosales Altuve, Grenddy Adrián Perozo Rincón, Gabriel Alejandro Cichero Konarek (44.Alexander David González Sibulo), Juan Fernando Arango Sáenz, César Eduardo González Amais (70.Yohandry José Orozco Cujía), Franklin José Lucena Peña, Luis Manuel Seijas Gunther (79.Rómulo Otero Vásquez), José Salomón Rondón Giménez, Josef Alexander Martínez. Trainer: César Alejandro Farías Acosta.
Goals: 1-0 Eduardo Jesús Vargas Rojas (10), 2-0 Marcos Andrés González Salazar (30), 3-0 Arturo Erasmo Vidal Pardo (85).

Cautions: Oswaldo Augusto Vizcarrondo Araujo, Grenddy Adrián Perozo Rincón, Roberto José Rosales Altuve.

06.09.2013, Estadio Monumental, Lima; Attendance: 39,222
Referee: Patricio Loustau (Argentina)

PERU - URUGUAY 1-2(0-1)

PER: Raúl Omar Fernández Valverde, Alberto Junior Rodríguez Valdelomar, Christian Guillermo Martín Ramos Garagay, Luis Jan Piers Advíncula Castrillón (65.Jhoel Alexander Herrera Zegarra), Paulo Rinaldo Cruzado Durand, Josepmir Aarón Ballón Villacorta (46.Juan Manuel Vargas Risco), Luis Alberto Ramírez Lucay (66.Cristopher Paolo César Hurtado Huertas), Víctor Yoshimar Yotún Flores, Jefferson Agustín Farfán Guadalupe, José Paolo Guerrero Gonzáles, Claudio Miguel Pizarro Bosio. Trainer: Sergio Apraham Markarián Abrahamian (Uruguay).
URU: Néstor Fernando Muslera Micol, Diego Alfredo Lugano Morena, Victorio Maximiliano Pereira Páez, José Martín Cáceres Silva (81.Jorge Ciro Fucile Perdomo), Diego Roberto Godín Leal, Cristian Gabriel Rodríguez Barotti, Walter Alejandro Gargano Guevara (70.Álvaro Rafael González Luengo), Egidio Raúl Arévalo Ríos, Luis Alberto Suárez Díaz, Diego Martín Forlán Corazzo (25.Christian Ricardo Stuani Curbelo), Edinson Roberto Cavani Gómez. Trainer: Óscar Wáshington Tabárez Silva.
Goals: 0-1 Luis Alberto Suárez Díaz (43 penalty), 0-2 Luis Alberto Suárez Díaz (67), 1-2 Jefferson Agustín Farfán Guadalupe (84).
Cautions: Luis Jan Piers Advíncula Castrillón, Jefferson Agustín Farfán Guadalupe / Diego Alfredo Lugano Morena, Diego Roberto Godín Leal, Edinson Roberto Cavani Gómez.
Sent off: Víctor Yoshimar Yotún Flores (45+2).

10.09.2013, Estadio "Hernando Siles Zuazo", La Paz; Attendance: 12,043
Referee: Paulo César de Oliveira (Brazil)

BOLIVIA - ECUADOR 1-1(0-0)

BOL: Romel Javier Quiñónez Suárez, Ronald Raldes Balcázar, Edward Mauro Zenteno Álvarez, Marvin Orlando Bejarano Jiménez (46.Jaime Darío Arrascaita Iriondo), Alejandro Saúl Chumacero Bracamonte (74.Leandro Marcelo Maygua Ríos), Rudy Alejandro Cardozo Fernández, Diego Bejarano Ibañez, Juan Carlos Arce Justiniano, Diego Aroldo Cabrera Flores, Wálter Veizaga Argote, Pedro Jesús Azogue Rojas (46.Marcelo Moreno Martins). Trainer: Francisco Xabier Azcargorta Uriarte (Spain).
ECU: Alexander Domínguez Carabalí, Jorge Daniel Guagua Tamayo, Walter Orlando Ayoví Corozo, Juan Carlos Paredes Reasco, Frickson Rafael Erazo Vivero, Segundo Alejandro Castillo Nazareno (65.Christian Fernando Noboa Tello), Luis Fernando Saritama Padilla, Luis Antonio Valencia Mosquera, Jaime Javier Ayoví Corozo (50.Alex Renato Ibarra Mina), Felipe Salvador Caicedo Corozo (73.Joffre David Guerrón Méndez), Jefferson Antonio Montero Vite. Trainer: Reinaldo Rueda Rivera (Colombia).
Goals: 1-0 Jaime Darío Arrascaita Iriondo (47), 1-1 Felipe Salvador Caicedo Corozo (58).

10.09.2013, Estadio Centenario, Montevideo; Attendance: 51,000
Referee: Antonio Javier Arias Alvarenga (Paraguay)

URUGUAY - COLOMBIA 2-0(0-0)

URU: Néstor Fernando Muslera Micol, Jorge Ciro Fucile Perdomo, Andrés Scotti Ponce de León, Victorio Maximiliano Pereira Páez, José María Giménez de Vargas, Cristian Gabriel Rodríguez Barotti (71.Gastón Ezequiel Ramírez Pereyra), Álvaro Rafael González Luengo (46.Walter Alejandro Gargano Guevara), Egidio Raúl Arévalo Ríos, Marcelo Nicolás Lodeiro Benítez (46.Christian Ricardo Stuani Curbelo), Luis Alberto Suárez Díaz, Edinson Roberto Cavani Gómez. Trainer: Óscar Wáshington Tabárez Silva.
COL: David Ospina Ramírez, Mario Alberto Yepes Díaz, Luis Amaranto Perea Mosquera, John Stefan Medina Ramírez, Abel Enrique Aguilar Tapias (80.Aldo Leão Ramírez), Juan Camilo Zúñiga Mosquera, Carlos Alberto Sánchez Moreno (86.Jackson Arley Martínez Valencia), Fredy Alejandro Guarín Vásquez, James David Rodríguez Rubio, Radamel Falcao García Zárate, Teófilo Antonio Gutiérrez Roncancio (69.Juan Guillermo Cuadrado Bello). Trainer: José Néstor Pékerman (Argentina).
Goals: 1-0 Edinson Roberto Cavani Gómez (77), 2-0 Christian Ricardo Stuani Curbelo (81).
Cautions: Victorio Maximiliano Pereira Páez, Christian Ricardo Stuani Curbelo / John Stefan Medina

Ramírez, James David Rodríguez Rubio.

10.09.2013, Estadio Olímpico "General José Antonio Anzoátegui", Puerto la Cruz; Attendance: 20,049
Referee: Néstor Fabián Pitana (Argentina)

VENEZUELA - PERU **3-2(1-1)**

VEN: Daniel Hernández Santos, Fernando Gabriel Amorebieta Mardaras, Oswaldo Augusto Vizcarrondo Araujo, Roberto José Rosales Altuve, Alexander David González Sibulo, Juan Fernando Arango Sáenz (86.Fernando Luis Aristeguieta de Luca), César Eduardo González Amais (68.Rómulo Otero Vásquez), Yohandry José Orozco Cujía, Tomás Eduardo Rincón Hernández, José Salomón Rondón Giménez, Josef Alexander Martínez (75.Franklin José Lucena Peña). Trainer: César Alejandro Farías Acosta.

PER: Raúl Omar Fernández Valverde, Alberto Junior Rodríguez Valdelomar, Jhoel Alexander Herrera Zegarra (14.Luis Jan Piers Advíncula Castrillón), Carlos Augusto Zambrano Ochandarte, Paulo Rinaldo Cruzado Durand (63.Luis Alberto Ramírez Lucay), Cristopher Paolo César Hurtado Huertas, Carlos Augusto Lobatón Espejo, Edwin Retamoso Palomino, Juan Manuel Vargas Risco, Claudio Miguel Pizarro Bosio (64.José Paolo Guerrero Gonzáles), André Martín Carrillo Díaz. Trainer: Sergio Apraham Markarián Abrahamian (Uruguay).

Goals: 0-1 Cristopher Paolo César Hurtado Huertas (20), 1-1 José Salomón Rondón Giménez (37), 2-1 César Eduardo González Amais (62 penalty), 3-1 Rómulo Otero Vásquez (77), 3-2 Carlos Augusto Zambrano Ochandarte (87).

Cautions: César Eduardo González Amais, Rómulo Otero Vásquez / Carlos Augusto Lobatón Espejo, Luis Jan Piers Advíncula Castrillón, Paulo Rinaldo Cruzado Durand, Carlos Augusto Zambrano Ochandarte, Raúl Omar Fernández Valverde, Cristopher Paolo César Hurtado Huertas.

10.09.2013, Estadio Defensores del Chaco, Asunción; Attendance: 27,000
Referee: Enrique Roberto Osses Zencovich (Chile)

PARAGUAY - ARGENTINA **2-5(1-2)**

PAR: Roberto Junior Fernández Torres, Paulo César da Silva Barrios, Salustiano Antonio Candia Galeano, Marcos Antonio Cáceres Centurión, Miguel Ángel Ramón Samudio, Cristian Miguel Riveros Núñez, Jonathan Fabbro (55.Jorge Luis Rojas Mendoza), Víctor Hugo Ayala Núñez, Richard Ortíz Busto (21.Sergio Daniel Aquino; 46.Óscar David Romero Villamayor), Roque Luis Santa Cruz Cantero, José Ariel Núñez Portelli. Trainer: Víctor Genés.

ARG: Sergio Germán Romero, Fabricio Coloccini, Pablo Javier Zabaleta Girod, José María Basanta Pavone, Hugo Armando Campagnaro, Lucas Rodrigo Biglia, Fernando Rubén Gago (86.Maximiliano Rubén Rodríguez), Ángel Fabián di María Hernández, Rodrigo Sebastián Palacio (65.Ezequiel Iván Lavezzi), Lionel Andrés Messi, Sergio Leonel Agüero del Castillo (77.Éver Maximiliano David Banega). Trainer: Alejandro Sabella.

Goals: 0-1 Lionel Andrés Messi (12 penalty), 1-1 José Ariel Núñez Portelli (17), 1-2 Sergio Leonel Agüero del Castillo (32), 1-3 Ángel Fabián di María Hernández (50), 1-4 Lionel Andrés Messi (53 penalty), 2-4 Roque Luis Santa Cruz Cantero (86), 2-5 Maximiliano Rubén Rodríguez (90).

Cautions: Roberto Junior Fernández Torres / Pablo Javier Zabaleta Girod.

11.10.2013, Estadio Metropolitano "Roberto Meléndez", Barranquilla; Attendance: 40,388
Referee: Paulo César de Oliveira (Brazil)

COLOMBIA - CHILE 3-3(0-3)

COL: David Ospina Ramírez, Mario Alberto Yepes Díaz, Luis Amaranto Perea Mosquera, John Stefan Medina Ramírez (46.Fredy Alejandro Guarín Vásquez), Abel Enrique Aguilar Tapias (46.Macnelly Torres Berrío), Carlos Alberto Sánchez Moreno (67.Carlos Arturo Bacca Ahumada), Pablo Estifer Armero, Juan Guillermo Cuadrado Bello, James David Rodríguez Rubio, Radamel Falcao García Zárate, Teófilo Antonio Gutiérrez Roncancio. Trainer: José Néstor Pékerman (Argentina).

CHI: Claudio Andrés Bravo Muñoz, Marcos Andrés González Salazar, Gonzalo Alejandro Jara Reyes, Eugenio Esteban Mena Reveco, Jorge Luis Valdivia Toro (61.Jean André Emanuel Beausejour Coliqueo), Arturo Erasmo Vidal Pardo, Mauricio Aníbal Isla Isla (53.José Manuel Rojas Bahamondes), Gary Alexis Medel Soto, Carlos Emilio Carmona Tello, Alexis Alejandro Sánchez Sánchez, Eduardo Jesús Vargas Rojas (69.Francisco Andrés Silva Gajardo). Trainer: Jorge Luis Sampaoli Moya (Argentina).

Goals: 0-1 Arturo Erasmo Vidal Pardo (19 penalty), 0-2 Alexis Alejandro Sánchez Sánchez (22), 0-3 Alexis Alejandro Sánchez Sánchez (29), 1-3 Teófilo Antonio Gutiérrez Roncancio (69), 2-3 Radamel Falcao García Zárate (74 penalty), 3-3 Radamel Falcao García Zárate (83 penalty).

Cautions: Pablo Estifer Armero, David Ospina Ramírez, Juan Guillermo Cuadrado Bello, Mario Alberto Yepes Díaz, Fredy Alejandro Guarín Vásquez, Radamel Falcao García Zárate / Mauricio Aníbal Isla Isla, Carlos Emilio Carmona Tello, Francisco Andrés Silva Gajardo, Claudio Andrés Bravo Muñoz.

Sent off: Carlos Emilio Carmona Tello (66).

11.10.2013, Estadio Olimpico "Atahualpa", Quito; Attendance: 32,996
Referee: Sandro Meira Ricci (Brazil)

ECUADOR - URUGUAY 1-0(1-0)

ECU: Alexander Domínguez Carabalí, Jorge Daniel Guagua Tamayo, Walter Orlando Ayoví Corozo, Juan Carlos Paredes Reasco, Frickson Rafael Erazo Vivero, Segundo Alejandro Castillo Nazareno, Luis Antonio Valencia Mosquera, Christian Fernando Noboa Tello, Enner Remberto Valencia Lastra (71.Joao Robin Rojas Mendoza; 90.Alex Leonardo Bolaños Reascos), Felipe Salvador Caicedo Corozo, Jefferson Antonio Montero Vite (82.Alex Renato Ibarra Mina). Trainer: Reinaldo Rueda Rivera (Colombia).

URU: Néstor Fernando Muslera Micol, Diego Alfredo Lugano Morena, Jorge Ciro Fucile Perdomo, Victorio Maximiliano Pereira Páez (65.Diego Martín Forlán Corazzo), Diego Roberto Godín Leal, José María Giménez de Vargas, Cristian Gabriel Rodríguez Barotti (78.Gastón Ezequiel Ramírez Pereyra), Walter Alejandro Gargano Guevara (72.Alejandro Daniel Silva González), Egidio Raúl Arévalo Ríos, Luis Alberto Suárez Díaz, Edinson Roberto Cavani Gómez. Trainer: Óscar Wáshington Tabárez Silva.

Goal: 1-0 Jefferson Antonio Montero Vite (30).

Cautions: Diego Alfredo Lugano Morena, Egidio Raúl Arévalo Ríos.

11.10.2013, Estadio Polideportivo de Pueblo Nuevo, San Cristóbal; Attendance: 27,227
Referee: Víctor Hugo Carrillo Casanova (Peru)

VENEZUELA - PARAGUAY 1-1(0-1)

VEN: Daniel Hernández Santos, Fernando Gabriel Amorebieta Mardaras, Oswaldo Augusto Vizcarrondo Araujo, Roberto José Rosales Altuve, Alexander David González Sibulo (77.Luis Manuel Seijas Gunther), Juan Fernando Arango Sáenz, Franklin José Lucena Peña, Yohandry José Orozco Cujía, Rómulo Otero Vásquez (64.Fernando Luis Aristeguieta de Luca), Nicolás Ladislao Fedor Flores, Josef Alexander Martínez (71.Louis Angelo Peña Puentes). Trainer: César Alejandro Farías Acosta.

PAR: Justo Wilmar Villar Viveros, Paulo César da Silva Barrios, Carlos Bonet Cáceres, Gustavo Raúl Gómez Portillo, Júnior Osmar Ignacio Alonso Mujica, Víctor Javier Cáceres Centurión, Víctor Hugo Ayala Núñez, Luis Alcides Miño Muñoz (86.Jorge Luis Rojas Mendoza), Roque Luis Santa Cruz Cantero, Óscar René Cardozo Marín (66.Fidencio Oviedo Domínguez), Édgar Milciades Benítez Santander (57.Óscar David Romero Villamayor). Trainer: Víctor Genés.

Goals: 0-1 Édgar Milciades Benítez Santander (28), 1-1 Luis Manuel Seijas Gunther (82).

Cautions: Josef Alexander Martínez / Óscar David Romero Villamayor.

11.10.2013, Estadio Monumental „Antonio Vespucio Liberti“, Buenos Aires; Attendance: 28,977
Referee: Carlos Alfredo Vera Rodríguez (Ecuador)
ARGENTINA - PERU **3-1(2-1)**
ARG: Sergio Germán Romero, Pablo Javier Zabaleta Girod, Ezequiel Marcelo Garay González, Federico Fernández, Faustino Marcos Alberto Rojo, Lucas Rodrigo Biglia, Ángel Fabián di María Hernández (90+1.Leandro Daniel Somoza), Éver Maximiliano David Banega, Rodrigo Sebastián Palacio (80.Erik Manuel Lamela), Sergio Leonel Agüero del Castillo, Ezequiel Iván Lavezzi (87.Maximiliano Rubén Rodríguez). Trainer: Alejandro Sabella.
PER: Diego Alonso Penny Valdez, Néstor Alonso Duarte Carassa, Gianmarco Gambetta Sponza, Edwin Alexi Gómez Gutiérrez (46.Cristian Benavente Bristol), Roberto Efraín Koichi Aparicio Mori, Josepmir Aarón Ballón Villacorta, Luis Alberto Ramírez Lucay (84.José Yordy Reyna Serna), Cristopher Paolo César Hurtado Huertas, Juan Manuel Vargas Risco, Claudio Miguel Pizarro Bosio, André Martín Carrillo Díaz (69.Óscar Christopher Vílchez Soto). Trainer: Sergio Apraham Markarián Abrahamian (Uruguay).
Goals: 0-1 Claudio Miguel Pizarro Bosio (21), 1-1 Ezequiel Iván Lavezzi (23), 2-1 Ezequiel Iván Lavezzi (35), 3-1 Rodrigo Sebastián Palacio (47).
Cautions: Sergio Leonel Agüero del Castillo / Roberto Efraín Koichi Aparicio Mori.

15.10.2013, Estadio Defensores del Chaco, Asunción; Attendance: 7,142
Referee: Diego Hernán Abal (Argentina)
PARAGUAY - COLOMBIA **1-2(1-1)**
PAR: Justo Wilmar Villar Viveros, Paulo César da Silva Barrios, Salustiano Antonio Candia Galeano, Carlos Bonet Cáceres (46.Óscar René Cardozo Marín), Gustavo Raúl Gómez Portillo, Sergio Daniel Aquino, Fidencio Oviedo Domínguez, Óscar David Romero Villamayor (77.David Ariel Mendieta Chávez), Jorge Luis Rojas Mendoza, Roque Luis Santa Cruz Cantero, José Ariel Núñez Portelli (62.Arnaldo Antonio Sanabria Ayala). Trainer: Víctor Genés.
COL: David Ospina Ramírez, Mario Alberto Yepes Díaz, Cristián Eduardo Zapata Valencia, Santiago Arias Naranjo, Macnelly Torres Berrío (37.Aldo Leão Ramírez), Carlos Alberto Sánchez Moreno, Pablo Estifer Armero, Fredy Alejandro Guarín Vásquez, James David Rodríguez Rubio (90.Alexander Mejía Sabalsa), Jackson Arley Martínez Valencia, Carlos Arturo Bacca Ahumada (66.Juan Fernando Quintero Paniagua). Trainer: José Néstor Pékerman (Argentina).
Goals: 1-0 Jorge Luis Rojas Mendoza (7), 1-1 Mario Alberto Yepes Díaz (38), 1-2 Mario Alberto Yepes Díaz (56).
Cautions: José Ariel Núñez Portelli, Gustavo Raúl Gómez Portillo / Fredy Alejandro Guarín Vásquez, Carlos Alberto Sánchez Moreno.
Sent off: Fredy Alejandro Guarín Vásquez (32).

15.10.2013, Estadio Nacional „Julio Martínez Prádanos“, Santiago; Attendance: 47,458
Referee: Leandro Pedro Vuaden (Brazil)
CHILE - ECUADOR **2-1(2-0)**
CHI: Claudio Andrés Bravo Muñoz, Marcos Andrés González Salazar, Eugenio Esteban Mena Reveco, Jorge Luis Valdivia Toro (89.Mauricio Ricardo Pinilla Ferrera), Arturo Erasmo Vidal Pardo, Mauricio Aníbal Isla Isla, Marcelo Alfonso Díaz Rojas, Gary Alexis Medel Soto, Charles Mariano Aránguiz Sandoval (76.Matías Ariel Fernández Fernández), Alexis Alejandro Sánchez Sánchez, Eduardo Jesús Vargas Rojas (86.Jean André Emanuel Beausejour Coliqueo). Trainer: Jorge Luis Sampaoli Moya (Argentina).
ECU: Alexander Domínguez Carabalí, Jorge Daniel Guagua Tamayo, Walter Orlando Ayoví Corozo, Juan Carlos Paredes Reasco, Frickson Rafael Erazo Vivero, Segundo Alejandro Castillo Nazareno, Luis Antonio Valencia Mosquera, Christian Fernando Noboa Tello, Enner Remberto Valencia Lastra (72.Jaime Javier Ayoví Corozo), Felipe Salvador Caicedo Corozo (89.Alex Renato Ibarra Mina), Jefferson Antonio Montero Vite (84.Fidel Francisco Martínez Tenorio). Trainer: Reinaldo Rueda Rivera (Colombia).
Goals: 1-0 Alexis Alejandro Sánchez Sánchez (35), 2-0 Gary Alexis Medel Soto (38), 2-1 Felipe

Salvador Caicedo Corozo (66).
Cautions: Alexis Alejandro Sánchez Sánchez, Charles Mariano Aránguiz Sandoval / Frickson Rafael Erazo Vivero, Luis Antonio Valencia Mosquera, Jaime Javier Ayoví Corozo.

15.10.2013, Estadio Centenario, Montevideo; Attendance: 55,000
Referee: Marcelo de Lima Henrique (Brazil)
URUGUAY - ARGENTINA 3-2(2-2)
URU: Néstor Fernando Muslera Micol, Diego Alfredo Lugano Morena, Jorge Ciro Fucile Perdomo, Victorio Maximiliano Pereira Páez, Diego Roberto Godín Leal, Diego Fernando Pérez Aguado (46.Gastón Ezequiel Ramírez Pereyra), Cristian Gabriel Rodríguez Barotti, Egidio Raúl Arévalo Ríos, Luis Alberto Suárez Díaz, Edinson Roberto Cavani Gómez, Christian Ricardo Stuani Curbelo (90.José María Giménez de Vargas). Trainer: Óscar Wáshington Tabárez Silva.
ARG: Sergio Germán Romero, Sebastián Enrique Domínguez, José María Basanta Pavone, Hugo Armando Campagnaro, Federico Fernández, Maximiliano Rubén Rodríguez, Lucas Rodrigo Biglia, Augusto Matías Fernández (82.Mauro Emanuel Icardi Rivero), Éver Maximiliano David Banega (68.Leandro Daniel Somoza), Rodrigo Sebastián Palacio, Erik Manuel Lamela (76.José Ernesto Sosa). Trainer: Alejandro Sabella.
Goals: 1-0 Cristian Gabriel Rodríguez Barotti (6), 1-1 Maximiliano Rubén Rodríguez (14), 2-1 Luis Alberto Suárez Díaz (34 penalty), 2-2 Maximiliano Rubén Rodríguez (41), 3-2 Edinson Roberto Cavani Gómez (49).
Cautions: Erik Manuel Lamela.

15.10.2013, Estadio Nacional, Lima; Attendance: *played behind closed doors*
Referee: Enrique Cáceres Villafante (Paraguay)
PERU - BOLIVIA 1-1(1-1)
PER: Diego Alonso Penny Valdez, Néstor Alonso Duarte Carassa, Carlos Augusto Zambrano Ochandarte, Luis Jan Piers Advíncula Castrillón, Josepmir Aarón Ballón Villacorta, Carlos Augusto Lobatón Espejo, Víctor Yoshimar Yotún Flores, Juan Manuel Vargas Risco, Cristian Benavente Bristol (46.José Yordy Reyna Serna), Claudio Miguel Pizarro Bosio, Irven Beybe Ávila Acero (60.André Martín Carrillo Díaz). Trainer: Sergio Apraham Markarián Abrahamian (Uruguay).
BOL: Romel Javier Quiñónez Suárez, Ronald Raldes Balcázar, Edward Mauro Zenteno Álvarez, Luis Alberto Gutiérrez Herrera, Marvin Orlando Bejarano Jiménez, José Luis Chávez Sánchez, Diego Bejarano Ibáñez (86.Edemir Rodríguez Mercado), Danny Brayhan Bejarano Yañez (46.Juan Carlos Arce Justiniano), Marcelo Moreno Martins, Edivaldo Rojas Hermoza (74.Jaime Darío Arrascaita Iriondo), Wálter Veizaga Argote. Trainer: Francisco Xabier Azcargorta Uriarte (Spain).
Goals: 1-0 Víctor Yoshimar Yotún Flores (19), 1-1 Diego Bejarano Ibáñez (45).
Cautions: Juan Manuel Vargas Risco, Carlos Augusto Lobatón Espejo / Marvin Orlando Bejarano Jiménez, Wálter Veizaga Argote.

NORTH, CENTRAL AMERICA AND CARIBBEAN

Three places in the Final Tournament are alocated for the CONCACAF national teams. A fourth CONCACAF national team would also reach the Final Tournament through Inter-confederation play-offs against an Oceanian national team.

35 (all FIFA-affiliated CONCACAF national associations) have entered the World Cup qualifiers. The March 2011 FIFA World Ranking was used to seed the 35 teams for the first three rounds.

Places 1-6 – Qualified for the Third Round
United States (FIFA World Rankings Place: 19), Mexico (27), Honduras (38), Jamaica (48), Costa Rica (53), Cuba (64).
Places 7-25 – Qualified for the Second Round
Panama (68), Canada (84), El Salvador (92), Grenada (94), Trinidad and Tobago (95), Haiti (99), Antigua and Barbuda (101), Guyana (109), Suriname (114), Saint Kitts and Nevis (119), Guatemala (125), Dominica (130), Puerto Rico (131), Barbados (137), Curaçao (146), Saint Vincent and the Grenadines (148), Cayman Islands (158), Nicaragua (164), Bermuda (165).
Places 26-35 – Competing in First Round
Belize (166-167), Dominican Republic (166-167), British Virgin Islands (177), Saint Lucia (182), Turks and Caicos Islands (193-194), Bahamas (193-194), Aruba (199), U.S. Virgin Islands (200), Anguilla (202-204), Montserrat (202-204).

The qualifying consists of 4 Rounds:

1st Round: 5 two-legged knock-out ties (played between 15 June and 17 July 2011), involving the 10 lowest-ranked teams according to FIFA World Rankings.

2nd Round: 6 groups with each 4 teams (19 CONCACAF teams placed 7-25 in the FIFA World Rankings joined by the 5 winners from the 1st Round). Each group winner will advance to the 3rd Round.

3rd Round: 3 groups with each 4 teams (Top-6 CONCACAF teams joined by the 6 group winners from the Second Round). Each group winner and runner-up will advance to the 4th Round.

4th Round: One group of 6 teams. Top-3 national teams will qualify to the Final Tournament 2014. Place 4 advance to the intercontinental Play-offs.

FIRST ROUND
(15.06.2011 – 17.07.2011)

Montserrat - **Belize**	2-5(1-1)	1-3(0-1)
Turks and Caicos Islands - **Bahamas**	0-4(0-2)	0-6(0-2)
US Virgin Islands – British Virgin Islands	2-0(1-0)	2-1(1-1)
Anguilla – **Dominican Republic**	0-2(0-2)	0-4(0-3)
Aruba – **Saint Lucia**	4-2(1-1)	2-4(1-2,2-4,2-4); 4-5 pen

15.06.2011, „Ato Boldon“ Stadium, Couva (Trinidad and Tobago); Attendance: 100
Referee: Bryan Willett (Antigua and Barbuda)
MONTSERRAT - BELIZE **2-5(1-1)**
MSR: Micah Hilton, Kendall Allen, Anthony James Griffith, Alex Dyer, Wayne Dyer (90.Nyron Dyer), Dale Lee, Darryl Roach, Albert Junior Hillyard Andrew Mendes, Julian Wade (76.Alexander Bramble), Leovan O'Garro, Jay-Lee Hodgson. Trainer: Kenneth Dyer.
BLZ: Shane Moody-Orio, Dalton Eiley, Ian Gaynair, Luis Méndez (46.Ryan Simpson), Elroy Smith, Vallan Symms, Everal Trapp, Deris Benavidez (64.David Trapp), Elroy Kuylen, Harrison Dwith Róchez (82.Daniel Jiménez), Deon McCaulay. Trainer: José de la Paz Herrera Ucles (Honduras).
Goals: 0-1 Deon McCaulay (24), 1-1 Jay-Lee Hodgson (44), 1-2 Harrison Dwith Róchez (50), 1-3 Elroy Kuylen (53), 1-4 Deon McCaulay (74), 1-5 Deon McCaulay (83), 2-5 Jay-Lee Hodgson (86).
Cautions: Jay-Lee Hodgson.

17.07.2011, Estadio Olímpico, San Pedro Sula (Honduras); Attendance: 150
Referee: Óscar Reyna (Guatemala)
BELIZE - MONTSERRAT **3-1(1-0)**
BLZ: Shane Moody-Orio, Ian Gaynair, Luis Méndez, Vallan Symms, Mario Villanueva, Elroy Kuylen, Ryan Simpson, Harrison Tasher, David Trapp (46.Deris Benavides), Daniel Jiménez (66.Evan Mariano), Deon McCaulay. Trainer: José de la Paz Herrera Ucles (Honduras).
MSR: Jermain Sweeney, Kendall Allen, Nyron Dyer (60.Dale Lee), Calvin Petrie, Clifford Joseph, Anthony James Griffith, Alex Dyer, Darryl Roach, Alexander Bramble (60.Denoy Campbell), Leovan O'Garro, Jay-Lee Hodgson. Trainer: Kenneth Dyer.
Goals: 1-0 Daniel Jiménez (23), 1-1 Jay-Lee Hodgson (58), 2-1 Deon McCaulay (59), 3-1 Luis Méndez (61).
Cautions: Mario Villanueva / Leovan O'Garro.
(Belize won 8-3 on aggregate)

02.07.2011, National Stadium, Providenciales; Attendance: 1,021
Referee: Hugo Cruz Álvarado (Costa Rica)
TURKS AND CAICOS ISLANDS - BAHAMAS **0-4(0-2)**
TCA: Raymondson Azemard, Duane Glinton (46.Spentz Francois), Woody Gibson, Kevin Speer (75.Lagneau Brumvert), Peter Glinton, Events Jean (67.James McKnight), George Brough, Lenford Singh, Gavin Glinton, Philip Shearer, Billy Forbes. Trainer: Gary Brough.
BAH: Raynaldo Sturrup, Anton Justin Sealey, Dana Matthew Veth, Shemord Thompson, Dwayne Forbes, Mackenson Altidor (76.Raymorn Sturrup), Demont Mitchell, Michael Bethel (76.Jonathan Sykes), Cameron Robert Hepple, Lesly St. Fleur (84.Jackner Louis), Nesley Jean. Trainer: Kevin Davies.
Goals: 0-1 Nesley Jean (32), 0-2 Cameron Robert Hepple (36 penalty), 0-3 Nesley Jean (61), 0-4 Jackner Louis (90).
Cautions: Lesly St. Fleur, Demont Mitchell.

09.07.2011, „Roscow A. L. Davies“ Soccer Field, Nassau; Attendance: 1,600
Referee: Javier Santos (Puerto Rico)

BAHAMAS - TURKS AND CAICOS ISLANDS 6-0(2-0)

BAH: Raynaldo Sturrup, Anton Justin Sealey, Dana Matthew Veth, Shemord Thompson, Dwayne Forbes, Mackenson Altidor (67.Raymorn Sturrup), Demont Mitchell, Cameron Robert Hepple, Michael Bethel (74.Andrew Pratt), Jonathan Sykes (46.Christopher Larson), Lesly St. Fleur. Trainer: Kevin Davies.

TCA: Ian Jones, Duane Glinton, Woody Gibson, Gavin Glinton, James Rene, Marco Fenelus, Kevin Speer (46.Peter Glinton), George Brough (75.Syed Hassan), Lenford Singh (72.James McKnight), Philip Shearer, Billy Forbes. Trainer: Gary Brough.

Goals: 1-0 Woody Gibson (4 own goal), 2-0 Lesly St. Fleur (17), 3-0 Lesly St. Fleur (64), 4-0 Lesly St. Fleur (73), 5-0 Lesly St. Fleur (84), 6-0 Lesly St. Fleur (90).

Cautions: Dwayne Forbes, Mackenson Altidor / Lenford Singh, Gavin Glinton.

(Bahamas won 10-0 on aggregate)

03.07.2011, „Lionel Roberts“ Park, Charlotte Amalie; Attendance: 350
Referee: Mauricio Navarro (Canada)

US VIRGIN ISLANDS - BRITISH VIRGIN ISLANDS 2-0(1-0)

VIR: Dillon Pieffer, Derrick Smith, Alberto Van Gurp, Ayinde Augustus, Kimani George, Kai Schuster, MacDonald Taylor, Reid William Klopp, Dwayne Thomas (62.Michael Beharry), Junior Laurencin (74.Alexander Nissman), Alderman Rowe Nicholas Lesmond (87.Adam Fuller). Trainer: Keith Griffith (Barbados).

VGB: Dowlyn Daly, Jhon Samuel, Errol Wellington, Javier Smith (42.Andy Davis), Vanquever Frett (68.Gregory James), Jevon Demming, Troy Kavon Caesar, Joel Fahie (54.Carlos Septus), Christopher Telemache, Chevon Russell, Trevor Peters. Trainer: Avondale Williams.

Goals: 1-0 Alderman Rowe Nicholas Lesmond (7), 2-0 Reid William Klopp (57).

Cautions: Alderman Rowe Nicholas Lesmond, Kimani George.

Sent off: Jhon Samuel (60).

10.07.2011, Sherly Ground, Road Town; Attendance: 600
Referee: Kevin Morrison (Jamaica)

BRITISH VIRGIN ISLANDS - US VIRGIN ISLANDS 1-2(1-1)

VGB: Dowlyn Daly, Gregory James, Javier Smith (76.Errol Wellington), Vanquever Frett (55.Christopher Telemache), Jevon Demming, Troy Kavon Caesar, Joel Fahie, Carlos Septus (81.Frandy Felix), Andy Davis, Chevon Russell, Trevor Peters. Trainer: Avondale Williams.

VIR: Dillon Pieffer, Ayinde Augustus, Alberto Van Gurp, Kimani George (46.Lishati-Shumba Bailey), Derrick Smith, MacDonald Taylor, Dwayne Thomas (75.Wilbert Pierre), Reid William Klopp, Michael Beharry (46.Alexander Nissman), Junior Laurencin, Alderman Rowe Nicholas Lesmond. Trainer: Terrence Jones.

Goals: 0-1 Dwayne Thomas (2), 1-1 Trevor Peters (38), 1-2 Reid William Klopp (90).

(US Virgin Islands won 4-1 on aggregate)

08.07.2011, Estadio Panamericano, San Cristóbal (Dominican Republic); Attendance: 1,000
Referee: Neal Brizan (Trinidad and Tobago)

ANGUILLA - DOMINICAN REPUBLIC 0-2(0-2)

AIA: Ryan Kelvin Liddie, Leon Jeffers, Kieran Kentish (56.Damian Bailey), Kevin Hawley, Adonijah Richardson, Desroy Findlay, Kenny Williams, Girdon Connor, André Griffith (20.Khaloni Richardson), Terrence Rodgers, Javille Brooks (82.Ikenya Browne). Trainer: Colin Johnson.
DOM: Miguel Lloyd, Johan Alberto Cruz De La Cruz, César García Peralta, Rafael Ramírez Estasa, Kelvin De Jesús Severino Sosa, Rafael Leonardo Flores (56.Mikhail Meyreles Pérez), Domingo Antonio Peralta Florencio (75.Manuel Pérez), Johan Sánchez, Jonathan Rafael Faña Frias, Darly Noemi Batista (89.Fernando Casanova), Kelvin Rafael Rodríguez Pichardo. Trainer: Clemente Domingo Hernández (Cuba).
Goals: 0-1 Domingo Antonio Peralta Florencio (7), 0-2 Jonathan Rafael Faña Frias (42).
Cautions: Leon Jeffers / Kelvin De Jesús Severino Sosa.

10.07.2011, Estadio Panamericano, San Cristóbal; Attendance: 1,500
Referee: Marco Daniel Brea Despaigne (Cuba)

DOMINICAN REPUBLIC - ANGUILLA 4-0(3-0)

DOM: Miguel Lloyd, Johan Alberto Cruz De La Cruz, César García Peralta, Francisco Ubiera, Rafael Ramírez Estasa, Kelvin De Jesús Severino Sosa (64.Erick Ozuna López), Inoel Navarro González (71.Ruddy Encarnación), Domingo Antonio Peralta Florencio (60.Manuel Pérez), Johan Sánchez, Jonathan Rafael Faña Frias, Kelvin Rafael Rodríguez Pichardo. Trainer: Clemente Domingo Hernández (Cuba).
AIA: Ryan Kelvin Liddie, Leon Jeffers, Desroy Findlay, Khaloni Richardson, Adonijah Richardson, Kevin Hawley (87.Glenford Hughes), Kenny Williams, Girdon Connor, Damian Bailey (64.Ikenya Browne), Terrence Rodgers, Javille Brooks (76.Jermain Hodge). Trainer: Colin Johnson.
Goals: 1-0 Inoel Navarro González (18), 2-0 Johan Sánchez (27), 3-0 Inoel Navarro González (42), 4-0 Jonathan Rafael Faña Frias (58).
Cautions: Adonijah Richardson.
(Dominican Republic won 6-0 on aggregate)

08.07.2011, „Guillermo Prospero Trinidad“ Stadium, Oranjestad; Attendance: 300
Referee: Nolan Foster (Cayman Islands)

ARUBA - SAINT LUCIA 4-2(1-1)

ARU: Eric Abdul, François Croes, Theric Ruiz, Roman Aparicio, Giovanni Thode, Raymond Baten, Erik Santos de Gouveia (86.Sylvester Schwengle), David Abdul, Carlos Quandt, Maurice Escalona (62.Frederick Gomez), Rensy Barradas (68.Jelano Cruden). Trainer: Elvis Albertus.
LCA: Iran Cassius, Bernard Edward, Kurt Frederick, Vernus Abbot, Pernal Williams, Enderson George, Zaine Pierre (69.Shervon Jack), Kevin Edward, Guy George, Jamil Joseph (26.Cliff Valcin), Tremain Paul (86.Nathan Justin). Trainer: Alain Providence.
Goals: 1-0 Erik Santos de Gouveia (13), 1-1 Kevin Edward (20), 1-2 Cliff Valcin (46), 2-2 Maurice Escalona (48), 3-2 Frederick Gomez (76), 4-2 David Abdul (85).
Cautions: Raymond Baten / Guy George, Kurt Frederick, Pernal Williams, Kevin Edward, Cliff Valcin.
Sent off: Bernard Edward (83).

12.07.2011, „Mindoo Philip" Park, Castries; Attendance: 500
Referee: Stanley Lancaster (Guyana)

SAINT LUCIA - ARUBA **4-2(2-1,4-2)**
5-4 on penalties

LCA: Iran Cassius, Fabian Joseph, Kurt Frederick, Pernal Williams, Vernus Abbot, Nathan Justin, Enderson George (66.Eden Charles), Zaine Pierre, Hiram Hunte, Guy George (56.Kevin Edward), Jamil Joseph (84.Tremain Paul). Trainer: Alain Providence.
ARU: Eric Abdul, François Croes, Theric Ruiz (66.Annuar Kock), Raymond Baten, Juan Valdez, Roman Aparicio, Frederick Gomez, Erik Santos de Gouveia (60.Jelano Cruden), Carlos Quandt (37.Sylvester Schwengle), Rensy Barradas, Jean-Luc Bergen. Trainer: Elvis Albertus.
Goals: 1-0 Jamil Joseph (19), 2-0 Jamil Joseph (29), 2-1 Frederick Gomez (44), 3-1 Jamil Joseph (71), 3-2 Rensy Barradas (76), 4-2 Kurt Frederick (74).
Penalties: Zaine Pierre 1-0; Jean-Luc Bergen 1-1; Nathan Justin 2-1; Raymond Baten 2-2; Kurt Frederick 3-2; Rensy Barradas 3-3; Kevin Edward 4-3; Frederick Gomez 4-4; Pernal Williams 5-4; Jelano Cruden (missed).
Cautions: Nathan Justin, Jamil Joseph / Erik Santos de Gouveia, Juan Valdez, Eric Abdul, François Croes, Jean-Luc Bergen.
(Saint Lucia won 5-4 on penalties (after 6-6 on aggregate))

SECOND ROUND
(02.09.2011 – 15.11.2011)

The 24 teams were seeded into 4 pots:

Pot 1: Panama, Canada, El Salvador, Grenada, Trinidad and Tobago, Haiti.
Pot 2: Antigua and Barbuda, Guyana, Suriname, Saint Kitts and Nevis, Guatemala, Dominica.
Pot 3: Puerto Rico, Barbados, Curaçao, Saint Vincent and the Grenadines, Cayman Islands, Nicaragua.
Pot 4: Bermuda, Belize, Dominican Republic, Saint Lucia, Bahamas, U.S. Virgin Islands.

The six qualifying groups of the 2nd Round were as follows:

GROUP A	GROUP B	GROUP C
El Salvador	Trinidad and Tobago	Panama
Suriname	Guyana	Dominica
Cayman Islands	Barbados	Nicaragua
Dominican Republic	Bermuda	Bahamas

GROUP D	GROUP E	GROUP F
Canada	Grenada	Haiti
Saint Kitts and Nevis	Guatemala	Antigua and Barbuda
Puerto Rico	Saint Vincent and the Grenadines	Curaçao
Saint Lucia	Belize	U.S. Virgin Islands

GROUP A

02.09.2011	Paramaribo	Suriname – Cayman Islands	1-0(1-0)
02.09.2011	San Salvador	El Salvador - Dominican Republic	3-2(0-0)
06.09.2011	San Cristóbal	Cayman Islands - El Salvador	1-4(0-0)
06.09.2011	George Town	Dominican Republic - Suriname	1-1(0-1)
07.10.2011	San Cristóbal	Dominican Republic - El Salvador	1-2(0-1)
07.10.2011	George Town	Cayman Islands - Suriname	0-1(0-0)
11.10.2011	Paramaribo	Suriname - Dominican Republic	1-3(0-1)
11.10.2011	San Salvador	El Salvador - Cayman Islands	4-0(3-0)
11.11.2011	San Cristóbal	Dominican Republic - Cayman Islands	4-0(2-0)
11.11.2011	Paramaribo	Suriname - El Salvador	1-3(0-1)
14.11.2011	George Town	Cayman Islands - Dominican Republic	1-1(0-1)
15.11.2011	San Salvador	El Salvador - Suriname	4-0(1-0)

FINAL STANDINGS

1.	**El Salvador**	6	6	0	0	20	-	5	18
2.	Dominican Republic	6	2	2	2	12	-	8	8
3.	Suriname	6	2	1	3	5	-	11	7
4.	Cayman Islands	6	0	1	5	2	-	15	1

02.09.2011, „André Kamperveen“ Stadion, Paramaribo; Attendance: 1,000
Referee: Adrian Skeete (Barbados)
SURINAME – CAYMAN ISLANDS 1-0(1-0)
SUR: Obrendo Huiswoud, Naldo Kwasie, Giovanni Alleyne, Marlon Felter, Friso Mando, Fabian van Dijk (79.Jermain Sergio van Dijk), Giovanni Waal, Gregory Pokie, Orfeo Anautan (46.Stefano Rijssel), Milton Pinas, Giovanni Drenthe (46.Evani Esperance). Trainer: Kenneth Jaliens.
CAY: Anthony Ramon Sealy, Donovan Jedd Ebanks, Luigi Malcolm Hernández, Benjamin Cupid, Leighton Elliott, Andre McFarlane (85.Donald Solomon), Ian Lindo (88.Demion Denzel Williams), Jairo Sánchez (71.Dwayne Wright), Mario René Carter, Mark Ebanks, Theron Wood. Trainer: Carl Brown.
Goal: 1-0 Friso Mando (11 penalty).
Cautions: Leighton Elliott, Theron Wood, Luigi Malcolm Hernández.

02.09.2011, Estadio Cuscatlán, San Salvador; Attendance: 25,272
Referee: Luis Rodríguez De La Rosa (Panama)
EL SALVADOR - DOMINICAN REPUBLIC 3-2(0-0)
SLV: Juan José Gómez, Moisés Xavier García Orellana, Alexander Escobar Rosales, Víctor Samuel Turcios Pacheco, Carlos Romeo Monteagudo Alfaro (65.Edwin Ernesto Sánchez Vigil), Dennis Jonathan Alas Morales, Jaime Enrique Alas Morales, William Osael Romero Castillo, Herbert Arnoldo Sosa Burgos (65.José Arturo Álvarez Hernández), Christian Javier Bautista, Rodolfo Antonio Zelaya García (86.Mark Léster Blanco Pineda). Trainer: Rubén Israel (Uruguay).
DOM: Miguel Lloyd, Johan Alberto Cruz De La Cruz, César García Peralta, César Ledesma, Rafael Ramírez Estasa (66.Hansley Alexander Martínez García), Francisco Ubiera, Kelvin De Jesús Severino Sosa, Kelvin Rafael Rodríguez Pichardo (75.Domingo Antonio Peralta Florencio), Inoel Navarro González (73.Fernando Casanova), Vinicio Edwards Espinal Marte, Jonathan Rafael Faña Frias. Trainer: Clemente Domingo Hernández (Cuba).
Goals: 1-0 Rodolfo Antonio Zelaya García (54), 2-0 Christian Javier Bautista (64), 2-1 Johan Alberto Cruz De La Cruz (66), 3-1 Rodolfo Antonio Zelaya García (78), 3-2 Domingo Antonio Peralta Florencio (89).
Cautions: Rodolfo Antonio Zelaya García, Jaime Enrique Alas Morales / Francisco Ubiera, Rafael Ramírez Estasa.
Sent off: Francisco Ubiera (57).

06.09.2011, „Truman Bodden Stadium", George Town; Attendance: 2,200
Referee: Elmar Lizardo Rodas Hernández (Guatemala)
CAYMAN ISLANDS - EL SALVADOR 1-4(0-0)
CAY: Anthony Ramon Sealy, Donovan Jedd Ebanks, Luigi Malcolm Hernández, Andre McFarlane, Donald Solomon, Benjamin Cupid, Ian Lindo, Jairo Sánchez (62.Demion Denzel Williams), Dion Brandon (85.Derrin Ebanks), Mark Ebanks (78.Tex Whitelocke), Theron Wood. Trainer: Carl Brown.
SLV: Dagoberto Portillo Gamero, Moisés Xavier García Orellana, Luis Alonso Anaya Merino, Víctor Samuel Turcios Pacheco, Carlos Romeo Monteagudo Alfaro, Dennis Jonathan Alas Morales, Jaime Enrique Alas Morales (56.José Arturo Álvarez Hernández), William Osael Romero Castillo, Andrés Alexander Flores Mejía (68.Edwin Ernesto Sánchez Vigil), Christian Javier Bautista (68.Rafael Edgardo Burgos), Rodolfo Antonio Zelaya García. Trainer: Rubén Israel (Uruguay).
Goals: 0-1 Christian Javier Bautista (49), 0-2 Luis Alonso Anaya Merino (62), 1-2 Mark Ebanks (73 penalty), 1-3 Luis Alonso Anaya Merino (80), 1-4 Moisés Xavier García Orellana (90+3).

06.09.2011, Estadio Panamericano, San Cristóbal; Attendance: 2,300
Referee: Raul Edgardo Castro Zuñíga (Honduras)
DOMINICAN REPUBLIC - SURINAME 1-1(0-1)
DOM: Miguel Lloyd, Johan Alberto Cruz De La Cruz, César García Peralta, César Ledesma (90.Hansley Alexander Martínez García), Rafael Ramírez Estasa, Kelvin De Jesús Severino Sosa, Domingo Antonio Peralta Florencio, Vinicio Edwards Espinal Marte, Jonathan Rafael Faña Frias, Fernando Casanova (64.Inoel Navarro González), Kelvin Rafael Rodríguez Pichardo (56.Erick Ozuna López). Trainer: Clemente Domingo Hernández (Cuba).
SUR: Obrendo Huiswoud, Naldo Kwasie (78.Joel Baja), Giovanni Alleyne, Marlon Felter, Friso Mando, Fabian van Dijk, Giovanni Waal, Gregory Pokie, Milton Pinas (69.Orfeo Anautan), Stefano Rijssel, Evani Esperance (79.Giovanni Drenthe). Trainer: Kenneth Jaliens.
Goals: 0-1 Friso Mando (25 penalty), 1-1 Erick Ozuna López (68).
Cautions: Fernando Casanova, Rafael Ramírez Estasa, Jonathan Rafael Faña Frias / Stefano Rijssel, Naldo Kwasie, Gregory Pokie.

07.10.2011, Estadio Panamericano, San Cristóbal; Attendance: 2,323
Referee: Ricardo Cerdas Sánchez (Costa Rica)
DOMINICAN REPUBLIC - EL SALVADOR 1-2(0-1)
DOM: Miguel Lloyd, Johan Alberto Cruz De La Cruz, Ernesto Manuel Cabrera Jiménez, César García Peralta, César Ledesma (49.Kelvin Rafael Rodríguez Pichardo), Francisco Ubiera, Kelvin De Jesús Severino Sosa, Inoel Navarro González (66.Domingo Antonio Peralta Florencio), Erick Ozuna López, Jonathan Rafael Faña Frias, Fernando Casanova (44.Rafael Leonardo Flores). Trainer: Clemente Domingo Hernández (Cuba).
SLV: Dagoberto Portillo Gamero, Moisés Xavier García Orellana, Luis Alonso Anaya Merino, Víctor Samuel Turcios Pacheco, Carlos Romeo Monteagudo Alfaro, Dennis Jonathan Alas Morales, Jaime Enrique Alas Morales (72.Herbert Arnoldo Sosa Burgos), William Osael Romero Castillo, Ramón Alfredo Sánchez Paredes (58.Edwin Ernesto Sánchez Vigil), Christian Javier Bautista (58.Rafael Edgardo Burgos), Mark Léster Blanco Pineda. Trainer: Rubén Israel (Uruguay).
Goals: 0-1 William Osael Romero Castillo (38 penalty), 1-1 Erick Ozuna López (54), 1-2 Mark Léster Blanco Pineda (67).
Cautions: Fernando Casanova, Domingo Antonio Peralta Florencio, Johan Alberto Cruz De La Cruz / Dagoberto Portillo Gamero, Víctor Samuel Turcios Pacheco.
Sent off: Ernesto Manuel Cabrera Jiménez (36).

07.10.2011, „Truman Bodden Stadium", George Town; Attendance: 2,100
Referee: Edvin Jurisevic (United States)
CAYMAN ISLANDS - SURINAME 0-1(0-0)
CAY: Miguel Pitta, Donovan Jedd Ebanks (67.Raheem Robinson), Michael Johnson, Luigi Malcolm Hernández, Benjamin Cupid, Nicholas Phillip Ebanks, Donald Solomon, Dion Brandon, Ian Lindo (52.Demion Denzel Williams), Mark Ebanks (41.Andre McFarlane), Theron Wood. Trainer: Carl Brown.
SUR: Obrendo Huiswoud, Naldo Kwasie, Giovanni Alleyne, Marlon Felter, Friso Mando, Stefano Baneti (72.Jermain Sergio van Dijk), Giovanni Waal, Gregory Pokie (89.Fabian van Dijk), Stefano Rijssel, Milton Pinas (78.Orfeo Anautan), Giovanni Drenthe. Trainer: Kenneth Jaliens.
Goal: 0-1 Giovanni Drenthe (57).
Cautions: Mark Ebanks, Benjamin Cupid.
Sent off: Miguel Pitta (87).

11.10.2011, „André Kamperveen" Stadion, Paramaribo; Attendance: 1,200
Referee: Paul Ward (Canada)
SURINAME - DOMINICAN REPUBLIC 1-3(0-1)
SUR: Obrendo Huiswoud, Naldo Kwasie, Giovanni Alleyne, Marlon Felter, Friso Mando, Stefano Baneti (54.Jermain Sergio van Dijk), Giovanni Waal (77.Jetro Fer), Gregory Pokie, Stefano Rijssel, Milton Pinas (52.Orfeo Anautan), Giovanni Drenthe. Trainer: Kenneth Jaliens.
DOM: Miguel Lloyd, Johan Alberto Cruz De La Cruz, Francisco Ubiera, César Ledesma, César García Peralta, Rafael Ramírez Estasa, Kelvin De Jesús Severino Sosa, Inoel Navarro González (65.Kelvin Rafael Rodríguez Pichardo), Rafael Leonardo Flores, Erick Ozuna López (79.Domingo Antonio Peralta Florencio), Jonathan Rafael Faña Frias (90.Hansley Alexander Martínez García). Trainer: Clemente Domingo Hernández (Cuba).
Goals: 0-1 Jonathan Rafael Faña Frias (9), 0-2 Erick Ozuna López (47), 0-3 Erick Ozuna López (76), 1-3 Naldo Kwasie (81).
Cautions: Gregory Pokie, Orfeo Anautan / Jonathan Rafael Faña Frias, Francisco Ubiera, Erick Ozuna López.

11.10.2011, Estadio Cuscatlán, San Salvador; Attendance: 17,570
Referee: Hugo Cruz Alvarado (Costa Rica)
EL SALVADOR - CAYMAN ISLANDS 4-0(3-0)
SLV: Dagoberto Portillo Gamero, Moisés Xavier García Orellana, Steven Francis Gordon Purdy, Víctor Samuel Turcios Pacheco, Carlos Romeo Monteagudo Alfaro, Dennis Jonathan Alas Morales, Jaime Enrique Alas Morales, William Osael Romero Castillo (72.Herbert Arnoldo Sosa Burgos), Andrés Alexander Flores Mejía (79.Edwin Ernesto Sánchez Vigil), Rafael Edgardo Burgos (61.Christian Javier Bautista), Mark Léster Blanco Pineda. Trainer: Rubén Israel (Uruguay).
CAY: Anthony Ramon Sealy, Donovan Jedd Ebanks, Dion Brandon, Donald Solomon, Benjamin Cupid, Michael Johnson (87.Darvin Watson), Luigi Malcolm Hernández, Andre McFarlane, Alfredo Challenger (46.Demion Denzel Williams), Mark Ebanks (74.Derrin Ebanks), Theron Wood. Trainer: Carl Brown.
Goals: 1-0 Víctor Samuel Turcios Pacheco (6), 2-0 Steven Francis Gordon Purdy (13), 3-0 Jaime Enrique Alas Morales (45), 4-0 Herbert Arnoldo Sosa Burgos (88).
Cautions: Benjamin Cupid, Luigi Malcolm Hernández, Donald Solomon.

11.11.2011, Estadio Panamericano, San Cristóbal; Attendance: 1,000
Referee: José René Guerrero (Nicaragua)
DOMINICAN REPUBLIC - CAYMAN ISLANDS 4-0(2-0)
DOM: Miguel Lloyd (46.Wellington Agramonte), Johan Alberto Cruz De La Cruz, César García Peralta, Yohan Manuel Peña, Rafael Ramírez Estasa, Kelvin De Jesús Severino Sosa, Inoel Navarro González (74.Jack Michel Morillo), Domingo Antonio Peralta Florencio (57.Jimmy Reyes Bautista), Rafael Leonardo Flores, Erick Ozuna López, Kelvin Rafael Rodríguez Pichardo. Trainer: Clemente Domingo Hernández (Cuba).
CAY: Miguel Pitta, Donovan Jedd Ebanks, Andre McFarlane, Donald Solomon, Dion Brandon, Ian Lindo (65.Kemar Scott), Nicholas Phillip Ebanks, Derrin Ebanks (37.Matthew Suberan), Raheem Robinson, Jorronie McLean (59.Darvin Watson), Theron Wood. Trainer: Carl Brown.
Goals: 1-0 Inoel Navarro González (17), 2-0 Erick Ozuna López (38), 3-0 Kelvin Rafael Rodríguez Pichardo (64), 4-0 Jack Michel Morillo (79).
Cautions: Inoel Navarro González / Matthew Suberan, Darvin Watson.

11.11.2011, „André Kamperveen Stadion", Paramaribo; Attendance: 500
Referee: Marco Daniel Brea Despaigne (Cuba)
SURINAME - EL SALVADOR 1-3(0-1)
SUR: Obrendo Huiswoud, Naldo Kwasie, Jetro Fer, Marlon Felter, Friso Mando (80.Rocky Kaise), Stefano Baneti (82.Wirinder Somai), Giovanni Waal (69.Orfeo Anautan), Fabian van Dijk, Stefano Rijssel, Evani Esperance, Giovanni Drenthe. Trainer: Kenneth Jaliens.
SLV: Dagoberto Portillo Gamero, Moisés Xavier García Orellana, Steven Francis Gordon Purdy, Víctor Samuel Turcios Pacheco, Carlos Romeo Monteagudo Alfaro, Dennis Jonathan Alas Morales, Jaime Enrique Alas Morales (64.Christian Giovanni Castillo Martínez), William Osael Romero Castillo, Andrés Alexander Flores Mejía (61.Edwin Ernesto Sánchez Vigil), Eliseo Antonio Quintanilla Ortíz, Mark Léster Blanco Pineda (72.Walter Fabricio Soto Pineda). Trainer: Rubén Israel (Uruguay).
Goals: 0-1 Mark Léster Blanco Pineda (21), 0-2 Mark Léster Blanco Pineda (58), 0-3 Edwin Ernesto Sánchez Vigil (78), 1-3 Evani Esperance (81).
Cautions: Jetro Fer, Friso Mando.

14.11.2011, „Truman Bodden Stadium", George Town; Attendance: 1,750
Referee: James Matthew (Saint Kitts and Nevis)
CAYMAN ISLANDS - DOMINICAN REPUBLIC 1-1(0-1)
CAY: Miguel Pitta, Donovan Jedd Ebanks, Luigi Malcolm Hernández, Andre McFarlane, Donald Solomon, Ian Lindo (66.Raheem Robinson), Dion Brandon, Jairo Sánchez, Tex Whitelocke (78.Darvin Watson), Mark Ebanks (89.Alfredo Challenger), Theron Wood. Trainer: Carl Brown.
DOM: Wellington Agramonte, Johan Alberto Cruz De La Cruz, César García Peralta, Yohan Manuel Peña (81.Rafael Ramírez Estasa), Kelvin De Jesús Severino Sosa, Inoel Navarro González (68.Rafael Leonardo Flores), Hansley Alexander Martínez García, Erick Ozuna López (90.Domingo Antonio Peralta Florencio), Jimmy Reyes Bautista, Jonathan Rafael Faña Frias, Kelvin Rafael Rodríguez Pichardo. Trainer: Clemente Domingo Hernández (Cuba).
Goals: 0-1 César García Peralta (41), 1-1 Mark Ebanks (72).
Cautions: Theron Wood, Mark Ebanks.

15.11.2011, Estadio Cuscatlán, San Salvador; Attendance: 9,659
Referee: Javier Santos (Puerto Rico)

EL SALVADOR - SURINAME **4-0(1-0)**

SLV: Dagoberto Portillo Gamero, Moisés Xavier García Orellana, Steven Francis Gordon Purdy, Víctor Samuel Turcios Pacheco, Carlos Romeo Monteagudo Alfaro, Dennis Jonathan Alas Morales, Jaime Enrique Alas Morales, William Osael Romero Castillo, Christian Giovanni Castillo Martínez (57.Edwin Ernesto Sánchez Vigil), Eliseo Antonio Quintanilla Ortíz (71.Ramón Alfredo Sánchez Paredes), Mark Léster Blanco Pineda (67.Rafael Edgardo Burgos). Trainer: Rubén Israel (Uruguay).

SUR: Ronny Aloema, Marlon Felter, Naldo Kwasie, Stefano Baneti, Jetro Fer, Friso Mando, Fabian van Dijk, Giovanni Waal (78.Wirinder Somai), Stefano Rijssel, Evani Esperance (70.Rocky Kaise), Giovanni Drenthe (46.Orfeo Anautan). Trainer: Kenneth Jaliens.

Goals: 1-0 William Osael Romero Castillo (33), 2-0 William Osael Romero Castillo (62), 3-0 Rafael Edgardo Burgos (76), 4-0 Rafael Edgardo Burgos (83).

Cautions: Eliseo Antonio Quintanilla Ortíz / Stefano Baneti.

GROUP B

02.09.2011	Port Of Spain	Trinidad and Tobago - Bermuda	1-0(1-0)
02.09.2011	Providence	Guyana - Barbados	2-0(1-0)
06.09.2011	Bridgetown	Barbados - Trinidad and Tobago	0-2(0-1)
06.09.2011	Providence	Guyana - Bermuda	2-1(0-0)
07.10.2011	Bridgetown	Barbados - Guyana	0-2(0-0)
07.10.2011	Devonshire Parish	Bermuda - Trinidad and Tobago	2-1(0-0)
11.10.2011	Port Of Spain	Trinidad and Tobago - Barbados	4-0(1-0)
11.10.2011	Devonshire Parish	Bermuda - Guyana	1-1(0-0)
11.11.2011	Providence	Guyana - Trinidad and Tobago	2-1(1-0)
11.11.2011	Devonshire Parish	Bermuda - Barbados	2-1(1-1)
14.11.2011	Devonshire Parish	Barbados - Bermuda	1-2(0-0)
15.11.2011	Port Of Spain	Trinidad and Tobago - Guyana	2-0(0-0) Awarded 3-0

FINAL STANDINGS

1.	**Guyana**	6	4	1	1	9 - 6	13
2.	Trinidad and Tobago	6	4	0	2	12 - 4	12
3.	Bermuda	6	3	1	2	8 - 7	10
4.	Barbados	6	0	0	6	2 - 14	0

02.09.2011, „Hasely Crawford" Stadium, Port of Spain; Attendance: 6,000
Referee: Jafeth Perea (Panama)
TRINIDAD AND TOBAGO - BERMUDA 1-0(1-0)
TRI: Anthony Randolph Warner, Anthony Wolfe, Julius James, Seon Power, Akenhaton Carlos Edwards, Christopher Birchall, Hayden Tinto, Khaleem Hyland (36.Keon Kelly Daniel), Kenwyne Joel Jones (82.Clyde Leon), Stern John (53.Lester Stefan Peltier), Darryl Bevon Roberts. Trainer: Otto Pfister (Germany).
BER: Frederick Michael George Hall, Seion Darrell, Kamen Tucker, Roger Lee, DeVrae Tankard (62.Damon Ming), Reggie Lambe, Tyrell Allan Burgess (62.Lashun Dill), Taurean André Manders, Devaun Samuel DeGraff, Khano Smith, Nahki Wells (77.Zeiko Lewis). Trainer: Devarr Boyles.
Goal: 1-0 Kenwyne Joel Jones (45).
Cautions: Reggie Lambe.

02.09.2011, Providence Stadium, Providence; Attendance: 4,500
Referee: Canaan St. Catherine (Saint Lucia)
GUYANA - BARBADOS 2-0(1-0)
GUY: Ronson Williams, Jake Alexander Newton, Walter Andre Moore, Christopher Bourne (70.Travis Grant), Christopher Ronald Nurse, Dwain Jacobs, Charles Roylon Pollard, Kayode McKinnon, Shawn Beveney, Gregory Richardson (89.Anthony Abrams), Vurlon Mills (78.Trayon Bobb). Trainer: Jamaal Shabazz (Trinidad and Tobago).
BRB: Jason Boxhill, Barry Skeete, Omar Archer, Jason Lovell, Carl Joseph (38.Louis Alexander Moss), Renaldo Marquez, Norman Forde, Craig Worrell, Jonathan David Nurse, Kadeem Atkins (46.Dwayne Mars), Riviere Williams (77.Kyle Gibson). Trainer: Collin Forde.
Goals: 1-0 Shawn Beveney (26), 2-0 Charles Roylon Pollard (73).
Cautions: Christopher Ronald Nurse, Gregory Richardson / Barry Skeete, Norman Forde.

06.09.2011, Barbados National Stadium, Bridgetown; Attendance: 775
Referee: Elmer Arturo Bonilla (El Salvador)
BARBADOS - TRINIDAD AND TOBAGO **0-2(0-1)**
BRB: Jason Boxhill, Barry Skeete, Omar Archer (40.Rommelle Burgess), Johnathan Straker, Renaldo Marquez, Norman Forde, Ramuel Miller, Mario Harte (68.Kyle Gibson), Louis Alexander Moss (61.Kadeem Atkins), Jonathan David Nurse, Riviere Williams. Trainer: Collin Forde.
TRI: Marvin Phillip, Anthony Wolfe, Julius James, Seon Power, Akenhaton Carlos Edwards, Christopher Birchall (67.Khaleem Hyland), Hayden Tinto (90.Densill Theobald), Keon Kelly Daniel, Clyde Leon, Kenwyne Joel Jones, Darryl Bevon Roberts (75.Lester Stefan Peltier). Trainer: Otto Pfister (Germany).
Goals: 0-1 Keon Kelly Daniel (17), 0-2 Darryl Bevon Roberts (67).

06.09.2011, Providence Stadium, Providence; Attendance: 3,500
Referee: Mark Geiger (United States)
GUYANA - BERMUDA **2-1(0-0)**
GUY: Ronson Williams, Jake Alexander Newton, Walter Andre Moore, Christopher Bourne, Dwain Jacobs, Christopher Ronald Nurse, Travis Grant (82.Eusi Phillips), Charles Roylon Pollard, Kayode McKinnon, Shawn Beveney (70.Gregory Richardson), Vurlon Mills (90.Anthony Benfield). Trainer: Jamaal Shabazz (Trinidad and Tobago).
BER: Frederick Michael George Hall, Seion Darrell, Kamen Tucker, Roger Lee, DeVrae Tankard, Reggie Lambe (67.Angelo Simmons), Taurean André Manders, Devaun Samuel DeGraff, Nahki Wells (85.Quadir Maynard), Khano Smith, John Barry Nusum (61.Tyrell Allan Burgess). Trainer: Devarr Boyles.
Goals: 1-0 Vurlon Mills (50), 2-0 Vurlon Mills (60), 2-1 Khano Smith (90).
Cautions: Dwain Jacobs, Christopher Bourne / Khano Smith, Reggie Lambe, Roger Lee.

07.10.2011, Barbados National Stadium, Bridgetown; Attendance: 2,500
Referee: Alain Georges (Haiti)
BARBADOS - GUYANA **0-2(0-0)**
BRB: Jason Boxhill, Emmerson Orlando Boyce, Barry Skeete, Johnathan Straker, Ramuel Miller, Rommelle Burgess, Norman Forde, Renaldo Marquez (80.Dwayne Griffith), Tristan Parris (57.Kyle Gibson), Neil Anthony Cory Harvey, Diquan Adamson (69.Louis Alexander Moss). Trainer: Collin Forde.
GUY: Ronson Williams, Leon Cort, Charles Roylon Pollard, Jake Alexander Newton, Walter Andre Moore, Ricky Ulric Shakes (61.Anthony Abrams), Dwain Jacobs, Christopher Ronald Nurse, Shawn Beveney (80.Travis Grant), Kayode McKinnon, Howard Newton (71.Alinani Mounter). Trainer: Jamaal Shabazz (Trinidad and Tobago).
Goals: 0-1 Anthony Abrams (73), 0-2 Christopher Ronald Nurse (87).
Cautions: Ramuel Miller / Ricky Ulric Shakes, Christopher Ronald Nurse.

07.10.2011, Bermuda National Stadium, Devonshire Parish; Attendance: 2,243
Referee: Jeffrey Solís Calderón (Costa Rica)
BERMUDA - TRINIDAD AND TOBAGO **2-1(0-0)**
BER: Frederick Michael George Hall, Kamen Tucker, Tyrell Allan Burgess, DeVrae Tankard, Lashun Dill (67.Damon Ming), Kwame Steede, Taurean André Manders (85.Seion Darrell), Khano Smith, Antwan Russell, Nahki Wells (79.Christopher Caisey), John Barry Nusum. Trainer: Devarr Boyles.
TRI: Marvin Phillip, Akeem Adams, Julius James, Osei Telesford, Seon Power, Khaleem Hyland, Keon Kelly Daniel (67.Kevaughn Connell Ramsawack), Kevin Molino, Hayden Tinto (34.Hughton Hector), Lester Stefan Peltier, Stern John (59.Devon Jorsling). Trainer: Otto Pfister (Germany).
Goals: 1-0 Antwan Russell (52), 2-0 Nahki Wells (63), 2-1 Kevin Molino (82).
Cautions: Antwan Russell / Khaleem Hyland.
Sent off: Tahj-Michael Bell (30, on the bench).

11.10.2011, „Hasely Crawford" Stadium, Port of Spain; Attendance: 3,000
Referee: Raymond Bogle (Jamaica)

TRINIDAD AND TOBAGO - BARBADOS 4-0(1-0)

TRI: Marvin Phillip, Akeem Adams, Julius James, Osei Telesford, Seon Power, Khaleem Hyland, Kevin Molino (76.Kendall Maurice Jagdeosingh), Keon Kelly Daniel (46.Hayden Tinto), Lester Stefan Peltier, Stern John, Devon Jorsling (46.Hughton Hector). Trainer: Otto Pfister (Germany).

BRB: Jason Boxhill, Emmerson Orlando Boyce, Barry Skeete, Sheridan Grosvenor, Rommelle Burgess (46.Tristan Parris), Carl Joseph (24.Diquan Adamson), Renaldo Marquez (64.Dwayne Griffith), Norman Forde, Ramuel Miller, John Parris, Neil Anthony Cory Harvey. Trainer: Collin Forde.

Goals: 1-0 Lester Stefan Peltier (6), 2-0 Lester Stefan Peltier (55), 3-0 Lester Stefan Peltier (63), 4-0 Hughton Hector (90).

Cautions: Osei Telesford / Carl Joseph, Diquan Adamson.

11.10.2011, Bermuda National Stadium, Devonshire Parish; Attendance: 2,573
Referee: Rudolph Angela (Aruba)

BERMUDA - GUYANA 1-1(0-0)

BER: Frederick Michael George Hall, Tyrell Allan Burgess, Taurean André Manders, Antwan Russell (57.Devaun Samuel DeGraff), Kwame Steede, Khano Smith, Reggie Lambe (85.Angelo Simmons), DeVrae Tankard (62.Quadir Maynard), Kamen Tucker, Nahki Wells, John Barry Nusum. Trainer: Devarr Boyles.

GUY: Ronson Williams, Jake Alexander Newton, Leon Cort, Charles Roylon Pollard, Walter Andre Moore, Howard Newton (72.Anthony Abrams), Dwain Jacobs, Shawn Beveney, Kayode McKinnon, Travis Grant (85.Alinani Mounter), Vurlon Mills (59.Ricky Ulric Shakes). Trainer: Jamaal Shabazz (Trinidad and Tobago).

Goals: 1-0 John Barry Nusum (71), 1-1 Ricky Ulric Shakes (81).

Cautions: Antwan Russell.

11.11.2011, Providence Stadium, Providence; Attendance: 18,000
Referee: Enrico Wijngaarde (Suriname)

GUYANA - TRINIDAD AND TOBAGO 2-1(1-0)

GUY: Ronson Williams, Jake Alexander Newton, Leon Cort, Walter Andre Moore, Charles Roylon Pollard, Christopher Ronald Nurse, Carl Cort, Dwain Jacobs (75.Christopher Bourne), Kayode McKinnon (81.Travis Grant), Ricky Ulric Shakes, Gregory Richardson (60.Vurlon Mills). Trainer: Jamaal Shabazz (Trinidad and Tobago).

TRI: Marvin Phillip, Akeem Adams, Julius James, Seon Power, Christopher Birchall (38.Hughton Hector), Khaleem Hyland, Akenhaton Carlos Edwards, Lester Stefan Peltier (57.Stern John), Kevin Molino, Keon Kelly Daniel (55.Kendall Maurice Jagdeosingh), Kenwyne Joel Jones. Trainer: Otto Pfister (Germany).

Goals: 1-0 Ricky Ulric Shakes (10), 2-0 Leon Cort (81), 2-1 Kenwyne Joel Jones (90+3).

Cautions: Vurlon Mills, Christopher Bourne / Kevin Molino.

11.11.2011, Bermuda National Stadium, Devonshire Parish; Attendance: 1,000
Referee: Otto Ramón Barrios Díaz (Guatemala)

BERMUDA - BARBADOS 2-1(1-1)

BER: Mykal Crockwell (46.Dale Eve), Tyrell Allan Burgess, Damon Ming, Taurean André Manders, Domico Coddington, Devaun Samuel DeGraff (69.Angelo Simmons), Kwame Steede, DeVrae Tankard, Khano Smith, Quadir Maynard (62.Reggie Lambe), John Barry Nusum. Trainer: Devarr Boyles.

BRB: Jason Boxhill, Barry Skeete, Johnathan Straker, Rommelle Burgess (32.John Parris), Sheridan Grosvenor, Renaldo Marquez, Norman Forde, Kyle Gibson (25.Bentley Springer), Ramuel Miller, Dwayne Griffith (75.Dwayne Mars), Diquan Adamson. Trainer: Collin Forde.

Goals: 0-1 Diquan Adamson (7), 1-1 Khano Smith (28 penalty), 2-1 Kwame Steede (49).

Cautions: Tyrell Allan Burgess, DeVrae Tankard / Norman Forde, Renaldo Marquez, Diquan Adamson.

Sent off: Jason Boxhill (25).

14.11.2011, Bermuda National Stadium, Devonshire Parish (Bermuda); Attendance: 1,000
Referee: Roberto Moreno (Panama)
BARBADOS - BERMUDA 1-2(0-0)
BRB: Bentley Springer, Barry Skeete (80.Jason Lovell), Johnathan Straker, Sheridan Grosvenor, John Parris, Renaldo Marquez, Mario Harte (76.Dwayne Mars), Ramuel Miller, Dwayne Griffith, Kyle Gibson, Tristan Parris (69.Carl Joseph). Trainer: Collin Forde.
BER: Tahj-Michael Bell, Tyrell Allan Burgess, Taurean André Manders, Domico Coddington (56.Antwan Russell), Lashun Dill (65.Angelo Simmons), Devaun Samuel DeGraff, Kwame Steede, DeVrae Tankard, Khano Smith, John Barry Nusum (56.Damon Ming), Nahki Wells. Trainer: Devarr Boyles.
Goals: 0-1 Nahki Wells (46), 0-2 Khano Smith (72 penalty), 1-2 Sheridan Grosvenor (90+2).
Cautions: Tristan Parris, John Parris, Bentley Springer, Jason Lovell / John Barry Nusum, Khano Smith.

15.11.2011, „Hasely Crawford" Stadium, Port of Spain; Attendance: 2,000
Referee: Marlon Alfonso Mejía Carillo (El Salvador)
TRINIDAD AND TOBAGO - GUYANA 2-0(0-0)*
TRI: Marvin Phillip, Carlyle Mitchell, Akeem Adams, Osei Telesford, Seon Power, Akenhaton Carlos Edwards, Lester Stefan Peltier, Hughton Hector, Kevin Molino, Kendall Maurice Jagdeosingh, Kenwyne Joel Jones (81.Hayden Tinto). Trainer: Otto Pfister (Germany).
GUY: Richard Reynolds, Jake Alexander Newton, Christopher Bourne, Leon Cort, Walter Andre Moore, Dwain Jacobs, Charles Roylon Pollard (46.Taylor Benjamin), Anthony Benfield (62.Alinani Mounter), Travis Grant, Dwight Peters, Vurlon Mills (69.Colin Nelson). Trainer: Jamaal Shabazz (Trinidad and Tobago).
Goals: 1-0 Kenwyne Joel Jones (59), 2-0 Lester Stefan Peltier (69).
Cautions: Seon Power / Walter Andre Moore.
Please note: FIFA awarded a 3-0 win for Trinidad and Tobago.

GROUP C

Bahamas withdrew.

02.09.2011	Roseau	Dominica - Nicaragua	0-2(0-2)
06.09.2011	Managua	Nicaragua - Panama	1-2(1-1)
07.10.2011	Roseau	Dominica - Panama	0-5(0-2)
11.10.2011	Ciudad de Panamá	Panama - Nicaragua	5-1(1-0)
11.11.2011	Managua	Nicaragua - Dominica	1-0(0-0)
15.11.2011	Ciudad de Panamá	Panama - Dominica	3-0(2-0)

FINAL STANDINGS

1.	**Panama**	4	4	0	0	15 - 2	12
2.	Nicaragua	4	2	0	2	5 - 7	6
3.	Dominica	4	0	0	4	0 - 11	0

02.09.2011, Windsor Park, Roseau; Attendance: 3,000
Referee: Valdin Legister (Jamaica)
DOMINICA - NICARAGUA 0-2(0-2)
DMA: Glenson Prince, Elmond Derrick, Calvin Christopher, Jerome Thomas, Prince Austrie (69.Hubert Prince), Rashid Bertrand, Chad Bertrand, Euclid Bertrand (67.Craig Reid), Mitchell Joseph, Glensworth Elizee (75.Lester Langlais), Kurlson Benjamin. Trainer: Kirt Hector.
NCA: Denis Jesús Espinoza Camacho, Salvador Antonio García Acuña, Donald José Parrales Valverde, Josué Abraham Quijano Potosme, Maximo Arturo Gámez, Juan Ramón Barrera Pérez (75.Axel Mathias Villanueva Sandoval), Félix Eliud Zeledón Zeledón, Félix Dorian Rodríguez, Raúl Moisés Leguías Ávila, Daniel Salvador Reyes Avellán (68.Norfran Adán Lazo Morales), Samuel Israel Wilson Rostrán (89.Elvis Ángel Figueroa Pinell). Trainer: Enrique Llena León (Spain).
Goals: 0-1 Raúl Moisés Leguías Ávila (1), 0-2 Félix Dorian Rodríguez (36).
Cautions: Prince Austrie, Calvin Christopher, Chad Bertrand.

06.09.2011, Estadio Nacional de Fútbol, Managua; Attendance: 10,521
Referee: Oscar Reyna (Guatemala)
NICARAGUA - PANAMA 1-2(1-1)
NCA: Denis Jesús Espinoza Camacho, Salvador Antonio García Acuña, Manuel Salvador Gutiérrez Castro (52.Josué Abraham Quijano Potosme), David Sebastián Solórzano Sánchez, Daniel Zuñiga (62.Daniel Salvador Reyes Avellán), Juan Ramón Barrera Pérez (71.Axel Mathias Villanueva Sandoval), Maximo Arturo Gámez, Félix Eliud Zeledón Zeledón, Félix Dorian Rodríguez, Raúl Moisés Leguías Ávila, Samuel Israel Wilson Rostrán. Trainer: Enrique Llena León (Spain).
PAN: Jaime Manuel Penedo Cano, Eduardo César Dasent Paz, Adolfo Abdiel Machado, Román Aureliano Torres Morcillo, Luis Alfonso Henríquez Ledezma, Gabriel Enrique Gómez Giron, Amílcar Henríquez Espinosa, Nelson Alberto Barahona Collins (70.Gabriel Arturo Torres Tejada; 90.Eybir Bonaga Cerrud), Armando Cooper, Blas Antonio Miguel Pérez Ortega, Luis Carlos Tejada Hansell (88.Aníbal Cesis Godoy). Trainer: Jorge Luis Dely Valdes.
Goals: 0-1 Luis Carlos Tejada Hansell (7), 1-1 Román Aureliano Torres Morcillo (18 own goal), 1-2 Blas Antonio Miguel Pérez Ortega (50).
Cautions: Félix Eliud Zeledón Zeledón, Félix Dorian Rodríguez / Armando Cooper.

07.10.2011, Windsor Park, Roseau; Attendance: 4,000
Referee: Enrico Wijngaarde (Suriname)
DOMINICA - PANAMA **0-5(0-2)**
DMA: Glenson Prince, Prince Austrie, Hubert Prince, Calvin Christopher, Malcolm Joseph, Jerome Thomas (60.Craig Reid), Jonathan Abel, Rashid Bertrand (57.Joslyn Prince), Chad Bertrand, Kelly Peters, Mitchell Joseph (67.Lester Langlais). Trainer: Kirt Hector.
PAN: Jaime Manuel Penedo Cano, Felipe Abdiel Baloy Ramírez, Eduardo César Dasent Paz, Eric Davis, Roderick Miller, Ricardo Enrique Buitrago Medina, Eybir Bonaga Cerrud, Gabriel Enrique Gómez Giron, Johnny Ruíz (63.Alberto Abdiel Quintero Medina), Amir Waithe, Luis Carlos Tejada Hansell (54.Blas Antonio Miguel Pérez Ortega). Trainer: Jorge Luis Dely Valdes.
Goals: 0-1 Amir Waithe (26), 0-2 Luis Carlos Tejada Hansell (34), 0-3 Blas Antonio Miguel Pérez Ortega (55), 0-4 Ricardo Buitrago (62), 0-5 Amir Waithe (88).
Cautions: Calvin Christopher / Ricardo Enrique Buitrago Medina, Johnny Ruíz.

11.10.2011, Estadio „Rommel Fernández“, Ciudad de Panamá; Attendance: 10,846
Referee: Edenilson Ventura (El Salvador)
PANAMA - NICARAGUA **5-1(1-0)**
PAN: Jaime Manuel Penedo Cano, Felipe Abdiel Baloy Ramírez, Adolfo Abdiel Machado, Román Aureliano Torres Morcillo, Gabriel Enrique Gómez Giron, Amílcar Henríquez Espinosa, Alberto Abdiel Quintero Medina (70.Amir Waithe), Nelson Alberto Barahona Collins, Armando Cooper, Blas Antonio Miguel Pérez Ortega, Luis Carlos Tejada Hansell (82.Luis Gabriel Rentería). Trainer: Jorge Luis Dely Valdes.
NCA: Denis Jesús Espinoza Camacho, Maximo Arturo Gámez, Salvador Antonio García Acuña, Donald José Parrales Valverde, Josué Abraham Quijano Potosme, David Sebastián Solórzano Sánchez (52.Norfran Adán Lazo Morales), Juan Ramón Barrera Pérez, Félix Eliud Zeledón Zeledón (74.Daniel Salvador Reyes Avellán), Félix Dorian Rodríguez, Raúl Moisés Leguías Ávila, Samuel Israel Wilson Rostrán (61.Marcos Méndez). Trainer: Enrique Llena León (Spain).
Goals: 1-0 Luis Carlos Tejada Hansell (29), 2-0 Blas Antonio Miguel Pérez Ortega (49), 3-0 Blas Antonio Miguel Pérez Ortega (52), 4-0 Luis Carlos Tejada Hansell (64), 5-0 Blas Antonio Miguel Pérez Ortega (87), 5-1 Daniel Salvador Reyes Avellán (89).
Cautions: David Sebastián Solórzano Sánchez, Salvador Antonio García Acuña, Maximo Arturo Gámez.

11.11.2011, Estadio Nacional de Fútbol, Managua; Attendance: 2,100
Referee: Hugo Cruz Alvarado (Costa Rica)
NICARAGUA - DOMINICA **1-0(0-0)**
NCA: Denis Jesús Espinoza Camacho, Maximo Arturo Gámez, Salvador Antonio García Acuña, Donald José Parrales Valverde, Josué Abraham Quijano Potosme, Juan Ramón Barrera Pérez, Medardo Antonio Martínez Morales (57.Elvis Ángel Figueroa Pinell), Félix Eliud Zeledón Zeledón, Félix Dorian Rodríguez, Raúl Moisés Leguías Ávila (78.Ricardo Antonio Vega), Samuel Israel Wilson Rostrán (88.Marcos Méndez). Trainer: Enrique Llena León (Spain).
DMA: Glenson Prince, Prince Austrie, Elmond Derrick, Craig Reid, Hubert Prince (46.Jerome Thomas), Colin Bernard, Jonathan Abel, Rashid Bertrand, Chad Bertrand (80.Joslyn Prince), Mitchell Joseph, Kelly Peters (63.Kurlson Benjamin). Trainer: Kirt Hector.
Goal: 1-0 Raúl Moisés Leguías Ávila (57).
Cautions: Donald José Parrales Valverde / Mitchell Joseph, Colin Bernard, Chad Bertrand.

15.11.2011, Estadio „Rommel Fernández", Ciudad de Panamá; Attendance: 8,000
Referee: Terry Vaughn (United States)

PANAMA - DOMINICA **3-0(2-0)**

PAN: Kevin Melgar, Felipe Abdiel Baloy Ramírez, Roderick Miller, Sergio Thompson (67.Marcos Aníbal Sánchez Mullins), Rolando Antonio Algandona Teja, Ricardo Enrique Buitrago Medina, Aníbal Cesis Godoy, Gabriel Enrique Gómez Giron, Federico Marines (63.Johnny Ruíz), Armando Cooper, Rolando Manrique Blackburn Ortega (76.Blas Antonio Miguel Pérez Ortega). Trainer: Jorge Luis Dely Valdes.

DMA: Glenson Prince, Prince Austrie, Calvin Christopher, Craig Reid, Elmond Derrick, Colin Bernard, Joslyn Prince (46.Mitchell Joseph), Lester Langlais (84.Jerome Thomas), Jonathan Abel, Euclid Bertrand (73.Rashid Bertrand), Kurlson Benjamin. Trainer: Kirt Hector.

Goals: 1-0 Rolando Manrique Blackburn Ortega (7), 2-0 Ricardo Enrique Buitrago Medina (21), 3-0 Blas Antonio Miguel Pérez Ortega (84).

GROUP D

02.09.2011	Basseterre	Saint Kitts and Nevis - Puerto Rico	0-0
02.09.2011	Toronto	Canada - Saint Lucia	4-1(1-1)
06.09.2011	Gros Islet	Saint Lucia - Saint Kitts and Nevis	2-4(0-4)
06.09.2011	Bayamón	Puerto Rico - Canada	0-3(0-1)
07.10.2011	Bayamón	Puerto Rico - Saint Kitts and Nevis	1-1(1-0)
07.10.2011	Gros Islet	Saint Lucia - Canada	0-7(0-4)
11.10.2011	Toronto	Canada - Puerto Rico	0-0
11.10.2011	Basseterre	Saint Kitts and Nevis - Saint Lucia	1-1(0-0)
11.11.2011	Basseterre	Saint Kitts and Nevis - Canada	0-0
11.11.2011	Bayamón	Saint Lucia - Puerto Rico	0-4(0-2)
15.11.2011	Mayagüez	Puerto Rico - Saint Lucia	3-0(1-0)
15.11.2011	Toronto	Canada - Saint Kitts and Nevis	4-0(3-0)

FINAL STANDINGS

1.	**Canada**	6	4	2	0	18 - 1	14
2.	Puerto Rico	6	2	3	1	8 - 4	9
3.	Saint Kitts and Nevis	6	1	4	1	6 - 8	7
4.	Saint Lucia	6	0	1	5	4 - 23	1

02.09.2011, Warner Park, Basseterre; Attendance: 2,500
Referee: Ricardo Arellano Nieves (Mexico)
SAINT KITTS AND NEVIS - PUERTO RICO 0-0
SKN: Akil Byron, Kareem Harris, Joel Jeffers, Kareem Mitchum, Mudassa Howe, Orlando Mitchum, Gerard Williams, Ian Lake (68.Joeski Williams), Keith Jerome Gumbs (81.Tishan Hanley), Alexis Saddler (62.Devaughn Elliott), Jevon Francis. Trainer: Clinton Percival.
PUR: Terence Boss, John Krause, Cristian Arrieta, Alexis Rivera Curet (79.Jorge Rodríguez), Richard Andrew Martínez, Scott Horta, Scott Jones, Petter Enrique Villegas España (64.Tyler Linden Wilson), Noah Delgado, Andrés Pérez, Christopher Megaloudis (86.Héctor Omar Ramos Lebron). Trainer: Jeaustin Campos Madriz (Costa Rica).
Cautions: Mudassa Howe, Keith Jerome Gumbs / John Krause, Scott Jones.

02.09.2011, BMO Field, Toronto; Attendance: 11,500
Referee: Jair Marrufo (United States)
CANADA - SAINT LUCIA 4-1(1-1)
CAN: Lars Justin Hirschfeld, André Robert Hainault, Kevin James McKenna, Ante Jazić, Jonathan Beaulieu-Bourgault, Julien Bobby de Guzman, Atiba Hutchinson (69.William David Johnson), Joshua Christopher Simpson (69.Tosaint Antony Ricketts), Dwayne Anthony de Rosario, Iain Edward Hume (82.Marcus Haber), Simeon Alexander Jackson. Trainer: Stephen Hart (Trinidad & Tobago).
LCA: Iran Cassius, Bernard Edward (29.Fabian Joseph), Kurt Frederick, Pernal Williams, Hiram Hunte, Enderson George, Zaine Pierre (69.Cliff Valcin), Nathan Justin, Guy George (50.Kevin Edward), Tremain Paul, Jamil Joseph. Trainer: Alain Providence.
Goals: 1-0 Joshua Christopher Simpson Simpson (6), 1-1 Tremain Paul (7), 2-1 Dwayne Anthony de Rosario (50 penalty), 3-1 Joshua Christopher Simpson (61), 4-1 William David Johnson (90+1).
Cautions: Pernal Williams, Hiram Hunte.
Sent off: Pernal Williams (87).

06.09.2011, Beausejour Stadium, Gros Islet; Attendance: 2,005
Referee: Kevin Thomas (Jamaica)
SAINT LUCIA - SAINT KITTS AND NEVIS 2-4(0-4)
LCA: Iran Cassius, Bernard Edward, Kurt Frederick, Vernus Abbot, Hiram Hunte (56.Kevin Edward), Nathan Justin, Enderson George (58.Decoursey Simon), Zaine Pierre, Guy George (67.Cliff Valcin), Tremain Paul, Jamil Joseph. Trainer: Alain Providence.
SKN: Akil Byron, Kareem Harris, Joel Jeffers, Mudassa Howe, Kareem Mitchum, Gerard Williams, Orlando Mitchum (73.Tiran Hanley), Joeski Williams (70.Errol O'Loughlin), Devaughn Elliott (79.Alexis Saddler), Ian Lake, Jevon Francis. Trainer: Clinton Percival.
Goals: 0-1 Ian Lake (7), 0-2 Jevon Francis (12), 0-3 Orlando Mitchum (15), 0-4 Devaughn Elliott (44), 1-4 Zaine Pierre (65), 2-4 Cliff Valcin (84).
Cautions: Bernard Edward, Jamil Joseph / Ian Lake.

06.09.2011, Estadio „Juan Ramón Loubriel", Bayamón; Attendance: 4,000
Referee: Enrico Wijngaarde (Suriname)
PUERTO RICO - CANADA 0-3(0-1)
PUR: Eric Reyes, John Krause, Richard Andrew Martínez, Scott Horta, Alexis Rivera Curet, Cristian Arrieta (46.Héctor Omar Ramos Lebron), Noah Delgado, Scott Jones, Andrés Pérez (81.Jorge Rodríguez), Andrés Nicolás Cabrero Gómez, Christopher Megaloudis (57.Tyler Linden Wilson). Trainer: Jeaustin Campos Madriz (Costa Rica).
CAN: Lars Justin Hirschfeld, David Edward Edgar, André Robert Hainault, Kevin James McKenna, Michael Klukowski, Julien Bobby de Guzman, Terence Dunfield (62.Simeon Alexander Jackson), Joshua Christopher Simpson (83.Tosaint Antony Ricketts), Dwayne Anthony de Rosario, Iain Edward Hume, William David Johnson. Trainer: Stephen Hart (Trinidad & Tobago).
Goals: 0-1 Iain Edward Hume (42), 0-2 Simeon Alexander Jackson (84), 0-3 Tosaint Antony Ricketts (90+3).
Cautions: David Edward Edgar, Terence Dunfield.

07.10.2011, Estadio „Juan Ramón Loubriel", Bayamón; Attendance: 2,500
Referee: Neal Brizan (Trinidad and Tobago)
PUERTO RICO - SAINT KITTS AND NEVIS 1-1(1-0)
PUR: Brandon Saldaña, Richard Andrew Martínez, Alexis Rivera Curet, Scott Horta, Cristian Arrieta, Petter Enrique Villegas España, Scott Jones, Andrés Pérez (87.Marco Vélez), Andrés Nicolás Cabrero Gómez, Julian Cardona (53.Tyler Linden Wilson), Christopher Megaloudis (73.Noah Delgado). Trainer: Jeaustin Campos Madriz (Costa Rica).
SKN: Akil Byron, Kareem Harris, Gerard Williams, Kareem Mitchum, Joel Jeffers, Orlando Mitchum, Joeski Williams (60.Alexis Saddler), Thrizen Leader, Devaughn Elliott (57.George Isaac), Ian Lake (77.Terrance Warde), Jevon Francis. Trainer: Clinton Percival.
Goals: 1-0 Andrés Nicolás Cabrero Gómez (37), 1-1 Ian Lake (59).
Cautions: Andrés Pérez, Cristian Arrieta / Thrizen Leader.

07.10.2011, Beausejour Stadium, Gros Islet; Attendance: 1,005
Referee: Rolando Vidal (Panama)
SAINT LUCIA - CANADA 0-7(0-4)
LCA: Pessius Polius, Bernard Edward, Kurt Frederick, Pernal Williams, Vernus Abbot (74.Andreas Willie), Germal Valcin, Enderson George, Guy George (46.Kevin Edward), Cliff Valcin, Decoursey Simon (46.Jamil Joseph), Tremain Paul. Trainer: Alain Providence.
CAN: Kyriakos Stamatopoulos, David Edward Edgar, John Adam Straith, Ante Jazić, Julien Bobby de Guzman, Nikolas William Ledgerwood, Dwayne Anthony de Rosario (55.Joshua Christopher Simpson), Iain Edward Hume, William David Johnson (17.Terence Dunfield), Simeon Alexander Jackson (72.Ashtone Morgan), Olivier Occéan. Trainer: Stephen Hart (Trinidad & Tobago).
Goals: 0-1 Simeon Alexander Jackson (19), 0-2 Simeon Alexander Jackson (27), 0-3 Olivier Occéan (35), 0-4 Simeon Alexander Jackson (39), 0-5 Olivier Occéan (52), 0-6 Iain Edward Hume (73), 0-7 Iain Edward Hume (86).

11.10.2011, BMO Field, Toronto; Attendance: 12,178
Referee: Stanley Lancaster (Guyana)
CANADA - PUERTO RICO 0-0
CAN: Lars Justin Hirschfeld, David Edward Edgar, John Adam Straith, Ante Jazić, Julien Bobby de Guzman, Terence Dunfield, Nikolas William Ledgerwood, Joshua Christopher Simpson, Dwayne Anthony de Rosario, Iain Edward Hume (34.Olivier Occéan), Simeon Alexander Jackson (70.Tosaint Antony Ricketts). Trainer: Stephen Hart (Trinidad & Tobago).
PUR: Brandon Saldaña, Richard Andrew Martínez, Scott Horta, Alexis Rivera Curet, Cristian Arrieta, Petter Enrique Villegas España (57.Marco Vélez), Andrés Pérez, Scott Jones, Andrés Nicolás Cabrero Gómez, Héctor Omar Ramos Lebron (87.Stephan Barea), Tyler Linden Wilson (78.Christopher Megaloudis). Trainer: Jeaustin Campos Madriz (Costa Rica).
Cautions: Julien Bobby de Guzman / Andrés Pérez, Marco Vélez.

11.10.2011, Warner Park, Basseterre; Attendance: 1,000
Referee: Adrian Skeete (Barbados)
SAINT KITTS AND NEVIS - SAINT LUCIA 1-1(0-0)
SKN: Akil Byron, Kareem Harris, Joel Jeffers, Kareem Mitchum, Gerard Williams, Orlando Mitchum (69.Tiran Hanley), George Isaac, Thrizen Leader, Devaughn Elliott (73.Alexis Saddler), Ian Lake, Jevon Francis (61.Tishan Hanley). Trainer: Clinton Percival.
LCA: Iran Cassius, Kurt Frederick, Pernal Williams (55.Fabian Joseph), Nathan Justin, Germal Valcin, Kevin Edward, Enderson George (63.Decoursey Simon), Guy George, Cliff Valcin, Tremain Paul, Jamil Joseph (89.Vernus Abbot). Trainer: Alain Providence.
Goals: 0-1 Cliff Valcin (74), 1-1 Ian Lake (83).
Cautions: Pernal Williams.

11.11.2011, Warner Park, Basseterre; Attendance: 4,000
Referee: Elmer Arturo Bonilla (El Salvador)
SAINT KITTS AND NEVIS - CANADA 0-0
SKN: Akil Byron, Kareem Harris, Kareem Mitchum, Joel Jeffers, Gerard Williams, George Isaac, Akil Grier (63.Orlando Mitchum), Thrizen Leader, Errol O'Loughlin (87.Terrance Warde), Ian Lake (68.Matthew Anthony Berkeley), Keith Jerome Gumbs. Trainer: Clinton Percival.
CAN: Lars Justin Hirschfeld, David Edward Edgar, John Adam Straith, Ante Jazić, Michael Klukowski, Jonathan Beaulieu-Bourgault, Julien Bobby de Guzman, Joshua Christopher Simpson, Dwayne Anthony de Rosario (80.Olivier Occéan), William David Johnson (60.Tosaint Antony Ricketts), Simeon Alexander Jackson. Trainer: Stephen Hart (Trinidad & Tobago).

11.11.2011, Estadio „Juan Ramón Loubriel", Bayamón (Puerto Rico); Attendance: 350
Referee: Kenville Holder (Cayman Islands)
SAINT LUCIA - PUERTO RICO 0-4(0-2)
LCA: Iran Cassius, Kurt Frederick, Nathan Justin, Germal Valcin (46.Fabian Joseph), Pernal Williams, Enderson George, Kevin Edward, Guy George, Cliff Valcin (69.Vernus Abbot), Tremain Paul, Decoursey Simon (87.Teran John). Trainer: Alain Providence.
PUR: Eric Reyes, John Krause, Scott Horta, Richard Andrew Martínez, Alexis Rivera Curet, Cristian Arrieta, Noah Delgado (64.Tyler Linden Wilson), Joseph Marrero (73.Esdras Méndez), Scott Jones, Andrés Nicolás Cabrero Gómez, Héctor Omar Ramos Lebron (85.Gadiel Figueroa Robles). Trainer: Jeaustin Campos Madriz (Costa Rica).
Goals: 0-1 Cristian Arrieta (4), 0-2 Héctor Omar Ramos Lebron (14), 0-3 Héctor Omar Ramos Lebron (46), 0-4 Andrés Nicolás Cabrero Gómez (54).
Cautions: Scott Jones.
Sent off: Kevin Edward (82), Richard Andrew Martínez (82).

14.11.2011, Mayagüez Athletics Stadium, Mayagüez; Attendance: 1,050
Referee: Bryan Willett (Antigua and Barbuda)
PUERTO RICO - SAINT LUCIA 3-0(1-0)
PUR: Brandon Saldaña, John Krause, Alexis Rivera Curet, Cristian Arrieta, Scott Horta, Noah Delgado (90.Álvaro Betancourt), Joseph Marrero, Gadiel Figueroa Robles (71.Gustavo Rivera), Andrés Pérez, Andrés Nicolás Cabrero Gómez, Héctor Omar Ramos Lebron (90.Alex Oikkonen). Trainer: Jeaustin Campos Madriz (Costa Rica).
LCA: Iran Cassius, Fabian Joseph, Kurt Frederick, Vernus Abbot, Nathan Justin, Enderson George, Rickson Augustin, Teran John (88.Decoursey Simon), Andreas Willie, Cliff Valcin, Tremain Paul. Trainer: Alain Providence.
Goals: 1-0 Héctor Omar Ramos Lebron (13), 2-0 Héctor Omar Ramos Lebron (85), 3-0 Joseph Marrero (87).

15.11.2011, BMO Field, Toronto; Attendance: 10,235
Referee: Ricardo Cerdas Sánchez (Costa Rica)
CANADA - SAINT KITTS AND NEVIS 4-0(3-0)
CAN: Kyriakos Stamatopoulos, David Edward Edgar, Ashtone Morgan, John Adam Straith, Patrice Bernier (82.Jonathan Beaulieu-Bourgault), Nikolas William Ledgerwood (70.Nana Attakora-Gyan), Joshua Christopher Simpson, Dwayne Anthony de Rosario, William David Johnson, Olivier Occéan (70.Simeon Alexander Jackson), Tosaint Antony Ricketts. Trainer: Stephen Hart (Trinidad & Tobago).
SKN: Akil Byron, Joel Jeffers, Kareem Mitchum, Kareem Harris, Gerard Williams, George Isaac (65.Orlando Mitchum), Akil Grier (59.Tiran Hanley), Thrizen Leader, Errol O'Loughlin, Keith Jerome Gumbs, Ian Lake (58.Matthew Anthony Berkeley). Trainer: Clinton Percival.
Goals: 1-0 Olivier Occéan (27), 2-0 Dwayne Anthony de Rosario (35 penalty), 3-0 Joshua Christopher Simpson (45), 4-0 Tosaint Antony Ricketts (88).
Cautions: Ashtone Morgan, Nana Attakora-Gyan / Kareem Mitchum, Akil Grier, Kareem Harris.

GROUP E

02.09.2011	Cdad de Guatemala	Guatemala - Saint Vincent and the Grenadines	4-0(2-0)
02.09.2011	St. George's	Grenada - Belize	0-3(0-2)
06.09.2011	Belmopan	Belize - Guatemala	1-2(0-1)
18.09.2011	Kingstown	Saint Vincent and the Grenadines - Grenada	2-1(1-0)
07.10.2011	Kingstown	Saint Vincent and the Grenadines - Guatemala	0-3(0-1)
07.10.2011	Belmopan	Belize - Grenada	1-4(0-2)
11.10.2011	Cdad de Guatemala	Guatemala - Belize	3-1(1-1)
15.10.2011	St. George's	Grenada - Saint Vincent and the Grenadines	1-1(0-0)
11.11.2011	Cdad de Guatemala	Guatemala - Grenada	3-0(3-0)
11.11.2011	Belmopan	Belize - Saint Vincent and the Grenadines	1-1(1-1)
15.11.2011	Kingstown	Saint Vincent and the Grenadines - Belize	0-2(0-0)
15.11.2011	St. George's	Grenada - Guatemala	1-4(1-0)

FINAL STANDINGS

1.	**Guatemala**	6	6	0	0	19	-	3	18
2.	Belize	6	2	1	3	9	-	10	7
3.	Saint Vincent and the Grenadines	6	1	2	3	4	-	12	5
4.	Grenada	6	1	1	4	7	-	14	4

02.09.2011, Estadio Nacional „Mateo Flores", Ciudad de Guatemala; Attendance: 24,000
Referee: Erick Rigoberto Andino Medina (Honduras)
GUATEMALA - SAINT VINCENT AND THE GRENADINES 4-0(2-0)
GUA: Ricardo Antonio Jérez Figueroa, Gustavo Adolfo Cabrera Marroquín, Yony Wilson Flores Monroy, Cristian Jafeth Noriega Santizo, Jhonathan Winibakcer López Mejicanos (46.Mario Rafael Rodríguez Rodríguez), Marco Pablo Pappa Ponce (67.Freddy Alexander García Carrera), Gonzalo Antonio Romero Paz, Fredy Williams Thompson León, Wilfred Armando Velásquez González, Jairo Randolfo Arreola Silva, Minor Ignacio López Campollo (46.Tránsito Eduardo Montepeque Linares). Trainer: Ever Hugo Almeida Almada (Paraguay).
VIN: Dwayne Sandy, Keith James, Reginald Richardson, Cornelius Huggins, Roy Richards, Emerald George (51.Norrel George), Chad Balcombe, Devon Browne, Wendell Cuffy (56.Gregson Hazell), Myron Samuel, Shandel Samuel (83.Durwin Ross). Trainer: Colwyn Roger Rowe (England).
Goals: 1-0 Marco Pablo Pappa Ponce (14), 2-0 Yony Wilson Flores Monroy (30), 3-0 Mario Rafael Rodríguez Rodríguez (52), 4-0 Freddy Alexander García Carrera (71).
Cautions: Emerald George, Keith James, Chad Balcombe.
Sent off: Devon Browne (88).

02.09.2011, Grenada National Stadium, St. George's; Attendance: 2,600
Referee: David Rubalcaba (Cuba)
GRENADA - BELIZE 0-3(0-2)
GRN: Shemel Louison, David Cyrus, Raymond Dominique Alleyne, Kareem Joseph, Rickel Rick Leron Augustine, Shane Rennie, Wendell Rennie (78.Kevin Wellington), Junior Williams, Clive Naive Murray, Elliott Grant Charles (64.Lyndon Joseph), Ettienne Richardson (46.Nicko Williams). Trainer: Franklyn Simpson (Trinidad and Tobago).
BLZ: Shane Moody-Orio, Dalton Eiley, Ian Gaynair, Luis Méndez (65.Everal Trapp), Vallan Symms, Elroy Kuylen (88.David Trapp), Víctor Morales, Harrison Dwith Róchez, Ryan Simpson (74.Elroy Smith), Daniel Jiménez, Deon McCaulay. Trainer: José de la Paz Herrera Ucles (Honduras).
Goals: 0-1 Deon McCaulay (11), 0-2 Harrison Dwith Róchez (35), 0-3 Deon McCaulay (79).
Cautions: Shane Rennie, Elliott Grant Charles / Elroy Kuylen.

06.09.2011, FFB Field, Belmopan; Attendance: 3,027
Referee: Marlon Alfonso Mejía Carillo (El Salvador)

BELIZE - GUATEMALA 1-2(0-1)

BLZ: Shane Moody-Orio, Dalton Eiley, Ian Gaynair, Luis Méndez (46.Daniel Jiménez), Elroy Smith (46.Víctor Morales), Vallan Symms, Everal Trapp (67.Harrison Tasher), Elroy Kuylen, Harrison Dwith Róchez, Ryan Simpson, Deon McCaulay. Trainer: José de la Paz Herrera Ucles (Honduras).
GUA: Ricardo Antonio Jérez Figueroa, Gustavo Adolfo Cabrera Marroquín, Yony Wilson Flores Monroy, Rafael Humberto Morales de León, Cristian Jafeth Noriega Santizo, Jhonathan Winibakcer López Mejicanos (46.Marvin Tomás Ávila Sánchez), Marco Pablo Pappa Ponce, Mario Rafael Rodríguez Rodríguez (65.Freddy Alexander García Carrera), Fredy Williams Thompson León, Wilfred Armando Velásquez González (46.Minor Ignacio López Campollo), Jairo Randolfo Arreola Silva. Trainer: Ever Hugo Almeida Almada (Paraguay).
Goals: 0-1 Gustavo Adolfo Cabrera Marroquín (4), 0-2 Minor Ignacio López Campollo (75), 1-2 Deon McCaulay (77).
Cautions: Ryan Simpson / Cristian Jafeth Noriega Santizo.

18.09.2011, Arnos Vale Stadium, Kingstown; Attendance: 2,500
Referee: Paul Ward (Canada)

SAINT VINCENT AND THE GRENADINES - GRENADA 2-1(1-0)

VIN: Dwayne Sandy, Cornelius Huggins, Reginald Richardson, Roy Richards, Shorn Lowman, Jolanshoy Lamon McDowall, Shemol Trimmingham, Cornelius Stewart, Wendell Cuffy (68.Shandel Samuel), Damal Francis (61.Emerald George), Myron Samuel (83.Darren Hamlett). Trainer: Colwyn Roger Rowe (England).
GRN: Desmond Noel, Michael Mark, Cassim Langaigne, Marc Marshall (34.Dwayne Leo), Craig Aaron Rocastle, Anthony Augustine, Shane Rennie, Clive Naive Murray (75.Ashton Henry), Kyle Joseph (46.Junior Williams), Elliott Grant Charles, Marcus Julien. Trainer: Franklyn Simpson (Trinidad and Tobago).
Goals: 1-0 Myron Samuel (22), 2-0 Cornelius Stewart (72), 2-1 Cassim Langaigne (76).
Cautions: Shorn Lowman, Cornelius Stewart, Shemol Trimmingham, Darren Hamlett / Cassim Langaigne, Michael Mark.

07.10.2011, Arnos Vale Stadium, Kingstown; Attendance: 3,000
Referee: Marco Daniel Brea Despaigne (Cuba)

SAINT VINCENT AND THE GRENADINES - GUATEMALA 0-3(0-1)

VIN: Dwayne Sandy, Shorn Lowman, Cornelius Huggins, Reginald Richardson, Roy Richards, Shemol Trimmingham, Wendell Cuffy (64.Emerald George), Damal Francis (70.Romano Snagg), Jolanshoy Lamon McDowall, Cornelius Stewart, Myron Samuel (78.Shandel Samuel). Trainer: Colwyn Roger Rowe (England).
GUA: Ricardo Antonio Jérez Figueroa, Gustavo Adolfo Cabrera Marroquín, Yony Wilson Flores Monroy, Carlos Eduardo Gallardo Nájera, Cristian Jafeth Noriega Santizo, José Manuel Contreras y Contreras (60.Edwin Rafael González Ávalos), Jhonathan Winibakcer López Mejicanos (36.Dwight Anthony Pezzarossi García), Mario Rafael Rodríguez Rodríguez, Fredy Williams Thompson León, Wilfred Armando Velásquez González, Minor Ignacio López Campollo (65.Marvin Tomás Ávila Sánchez). Trainer: Ever Hugo Almeida Almada (Paraguay).
Goals: 0-1 Mario Rafael Rodríguez Rodríguez (44), 0-2 Mario Rafael Rodríguez Rodríguez (57), 0-3 Dwight Anthony Pezzarossi García (75).
Cautions: Cornelius Huggins, Cornelius Stewart, Jolanshoy Lamon McDowall.

07.10.2011, FFB Field, Belmopan; Attendance: 1,200
Referee: Franklin Jarquín (Nicaragua)

BELIZE - GRENADA **1-4(0-2)**

BLZ: Shane Moody-Orio, Dalton Eiley, Ian Gaynair, Elroy Smith, Elroy Kuylen, Víctor Morales, Harrison Dwith Róchez, Harrison Tasher, Orlando Jiménez (46.Ryan Simpson), Daniel Jiménez, Deon McCaulay (83.Evan Mariano). Trainer: José de la Paz Herrera Ucles (Honduras).

GRN: Josh Charles, Michael Mark, Cassim Langaigne, Anthony Augustine, Kimroy Redhead (72.Dwayne Leo), Ashton Henry, Craig Aaron Rocastle, Kyle Joseph (84.Raymond Dominique Alleyne), Shane Rennie, Clive Naive Murray, Marcus Julien. Trainer: Franklyn Simpson (Trinidad and Tobago).

Goals: 0-1 Shane Rennie (37), 0-2 Marcus Julien (41), 0-3 Kyle Joseph (50), 0-4 Clive Naive Murray (80), 1-4 Ryan Simpson (90).

Cautions: Elroy Kuylen, Orlando Jiménez, Harrison Dwith Róchez, Víctor Morales / Kimroy Redhead, Craig Aaron Rocastle.

11.10.2011, Estadio Nacional „Mateo Flores", Ciudad de Guatemala; Attendance: 21,107
Referee: José Peñaloza Soto (Mexico)

GUATEMALA - BELIZE **3-1(1-1)**

GUA: Ricardo Antonio Jérez Figueroa, Gustavo Adolfo Cabrera Marroquín, Yony Wilson Flores Monroy, Carlos Eduardo Gallardo Nájera, Cristian Jafeth Noriega Santizo (46.José Manuel Contreras y Contreras), Marco Pablo Pappa Ponce (46.Jhonathan Winibakcer López Mejicanos), Mario Rafael Rodríguez Rodríguez, Fredy Williams Thompson León, Wilfred Armando Velásquez González, Dwight Anthony Pezzarossi García (46.Minor Ignacio López Campollo), Carlos Humberto Ruíz Gutiérrez. Trainer: Ever Hugo Almeida Almada (Paraguay).

BLZ: Shane Moody-Orio (67.Woodrow West), Dalton Eiley (22.Everal Trapp), Ian Gaynair, Elroy Smith, Víctor Morales, Harrison Dwith Róchez, Ryan Simpson, Harrison Tasher (54.Luis Méndez), David Trapp, Daniel Jiménez, Deon McCaulay. Trainer: José de la Paz Herrera Ucles (Honduras).

Goals: 1-0 Carlos Eduardo Gallardo Nájera (6 penalty), 1-1 Deon McCaulay (31), 2-1 Minor Ignacio López Campollo (65), 3-1 Carlos Humberto Ruíz Gutiérrez (81).

Cautions: Dwight Anthony Pezzarossi García / Harrison Tasher, Shane Moody-Orio, Ryan Simpson.

Sent off: Everal Trapp (76).

11.10.2011, Grenada National Stadium, St. George's; Attendance: 2,000
Referee: Bryan Willett (Antigua and Barbuda)

GRENADA - SAINT VINCENT AND THE GRENADINES **1-1(0-0)**

GRN: Josh Charles, Anthony Augustine (88.Lyndon Joseph), Michael Mark, Patrick Modeste, Cassim Langaigne, Ashton Henry, Kevin Wellington (55.Clive Naive Murray), Kimroy Redhead (66.Kyle Joseph), Shane Rennie, Craig Aaron Rocastle, Marcus Julien. Trainer: Franklyn Simpson (Trinidad and Tobago).

VIN: Dwayne Sandy, Cornelius Huggins, Reginald Richardson, Roy Richards, Shorn Lowman, Jolanshoy Lamon McDowall, Shemol Trimmingham, Wendell Cuffy, Emerald George (80.Chad Balcombe), Myron Samuel (89.Durwin Ross), Shandel Samuel. Trainer: Colwyn Roger Rowe (England).

Goals: 0-1 Myron Samuel (62), 1-1 Clive Naive Murray (90+2).

11.11.2011, Estadio Nacional „Mateo Flores“, Ciudad de Guatemala; Attendance: 13,710
Referee: Neal Brizan (Trinidad and Tobago)
GUATEMALA - GRENADA 3-0(3-0)
GUA: Juan José Paredes Guzmán, Gustavo Adolfo Cabrera Marroquín, Yony Wilson Flores Monroy, Cristian Jafeth Noriega Santizo, Freddy Alexander García Carrera (75.Lisandro Francisco Pérez), Jhonathan Winibakcer López Mejicanos, Ángelo Alfonso Padilla, Guillermo Ramírez Ortega, Fredy Williams Thompson León (46.José Carlos Castillo), Wilfred Armando Velásquez González, Minor Ignacio López Campollo (46.Carlos Andrés Villa Perdomo). Trainer: Ever Hugo Almeida Almada (Paraguay).
GRN: Josh Charles, Michael Mark, Cassim Langaigne, Raymond Dominique Alleyne, Kyle Joseph, Finbar Williams, Shane Rennie, Kimroy Redhead (90.Kevin Wellington), Kareem Joseph (64.Lyndon Joseph; 71.Claude James), Clive Naive Murray, Marcus Julien. Trainer: Franklyn Simpson (Trinidad and Tobago).
Goals: 1-0 Freddy Alexander García Carrera (1), 2-0 Freddy Alexander García Carrera (31), 3-0 Ángelo Alfonso Padilla (45).
Cautions: Cristian Jafeth Noriega Santizo / Marcus Julien.

11.11.2011, FFB Field, Belmopan; Attendance: 300
Referee: Adrian Skeete (Barbados)
BELIZE - SAINT VINCENT AND THE GRENADINES 1-1(1-1)
BLZ: Woodrow West, Dalton Eiley, Ian Gaynair, Elroy Smith, Vallan Symms, Elroy Kuylen, Víctor Morales (84.Luis Méndez), Harrison Dwith Róchez (86.Evan Mariano), Harrison Tasher, David Trapp (61.Daniel Jiménez), Deon McCaulay. Trainer: José de la Paz Herrera Ucles (Honduras).
VIN: Dwayne Sandy, Cornelius Huggins, Roy Richards, Reginald Richardson, Cornelius Stewart, Chad Balcombe, Jolanshoy Lamon McDowall, Shemol Trimmingham, Wendell Cuffy (75.Romano Snagg), Myron Samuel (90.Durwin Ross), Shandel Samuel (60.Akeeno Hazelwood). Trainer: Colwyn Roger Rowe (England).
Goals: 0-1 Cornelius Stewart (11), 1-1 Deon McCaulay (22)
Cautions: Ian Gaynair / Jolanshoy Lamon McDowall, Shemol Trimmingham, Akeeno Hazelwood, Chad Balcombe, Cornelius Huggins.
Sent off: Shemol Trimmingham (89).

15.11.2011, Arnos Vale Stadium, Kingstown; Attendance: 500
Referee: Kevin Thomas (Jamaica)
SAINT VINCENT AND THE GRENADINES - BELIZE 0-2(0-0)
VIN: Dwayne Sandy, Shorn Lowman, Reginald Richardson, Roy Richards, Geroni Peters, Cornelius Stewart, Darren Hamlett (79.Damal Francis), Akeeno Hazelwood (60.Wendell Cuffy), Romano Snagg (52.Shandel Samuel), Myron Samuel, Durwin Ross. Trainer: Colwyn Roger Rowe (England).
BLZ: Woodrow West, Dalton Eiley, Ian Gaynair, Vallan Symms, Everal Trapp, Elroy Kuylen, Víctor Morales, Ryan Simpson (88.Khalil Velasquez), David Trapp, Daniel Jiménez, Deon McCaulay. Trainer: José de la Paz Herrera Ucles (Honduras).
Goals: 0-1 Deon McCaulay (78), 0-2 Deon McCaulay (81 penalty).
Cautions: Roy Richards, Reginald Richardson / Ian Gaynair, Everal Trapp.

15.11.2011, Grenada National Stadium, St. George's; Attendance: 200
Referee: Rudolph Angela (Aruba)
GRENADA - GUATEMALA **1-4(1-0)**
GRN: Josh Charles, Michael Mark, Cassim Langaigne, Kareem Joseph (86.Alec Jones), Nicko Williams, Kyle Joseph (69.Kimroy Redhead), Lyndon Joseph, Shane Rennie, Finbar Williams, Clive Naive Murray, Marcus Julien. Trainer: Franklyn Simpson (Trinidad and Tobago).
GUA: Ricardo Antonio Jérez Figueroa, Gustavo Adolfo Cabrera Marroquín, Carlos Mauricio Castrillo Alonzo, Yony Wilson Flores Monroy, Carlos Eduardo Gallardo Nájera, Marvin Tomás Ávila Sánchez (46.Freddy Alexander García Carrera), José Carlos Castillo, Jhonathan Winibakcer López Mejicanos (46.Ángelo Alfonso Padilla), Fredy Williams Thompson León, Jorge Eduardo Estrada Hidalgo (46.Guillermo Ramírez Ortega), Minor Ignacio López Campollo. Trainer: Ever Hugo Almeida Almada (Paraguay).
Goals: 1-0 Shane Rennie (37 penalty), 1-1 Nicko Williams (67 own goal), 1-2 Fredy Williams Thompson León (78), 1-3 Guillermo Ramírez Ortega (85), 1-4 Lyndon Joseph (90+2 own goal).
Cautions: Cassim Langaigne.
Sent off: Cassim Langaigne (62).

GROUP F

02.09.2011	St. John's	Antigua and Barbuda - Curaçao	5-2(2-1)
02.09.2011	Port-au-Prince	Haiti - US Virgin Islands	6-0(3-0)
06.09.2011	Frederiksted	US Virgin Islands - Antigua and Barbuda	1-8(0-2)
06.09.2011	Willemstad	Curaçao - Haiti	2-4(2-1)
07.10.2011	Willemstad	Curaçao - Antigua and Barbuda	0-1(0-0) Awarded 0-3
07.10.2011	Frederiksted	US Virgin Islands - Haiti	0-7(0-2)
11.10.2011	St. John's	Antigua and Barbuda - US Virgin Islands	10-0(5-0)
11.10.2011	Port-au-Prince	Haiti - Curaçao	2-2(1-2)
11.11.2011	Frederiksted	US Virgin Islands - Curaçao	0-3(0-3)
11.11.2011	St. John's	Antigua and Barbuda - Haiti	1-0(0-0)
15.11.2011	Willemstad	Curaçao - US Virgin Islands	6-1(2-0)
15.11.2011	Port-au-Prince	Haiti - Antigua and Barbuda	2-1(0-1)

FINAL STANDINGS

1.	**Antigua and Barbuda**	6	5	0	1	28	-	5	15
2.	Haiti	6	4	1	1	21	-	6	13
3.	Curaçao	6	2	1	3	15	-	15	7
4.	US Virgin Islands	6	0	0	6	2	-	40	0

02.09.2011, „Sir Vivian Richards" Stadium, North Sound; Attendance: 2,000
Referee: Javier Santos (Puerto Rico)
ANTIGUA AND BARBUDA - CURAÇAO 5-2(2-1)
ATG: Javid Joseph, Ranjae Christian, Marc Ellis Joseph, George Dublin, Roy Gregory, Justin Vincent Cochrane (78.Karanja Mack), Lawson Robinson (85.Stephan Smith), Quentin Griffith, Tamarley Thomas (69.Gayson Gregory), Randolph Burton, Peter Byers. Trainer: Thomas David Curtis (England).
CUW: Wencho Farrell, Ryangelo Cijntje, Cuco Martina, Bryan Anastatia (46.Raynick Damasco), Anton Jongsma, Angelo Zimmerman (70.Orin de Waard), Christy Bonevacia, Sorandley Tomsjansen, Dyron Rudolph Daal (64.Gillian Justiana), Rihairo Meulens, Richmar Simon Sabino Siberie. Trainer: Manuel Reinaldo Bilches (Argentina).
Goals: 0-1 Rihairo Meulens (9), 1-1 Marc Ellis Joseph (42), 2-1 Quentin Griffith (45), 3-1 Tamarley Thomas (54), 3-2 Richmar Simon Sabino Siberie (74), 4-2 Peter Byers (75), 5-2 Peter Byers (80).
Cautions: Bryan Anastatia, Christy Bonevacia, Dyron Rudolph Daal.

02.09.2011, Stade „Sylvio Cator", Port-au-Prince; Attendance: 12,000
Referee: Hugo Cruz Alvarado (Costa Rica)
HAITI - US VIRGIN ISLANDS 6-0(3-0)
HAI: Steward Ceus, Kevin Pierre Lafrance, Jean-Jacques Pierre, Judelin Aveska, Wild-Donald Guerrier, Kennel Listner Pierre-Louis (46.Gary Ambroise), Charles Hérold (46.Jean-Sony Alcenat), Jean Monuma-Constant, James Marcelin, Jean-Eudes Maurice, Kervens Belfort Fils (46.Jean-Marc Alexandre). Trainer: Edson Araujo Tavares (Brazil).
VIR: Carlos Claxton, Ayinde Augustus, Lishati-Shumba Bailey (66.Kellen Ganiko), John Phillip, Alberto Van Gurp, Derrick Smith, Jamie Browne (46.Alexander Nissman), Dwayne Thomas, Reid William Klopp, Junior Laurencin (72.Joseph Limeburner), Andres Caesar. Trainer: Terrence Jones.
Goals: 1-0 James Marcelin (18), 2-0 Jean-Eudes Maurice (27), 3-0 Kennel Listner Pierre-Louis (44), 4-0 Jean Monuma-Constant (61), 5-0 Jean-Marc Alexandre (65), 6-0 Jean-Marc Alexandre (79).
Cautions: Charles Hérold, Jean Monuma-Constant.

06.09.2011, „Paul E. Joseph“ Stadium, Frederiksted; Attendance: 250
Referee: Stanley Lancaster (Guyana)
US VIRGIN ISLANDS - ANTIGUA AND BARBUDA 1-8(0-2)
VIR: Dillon Pieffer, Ayinde Augustus, Lishati-Shumba Bailey, Alberto Van Gurp, Derrick Smith, Keithroy Cornelius, Jamie Browne, Dwayne Thomas (71.John Phillip), Kellen Ganiko (57.Alexander Nissman), Junior Laurencin (63.Chad Walter), Andres Caesar. Trainer: Terrence Jones.
ATG: Javid Joseph, Ranjae Christian, Roy Gregory, Justin Vincent Cochrane (72.Jamie Thomas), Lawson Robinson, George Dublin, Quentin Griffith, Karanja Mack, Akeem Thomas (57.Kerry Kadie Skepple), Randolph Burton, Peter Byers (86.Elvis Thomas). Trainer: Thomas David Curtis (England).
Goals: 0-1 Ranjae Christian (18), 0-2 Peter Byers (38 penalty), 0-3 Justin Vincent Cochrane (47), 1-3 Jamie Browne (49), 1-4 Peter Byers (51), 1-5 George Dublin (54), 1-6 Peter Byers (57), 1-7 Randolph Burton (68), 1-8 Randolph Burton (74).
Cautions: Justin Vincent Cochrane, Karanja Mack.

06.09.2011, Stadion „Ergilio Hato“, Willemstad; Attendance: 5,000
Referee: Jeffrey Solís Calderón (Costa Rica)
CURAÇAO - HAITI 2-4(2-1)
CUW: Wencho Farrell (65.Rowendy Sumter), Ryangelo Cijntje, Cuco Martina, Javier Martina, Anton Jongsma, Angelo Zimmerman (83.Raynick Damasco), Christy Bonevacia, Shanon Carmelia, Gillian Justiana, Orin de Waard (57.Gersinio Constancia), Richmar Simon Sabino Siberie. Trainer: Manuel Reinaldo Bilches (Argentina).
HAI: Steward Ceus, Kevin Pierre Lafrance (46.Kervens Belfort Fils), Jean-Jacques Pierre, Judelin Aveska, Wild-Donald Guerrier, Kennel Listner Pierre-Louis (69.Jean Monuma-Constant), Jean-Sony Alcenat, Charles Hérold, James Marcelin, Jean-Marc Alexandre, Jean-Eudes Maurice (80.Gary Ambroise). Trainer: Edson Araujo Tavares (Brazil).
Goals: 1-0 Orin de Waard (12), 1-1 Kevin Pierre Lafrance (37), 2-1 Angelo Zimmerman (43), 2-2 James Marcelin (58), 2-3 Wild-Donald Guerrier (61), 2-4 Angelo Zimmerman (75 own goal).
Cautions: Christy Bonevacia / Kevin Pierre Lafrance, Kervens Belfort Fils.

07.10.2011, Stadion „Ergilio Hato“, Willemstad; Attendance: 2,563
Referee: Oscar Reyna (Guatemala)
CURAÇAO - ANTIGUA AND BARBUDA 0-1(0-0)*
CUW: Rugenio Josephia, Ryangelo Cijntje, Hubertson Pauletta (79.Javier Martina), Cuco Martina, Nuelson Wau, Christy Bonevacia (83.Everon Espacia), Shanon Carmelia, Orlando Smeekes, Sendley Bito, Dyron Rudolph Daal, Richmar Simon Sabino Siberie (87.Mirco Colina). Trainer: Manuel Reinaldo Bilches (Argentina).
ATG: Molvin James, Akeem Thomas (89.Brian Edwards), George Dublin, Marc Ellis Joseph, Quentin Griffith, Mikele Benjamin Leigertwood, Tamarley Thomas (83.Ranjae Christian), Randolph Burton, Kieran Zac Murtagh, Lawson Robinson, Peter Byers. Trainer: Thomas David Curtis (England).
Goal: 0-1 Tamarley Thomas (73).
Cautions: Dyron Rudolph Daal / Randolph Burton.
**Please note:* FIFA awarded a 3-0 win gor Antigua and Barbuda.*

07.10.2011, „Paul E. Joseph“ Stadium, Frederiksted; Attendance: 406
Referee: Kenville Holder (Cayman Islands)
US VIRGIN ISLANDS - HAITI **0-7(0-2)**
VIR: Dillon Pieffer, Ayinde Augustus, Lishati-Shumba Bailey, Kellen Ganiko, Clifford Adams, Keithroy Cornelius (88.Andre Christof Thomas), Dusty Good, Garrick Mathurin (87.Chad Walter), Michael Beharry (46.Adam Fuller), Dwayne Trimm, Dereck Villafana. Trainer: Terrence Jones.
HAI: Steward Ceus, Kim Jaggy, Jean-Jacques Pierre, Judelin Aveska, Frantz Bertin, Kennel Listner Pierre-Louis, Réginal Goreux, Charles Hérold (46.Peterson Joseph), James Marcelin (46.Jean-Sony Alcenat), Jean-Marc Alexandre (46.Kervens Belfort Fils), Jean-Eudes Maurice. Trainer: Edson Araujo Tavares (Brazil).
Goals: 0-1 Jean-Eudes Maurice (5), 0-2 Kim Jaggy (11), 0-3 Réginal Goreux (57), 0-4 Réginal Goreux (64), 0-5 Jean-Eudes Maurice (65 penalty), 0-6 Kervens Belfort Fils (73 penalty), 0-7 Jean-Eudes Maurice (82).
Cautions: Garrick Mathurin, Clifford Adams, Dillon Pieffer / Jean-Eudes Maurice.

11.10.2011, „Sir Vivian Richards“ Stadium, North Sound; Attendance: 1,500
Referee: James Matthew (Saint Kitts and Nevis)
ANTIGUA AND BARBUDA - US VIRGIN ISLANDS **10-0(5-0)**
ATG: Molvin James, George Dublin, Marc Ellis Joseph, Ranjae Christian, Kieran Zac Murtagh, Quentin Griffith, Karanja Mack, Tamarley Thomas, Randolph Burton (78.Jamie Thomas), Lawson Robinson (60.Kerry Kadie Skepple), Peter Byers (74.Elvis Thomas). Trainer: Thomas David Curtis (England).
VIR: Dillon Pieffer, Ayinde Augustus, Lishati-Shumba Bailey, Alberto Van Gurp, Kellen Ganiko, Clifford Adams (46.Joseph Limeburner), Keithroy Cornelius, Dusty Good (68.Adam Fuller), Garrick Mathurin (60.Chad Walter), Michael Beharry, Dwayne Trimm. Trainer: Terrence Jones.
Goals: 1-0 Tamarley Thomas (7), 2-0 Peter Byers (24), 3-0 Peter Byers (31), 4-0 Peter Byers (40), 5-0 Tamarley Thomas (41), 6-0 Randolph Burton (55), 7-0 Randolph Burton (65), 8-0 Tamarley Thomas (78), 9-0 Jamie Thomas (86), 10-0 Kieran Zac Murtagh (90).

11.10.2011, Stade „Sylvio Cator“, Port-au-Prince; Attendance: 7,800
Referee: Leon Clarke (Saint Lucia)
HAITI - CURAÇAO **2-2(1-2)**
HAI: Steward Ceus, Kim Jaggy, Jean-Jacques Pierre, Frantz Bertin, Judelin Aveska (46.James Marcelin), Jean-Sony Alcenat, Réginal Goreux (66.Wild-Donald Guerrier), Charles Hérold, Peterson Joseph, Kervens Belfort Fils, Jean-Eudes Maurice. Trainer: Edson Araujo Tavares (Brazil).
CUW: Rugenio Josephia, Ryangelo Cijntje, Hubertson Pauletta, Cuco Martina, Nuelson Wau, Christy Bonevacia (84.Everon Espacia), Shanon Carmelia, Javier Martina (85.Mirco Colina), Orlando Smeekes (72.Charles Martina), Sendley Bito, Richmar Simon Sabino Siberie. Trainer: Manuel Reinaldo Bilches (Argentina).
Goals: 0-1 Richmar Simon Sabino Siberie (7), 0-2 Sendley Bito (14), 1-2 Jean-Eudes Maurice (25 penalty), 2-2 Kervens Belfort Fils (60).
Cautions: Charles Hérold / Ryangelo Cijntje, Cuco Martina, Everon Espacia.

11.11.2011, „Paul E. Joseph“ Stadium, Frederiksted; Attendance: 210
Referee: Mauricio Navarro (Canada)
US VIRGIN ISLANDS - CURAÇAO **0-3(0-3)**
VIR: Dillon Pieffer, Ayinde Augustus, Lishati-Shumba Bailey, Kellen Ganiko, Derrick Smith, Dwayne Thomas, Keithroy Cornelius, Chad Walter (82.Joseph Limeburner), Reid William Klopp (56.Garrick Mathurin), McCoy Livingston, Dwayne Trimm (72.Alex Washington). Trainer: Terrence Jones.
CUW: Rugenio Josephia, Ryangelo Cijntje (68.Joël Victoria), Hubertson Pauletta (30.Fernando Zimmerman), Cuco Martina, Glenciéne Gregoria, Christy Bonevacia, Shanon Carmelia (74.Frenly Servania), Everon Espacia, Daymon Lodovica, Sendley Bito, Richmar Simon Sabino Siberie. Trainer: Manuel Reinaldo Bilches (Argentina).
Goals: 0-1 Richmar Simon Sabino Siberie (8), 0-2 Richmar Simon Sabino Siberie (14), 0-3 Sendley

Bito (26).
Cautions: Dillon Pieffer, Dwayne Thomas / Shanon Carmelia.

11.11.2011, „Sir Vivian Richards" Stadium, North Sound; Attendance: 8,000
Referee: José Benigno Pineda Fernández (Honduras)
ANTIGUA AND BARBUDA - HAITI 1-0(0-0)
ATG: Molvin James, Marvin McCoy, George Dublin, Marc Ellis Joseph, Quentin Griffith (90.Karanja Mack), Tamarley Thomas, Mikele Benjamin Leigertwood, Kieran Zac Murtagh, Randolph Burton (90.Ranjae Christian), Lawson Robinson (76.Kerry Kadie Skepple), Peter Byers. Trainer: Thomas David Curtis (England).
HAI: Johnathan Placide, Judelin Aveska, Kim Jaggy (87.Wild-Donald Guerrier), Jean-Jacques Pierre, Lecsinel Jean-François, Jean-Sony Alcenat, Kennel Listner Pierre-Louis (84.Kervens Belfort Fils), Jeff Louis, Jean-Marc Alexandre, Jean Michel Alexandre Boucicaut (55.Sony Norde), Jean-Eudes Maurice. Trainer: Edson Araujo Tavares (Brazil).
Goal: 1-0 Kerry Kadie Skepple (81).
Cautions: Lawson Robinson, Peter Byers / Jean Michel Alexandre Boucicaut, Jean-Marc Alexandre, Judelin Aveska, Sony Norde.

15.11.2011, Stadion „Ergilio Hato", Willemstad; Attendance: 2,000
Referee: Valdin Legister (Jamaica)
CURAÇAO - US VIRGIN ISLANDS 6-1(2-0)
CUW: Rugenio Josephia, Ryangelo Cijntje, Cuco Martina, Glenciéne Gregoria, Christy Bonevacia, Shanon Carmelia, Fernando Zimmerman (43.Marcello Michelangel Anthony Pisas), Everon Espacia (81.Frenly Servania), Daymon Lodovica (56.Joël Victoria), Sendley Bito, Richmar Simon Sabino Siberie. Trainer: Manuel Reinaldo Bilches (Argentina).
VIR: Terrence Jones, Ayinde Augustus, Lishati-Shumba Bailey, Derrick Smith, Alberto Van Gurp, Kellen Ganiko (88.Andre Christof Thomas), Dwayne Thomas (69.Alex Washington), McCoy Livingston, Keithroy Cornelius, Reid William Klopp (77.Chad Walter), Dwayne Trimm. Trainer: Terrence Jones / Eustace Bailey.
Goals: 1-0 Shanon Carmelia (33), 2-0 Richmar Simon Sabino Siberie (40), 2-1 Keithroy Cornelius (51), 3-1 Everon Espacia (73), 4-1 Shanon Carmelia (78), 5-1 Richmar Simon Sabino Siberie (86), 6-1 Ryangelo Cijntje (90).
Cautions: Fernando Zimmerman.
Sent off: Rugenio Josephia (42).

15.11.2011, Stade „Sylvio Cator", Port-au-Prince; Attendance: 3,000
Referee: Baldomero Toledo (United States)
HAITI - ANTIGUA AND BARBUDA 2-1(0-1)
HAI: Johnathan Placide, Kim Jaggy, Jean-Jacques Pierre, Lecsinel Jean-François (46.Jean Monuma-Constant), Frantz Bertin, Judelin Aveska, Jean-Sony Alcenat, Jeff Louis (44.Ricardo Charles), Jean-Marc Alexandre, Kervens Belfort Fils, Jean-Eudes Maurice (80.Wild-Donald Guerrier). Trainer: Carlo Marcelin.
ATG: Molvin James, Karanja Mack, George Dublin, Quentin Griffith, Mikele Benjamin Leigertwood, Marc Ellis Joseph, Tamarley Thomas, Lawson Robinson (85.Eugene Kirwan), Justin Vincent Cochrane (62.Ranjae Christian), Randolph Burton, Peter Byers (78.Kerry Kadie Skepple). Trainer: Thomas David Curtis (England).
Goals: 0-1 Tamarley Thomas (10), 1-1 Judelin Aveska (60), 2-1 Kervens Belfort Fils (67).
Cautions: Frantz Bertin / Kerry Kadie Skepple.

THIRD ROUND
(08.06.2011 – 16.10.2012)

12 qualified teams were seeded into 3 pots:

Pot 1: United States, Mexico, Honduras.
Pot 2: Jamaica, Costa Rica, Cuba.
Pot 3: El Salvador, Guyana, Panama, Canada, Guatemala, Antigua and Barbuda.

The three qualifying groups of the 3rd Round are as follows:

GROUP A	GROUP B	GROUP C
United States	Mexico	Honduras
Jamaica	Costa Rica	Cuba
Guatemala	El Salvador	Panama
Antigua and Barbuda	Guyana	Canada

GROUP A

08.06.2012	Tampa	United States – Antigua and Barbuda	3-1(2-0)
08.06.2012	Kingston	Jamaica - Guatemala	2-1(1-0)
12.06.2012	North Sound	Antigua and Barbuda - Jamaica	0-0
12.06.2012	Cdad de Guatemala	Guatemala – United States	1-1(0-1)
07.09.2012	Kingston	Jamaica – United States	2-1(1-1)
07.09.2012	Cdad de Guatemala	Guatemala – Antigua and Barbuda	3-1(0-1)
11.09.2012	North Sound	Antigua and Barbuda – Guatemala	0-1(0-1)
11.09.2012	Columbus	United States – Jamaica	1-0(0-0)
12.10.2012	North Sound	Antigua and Barbuda – United States	1-2(1-1)
12.10.2012	Cdad de Guatemala	Guatemala – Jamaica	2-1(1-0)
16.10.2012	Kansas City	United States – Guatemala	3-1(3-1)
16.10.2012	Kingston	Jamaica – Antigua and Barbuda	4-1(2-0)

FINAL STANDINGS

1.	**United States**	6	4	1	1	11 - 6	13
2.	**Jamaica**	6	3	1	2	9 - 6	10
3.	Guatemala	6	3	1	2	9 - 8	10
4.	Antigua and Barbuda	6	0	1	5	4 - 13	1

08.06.2012, „Raymond James“ Stadium, Tampa; Attendance: 23,971
Referee: Hugo Cruz Alvarado (Costa Rica)
UNITED STATES – ANTIGUA AND BARBUDA 3-1(2-0)
USA: Timothy Matthew Howard, Steven Emil Cherundolo, Clarence Goodson, Carlos Manuel Bocanegra, José Francisco Torres Mezzell (57.Oguchialu Chijioke Onyewu Onyewu), Edu Maurice Edu Jr., Michael Sheehan Bradley, Jermaine Jones (81.Terrence Anthony Boyd), Landon Timothy Donovan, Clinton Drew Dempsey, Herculez Gomez Hurtado (80.Josmer Volmy Altidore). Trainer: Jürgen Klinsmann (Germany).
ATG: Molvin James, Marvin Anthony McCoy, George Dublin, Marc Ellis Joseph, Quentin Griffith, Mikele Benjamin Leigertwood, Lawson Robinson, Tamarley Thomas (83.Stephan Smith), Keiran Zac Murtagh (63.Peter Byers), Randolph Burton, Dexter Anthony Titus Blackstock. Trainer: Thomas David Curtis (England).
Goals: 1-0 Carlos Manuel Bocanegra (8), 2-0 Clinton Drew Dempsey (44 penalty), 2-1 Peter Byers (65), 3-1 Herculez Gomez Hurtado (72).

Cautions: Marc Ellis Joseph, Quentin Griffith.

08.06.2012, Independence Park, Kingston; Attendance: 14,000
Referee: Roberto Moreno (Panama)
JAMAICA - GUATEMALA **2-1(1-0)**
JAM: Donovan Ricketts (13.Dwayne Miller), Nyron Paul Henry Nosworthy, Adrian Joseph Mariappa, Lovel Palmer, Demar Constantine Phillips, Jason Morrison, JeVaughn Watson, Rodolph Austin, Luton George Shelton (69.Ricardo Dwayne Fuller), Dane Richards, Ryan Johnson (87.Tremaine Stewart). Trainer: Theodore Whitmore.
GUA: Ricardo Antonio Jérez Figueroa, Carlos Eduardo Gallardo Nájera, Erwin Armando Morales Hernández, Elías Enoc Vásquez Prera, Luis Ricardo Rodríguez Jérez, Wilfred Armando Velásquez González, Marco Pablo Pappa Ponce (46.Mario Rafael Rodríguez Rodríguez), Jhonathan Winibakcer López Mejicanos, Alejandro Miguel Galindo (46.José Manuel Contreras y Contreras), Jairo Randolfo Arreola Silva (46.Dwight Anthony Pezzarossi García), Carlos Humberto Ruíz Gutiérrez. Trainer: Ever Hugo Almeida Almada (Paraguay).
Goals: 1-0 Demar Constantine Phillips (40), 2-0 Ryan Johnson (46), 2-1 Dwight Anthony Pezzarossi García (90+2).

12.06.2012, „Sir Vivian Richards" Stadium, North Sound; Attendance: 8,500
Referee: Stanley Lancaster (Guyana)
ANTIGUA AND BARBUDA - JAMAICA **0-0**
ATG: Molvin James, Marvin Anthony McCoy, George Dublin, Marc Ellis Joseph, Quentin Griffith, Lawson Robinson, Keiran Zac Murtagh (73.Stephan Smith), Mikele Benjamin Leigertwood, Tamarley Thomas (88.Joshua Kevin Stanley Parker), Randolph Burton, Peter Byers. Trainer: Thomas David Curtis (England).
JAM: Dwayne Miller, Nyron Paul Henry Nosworthy, Jason Morrison, Lovel Palmer, Adrian Joseph Mariappa, Demar Constantine Phillips, JeVaughn Watson, Rodolph Austin, Luton George Shelton (64.Tremaine Stewart), Dane Richards (74.Errol Anthony Stevens), Ryan Johnson (87.Ricardo Dwayne Fuller). Trainer: Theodore Whitmore.
Cautions: Marc Ellis Joseph / Jason Morrison.

12.06.2012, Estadio Nacional „Mateo Flores", Ciudad de Guatemala; Attendance: 18,000
Referee: Joel Antonio Aguilar Chicas (El Salvador)
GUATEMALA – UNITED STATES **1-1(0-1)**
GUA: Ricardo Antonio Jérez Figueroa, Carlos Eduardo Gallardo Nájera, Erwin Armando Morales Hernández, Elías Enoc Vásquez Prera, José Manuel Contreras y Contreras (46.Marco Pablo Pappa Ponce), Luis Ricardo Rodríguez Jérez, Carlos Fernando Figueroa Martínez (46.Manuel Antonio León Sandoval), Wilfred Armando Velásquez González, Carlos Humberto Ruíz Gutiérrez, Mario Rafael Rodríguez Rodríguez (46.Dwight Anthony Pezzarossi García), Marvin Tomás Ávila Sánchez. Trainer: Ever Hugo Almeida Almada (Paraguay).
USA: Timothy Matthew Howard, Steven Emil Cherundolo, Clarence Goodson (46.Geoffrey Scott Cameron), Carlos Manuel Bocanegra, Fabian Johnson, Edu Maurice Edu Jr., Michael Sheehan Bradley, Jermaine Jones, Landon Timothy Donovan (90+3.Kyle Robert Beckerman), Clinton Drew Dempsey, Herculez Gomez Hurtado (64.Josmer Volmy Altidore). Trainer: Jürgen Klinsmann (Germany).
Goals: 0-1 Clinton Drew Dempsey (40), 1-1 Marco Pablo Pappa Ponce (83).
Cautions: Luis Ricardo Rodríguez Jérez, Marco Pablo Pappa Ponce / Clarence Goodson, Michael Sheehan Bradley, Edu Maurice Edu Jr., Fabian Johnson.

07.09.2012, Independence Park, Kingston; Attendance: 25,000
Referee: Marco Antonio Rodríguez Moreno (Mexico)
JAMAICA - UNITED STATES 2-1(1-1)
JAM: Dwayne Miller, Nyron Paul Henry Nosworthy, Jermaine Taylor, Jason Morrison, Adrian Joseph Mariappa, JeVaughn Watson, Lovel Palmer, Rodolph William Austin, Kavin Bryan (63.Darren Mattocks), Luton George Shelton (83.Joel Senior), Ryan Johnson (90.Omar Cummings). Trainer: Theodore Whitmore.
USA: Timothy Matthew Howard, Clarence Goodson, Michael Parkhurst, Fabian Johnson, Geoffrey Scott Cameron, Clint Drew Dempsey, Jermaine Jones, Kyle Robert Beckerman (58.Daniel Williams), Edu Maurice Edu Jr. (71.Terrence Anthony Boyd), Hérculez Gómez Hurtado, Josmer Volmy Altidore (71.Dane Brekken Shea). Trainer: Jürgen Klinsmann (Germany).
Goals: 0-1 Clint Drew Dempsey (1), 1-1 Rodolph William Austin (24), 2-1 Luton George Shelton (61).
Cautions: JeVaughn Watson / Clarence Goodson, Jermaine Jones.

07.09.2012, Estadio "Mateo Flores", Ciudad de Guatemala; Attendance: 8,000
Referee: Marco Daniel Brea Despaigne (Cuba)
GUATEMALA - ANTIGUA AND BARBUDA 3-1(0-1)
GUA: Ricardo Antonio Jérez Figueroa, Carlos Eduardo Gallardo Nájera, Erwin Armando Morales Hernández, Luis Ricardo Rodríguez Jérez, José Manuel Contreras y Contreras (71.Henry David López Guerra), Manuel Antonio León Sandoval, Gonzalo Antonio Romero Paz (46.Marco Tulio Ciani Barillas), Jhonathan Winibakcer López Mejicanos (46.Dwight Anthony Pezzarossi García), Carlos Humberto Ruíz Gutiérrez, Mario Rafael Rodríguez Rodríguez, Marco Pablo Pappa Ponce. Trainer: Ever Hugo Almeida Almada (Paraguay).
ATG: Molvin James, Zaine Francis-Angol (82.Moses Ashikodi), George Dublin, Ranjae Christian, Akeem Thomas, Quinton Griffith, Lawson Robinson, Tamarley Thomas, Kieran Zac Murtagh (70.Stephan Smith), Randolph Burton (78.Keita DeCastro), Peter Byers. Trainer: Thomas David Curtis (England).
Goals: 0-1 Peter Byers (39), 1-1 Carlos Humberto Ruíz Gutiérrez (60), 2-1 Carlos Humberto Ruíz Gutiérrez (79), 3-1 Dwight Anthony Pezzarossi García (90+1).
Cautions: Luis Ricardo Rodríguez Jérez / Molvin James, Quinton Griffith, Lawson Robinson, Ranjae Christian.
Sent off: Molvin James (76).

11.09.2012, "Sir Vivian Richards" Stadium, North Sound; Attendance: 5,000
Referee: David Gantar (Canada)
ANTIGUA AND BARBUDA - GUATEMALA 0-1(0-1)
ATG: Keita DeCastro, Luke Blakely, Zaine Francis-Angol, George Dublin, Marc Ellis Joseph, Ranjae Christian, Lawson Robinson (58.Stephan Smith), Kieran Zac Murtagh, Tamarley Thomas (75.James Luke Newton Walker), Randolph Burton (89.Moses Ashikodi), Peter Byers. Trainer: Thomas David Curtis (England).
GUA: Ricardo Antonio Jérez Figueroa, Claudio Josué Albizuris Aguilár, Carlos Eduardo Gallardo Nájera (54.Jhonathan Winibakcer López Mejicanos), Erwin Armando Morales Hernández, Rubén Darío Morales Pereira, José Manuel Contreras y Contreras, Manuel Antonio León Sandoval, Carlos Humberto Ruíz Gutiérrez, Mario Rafael Rodríguez Rodríguez (64.Carlos Fernando Figueroa Martínez), Dwight Anthony Pezzarossi García (82.Jean Jonathan Márquez Orellana), Marco Pablo Pappa Ponce. Trainer: Ever Hugo Almeida Almada (Paraguay).
Goal: 0-1 Carlos Humberto Ruíz Gutiérrez (25).
Cautions: Peter Byers, Lawson Robinson, Randolph Burton, Ranjae Christian / Jhonathan Winibakcer López Mejicanos, Carlos Humberto Ruíz Gutiérrez.

11.09.2012, Columbus Crew Stadium, Columbus; Attendance: 23,881
Referee: José Benigno Pineda Fernández (Honduras)
UNITED STATES - JAMAICA **1-0(0-0)**
USA: Timothy Matthew Howard, Carlos Manuel Bocanegra, Fabian Johnson, Geoffrey Scott Cameron, Steven Emil Cherundolo, Clint Drew Dempsey, Jermaine Jones, José Francisco Torres Mezzell (67.Dane Brekken Shea), Daniel Williams, Graham Jonathan Zusi (72.Edu Maurice Edu Jr.), Hérculez Gómez Hurtado (80.Josmer Volmy Altidore). Trainer: Jürgen Klinsmann (Germany).
JAM: Dwayne Miller, Nyron Paul Henry Nosworthy, Adrian Joseph Mariappa, Jermaine Taylor, Jason Morrison, Omar Cummings (77.Dane Richards), Lovel Palmer, JeVaughn Watson (75.Tremaine Stewart), Rodolph William Austin, Luton George Shelton (66.Kavin Bryan), Ryan Johnson. Trainer: Theodore Whitmore.
Goal: 1-0 Hérculez Gómez Hurtado (55).
Cautions: Graham Jonathan Zusi / Lovel Palmer.

12.10.2012, "Sir Vivian Richards" Stadium, North Sound; Attendance: 7,000
Referee: Neal Brizan (Trinidad and Tobago)
ANTIGUA AND BARBUDA - UNITED STATES **1-2(1-1)**
ATG: Molvin James, Luke Blakely, Zaine Francis-Angol, George Dublin, Akeem Thomas, Marc Ellis Joseph, Quinton Griffith, Tamarley Thomas, Randolph Burton (90.Moses Ashikodi), Dexter Anthony Titus Blackstock, Peter Byers (88.Stephan Smith). Trainer: Thomas David Curtis (England).
USA: Timothy Matthew Howard, Carlos Manuel Bocanegra, Clarence Goodson, Geoffrey Scott Cameron, Steven Emil Cherundolo, Clint Drew Dempsey, Michael Sheehan Bradley, Daniel Williams (56.Jermaine Jones), Graham Jonathan Zusi (78.Sacha Bryan Klještan), Edward Abraham Johnson, Hérculez Gómez Hurtado (73.Alan Gordon). Trainer: Jürgen Klinsmann (Germany).
Goals: 0-1 Edward Abraham Johnson (20), 1-1 Dexter Anthony Titus Blackstock (25), 1-2 Edward Abraham Johnson (90).
Cautions: Tamarley Thomas, Dexter Anthony Titus Blackstock / Jermaine Jones.

12.10.2012, Estadio "Mateo Flores", Ciudad de Guatemala; Attendance: 20,717
Referee: Roberto García Orozco (Mexico)
GUATEMALA - JAMAICA **2-1(1-0)**
GUA: Ricardo Antonio Jérez Figueroa, Erwin Armando Morales Hernández, Elías Enoc Vásquez Prera, Rubén Darío Morales Pereira, José Manuel Contreras y Contreras, Carlos Fernando Figueroa Martínez (74.Marco Tulio Ciani Barillas), Manuel Antonio León Sandoval, Jhonathan Winibakcer López Mejicanos, Carlos Humberto Ruíz Gutiérrez, Marco Pablo Pappa Ponce (67.Dwight Anthony Pezzarossi García), Minor Ignacio López Campollo (65.Gregory Lester Ruíz David). Trainer: Ever Hugo Almeida Almada (Paraguay).
JAM: Dwayne Miller, Nyron Paul Henry Nosworthy, Shavar Thomas, Jermaine Taylor, Jason Morrison, Jermaine Hue (82.Tremaine Stewart), Lovel Palmer, JeVaughn Watson (41.Dane Richards), Demar Phillips, Luton George Shelton, Ryan Johnson (75.Omar Cummings). Trainer: Theodore Whitmore.
Goals: 1-0 Carlos Fernando Figueroa Martínez (15), 1-1 Luton George Shelton (60 penalty), 2-1 Carlos Humberto Ruíz Gutiérrez (85).
Cautions: Minor Ignacio López Campollo, José Manuel Contreras y Contreras, Marco Tulio Ciani Barillas / Nyron Paul Henry Nosworthy, Jason Morrison.

16.10.2012, Livestrong Sporting Park, Kansas City; Attendance: 16,947
Referee: Roberto Moreno (Panama)
UNITED STATES - GUATEMALA 3-1(3-1)
USA: Timothy Matthew Howard, Carlos Manuel Bocanegra, Michael Parkhurst, Geoffrey Scott Cameron, Steven Emil Cherundolo, Clint Drew Dempsey, Michael Sheehan Bradley, Daniel Williams, Graham Jonathan Zusi (77.Edu Maurice Edu Jr.), Edward Abraham Johnson (89.Joe Benny Corona Crespín), Hérculez Gómez Hurtado (65.Sacha Bryan Klještan). Trainer: Jürgen Klinsmann (Germany).
GUA: Ricardo Antonio Jérez Figueroa, Erwin Armando Morales Hernández, Rafael Humberto Morales de León, Elías Enoc Vásquez Prera, José Manuel Contreras y Contreras, Carlos Fernando Figueroa Martínez (46.Marco Pablo Pappa Ponce), Wilfred Armando Velásquez González, Manuel Antonio León Sandoval, Jhonathan Winibakcer López Mejicanos, Carlos Humberto Ruíz Gutiérrez (88.Dwight Anthony Pezzarossi García), Mario Rafael Rodríguez Rodríguez (46.Minor Ignacio López Campollo). Trainer: Ever Hugo Almeida Almada (Paraguay).
Goals: 0-1 Carlos Humberto Ruíz Gutiérrez (5), 1-1 Carlos Manuel Bocanegra (10), 2-1 Clint Drew Dempsey (18), 3-1 Clint Drew Dempsey (36).
Cautions: Clint Drew Dempsey / Elías Enoc Vásquez Prera.

16.10.2012, Independence Park, Kingston; Attendance: 8,000
Referee: Wálter Enrique Quesada Cordero (Costa Rica)
JAMAICA - ANTIGUA AND BARBUDA 4-1(2-0)
JAM: Dwayne Miller, Nyron Paul Henry Nosworthy, Jermaine Taylor, Lovel Palmer, Demar Phillips, Jermaine Hue, Rodolph William Austin, Dane Richards, Tremaine Stewart (84.JeVaughn Watson), Luton George Shelton (58.Joel Senior), Ryan Johnson (69.Omar Cummings). Trainer: Theodore Whitmore.
ATG: Molvin James, Luke Blakely (83.Kemoy Alexander), Zaine Francis-Angol, George Dublin, Marc Ellis Joseph, Lawson Robinson, Quinton Griffith, Tamarley Thomas, Randolph Burton (75.Stephan Smith), Dexter Anthony Titus Blackstock (83.Ranjae Christian), Peter Byers. Trainer: Thomas David Curtis (England).
Goals: 1-0 Demar Phillips (16), 2-0 Nyron Paul Henry Nosworthy (18), 2-1 Quinton Griffith (61), 3-1 Dane Richards (77), 4-1 Dane Richards (88).
Cautions: Tamarley Thomas.

GROUP B

08.06.2012	Ciudad de México	Mexico - Guyana	3-1(2-0)
08.06.2012	San José	Costa Rica – El Salvador	2-2(2-1)
12.06.2012	Providence	Guyana – Costa Rica	0-4(0-2)
12.06.2012	San Salvador	El Salvador - Mexico	1-2(0-0)
07.09.2012	San Salvador	El Salvador – Guyana	2-2(2-1)
07.09.2012	San José	Costa Rica – Mexico	0-2(0-1)
11.09.2012	Providence	Guyana – El Salvador	2-3(1-1)
11.09.2012	Ciudad de México	Mexico – Costa Rica	1-0(0-0)
12.10.2012	Houston	Guyana – Mexico	0-5(0-0)
12.10.2012	San Salvador	El Salvador – Costa Rica	0-1(0-1)
16.10.2012	San José	Costa Rica – Guyana	7-0(2-0)
16.10.2012	Torreón	Mexico – El Salvador	2-0(0-0)

FINAL STANDINGS

1.	**Mexico**	6	6	0	0	15 - 2	18
2.	**Costa Rica**	6	3	1	2	14 - 5	10
3.	El Salvador	6	1	2	3	8 - 11	5
4.	Guyana	6	0	1	5	5 - 24	1

08.06.2012, Estadio Azteca, Ciudad de México; Attendance: 80,401
Referee: Javier Santos (Puerto Rico)
MEXICO - GUYANA **3-1(2-0)**
MEX: José de Jesús Corona Rodríguez, Francisco Javier Rodríguez Pinedo, Carlos Arnoldo Salcido Flores, Héctor Alfredo Moreno Herrera, Severo Efraín Meza Mayorga, José Andrés Guardado Hernández, Pablo Edson Barrera Acosta (66.Édgar Bismarck Estuardo Andrade Rentería), Jesús Eduardo Zavala Castañeda, Jesús Aldo de Nigris Guajardo (81.Jorge Emmanuel Torres Nilo), Giovani dos Santos Ramírez (61.Ángel Eduardo Reyna Martínez), Javier Hernández Balcázar. Trainer: José Manuel de la Torre Menchaca.
GUY: Ronson Williams, Jake Alexander Newton, Leon Cort, John Paul Rodrigues, Walter Andre Moore, Kester Jacobs, Howard Newton (46.Gregory Richardson), Christopher Ronald Nurse, Kayode McKinnon, Ricky Ulric Shakes (71.Dwight Peters), Carl Edward Richard Cort (80.Anthony Abrams). Trainer: Jamaal Shabazz (Trinidad and Tobago).
Goals: 1-0 Carlos Arnoldo Salcido Flores (11), 2-0 Giovani dos Santos Ramírez (15), 3-0 Javier Hernández Balcázar (51), 3-1 Héctor Alfredo Moreno Herrera (62 own goal).
Cautions: Christopher Ronald Nurse, Howard Newton.

08.06.2012, Estadio Nacional de Costa Rica, San José; Attendance: 23,701
Referee: Walter Alexander López Castellanos (Guatemala)
COSTA RICA – EL SALVADOR **2-2(2-1)**
CRC: Keylor Antonio Navas Gamboa, Míchael Umaña Corrales, Roy Miller Hernández, Bryan Oviedo Jiménez, José Andrés Salvatierra López, Michael Barrantes Rojas, Randall Azofeifa Corrales (90.Olman Vargas López), Celso Borges Mora (46.Óscar Emilio Rojas Ruíz), Álvaro Alberto Saborío Chacón, Randall Brenes Moya (67.Mauricio Castillo Contreras), Joel Nathaniel Campbell Samuels. Trainer: Jorge Luis Pinto Afanador (Colombia).
SLV: Benji Oldai Villalobos Segovia, Moisés Xavier García Orellana, Steven Francis Gordon Purdy, Víctor Samuel Turcios Pacheco, Alfredo Alberto Pacheco, Dennis Jonathan Alas Morales, Ramón Alfredo Sánchez Paredes (60.Elder José Figueroa Sarmiento), William Osael Romero Castillo (85.Eliseo Antonio Quintanilla Ortíz), Jaime Enrique Alas Morales, José Isidro Gutiérrez Vásquez, Rafael Edgardo Burgos (78.Mark Léster Blanco Pineda). Trainer: Rubén Israel (Uruguay).
Goals: 1-0 Álvaro Alberto Saborío Chacón (10), 2-0 Joel Nathaniel Campbell Samuels (16), 2-1 José Isidro Gutiérrez Vásquez (24), 2-2 William Osael Romero Castillo (55)

Cautions: Álvaro Alberto Saborío Chacón, Michael Barrantes Rojas, José Andrés Salvatierra López, Míchael Umaña Corrales, Óscar Emilio Rojas Ruíz / Alfredo Alberto Pacheco, Moisés Xavier García Orellana, Dennis Jonathan Alas Morales, Benji Oldai Villalobos Segovia, Víctor Samuel Turcios Pacheco.

12.06.2012, Providence Stadium, Providence; Attendance: 11,000
Referee: Marco Daniel Brea Despaigne (Cuba)
GUYANA – COSTA RICA **0-4(0-2)**
GUY: Ronson Williams, Jake Alexander Newton (78.Dwight Peters), John Paul Rodrigues, Leon Cort, Walter Andre Moore, Ricky Ulric Shakes, Christopher Ronald Nurse, Gregory Richardson, Kayode McKinnon, Kester Jacobs (46.Christopher Bourne), Carl Edward Richard Cort (62.Anthony Abrams). Trainer: Jamaal Shabazz (Trinidad and Tobago).
CRC: Keylor Antonio Navas Gamboa, Roy Miller Hernández, Bryan Oviedo Jiménez, Geancarlo González Castro, José Andrés Salvatierra López (73.Heiner Mora), Michael Barrantes Rojas, Óscar Emilio Rojas Ruíz, José Miguel Cubero Loria, Mauricio Castillo Contreras (59.Porfirio López Meza), Álvaro Alberto Saborío Chacón (80.Celso Borges Mora), Joel Nathaniel Campbell Samuels. Trainer: Jorge Luis Pinto Afanador (Colombia).
Goals: 0-1 Álvaro Alberto Saborío Chacón (19), 0-2 Álvaro Alberto Saborío Chacón (26), 0-3 Álvaro Alberto Saborío Chacón (52), 0-4 Joel Nathaniel Campbell Samuels (78).
Cautions: Kayode McKinnon, Gregory Richardson, Anthony Abrams / Joel Nathaniel Campbell Samuels, Roy Miller Hernández, Porfirio López Meza, Geancarlo González Castro.

12.06.2012, Estadio Cuscatlán, San Salvador; Attendance: 29,712
Referee: José Benigno Pineda Fernández (Honduras)
EL SALVADOR - MEXICO **1-2(0-0)**
SLV: Benji Oldai Villalobos Segovia, Moisés Xavier García Orellana, Steven Francis Gordon Purdy, Víctor Samuel Turcios Pacheco, Alfredo Alberto Pacheco, Dennis Jonathan Alas Morales, Ramón Alfredo Sánchez Paredes, William Osael Romero Castillo (79.Eliseo Antonio Quintanilla Ortíz), Jaime Enrique Alas Morales, José Isidro Gutiérrez Vásquez (84.Nelson Wilfredo Bonilla Sánchez), Rafael Edgardo Burgos (68.Mark Léster Blanco Pineda). Trainer: Rubén Israel (Uruguay).
MEX: José de Jesús Corona Rodríguez, Francisco Javier Rodríguez Pinedo, Carlos Arnoldo Salcido Flores, Severo Efraín Meza Mayorga, Jorge Emmanuel Torres Nilo, Héctor Alfredo Moreno Herrera, José Andrés Guardado Hernández (67.Édgar Bismarck Estuardo Andrade Rentería), Pablo Edson Barrera Acosta (87.Hugo Ayala Castro), Jesús Eduardo Zavala Castañeda, Giovani dos Santos Ramírez (68.Ángel Eduardo Reyna Martínez), Javier Hernández Balcázar. Trainer: José Manuel de la Torre Menchaca.
Goals: 0-1 Jesús Eduardo Zavala Castañeda (60), 1-1 Alfredo Alberto Pacheco (65), 1-2 Héctor Alfredo Moreno Herrera (82).
Cautions: Moisés Xavier García Orellana, Ramón Alfredo Sánchez Paredes / Francisco Javier Rodríguez Pinedo.

07.09.2012, Estadio Cuscatlán, San Salvador; Attendance: 24,000
Referee: Jair Marrufo (United States)
EL SALVADOR – GUYANA **2-2(2-1)**
SLV: Dagoberto Portillo Gamero, Elder José Figueroa Sarmiento, Alfredo Alberto Pacheco (87.Jonathan Josué Águila Joya), Steven Francis Gordon Purdy, Jaime Enrique Alas Morales, Christian Giovanni Castillo Martínez (68.Dennis Jonathan Alas Morales), Darwin Adelso Cerén Delgado, José Isidro Gutiérrez Vásquez, William Osael Romero Castillo (90+3.Carlos Romeo Monteagudo Alfaro), Eliseo Antonio Quintanilla Ortíz, Rafael Edgardo Burgos. Trainer: Juan de Dios Castillo González (Mexico).
GUY: Richard Reynolds, John Paul Rodrigues, Jamaal Smith, Charles Roylon Pollard, Walter Andre Moore, Ricky Ulric Shakes, Nick Millington (65.Dwain Jacobs), Trayon Bobb (77.Shawn Beveney), Christopher Ronald Nurse, Gregory Richardson, Vurlon Mills (61.Kayode McKinnon). Trainer: Jamaal Shabazz (Trinidad and Tobago).
Goals: 1-0 José Isidro Gutiérrez Vásquez (3), 1-1 Trayon Bobb (16), 2-1 William Osael Romero

Castillo (28), 2-2 Trayon Bobb (53).
Cautions: Walter Andre Moore, Richard Reynolds.

07.09.2012, Estadio Nacional de Costa Rica, San José; Attendance: 32,500
Referee: Roberto Moreno (Panama)
COSTA RICA - MEXICO **0-2(0-1)**
CRC: Keylor Antonio Navas Gamboa, Jhonny Acosta Zamora, José Andrés Salvatierra López, Michael Umaña Corrales (63.Randall Brenes Moya), Geancarlo González Castro, Bryan Josué Oviedo Jiménez, Michael Barrantes Rojas (46.Óscar Emilio Rojas Ruíz), José Miguel Cubero Loria, Cristian Bolaños Navarro, Joël Nathaniel Campbell Samuels (72.Rodney Wallace), Álvaro Alberto Saborío Chacón. Trainer: Jorge Luis Pinto Afanador (Colombia).
MEX: José de Jesús Corona Rodríguez, Francisco Javier Rodríguez Pinedo, Jorge Emmanuel Torres Nilo, Héctor Alfredo Moreno Herrera, Severo Efraín Meza Mayorga (36.Israel Sabdi Jiménez Nañez), Javier Ignacio Aquino Carmona (84.Hugo Ayala Castro), José Andrés Guardado Hernández, Carlos Arnoldo Salcido Flores, Jesús Eduardo Zavala Castañeda, Oribe Peralta Morones, Javier Hernández Balcázar (76.Marco Jhonfai Fabián de la Mora). Trainer: José Manuel de la Torre Menchaca.
Goals: 0-1 Carlos Arnoldo Salcido Flores (43), 0-2 Jesús Eduardo Zavala Castañeda (52).
Cautions: Michael Umaña Corrales, José Miguel Cubero Loria / Carlos Arnoldo Salcido Flores.

11.09.2012, Providence Stadium, Providence; Attendance: 4,141
Referee: Raymond Bogle (Jamaica)
GUYANA - EL SALVADOR **2-3(1-1)**
GUY: Richard Reynolds, John Paul Rodrigues (86.Dwight Peters), Charles Roylon Pollard, Jamaal Smith, Walter Andre Moore, Ricky Ulric Shakes (77.Dwain Jacobs), Nick Millington (79.Kayode McKinnon), Trayon Bobb, Christopher Ronald Nurse, Carl Edward Richard Cort, Gregory Richardson. Trainer: Jamaal Shabazz (Trinidad and Tobago).
SLV: Dagoberto Portillo Gamero, Moisés Xavier García Orellana, Milton Alexander Molina Miguel, Carlos Romeo Monteagudo Alfaro, Dennis Jonathan Alas Morales, Jaime Enrique Alas Morales, Darwin Adelso Cerén Delgado (75. Alexander Vidal Larín Hernández), José Isidro Gutiérrez Vásquez, William Osael Romero Castillo (89.Christian Giovanni Castillo Martínez), Eliseo Antonio Quintanilla Ortíz (80.Ramón Alfredo Sánchez Paredes), Rafael Edgardo Burgos. Trainer: Juan de Dios Castillo González (Mexico).
Goals: 1-0 Gregory Richardson (1), 1-1 William Osael Romero Castillo (13), 1-2 Jaime Enrique Alas Morales (51), 2-2 Christopher Ronald Nurse (62), 2-3 Rafael Edgardo Burgos (77).
Cautions: Darwin Adelso Cerén Delgado, Eliseo Antonio Quintanilla Ortíz, Milton Alexander Molina Miguel.

11.09.2012, Estadio Azteca, Ciudad de México; Attendance: 44,007
Referee: Courtney Campbell (Jamaica)
MEXICO - COSTA RICA **1-0(0-0)**
MEX: José de Jesús Corona Rodríguez, Francisco Javier Rodríguez Pinedo, Jorge Emmanuel Torres Nilo (62.Hiram Ricardo Mier Alanis), Héctor Alfredo Moreno Herrera, Severo Efraín Meza Mayorga, Javier Ignacio Aquino Carmona (67.Elías Hernán Hernández Jacuinde), José Andrés Guardado Hernández, Carlos Arnoldo Salcido Flores, Jesús Eduardo Zavala Castañeda, Oribe Peralta Morones (81.Gerardo Torrado Díez de Bonilla), Javier Hernández Balcázar. Trainer: José Manuel de la Torre Menchaca.
CRC: Keylor Antonio Navas Gamboa, Jhonny Acosta Zamora, Gabriel Badilla Segura, José Andrés Salvatierra López, Pedro Luis Leal Valencia (73.Rodney Wallace), Geancarlo González Castro, José Miguel Cubero Loria, Yeltsin Ignacio Tejeda Valverde (76.Celso Borges Mora), Cristian Bolaños Navarro, Randall Brenes Moya, Joël Nathaniel Campbell Samuels (59.Álvaro Alberto Saborío Chacón). Trainer: Jorge Luis Pinto Afanador (Colombia).
Goal: 1-0 Javier Hernández Balcázar (61).
Cautions: Carlos Arnoldo Salcido Flores / Geancarlo González Castro, Gabriel Badilla Segura.

12.10.2012, BBVA Compass Stadium, Houston (United States); Attendance: 12,115
Referee: Walter Alexander López Castellanos (Guatemala)

GUYANA - MEXICO 0-5(0-0)

GUY: Derrick Carter, Walter Andre Moore, Dwain Jacobs, Charles Roylon Pollard, Jamaal Smith, Christopher Ronald Nurse, Nick Millington (73.Anthony Abrams), Trayon Bobb, Shawn Beveney (66.Kester Jacobs), Ricky Ulric Shakes (80.Dwight Peters), Gregory Richardson. Trainer: Jamaal Shabazz (Trinidad and Tobago).
MEX: Jonathan Emmanuel Orozco Domínguez, Francisco Javier Rodríguez Pinedo, Jorge Emmanuel Torres Nilo, Héctor Alfredo Moreno Herrera, Javier Ignacio Aquino Carmona, Israel Sabdi Jiménez Nañez (57.Elías Hernán Hernández Jacuinde), José Andrés Guardado Hernández, Antônio Naelson Matías „Sinha" (73.Ángel Eduardo Reyna Martínez), Gerardo Torrado Díez de Bonilla (39.Jorge Enríquez García), Oribe Peralta Morones, Javier Hernández Balcázar. Trainer: José Manuel de la Torre Menchaca.
Goals: 0-1 José Andrés Guardado Hernández (78), 0-2 Oribe Peralta Morones (79), 0-3 Charles Roylon Pollard (82 own goal), 0-4 Javier Hernández Balcázar (84), 0-5 Ángel Eduardo Reyna Martínez (86).
Cautions: Derrick Carter, Trayon Bobb, Christopher Ronald Nurse.

12.10.2012, Estadio Cuscatlán, San Salvador; Attendance: 35,082
Referee: Mark Geiger (United States)

EL SALVADOR - COSTA RICA 0-1(0-1)

SLV: Dagoberto Portillo Gamero, Moisés Xavier García Orellana, José Mardoqueo Henríquez Dubón, Alfredo Alberto Pacheco, Dennis Jonathan Alas Morales, Jaime Enrique Alas Morales, José Isidro Gutiérrez Vásquez (61.Christian Giovanni Castillo Martínez), William Osael Romero Castillo, Eliseo Antonio Quintanilla Ortíz, Rafael Edgardo Burgos (22.Nelson Wilfredo Bonilla Sánchez), Rodolfo Antonio Zelaya García (68.Cristian Javier Bautista). Trainer: Juan de Dios Castillo González (Mexico).
CRC: Keylor Antonio Navas Gamboa, Jhonny Acosta Zamora, Roy Miller Hernández, Cristian Esteban Gamboa Luna, Michael Umaña Corrales, Bryan Josué Oviedo Jiménez, José Miguel Cubero Loria, Yeltsin Ignacio Tejeda Valverde (54.Michael Barrantes Rojas), Cristian Bolaños Navarro, Bryan Jafet Ruíz González (46.Randall Brenes Moya), Álvaro Alberto Saborío Chacón (82.Rodney Wallace). Trainer: Jorge Luis Pinto Afanador (Colombia).
Goal: 0-1 José Miguel Cubero Loria (31).
Cautions: José Mardoqueo Henríquez Dubón, José Isidro Gutiérrez Vásquez / Bryan Josué Oviedo Jiménez, Jhonny Acosta Zamora, Michael Umaña Corrales.
Sent off: Eliseo Antonio Quintanilla Ortíz (87), Alfredo Alberto Pacheco (90+2).

16.10.2012, Estadio Nacional de Costa Rica, San José; Attendance: 27,500
Referee: Héctor Francisco Rodríguez Hernández (Honduras)

COSTA RICA - GUYANA 7-0(2-0)

CRC: Keylor Antonio Navas Gamboa, Roy Miller Hernández, Cristian Esteban Gamboa Luna, Geancarlo González Castro, Bryan Josué Oviedo Jiménez, Michael Barrantes Rojas, José Miguel Cubero Loria, Allen Esteban Guevara Zúñiga (58.Celso Borges Mora), Cristian Bolaños Navarro (75.Yeltsin Ignacio Tejeda Valverde), Randall Brenes Moya (69.Joël Nathaniel Campbell Samuels), Álvaro Alberto Saborío Chacón. Trainer: Jorge Luis Pinto Afanador (Colombia).
GUY: Derrick Carter, Walter Andre Moore, Jamaal Smith, Charles Roylon Pollard, Kester Jacobs (83.Daniel Wilson), Dwain Jacobs, Nick Millington, Trayon Bobb (45.Colin Nelson), Vurlon Mills (62.Brandon Beresford), Ricky Ulric Shakes, Gregory Richardson. Trainer: Jamaal Shabazz (Trinidad and Tobago).
Goals: 1-0 Randall Brenes Moya (10), 2-0 Cristian Esteban Gamboa Luna (14), 3-0 Randall Brenes Moya (48), 4-0 Álvaro Alberto Saborío Chacón (51 penalty), 5-0 Cristian Bolaños Navarro (61), 6-0 Celso Borges Mora (70), 7-0 Álvaro Alberto Saborío Chacón (77).
Cautions: Trayon Bobb, Walter Andre Moore, Jamaal Smith, Gregory Richardson.
Sent off: Walter Andre Moore (51).

16.10.2012, Estadio Corona, Torreón; Attendance: 26,333
Referee: Jafeth Perea Amador (Panama)
MEXICO – EL SALVADOR 2-0(0-0)
MEX: Alfredo Talavera Díaz, Francisco Javier Rodríguez Pinedo, Adrián Alexei Aldrete Rodríguez, Joel Adrián Huiqui Andrade, Severo Efraín Meza Mayorga, José Andrés Guardado Hernández (68.Héctor Miguel Herrera López), Ángel Eduardo Reyna Martínez, Jorge Enríquez García, Carlos Alberto Peña Rodríguez (59.Elías Hernán Hernández Jacuinde), Oribe Peralta Morones, Jesús Aldo de Nigris Guajardo (61.Javier Hernández Balcázar). Trainer: José Manuel de la Torre Menchaca.
SLV: Dagoberto Portillo Gamero, Moisés Xavier García Orellana, José Mardoqueo Henríquez Dubón, Steven Francis Gordon Purdy, Carlos Romeo Monteagudo Alfaro, Darwin Adelso Cerén Delgado (85.Ramón Ulises Flores Aguirre), Dennis Jonathan Alas Morales, Christian Giovanni Castillo Martínez, William Osael Romero Castillo (68. Alexander Vidal Larín Hernández), Jaime Enrique Alas Morales, Jonathan Josué Águila Joya (74.Nelson Wilfredo Bonilla Sánchez). Trainer: Juan de Dios Castillo González (Mexico).
Goals: 1-0 Oribe Peralta Morones (64), 2-0 Javier Hernández Balcázar (85).

GROUP C

08.06.2012	Ciudad de la Habana	Cuba - Canada	0-1(0-0)
08.06.2012	San Pedro Sula	Honduras - Panama	0-2(0-0)
12.06.2012	Toronto	Canada - Honduras	0-0
12.06.2012	Ciudad de Panamá	Panama - Cuba	1-0(0-0)
07.09.2012	Ciudad de la Habana	Cuba – Honduras	0-3(0-1)
07.09.2012	Toronto	Canada – Panama	1-0(0-0)
11.09.2012	Ciudad de Panamá	Panama – Canada	2-0(1-0)
11.09.2012	San Pedro Sula	Honduras – Cuba	1-0(1-0)
12.10.2012	Toronto	Canada – Cuba	3-0(1-0)
12.10.2012	Ciudad de Panamá	Panama – Honduras	0-0
16.10.2012	Ciudad de la Habana	Cuba – Panama	1-1(1-0)
16.10.2012	San Pedro Sula	Honduras – Canada	8-1(4-0)

FINAL STANDINGS

1.	**Honduras**	6	3	2	1	12	-	3	11
2.	**Panama**	6	3	2	1	6	-	2	11
3.	Canada	6	3	1	2	6	-	10	10
4.	Cuba	6	0	1	5	1	-	10	1

08.06.2012, Estadio „Pedro Marrero", Ciudad de la Habana; Attendance: 7,000
Referee: Courtney Campbell (Jamaica)
CUBA - CANADA **0-1(0-0)**
CUB: Odisnel Cooper Despaigne, Yénier Márquez Molina, Joel Colomé Valencia, Reysánder Fernández Cervantes, Marcel Hernández Campanioni, Carlos Domingo Francisco Serrano, Alianni Urgellés (80.Jorge Luis Corrales Cordero), Dalain Aira Fernández (77.Roberto Linares Balmaseda), Alberto Gómez (74.Adonis Ramos), Ariel Pedro Martínez González, Alain Alfredo Cervantes O'Farril. Trainer: Alexander González.
CAN: Lars Justin Hirschfeld, Kevin James McKenna, David Edward Edgar, Ante Jazić, André Robert Hainault, William David Johnson, Julien Bobby de Guzman (69.Atiba Hutchinson), Dwayne Anthony de Rosario, Nikolas William Ledgerwood, Tosaint Antony Ricketts (65.Milan Borjan), Olivier Occéan (81.Simeon Alexander Jackson). Trainer: Stephen Hart (Trinidad & Tobago).
Goal: 0-1 Olivier Occéan (54).
Cautions: Alberto Gómez / Ante Jazić, William David Johnson.
Sent off: Lars Justin Hirschfeld (70).

08.06.2012, Estadio Olímpico Metropolitano, San Pedro Sula; Attendance: 28,215
Referee: Mark Geiger (United States)
HONDURAS - PANAMA **0-2(0-0)**
HON: Noel Eduardo Valladares Bonilla, Maynor Alexis Figueroa Róchez, Emilio Arturo Izaguirre Girón, Mauricio Alberto Sabillón Peña, Johnny Harold Leverón Uclés, Víctor Salvador Bernárdez Blanco, Oscar Boniek García Ramírez, Wilson Roberto Palacios Suazo (46.Anthony Rubén Lozano Colón), Edder Gerardo Delgado Zerón, Carlos Will Mejía García (63.Kervin Christopfer Johnson Allen), Carlos Yaír Costly Molina. Trainer: Luis Fernando Suárez (Colombia).
PAN: Jaime Manuel Penedo Cano, Felipe Abdiel Baloy Ramírez, Jean Carlos Cedeño, Luis Alfonso Henríquez Ledezma, Román Aureliano Torres Morcillo, Juan De Dios Pérez Quijada (73.Nelson Alberto Barahona Collins), Amílcar Henríquez Espinosa, Armando Cooper, Alberto Abdiel Quintero Medina (64.Marcos Aníbal Sánchez Mullins), Blas Antonio Miguel Pérez Ortega, Luis Gabriel Rentería (84.Aníbal Cesis Godoy). Trainer: Jorge Luis Dely Valdes.

Goals: 0-1 Blas Antonio Miguel Pérez Ortega (65), 0-2 Blas Antonio Miguel Pérez Ortega (81).
Cautions: Alberto Abdiel Quintero Medina.

12.06.2012, BMO Field, Toronto; Attendance: 16,132
Referee: Enrico Wijngarde (Suriname)
CANADA - HONDURAS **0-0**
CAN: Milan Borjan, Kevin James McKenna, David Edward Edgar, Ante Jazić, André Robert Hainault, William David Johnson, Julien Bobby de Guzman, Kevin James McKenna, Atiba Hutchinson (87.Simeon Alexander Jackson), Nikolas William Ledgerwood (71.Tosaint Antony Ricketts), Olivier Occéan (84.Iain Edward Hume). Trainer: Stephen Hart (Trinidad & Tobago).
HON: Noel Eduardo Valladares Bonilla, Maynor Alexis Figueroa Róchez, Emilio Arturo Izaguirre Girón, Mauricio Alberto Sabillón Peña, Juan Carlos García Álvarez, Víctor Salvador Bernárdez Blanco, Oscar Boniek García Ramírez, Wilson Roberto Palacios Suazo, Roger Espinoza Ramírez, Carlos Yaír Costly Molina, Anthony Rubén Lozano Colón (72.Óscar David Suazo Velázquez).Trainer: Luis Fernando Suárez (Colombia).
Cautions: Kevin James McKenna, Kevin James McKenna, Olivier Occéan / Maynor Alexis Figueroa Róchez, Mauricio Alberto Sabillón Peña.

12.06.2012, Estadio „Rommel Fernández", Ciudad de Panamá; Attendance: 21,000
Referee: Mark Geiger (United States)
PANAMA - CUBA **1-0(0-0)**
PAN: Jaime Manuel Penedo Cano, Felipe Abdiel Baloy Ramírez, Jean Carlos Cedeño, Luis Alfonso Henríquez Ledezma, Román Aureliano Torres Morcillo, Nelson Alberto Barahona Collins (75.Juan De Dios Pérez Quijada), Amílcar Henríquez Espinosa, Armando Cooper, Alberto Abdiel Quintero Medina, Blas Antonio Miguel Pérez Ortega (46.Edwin Enrique Aguilar Samaniego), Luis Gabriel Rentería (59.Luis Carlos Tejada Hansell). Trainer: Jorge Luis Dely Valdes.
CUB: Odisnel Cooper Despaigne, Yénier Márquez Molina, Joel Colomé Valencia, Reysánder Fernández Cervantes, Marcel Hernández Campanioni, Carlos Domingo Francisco Serrano, Alianni Urgellés (87.Jorge Luis Corrales Cordero), Dalain Aira Fernández (69.Roberto Linares Balmaseda), Alberto Gómez, Ariel Pedro Martínez González (58.Adonis Ramos), Alain Alfredo Cervantes O'Farril. Trainer: Alexander González.
Goal: 1-0 Nelson Alberto Barahona Collins (57).
Cautions: Nelson Alberto Barahona Collins / Carlos Domingo Francisco Serrano, Reysánder Fernández Cervantes.

07.09.2012, Estadio "Pedro Marrero", Ciudad de la Habana; Attendance: 8,000
Referee: Wálter Enrique Quesada Cordero (Costa Rica)
CUBA – HONDURAS **0-3(0-1)**
CUB: Odisnel Cooper Despaigne, Carlos Domingo Francisco Serrano, Jorge Luis Corrales Cordero, Jorge Luis Clavelo Tejada, Yoel Colomé Valencia, Reysánder Fernández Cervantes, Marcel Hernández Campanioni, Alberto Gómez Carbonell (83.Roberto Linares Balsameda), Rúslan Roberto Batista Machado (71.Sander Fernández Cervantes), Yaudel Lahera García, Ariel Pedro Martínez González (53.Jaime Colomé Valencia). Trainer: Alexander González.
HON: Noel Eduardo Valladares Bonilla, Maynor Alexis Figueroa Róchez, Emilio Arturo Izaguirre Girón, Juan Carlos García Álvarez (15.Mario Roberto Martínez Hernández), Víctor Salvador Bernárdez Blanco, Oscar Boniek García Ramírez, Wilson Roberto Palacios Suazo (81.Jorge Aarón Claros Juárez), Edder Gerardo Delgado Zerón, Arnold Fabián Peralta Sosa, Georgie Wilson Welcome Collins (89.Marvin Antonio Chávez), Jerry Ricardo Bengtson Bodden. Trainer: Luis Fernando Suárez (Colombia).
Goals: 0-1 Jerry Ricardo Bengtson Bodden (33), 0-2 Víctor Salvador Bernárdez Blanco (62), 0-3 Marvin Antonio Chávez (90+3).

07.09.2012, BMO Field, Toronto; Attendance: 17,586
Referee: Jeffrey Solís Calderón (Costa Rica)
CANADA - PANAMA **1-0(0-0)**
CAN: Lars Justin Hirschfeld, David Edward Edgar, André Robert Hainault, Kevin James McKenna, Ante Jazić, Julien Bobby de Guzman, Atiba Hutchinson, Dwayne Anthony de Rosario, William Johnson (70.Patrice Bernier), Simeon Alexander Jackson (86.Marcel de Jong), Olivier Occéan (66.Tosaint Antony Ricketts). Trainer: Stephen Hart (Trinidad and Tobago).
PAN: Jaime Manuel Penedo Cano, Felipe Abdiel Baloy Ramírez, Luis Alfonso Henríquez Ledezma, Román Aureliano Torres Morcillo, Juan De Dios Pérez Quijada (78.Aníbal Cesis Godoy), Nelson Alberto Barahona Collins (63.Armando Cooper), Amílcar Henríquez Espinosa, Alberto Abdiel Quintero Medina, Jean Carlos Cedeño, Luis Carlos Tejada Hansell (84.Rolando Manrique Blackburn Ortega), Blas Antonio Miguel Pérez Ortega. Trainer: Jorge Luis Dely Valdes.
Goal: 1-0 Dwayne Anthony de Rosario (77).
Cautions: William Johnson, Simeon Alexander Jackson / Amílcar Henríquez Espinosa, Jean Carlos Cedeño, Armando Cooper.

11.09.2012, Estadio "Rommel Fernández", Ciudad de Panamá; Attendance: 20,000
Referee: Élmer Arturo Bonilla Ruiz (El Salvador)
PANAMA - CANADA **2-0(1-0)**
PAN: Jaime Manuel Penedo Cano, Felipe Abdiel Baloy Ramírez, Luis Alfonso Henríquez Ledezma, Román Aureliano Torres Morcillo, Eduardo César Dasent Paz, Gabriel Enrique Gómez Giron, Amílcar Henríquez Espinosa, Armando Cooper (86.Nelson Alberto Barahona Collins), Alberto Abdiel Quintero Medina (75.Jairo Armando Glaize Yau), Blas Antonio Miguel Pérez Ortega, Rolando Manrique Blackburn Ortega (69.Aníbal Cesis Godoy). Trainer: Jorge Luis Dely Valdes.
CAN: Lars Justin Hirschfeld, David Edward Edgar (78.Nicolas William Ledgerwood), André Robert Hainault, Kevin James McKenna, Ante Jazić, Marcel de Jong, Patrice Bernier (79.Pedro Miguel Salgadinho Pacheco de Melo), Julien Bobby de Guzman, Atiba Hutchinson, Dwayne Anthony de Rosario (21.Tosaint Antony Ricketts), Simeon Alexander Jackson. Trainer: Stephen Hart (Trinidad and Tobago).
Goals: 1-0 Rolando Manrique Blackburn Ortega (23), 2-0 Blas Antonio Miguel Pérez Ortega (57).

11.09.2012, Estadio Olímpico Metropolitano, San Pedro Sula; Attendance: 12,000
Referee: Walter Alexander López Castellanos (Guatemala)
HONDURAS - CUBA **1-0(1-0)**
HON: Noel Eduardo Valladares Bonilla, Maynor Alexis Figueroa Róchez, Emilio Arturo Izaguirre Girón, Mauricio Alberto Sabillón Peña, Víctor Salvador Bernárdez Blanco, Oscar Boniek García Ramírez, Wilson Roberto Palacios Suazo (89.Orlin Orlando Peralta Gonzáles), Roger Espinoza Ramírez, Marvin Antonio Chávez (56.Mario Roberto Martínez Hernández), Georgie Wilson Welcome Collins (72.Arnold Fabián Peralta Sosa), Jerry Ricardo Bengtson Bodden. Trainer: Luis Fernando Suárez (Colombia).
CUB: Odelín Molina Hernández, Carlos Domingo Francisco Serrano, Jorge Luis Corrales Cordero, Jorge Luis Clavelo Tejada, Yoel Colomé Valencia, Marcel Hernández Campanioni (58.Ariel Pedro Martínez González), Jaime Colomé Valencia, Yaudel Lahera García (85.Roberto Linares Balsameda), Reysánder Fernández Cervantes, Rúslan Roberto Batista Machado, Alberto Gómez Carbonell (82.Adonis Ramos Soler). Trainer: Alexander González.
Goal: 1-0 Jerry Ricardo Bengtson Bodden (33).
Cautions: Jorge Luis Corrales Cordero.

12.10.2012, BMO Field, Toronto; Attendance: 17,712
Referee: Javier Santos (Puerto Rico)
CANADA – CUBA **3-0(1-0)**
CAN: Lars Justin Hirschfeld, David Edward Edgar (79.Nicolas William Ledgerwood), André Robert Hainault, Kevin James McKenna, Ante Jazić, Julien Bobby de Guzman, Atiba Hutchinson, William Johnson (82.Pedro Miguel Salgadinho Pacheco de Melo), Simeon Alexander Jackson, Olivier Occéan, Tosaint Antony Ricketts (86.Iain Edward Hume). Trainer: Stephen Hart (Trinidad and Tobago).
CUB: Odelín Molina Hernández, Carlos Domingo Francisco Serrano, Jorge Luis Clavelo Tejada, José Dairon Macías Cardenas, Jaime Colomé Valencia, Yoel Colomé Valencia, Yaudel Lahera García, Alberto Gómez Carbonell, Adonis Ramos Soler, Rúslan Roberto Batista Machado, Roberto Linares Balsameda. Trainer: Alexander González.
Goals: 1-0 Tosaint Antony Ricketts (14), 2-0 William Johnson (73), 3-0 David Edward Edgar (78).
Cautions: André Robert Hainault.
Sent off: Roberto Linares Balsameda (71), Olivier Occéan (73).

12.10.2012, Estadio "Rommel Fernández", Ciudad de Panamá; Attendance: 27,000
Referee: Joel Antonio Aguilar Chicas (El Salvador)
PANAMA – HONDURAS **0-0**
PAN: Jaime Manuel Penedo Cano, Felipe Abdiel Baloy Ramírez, Luis Alfonso Henríquez Ledezma, Román Aureliano Torres Morcillo, Eduardo César Dasent Paz (88.Jean Carlos Cedeño), Gabriel Enrique Gómez Giron, Amílcar Henríquez Espinosa, Armando Cooper (76.Jairo Armando Glaize Yau), Alberto Abdiel Quintero Medina (57.Nelson Alberto Barahona Collins), Luis Carlos Tejada Hansell, Blas Antonio Miguel Pérez Ortega. Trainer: Jorge Luis Dely Valdes.
HON: Donis Salatiel Escober Izaguirre, Maynor Alexis Figueroa Róchez, Emilio Arturo Izaguirre Girón, Víctor Salvador Bernárdez Blanco, Oscar Boniek García Ramírez, Jorge Aarón Claros Juárez, Luis Fernando Garrido, Mario Roberto Martínez Hernández (82.Marvin Antonio Chávez), Arnold Fabián Peralta Sosa, Carlos Yaír Costly Molina, Jerry Ricardo Bengtson Bodden. Trainer: Luis Fernando Suárez (Colombia).
Cautions: Blas Antonio Miguel Pérez Ortega / Arnold Fabián Peralta Sosa.

16.10.2012, Estadio "Pedro Marrero", Ciudad de la Habana; Attendance: 3,500
Referee: Stanley Lancaster (Guyana)
CUBA – PANAMA **1-1(1-0)**
CUB: Andy Ramos Gómez, Carlos Domingo Francisco Serrano, Jorge Luis Corrales Cordero, Yoel Colomé Valencia, Arturo Adrián Diz Pe, José Dairon Macías Cardenas, Ariel Pedro Martínez González (90.Daniel Eduardo Luís Sáez), Yaudel Lahera García (73.Maykel Alejandro Reyes Azquy), Aliannis Urgellés Montoya, Alberto Gómez Carbonell, Rúslan Roberto Batista Machado (72.Adonis Ramos Soler). Trainer: Alexander González.
PAN: Jaime Manuel Penedo Cano, Felipe Abdiel Baloy Ramírez, Luis Alfonso Henríquez Ledezma, Román Aureliano Torres Morcillo, Eduardo César Dasent Paz, Gabriel Enrique Gómez Giron (74.Jairo Armando Glaize Yau), Nelson Alberto Barahona Collins, Amílcar Henríquez Espinosa (65.Aníbal Cesis Godoy), Armando Cooper, Luis Carlos Tejada Hansell (46.Rolando Manrique Blackburn Ortega), Blas Antonio Miguel Pérez Ortega. Trainer: Jorge Luis Dely Valdes.
Goals: 1-0 Alberto Gómez Carbonell (37), 1-1 Nelson Alberto Barahona Collins (77).
Cautions: Yoel Colomé Valencia.

16.10.2012, Estadio Olímpico Metropolitano, San Pedro Sula; Attendance: 38,000
Referee: Mauricio Morales (Mexico)

HONDURAS - CANADA **8-1(4-0)**

HON: Donis Salatiel Escober Izaguirre (75.José Alberto Mendoza Posas), Maynor Alexis Figueroa Róchez, Emilio Arturo Izaguirre Girón (75.Juan Carlos García Álvarez), Víctor Salvador Bernárdez Blanco, Oscar Boniek García Ramírez (77.Wilmer Crisanto Casildo), Jorge Aarón Claros Juárez, Luis Fernando Garrido, Mario Roberto Martínez Hernández, Arnold Fabián Peralta Sosa, Carlos Yaír Costly Molina, Jerry Ricardo Bengtson Bodden. Trainer: Luis Fernando Suárez (Colombia).

CAN: Lars Justin Hirschfeld, David Edward Edgar, André Robert Hainault, Kevin James McKenna, Michael Klukowski, Julien Bobby de Guzman, Atiba Hutchinson, Nicolas William Ledgerwood (46.Iain Edward Hume), William Johnson, Simeon Alexander Jackson (64.Lucas Daniel Cavallini), Tosaint Antony Ricketts. Trainer: Stephen Hart (Trinidad and Tobago).

Goals: 1-0 Jerry Ricardo Bengtson Bodden (7), 2-0 Jerry Ricardo Bengtson Bodden (17), 3-0 Carlos Yaír Costly Molina (29), 4-0 Mario Roberto Martínez Hernández (33), 5-0 Carlos Yaír Costly Molina (48), 6-0 Mario Roberto Martínez Hernández (62), 6-1 Iain Edward Hume (77), 7-1 Jerry Ricardo Bengtson Bodden (83), 8-1 Carlos Yaír Costly Molina (89).

Cautions: Víctor Salvador Bernárdez Blanco, Carlos Yaír Costly Molina / David Edward Edgar.

FOURTH ROUND
(08.06.2013 – 15.10.2013)

06.02.2013	San Pedro Sula	Honduras - United States	2-1(1-1)
06.02.2013	Ciudad de Panamá	Panama - Costa Rica	2-2(2-1)
06.02.2013	Ciudad de México	Mexico - Jamaica	0-0
22.03.2013	San Pedro Sula	Honduras - Mexico	2-2(0-1)
22.03.2013	Kingston	Jamaica - Panama	1-1(1-0)
22.03.2013	Commerce City	United States - Costa Rica	1-0(1-0)
26.03.2013	San José	Costa Rica - Jamaica	2-0(1-0)
26.03.2013	Ciudad de Panamá	Panama - Honduras	2-0(1-0)
26.03.2013	Ciudad de México	Mexico - United States	0-0
04.06.2013	Kingston	Jamaica - Mexico	0-1(0-0)
07.06.2013	Kingston	Jamaica - United States	1-2(0-1)
07.06.2013	San José	Costa Rica - Honduras	1-0(1-0)
07.06.2013	Ciudad de Panamá	Panama - Mexico	0-0
11.06.2013	Ciudad de México	Mexico - Costa Rica	0-0
11.06.2013	Tegucigalpa	Honduras - Jamaica	2-0(1-0)
11.06.2013	Seattle	United States - Panama	2-0(1-0)
18.06.2013	Sandy	United States - Honduras	1-0(0-0)
18.06.2013	San José	Costa Rica - Panama	2-0(0-0)
06.09.2013	Ciudad de México	Mexico - Honduras	1-2(1-0)
06.09.2013	San José	Costa Rica - United States	3-1(2-1)
06.09.2013	Ciudad de Panamá	Panama - Jamaica	0-0
10.09.2013	Kingston	Jamaica - Costa Rica	1-1(0-0)
10.09.2013	Columbus	United States - Mexico	2-0(0-0)
10.09.2013	Tegucigalpa	Honduras - Panama	2-2(1-0)
11.10.2013	San Pedro Sula	Honduras - Costa Rica	1-0(0-0)
11.10.2013	Kansas City	United States - Jamaica	2-0(0-0)
11.10.2013	Ciudad de México	Mexico - Panama	2-1(1-0)
15.10.2013	San José	Costa Rica - Mexico	2-1(1-1)
15.10.2013	Kingston	Jamaica - Honduras	2-2(1-2)
15.10.2013	Ciudad de Panamá	Panama - United States	2-3(1-0)

FINAL STANDINGS

1.	**UNITED STATES**	10	7	1	2	15 - 8	22
2.	**COSTA RICA**	10	5	3	2	13 - 7	18
3.	**HONDURAS**	10	4	3	3	13 - 12	15
4.	**Mexico**	10	2	5	3	7 - 9	11
5.	Panama	10	1	5	4	10 - 14	8
6.	Jamaica	10	0	5	5	5 - 13	5

United States, Costa Rica and Honduras qualified for the FIFA World Cup final tournament.
Mexico qualified for the Intercontinental play-offs against the Oceania winner (New Zealand).

06.02.2013, Estadio Olímpico Metropolitano, San Pedro Sula; Attendance: 32,000
Referee: Wálter Enrique Quesada Cordero (Costa Rica)
HONDURAS - UNITED STATES **2-1(1-1)**
HON: Noel Eduardo Valladares Bonilla, Maynor Alexis Figueroa Róchez, Juan Carlos García Álvarez, Víctor Salvador Bernárdez Blanco, Oscar Boniek García Ramírez, Roger Espinoza Ramírez, Luis Fernando Garrido, Mario Roberto Martínez Hernández, Arnold Fabián Peralta Sosa, Carlos Yaír Costly Molina (90+3.Georgie Wilson Welcome Collins), Jerry Ricardo Bengtson Bodden (84.Jorge Aarón Claros Juárez). Trainer: Luis Fernando Suárez (Colombia).
USA: Timothy Matthew Howard, Fabian Johnson, Geoffrey Scott Cameron, Timothy Chandler, Omar Gonzalez, Clint Drew Dempsey, Jermaine Jones (67.Graham Jonathan Zusi), Michael Sheehan Bradley, Daniel Williams (58.Edu Maurice Edu Jr.), Edward Abraham Johnson (59.Sacha Bryan Klještan), Josmer Volmy Altidore. Trainer: Jürgen Klinsmann (Germany).
Goals: 0-1 Clint Drew Dempsey (36), 1-1 Juan Carlos García Álvarez (40), 2-1 Jerry Ricardo Bengtson Bodden (79).

06.02.2013, Estadio "Rommel Fernández", Ciudad de Panamá; Attendance: 25,000
Referee: Francisco Chacón Gutiérrez (Mexico)
PANAMA - COSTA RICA **2-2(2-1)**
PAN: Jaime Manuel Penedo Cano, Felipe Abdiel Baloy Ramírez, Luis Alfonso Henríquez Ledezma (70.Aníbal Cesis Godoy), Román Aureliano Torres Morcillo, Carlos Gabriel Rodríguez Orantes, Leonel Parris, Rolando Emilio Escobar Batista (64.Luis Gabriel Rentería), Gabriel Enrique Gómez Giron, Armando Cooper (87.Jairo Armando Glaize Yau), Marcos Aníbal Sánchez Mullins, Blas Antonio Miguel Pérez Ortega. Trainer: Jorge Luis Dely Valdes.
CRC: Patrick Alberto Pemberton Bernard, Christopher Meneses Barrantes, José Andrés Salvatierra López (68.Cristian Esteban Gamboa Luna), Michael Umaña Corrales, Geancarlo González Castro, Cristian Bolaños Navarro, Celso Borges Mora (57.Michael Barrantes Rojas), Eithel Ariel Rodríguez, Bryan Jafet Ruíz González, Randall Brenes Moya (46.Joël Nathaniel Campbell Samuels), Álvaro Alberto Saborío Chacón. Trainer: Jorge Luis Pinto Afanador (Colombia).
Goals: 1-0 Luis Alfonso Henríquez Ledezma (15), 2-0 Román Aureliano Torres Morcillo (26), 2-1 Álvaro Alberto Saborío Chacón (39), 2-2 Bryan Jafet Ruíz González (84).
Cautions: Felipe Abdiel Baloy Ramírez / Celso Borges Mora, Cristian Bolaños Navarro.

06.02.2013, Estadio Azteca, Ciudad de México; Attendance: 43,002
Referee: Mark Geiger (United States)
MEXICO - JAMAICA **0-0**
MEX: José de Jesús Corona Rodríguez, Francisco Javier Rodríguez Pinedo, Paul Nicolás Aguilar Rojas, Jorge Emmanuel Torres Nilo, Héctor Alfredo Moreno Herrera, José Andrés Guardado Hernández (80.Marco Jhonfai Fabián de la Mora), Carlos Arnoldo Salcido Flores, Héctor Miguel Herrera López (67.Ángel Eduardo Reyna Martínez), Oribe Peralta Morones, Giovani dos Santos Ramírez (46.Javier Ignacio Aquino Carmona), Javier Hernández Balcázar. Trainer: José Manuel de la Torre Menchaca.
JAM: Donovan Ricketts, Jermaine Taylor, Nyron Paul Henry Nosworthy, Adrian Joseph Mariappa, Demar Constantine Phillips, Marvin Conrad Elliott, Rodolph William Austin, Joel Joshua Frederick Melvin McAnuff, Jermaine Johnson (53.Theo Larayan Ronaldo Robinson), Garath James McCleary (84.Omar Daley), Ryan Johnson (80.Tremaine Stewart). Trainer: Theodore Whitmore.
Cautions: Héctor Alfredo Moreno Herrera / Jermaine Johnson.

22.03.2013, Estadio Olímpico Metropolitano, San Pedro Sula; Attendance: 38,500
Referee: Courtney Campbell (Jamaica)

HONDURAS - MEXICO **2-2(0-1)**

HON: Noel Eduardo Valladares Bonilla, Maynor Alexis Figueroa Róchez, Emilio Arturo Izaguirre Girón (60.Jerry Nelson Palacios Suazo), Víctor Salvador Bernárdez Blanco, Oscar Boniek García Ramírez, Roger Espinoza Ramírez, Luis Fernando Garrido, Mario Roberto Martínez Hernández (83.Carlos Israel Discua Castellanos), Arnold Fabián Peralta Sosa, Carlos Yaír Costly Molina, Jerry Ricardo Bengtson Bodden. Trainer: Luis Fernando Suárez (Colombia).

MEX: Francisco Guillermo Ochoa Magaña, Francisco Javier Rodríguez Pinedo, Jorge Emmanuel Torres Nilo, Héctor Alfredo Moreno Herrera, Severo Efraín Meza Mayorga, Javier Ignacio Aquino Carmona (87.Héctor Miguel Herrera López), José Andrés Guardado Hernández, Carlos Arnoldo Salcido Flores, Jesús Eduardo Zavala Castañeda, Giovani dos Santos Ramírez (76.Raúl Alonso Jiménez Rodríguez), Javier Hernández Balcázar (65.Omar Bravo Tordecillas). Trainer: José Manuel de la Torre Menchaca.

Goals: 0-1 Javier Hernández Balcázar (28), 0-2 Javier Hernández Balcázar (54), 1-2 Carlos Yaír Costly Molina (77), 2-2 Jerry Ricardo Bengtson Bodden (80).

Cautions: Jorge Emmanuel Torres Nilo, Francisco Javier Rodríguez Pinedo.

22.03.2013, Independence Park, Kingston; Attendance: 25,000
Referee: Héctor Francisco Rodríguez Hernández (Honduras)

JAMAICA - PANAMA **1-1(1-0)**

JAM: Donovan Ricketts, Jermaine Taylor, Nyron Paul Henry Nosworthy (45.Omar Daley), Adrian Joseph Mariappa, Demar Constantine Phillips, Marvin Conrad Elliott, Rodolph William Austin, Luton George Shelton, Joel Joshua Frederick Melvin McAnuff (78.Jermaine Johnson), Garath James McCleary, Jermaine Paul Alexander Beckford (65.Theo Larayan Ronaldo Robinson). Trainer: Theodore Whitmore.

PAN: Luis Ricardo Mejía Cajar, Felipe Abdiel Baloy Ramírez, Luis Alfonso Henríquez Ledezma, Román Aureliano Torres Morcillo, Leonel Parris, Rolando Emilio Escobar Batista (63.Nelson Alberto Barahona Collins), Gabriel Enrique Gómez Giron (78.Alberto Abdiel Quintero Medina), Armando Cooper (54.Aníbal Cesis Godoy), Marcos Aníbal Sánchez Mullins, Luis Carlos Tejada Hansell, Blas Antonio Miguel Pérez Ortega. Trainer: Jorge Luis Dely Valdes.

Goals: 1-0 Marvin Conrad Elliott (23), 1-1 Luis Alfonso Henríquez Ledezma (66).

Cautions: Jermaine Paul Alexander Beckford, Demar Constantine Phillips, Luton George Shelton, Omar Daley, Garath James McCleary / Marcos Aníbal Sánchez Mullins, Gabriel Enrique Gómez Giron, Alberto Abdiel Quintero Medina.

22.03.2013, Dick's Sporting Goods Park, Commerce City; Attendance: 19,734
Referee: Joel Antonio Aguilar Chicas (El Salvador)

UNITED STATES - COSTA RICA **1-0(1-0)**

USA: Bradley Edwin Guzan, Clarence Goodson, Geoffrey Scott Cameron, Omar Gonzalez, Jermaine Jones (81.Edu Maurice Edu Jr.), DaMarcus Lamont Beasley, Clint Drew Dempsey, Michael Sheehan Bradley, Graham Jonathan Zusi (73.Edward Abraham Johnson), Hérculez Gómez Hurtado (90+4.Kyle Robert Beckerman), Josmer Volmy Altidore. Trainer: Jürgen Klinsmann (Germany).

CRC: Keylor Antonio Navas Gamboa, Roy Miller Hernández, Cristian Esteban Gamboa Luna (81.Juan Diego Madrigal Espinoza), Michael Umaña Corrales, Geancarlo González Castro, Bryan Josué Oviedo Jiménez (73.Diego Gerardo Calvo Fonseca), Michael Barrantes Rojas, Cristian Bolaños Navarro (61.Joël Nathaniel Campbell Samuels), Eithel Ariel Rodríguez, Bryan Jafet Ruíz González, Álvaro Alberto Saborío Chacón. Trainer: Jorge Luis Pinto Afanador (Colombia).

Goal: 1-0 Clint Drew Dempsey (16).

Cautions: Roy Miller Hernández, Geancarlo González Castro.

26.03.2013, Estadio Nacional de Costa Rica, San José; Attendance: 32,427
Referee: Enrico Wijngaarde (Suriname)

COSTA RICA - JAMAICA 2-0(1-0)

CRC: Keylor Antonio Navas Gamboa, Cristian Esteban Gamboa Luna, Michael Umaña Corrales, Geancarlo González Castro, Bryan Josué Oviedo Jiménez, Michael Barrantes Rojas (83.Celso Borges Mora), Osvaldo Rodríguez Flores (58.Diego Gerardo Calvo Fonseca), Eithel Ariel Rodríguez, Bryan Jafet Ruíz González, Joël Nathaniel Campbell Samuels (86.Jhonny Acosta Zamora), Álvaro Alberto Saborío Chacón. Trainer: Jorge Luis Pinto Afanador (Colombia).
JAM: Donovan Ricketts, Lloyd Colin Doyley, Jermaine Taylor, Adrian Joseph Mariappa, Demar Constantine Phillips, Marvin Conrad Elliott, Rodolph William Austin, Joel Joshua Frederick Melvin McAnuff, Luton George Shelton (61.Jermaine Johnson), Garath James McCleary (77.Dane Richards), Jermaine Paul Alexander Beckford (62.Theo Larayan Ronaldo Robinson). Trainer: Theodore Whitmore.
Goals: 1-0 Michael Umaña Corrales (22), Diego Gerardo Calvo Fonseca (82).
Cautions: Eithel Ariel Rodríguez, Michael Umaña Corrales / Jermaine Taylor, Jermaine Johnson.

26.03.2013, Estadio "Rommel Fernández", Ciudad de Panamá; Attendance: 18,253
Referee: Jair Marrufo (United States)

PANAMA - HONDURAS 2-0(1-0)

PAN: Luis Ricardo Mejía Cajar, Felipe Abdiel Baloy Ramírez, Luis Alfonso Henríquez Ledezma (80.Harold Oshkaly Cummings Segura), Román Aureliano Torres Morcillo, Carlos Gabriel Rodríguez Orantes, Leonel Parris (90+2.Juan De Dios Pérez Quijada), Gabriel Enrique Gómez Giron, Marcos Aníbal Sánchez Mullins, Aníbal Cesis Godoy, Luis Carlos Tejada Hansell (65.Nelson Alberto Barahona Collins), Blas Antonio Miguel Pérez Ortega. Trainer: Jorge Luis Dely Valdes.
HON: Noel Eduardo Valladares Bonilla, Maynor Alexis Figueroa Róchez, Juan Carlos García Álvarez, Víctor Salvador Bernárdez Blanco, Oscar Boniek García Ramírez, Roger Espinoza Ramírez, Luis Fernando Garrido, Mario Roberto Martínez Hernández, Arnold Fabián Peralta Sosa (60.Jerry Nelson Palacios Suazo), Carlos Yaír Costly Molina, Jerry Ricardo Bengtson Bodden (83.Roger Fabricio Rojas Lazo). Trainer: Luis Fernando Suárez (Colombia).
Goals: 1-0 Luis Carlos Tejada Hansell (2), 2-0 Blas Antonio Miguel Pérez Ortega (75).

26.03.2013, Estadio Azteca, Ciudad de México; Attendance: 85,500
Referee: Walter Alexander López Castellanos (Guatemala)

MEXICO - UNITED STATES 0-0

MEX: Francisco Guillermo Ochoa Magaña, Jorge Emmanuel Torres Nilo (72.Ángel Eduardo Reyna Martínez), Héctor Alfredo Moreno Herrera, Severo Efraín Meza Mayorga, Javier Ignacio Aquino Carmona (81.Omar Bravo Tordecillas), Diego Antonio Reyes Rosales, José Andrés Guardado Hernández, Carlos Arnoldo Salcido Flores, Jesús Eduardo Zavala Castañeda, Giovani dos Santos Ramírez, Javier Hernández Balcázar. Trainer: José Manuel de la Torre Menchaca.
USA: Bradley Edwin Guzan, Geoffrey Scott Cameron, Matt Besler, Omar Gonzalez, DaMarcus Lamont Beasley, Clint Drew Dempsey, Michael Sheehan Bradley, Edu Maurice Edu Jr., Graham Jonathan Zusi (82.Dane Brekken Shea), Hérculez Gómez Hurtado (71.Bradley Joseph Davis), Josmer Volmy Altidore (46.Edward Abraham Johnson). Trainer: Jürgen Klinsmann (Germany).
Cautions: DaMarcus Lamont Beasley, Matt Besler, Bradley Joseph Davis.

04.06.2013, Independence Park, Kingston; Attendance: 16,483
Referee: Joel Antonio Aguilar Chicas (El Salvador)
JAMAICA - MEXICO 0-1(0-0)
JAM: Donovan Ricketts, Alvas Elvis Powell, Adrian Joseph Mariappa, O'Brian Woodbine, Jermaine Hue, Daniel Gordon, Marvin Conrad Elliott, Rodolph William Austin (76.Keammar Rudolph Daley), JeVaughn Watson (62.Darren Mattocks), Garath James McCleary, Ryan Johnson (62.Jermaine Paul Alexander Beckford). Trainer: Theodore Whitmore.
MEX: José de Jesús Corona Rodríguez, Francisco Javier Rodríguez Pinedo, Severo Efraín Meza Mayorga, Diego Antonio Reyes Rosales, José Andrés Guardado Hernández, Gerardo Torrado Díez de Bonilla, Carlos Arnoldo Salcido Flores, Jesús Eduardo Zavala Castañeda, Pablo Edson Barrera Acosta (59.Gerardo Flores Zúñiga), Jesús Aldo de Nigris Guajardo (67.Giovani dos Santos Ramírez), Javier Hernández Balcázar (86.Raúl Alonso Jiménez Rodríguez). Trainer: José Manuel de la Torre Menchaca.
Goal: 0-1 Jesús Aldo de Nigris Guajardo (48).
Cautions: Alvas Elvis Powell / Gerardo Torrado Díez de Bonilla.

07.06.2013, Independence Park, Kingston; Attendance: 12,130
Referee: Roberto Moreno (Panama)
JAMAICA - UNITED STATES 1-2(0-1)
JAM: Donovan Ricketts, Alvas Elvis Powell, Adrian Joseph Mariappa, O'Brian Woodbine, Jermaine Hue (70.Jermaine Paul Alexander Beckford), Daniel Gordon, Marvin Conrad Elliott, Rodolph William Austin, Jermaine Johnson (68.Theo Larayan Ronaldo Robinson), Garath James McCleary (74.Omar Daley), Ryan Johnson. Trainer: Theodore Whitmore.
USA: Timothy Matthew Howard, Matt Besler, Omar Gonzalez, DaMarcus Lamont Beasley, Fabian Johnson (76.Edgar Eduardo Castillo Carrillo), Jermaine Jones (59.Geoffrey Scott Cameron), Clint Drew Dempsey, Michael Sheehan Bradley, Bradley Ray Evans, Graham Jonathan Zusi, Josmer Volmy Altidore (83.Edward Abraham Johnson). Trainer: Jürgen Klinsmann (Germany).
Goals: 0-1 Josmer Volmy Altidore (30), 1-1 Jermaine Paul Alexander Beckford (89), 1-2 Bradley Ray Evans (90+2).
Cautions: Graham Jonathan Zusi, Bradley Ray Evans.

07.06.2013, Estadio Nacional de Costa Rica, San José; Attendance: 35,000
Referee: Walter Alexander López Castellanos (Guatemala)
COSTA RICA - HONDURAS 1-0(1-0)
CRC: Keylor Antonio Navas Gamboa, Roy Miller Hernández, Cristian Esteban Gamboa Luna, Geancarlo González Castro, Christopher Meneses Barrantes, Celso Borges Mora, Eithel Ariel Rodríguez, Cristian Bolaños Navarro (81.Kendall Jamaal Waston Manley), Bryan Jafet Ruíz González (69.Diego Gerardo Calvo Fonseca), Jairo Arrieta Obando (57.Álvaro Alberto Saborío Chacón), Joël Nathaniel Campbell Samuels. Trainer: Jorge Luis Pinto Afanador (Colombia).
HON: Noel Eduardo Valladares Bonilla, Juan Carlos García Álvarez (72.Emilio Arturo Izaguirre Girón), Víctor Salvador Bernárdez Blanco, Osman Danilo Chávez Guity, Oscar Boniek García Ramírez, Wilson Roberto Palacios Suazo, Roger Espinoza Ramírez, Luis Fernando Garrido (57.Andy Najar Rodríguez), Arnold Fabián Peralta Sosa, Carlos Yaír Costly Molina, Jerry Ricardo Bengtson Bodden (61.Jerry Nelson Palacios Suazo). Trainer: Luis Fernando Suárez (Colombia).
Goal: 1-0 Roy Miller Hernández (25).
Cautions: Keylor Antonio Navas Gamboa, Eithel Ariel Rodríguez / Luis Fernando Garrido, Roger Espinoza Ramírez, Carlos Yaír Costly Molina.

07.06.2013, Estadio "Rommel Fernández", Ciudad de Panamá; Attendance: 27,100
Referee: Wálter Enrique Quesada Cordero (Costa Rica)
PANAMA - MEXICO 0-0
PAN: Jaime Manuel Penedo Cano, Felipe Abdiel Baloy Ramírez, Luis Alfonso Henríquez Ledezma, Román Aureliano Torres Morcillo, Carlos Gabriel Rodríguez Orantes, Leonel Parris, Gabriel Enrique Gómez Giron (59.Armando Cooper), Amílcar Henríquez Espinosa, Marcos Aníbal Sánchez Mullins, Luis Carlos Tejada Hansell (79.Nelson Alberto Barahona Collins), Blas Antonio Miguel Pérez Ortega (71.Rolando Manrique Blackburn Ortega). Trainer: Jorge Luis Dely Valdes.
MEX: José de Jesús Corona Rodríguez, Francisco Javier Rodríguez Pinedo, Héctor Alfredo Moreno Herrera, Severo Efraín Meza Mayorga, Javier Ignacio Aquino Carmona (73.Gerardo Flores Zúñiga), José Andrés Guardado Hernández, Gerardo Torrado Díez de Bonilla, Carlos Arnoldo Salcido Flores, Jesús Eduardo Zavala Castañeda, Giovani dos Santos Ramírez (68.Ángel Eduardo Reyna Martínez), Javier Hernández Balcázar (80.Jesús Aldo de Nigris Guajardo). Trainer: José Manuel de la Torre Menchaca.
Cautions: Román Aureliano Torres Morcillo / Gerardo Flores Zúñiga.

11.06.2013, Estadio Azteca, Ciudad de México; Attendance: 65,753
Referee: Mark Geiger (United States)
MEXICO - COSTA RICA 0-0
MEX: José de Jesús Corona Rodríguez, Francisco Javier Rodríguez Pinedo, Héctor Alfredo Moreno Herrera, Gerardo Flores Zúñiga, Héctor Miguel Herrera López (75.Giovani dos Santos Ramírez), José Andrés Guardado Hernández, Carlos Arnoldo Salcido Flores, Jesús Eduardo Zavala Castañeda, Pablo Edson Barrera Acosta (46.Javier Ignacio Aquino Carmona), Jesús Aldo de Nigris Guajardo (54.Raúl Alonso Jiménez Rodríguez), Javier Hernández Balcázar. Trainer: José Manuel de la Torre Menchaca.
CRC: Keylor Antonio Navas Gamboa, Michael Umaña Corrales, Júnior Enrique Díaz Campbell, Cristian Esteban Gamboa Luna, Geancarlo González Castro, Jhonny Acosta Zamora, Michael Barrantes Rojas (76.Celso Borges Mora), Cristian Bolaños Navarro (66.Kenny Martin Cunningham Brown), Yeltsin Ignacio Tejeda Valverde, Bryan Jafet Ruíz González, Joël Nathaniel Campbell Samuels (86.Álvaro Alberto Saborío Chacón). Trainer: Jorge Luis Pinto Afanador (Colombia).
Cautions: Javier Hernández Balcázar, Héctor Alfredo Moreno Herrera / Cristian Esteban Gamboa Luna.

11.06.2013, Estadio „Tiburcio Carías Andino", Tegucigalpa; Attendance: 29,000
Referee: Marco Antonio Rodríguez Moreno (Mexico)
HONDURAS - JAMAICA 2-0(1-0)
HON: Noel Eduardo Valladares Bonilla, Emilio Arturo Izaguirre Girón (85.Juan Carlos García Álvarez), Víctor Salvador Bernárdez Blanco, Juan Pablo Montes Montes, Oscar Boniek García Ramírez (29.Marvin Antonio Chávez), Wilson Roberto Palacios Suazo, Roger Espinoza Ramírez, Luis Fernando Garrido, Mario Roberto Martínez Hernández (85.Jorge Aarón Claros Juárez), Arnold Fabián Peralta Sosa, Roger Fabricio Rojas Lazo. Trainer: Luis Fernando Suárez (Colombia).
JAM: Donovan Ricketts, Alvas Elvis Powell, Adrian Joseph Mariappa, O'Brian Woodbine, JeVaughn Watson (61.Darren Mattocks), Daniel Gordon, Marvin Conrad Elliott, Rodolph William Austin, Jermaine Johnson (73.Damian Williams), Ryan Johnson (61.Theo Larayan Ronaldo Robinson), Jermaine Paul Alexander Beckford. Trainer: Theodore Whitmore.
Goals: 1-0 Oscar Boniek García Ramírez (10), 2-0 Roger Fabricio Rojas Lazo (88).
Cautions: Luis Fernando Garrido, Víctor Salvador Bernárdez Blanco, Marvin Antonio Chávez / O'Brian Woodbine, Jermaine Johnson, Adrian Joseph Mariappa.
Sent off: Adrian Joseph Mariappa (77).

11.06.2013, CenturyLink Field, Seattle; Attendance: 40,847
Referee: Roberto García Orozco (Mexico)
UNITED STATES - PANAMA 2-0(1-0)
USA: Timothy Matthew Howard, Matt Besler, Geoffrey Scott Cameron, Omar Gonzalez, DaMarcus Lamont Beasley, Fabian Johnson (87.Bradley Joseph Davis), Clint Drew Dempsey, Michael Sheehan Bradley, Bradley Ray Evans, Edward Abraham Johnson (87.Joe Benny Corona Crespín), Josmer Volmy Altidore (90+1.Stuart Alistair Holden). Trainer: Jürgen Klinsmann (Germany).
PAN: Jaime Manuel Penedo Cano, Felipe Abdiel Baloy Ramírez, Román Aureliano Torres Morcillo, Carlos Gabriel Rodríguez Orantes, Leonel Parris, Amílcar Henríquez Espinosa (78.Gabriel Arturo Torres Tejada), Armando Cooper (60.Nelson Alberto Barahona Collins), Alberto Abdiel Quintero Medina, Marcos Aníbal Sánchez Mullins, Aníbal Cesis Godoy (60.Rolando Manrique Blackburn Ortega), Luis Carlos Tejada Hansell. Trainer: Jorge Luis Dely Valdes.
Goals: 1-0 Josmer Volmy Altidore (36), 2-0 Edward Abraham Johnson (53).
Cautions: Josmer Volmy Altidore, Geoffrey Scott Cameron, DaMarcus Lamont Beasley, Timothy Matthew Howard / Marcos Aníbal Sánchez Mullins.

18.06.2013, Rio Tinto Stadium, Sandy; Attendance: 20,250
Referee: Enrico Wijngaarde (Suriname)
UNITED STATES - HONDURAS 1-0(0-0)
USA: Timothy Matthew Howard, Matt Besler, Omar Gonzalez, Fabian Johnson, Clint Drew Dempsey, Jermaine Jones (74.Geoffrey Scott Cameron), Michael Sheehan Bradley, Bradley Ray Evans, Graham Jonathan Zusi (74.Bradley Joseph Davis), Edward Abraham Johnson (87.Edgar Eduardo Castillo Carrillo), Josmer Volmy Altidore. Trainer: Jürgen Klinsmann (Germany).
HON: Noel Eduardo Valladares Bonilla, Emilio Arturo Izaguirre Girón, Juan Pablo Montes Montes, José David Velásquez Colón, Jorge Aarón Claros Juárez, Wilson Roberto Palacios Suazo, Roger Espinoza Ramírez, Mario Roberto Martínez Hernández (69.Marvin Antonio Chávez), Arnold Fabián Peralta Sosa (76.Oscar Boniek García Ramírez), Andy Najar Rodríguez, Carlos Yaír Costly Molina (33.Roger Fabricio Rojas Lazo). Trainer: Luis Fernando Suárez (Colombia).
Goal: 1-0 Josmer Volmy Altidore (73).
Cautions: Jermaine Jones / Arnold Fabián Peralta Sosa, Wilson Roberto Palacios Suazo, José David Velásquez Colón.

18.06.2013, Estadio Nacional de Costa Rica, San José; Attendance: 35,000
Referee: Courtney Campbell (Jamaica)
COSTA RICA - PANAMA 2-0(0-0)
CRC: Keylor Antonio Navas Gamboa, Michael Umaña Corrales, Júnior Enrique Díaz Campbell, Cristian Esteban Gamboa Luna, Geancarlo González Castro, Celso Borges Mora, Eithel Ariel Rodríguez, Cristian Bolaños Navarro (65.Kenny Martin Cunningham Brown), Bryan Jafet Ruíz González (86.Roy Miller Hernández), Álvaro Alberto Saborío Chacón, Joël Nathaniel Campbell Samuels (83.Diego Gerardo Calvo Fonseca). Trainer: Jorge Luis Pinto Afanador (Colombia).
PAN: Jaime Manuel Penedo Cano, Felipe Abdiel Baloy Ramírez, Luis Alfonso Henríquez Ledezma (75.Roderick Miller), Román Aureliano Torres Morcillo, Leonel Parris, Rolando Emilio Escobar Batista, Amílcar Henríquez Espinosa, Armando Cooper, Alberto Abdiel Quintero Medina (58.Nelson Alberto Barahona Collins), Luis Carlos Tejada Hansell, Blas Antonio Miguel Pérez Ortega (69.Gabriel Arturo Torres Tejada). Trainer: Jorge Luis Dely Valdes.
Goals: 1-0 Bryan Jafet Ruíz González (47), 2-0 Celso Borges Mora (51).
Cautions: Eithel Ariel Rodríguez, Bryan Jafet Ruíz González / Blas Antonio Miguel Pérez Ortega, Felipe Abdiel Baloy Ramírez.

06.09.2013, Estadio Azteca, Ciudad de México; Attendance: 73,981
Referee: Roberto Moreno (Panama)
MEXICO - HONDURAS 1-2(1-0)
MEX: José de Jesús Corona Rodríguez, Héctor Alfredo Moreno Herrera, Severo Efraín Meza Mayorga, Diego Antonio Reyes Rosales, Gerardo Torrado Díez de Bonilla (69.Javier Hernández Balcázar), Carlos Arnoldo Salcido Flores, Fernando Enrique Arce Ruiz, Christian Estuardo Giménez (56.José Andrés Guardado Hernández), Ángel Eduardo Reyna Martínez (66.Javier Ignacio Aquino Carmona), Oribe Peralta Morones, Giovani dos Santos Ramírez. Trainer: José Manuel de la Torre Menchaca.
HON: Noel Eduardo Valladares Bonilla, Maynor Alexis Figueroa Róchez, Emilio Arturo Izaguirre Girón, Víctor Salvador Bernárdez Blanco, Brayan Antonio Beckeles, Oscar Boniek García Ramírez (60.Edgard Anthony Álvarez Reyes), Wilson Roberto Palacios Suazo, Roger Aníbal Espinoza Ramírez, Luis Fernando Garrido, Andy Najar Rodríguez (46.Jerry Ricardo Bengtson Bodden), Carlos Yaír Costly Molina (80.Marvin Antonio Chávez). Trainer: Luis Fernando Suárez (Colombia).
Goals: 1-0 Oribe Peralta Morones (5), 1-1 Jerry Ricardo Bengtson Bodden (63), 1-2 Carlos Yaír Costly Molina (66).
Cautions: Gerardo Torrado Díez de Bonilla / Víctor Salvador Bernárdez Blanco, Oscar Boniek García Ramírez, Carlos Yaír Costly Molina.

06.09.2013, Estadio Nacional de Costa Rica, San José; Attendance: 35,000
Referee: Marco Antonio Rodríguez Moreno (Mexico)
COSTA RICA - UNITED STATES 3-1(2-1)
CRC: Keylor Antonio Navas Gamboa, Míchael Umaña Corrales, Bryan Josué Oviedo Jiménez, Cristian Esteban Gamboa Luna, Geancarlo González Castro, Jhonny Acosta Zamora, Celso Borges Mora, Cristian Bolaños Navarro (86.Randall Brenes Moya), Yeltsin Ignacio Tejeda Valverde (73.José Miguel Cubero Loria), Bryan Jafet Ruíz González (80.Álvaro Alberto Saborío Chacón), Joël Nathaniel Campbell Samuels. Trainer: Jorge Luis Pinto Afanador (Colombia).
USA: Timothy Matthew Howard, DaMarcus Lamont Beasley, Fabian Marco Johnson (71.Josmer Volmy Altidore), Geoffrey Scott Cameron, Michael Orozco Fiscal, Matt Besler, Omar González, Jermaine Jones, Graham Jonathan Zusi (58.Edward Abraham Johnson), Clinton Drew Dempsey (90.Aron Jóhannsson), Landon Timothy Donovan. Trainer: Jürgen Klinsmann (Germany).
Goals: 1-0 Jhonny Acosta Zamora (2), 2-0 Celso Borges Mora (10), 2-1 Clinton Drew Dempsey (43 penalty), 3-1 Joël Nathaniel Campbell Samuels (75).
Cautions: Míchael Umaña Corrales, Cristian Bolaños Navarro, Keylor Antonio Navas Gamboa / Geoffrey Scott Cameron, Matt Besler, Josmer Volmy Altidore.

06.09.2013, Estadio "Rommel Fernández", Ciudad de Panamá; Attendance: 20,000
Referee: Walter Alexander López Castellanos (Guatemala)
PANAMA - JAMAICA 0-0
PAN: Jaime Manuel Penedo Cano, Luis Alfonso Henríquez Ledezma, Román Aureliano Torres Morcillo, Carlos Gabriel Rodríguez Orantes (46.Harold Oshkaly Cummings Segura), Roberto Leandro Chen Rodríguez, Gabriel Enrique Gómez Giron (76.Jairo Joseth Jiménez Robles), Alberto Abdiel Quintero Medina, Marcos Aníbal Sánchez Mullins, Aníbal Cesis Godoy, Gabriel Arturo Torres Tejada, Cecilio Alfonso Waterman Ruíz (66.Alcibíades Rojas McRay). Trainer: Jorge Luis Dely Valdes.
JAM: Donovan Ricketts, Lloyd Colin Doyley, Westley Nathan Morgan, Alvas Elvis Powell (44.O'Brian Woodbine), Shaun Michael Cummings, Jermaine Taylor, Rodolph William Austin, Joel Joshua Frederick Melvin McAnuff, Luton George Shelton (75.Jermaine Johnson), Garath James McCleary, Marlon Francis King (63.Marvin Conrad Elliott). Trainer: Winfried Schäfer (Germany).
Cautions: Román Aureliano Torres Morcillo / Marlon Francis King, Rodolph William Austin, Donovan Ricketts.
Sent off: Rodolph William Austin (58).

10.09.2013, Independence Park, Kingston; Attendance: 6,100
Referee: Jair Marrufo (United States)
JAMAICA - COSTA RICA **1-1(0-0)**
JAM: Richard McCallum, Lloyd Colin Doyley, Westley Nathan Morgan, Adrian Joseph Mariappa, Shaun Michael Cummings, Jermaine Taylor, Marvin Conrad Elliott (83.Christopher Charles Humphrey), Garath James McCleary, Joel Joshua Frederick Melvin McAnuff, Luton George Shelton (46.Jermaine Paul Alexander Beckford), Marlon Francis King (68.Jermaine Anderson). Trainer: Winfried Schäfer (Germany).
CRC: Patrick Alberto Pemberton Bernard, Míchael Umaña Corrales, Júnior Enrique Díaz Campbell, Cristian Esteban Gamboa Luna, Geancarlo González Castro, Jhonny Acosta Zamora, Celso Borges Mora, Yeltsin Ignacio Tejeda Valverde (57.José Miguel Cubero Loria), Bryan Jafet Ruíz González, Joël Nathaniel Campbell Samuels (79.Carlos Johnson Carpio), Diego Gerardo Calvo Fonseca (68.Randall Brenes Moya). Trainer: Jorge Luis Pinto Afanador (Colombia).
Goals: 0-1 Randall Brenes Moya (74), 1-1 Jermaine Anderson (90+2).

10.09.2013, Columbus Crew Stadium, Columbus; Attendance: 24,584
Referee: Courtney Campbell (Jamaica)
UNITED STATES - MEXICO **2-0(0-0)**
USA: Timothy Matthew Howard, DaMarcus Lamont Beasley, Clarence Edgar Goodson, Fabian Marco Johnson (46.Michael Finlay Parkhurst), Omar González, Edward Abraham Johnson (76.Mikkel Morgenstar Pålssønn Diskerud), Jermaine Jones, Kyle Robert Beckerman, Alejandro Bedoya (84.Graham Jonathan Zusi), Clinton Drew Dempsey, Landon Timothy Donovan. Trainer: Jürgen Klinsmann (Germany).
MEX: José de Jesús Corona Rodríguez, José Andrés Guardado Hernández, Héctor Alfredo Moreno Herrera, Hiram Ricardo Mier Alanis, Diego Antonio Reyes Rosales, Carlos Arnoldo Salcido Flores (77.Ángel Eduardo Reyna Martínez), Fernando Enrique Arce Ruiz (69.Oribe Peralta Morones), Christian Estuardo Giménez (55.Héctor Miguel Herrera López), Jesús Eduardo Zavala Castañeda, Giovani dos Santos Ramírez, Javier Hernández Balcázar. Trainer: Luis Fernando Tena Garduño.
Goals: 1-0 Edward Abraham Johnson (49), 2-0 Landon Timothy Donovan (78).
Cautions: Alejandro Bedoya, Landon Timothy Donovan.

10.09.2013, Estadio Nacional "Tiburcio Carías Andino", Tegucigalpa; Attendance: 26,582
Referee: Mark Geiger (United States)
HONDURAS - PANAMA **2-2(1-0)**
HON: Noel Eduardo Valladares Bonilla, Maynor Alexis Figueroa Róchez, Emilio Arturo Izaguirre Girón, Víctor Salvador Bernárdez Blanco, Brayan Antonio Beckeles, Oscar Boniek García Ramírez (81.Edgard Anthony Álvarez Reyes), Wilson Roberto Palacios Suazo, Roger Aníbal Espinoza Ramírez, Luis Fernando Garrido, Carlos Yaír Costly Molina, Jerry Ricardo Bengtson Bodden (90.Georgie Wilson Welcome Collins). Trainer: Luis Fernando Suárez (Colombia).
PAN: Jaime Manuel Penedo Cano, Felipe Abdiel Baloy Ramírez, Luis Alfonso Henríquez Ledezma, Harold Oshkaly Cummings Segura, Roberto Leandro Chen Rodríguez, Gabriel Enrique Gómez Giron (62.Aníbal Cesis Godoy), Amílcar Henríquez Espinosa, Alberto Abdiel Quintero Medina (47.Jairo Joseth Jiménez Robles), Marcos Aníbal Sánchez Mullins (78.Alcibíades Rojas McRay), Blas Antonio Miguel Pérez Ortega, Gabriel Arturo Torres Tejada. Trainer: Jorge Luis Dely Valdes.
Goals: 1-0 Carlos Yaír Costly Molina (28), 1-1 Gabriel Arturo Torres Tejada (50), 2-1 Wilson Roberto Palacios Suazo (62), 2-2 Roberto Leandro Chen Rodríguez (90+1).
Cautions: Luis Fernando Garrido, Emilio Arturo Izaguirre Girón / Roberto Leandro Chen Rodríguez, Alberto Abdiel Quintero Medina, Felipe Abdiel Baloy Ramírez, Gabriel Arturo Torres Tejada.

11.10.2013, Estadio Olímpico Metropolitano, San Pedro Sula; Attendance: 38,500
Referee: Jair Marrufo (United States)
HONDURAS - COSTA RICA 1-0(0-0)
HON: Noel Eduardo Valladares Bonilla, Maynor Alexis Figueroa Róchez, Emilio Arturo Izaguirre Girón (79.Juan Carlos García Álvarez), Víctor Salvador Bernárdez Blanco, Oscar Boniek García Ramírez, Wilson Roberto Palacios Suazo (58.Andy Najar Rodríguez), Roger Aníbal Espinoza Ramírez, Luis Fernando Garrido, Arnold Fabián Peralta Sosa, Carlos Yaír Costly Molina, Jerry Ricardo Bengtson Bodden (74.Jorge Aarón Claros Juárez). Trainer: Luis Fernando Suárez (Colombia).
CRC: Keylor Antonio Navas Gamboa, Míchael Umaña Corrales, Júnior Enrique Díaz Campbell, Cristian Esteban Gamboa Luna, Geancarlo González Castro, Jhonny Acosta Zamora, Celso Borges Mora, Cristian Bolaños Navarro (70.Diego Gerardo Calvo Fonseca), José Miguel Cubero Loria, Bryan Jafet Ruíz González (61.Joël Nathaniel Campbell Samuels), Álvaro Alberto Saborío Chacón (70.Víctor Núñez Rodríguez). Trainer: Jorge Luis Pinto Afanador (Colombia).
Goal: 1-0 Jerry Ricardo Bengtson Bodden (64).
Cautions: Jerry Ricardo Bengtson Bodden.

11.10.2013, Sporting Park, Kansas City; Attendance: 18,467
Referee: Elmer Arturo Bonilla (El Salvador)
UNITED STATES - JAMAICA 2-0(0-0)
USA: Timothy Matthew Howard, DaMarcus Lamont Beasley (66.Edgar Eduardo Castillo Carrillo), Geoffrey Scott Cameron, Matt Besler, Jermaine Jones, Bradley Ray Evans, Mikkel Morgenstar Pålssønn Diskerud, Alejandro Bedoya, Landon Timothy Donovan (46.Graham Jonathan Zusi), Josmer Volmy Altidore, Aron Jóhannsson (72.Sacha Bryan Klještan). Trainer: Jürgen Klinsmann (Germany).
JAM: Duwayne Oriel Kerr, Lloyd Colin Doyley, Westley Nathan Morgan, Adrian Joseph Mariappa, Demar Constantine Phillips, Joel Joshua Frederick Melvin McAnuff, JeVaughn Watson (72.Theo Larayan Ronaldo Robinson), Rodolph William Austin, Deshorn Brown, Ryan Johnson (84.Jermaine Anderson), Darren Mattocks. Trainer: Winfried Schäfer (Germany).
Goals: 1-0 Graham Jonathan Zusi (77), 2-0 Josmer Volmy Altidore (80).
Cautions: Sacha Bryan Klještan / Jermaine Anderson.

11.10.2013, Estadio Azteca, Ciudad de México; Attendance: 90,758
Referee: Joel Antonio Aguilar Chicas (El Salvador)
MEXICO - PANAMA 2-1(1-0)
MEX: Francisco Guillermo Ochoa Magaña, Rafael Márquez Álvarez, Hugo Ayala Castro, Jorge Emmanuel Torres Nilo, Miguel Arturo Layún Prado, Jesús Eduardo Zavala Castañeda (82.Raúl Alonso Jiménez Rodríguez), Javier Ignacio Aquino Carmona (65.Christian Estuardo Giménez), Carlos Alberto Peña Rodríguez, Oribe Peralta Morones, Giovani dos Santos Ramírez (70.Fernando Enrique Arce Ruiz), Javier Hernández Balcázar. Trainer: Víctor Manuel Vucetich Rojas.
PAN: Jaime Manuel Penedo Cano, Felipe Abdiel Baloy Ramírez, Luis Alfonso Henríquez Ledezma, Román Aureliano Torres Morcillo, Harold Oshkaly Cummings Segura, Gabriel Enrique Gómez Giron (68.Luis Carlos Tejada Hansell), Amílcar Henríquez Espinosa, Alberto Abdiel Quintero Medina, Marcos Aníbal Sánchez Mullins (75.Jairo Joseth Jiménez Robles), Aníbal Cesis Godoy, Blas Antonio Miguel Pérez Ortega (79.Gabriel Arturo Torres Tejada). Trainer: Jorge Luis Dely Valdes.
Goals: 1-0 Oribe Peralta Morones (39), 1-1 Luis Carlos Tejada Hansell (81), 2-1 Raúl Alonso Jiménez Rodríguez (85).
Cautions: Oribe Peralta Morones, Jesús Eduardo Zavala Castañeda / Harold Oshkaly Cummings Segura.

15.10.2013, Estadio Nacional de Costa Rica, San José; Attendance: 35,000
Referee: Walter Alexander López Castellanos (Guatemala)

COSTA RICA - MEXICO **2-1(1-1)**

CRC: Keylor Antonio Navas Gamboa, Míchael Umaña Corrales, Bryan Josué Oviedo Jiménez, Cristian Esteban Gamboa Luna, Geancarlo González Castro, Jhonny Acosta Zamora, Celso Borges Mora, Cristian Bolaños Navarro, Yeltsin Ignacio Tejeda Valverde (72.José Miguel Cubero Loria), Bryan Jafet Ruíz González (49.Álvaro Alberto Saborío Chacón), Joël Nathaniel Campbell Samuels (77.Michael Barrantes Rojas). Trainer: Jorge Luis Pinto Afanador (Colombia).

MEX: Francisco Guillermo Ochoa Magaña, Rafael Márquez Álvarez, Hugo Ayala Castro, Jorge Emmanuel Torres Nilo (73.Isaác Brizuela Muñoz), Miguel Arturo Layún Prado, Christian Estuardo Giménez, Jesús Eduardo Zavala Castañeda, Javier Ignacio Aquino Carmona (66.Giovani dos Santos Ramírez), Carlos Alberto Peña Rodríguez, Oribe Peralta Morones, Javier Hernández Balcázar (60.Raúl Alonso Jiménez Rodríguez). Trainer: Víctor Manuel Vucetich Rojas.

Goals: 1-0 Bryan Jafet Ruíz González (24), 1-1 Oribe Peralta Morones (28), 2-1 Álvaro Alberto Saborío Chacón (63).

Cautions: Bryan Josué Oviedo Jiménez, Jhonny Acosta Zamora, Keylor Antonio Navas Gamboa / Jorge Emmanuel Torres Nilo, Rafael Márquez Álvarez.

15.10.2013, Independence Park, Kingston; Attendance: 6,000
Referee: Mark Geiger (United States)

JAMAICA - HONDURAS **2-2(1-2)**

JAM: Duwayne Oriel Kerr, Lloyd Colin Doyley (59.Alvas Elvis Powell), Westley Nathan Morgan, Adrian Joseph Mariappa, Demar Constantine Phillips, Joel Joshua Frederick Melvin McAnuff, Rodolph William Austin, JeVaughn Watson, Darren Mattocks (62.Theo Larayan Ronaldo Robinson), Deshorn Brown (77.Ryan Johnson), Jermaine Anderson.Trainer: Winfried Schäfer (Germany).

HON: Noel Eduardo Valladares Bonilla, Maynor Alexis Figueroa Róchez, Emilio Arturo Izaguirre Girón, Víctor Salvador Bernárdez Blanco, Brayan Antonio Beckeles, Oscar Boniek García Ramírez, Jorge Aarón Claros Juárez, Roger Aníbal Espinoza Ramírez (89.Arnold Fabián Peralta Sosa), Luis Fernando Garrido, Andy Najar Rodríguez (64.Wilson Roberto Palacios Suazo), Carlos Yaír Costly Molina (86.Jerry Ricardo Bengtson Bodden). Trainer: Luis Fernando Suárez (Colombia).

Goals: 0-1 Carlos Yaír Costly Molina (2), 1-1 Jorge Aarón Claros Juárez (3 own goal), 1-2 Maynor Alexis Figueroa Róchez (32), 2-2 Rodolph William Austin (59 penalty).

Cautions: Rodolph William Austin, Demar Constantine Phillips, JeVaughn Watson / Brayan Antonio Beckeles, Noel Eduardo Valladares Bonilla.

15.10.2013, Estadio "Rommel Fernández", Ciudad de Panamá; Attendance: 18,254
Referee: Courtney Campbell (Jamaica)

PANAMA - UNITED STATES **2-3(1-0)**

PAN: Jaime Manuel Penedo Cano, Felipe Abdiel Baloy Ramírez, Luis Alfonso Henríquez Ledezma, Román Aureliano Torres Morcillo, Carlos Gabriel Rodríguez Orantes (72.Jairo Joseth Jiménez Robles), Gabriel Enrique Gómez Giron (72.Roberto Leandro Chen Rodríguez), Amílcar Henríquez Espinosa, Alberto Abdiel Quintero Medina, Marcos Aníbal Sánchez Mullins (78.Luis Carlos Tejada Hansell), Blas Antonio Miguel Pérez Ortega, Gabriel Arturo Torres Tejada. Trainer: Jorge Luis Dely Valdes.

USA: Bradley Edwin Guzan, Clarence Edgar Goodson, Edgar Eduardo Castillo Carrillo, Michael Orozco Fiscal, Sacha Bryan Klještan, Kyle Robert Beckerman, Bradley Ray Evans (56.Bradley Joseph Davis), Graham Jonathan Zusi, Mikkel Morgenstar Pålssønn Diskerud (62.Aron Jóhannsson), Alejandro Bedoya, Josmer Volmy Altidore (76.Terrence Anthony Boyd). Trainer: Jürgen Klinsmann (Germany).

Goals: 1-0 Gabriel Arturo Torres Tejada (18), 1-1 Michael Orozco Fiscal (64), 2-1 Luis Carlos Tejada Hansell (83), 2-2 Graham Jonathan Zusi (90+3), 2-3 Aron Jóhannsson (90+4).

Cautions: Román Aureliano Torres Morcillo, Luis Carlos Tejada Hansell,

Sent off: Luis Carlos Tejada Hansell (90).

AFRICA

52 (of 53 national associations affiliated to CAF) have entered the African World Cup qualifiers. The FIFA World Ranking from July 2011 was used to seed the 52 teams for the first two rounds, which was drawn in Brazil on 30 July 2011. The used qualifying format was as follows:

1st Round: 12 two-legged knock-out ties (played on 11 and 15 November 2011), involving the 24 lowest-ranked teams according to FIFA World Rankings.

2nd Round: 10 groups with each 4 teams (top 28 ranked CAF teams joined by the 12 winners from the 1st Round), each group winner will advance to the 3rd Round.

3rd Round: 5 two-legged knock-out ties to determine the five national teams which will qualify to the Final Tournament 2014.

FIRST ROUND
(11.11.2011 – 15.11.2011)

Chad - **Tanzania**	1-2(1-1)	1-0(0-0)
Comoros - **Mozambique**	0-1(0-0)	1-4(0-1)
Djibouti - **Namibia**	0-4(0-1)	0-4(0-2)
Equatorial Guinea - Madagascar	2-0(1-0)	1-2(1-0)
Eritrea - **Rwanda**	1-1(1-0)	1-3(0-1)
Guinea-Bissau - **Togo**	1-1(1-1)	0-1(0-1)
Lesotho - Burundi	1-0(0-0)	2-2(2-1)
Seychelles - **Kenya**	0-3(0-1)	0-4(0-3)
São Tomé and Príncipe - **Congo**	0-5(0-3)	1-1(0-0)
Somalia - **Ethiopia**	0-0	0-5(0-1)
Swaziland – **D.R. Congo**	1-3(0-2)	1-5(0-1)

Liberia qualified for the 2nd Round (Mauritius withdrew)

11.11.2011, Stade Omnisports „Idriss Mahamat Ouya“, N'Djaména; Attendance: 10,000
Referee: Bunmi Ogunkolade (Nigeria)

CHAD - TANZANIA **1-2(1-1)**

CHA: Brice Mabaya II, Nassama Asselme (44.César Abaya), Armand Djérabé, Sylvain Félix Doubam, Herman Doumdé, Ferdinand Gassina, Yaya Kerim, Hassan Hissein, Mahamat Ahmat Labbo (82.Rodrigue Ninga Casimir), Karl Max Barthélémy (70.Appolinaire Djingabeye), Ezechiel N'Douassel. Trainer: Moudou Kouta.

TAN: Juma Kaseja, Aggrey Morris, Abdi Kassim Sadalla (69.Hamadi Nurdin Bakari), Said Idrissa Rajabu, Juma Saidi Nyoso, Shomari Kapombe, Nizar Khalfan (66.Thomas Ulimwengu), Godfrey Taita Magina, Henry Joseph Shindika, Mrisho Alfani Ngasa, Mbwana Aly Samatta (81.Mohammed Rajab). Trainer: Jan Børge Poulsen (Denmark).

Goals: Mahamat Ahmat Labbo (12).

Cautions: César Abaya, Ezechiel N'Douassel / Mrisho Alfani Ngasa, Said Idrissa Rajabu.

15.11.2011, „Benjamin Mkapa“ National Stadium, Dar es Salaam; Attendance: 42,700
Referee: Hamada Nampiandraza (Madagascar)

TANZANIA - CHAD **0-1(0-0)**

TAN: Juma Kaseja, Shomari Kapombe, Said Idrissa Rajabu, Juma Saidi Nyoso, Aggrey Morris, Shaban Mussa Nditi, Henry Joseph Shindika (72.Abdi Kassim Sadalla), Mbwana Aly Samatta, Nizar Khalfan (62.Hamadi Nurdin Bakari), Mrisho Alfani Ngasa, Hussein Javu (77.Mohammed Rajab). Trainer: Jan Børge Poulsen (Denmark).

CHA: Brice Mabaya II, Sylvain Félix Doubam, Habib Mahamat Saleh (81.Karl Max Barthélémy), Yaya Kerim (72.Appolinaire Djingabeye), Herman Doumdé, Ferdinand Gassina, Mahamat Ahmat Labbo, Yves Maldjilam, César Abaya, Mahamat Ada, Hassan Hissein (75.Mahamat Issa Abakar) Trainer: Moudou Kouta.

Goal: Mahamat Ahmat Labbo (47).

Cautions: Yves Maldjilam, Sylvain Félix Doubam, Mahamat Ahmat Labbo.

*(**Tanzania** won on away goals rule (2-2 on aggregate))*

11.11.2011, Stade „Said Mohamed Cheikh“, Mitsamiouli; Attendance: 3,000
Referee: David Jane (Lesotho)

COMOROS - MOZAMBIQUE **0-1(0-0)**

COM: Mahamoud Mroivili, Ibrahim Rachidi, Nadjim Abdou, Ali M'Madi, Youssouf M'Changama (83.Nakibou Aboubakari), Ibrahim Iyad, Fouad Rachid, Djamal Mohamed, Benhamadi Ybnou Charaf (59.Samir Bertin d'Avesnes), Moubarak Abdallah Mfoihaya (90.Halifa Soulé), Mogni Youssouf. Trainer: Ali Mbaé Camara.

MOZ: João Raphael Kapango (75.Victor Soares „Soarito“), Dario Ivan Khan, Edson André Sitoe „Mexer“, Francisco Muchanga, Zainadine Abdula Chavango Júnior, Martinho Martins Mukana „Paíto“, Daniel Almiro Lobo „Miro“, Stélio Ernesto „Telinho“, Eduardo Jumisse (67.Francisco Massinga „Whiskey“), Jeremias Jorge Sitoe „Jerry“, Apson Sonito Manjate (67.Josemar Tiago Machaisse). Trainer: Gert Engels (Germany).

Goal: 0-1 Daniel Almiro Lobo „Miro“ (56 penalty).

Cautions: Ibrahim Rachidi, Ali M'Madi / Apson Sonito Manjate, Eduardo Jumisse, Stélio Ernesto „Telinho“,Daniel Almiro Lobo „Miro“.

15.11.2011, Estádio do Zimpeto, Maputo; Attendance: 10,000
Referee: Ruzive Ruzive (Zimbabwe)

MOZAMBIQUE - COMOROS **4-1(2-0)**

MOZ: João Raphael Kapango, Edson André Sitoe „Mexer“, Francisco Muchanga, Francisco Massinga „Whiskey“, Zainadine Abdula Chavango Júnior, Martinho Martins Mukana „Paíto“, Daniel Almiro Lobo „Miro“ (72.Clésio Bauque), Momed Antonio Hagy (90+1.Antonio Machava), Stélio Ernesto „Telinho“, Elias Gaspar Pelembe „Dominguês“, Jeremias Jorge Sitoe „Jerry“ (87.Ivan Esculuades „Maninho“). Trainer: Gert Engels (Germany).

COM: Mohamed Hassani Mbalia, Mahamoud Ali M'Changama, Nadjim Abdou, Ali Mourade (59.Nakibou Aboubakari), Youssouf M'Changama, Ibrahim Rachidi, Ibrahim Iyad, Fouad Rachid (72.Djamal Mohamed), Ali M'Madi (88.Halifa Soulé), Mogni Youssouf, Moubarak Abdallah Mfoihaya. Trainer: Ali Mbaé Camara.

Goals: 1-0 Elias Gaspar Pelembe „Dominguês“ (26), 2-0 Jeremias Jorge Sitoe „Jerry“ (44), 3-0 Francisco Massinga „Whiskey“ (58), 3-1 Mogni Youssouf (72), 4-1 Clésio Bauque (81).

Cautions: Momed Antonio Hagy / Mohamed Hassani Mbalia.

*(**Mozambique** won 5-1 on aggregate)*

11.11.2011, Stade National Gouled, Djibouti; Attendance: 3,000
Referee: Tessema Bamlak (Ethiopia)
DJIBOUTI - NAMIBIA 0-4(0-1)
DJI: Youssouf Abdourahman, Hassan Abdoulrahman, Daher Mohamed Kadar, Abchir Iqueh Houssein, Abdi Hassan Mohamed Kadar, Mousa Warsama (77.Darar Aboubaker Djamé), Moussa Hirir (90.Ahmed Hassan Daoud), Mohamed Liban Issa, Abdallah Mohamed, Mohamed Ahmed Id (59.Galal Ramzi), Omar Elmi Aboubaker. Trainer: Gharsalli Noureddine (Tunisia).
NAM: Virgil Vries, Da Costa Angula, Teberius Lombaard, Willem Mwedihanga, Bryan Bantam, Larry Horaeb, Heinrich Isaacks (66.Willy Stephanus), Petrus Shitembi, Henrico Botes (46.Lazarus Kaimbi), Tangeni Shipahu (71.Sidney Urikhob), Rudolph Bester. Trainer: Bernard Kaanjuka.
Goals: 0-1 Rudolph Bester (13), 0-2 Lazarus Kaimbi (50), 0-3 Rudolph Bester (52), 0-4 Sidney Urikhob (88).
Cautions: Mohamed Liban Issa / Heinrich Isaacks, Lazarus Kaimbi,

15.11.2011, „Sam Nujoma“ Stadium, Windhoek; Attendance: 2,145
Referee: Samuel Chirinda (Mozambique)
NAMIBIA - DJIBOUTI 4-0(2-0)
NAM: Ephraim Tjihonge, Da Costa Angula, Willem Mwedihanga, Steven Sabatha, Bryan Bantam (61.Willy Stephanus), Larry Horaeb, Heinrich Isaacks, Ronald Ketjijere, Lazarus Kaimbi, Tangeni Shipahu (61.Petrus Shitembi), Rudolph Bester (78.Sidney Urikhob). Trainer: Bernard Kaanjuka.
DJI: Youssouf Abdourahman, Daoud Wais, Abchir Iqueh Houssein, Hassan Djama Ilyass, Mousa Warsama (61.Mohamed Ahmed Id), Daher Mohamed Kadar, Abdi Hassan Mohamed Kadar (63.Miad Nour Charmake), Ahmed Moumin Mahdi (46.Abdallah Mohamed), Ahmed Hassan Daoud, Mohamed Liban Issa, Omar Elmi Aboubaker. Trainer: Gharsalli Noureddine (Tunisia).
Goals: 1-0 Heinrich Isaacks (17), 2-0 Lazarus Kaimbi (34), 3-0 Lazarus Kaimbi (60), 4-0 Sidney Urikhob (83).
Cautions: Lazarus Kaimbi / Daher Mohamed Kadar, Miad Nour Charmake.
*(**Namibia** won 8-0 on aggregate)*

11.11.2011, Nuevo Estadio de Malabo, Malabo; Attendance: 10,000
Referee: Eric Otogo-Castane (Gabon)
EQUATORIAL GUINEA - MADAGASCAR 2-0(1-0)
EQG: Felipe Ovono Mbang, José Bokung Alogo „Colin“, Lawrence Sokota Doe, Eusebio Peque Edjang Nguema (77.Daniel Vladmir Ekedo Chigozirim), Rui Fernando Da Gracia Gomes, Armando Sipoto Bohale Aqueriaco „Sipo“, Viera Ellong Doualla, Samuel Bertrand Itondo Eyoum (67.Juanito Eyama Ndong), Juvenal Edjogo-Owono Montalbán (62.Thierry Fidjeu Tazemeta), Ben Konaté, Iban Iyanga Travieso „Randy“. Trainer: Henri Michel (France).
MAD: Jean Dieu-Donné Randrianasolo, Urbain Hassina Andriamampionona, Abdourahamany Mohamed, Michael Randrianantenaina (56.Edgar Nandrasana), Lalaina Nomenjanahary, Baggio Rakotonomenjanahary, Josoa Razafimahatratra, José Jean Tigana Razafimandimby (60.Ferdinand Falimery Ramanamahefa), Johann Paul, Arsène Faed (78.Jimmy Simouri), Paulin Voavy. Trainer: Frank Rajaonarisamba.
Goals: 1-0 Juvenal Edjogo-Owono Montalbán (20 penalty), 2-0 Iban Iyanga Travieso „Randy“ (74 penalty).
Cautions: Viera Ellong Doualla, Iban Iyanga Travieso „Randy“ / Baggio Rakotonomenjanahary, Jean Dieu-Donné Randrianasolo.

15.11.2011, Mahamasina Municipal Stadium, Antananarivo; Attendance: 5,000
Referee: Parmendra Nunkoo (Mauritius)

MADAGASCAR - EQUATORIAL GUINEA **2-1(0-1)**

MAD: Robin Jean Claude Rakotonirina, Lalaina Nomenjanahary, Vonjiniaina Jules Razafimahatratra, Abdourahamany Mohamed, Edgar Nandrasana, Baggio Rakotonomenjanahary, José Jean Tigana Razafimandimby (62.Ferdinand Falimery Ramanamahefa), Johann Paul, Arsène Faed (46.Jimmy Simouri), Yvan Rajoarimanana (81.Boto Fagnorena), Paulin Voavy.Trainer: Frank Rajaonarisamba.

EQG: Felipe Ovono Mbang, José Bokung Alogo „Colin", Armando Sipoto Bohale Aqueriaco „Sipo", Lawrence Sokota Doe, Rui Fernando Da Gracia Gomes, Juvenal Edjogo-Owono Montalbán (77.Thierry Fidjeu Tazemeta), Juanito Eyama Ndong, Ben Konaté, Viera Ellong Doualla (64.Iban Iyanga Travieso „Randy"), Daniel Vladmir Ekedo Chigozirim, Narcisse Ekanga Amia (88.Samuel Bertrand Itondo Eyoum). Trainer: Henri Michel (France).

Goals: 0-1 Viera Ellong Doualla (24), 1-1 Yvan Rajoarimanana (70), 2-1 Ferdinand Falimery Ramanamahefa (90+3).

Cautions: Lalaina Nomenjanahary, Johann Paul / Juanito Eyama Ndong, Ben Konaté.

*(**Equatorial Guinea** won 3-2 on aggregate)*

11.11.2011, Cicero Stadium, Asmara; Attendance: 6,000
Referee: Mahamadou Keita (Mali)

ERITREA - RWANDA **1-1(1-0)**

ERI: Samuel Alazar, Merhawi Kesete, Essey Kiflom, Ahmed Abdurhman (55.Surafiel Tesfamicael; 84.Daniel Alexander), Yohannes Nega, Medhanie Redie, Hermon Tecleab, Tesfalem Tekle, Abraham Tedros (66.Haile Goitom), Yohannes Tilahun, Yonathan Solomo. Trainer: Negash Teklit.

RWA: Jean-Claude Ndori, Mao Kalisa, Ismaël Nshutiyamagara, Eric Gasana Mbuyu Twite, Jean-Baptiste Mugiraneza, Frédéric Ndaka, Haruna Niyonzima, Hussein Sibomana, Olivier Karekezi (50.Elias Uzamukunda), Labama Kamana Bokota, Meddie Kagere. Trainer: Milutin Sredojević (Serbia).

Goals: 1-0 Tesfalem Tekle (35), 1-1 Elias Uzamukunda (52).

15.11.2011, Stade Amahoro, Kigali; Attendance: 10,000
Referee: Joshua Bondo (Botswana)

RWANDA - ERITREA **3-1(1-0)**

RWA: Jean-Claude Ndori, Mao Kalisa, Eric Gasana Mbuyu Twite, Albert Ngabo, Jean-Baptiste Mugiraneza, Frédéric Ndaka, Haruna Niyonzima, Hussein Sibomana (80.Emery Bayisenge), Olivier Karekezi (76.Labama Kamana Bokota), Elias Uzamukunda (57.Jean-Claude Iranzi), Meddie Kagere. Trainer: Milutin Sredojević (Serbia).

ERI: Daniel Goitom, Haile Goitom (75.Surafiel Tesfamicael), Merhawi Kesete, Essey Kiflom, Daniel Alexander (88.Ahmed Abdurhman), Yohannes Nega, Tesfalem Tekle, Abraham Tedros, Yohannes Tilahun, Isaias Andberhian (77.Samuel Ghebrehiwet Tesfagabr), Yonathan Solomon. Trainer: Negash Teklit.

Goals: 1-0 Olivier Karekezi (4), 2-0 Jean-Claude Iranzi (71), 3-0 Labama Kamana Bokota (78), 3-1 Abraham Tedros (90).

Cautions: Mao Kalisa, Hussein Sibomana.

*(**Rwanda** won 4-2 on aggregate)*

11.11.2011, Estádio „Lino Correia", Bissau; Attendance: 3,000
Referee: Malang Diedhiou (Senegal)
GUINEA-BISSAU - TOGO 1-1(1-1)
GNB: Jonas Asvedo Mendes, Saido Indjai, Bruno João Nandinga Borges Fernandes, Édson Ricardo Nunes Correia, José Luís Mendes Lopes „Zezinho", Bacar Baldé, Bocundji Cá, Ibrahima So, Ivanildo Soares Cassamá (6.Muhammad Youssuf Candé „Mamadú Candé"), Basile Salomon Pereira de Carvalho (78.Aílton Pedro Mota Pereira), Leocísio Sami (74.Almani Samori da Silva Moreira). Trainer: Luís Maria Cabral Norton de Matos (Portugal).
TOG: Mawugbe Atsou, Daré Nibombé, Serge Ognadon Akakpo, Abdul-Gafar Mamah, Jacques Alaixys Romao, Komlan Amewou, Zakari Morou, Kossi Prince Segbefia (68.Floyd Ayité), Serge Gakpé (55.Sename Dové Wome Dobe), Kondo Arimiyaou, Abdoulrazak Boukari (81.Ayara Samoudini). Trainer: Didier Six (France).
Goals: 0-1 Serge Gakpé (32), 1-1 Basile Salomon Pereira de Carvalho (38).
Cautions: Basile Salomon Pereira de Carvalho / Zakari Morou.

15.11.2011, Stade de Kégué, Lomé; Attendance: 25,000
Referee: Mal Souley Mohamadou (Cameroon)
TOGO - GUINEA-BISSAU 1-0(1-0)
TOG: Kossi Agassa, Daré Nibombé, Sadat Ouro-Akoriko, Serge Ognadon Akakpo, Abdul-Gafar Mamah, Jacques Alaixys Romao, Niasidji Donou Kokou, Kossi Prince Segbefia, Sename Dové Wome Dobe (59.Floyd Ayité), Serge Gakpé (79.Komlan Amewou), Sheyi Emmanuel Adebayor. Trainer: Didier Six (France).
GNB: Jonas Asvedo Mendes, Bruno João Nandinga Borges Fernandes, Saido Indjai, José Monteiro de Macedo, José Luís Mendes Lopes „Zezinho", Bacar Baldé, Bocundji Cá (46.Luciano Mendes Teixeira), Almani Samori da Silva Moreira (72.Aílton Pedro Mota Pereira), Ibrahima Baldé, Basile Salomon Pereira de Carvalho, Leocísio Sami (80.Dionísio Fernandes Mendes „Niche"). Trainer: Luís Maria Cabral Norton de Matos (Portugal).
Goal: 1-0 Serge Gakpé (2).
Cautions: Serge Gakpé / Ibrahima Baldé.
*(**Togo** won 2-1 on aggregate)*

11.11.2011, Setsoto National Stadium, Maseru; Attendance: 5,000
Referee: Rainhold Shikongo (Namibia)
LESOTHO - BURUNDI 1-0(0-0)
LES: Mohau Kuenane, Thabo Masualle, Bokang Mothoana, Moitheri Ntobo, Nkau Lerotholi, Motlalepula Mofolo (81.Lawrence Molengoane), Ralekoti Mokhahlane, Bushi Moletsane, Thulo Ranchobe (56.Thapelo Tale), Katleho Moleko, Lehlomela Ramabele. Trainer: Leslie Notsi.
BDI: Saidi Nduwimana, Gilbert Demunga Kaze, Valery Twite Nahayo, Floribert Tambwe Ndayisaba, Hassan Hakizimana, Emery Nimubona, Pierre Kwizera, Cédric Amissi, Dugary Ndabashinze, Laudy Mavugo (60.Denis Kalala Masumbuko), Saidi Ntibazonkiza. Trainer: Adel Amrouche (Algeria).
Goal: 1-0 Lehlomela Ramabele (82).
Cautions: Bokang Mothoana / Valery Twite Nahayo.

15.11.2011, Stade du „Prince Louis Rwagasore“, Bujumbura; Attendance: n/a
Referee: Anthony Ramsy Raphael (Malawi)
BURUNDI - LESOTHO **2-2(1-2)**
BDI: Saidi Nduwimana, Gilbert Demunga Kaze, Valery Twite Nahayo, Floribert Tambwe Ndayisaba, Karim Niizigiyimana (46.Claude Nahimana), Hassan Hakizimana, Faty Papy (71.Pierre Kwizera), Cédric Amissi, Dugary Ndabashinze (79.Didier Kayumbagu), Selemani Yamin Ndikumana, Saidi Ntibazonkiza. Trainer: Adel Amrouche (Algeria).
LES: Mohau Kuenane, Thabo Masualle, Bokang Mothoana, Moitheri Ntobo, Thabiso Maile, Nkau Lerotholi, Motlalepula Mofolo, Ralekoti Mokhahlane, Katleho Moleko (72.Tsoanelo Koetle), Lehlomela Ramabele (54.Thulo Ranchobe), Thapelo Tale (67.Dlomo Monaphati). Trainer: Leslie Notsi.
Goals: 0-1 Thapelo Tale (16), 0-2 Bokang Mothoana (22), 1-2 Cédric Amissi (29), 2-2 Selemani Yamin Ndikumana (88).
Cautions: Gilbert Demunga Kaze, Faty Papy, Saidi Ntibazonkiza, Didier Kayumbagu / Thabiso Maile, Thulo Ranchobe, Bokang Mothoana.
*(**Lesotho** won 3-2 on aggregate)*

11.11.2011, Stade Linité, Victoria; Attendance: 2,000
Referee: Denis Batte (Uganda)
SEYCHELLES - KENYA **0-3(0-1)**
SEY: Eric Nelson Sopha, Jonathan Bibi, Nigel Freminot (86.Brian Dorby), Jones Joubert, Allain Larue, Alex Nibourette, Don Annacoura, Henny Dufresne, Achille Henriette, Kevin Betsy, Nelson Laurence (75.Ryan Antat). Trainer: Ralph Jean-Louis.
KEN: Arnold Origi Otieno, Brian Mandela, Pascal Ochieng, James Wakhungu Situma, Jamal Mohammed, Titus Brian Mulama, Dennis Odhiambo, Victor Mugubi Wanyama, Stephen Waruru (71.Anthony Kimani Wanjohi), Bob Mugalia (80.Paul Were), Dennis Oliech (90+2.Collins Okoth). Trainer: Francis Kimanzi.
Goals: 0-1 Pascal Ochieng (41), 0-2 Anthony Kimani Wanjohi (75), 0-3 Dennis Oliech (81).
Cautions: Arnold Origi Otieno.

15.11.2011, Nyayo National Stadium, Nairobi; Attendance: 5,000
Referee: Victor Gomes (South Africa)
KENYA - SEYCHELLES **4-0(3-0)**
KEN: Arnold Origi Otieno, Brian Mandela, Pascal Ochieng, James Wakhungu Situma, Jamal Mohammed (82.Humphrey Ochieng Mieno), Titus Brian Mulama (59.Collins Okoth), Dennis Odhiambo, Victor Mugubi Wanyama, Dennis Oliech (59.Bob Mugalia), Kevin Kimani, Paul Were. Trainer: Francis Kimanzi.
SEY: Vincent Euphrasie, Jonathan Bibi, Ronny Marengo (46.Nigel Freminot), Brian Dorby (81.Lerooy Corallie), Jones Joubert, Allain Larue, Don Annacoura, Alex Nibourette, Achille Henriette (88.Dine Suzette), Kevin Betsy, Jude Nancy. Trainer: Ralph Jean-Louis.
Goals: 1-0 Brian Mandela (20), 2-0 Dennis Oliech (38), 3-0 Titus Brian Mulama (45), 4-0 Victor Mugubi Wanyama (76).
Cautions: Don Annacoura, Jonathan Bibi.
*(**Kenya** won 7-0 on aggregate)*

11.11.2011, Estádio Nacional 12 de Julho, São Tomé; Attendance: 3,000
Referee: Sosthene Ngbokaye (Central African Republic)
SÃO TOMÉ E PRINCIPE - CONGO 0-5(0-3)
STP: Dungue Lima (62.Nilson Taty), Denilson Afonso, Ódair Bom, Kilson Neto de Ceita, Aykemss Capela, Ibraimo Bengo (77.Reny Lima), Francisco Nay do Nascimento, Orgando dos Santos, Adilson Mendes, Joazhifel Soares (20.Juary Cardoso), José da Silva. Trainer: Gustave Nyoumba.
CGO: Barel Morial Mouko, Maël Lépicier, Oxence Dorian Mbani Madzou (65.Bruce Abdoulaye), Ugor N'Ganga, Francis N'Ganga, David Louhoungou, Prince Oniangué, Oscar Ewolo, Christopher Gaël Missilou (60.Harris Brandt Tchilimbou), Francis Chris Malonga Ntsayi, Ladislas Douniama. Trainer: Jean-Guy Wallemme (France).
Goals: 0-1 Christopher Gaël Missilou (3), 0-2 Ladislas Douniama (8), 0-3 Francis Chris Malonga Ntsayi (32), 0-4 Prince Oniangué (55), 0-5 Harris Brandt Tchilimbou (70).
Cautions: Kilson Neto de Ceita / Francis Chris Malonga Ntsayi.
Sent off: Kilson Neto de Ceita (88), Francis Chris Malonga Ntsayi (89).

15.11.2011, Stade Municipal, Pointe-Noire; Attendance: 12,000
Referee: Oumar Mahamat (Chad)
CONGO - SÃO TOMÉ E PRINCIPE 1-1(0-0)
CGO: Barel Morial Mouko, Bruce Abdoulaye, Maël Lépicier, Chancel Gombessa, Francis N'Ganga, David Louhoungou (42.Yven Moyo), Prince Oniangué (84.Césaire Gandzé), Oscar Ewolo, Ladislas Douniama, Matt Devlin Moussilou Massamba, Harris Brandt Tchilimbou (73.Percy Akoli). Trainer: Jean-Guy Wallemme (France).
STP: Alfonso Girael Pedroso, Denilson Afonso, Francisco Nay do Nascimento, Ibraimo Bengo (87.Ódair Bom), Aykemss Capela, Orgando dos Santos, Joazhifel Soares, Agilson Sole (83.Osvaldo Eduardo), Juary Cardoso, Jair Nunes (60.Adilson Mendes), José da Silva. Trainer: Gustave Nyoumba.
Goals: Orgando dos Santos (49).
Cautions: Bruce Abdoulaye / Francisco Nay do Nascimento.
*(**Congo** won 6-1 on aggregate)*

11.11.2011, Somhlolo National Stadium, Lobamba; Attendance: 785
Referee: Janny Sikazwe (Zambia)
SWAZILAND – D.R. CONGO 1-3(0-2)
SWA: Sandile Ginindza, Mudeni Mamba, Siyabonga Mdluli, Maqhawe Dlamini, Welile Siboniso Maseko (46.Darren Christie Melusi), Zweli Nxumalo (46.Sihawu Dlamini), Mthunzi Mkhontfo, Sibonginkosi Gamedze, Sandile Motsa, Colani Sikhondze, Barry Steenkamp (60.Sidumo Shongwe). Trainer: Obed Mlotsa.
CGO: Vumi Ley Matampi, Gladys Bokese, Issama Mpeko, Landry Mulemo, Tshiolola Tshinyama, Zola Matumona (70.Diego Kazadi Mutombo), Déo Kanda A Mukok, Christian Fuanda Luzolo Kinkela, Mapuata Cédric Makiadi (87.Pamphile Mihayo Kazembe), Alain Dioko Kaluyituka, Trésor Mputu Mabi. Trainer: Claude Marie François Le Roy (France).
Goals: 0-1 Alain Dioko Kaluyituka (18), 0-2 Trésor Mputu Mabi (24), 1-2 Sidumo Shongwe (65), 1-3 Gladys Bokese (73).
Cautions: Mudeni Mamba, Colani Sikhondze.

15.11.2011, Stade des Martyrs, Kinshasa; Attendance: 24,000
Referee: Jean Michel Moukoko (Congo)
D.R. CONGO - SWAZILAND 5-1(1-0)
CGO: Thierry Bolongo Ebengui, Gladys Bokese, Jean Kasusula Kiritsho (78.Patrick Mampuya), Issama Mpeko, Tshiolola Tshinyama, Zola Matumona, Alain Dioko Kaluyituka, Déo Kanda A Mukok, Mapuata Cédric Makiadi, Christian Fuanda Luzolo Kinkela (57.Yves Ilunga Diba), Trésor Mputu Mabi (72.Yves Angani Kayiba). Trainer: Claude Marie François Le Roy (France).
SWA: Sandile Ginindza, Mudeni Mamba, Siyabonga Mdluli, Sihawu Dlamini, Mthunzi Mkhontfo (74.Samkelo Gumbi), Sibonginkosi Gamedze, Juries Gama (49. Darren Christie Melusi), Sandile Motsa, Zweli Msibi (49.Sidumo Shongwe), Colani Sikhondze, Barry Steenkamp. Trainer: Obed Mlotsa.
Goals: 1-0 Trésor Mputu Mabi (7), 2-0 Alain Dioko Kaluyituka (46), 3-0 Trésor Mputu Mabi (49), 4-0 Alain Dioko Kaluyituka (61), 4-1 Sidumo Shongwe (63), 5-1 Yves Ilunga Diba (66).
Cautions: Tshiolola Tshinyama / Sidumo Shongwe, Darren Christie Melusi.
*(**D.R. Congo** won 8-2 on aggregate)*

12.11.2011, Stade National Gouled, Djibouti (Djibouti); Attendance: 3,000
Referee: Mohamed Hassan Ourouke (Djibouti)
SOMALIA - ETHIOPIA 0-0
SOM: Khalid Ali Mursal, Abukar Nur Abdikarim, Ahmed Abdulkadir Dayib (78.Hussein Ibrahim Adan), Anwar Sadad Ibrahim, Sa'ad Salah Hussein, Ali Egal Yasin, Hassan Ali Mohamed, Mohamed Mohamud Said (67.Abdinur Mohamud), Ali Hassan Khalid, Osman Ibrahim Mohamed (46.Mohamed Ali Abdiaziz), Cisse Aadan Abshir. Trainer: Alfred Imonje (Kenya).
ETH: Binyam Habtamu, Abebaw Butako, Degu Debebe, Aynalem Hailu Reda, Tesfaye Seyoum (85.Tesfaye Bekele), Tesfaye Alebachew Gebre, Mesud Mohamed, Birhanu Bogale Boyzo, Dawit Berhanu Fekadu, Fikru Tefera Lemessa, Getaneh Kebede Gibeto (64.Umed Ukuri).Trainer: Sewnet Beshaw.
Cautions: Anwar Sadad Ibrahim / Fikru Tefera Lemessa.
Sent off: Tesfaye Alebachew Gebre (64).

15.11.2011, Addis Abeba Stadium, Addis Abeba; Attendance: 22,000
Referee: Med Said Kordi (Tunisia)
ETHIOPIA - SOMALIA 5-0(1-0)
ETH: Binyam Habtamu, Abebaw Butako, Degu Debebe, Alula Girma Mekonnen, Birhanu Bogale Boyzo, Aynalem Hailu Reda, Shimelis Bekele Godo, Yared Zinabu Showaatir, Dawit Berhanu Fekadu (46.Mesud Mohamed; 82.Tesfaye Bekele), Fikru Tefera Lemessa (63.Getaneh Kebede Gibeto), Umed Ukuri. Trainer: Sewnet Beshaw.
SOM: Khalid Ali Mursal, Ahmed Abdulkadir Dayib, Hussein Ibrahim Adan, Anwar Sadad Ibrahim, Sa'ad Salah Hussein, Ali Egal Yasin, Hassan Ali Mohamed, Ali Abdulkadir (60.Abdullahi Nur Dek), Ali Hassan Khalid (46.Abdinur Mohamud), Mohamed Ali Abdiaziz (79.Osman Ibrahim Mohamed), Cisse Aadan Abshir. Trainer: Alfred Imonje (Kenya).
Goals: 1-0 Umed Ukuri (5), 2-0 Shimelis Bekele Godo (62), 3-0 Shimelis Bekele Godo (65), 4-0 Getaneh Kebede Gibeto (87), 5-0 Getaneh Kebede Gibeto (90).
Cautions: Birhanu Bogale Boyzo / Ali Hassan Khalid, Ali Abdulkadir, Abdinur Mohamud, Ahmed Abdulkadir Dayib.
*(**Ethiopia** won 5-0 on aggregate)*

Liberia *qualified for the 2nd Round (Mauritius withdrew)*

SECOND ROUND

GROUP A

02.06.2012	Bangui	Central African Republic - Botswana	2-0(1-0)
03.06.2012	Rustenburg	South Africa - Ethiopia	1-1(0-1)
09.06.2012	Gaborone	Botswana - South Africa	1-1(1-1)
10.06.2012	Addis Abeba	Ethiopia - Central African Republic	2-0(1-0)
23.03.2013	Cape Town	South Africa - Central African Republic	2-0(1-0)
24.03.2013	Addis Abeba	Ethiopia - Botswana	1-0(0-0)
08.06.2013	Lobatse	Botswana - Ethiopia	1-2(0-2); Awarded 3-0
08.06.2013	Yaoundé (CMR)	Central African Republic - South Africa	0-3(0-2)
15.06.2013	Lobatse	Botswana - Central African Republic	3-2(1-1)
16.06.2013	Addis Abeba	Ethiopia - South Africa	2-1(1-1)
07.09.2013	Durban	South Africa - Botswana	4-1(2-0)
07.09.2013	Brazzaville (CGO)	Central African Republic - Ethiopia	1-2(1-0)

FINAL STANDINGS

1.	Ethiopia	6	4	1	1	8 - 6	13
2.	South Africa	6	3	2	1	12 - 5	11
3.	Botswana	6	2	1	3	8 - 10	7
4.	Central African Republic	6	1	0	5	5 - 12	3

Ethiopia qualified for the Third Round.

02.06.2012, Stade "Barthelemy Boganda", Bangui; Attendance: 20,000
Referee: Bernard Camille (Seychelles)

CENTRAL AFRICAN REPUBLIC - BOTSWANA 2-0(1-0)

CTA: Geoffrey Lembet, Manassé Ruben Enza Yamissi, Salif Kéïta, Kelly Alexandre Youga (77.Thérence Kéthévoama), Clovis-Franklin Anzité, Éloge Ethisse Enza Yamissi, Romaric Lignanzi, Eudes Dagoulou (79.Destin Amorese), Foxi Kéthévoama (71.David Manga Lembe), Evans Kondogbia, Hilaire Roméo Verdi Momi. Trainer: Hervé Lougoundji.

BOT: Kabelo Dambe, Ndiapo Letsholathebe, Oscar Obuile Ncenga, Mmusa Ohilwe, Edwin Olerile, Joel Mogorosi (66.Phenyo Mongala), Boitumelo Mafoko, Jackie Mothatego (59.Tshepo Motlhabankwe), Ofentse Nato, Lemponye Tshireletso, Jérôme Ramatlhokwane. Trainer: Stanley Hunter Tshosane.

Goals: 1-0 Foxi Kéthévoama (18), 2-0 Foxi Kéthévoama (47).

Cautions: Ndiapo Letsholathebe.

03.06.2012, Royal Bafokeng Stadium, Rustenburg; Attendance: 13,611
Referee: Hamada Nampiandraza (Madagascar)

SOUTH AFRICA - ETHIOPIA 1-1(0-1)

RSA: Itumeleng Isaack Khune, Morgan Leonard Gould, Bongani Sandile Khumalo, Siboniso Pa Gaxa, Peter Tsepo Masilela (35.Punch Jan Masenamela), Reneilwe Letsholonyane (46.Matthews Oupa Manyisa), Thanduyise Khuboni (73.Teko Tsholofelo Modise), Steven Jerome Pienaar, Lawrence Siphiwe Tshabalala, Siyabonga Eugene Nomvethe, Katlego Abel Mphela. Trainer: Pitso John Mosimane.

ETH: Sisay Bancha Basa, Abebaw Butako, Degu Debebe, Alula Girma Mekonnen (71.Aynalem Hailu Reda), Moges Ceuyon, Asrat Megersa Gobena, Menyahel Teshome Beyene, Biyadigligm Zewc, Gebryes Adane, Salaheldin Said, Addis Tekle. Trainer: Sewnet Beshaw.

Goals: 0-1 Salaheldin Said (28), 1-1 Katlego Abel Mphela (77).

Cautions: Bongani Sandile Khumalo / Abebaw Butako, Menyahel Teshome Beyene, Sisay Bancha Basa, Addis Tekle.

09.06.2012, University of Botswana Stadium, Gaborone; Attendance: 7,500
Referee: Mahamadou Keita (Mali)
BOTSWANA - SOUTH AFRICA 1-1(1-1)
BOT: Kabelo Dambe, Ndiapo Letsholathebe, Tshepo Motlhabankwe, Mmusa Ohilwe, Mompati Thuma, Joel Mogorosi, Patrick Motsepe (84.Kekaetswe Moloi), Ofentse Nato, Mogakolodi Ngele (59.Moemedi Moatlhaping), Lemponye Tshireletso (63.Phenyo Mongala), Jérôme Ramatlhokwane. Trainer: Stanley Hunter Tshosane.
RSA: Itumeleng Isaack Khune, Morgan Leonard Gould, Bongani Sandile Khumalo, Punch Jan Masenamela (62.Mzikayise Mashaba), Calvin Anele Ngcongca, Thanduyise Khuboni, Matthews Oupa Manyisa, Steven Jerome Pienaar, Lawrence Siphiwe Tshabalala (68.Teko Tsholofelo Modise), Siyabonga Eugene Nomvethe (62.Tokelo Anthony Rantie), Katlego Abel Mphela. Trainer: Stephen Mbuyiselo Komphela.
Goals: 0-1 Morgan Leonard Gould (15), 1-1 Ofentse Nato (38).
Cautions: Ndiapo Letsholathebe / Punch Jan Masenamela.

10.06.2012, Addis Abeba Stadium, Addis Abeba; Attendance: 25,000
Referee: Anthony Ramsy Raphael (Malawi)
ETHIOPIA - CENTRAL AFRICAN REPUBLIC 2-0(1-0)
ETH: Sisay Bancha Basa, Abebaw Butako, Degu Debebe, Adane Girma Gebreyes, Alula Girma Mekonnen, Tesfaye Seyoum (60.Shimelis Bekele Godo), Asrat Megersa Gobena (82.Birhanu Bogale Boyzo), Menyahel Teshome Beyene, Biyadigligm Zewc, Salaheldin Said, Addis Tekle (62.Messiud Mohamed Mussa). Trainer: Sewnet Beshaw.
CTA: Geoffrey Lembet, Manassé Ruben Enza Yamissi, Salif Kéïta, Thérence Kéthévoama (68.Fernander Kassaï), Brice Zimbori-Auzingoni, Éloge Ethisse Enza Yamissi (78.Mamadi Saoudi), Clovis-Franklin Anzité, Romaric Lignanzi, Eudes Dagoulou (66.Gervais Kago), Foxi Kéthévoama, Hilaire Roméo Verdi Momi. Trainer: Hervé Lougoundji.
Goals: 1-0 Salaheldin Said (38), 2-0 Salaheldin Said (88).
Cautions: Tesfaye Seyoum / Hilaire Roméo Verdi Momi, Salif Kéïta, Foxi Kéthévoama, Clovis-Franklin Anzité.

23.03.2013, Cape Town Stadium, Cape Town; Attendance: 36,740
Referee: Ali Kalyango (Uganda)
SOUTH AFRICA - CENTRAL AFRICAN REPUBLIC 2-0(1-0)
RSA: Itumeleng Isaack Khune, Calvin Anele Ngcongca, Morgan Leonard Gould, Thabo Nthethe, Thabo Matlaba, Dean Furman (43.Kagiso Evidence Dikgacoi), Thuso Phala (54.Lawrence Siphiwe Tshabalala), Reneilwe Letsholonyane, May Siphiwe Mahlangu, Bernard Melvin Parker, Tokelo Anthony Rantie (65.Matthews Oupa Manyisa). Trainer: Gordon George Igesund.
CTA: Geoffrey Lembet, Kelly Alexandre Youga, Clovis-Franklin Anzité, Manassé Ruben Enza Yamissi (83.Fernander Kassaï), Salif Kéïta, Brice Nicaise Zimbori-Auzingoni, Éloge Ethisse Enza Yamissi, Romaric Lignanzi (57.Vianney Mabidé), Foxi Kéthévoama, David Manga Lembe (65.Hilaire Roméo Verdi Momie), Josué Kossingou Balamandji. Trainer: Hervé Lougoundji.
Goals: 1-0 Thabo Matlaba (33), 2-0 Bernard Melvin Parker (71).
Cautions: Itumeleng Isaack Khune / Josué Kossingou Balamandji.

24.03.2013, Addis Abeba Stadium, Addis Abeba; Attendance: 22,000
Referee: Rédouane Jiyed (Morocco)

ETHIOPIA - BOTSWANA 1-0(0-0)

ETH: Jemal Tassew Bushra, Alula Girma Mekonnen, Abebaw Butako, Aynalem Hailu Reda, Degu Debebe, Siyoum Tesfaye (70.Behailu Assefa), Adane Girma Gebreyes (46.Getaneh Kebede Gebeto), Menyahel Teshome Beyene, Addis Hintsa, Salaheldin Ahmed Said, Shimelis Bekele Godo. Trainer: Sewnet Beshaw.

BOT: Kabelo Dambe, Tshepo Motlhabankwe, Oscar Obuile Ncenga, Mmusa Ohilwe, Mompati Thuma, Joel Mogorosi, Alphonse Modisaotsile (51.Abednico Powell), Ofentse Nato, Lemponye Tshireletso (78.Galabgwe Moyana), Moemedi Moatlhaping (72.Tebogo Sembowa), Jérôme Ramatlhokwane. Trainer: Stanley Hunter Tshosane.

Goal: 1-0 Getaneh Kebede Gebeto (89).

Cautions: Menyahel Teshome Beyene, Jemal Tassew Bushra / Ofentse Nato, Jérôme Ramatlhokwane, Moemedi Moatlhaping.

08.06.2013, Lobatse Stadium, Lobatse; Attendance: 5,000
Referee: Dennis Batte (Uganda)

BOTSWANA - ETHIOPIA 1-2(0-2)

BOT: Kabelo Dambe, Ndiapo Letsholathebe (50.Oscar Obuile Ncenga), Tshepo Motlhabankwe, Edwin Olerile, Mompati Thuma, Joel Mogorosi (63.Galabgwe Moyana), Joel Jackie Mothatego, Dirang Moloi, Phenyo David Mongala, Mogakolodi Ngele, Jérôme Ramatlhokwane (60.Tebogo Sembowa). Trainer: Stanley Hunter Tshosane.

ETH: Jemal Tassew Bushra, Abebaw Butako, Aynalem Hailu Reda, Siyoum Tesfaye, Biadglegn Elias, Menyahel Teshome Beyene (69.Behailu Assefa), Asrat Megersa Gobena, Addis Hintsa, Salaheldin Ahmed Said (79.Dawit Fekadu), Getaneh Kebede Gebeto, Shimelis Bekele Godo (80.Adane Girma Gebreyes). Trainer: Sewnet Beshaw.

Goals: 0-1 Getaneh Kebede Gebeto (34), 0-2 Salaheldin Ahmed Said (45), 1-2 Tebogo Sembowa (76).

Cautions: Asrat Megersa Gobena, Aynalem Hailu Reda.

Please note: The match was awarded 3-0 for Botswana by FIFA because Ethiopia fielded an ineligible player (Minyahil Teshome).

08.06.2013, Stade Omnisports „Ahmadou-Ahidjo“ Yaoundé (Cameroon); Attendance: 7,000
Referee: William Agbovi (Ghana)

CENTRAL AFRICAN REPUBLIC - SOUTH AFRICA 0-3(0-2)

CTA: Emmanuel Yezzoat, Kelly Alexandre Youga, Clovis-Franklin Anzité, Salif Kéïta, Brice Nicaise Zimbori-Auzingoni (78.Moussa Limane), Éloge Ethisse Enza Yamissi, Romaric Lignanzi (54.Thérence Kéthévoama), Ralph Amores Dertin (67.Arnold Gervais Kago), Foxi Kéthévoama, Josué Kossingou Balamandji, Hilaire Roméo Verdi Momie. Trainer: Hervé Lougoundji.

RSA: Itumeleng Isaack Khune, Calvin Anele Ngcongca, Thabo Nthethe, Ricardo Nuno dos Santos Nunes, Molomowanadou Eric Mathoho, Dean Furman, Lawrence Siphiwe Tshabalala, Reneilwe Letsholonyane, May Siphiwe Mahlangu (80.Thandani Ntshumayelo), Bernard Melvin Parker (63.Katlego Evidence Mashego), Tokelo Anthony Rantie (57.Matthews Oupa Manyisa). Trainer: Gordon George Igesund.

Goals: 0-1 Bernard Melvin Parker (26), 0-2 Lawrence Siphiwe Tshabalala (41), 0-3 Katlego Evidence Mashego (90).

Cautions: Kelly Alexandre Youga, Clovis-Franklin Anzité, Éloge Ethisse Enza Yamissi / Katlego Evidence Mashego.

15.06.2013, Lobatse Stadium, Lobatse; Attendance: 2,500
Referee: Juste Ephrem Zio (Burkina Faso)

BOTSWANA - CENTRAL AFRICAN REPUBLIC 3-2(1-1)

BOT: Kabelo Dambe, Tshepo Motlhabankwe, Oscar Obuile Ncenga (62.Joel Jackie Mothatego), Edwin Olerile, Mompati Thuma, Joel Mogorosi, Ofentse Nato, Dirang Moloi, Phenyo David Mongala (31.Lemponye Tshireletso), Mogakolodi Ngele, Jérôme Ramatlhokwane (72.Tebogo Sembowa). Trainer: Stanley Hunter Tshosane.

CTA: Prince Samolah, Kelly Alexandre Youga, Ali Calvin Tolmbaye, Thérence Kéthévoama, Salif Kéïta, Brice Nicaise Zimbori-Auzingoni, Éloge Ethisse Enza Yamissi, Ralph Amores Dertin (43.Amos Youga), Foxi Kéthévoama, Josué Kossingou Balamandji (88.Romaric Lignanzi), Hilaire Roméo Verdi Momie (86.Arnold Gervais Kago). Trainer: Hervé Lougoundji.

Goals: 0-1 Brice Nicaise Zimbori-Auzingoni (29), 1-1 Jérôme Ramatlhokwane (41), 1-2 Brice Nicaise Zimbori-Auzingoni (50), 2-2 Mogakolodi Ngele (74), 3-2 Ofentse Nato (86).

Cautions: Mompati Thuma / Hilaire Roméo Verdi Momie

Sent off: Ali Calvin Tolmbaye (36).

16.06.2013, Addis Abeba Stadium, Addis Abeba; Attendance: 22,000
Referee: Mohamed Farouk Mahmoud (Egypt)

ETHIOPIA - SOUTH AFRICA 2-1(1-1)

ETH: Jemal Tassew Bushra, Abebaw Butako (79.Birhanu Bogale Boyzo), Aynalem Hailu Reda, Siyoum Tesfaye, Biadglegn Elias, Menyahel Teshome Beyene (63.Behailu Assefa), Asrat Megersa Gobena, Addis Hintsa, Salaheldin Ahmed Said, Getaneh Kebede Gebeto, Shimelis Bekele Godo (56.Adane Girma Gebreyes). Trainer: Sewnet Beshaw.

RSA: Itumeleng Isaack Khune, Calvin Anele Ngcongca, Thabo Nthethe, Tebogo Joseph Langerman (79.Katlego Evidence Mashego), Molomowanadou Eric Mathoho, Dean Furman, Lawrence Siphiwe Tshabalala, Thuso Phala (52.Tokelo Anthony Rantie), Reneilwe Letsholonyane, May Siphiwe Mahlangu (66.Tlou Segolela), Bernard Melvin Parker. Trainer: Gordon George Igesund.

Goals: 0-1 Bernard Melvin Parker (34), 1-1 Getaneh Kebede Gebeto (43), 2-1 Bernard Melvin Parker (70 own goal).

Cautions: Addis Hintsa, Aynalem Hailu Reda, Jemal Tassew Bushra.

07.09.2013, "Moses Mabhida" Stadium, Durban; Attendance: 28,712
Referee: Badara Diatta (Senegal)

SOUTH AFRICA - BOTSWANA 4-1(2-0)

RSA: Itumeleng Isaack Khune, Calvin Anele Ngcongca, Bongani Sandile Khumalo, Thabo Nthethe, Thabo Matlaba, Dean Furman, Kagiso Evidence Dikgacoi (66.Andile Ernest Jali), Lawrence Siphiwe Tshabalala (88.Daine Marcelle Klate), Kermit Romeo Erasmus (58.Bongani Zungu), Bernard Melvin Parker, Tokelo Anthony Rantie. Trainer: Gordon George Igesund.

BOT: Kabelo Dambe, Tshepo Motlhabankwe, Edwin Olerile, Mompati Thuma (59.Gaopatwe Seosenyeng), Joel Mogorosi, Joel Jackie Mothatego (46.Lemponye Tshireletso), Galabgwe Moyana (46.Dirang Moloi), Ofentse Nato, Mogogi Gabonamong, Mogakolodi Ngele, Jérôme Ramatlhokwane. Trainer: Stanley Hunter Tshosane.

Goals: 1-0 Kermit Romeo Erasmus (28), 2-0 Dean Furman (45+1), 2-1 Jérôme Ramatlhokwane (73), 3-1 Bernard Melvin Parker (84), 4-1 Bernard Melvin Parker (89 penalty).

Cautions: Joel Jackie Mothatego, Tshepo Motlhabankwe, Dirang Moloi.

07.09.2013, Stade "Alphonse Massemba-Débat", Brazzaville (Congo); Attendance: 1,500
Referee: Mohamed Benouza (Algeria)

CENTRAL AFRICAN REPUBLIC - ETHIOPIA 1-2(1-0)

CTA: Prince Samolah, Kelly Alexandre Youga, Clovis-Franklin Anzité, Thérence Kéthévoama, Salif Kéïta (55.Romaric Lignanzi), Brice Nicaise Zimbori-Auzingoni, Ralph Amores Dertin (64.Chris Igor N'Goyos), Arnold Gervais Kago, Foxi Kéthévoama, Josué Kossingou Balamandji (83.Moussa Limane), Evans Kondogbia. Trainer: Hervé Lougoundji.

ETH: Sisay Bancha Basa, Abebaw Butako, Degu Debebe, Siyoum Tesfaye, Saladin Bargecho, Adane Girma Gebreyes, Menyahel Teshome Beyene, Asrat Megersa Gobena, Oumed Oukri (46.Behailu Assefa), Salaheldin Ahmed Said, Shimelis Bekele Godo. Trainer: Sewnet Beshaw.

Goals: 1-0 Salif Kéïta (22), 1-1 Menyahel Teshome Beyene (48), 1-2 Salaheldin Ahmed Said (61).

Cautions: Foxi Kéthévoama, Brice Nicaise Zimbori-Auzingoni.

GROUP B

02.06.2012	Freetown	Sierra Leone - Cape Verde	2-1(2-0)
02.06.2012	Monastir	Tunisia - Equatorial Guinea	3-1(0-1)
09.06.2012	Malabo	Equatorial Guinea - Sierra Leone	2-2(2-2)
09.06.2012	Praia	Cape Verde - Tunisia	1-2(1-1)
23.03.2013	Radès	Tunisia - Sierra Leone	2-1(0-0)
24.03.2013	Malabo	Equatorial Guinea - Cape Verde	4-3(2-2); Awarded 0-3
08.06.2013	Freetown	Sierra Leone - Tunisia	2-2(1-0)
08.06.2013	Praia	Cape Verde - Equatorial Guinea	2-1(1-0); Awarded 3-0
15.06.2013	Praia	Cape Verde - Sierra Leone	1-0(1-0)
16.06.2013	Malabo	Equatorial Guinea - Tunisia	1-1(1-0)
07.09.2013	Freetown	Sierra Leone - Equatorial Guinea	3-2(2-0)
07.09.2013	Radès	Tunisia - Cape Verde	0-2(0-2); Awarded 3-0

FINAL STANDINGS

1.	Tunisia	6	4	2	0	13	-	6	14
2.	Cape Verde	6	3	0	3	9	-	7	9
3.	Sierra Leone	6	2	2	2	10	-	10	8
4.	Equatorial Guinea	6	0	2	4	6	-	15	2

Tunisia qualified for the Third Round.

02.06.2012, National Stadium, Freetown; Attendance: 25,000
Referee: William Agbovi (Ghana)

SIERRA LEONE - CAPE VERDE 2-1(2-0)

SLE: Christian Caulker, Ibrahim Marcel Koroma, Umaru Bangura, Ibrahim Obreh Kargbo, Mo Kamara, Samuel Barlay, Sheriff Awilo Suma, Mohamed Bangura, Ibrahim Teteh Bangura (88.Khalifa Jabbie), Alhassan Kamara (72.Mohamed Kallon), Kei Kamara. Trainer: Lars-Olof Mattsson (Sweden).

CPV: Ernesto da Conceição Soares, Carlos Emanuel Soares Tavares "Carlitos", Fernando Maria Neves "Nando", Fernando Lopes dos Santos Varela, Ianique dos Santos Tavares "Stopira", Walder Alves Souto Amado "Ronny" (59.Jorge Djaniny Tavares Semedo), Elvis Manuel Monteiro Macedo "Babanco", Sténio Nivaldo Matos dos Santos, Odair Júnior Lopes Fortes (60.Marco Paulo da Silva Soares), Héldon Augusto Almeida Ramos "Nhuck", José Luís Mendes Andrade "Zé Luis". Trainer: Ulisses Indalécio Silva Antunes "Lúcio Antunes".

Goals: 1-0 Mo Kamara (10), 2-0 Sheriff Awilo Suma (26), 2-1 José Luís Mendes Andrade "Zé Luis" (90+4).

Cautions: Walder Alves Souto Amado "Ronny", Héldon Augusto Almeida Ramos "Nhuck".

02.06.2012, Stade "Mustapha Ben Jannet", Monastir; Attendance: 10,000
Referee: Mehdi Abid Charef (Algeria)

TUNISIA - EQUATORIAL GUINEA 3-1(0-1)

TUN: Aymen Mathlouthi Balbouli, Ammar Jemal, Bilel Ifa, Anis Boussaïdi, Khalil Chemmam, Jamel Saihi (90.Hatten Baratli), Wissem Ben Yahia (46.Hamdi Harbaoui), Mejdi Traoui, Änis Ben-Hatira, Issam Jemâa (79.Chadi Hammami), Saber Khelifa. Trainer: Sami Trabelsi.

EQG: Emmanuel Danilo Clementino Silva, Lawrence Sokota Doe, Rui Fernando Da Gracia Gomes, Armando Sipoto Bohale Aqueriaco "Sipo", Juvenal Edjogo-Owono Montalbán (83.Alberto Edjogo Owono Montalbán), Ben Mamadou Konaté, Fernelly Castillo (73.Dani Jaer Micha), Daniel Vladmir Ekedo Chigozirim, Jean-Maxime Ndong Eyama "Juanito", Rubén Epitié Dyowe Roig (53.Narcisse Ekanga Amia), Iván Iyanga Travieso "Randy". Trainer: Gilson Paulo de Mello Filho (Brazil).

Goals: 0-1 Rubén Epitié Dyowe Roig (34), 1-1 Issam Jemâa (51), 2-1 Hamdi Harbaoui (56), 3-1 Chadi

Hammami (88).
Cautions: Saber Khelifa, Bilel Ifa / Ben Mamadou Konaté, Fernelly Castillo, Lawrence Sokota Doe.

09.06.2012, Nuevo Estadio de Malabo, Malabo; Attendance: 4,000
Referee: Adam Cordier (Chad)
EQUATORIAL GUINEA - SIERRA LEONE 2-2(2-2)
EQG: Emmanuel Danilo Clementino Silva, Lawrence Sokota Doe, Carolino Falcão Ronan (86.Armando Sipoto Bohale Aqueriaco "Sipo"), Rui Fernando Da Gracia Gomes, David Álvarez Aguirre "Kily", Juvenal Edjogo-Owono Montalbán (86.Alberto Edjogo Owono Montalbán), Rolan De la Cruz Biojó, Daniel Vladmir Ekedo Chigozirim (71.David Edu García Mitogo), Jean-Maxime Ndong Eyama "Juanito", Thierry Fidjeu Tazameta, Iván Iyanga Travieso "Randy". Trainer: Gilson Paulo de Mello Filho (Brazil).
SLE: Christian Caulker, Ibrahim Marcel Koroma, Umaru Bangura, Ibrahim Obreh Kargbo, Mo Kamara, Samuel Barlay, Sheriff Awilo Suma, Mohamed Bangura, Ibrahim Teteh Bangura (67.Khalifa Jabbie), Alhassan Kamara (46.Mohamed Kallon), Kei Kamara. Trainer: Lars-Olof Mattsson (Sweden).
Goals: 1-0 Juvenal Edjogo-Owono Montalbán (14), 1-1 Samuel Barlay (23), 1-2 Ibrahim Teteh Bangura (25), 2-2 Juvenal Edjogo-Owono Montalbán (40).
Cautions: David Álvarez Aguirre "Kily", David Edu García Mitogo / Sheriff Awilo Suma, Umaru Bangura.

09.06.2012, Estádio da Várzea, Praia; Attendance: 3,600
Referee: Rédouane Jiyed (Morocco)
CAPE VERDE - TUNISIA 1-2(1-1)
CPV: Ernesto da Conceição Soares, Carlos Emanuel Soares Tavares "Carlitos", Fernando Maria Neves "Nando", Fernando Lopes dos Santos Varela, Ianique dos Santos Tavares "Stopira", Walder Alves Souto Amado "Ronny", Marco Paulo da Silva Soares (74.Luís Carlos Amada Soares "Platini"), Elvis Manuel Monteiro Macedo "Babanco", Odair Júnior Lopes Fortes (63.Jorge Djaniny Tavares Semedo), Héldon Augusto Almeida Ramos "Nhuck" (55.Ryan Isaac Mendes da Graça), José Luís Mendes Andrade "Zé Luis". Trainer: Ulisses Indalécio Silva Antunes "Lúcio Antunes".
TUN: Aymen Mathlouthi Balbouli, Walid Hichri, Ammar Jemal, Anis Boussaïdi, Khalil Chemmam, Chadi Hammami, Mejdi Traoui, Änis Ben-Hatira (58.Wissem Ben Yahia), Hamdi Harbaoui (73.Wajdi Bouazzi), Issam Jemâa, Saber Khelifa. Trainer: Sami Trabelsi.
Goals: 0-1 Saber Khelifa (14), 1-1 Odair Júnior Lopes Fortes (26), 1-2 Issam Jemâa (46).
Cautions: Héldon Augusto Almeida Ramos "Nhuck" / Wissem Ben Yahia, Issam Jemâa, Ammar Jemal.

23.03.2013, Stade Olympique de Radès, Radès; Attendance: 10,000
Referee: Mal Souley Mohamadou (Cameroon)
TUNISIA - SIERRA LEONE 2-1(0-0)
TUN: Moez Ben Chérifia, Sofian Chahed, Karim Haggui, Yassine Salim Mikari, Aymen Abdennour, Khaled Mouelhi, Mejdi Traoui, Issam Jemâa (59.Wahbi Khazri), Saber Khelifa, Oussama Darragi (76.Wissem Ben Yahia), Youssef Msakni (86.Taha Yassine Khenissi). Trainer: Nabil Maâloul.
SLE: Christian Caulker, Sheriff Suma, Umaru Bangura, Mustapha Dumbuya, Samuel Barlay, Mohamed Kamara, Ibrahim Marcel Koroma, Rodney Strasser (76.Ibrahim Teteh Bangura), Khalifa Jabbie, Kei Ansu Kamara, Julius Gibrilla Woobay (69.Alhassan Kamara). Trainer: Lars-Olof Mattsson (Sweden).
Goals: 1-0 Oussama Darragi (57), 2-0 Wahbi Khazri (72), 2-1 Alhassan Kamara (74).
Cautions: Issam Jemâa / Ibrahim Marcel Koroma, Christian Caulker.

24.03.2013, Estadio de Malabo, Malabo; Attendance: 8,000
Referee: Mahamadou Keita (Mali)
EQUATORIAL GUINEA - CAPE VERDE 4-3(2-2)*
EQB: Emmanuel Danilo Clementino Silva, Lawrence Sokota Doe (46.Ben Mamadou Konaté), Baba Issaka, Rui Fernando Da Gracia Gomes, Fousseny Kamissoko, Claudiney Ramos „Rincón", Diouzer da Cruz dos Santos „Dio", Emilio Nsue López, Judson Augusto do Bonfim Santos (46.César Augusto Rivas Lasso), Iván Iyanga Travieso „Randy", Ricardo Martins Pereira „Ricardinho" (67.Jonatas Paulino da Silva Inacio „Obina"). Trainer: Andoni Goikoetxea Olaskoaga (Spain).
CPV: Josimar Dias Vózinha, Odysseu Guy Ramos, Fernando Lopes dos Santos Varela, Carlos Emanuel Soares Tavares „Carlitos" (66.Armindo Rodrigues Mendes Furtado „Brito"), Nivaldo Alves Freitas Santos (81.Ramilton Jorge Santos do Rosário „Rambé"), Toni Santos Varela Monteiro (66.David Mendes da Silva), Marco Paulo da Silva Soares, Elvis Manuel Monteiro Macedo „Babanco", Luís Carlos Amada Soares „Platini", Júlio Tavares, Jorge Djaniny Tavares Semedo. Trainer: Ulisses Indalécio Silva Antunes "Lúcio Antunes".
Goals: 1-0 Emilio Nsue López (3), 1-1 Jorge Djaniny Tavares Semedo (5), 2-1 Emilio Nsue López (16 penalty), 2-2 Luís Carlos Amada Soares „Platini" (18), 3-2 Emilio Nsue López (78), 3-3 Jorge Djaniny Tavares Semedo (84), 4-3 Claudiney Ramos „Rincón" (87).
Cautions: Lawrence Sokota Doe, Jonatas Paulino da Silva Inacio „Obina",Emilio Nsue López / Marco Paulo da Silva Soares, Júlio Tavares, Luís Carlos Amada Soares „Platini".
Sent off: Fernando Lopes dos Santos Varela (88).
**Please note*: Equatorial Guinea fielded the ineligible player Emilio Nsue López. FIFA awarded Cape Verde a 3–0 win.*

08.06.2013, National Stadium, Freetown; Attendance: 20,000
Referee: Eric Otogo-Castane (Gabon)
SIERRA LEONE - TUNISIA 2-2(1-0)
SLE: Ibrahim Tarawally, Ibrahim Kargbo, Sheriff Suma, Umaru Bangura, Mustapha Dumbuya, Mohamed Kamara, John Kamara (59.Samuel Barlay), George Davies (75.Ibrahim Teteh Bangura), Kei Ansu Kamara, Mohamed Bangura, Alhassan Kamara (85.Alfred Sankoh). Trainer: Jonathan McKinstry (Northern Ireland).
TUN: Moez Ben Chérifia, Sofian Chahed (46.Sameh Derbali), Karim Haggui, Yassine Salim Mikari (46.Oussama Darragi), Aymen Abdennour, Khalil Chemmam, Hocine Ragued, Chadi Hammami (83.Youssef Msakni), Ferjani Sassi, Salema Kasdaoui, Fakhreddine Ben Youssef. Trainer: Nabil Maâloul.
Goals: 1-0 Kei Ansu Kamara (38), 1-1 Oussama Darragi (55 penalty), 2-1 Sheriff Suma (70), 2-2 Fakhreddine Ben Youssef (89).
Cautions: Sheriff Suma, Ibrahim Tarawally / Aymen Abdennour, Fakhreddine Ben Youssef, Karim Haggui.

08.06.2013, Estádio da Várzea, Praia; Attendance: 3,500
Referee: Helder Martins de Carvalho (Angola)
CAPE VERDE - EQUATORIAL GUINEA 2-1(1-0)*
CPV: Josimar Dias Vózinha, Admilson Estaline Dias Barros „Gegé", Nivaldo Alves Freitas Santos, Carlos Emanuel Soares Tavares „Carlitos", Carlos Daniel Silveira da Graça „Kay", Toni Santos Varela Monteiro, Marco Paulo da Silva Soares, Elvis Manuel Monteiro Macedo „Babanco" (83.David Mendes da Silva), Luís Carlos Amada Soares „Platini" (10.Júlio Tavares), Héldon Augusto Almeida Ramos „Nhuck" (71.Carlos Lima „Calú"), Jorge Djaniny Tavares Semedo. Trainer: Ulisses Indalécio Silva Antunes "Lúcio Antunes".
EQB: Emmanuel Danilo Clementino Silva, Jimmy Bermúdez Valencia, Rui Fernando Da Gracia Gomes, Armando Sipoto Bohale Aqueriaco „Sipo", Carlos Akapo Martínez, Juvenal Edjogo-Owono Montalbán (84.Iván Iyanga Travieso „Randy"), Claudiney Ramos „Rincón", César Augusto Rivas Lasso (73.Judson Augusto do Bonfim Santos), Emilio Nsue López, Jonatas Paulino da Silva Inacio „Obina", Ricardo Martins Pereira „Ricardinho" (46.Diouzer da Cruz dos Santos „Dio"). Trainer: Andoni Goikoetxea Olaskoaga (Spain).

Goals: 1-0 Elvis Manuel Monteiro Macedo „Babanco" (17), 2-0 Jorge Djaniny Tavares Semedo (52), 2-1 Jonatas Paulino da Silva Inacio „Obina" (54).
Cautions: Emilio Nsue López, Rui Fernando Da Gracia Gomes.
**Please note*: Equatorial Guinea fielded the ineligible player Emilio Nsue López. FIFA awarded Cape Verde a 3–0 win.*

15.06.2013, Estádio da Várzea, Praia; Attendance: 3,500
Referee: Anthony Ramsy Raphael (Malawi)
CAPE VERDE - SIERRA LEONE 1-0(1-0)
CPV: Josimar Dias Vózinha, Admilson Estaline Dias Barros „Gegé", Nivaldo Alves Freitas Santos, Carlos Emanuel Soares Tavares „Carlitos", Carlos Daniel Silveira da Graça „Kay", Toni Santos Varela Monteiro (69.Carlos Lima „Calú"), Marco Paulo da Silva Soares, Elvis Manuel Monteiro Macedo „Babanco", Héldon Augusto Almeida Ramos „Nhuck" (69.Aires Marques Fernandes "Alex"), Júlio Tavares, Jorge Djaniny Tavares Semedo (86.David Mendes da Silva). Trainer: Ulisses Indalécio Silva Antunes "Lúcio Antunes".
SLE: Solomon Zombo Morris, Ibrahim Kargbo, Umaru Bangura, Ibrahim Marcel Koroma (66.Gibril Sankoh), Mustapha Dumbuya (74.Khalifa Jabbie), Mohamed Kamara, John Kamara, George Davies (66.Mustapha Bangura), Abdulai Hindolo Bell-Baggie, Mohamed Bangura, Alhassan Kamara. Trainer: Jonathan McKinstry (Northern Ireland).
Goal: 1-0 Héldon Augusto Almeida Ramos „Nhuck" (13).
Cautions: Carlos Emanuel Soares Tavares „Carlitos",Jorge Djaniny Tavares Semedo, Elvis Manuel Monteiro Macedo „Babanco" / Ibrahim Marcel Koroma, John Kamara, Ibrahim Kargbo.

16.06.2013, Estadio de Malabo, Malabo; Attendance: 8,000
Referee: Bernard Camille (Seychelles)
EQUATORIAL GUINEA - TUNISIA 1-1(1-0)
EQB: Emmanuel Danilo Clementino Silva, Jimmy Bermúdez Valencia, David Álvarez Aguirre „Kily" (69.Judson Augusto do Bonfim Santos), Armando Sipoto Bohale Aqueriaco „Sipo", Diosdado Mbele Mangué, Juvenal Edjogo-Owono Montalbán, Claudiney Ramos „Rincón", Diouzer da Cruz dos Santos „Dio", César Augusto Rivas Lasso (46.Carlos Akapo Martínez), Iván Iyanga Travieso „Randy", Jonatas Paulino da Silva Inacio „Obina" (89.Rodolfo Bodipo Díaz). Trainer: Andoni Goikoetxea Olaskoaga (Spain).
TUN: Moez Ben Chérifia, Karim Haggui, Sameh Derbali, Aymen Abdennour, Khalil Chemmam, Hocine Ragued (89.Chadi Hammami), Mejdi Traoui, Issam Jemâa (81.Ferjani Sassi), Saber Khelifa (71.Mohamed Amine Chermiti), Oussama Darragi, Fakhreddine Ben Youssef. Trainer: Nabil Maâloul.
Goals: 1-0 Juvenal Edjogo-Owono Montalbán (36 penalty), 1-1 Oussama Darragi (64 penalty).
Cautions: Claudiney Ramos „Rincón" / Fakhreddine Ben Youssef, Saber Khelifa.

07.09.2013, National Stadium, Freetown; Attendance: 3,000
Referee: Mohamed Hussein El Fadil (Sudan)
SIERRA LEONE - EQUATORIAL GUINEA 3-2(2-0)
SLE: Solomon Zombo Morris, Ibrahim Kargbo, Sheriff Suma, Umaru Bangura, Mustapha Dumbuya, Mohamed Kamara, Mustapha Bangura (75.Michael Lahoud), Rodney Strasser, Abdulai Hindolo Bell-Baggie (69.Kei Ansu Kamara), Mohamed Bangura, Alhassan Kamara (84.Ibrahim Teteh Bangura). Trainer: Jonathan McKinstry (Northern Ireland).
EQB: Carlos Bejarano, Jimmy Bermúdez Valencia, David Álvarez Aguirre „Kily", Armando Sipoto Bohale Aqueriaco „Sipo", Diosdado Mbele Mangué, Juvenal Edjogo-Owono Montalbán, Rolan De la Cruz Biojó, Ellong Doualla Viera (46.Floriano Claudino de Souza), Iván Bolado Palacios, Iván Iyanga Travieso "Randy" (59.Yoiver González Mosquera), Thierry Fidjeu Tazemata. Trainer: Andoni Goikoetxea Olaskoaga (Spain).
Goals: 1-0 Mustapha Bangura (21), 2-0 Ibrahim Kargbo (40 penalty), 3-0 Alhassan Kamara (70), 3-1 Juvenal Edjogo-Owono Montalbán (85), 3-2 Iván Bolado Palacios (88).
Cautions: Alhassan Kamara, Mustapha Dumbuya, Solomon Zombo Morris, Mohamed Bangura / Carlos Bejarano.

07.09.2013, Stade Olympique de Radès, Radès; Attendance: 9,000
Referee: Bakary Papa Gassama (Gambia)

TUNISIA - CAPE VERDE **0-2(0-2)***

TUN: Moez Ben Chérifia, Karim Haggui, Sameh Derbali (57.Samuel Allagui), Aymen Abdennour, Khalil Chemmam, Khaled Mouelhi, Mejdi Traoui (10.Ferjani Sassi), Wahbi Khazri, Issam Jemâa, Oussama Darragi (68.Zouheïr Dhaouadi), Youssef Msakni. Trainer: Nabil Maâloul.

CPV: Josimar Dias Vózinha, Fernando Lopes dos Santos Varela, Admilson Estaline Dias Barros „Gegé“ (66.Carlos Emanuel Soares Tavares „Carlitos“), Nivaldo Alves Freitas Santos, Carlos Daniel Silveira da Graça „Kay“, Marco Paulo da Silva Soares, Elvis Manuel Monteiro Macedo „Babanco“ (76.Toni Santos Varela Monteiro), Luís Carlos Amada Soares „Platini“, Carlos Lima „Calú“, Ryan Isaac Mendes da Graça, Héldon Augusto Almeida Ramos „Nhuck“ (70.Sidnei dos Reis Mariano “Sita”). Trainer: Ulisses Indalécio Silva Antunes "Lúcio Antunes".

Goals: 0-1 Luís Carlos Amada Soares „Platini“ (28), 0-2 Héldon Augusto Almeida Ramos „Nhuck“ (42).

Cautions: Karim Haggui, Aymen Abdennour, Wahbi Khazri / Josimar Dias Vózinha, Nivaldo Alves Freitas Santos.

*<u>Please note</u>: *Cape Verde fielded the player Fernando Lopes dos Santos Varela, who had been sent off in the match against Equatorial Guinea on 24 March 2013 and which had been given a four match suspension. FIFA awarded Tunisia a 3–0 win.*

GROUP C

02.06.2012	Bakau	Gambia - Morocco	1-1(1-0)
02.06.2012	Abidjan	Côte d'Ivoire - Tanzania	2-0(1-0)
09.06.2012	Marrakech	Morocco - Côte d'Ivoire	2-2(1-1)
10.06.2012	Dar es Salaam	Tanzania - Gambia	2-1(0-1)
23.03.2013	Abidjan	Côte d'Ivoire - Gambia	3-0(0-0)
24.03.2013	Dar es Salaam	Tanzania - Morocco	3-1(0-0)
08.06.2013	Bakau	Gambia - Côte d'Ivoire	0-3(0-1)
08.06.2013	Marrakech	Morocco - Tanzania	2-1(1-1)
15.06.2013	Marrakech	Morocco - Gambia	2-0(1-0)
16.06.2013	Dar es Salaam	Tanzania - Côte d'Ivoire	2-4(2-3)
07.09.2013	Bakau	Gambia - Tanzania	2-0(1-0)
07.09.2013	Abidjan	Côte d'Ivoire - Morocco	1-1(0-0)

Côte d’Ivoire qualified for the Third Round.

FINAL STANDINGS

1.	Côte d'Ivoire	6	4	2	0	15	-	5	14
2.	Morocco	6	2	3	1	9	-	8	9
3.	Tanzania	6	2	0	4	8	-	12	6
4.	Gambia	6	1	1	4	4	-	11	4

02.06.2012, Independence Stadium, Bakau; Attendance: 15,000
Referee: Néant Alioum (Cameroon)

GAMBIA - MOROCCO 1-1(1-0)

GAM: Christopher Allen, Kebba Ceesay (70.Lamin Samateh), Pa Saikou Kujabi, Mamadou Danso, Ousman Koli, Abdou Jammeh, Pa Modou Jagne (90+2.Saihou Gassama), Tijan Jaiteh, Demba Savage, Mustapha Jarju, Momodou Ceesay. Trainer: Luciano Mancini (Italy).

MAR: Nadir Lamyaghri, Ismail Belmaalem, Mehdi Benatia, Zakarya Bergdich, Ayoub El Khaliqi, Adil Hermach, Houssine Kharja, Karim Aït Fana (65.Youssef El Arabi), Abdelaziz Barrada (46.Nordin Amrabat), Younès Belhanda, Yassine Salhi (46.Hamza Abourazzouk). Trainer: Eric Maria Gerets (Belgium).

Goals: 1-0 Abdou Jammeh (15), 1-1 Houssine Kharja (76).

Cautions: Kebba Ceesay / Ayoub El Khaliqi.

02.06.2012, Stade "Félix Houphouët-Boigny", Abidjan; Attendance: 15,000
Referee: Slim Jedidi (Tunisia)

CÔTE D'IVOIRE - TANZANIA 2-0(1-0)

CIV: Boubacar Barry, Igor Lolo, Kolo Habib Touré, Kafoumba Coulibaly, Emmanuel Eboué, Siaka Tiéné, Jean-Jacques Gosso, Cheick Ismael Tioté (67.Didier Ya Konan), Gervais Yao Kouassi „Gervinho“ (65.Abdul-Kader Keïta), Salomon Armand Magloire Kalou (77.Max-Alain Gradel), Didier Yves Drogba Tébily. Trainer: Sabri Lamouchi (France).

TAN: Juma Kaseja, Aggrey Morris, Kelvin Patrick Yondani, Amir Mrisho Maftah, Shaban Mussa Nditi, Salum Abubakar (67.John Raphael Bocco), Shomari Kapombe, Mwinyi Kazimoto, Frank Raymond Domayo, Mrisho Alfani Ngasa, Mbwana Aly Samatta. Trainer: Kim Poulsen (Denmark).

Goals: 1-0 Salomon Armand Magloire Kalou (18), 2-0 Didier Yves Drogba Tébily (80).

Cautions: Igor Lolo / Aggrey Morris.

Sent off: Aggrey Morris (70).

09.06.2012, Stade de Marrakech, Marrakech; Attendance: 36,000
Referee: Gehad Grisha (Egypt)

MOROCCO - CÔTE D'IVOIRE 2-2(1-1)

MAR: Nadir Lamyaghri, Ayoub El Khaliqi, Mehdi Benatia, Ismail Belmaalem, Zakarya Bergdich, Issam El Adoua, Houssine Kharja, Abdelaziz Barrada, Chemseddine Chtibi (76.Nordin Amrabat), Karim Aït Fana (76.Yassine Salhi), Youssef El Arabi (64.Hamza Abourazzouk). Trainer: Eric Maria Gerets (Belgium).

CIV: Boubacar Barry, Jean-Jacques Gosso, Igor Lolo, Kolo Habib Touré, Siaka Tiéné, Cheick Ismael Tioté, Kafoumba Coulibaly, Salomon Armand Magloire Kalou, Abdul-Kader Keïta (46.Didier Ya Konan), Gervais Yao Kouassi „Gervinho“ (61.Max-Alain Gradel), Didier Yves Drogba Tébily (85.Wilfried Guemiand Bony). Trainer: Sabri Lamouchi (France).

Goals: 0-1 Salomon Armand Magloire Kalou (8), 1-1 Houssine Kharja (41), 1-2 Kolo Habib Touré (60), 2-2 Hamza Abourazzouk (89).

Cautions: Nordin Amrabat, Ayoub El Khaliqi / Cheick Ismael Tioté, Gervais Yao Kouassi „Gervinho“.

10.06.2012, "Benjamin Mkapa" National Stadium, Dar es Salaam; Attendance: 20,000
Referee: Ruzive Ruzive (Zimbabwe)

TANZANIA - GAMBIA 2-1(0-1)

TAN: Juma Kaseja, Erasto Edward Nyoni, Kelvin Patrick Yondani, Amir Mrisho Maftah, Haruna Moshi Shaban (56.John Raphael Bocco), Shaban Mussa Nditi, Shomari Kapombe, Mwinyi Kazimoto, Frank Raymond Domayo, Mrisho Alfani Ngasa, Mbwana Aly Samatta. Trainer: Kim Poulsen (Denmark).

GAM: Christopher Allen, Kebba Ceesay, Mamadou Danso, Ousman Koli, Abdou Jammeh, Pa Saikou Kujabi, Pa Modou Jagne, Saihou Gassama, Demba Savage, Mustapha Jarju, Momodou Ceesay (68.Ali Sowe). Trainer: Luciano Mancini (Italy).

Goals: 0-1 Momodou Ceesay (8), 1-1 Shomari Kapombe (60), 2-1 Erasto Edward Nyoni (84 penalty).

Cautions: Abdou Jammeh, Ousman Koli, Pa Modou Jagne.

23.03.2013, Stade “Félix Houphouët-Boigny”, Abidjan; Attendance: 20,000
Referee: Eric Otogo-Castane (Gabon)

CÔTE D'IVOIRE - GAMBIA 3-0(0-0)

CIV: Boubacar Barry, Arthur Etienne Boka, Souleymane Bamba (78.Kolo Habib Touré), Brou Benjamin Angoua, Alain Didier Zokora Deguy, Gnégnéri Yaya Touré, Cheik Ismael Tioté, Sereso Geoffroy Gonzaroua Die „Serey Die“ (65.Didier Ya Konan), Salomon Armand Magloire Kalou, Gervais Yao Kouassi „Gervinho“, Wilfried Guemiand Bony (75.Arouna Koné). Trainer: Sabri Lamouchi (France).

GAM: Christopher Allen, Abdou Jammeh, Mamadou Danso, Pa Modou Jagne, Lamin Samateh, Abdoulie Mansally (80.Omar Colley), Ebrima Sohna, Sainey Nyassi, Yankuba Ceesay, Saihou Gassama (63.Hamza Barry), Momodou Ceesay (46.Sulayman Marreh). Trainer: Luciano Mancini (Italy).

Goals: 1-0 Wilfried Guemiand Bony (51 penalty), 2-0 Gnégnéri Yaya Touré (57), 3-0 Salomon Armand Magloire Kalou (70).

Cautions: Alain Didier Zokora Deguy, Brou Benjamin Angoua, Gervais Yao Kouassi „Gervinho“ / Sainey Nyassi.

24.03.2013, „Benjamin Mkapa“ National Stadium, Dar es Salaam; Attendance: 40,000
Referee: Helder Martins de Carvalho (Angola)

TANZANIA - MOROCCO 3-1(0-0)

TAN: Juma Kaseja, Erasto Edward Nyoni, Aggrey Morris, Kelvin Patrick Yondani, Shomari Salum Kapombé, Amri Kiemba Ramadhan, Mwinyi Kazimoto (46.Thomas Emanuel Ulimwengu), Salum Abubakar, Frank Raymond Domayo, Mbwana Aly Samatta (90+3.John Raphael Bocco), Mrisho Alfani Ngasa (64.Athuman Idd). Trainer: Kim Poulsen (Denmark).

MAR: Nadir Lamyaghri, Younès Bellakhdar, Younès Hammal, Abderrahim Achchakir, Zakarya Bergdich, Issam El Adoua, Kamel Chafni, Abdelilah Hafidi (78.Nordin Amrabat), Abdelaziz Barrada (69.Brahim El Bahri), Chahir Belghazouani (57.Youssef El Arabi), Hamza Abourazzouk. Trainer: Rachid Taoussi.

Goals: 1-0 Thomas Emanuel Ulimwengu (46), 2-0 Mbwana Aly Samatta (67), 3-0 Mbwana Aly Samatta (79), 3-1 Youssef El Arabi (90+3).

Cautions: Abdelaziz Barrada, Younès Bellakhdar.

Sent off: Abderrahim Achchakir (81).

08.06.2013, Independence Stadium, Bakau; Attendance: 24,000
Referee: Janny Sikazwe (Zambia)

GAMBIA - CÔTE D'IVOIRE 0-3(0-1)

GAM: Christopher Allen, Abdou Jammeh (74.Pa Modou Jagne), Mamadou Danso, Omar Colley, Sulayman Marreh, Tijan Jaiteh, Ebrima Sohna, Sainey Nyassi, Mustapha Jarju (88.Abdoulie Mansally), Demba Savage, Momodou Ceesay (82.Ali Sowe). Trainer: Peter Bonu Johnson.

CIV: Boubacar Barry, Arthur Etienne Boka, Brou Benjamin Angoua, Serge Aurier, Christian Koffi Ndri „Romaric“ (46.Mathis Gazoa Kippersund Bolly), Alain Didier Zokora Deguy, Gnégnéri Yaya Touré, Cheik Ismael Tioté, Sereso Geoffroy Gonzaroua Die „Serey Die“ (84.Souleymane Bamba), Wilfried Guemiand Bony, Lacina Traoré (65.Giovanni-Guy Yann Sio). Trainer: Sabri Lamouchi (France).

Goals: 0-1 Lacina Traoré (12), 0-2 Wilfried Guemiand Bony (61), 0-3 Gnégnéri Yaya Touré (89).

Cautions: Omar Colley / Lacina Traoré, Cheik Ismael Tioté, Arthur Etienne Boka.

08.06.2013, Stade de Marrakech, Marrakech; Attendance: 15,000
Referee: Daniel Frazer Bennett (South Africa)

MOROCCO - TANZANIA 2-1(1-1)

MAR: Nadir Lamyaghri, Yassine Jebbour (33.Abdellatif Noussir), Issam El Adoua, Ahmed Kantari, Zakarya Bergdich, Adil Hermach, Kamel Chafni, Mounir Obbadi, Abdelaziz Barrada (62.Youssef Kaddioui), Youssef El Arabi, Abderrazak Hamdallah (75.Alharbi El Jadeyaoui). Trainer: Rachid Taoussi.

TAN: Juma Kaseja, Erasto Edward Nyoni, Aggrey Morris, Kelvin Patrick Yondani, Shomari Salum Kapombé, Mrisho Alfani Ngasa (46.Nadir Haroub), Amri Kiemba Ramadhan, Salum Abubakar, Frank Raymond Domayo, Mbwana Aly Samatta, Thomas Emanuel Ulimwengu (46.Khamis Mcha Khamis; 83.John Raphael Bocco). Trainer: Kim Poulsen (Denmark).

Goals: 0-1 Amri Kiemba Ramadhan (26), 1-1 Abderrazak Hamdallah (39 penalty), 2-1 Youssef El Arabi (51).

Cautions: Abderrazak Hamdallah, Mounir Obbadi, Zakarya Bergdich, Ahmed Kantari / Mrisho Alfani Ngasa.

Sent off: Aggrey Morris (38).

15.06.2013, Stade de Marrakech, Marrakech; Attendance: 15,000
Referee: Mohamed Hussein El Fadil (Sudan)

MOROCCO - GAMBIA **2-0(1-0)**

MAR: Mohamed Amsif, Issam El Adoua, Ahmed Kantari, Abdellatif Noussir, Zakarya Bergdich, Kamel Chafni, Abdelaziz Barrada (60.Mounir Obbadi), Younès Belhanda, Salaheddine Saidi (83.Abdelilah Hafidi), Youssef El Arabi, Abderrazak Hamdallah (70.Chahir Belghazouani). Trainer: Rachid Taoussi.

GAM: Baboucarr Sanyang, Abdou Jammeh, Lamin Samateh, Omar Colley, Pa Modou Jagne, Sulayman Marreh (90+2.Hamza Barry), Abdoulie Mansally, Tijan Jaiteh, Sainey Nyassi (53.Mustapha Jarju), Demba Savage, Ali Sowe (68.Saloum Faal). Trainer: Peter Bonu Johnson.

Goals: 1-0 Abdelaziz Barrada (3), 2-0 Younès Belhanda (51).

Cautions: Salaheddine Saidi / Sainey Nyassi.

16.06.2013, „Benjamin Mkapa“ National Stadium, Dar es Salaam; Attendance: 60,000
Referee: Mehdi Abid Charef (Algeria)

TANZANIA - CÔTE D'IVOIRE **2-4(2-3)**

TAN: Juma Kaseja, Erasto Edward Nyoni, Kelvin Patrick Yondani, Shomari Salum Kapombé (89.Khamis Mcha Khamis), Nadir Haroub, Amri Kiemba Ramadhan, Mwinyi Kazimoto (89.Vincent Barnabas Saramba), Salum Abubakar, Frank Raymond Domayo, Mbwana Aly Samatta, Thomas Emanuel Ulimwengu. Trainer: Kim Poulsen (Denmark).

CIV: Boubacar Barry, Arthur Etienne Boka, Souleymane Bamba, Serge Aurier, Alain Didier Zokora Deguy, Gnégnéri Yaya Touré, Sereso Geoffroy Gonzaroua Die „Serey Die“ (80.Christian Koffi Ndri „Romaric“), Jean-Jacques Gosso Gosso, Salomon Armand Magloire Kalou (65.Giovanni-Guy Yann Sio), Gervais Yao Kouassi „Gervinho“, Lacina Traoré (89.Wilfried Guemiand Bony). Trainer: Sabri Lamouchi (France).

Goals: 1-0 Amri Kiemba Ramadhan (2), 1-1 Lacina Traoré (13), 1-2 Gnégnéri Yaya Touré (23), 2-2 Thomas Emanuel Ulimwengu (34), 2-3 Gnégnéri Yaya Touré (43 penalty), 2-4 Wilfried Guemiand Bony (90+3).

Cautions: Erasto Edward Nyoni / Souleymane Bamba, Jean-Jacques Gosso Gosso, Sereso Geoffroy Gonzaroua Die „Serey Die“.

07.09.2013, Independence Stadium, Bakau; Attendance: 10,000
Referee: Hudu Munyemana (Rwanda)

GAMBIA - TANZANIA **2-0(1-0)**

GAM: Baboucarr Sanyang, Omar Colley, Sulayman Marreh, Tijan Jaiteh, Ebrima Sohna, Abdoulie Mansally, Hamza Barry (86.Assan Ceesay), Saloum Faal (89.Modou Jatta), Bubacarr Sanneh, Mustapha Jarju (77.Matarr Nyan), Momodou Ceesay. Trainer: Peter Bonu Johnson.

TAN: Juma Kaseja, Henry Joseph Shindika, Erasto Edward Nyoni (70.Charles Luhende), Vincent Barnabas Saramba, Mrisho Alfani Ngasa, Nadir Haroub, Amri Kiemba Ramadhan, Khamis Mcha Khamis (61.Juma Luzio), Haruni Athumani Chanongo, Frank Raymond Domayo, Happygod Simon Msuva. Trainer: Kim Poulsen (Denmark).

Goals: 1-0 Mustapha Jarju (44), 2-0 Mustapha Jarju (51).

07.09.2013, Stade "Félix Houphouët-Boigny", Abidjan; Attendance: 20,000
Referee: Bernard Camille (Seychelles)

CÔTE D'IVOIRE - MOROCCO 1-1(0-0)

CIV: Boubacar Barry, Siaka Tiéné (57.Serge Aurier), Brou Benjamin Angoua, Ousmane Viera Diarrassouba, Brice Dja Djé Djé, Christian Koffi Ndri „Romaric" (73.Wilfried Guemiand Bony), Gnégnéri Yaya Touré, Cheik Ismael Tioté (67.Didier Ya Konan), Didier Yves Drogba Tébily, Salomon Armand Magloire Kalou, Gervais Yao Kouassi „Gervinho". Trainer: Sabri Lamouchi (France).

MAR: Mohamed Amsif, Issam El Adoua, Zouhair Feddal, Mohamed Oulhaj, Abdellatif Noussir, Zakarya Bergdich, Abdelaziz Barrada (71.Mounir Obbadi), Younès Belhanda (80.Mohamed Ali Bemaamar), Omar El Kaddouri (89.Abdessalam Benjelloun), Salaheddine Saidi, Youssef El Arabi. Trainer: Rachid Taoussi.

Goals: 0-1 Youssef El Arabi (52), 1-1 Didier Yves Drogba Tébily (83 penalty).

Cautions: Cheik Ismael Tioté, Gnégnéri Yaya Touré / Abdelaziz Barrada, Zouhair Feddal, Mohamed Amsif.

GROUP D

01.06.2012	Kumasi	Ghana - Lesotho	7-0(3-0)
02.06.2012	Khartoum	Sudan - Zambia	2-0(0-0) Awarded 0-3
09.06.2012	Ndola	Zambia - Ghana	1-0(1-0)
10.06.2012	Maseru	Lesotho - Sudan	0-0
24.03.2013	Maseru	Lesotho - Zambia	1-1(0-0)
24.03.2013	Kumasi	Ghana - Sudan	4-0(2-0)
07.06.2013	Omdurman	Sudan - Ghana	1-3(1-1)
08.06.2013	Ndola	Zambia - Lesotho	4-0(1-0)
15.06.2013	Ndola	Zambia - Sudan	1-1(0-0)
16.06.2013	Maseru	Lesotho - Ghana	0-2(0-1)
06.09.2013	Kumasi	Ghana - Zambia	2-1(1-0)
08.09.2013	Omdurman	Sudan - Lesotho	1-3(1-1)

Ghana qualified for the Third Round.

FINAL STANDINGS

1.	Ghana	6	5	0	1	18 - 3	15
2.	Zambia	6	3	2	1	11 - 4	11
3.	Lesotho	6	1	2	3	4 - 15	5
4.	Sudan	6	0	2	4	3 - 14	2

01.06.2012, Baba Yara Stadium, Kumasi; Attendance: 38,000
Referee: Badara Diatta (Senegal)

GHANA - LESOTHO 7-0(3-0)

GHA: Adambathia Larsen Kwarasey, John Boye, Jerry Akaminko, Samuel Diadie Inkoom (63.Daniel Tawiah Opare), Harrison Afful, Emmanuel Agyemang-Badu, Derek Owusu Boateng (73.Anthony Gildas Kofi Annan), Kojo Asamoah, Sulleyman Ali Muntari (67.Christian Atsu Twasam), Dominic Adiyiah, Jordan Pierre Ayew. Trainer: James Kwesi Appiah.

LES: Phasumane Kholuoe, Nkau Lerotholi (80.Mabuti Potloane), Thabiso Maile, Thabo Masualle, Thapelo Mokhele, Tumelo Bereng (47.Katleho Moleko), Moitheri Ntobo, Tsoanelo Koetle, Ralekoti Mokhahlane, Dlomo Monaphathi (46.Bushi Moletsane), Thapelo Tale. Trainer: Leslie Notsi.

Goals: 1-0 Sulleyman Ali Muntari (15), 2-0 Dominic Adiyiah (24), 3-0 Jordan Pierre Ayew (45), 4-0 Dominic Adiyiah (49), 5-0 Christian Atsu Twasam (86), 6-0 Jordan Pierre Ayew (89), 7-0 Jerry Akaminko (90+1).

Cautions: Jordan Pierre Ayew / Tsoanelo Koetle.

Sent off: Tsoanelo Koetle (90).

02.06.2012, Khartoum Stadium, Khartoum; Attendance: 18,000
Referee: Aboubacar Bangoura (Guinea)

SUDAN - ZAMBIA 2-0(0-0)*

SDN: Abdallah El Muez Mahjoub, Musa Zuma Al Tayeb, Ballah Gabir Kortokaila, Amin Sami Abdallah Dama, Saifeldin Ali Idris Farah Masawi, Nasr Eldin Omer El Shigail, Alaa Eldin Yousif Ahmed Hado (80.Hamouda Ahmed El Bashir), Mohannad Tahir Osman, Bader El Din Abdalla El Doud Galag (55.Haitham Mostafa Ahmed Karar), Bakri Abdel Kader Makeen Al Madina (69.Mohamed Abdel Marhoum), Mudather Eltaib Ibrahim El Tahir. Trainer: Mohammed Abdallah Ahmed.

ZAM: Kennedy Mweene, Hichani Himoonde, Oswald Kalaba, Davies Nkausu, Thomas Nyirenda (55.James Chamanga), Nathan Sinkala, Stophira Sunzu, Isaac Chansa (65.William Njovu), Chisamba Lungu, Christopher Katongo, Emmanuel Mayuka (82.Felix Katongo). Trainer: Hervé Renard (France).

Goals: 1-0 Mohannad Tahir Osman (50), 2-0 Saifeldin Ali Idris Farah Masawi (73).

Cautions: Ballah Gabir Kortokaila, Nasr Eldin Omer El Shigail / Thomas Nyirenda, Nathan Sinkala.

**Please note:* *FIFA awarded Zambia a 3–0 win as a result of Sudan fielding the ineligible player Saifeldin Ali Idris Farah Masawi.*

09.06.2012, New Ndola Stadium, Ndola; Attendance: 40,000
Referee: Med Said Kordi (Tunisia)
ZAMBIA - GHANA 1-0(1-0)
ZAM: Kennedy Mweene, Hichani Himoonde, Emmanuel Mbola, Nathan Sinkala, Stophira Sunzu, Isaac Chansa, Chisamba Lungu, Rainford Kalaba, Felix Katongo (81.Francis Kasonde), Christopher Katongo, Emmanuel Mayuka (63.Jonas Sakuwaha). Trainer: Hervé Renard (France).
GHA: Adambathia Larsen Kwarasey, John Boye, Isaac Vorsah, Samuel Diadie Inkoom, Harrison Afful, Emmanuel Agyemang-Badu, Derek Owusu Boateng (65.Anthony Gildas Kofi Annan), Kojo Asamoah (55.Christian Atsu Twasam), Sulleyman Ali Muntari (79.Richard Mpong), Dominic Adiyiah, Jordan Pierre Ayew. Trainer: James Kwesi Appiah.
Goal: 1-0 Christopher Katongo (15).
Cautions: Felix Katongo / Harrison Afful, Christian Atsu Twasam.

10.06.2012, Setsoto Stadium, Maseru; Attendance: 4,000
Referee: Rainhold Shikongo (Namibia)
LESOTHO - SUDAN 0-0
LES: Phasumane Kholuoe, Nkau Lerotholi, Thabiso Maile, Thubo Masualle, Bokang Mothoana, Mohapi Ntobo, Motlalepula Mofolo (43.Ralekoti Mokhahlane), Bushi Moletsane (80.Molibel Janefeke), Katleho Moleko, Lehlomela Ramabele, Thapelo Tale. Trainer: Leslie Notsi.
SDN: Abdallah El Muez Mahjoub, Musa Zuma Al Tayeb, Ballah Gabir Kortokaila (65.Hassan Elhag El Taher), Mowaia Osman Bashir Koko, Mohamed Abdel Marhoum (61.Bakri Abdel Kader Makeen Al Madina), Amin Sami Abdallah Dama, Nasr Eldin Omer El Shigail, Haitham Mostafa Ahmed Karar, Mohannad Tahir Osman, Ramadan Agab Shareif Ferein, Mudather Eltaib Ibrahim El Tahir. Trainer: Mohammed Abdallah Ahmed.
Cautions: Lehlomela Ramabele, Thapelo Tale / Abdallah El Muez Mahjoub, Ramadan Agab Shareif Ferein.

24.03.2013, Setsoto Stadium, Maseru; Attendance: 15,000
Referee: Malang Diedhiou (Senegal)
LESOTHO - ZAMBIA 1-1(0-0)
LES: Mohau Koenane, Moitheri Ntobo, Bokang Mothoana, Thabo Masualle, Tlale Maile, Litsepe Marabe, Motlalepula Mofolo, Ralekoti Mokhahlane, Libie Mojela Letsie (76.Lehlomela Ramabele), Katleho Moleko, Tshepo Christy Lekhoana. Trainer: Makhetha Leslie Notsi.
ZAM: Kennedy Mweene, Hichani Himoonde, Joseph Musonda, Stophira Sunzu, Davies Nkausu, Isaac Chansa, Rainford Kalaba (62.Jonas Sakuwaha), Fwayo Tembo (56.Joshua Titima), Nathan Sinkala, Christopher Katongo, Collins Ntofontofo Mbesuma (79.William Njovu). Trainer: Hervé Renard (France).
Goals: 0-1 Collins Ntofontofo Mbesuma (74), 1-1 Litsepe Marabe (88).
Cautions: William Njovu.
Sent off: Kennedy Mweene (53).

24.03.2013, Baba Yara Stadium, Kumasi; Attendance: 38,000
Referee: Anthony Ramsy Raphael (Malawi)

GHANA - SUDAN **4-0(2-0)**

GHA: Abdul Fatawu Dauda, Isaac Vorsah, Harrison Afful, John Boye, Richard Kissi Boateng, Sulleyman Ali Muntari (52.Solomon Asante Wiafe), Kwadwo Asamoah, Wakaso Mubarak, Mohammed Rabiu Alhassan (66.Emmanuel Yaw Frimpong), Asamoah Gyan (53.Emmanuel Agyemang-Badu), Majeed Abdul Waris. Trainer: James Kwesi Appiah.

SDN: Abdallah El Muez Mahjoub, Mowaia Osman Bashir Koko, Amir Kamal Suliman, Ahmed Abdallah Adam, Alaa Eldin Yousif Ahmed Hado (46.Ragei Abdelati Abdallah), Saifeldin Ali Idris Farah Masawi, Ballah Gabir Kortokaila, Nizar Hamid Nassir Koko, Mohamed Moussa Idris (59.Mohamed Abd Al Momen Ankba Al Faki), Mohannad Tahir Osman (80.Mohamed Abdallah), Ramadan Agab Shareif Ferein. Trainer: Mohammed Abdallah Ahmed.

Goals: 1-0 Asamoah Gyan (19), 2-0 Wakaso Mubarak (38), 3-0 Majeed Abdul Waris (80), 4-0 Emmanuel Agyemang-Badu (83).

Cautions: Majeed Abdul Waris / Alaa Eldin Yousif Ahmed Hado, Nizar Hamid Nassir Koko.

07.06.2013, Al Merrikh Stadium, Omdurman; Attendance: 3,211
Referee: Ousmane Fall (Senegal)

SUDAN - GHANA **1-3(1-1)**

SDN: Ehab Mohamed Abdelfatah Zoghbair, Amir Kamal Suliman (81.Hassan Elhag El Taher), Ahmed Abdallah Adam, Faris Abdallah, Malik Mohammed, Ali El Noor (75.Adam Sayer Adam), Salah Ibrahim, Saifeldin Ali Idris Farah Masawi, Amin Ibrahim Anklo El Mani (64.Nadir El Tayeb), Nizar Hamid Nassir Koko, Mudather Eltaib Ibrahim El Tahir. Trainer: Mohammed Abdallah Ahmed.

GHA: Abdul Fatawu Dauda, Harrison Afful, John Boye, Jonathan Mensah, Richard Kissi Boateng, Sulleyman Ali Muntari, Albert Danquah Adomah (79.Rashid Sumaila), Wakaso Mubarak (42.Samuel Diadie Inkoom), Mohammed Rabiu Alhassan, Asamoah Gyan, Richmond Yiadom Boakye (61.Emmanuel Agyemang-Badu). Trainer: James Kwesi Appiah.

Goals: 0-1 Asamoah Gyan (20), 1-1 Mudather Eltaib Ibrahim El Tahir (26 penalty), 1-2 Asamoah Gyan (57), 1-3 Sulleyman Ali Muntari (83).

Cautions: Nizar Hamid Nassir Koko, Mudather Eltaib Ibrahim El Tahir / Asamoah Gyan, Wakaso Mubarak, Abdul Fatawu Dauda.

Sent off: Richard Kissi Boateng (25).

08.06.2013, "Levy Mwanawasa" Stadium, Ndola; Attendance: 36,000
Referee: Ali Lemghaifry (Mauritania)

ZAMBIA - LESOTHO **4-0(1-0)**

ZAM: Kennedy Mweene, Hichani Himoonde, Davies Nkausu, Noah Sikombe Chivuta (55.Fwayo Tembo), Kondwani Mtonga, Nathan Sinkala, Mukuka Mulenga, Christopher Katongo, Collins Ntofontofo Mbesuma (85.Bornwell Mwape), Jacob Mulenga (79.James Chamanga), Chisamba Lungu. Trainer: Hervé Renard (France).

LES: Mohau Koenane, Moitheri Ntobo, Nkau Lerotholi, Thabo Masualle, Tlale Maile, Ngoako Mapheelle, Litsepe Marabe (79.Lehlomela Ramabele), Motlalepula Mofolo, Ralekoti Mokhahlane (62.Libie Mojela Letsie), Katleho Moleko (62.Thulo Ranchobe), Tshepo Christy Lekhoana. Trainer: Makhetha Leslie Notsi.

Goals: 1-0 Jacob Mulenga (36), 2-0 Christopher Katongo (61), 3-0 Jacob Mulenga (63), 4-0 Collins Ntofontofo Mbesuma (83).

Cautions: Ngoako Mapheelle.

15.06.2013, "Levy Mwanawasa" Stadium, Ndola; Attendance: 37,200
Referee: Eric Otogo-Castane (Gabon)
ZAMBIA - SUDAN 1-1(0-0)
ZAM: Kennedy Mweene, Hichani Himoonde, Davies Nkausu (80.Emmanuel Mayuka), Noah Sikombe Chivuta (46.Fwayo Tembo), Kondwani Mtonga, Nathan Sinkala, Mukuka Mulenga, Christopher Katongo, Collins Ntofontofo Mbesuma (52.James Chamanga), Jacob Mulenga, Chisamba Lungu. Trainer: Hervé Renard (France).
SDN: Ehab Mohamed Abdelfatah Zoghbair, Hassan Elhag El Taher, Amir Kamal Suliman, Ahmed Abdallah Adam, Faris Abdallah, Malik Mohammed, Salah Ibrahim (81.Adam Sayer Adam), Saifeldin Ali Idris Farah Masawi, Amin Ibrahim Anklo El Mani (42.Nadir El Tayeb), Mudather Eltaib Ibrahim El Tahir (90+1.Omer Mahmoud Al Shuhair), Mohammed Koko. Trainer: Mohammed Abdallah Ahmed.
Goals: 1-0 Jacob Mulenga (69), 1-1 Salah Ibrahim (70).
Cautions: Jacob Mulenga / Ahmed Abdallah Adam.

16.06.2013, Setsoto Stadium, Maseru; Attendance: 1,961
Referee: Thierry Nkurunziza (Burundi)
LESOTHO - GHANA 0-2(0-1)
LES: Mohau Koenane (68.Phasumane Kholuoe), Moitheri Ntobo, Nkau Lerotholi, Thabo Masualle, Tlale Maile, Litsepe Marabe, Motlalepula Mofolo, Ralekoti Mokhahlane, Bushi Moletsane (86.Tsepo Seturumane), Lehlomela Ramabele (70.Katleho Moleko), Tshepo Christy Lekhoana. Trainer: Makhetha Leslie Notsi.
GHA: Abdul Fatawu Dauda, Harrison Afful, John Boye, Jonathan Mensah, Samuel Diadie Inkoom, Sulleyman Ali Muntari (64.Emmanuel Agyemang-Badu), Kwadwo Asamoah, Mohammed Rabiu Alhassan (90+4.Rashid Sumaila), Asamoah Gyan, Richmond Yiadom Boakye (61.Dominic Adiyiah), Christian Atsu Twasam. Trainer: James Kwesi Appiah.
Goals: 0-1 John Boye (45), 0-2 Asamoah Gyan (82).
Cautions: Nkau Lerotholi, Ralekoti Mokhahlane.

06.09.2013, Baba Yara Stadium, Kumasi; Attendance: 40,000
Referee: Djamel Haimoudi (Algeria)
GHANA - ZAMBIA 2-1(1-0)
GHA: Abdul Fatawu Dauda, Harrison Afful, John Boye, Jonathan Mensah, Daniel Tawiah Opare, Kwadwo Asamoah, Wakaso Mubarak (55.Christian Atsu Twasam), Mohammed Rabiu Alhassan (55.Michael Kojo Essien), Asamoah Gyan (80.Emmanuel Agyemang-Badu), André Morgan Rami Ayew, Majeed Abdul Waris. Trainer: James Kwesi Appiah.
ZAM: Kennedy Mweene, Hichani Himoonde (46.Fwayo Tembo), Joseph Musonda (47.Emmanuel Mbola), Stophira Sunzu, Davies Nkausu (77.James Chamanga), Rainford Kalaba, Kondwani Mtonga, Nathan Sinkala, Christopher Katongo, Emmanuel Mayuka, Chisamba Lungu. Trainer: Patrice Beaumelle (France).
Goals: 1-0 Majeed Abdul Waris (17), 2-0 Kwadwo Asamoah (60), 2-1 Nathan Sinkala (71).
Cautions: Daniel Tawiah Opare, Harrison Afful / Kondwani Mtonga.

08.09.2013, Al-Hilal Stadium, Omdurman; Attendance: 5,000
Referee: Sylvester Kirwa (Kenya)

SUDAN - LESOTHO **1-3(1-1)**

SDN: Ehab Mohamed Abdelfatah Zoghbair, Hassan Elhag El Taher, Amir Kamal Suliman, Ahmed Abdallah Adam, Faris Abdallah, Malik Mohammed, Ragei Abdelati Abdallah (67.Adam Sayer Adam), Nizar Hamid Nassir Koko, Nadir El Tayeb, Mohannad Tahir Osman, Bakri Abdel Kader Makeen Al Madina (46.Mudather Eltaib Ibrahim El Tahir). Trainer: Mohammed Abdallah Ahmed.

LES: Phasumane Kholuoe, Moitheri Ntobo, Bokang Mothoana, Nkau Lerotholi, Thabo Masualle, Jeremia Kamele, Tsoanelo Koetle, Bushi Moletsane, Katleho Moleko (46.Mabuti Potloane), Tshepo Christy Lekhoana (86.Mohau Tale), Tsepo Seturumane. Trainer: Makhetha Leslie Notsi.

Goals: 1-0 Bakri Abdel Kader Makeen Al Madina (2), 1-1 Tsepo Seturumane (45), 1-2 Tshepo Christy Lekhoana (75), 1-3 Tsoanelo Koetle (77).

Cautions: Ahmed Abdallah Adam, Malik Mohammed / Bokang Mothoana, Bushi Moletsane.

Sent off: Ahmed Abdallah Adam (63).

GROUP E

02.06.2012	Ouagadougou	Burkina Faso - Congo	0-0; Awarded 0-3
03.06.2012	Niamey	Niger - Gabon	0-0; Awarded 3-0
09.06.2012	Pointe -Noire	Congo - Niger	1-0(0-0)
09.06.2012	Libreville	Gabon - Burkina Faso	1-0(0-0)
23.03.2013	Pointe-Noire	Congo - Gabon	1-0(0-0)
23.03.2013	Ouagadougou	Burkina Faso - Niger	4-0(2-0)
08.06.2013	Franceville	Gabon - Congo	0-0
09.06.2013	Niamey	Niger - Burkina Faso	0-1(0-0)
15.06.2013	Pointe-Noire	Congo - Burkina Faso	0-1(0-1)
15.06.2013	Franceville	Gabon - Niger	4-1(1-1)
07.09.2013	Ouagadougou	Burkina Faso - Gabon	1-0(0-0)
07.09.2013	Niamey	Niger - Congo	2-2(1-0)

Burkina Faso qualified for the Third Round.

FINAL STANDINGS

1.	Burkina Faso	6	4	0	2	7 - 4	12
2.	Congo	6	3	2	1	7 - 3	11
3.	Gabon	6	2	1	3	5 - 6	7
4.	Niger	6	1	1	4	6 - 12	4

02.06.2012, Stade du 4 Août, Ouagadougou; Attendance: 23,904
Referee: Bouchaib El Ahrach (Morocco)

BURKINA FASO - CONGO 0-0*

BFA: Abdoulaye Soulama, Ibrahim Gnanou, Paul Kéba Koulibaly, Hervé Xavier Zengué, Mady Saïdou Panandétiguiri, Charles Kaboré (90+3.Djakaridja Koné), Ali Rabo, Abdou Razack Traoré (61.Beninwende Yann Jonathan Pitroipa), Alain Sibiri Traoré, Beli Moumouni Dagano, Préjuce Nigiumbe Nakoulma (81.Wilfred Benjamin Balima). Trainer: Paul Put (Belgium).
CGO: Barel Morial Mouko, Bruce Abdoulaye (77.Ulrich Nzamba Mombo), Maël Lépicier Tsonga, Francis N'Ganga, Fabry Destin Makita-Passy, Delvin Chanel N'Dinga, Fabrice N'Guessi Ondama, Césaire Gandzé, Ladislas Douniama (89.Harris Brandt Tchilimbou), Dyzaiss Lys Mouithys (67.Dzon Delarge), Matt Devlin Moussilou Massamba. Trainer: Jean-Guy Wallemme (France).
Cautions: Ibrahim Gnanou / Delvin Chanel N'Dinga.
**Please note*: FIFA awarded Congo a 3–0 win as a result of Burkina Faso fielding the ineligible player Hervé Xavier Zengué.*

03.06.2012, Stade "Général Seyni Kountché", Niamey; Attendance: 20,000
Referee: Djamel Haimoudi (Algeria)

NIGER - GABON 0-0*

NIG: Kassaly Daouda, Ismaël Eragae Alassane, Mohamed Bachar (80.Kamilou Daouda), Koffi Dan Kowa, Mohamed Francisco Chikoto, Mohamed Soumaïla, Lancina Abdoul Karim Konaté, Ibrahim Adamou (62.Issoufou Boubacar Garba), Olivier Harouna Bonnes, William Tonji N'Gounou (60.Alhassane Dante Issoufou), Ouwo Moussa Maâzou. Trainer: Rolland Courbis (France).
GAB: Didier Janvier Ovono Ebang, Rémy Nemet Ebanega Ekwa, Bruno Ecuélé Manga, Charly Moussono, Edmond Mouélé, Lloyd Palun, Paul Ulrich Kessany Zategwa, Lévy Clément Madinda (87.Merlin Abdoulaye Tandjigora), Bruno Mbanangoyé Zita (89.Romaric Rogombé), Henry Arnaud Antchouet Rebienot (65.Stéphane N'Guéma), Daniel Michel Cousin. Trainer: Paulo Jorge Rebelo Duarte (Portugal).
Cautions: Issoufou Boubacar Garba, Mohamed Francisco Chikoto / Paul Ulrich Kessany Zategwa, Lloyd Palun.

Please note: The FIFA Disciplinary Committee has sanctioned the Gabon FA for fielding an ineligible player, Charly Moussono. The match was awarded 3-0 in favour of Niger.

09.06.2012, Stade Municipal, Pointe-Noire; Attendance: 10,500
Referee: Hudu Munyemana (Rwanda)
CONGO - NIGER **1-0(0-0)**
CGO: Barel Morial Mouko, Maël Lépicier Tsonga, Ugor N'Ganga, Fabry Destin Makita-Passy, Ulrich Nzamba Mombo, Delvin Chanel N'Dinga, Fabrice N'Guessi Ondama, Dyzaiss Lys Mouithys (63.Harris Brandt Tchilimbou), Matt Devlin Moussilou Massamba (52.Christopher Gaël Missilou), Ladislas Douniama, Dzon Delarge (63.Francis Chris Malonga Ntsayi). Trainer: Jean-Guy Wallemme (France).
NIG: Kassaly Daouda, Ismaël Eragae Alassane, Mohamed Bachar, Koffi Dan Kowa, Mohamed Francisco Chikoto, Ouwo Moussa Maâzou (83.Alhassane Dante Issoufou), Mohamed Soumaïla, Lancina Abdoul Karim Konaté, Olivier Harouna Bonnes (67.Kamilou Daouda), Issoufou Boubacar Garba, Issa Mossi Moussa (55.Tidjani Amadou Moutari Kalala). Trainer: Rolland Courbis (France).
Goal: 1-0 Francis Chris Malonga Ntsayi (89).
Cautions: Francis Chris Malonga Ntsayi / Lancina Abdoul Karim Konaté, Mohamed Francisco Chikoto.
Sent off: Mohamed Francisco Chikoto (43).

09.06.2012, Stade d'Angondjé, Libreville; Attendance: 23,000
Referee: Ousmane Fall (Senegal)
GABON - BURKINA FASO **1-0(0-0)**
GAB: Didier Janvier Ovono Ebang, Rémy Nemet Ebanega Ekwa, Bruno Ecuélé Manga, Georges Ambourouet, Edmond Mouélé, Lloyd Palun, Lévy Clément Madinda (81.Alexander N'Doumbou), Bruno Mbanangoyé Zita (65.Merlin Abdoulaye Tandjigora), Pierre-Emerick Aubameyang, Daniel Michel Cousin (70.Romaric Rogombé), Stéphane N'Guéma. Trainer: Paulo Jorge Rebelo Duarte (Portugal).
BFA: Abdoulaye Soulama, Ibrahim Gnanou, Paul Kéba Koulibaly, Mady Saïdou Panandétiguiri, Mohamed Koffi, Charles Kaboré, Ali Rabo, Beninwende Yann Jonathan Pitroipa (88.Abdou Razack Traoré), Issiaka Ouédraogo (69.Beli Moumouni Dagano), Alain Sibiri Traoré (79.Wilfred Benjamin Balima), Préjuce Nigiumbe Nakoulma. Trainer: Paul Put (Belgium).
Goal: 1-0 Rémy Nemet Ebanega Ekwa (56).
Cautions: Bruno Mbanangoyé Zita / Mohamed Koffi, Charles Kaboré.

23.03.2013, Stade Municipal, Pointe-Noire; Attendance: 13,000
Referee: Bakary Papa Gassama (Gambia)
CONGO - GABON **1-0(0-0)**
CGO: Barel Morial Mouko, Veijeany Christopher Samba, Francis N'Ganga, Maël Lépicier Tsonga, Oscar Ewolo, Francis Chris Malonga Ntsayi (74.Ladislas Douniama), Delvin Chanel N'dinga, Prince Oniangué (88.Matt Devlin Moussilou Massamba), David Percy Aymeri Louhoungou, Fabrice N'Guessi Ondama (85.Césaire Gandzé), Dyzaiss Lys Mouithys Mickalad. Trainer: Kamel Djabour (France).
GAB: Didier Janvier Ovono Ebang, Aaron Billy Ondele Appindangoyé, Bruno Ecuélé Manga, Yrondu Musavu-King (65.Merlin Abdoulaye Tandjigora), Edmond Mouélé, Lloyd Palun, Levy Clément Madinda, André Ivan Biyogho Poko (66.Daniel Michel Cousin), Guelor Kaku Kanga (58.Éric Mouloungui), Pierre-Emerick Aubameyang, Romaric Rogombé. Trainer: Paulo Jorge Rebelo Duarte (Portugal).
Goal: 1-0 Veijeany Christopher Samba (61).
Cautions: David Percy Aymeri Louhoungou, Ladislas Douniama / André Ivan Biyogho Poko, Éric Mouloungui, Aaron Billy Ondele Appindangoyé, Romaric Rogombé.

23.03.2013, Stade du 4 Août, Ouagadougou; Attendance: 35,000
Referee: Noumandiez Doué (Côte d'Ivoire)
BURKINA FASO - NIGER 4-0(2-0)
BFA: Daouda Diakité, Mady Saïdou Panandétiguiri (46.Narcisse Bambara), Bakary Koné, Paul Kéba Koulibaly, Charles Kaboré, Florent Rouamba, Mohamed Koffi, Aristide Bancé (88.Steeve Yago), Beninwende Yann Jonathan Pitroipa, Wilfried Sanou (71.Abdou Razack Traoré), Préjuce Niguimbe Nakoulma. Trainer: Paul Put (Belgium).
NIG: Kassaly Daouda, Kader Amadou Dodo (46.Issoufou Boubacar Garba), Koffi Dan Kowa, Issiaka Koudizé, Kourouma Fatoukouma, Lancina Abdoul Karim Konaté, Boubacar Djibo Talatou, Abdoulmoumouni Adamou (46.Mohamed Bachar), Ouwo Moussa Maâzou, Issa Mossi Moussa (85.Ousmane Ahmeye Zeidine), Abdoulnasser Nomaou. Trainer: Gernot Rohr (Germany).
Goals: 1-0 Beninwende Yann Jonathan Pitroipa (3), 2-0 Aristide Bancé (34), 3-0 Charles Kaboré (77), 4-0 Préjuce Niguimbe Nakoulma (86).
Cautions: Narcisse Bambara, Charles Kaboré / Abdoulnasser Nomaou, Issiaka Koudizé, Kourouma Fatoukouma, Koffi Dan Kowa.

08.06.2013, Stade de Franceville, Franceville; Attendance: 27,500
Referee: Gehad Grisha (Egypt)
GABON - CONGO 0-0
GAB: Didier Janvier Ovono Ebang, Bruno Ecuélé Manga, Edmond Mouélé, Aaron Billy Ondele Appindangoyé, Merlin Abdoulaye Tandjigora, Levy Clément Madinda, André Ivan Biyogho Poko, Guelor Kaku Kanga (46.Benjamin Zé Ondo), Éric Mouloungui (74.Fabrice Do Marcolino Anguilet), Pierre-Emerick Aubameyang, Didier Ibrahim Ndong (83.Romaric Rogombé). Trainer: Paulo Jorge Rebelo Duarte (Portugal).
CGO: Barel Morial Mouko, Francis N'Ganga, Fabry Destin Makita-Passy, Maël Lépicier Tsonga, Oscar Ewolo (67.Jusly Gitel Hermelin Boukama-Kaya), Francis Chris Malonga Ntsayi, Delvin Chanel N'dinga, Prince Oniangué, Fabrice N'Guessi Ondama (43.Férébory Doré), Harris Brandt Tchilimbou (70.Césaire Gandzé), Herman Prestone Lakolo. Trainer: Kamel Djabour (France).
Cautions: Didier Ibrahim Ndong / Oscar Ewolo.

09.06.2013, Stade "Général Seyni Kountché", Niamey; Attendance: 18,000
Referee: Tessema Bamlak (Ethiopia)
NIGER - BURKINA FASO 0-1(0-0)
NIG: Kassaly Daouda, Ismaël Eragae Alassane (78.Abdoulnasser Nomaou), Koffi Dan Kowa, Issiaka Koudizé, Mohamed Francisco Chikoto, Mohamed Bachar, Kourouma Fatoukouma, Ali Mohamed (69.Boubacar Djibo Talatou), Lancina Abdoul Karim Konaté, Yacouba Seydou Ali (84.Tidjani Amadou Moutari Kalala), Ouwo Moussa Maâzou. Trainer: Gernot Rohr (Germany).
BFA: Abdoulaye Traoré Soulama, Mady Saïdou Panandétiguiri, Bakary Koné, Paul Kéba Koulibaly, Wilfred Benjamin Balima (58.Issiaka Ouédraogo), Florent Rouamba, Mohamed Koffi, Ali Rabo, Aristide Bancé (72.Bertrand Isidore Traoré), Beninwende Yann Jonathan Pitroipa (88.Djakaridja Koné), Préjuce Niguimbe Nakoulma. Trainer: Paul Put (Belgium).
Goal: 0-1 Beninwende Yann Jonathan Pitroipa (80).
Cautions: Ouwo Moussa Maâzou / Paul Kéba Koulibaly, Beninwende Yann Jonathan Pitroipa, Préjuce Niguimbe Nakoulma, Bakary Koné.

15.06.2013, Stade Municipal, Pointe-Noire; Attendance: 13,497
Referee: Rainhold Shikongo (Namibia)
CONGO - BURKINA FASO **0-1(0-1)**
CGO: Barel Morial Mouko, Francis N'Ganga, Fabry Destin Makita-Passy, Maël Lépicier Tsonga, Oscar Ewolo (37.Césaire Gandzé), Francis Chris Malonga Ntsayi (88.Lorry Nkolo), Delvin Chanel N'dinga, Prince Oniangué, Fabrice N'Guessi Ondama, Férébory Doré, Herman Prestone Lakolo (73.Dzon Delarge). Trainer: Kamel Djabour (France).
BFA: Daouda Diakité, Mady Saïdou Panandétiguiri, Bakary Koné, Paul Kéba Koulibaly, Abdou Razack Traoré (62.Djakaridja Koné), Charles Kaboré, Florent Rouamba, Mohamed Koffi, Aristide Bancé, Préjuce Niguimbe Nakoulma, Issiaka Ouédraogo. Trainer: Paul Put (Belgium).
Goal: 0-1 Aristide Bancé (38).
Cautions: Férébory Doré / Florent Rouamba, Paul Kéba Koulibaly, Issiaka Ouédraogo.

15.06.2013, Stade de Franceville, Franceville; Attendance: 12,000
Referee: Samuel Chirindza (Mozambique)
GABON - NIGER **4-1(1-1)**
GAB: Didier Janvier Ovono Ebang, Aaron Billy Ondele Appindangoyé, Bruno Ecuélé Manga, Edmond Mouélé, André Ivan Biyogho Poko (89.Willy Fils Aubameyang), Benjamin Zé Ondo, Étienne Alain Djissikadié (66.Éric Mouloungui), Pierre-Emerick Aubameyang, Daniel Michel Cousin (90.Guelor Kaku Kanga), Didier Ibrahim Ndong, Romaric Rogombé. Trainer: Paulo Jorge Rebelo Duarte (Portugal).
NIG: Rabo Kabara Saminou Gado, Koffi Dan Kowa, Issiaka Koudizé, Mohamed Francisco Chikoto, Mohamed Bachar (35.Amadou Hassane), Kourouma Fatoukouma, Ali Mohamed, Lancina Abdoul Karim Konaté, Yacouba Seydou Ali, Ouwo Moussa Maâzou (83.Ganiyu El Tadj Tijani), Alhassane Dante Issoufou (69.Issa Mossi Moussa). Trainer: Gernot Rohr (Germany).
Goals: 0-1 Yacouba Seydou Ali (14), 1-1 Pierre-Emerick Aubameyang (42 penalty), 2-1 Pierre-Emerick Aubameyang (87 penalty), 3-1 Bruno Ecuélé Manga (90+6), 4-1 Pierre-Emerick Aubameyang (90+7 penalty).
Cautions: André Ivan Biyogho Poko, Daniel Michel Cousin / Alhassane Dante Issoufou, Kourouma Fatoukouma, Koffi Dan Kowa, Ouwo Moussa Maâzou.
Sent off: Koffi Dan Kowa (80), Éric Mouloungui (83), Kourouma Fatoukouma (86).

07.09.2013, Stade du 4 Août, Ouagadougou; Attendance: 30,000
Referee: Rajindraparsad Seechurn (Mauritius)
BURKINA FASO - GABON **1-0(0-0)**
BFA: Daouda Diakité, Bakary Koné, Steeve Yago, Jean-Noël Lingani (78.Mady Saïdou Panandétiguiri), Charles Kaboré, Mohamed Koffi, Djakaridja Koné, Beninwende Yann Jonathan Pitroipa, Jonathan Sundy Zongo (77.Florent Rouamba), Préjuce Niguimbe Nakoulma, Issiaka Ouédraogo. Trainer: Paul Put (Belgium).
GAB: Didier Janvier Ovono Ebang, Bruno Ecuélé Manga, Henri Junior Ndong Ngaleu, Edmond Mouélé, Merlin Abdoulaye Tandjigora (55.Levy Clément Madinda), Lloyd Palun (75.Bonaventure Sokambi), Benjamin Zé Ondo, Daniel Michel Cousin (64.Fabrice Do Marcolino Anguilet), Pierre-Emerick Aubameyang, Romaric Rogombé, Didier Ibrahim Ndong. Trainer: Paulo Jorge Rebelo Duarte (Portugal).
Goal: 1-0 Préjuce Niguimbe Nakoulma (53).
Cautions: Steeve Yago / Merlin Abdoulaye Tandjigora, Benjamin Zé Ondo.

07.09.2013, Stade Général Seyni Kountché, Niamey; Attendance: 20,000
Referee: Koman Coulibaly (Mali)

NIGER - CONGO **2-2(1-0)**

NIG: Kassaly Daouda, Jean Marcelin Koné, Issiaka Koudizé, Mohamed Francisco Chikoto, Shehu Musa, Ali Mohamed, Lancina Abdoul Karim Konaté, Souleymane Dela Sacko, Yacouba Seydou Ali (87.Issoufou Boubacar Garba), Mahamane Cissé (71.Saïdou Idrissa), Kamilou Daouda (90.Issa Mossi Moussa).Trainer: Gernot Rohr (Germany).

CGO: Barel Morial Mouko, Veijeany Christopher Samba, Igor N'Ganga, Francis N'Ganga, Fabry Destin Makita-Passy, Oscar Ewolo (46.Férébory Doré), Francis Chris Malonga Ntsayi (62.Fabrice N'Guessi Ondama), Delvin Chanel N'dinga, Prince Oniangué, Ulrich Kapolongo, Ladislas Douniama (46.Junior Makiese Mouzita). Trainer: Kamel Djabour (France).

Goals: 1-0 Mahamane Cissé (35), 1-1 Fabrice N'Guessi Ondama (66), 2-1 Kamilou Daouda (70), 2-2 Ulrich Kapolongo (76).

Cautions: Mohamed Francisco Chikoto, Issiaka Koudizé, Kamilou Daouda, Lancina Abdoul Karim Konaté, Shehu Musa.

GROUP F

02.06.2012	Nairobi	Kenya - Malawi	0-0
03.06.2012	Calabar	Nigeria - namibia	1-0(0-0)
09.06.2012	Blantyre	Malawi - Nigeria	1-1(0-0)
09.06.2012	Windhoek	Namibia - Kenya	1-0(0-0)
23.03.2013	Calabar	Nigeria - Kenya	1-1(0-1)
23.03.2013	Windhoek	Namibia - Malawi	0-1(0-0)
05.06.2013	Blantyre	Malawi - Namibia	0-0
05.06.2013	Nairobi	Kenya - Nigeria	0-1(0-0)
12.06.2013	Blantyre	Malawi - Kenya	2-2(0-0)
12.06.2013	Windhoek	Namibia - Nigeria	1-1(0-0)
07.09.2013	Calabar	Nigeria - Malawi	2-0(1-0)
08.09.2013	Nairobi	Kenya - Namibia	1-0(1-0)

Nigeria qualified for the Third Round.

FINAL STANDINGS

1.	Nigeria	6	3	3	0	7 - 3	12
2.	Malawi	6	1	4	1	4 - 5	7
3.	Kenya	6	1	3	2	4 - 5	6
4.	Namibia	6	1	2	3	2 - 4	5

02.06.2012, Moi International Sports Centre, Nairobi; Attendance: 14,000
Referee: Eric Otogo-Castane (Gabon)
KENYA - MALAWI 0-0
KEN: Boniface Oluoch, Jockins Atudo Otieno, Brian Mandela, James Wakhungu Situma, Bernard Wanyama Mangoli, Jamal Mohammed (52.Titus Brian Mulama), Clifton Miheso, Kevin Kimani, Humphrey Ochieng Mieno (79.Paul Were Ooko), Patrick Oboya Onyango (66.Kepha Aswani), Dennis Oguta Oliech. Trainer: Francis Kimanzi.
MWI: Simplex Nthala Nthara, Limbikani Mzava, Forster Namwera, James Sangala, Moses Chavula, Davi John Banda, Chimango Kayira, Joseph Kamwendo, Russel Mwafulirwa (90.Zicco Mkanda), Robin Ngalande (37.John Banda), Atusaye Nyondo (54.Frank Banda). Trainer: Kinnah Phiri.
Cautions: Joseph Kamwendo, Simplex Nthala Nthara.

03.06.2012, "U. J. Esuene" Stadium, Calabar; Attendance: 10,000
Referee: Khalid Abdel Rahman (Sudan)
NIGERIA - NAMIBIA 1-0(0-0)
NGA: Vincent Enyeama, Efetobore Ambrose Emuobo, Azubuike Egwuekwe, Juwon Oshaniwa, Godfrey Oboabona, Nwankwo Emeka Obiorah (69.Henry Uche), Reuben Shalu Gabriel, Christantus Ejike Uzoenyi, Victor Moses (76.Kalu Uche), Ikechukwu Uche, John Chukwudi Utaka (61.Ahmed Musa). Trainer: Stephen Okechukwu Keshi.
NAM: Virgil Vries, Da Costa Angula, Denzil Haoseb, Willem Mwedihanga, Eslin Kamuhanga (89.Benson Shilongo), Heinrich Isaacks, Larry Horaeb, Ronald Ketjijere, Willy Stephanus (75.Hendrik Somaeb), Petrus Shitembi (86.Sidney Urikhob), Tangeni Shipahu. Trainer: Bernard Kaanjuka.
Goal: 1-0 Ikechukwu Uche (80).
Cautions: Godfrey Oboabona, Efetobore Ambrose Emuobo / Larry Horaeb, Da Costa Angula.

09.06.2012, Kamuzu Stadium, Blantyre; Attendance: 25,000
Referee: Rajindraparsad Seechurn (Mauritius)

MALAWI - NIGERIA 1-1(0-0)

MWI: Simplex Nthala Nthara, Limbikani Mzava, Forster Namwera, James Sangala, Moses Chavula, Davi John Banda, Chimango Kayira (57.Robert Ng'ambi), Joseph Kamwendo, Russel Mwafulirwa, Robin Ngalande (78.John Banda), Atusaye Nyondo (57.Chiukepo Msowoya). Trainer: Kinnah Phiri.
NGA: Vincent Enyeama, Efetobore Ambrose Emuobo, Azubuike Egwuekwe, Juwon Oshaniwa, Godfrey Oboabona, Nwankwo Emeka Obiorah, Reuben Shalu Gabriel, Christantus Ejike Uzoenyi, Victor Moses (72.Kalu Uche), Ikechukwu Uche, John Chukwudi Utaka. Trainer: Stephen Okechukwu Keshi.
Goals: 0-1 Reuben Shalu Gabriel (89), 1-1 John Banda (90+3).
Cautions: Moses Chavula / Efetobore Ambrose Emuobo.

09.06.2012, "Sam Nujoma" Stadium, Windhoek; Attendance: 12,000
Referee: Joshua Bondo (Botswana)

NAMIBIA - KENYA 1-0(0-0)

NAM: Virgil Vries, Da Costa Angula, Denzil Haoseb, Willem Mwedihanga, Larry Horaeb, Heinrich Isaacks, Eslin Kamuhanga, Ronald Ketjijere, Henrico Botes, Lazarus Kaimbi (80.Petrus Shitembi), Tangeni Shipahu (71.Willy Stephanus). Trainer: Bernard Kaanjuka.
KEN: Arnold Otieno Origi, Jockins Atudo Otieno, Brian Mandela, Joseph Shikokoti, James Wakhungu Situma, Collins Okoth, Dennis Nzomo (83.Jamal Mohammed), Kevin Opondo Ochieng (82.Patrick Osiako), Patrick Oboya Onyango (70.Clifton Miheso), Victor Mugabe Wanyama, Dennis Oguta Oliech. Trainer: Francis Kimanzi.
Goal: 1-0 Henrico Botes (85).
Cautions: Henrico Botes, Willem Mwedihanga / Patrick Oboya Onyango, Dennis Oguta Oliech.

23.03.2013, "U. J. Esuene" Stadium, Calabar; Attendance: 7,475
Referee: Joshua Bondo (Botswana)

NIGERIA - KENYA 1-1(0-1)

NGA: Vincent Enyeama, Uwa Elderson Echiéjilé, Kenneth Josiah Omeruo, Godfrey Itama Oboabona, Solomon Sesugh Kwambe, John Michael Nchekwube Obinna, Victor Moses (39.John Ogu Ugochukwu), Ogenyi Eddy Onazi, Sunday Mba (75.Nnamdi Chidiebere Oduamadi), Obafemi Akinwunmi Martins (60.Ahmed Musa), Aide Brown Ideye. Trainer: Stephen Okechukwu Keshi.
KEN: Arnold Origi Otieno, Brian Mandela Onyango, James Mulinge Munandi Ndeto, David Ochieng, David Owino Odhiambo, Jamal Mohammed (51.Peter Opiyo Odhiambo), Victor Mugabe Wanyama, Johanna Omolo, David Gateri (88.Edwin Lavatsa Jumba), Francis Kahata Nyambura, Dennis Oguta Oliech (75.Christian Bwamy). Trainer: Adel Amrouche (Algeria).
Goals: 0-1 Francis Kahata Nyambura (35), 1-1 Nnamdi Chidiebere Oduamadi (90+4).
Cautions: Uwa Elderson Echiéjilé / Johanna Omolo, Dennis Oguta Oliech, Francis Kahata Nyambura, Arnold Origi Otieno.

23.03.2013, „Sam Nujoma" Stadium, Windhoek; Attendance: 5,000
Referee: Med Said Kordi (Tunisia)

NAMIBIA - MALAWI 0-1(0-0)

NAM: Virgil Vries, Da Costa Angula, Willem Mwedihanga, Larry Horaeb, Ronald Ketjijere, Jamuovandu Ngatjizeko, Manfred Starke (55.Petrus Shitembi), Henrico Botes, Rudolph Bester (62.Willy Stephanus), Lazarus Kaimbi, Tangeni Shipahu (85.Sidney Urikhob). Trainer: Bernard Kaanjuka.
MWI: Owen Chaima, Limbikani Mzava, Harry Nyirenda, James Sangala, Moses Chavula, Robert Ng'ambi, Douglas Chirambo (25.Ndaziona Chatsalira), Fisher Kondowe, Joseph Kamwendo, Zicco Mkanda (82.Chimango Kayira), Atusaye Nyondo (59.Gabadin Mhango). Trainer: Edington Ng'onamo.
Goal: 0-1 Gabadin Mhango (71).
Cautions: Ronald Ketjijere, Lazarus Kaimbi, Henrico Botes / Douglas Chirambo, Harry Nyirenda.

05.06.2013, Kamuzu Stadium, Blantyre; Attendance: 17,000
Referee: Koman Coulibaly (Mali)

MALAWI - NAMIBIA **0-0**

MWI: Charles Swini, Limbikani Mzava, Harry Nyirenda, Moses Chavula, Robert Ng'ambi, Bongani Kaipa, Douglas Chirambo (80.Davi John Banda), Fisher Kondowe (76.Gastin Simukonda), Joseph Kamwendo, Robin Ngalande, Atusaye Nyondo (30.Essau Boxer Kanyenda). Trainer: Edington Ng'onamo.

NAM: Virgil Vries, Da Costa Angula, Denzil Haoseb, Willem Mwedihanga, Larry Horaeb, Freedom Puriza, Manfred Starke (68.Pineas Jacob), Neville Tjiueza, Petrus Shitembi, Lazarus Kaimbi (78.Roger Katjiteo), Tangeni Shipahu (89.Deon Hotto Kavendji). Trainer: Roger Lennart Palmgren (Sweden).

Cautions: Fisher Kondowe / Neville Tjiueza, Da Costa Angula.

05.06.2013, Moi International Sports Centre, Nairobi; Attendance: 30,000
Referee: Noumandiez Doué (Côte d'Ivoire)

KENYA - NIGERIA **0-1(0-0)**

KEN: Duncan Ochieng, Brian Mandela Onyango, James Mulinge Munandi Ndeto, David Ochieng, David Owino Odhiambo (90+2.Andrew Murunga), Jamal Mohammed, Victor Mugabe Wanyama, Johanna Omolo, Francis Kahata Nyambura, Peter Opiyo Odhiambo (75.Patrick Osiako), Kepha Aswani (53.Stephen Waruru). Trainer: Adel Amrouche (Algeria).

NGA: Vincent Enyeama, Uwa Elderson Echiéjilé, Efetobore Ambrose Emuobo, Kenneth Josiah Omeruo, Godfrey Itama Oboabona, John Michael Nchekwube Obinna, Ogenyi Eddy Onazi, Sunday Mba (56.John Ogu Ugochukwu), Aide Brown Ideye (68.Anthony Ujah), Ahmed Musa, Nnamdi Chidiebere Oduamadi (87.Fegor Ogude). Trainer: Stephen Okechukwu Keshi.

Goal: 0-1 Ahmed Musa (80).

Cautions: Johanna Omolo, James Mulinge Munandi Ndeto, Duncan Ochieng, David Owino Odhiambo / Ogenyi Eddy Onazi.

12.06.2013, Kamuzu Stadium, Blantyre; Attendance: 13,000
Referee: Ali Mohamed Adelaïd (Comoros)

MALAWI - KENYA **2-2(0-0)**

MWI: Charles Swini, Limbikani Mzava, Harry Nyirenda, James Sangala, Moses Chavula, Davi John Banda (35.Chimango Kayira), Robert Ng'ambi, John Banda (35.Gabadin Mhango), Joseph Kamwendo, Essau Boxer Kanyenda (55.Chiukepo Msowoya), Robin Ngalande. Trainer: Edington Ng'onamo.

KEN: Duncan Ochieng, Brian Mandela Onyango, James Mulinge Munandi Ndeto, David Ochieng, David Owino Odhiambo, Jamal Mohammed, Patrick Osiako, Francis Kahata Nyambura (68.Patrick Kennedy Otieno), Edwin Lavatsa Jumba, Peter Opiyo Odhiambo (52.Jockins Atudo Otieno), Andrew Murunga (72.Paul Were Ooko). Trainer: Adel Amrouche (Algeria).

Goals: 1-0 Robin Ngalande (47), 1-1 Andrew Murunga (53), 2-1 Robert Ng'ambi (81), 2-2 Moses Chavula (88 own goal).

Cautions: Andrew Murunga, Brian Mandela Onyango, James Mulinge Munandi Ndeto.

12.06.2013, „Sam Nujoma" Stadium, Windhoek; Attendance: 9,000
Referee: Mensur Maeruf (Eritrea)

NAMIBIA - NIGERIA **1-1(0-0)**

NAM: Virgil Vries, Larry Horaeb, Willem Mwedihanga, Cris Katjiukua, Freedom Puriza, Denzil Haoseb, Neville Tjiueza, Pineas Jacob (78.Willy Stephanus), Petrus Shitembi, Lazarus Kaimbi (69.Deon Hotto Kavendji), Tangeni Shipahu (90+3.Sidney Urikhob). Trainer: Ricardo Mannetti.

NGA: Vincent Enyeama, Uwa Elderson Echiéjilé, Efetobore Ambrose Emuobo, Kenneth Josiah Omeruo, Godfrey Itama Oboabona, John Michael Nchekwube Obinna, Ogenyi Eddy Onazi (72.John Ogu Ugochukwu), Sunday Mba (89.Fegor Ogude), Anthony Ujah, Ahmed Musa, Nnamdi Chidiebere Oduamadi. Trainer: Stephen Okechukwu Keshi.

Goals: 1-0 Deon Hotto Kavendji (77), 1-1 Godfrey Itama Oboabona (82).

Cautions: Lazarus Kaimbi, Denzil Haoseb.

07.09.2013, "U. J. Esuene" Stadium, Calabar; Attendance: 8,000
Referee: Hamada Nampiandraza (Madagascar)

NIGERIA - MALAWI **2-0(1-0)**

NGA: Vincent Enyeama, Uwa Elderson Echiéjilé, Efetobore Ambrose Emuobo, Godfrey Itama Oboabona, Azubuike Emanuel Egwuekwe, John Michael Nchekwube Obinna, Victor Moses (71.Emmanuel Nosakhare Igiebor), Ogenyi Eddy Onazi, Emmanuel Chinenye Emenike (84.Foluwashola Ameobi), Ahmed Musa, Nnamdi Chidiebere Oduamadi (88.Uche Innocent Nwofor). Trainer: Stephen Okechukwu Keshi.

MWI: Simplex Nthala Nthara, Limbikani Mzava, Forster Namwera, James Sangala, Moses Chavula, Davi John Banda (61.Douglas Chirambo), Chimango Kayira, Joseph Kamwendo, Russel Mwaafulirwa, Robin Ngalande (74.John Banda), Atusaye Nyondo. Trainer: Tom Saintfiet (Belgium).

Goals: 1-0 Emmanuel Chinenye Emenike (45+1), 2-0 Victor Moses (50 penalty).

Cautions: Emmanuel Chinenye Emenike / Limbikani Mzava, Moses Chavula, James Sangala.

Sent off: Limbikani Mzava (53).

08.09.2013, Moi International Sports Centre, Nairobi; Attendance: 20,000
Referee: Gehad Grisha (Egypt)

KENYA - NAMIBIA **1-0(1-0)**

KEN: Duncan Ochieng, Jockins Atudo Otieno, Aboud Omar, Brian Mandela Onyango (62.Peter Opiyo Odhiambo), David Ochieng, David Owino Odhiambo, Jamal Mohammed, Victor Mugabe Wanyama, Francis Kahata Nyambura, Edwin Lavatsa Jumba (36.Allan Wanga Wetende), Dennis Oguta Oliech (87.Jesse Were). Trainer: Adel Amrouche (Algeria).

NAM: Ephraim Tjihonge, Larry Horaeb, Willem Mwedihanga, Cris Katjiukua, Freedom Puriza, Denzil Haoseb, Heinrich Isaacks (78.Deon Hotto Kavendji), Willy Stephanus, Petrus Shitembi (88.Riaan Cloete), Pineas Jacob, Jerome Louise (65.Roger Katjiteo). Trainer: Ricardo Mannetti.

Goal: 1-0 David Owino Odhiambo (6).

Cautions: David Ochieng, David Owino Odhiambo.

GROUP G

01.06.2012	Alexandria	Egypt - Mozambique	2-0(0-0)
03.06.2012	Harare	Zimbabwe - Guinea	0-1(0-1)
10.06.2012	Maputo	Mozambique - Zimbabwe	0-0
10.06.2012	Conakry	Guinea - Egypt	2-3(1-0)
24.03.2013	Maputo	Mozambique - Guinea	0-0
26.03.2013	Alexandria	Egypt - Zimbabwe	2-1(0-0)
09.06.2013	Harare	Zimbabwe - Egypt	2-4(1-2)
09.06.2013	Conakry	Guinea - Mozambique	6-1(3-1)
16.06.2013	Maputo	Mozambique - Egypt	0-1(0-1)
16.06.2013	Conakry	Guinea - Zimbabwe	1-0(1-0)
08.09.2013	Harare	Zimbabwe - Mozambique	1-1(1-0)
10.09.2013	El Gouna	Egypt - Guinea	4-2(1-1)

Egypt qualified for the Third Round.

FINAL STANDINGS

1.	Egypt	6	6	0	0	16	-	7	18
2.	Guinea	6	3	1	2	12	-	8	10
3.	Mozambique	6	0	3	3	2	-	10	3
4.	Zimbabwe	6	0	2	4	4	-	9	2

01.06.2012, Borg El Arab Stadium, Alexandria; Attendance: n/a
Referee: Sylvester Kirwa (Kenya)
EGYPT - MOZAMBIQUE 2-0(0-0)
EGY: Essam Kamal Tawfik El-Hadary, Ahmed Eissa Elmohamady Abdel-Fattah, Ahmed El Sayed Hegazy, Mahmoud Fathallah Abdo, Mohamed Abdel Marhoum Shafy, Hosny Abd Rabo Abd El Motaleb Ibrahim (79.Ashour El Teki), Mohamed El Nenny, Mohamed Salah Ghaly, Mohamed Aboutrika, Ahmed Temsah (65.Ibrahim Salah Abdel-Fattah), Mohamed Nagy Ismail Asl "Geddo" (46.Mohamed Abdullah Zidan). Trainer: Robert Bradley (United States).
MOZ: João Raphael Kapango, Zainadine Abdula Chavango Júnior, Edson André Sitoe „Mexer“, Francisco "Chico" Muchanga, Martinho Martins Mukana „Paíto“, Francisco Massinga „Whiskey“ (76.Carlos Bernardo Chimomole "Carlitos"), Simão Mate Junior, Stélio Ernesto „Telinho“, Eduardo Jumisse (69.António Alberto Diogo), Daniel Almiro Lobo "Miró", Jeremias Jorge Sitoe „Jerry“. Trainer: Gert Engels (Germany).
Goals: 1-0 Mahmoud Fathallah Abdo (56), 2-0 Mohamed Abdullah Zidan (63).
Cautions: Ibrahim Salah Abdel-Fattah / Zainadine Abdula Chavango Júnior.

03.06.2012, National Sports Stadium, Harare; Attendance: 30,000
Referee: Rajindraparsad Seechurn (Mauritius)
ZIMBABWE - GUINEA 0-1(0-1)
ZIM: Tapuwa Kapini, Esrom Nyandoro, Carlington Nyadombo, Tinashe Nengomasha, Vusumuzi Nyoni, Oscar Machapa, Takesure Chinyama (67.Terrence Mandaza), Khama Billiat (74.Denver Mukamba), Archford Uche Gutu (33.Willard Katsande), Knowledge Musona, Ovidy Obvious Karuru. Trainer: Norman Takanyariwa Mapeza.
GUI: Naby-Moussa Yattara, Oumar Kalabane, Kamil Zayatte, Ibrahima Diallo, Lanfia Camara, Thierno Lamine Bah, Habib-Jean Baldé, Naby Soumah (75.Alhassane Bangoura), Ibrahima Traoré, Abdoulaye Sadio Diallo, Abdoul Razzagui Camara (67.Idrissa Sylla). Trainer: Michel Dussuyer (France).
Goal: 0-1 Ibrahima Traoré (27).
Cautions: Vusumuzi Nyoni, Tinashe Nengomasha / Naby Soumah, Ibrahima Diallo.

10.06.2012, Estádio do Zimpeto, Maputo; Attendance: 26,000
Referee: Ali Kalyango (Uganda)
MOZAMBIQUE - ZIMBABWE 0-0
MOZ: Nelson Pinto, Edson André Sitoe „Mexer“ (46.Hélder Pelembe), Francisco "Chico" Muchanga, Zainadine Abdula Chavango Júnior, Martinho Martins Mukana „Paíto“, Daniel Almiro Lobo "Miró", Simão Mate Junior, Francisco Massinga „Whiskey“ (60.João Xavier Mazive), Stélio Ernesto „Telinho“, Elias Gaspar Pelembe „Dominguês“, Jeremias Jorge Sitoe „Jerry“ (78.Ruben Pamara). Trainer: Gert Engels (Germany).
ZIM: Tapuwa Kapini, Carlington Nyadombo, Onismor Bhasera, Vusumuzi Nyoni, Tinashe Nengomasha, Esrom Nyandoro, Oscar Machapa, Ovidy Obvious Karuru (53.Denver Mukamba), Willard Katsande, Takesure Chinyama (61.Terrence Mandaza), Knowledge Musona (87.Khama Billiat). Trainer: Norman Takanyariwa Mapeza.
Cautions: Elias Gaspar Pelembe „Dominguês“ / Oscar Machapa.

10.06.2012, Stade du 28 Septembre, Conakry; Attendance: 14,000
Referee: Néant Alioum (Cameroon)
GUINEA - EGYPT 2-3(1-0)
GUI: Naby-Moussa Yattara, Ibrahima Sory Conté (67.Abdul Aziz Keita), Habib-Jean Baldé, Oumar Kalabane, Ibrahima Diallo (62.Ibrahima Sory Bangoura), Mamoudou Mara, Mamadou Diouldé Bah, Ibrahima Traoré, Naby Soumah, Abdoul Razzagui Camara, Abdoulaye Sadio Diallo (77.Alhassane Bangoura). Trainer: Michel Dussuyer (France).
EGY: Essam Kamal Tawfik El-Hadary, Ali Fathi, Ahmed El Sayed Hegazy, Mahmoud Fathallah Abdo, Mohamed Abdel Marhoum Shafy, Mohamed Ali Abu El Yazid Shawky (40.Ahmed Temsah), Hosny Abd Rabo Abd El Motaleb Ibrahim, Mohamed El Nenny, Mohamed Salah Ghaly, Mohamed Aboutrika (86.Hossam El Sayed El Metwaly Ghaly), Mohamed Nagy Ismail Asl "Geddo" (59.Mohamed Abdullah Zidan). Trainer: Robert Bradley (United States).
Goals: 1-0 Abdoul Razzagui Camara (20 penalty), 1-1 Mohamed Aboutrika (58), 1-2 Mohamed Aboutrika (67), 2-2 Alhassane Bangoura (88), 2-3 Mohamed Salah Ghaly (90+5).
Cautions: Ibrahima Diallo, Ibrahima Traoré / Hosny Abd Rabo Abd El Motaleb Ibrahim.
Sent off: Naby-Moussa Yattara (64).

24.03.2013, Estádio do Zimpeto, Maputo; Attendance: 25,000
Referee: Mohamed Hussein El Fadil (Sudan)
MOZAMBIQUE - GUINEA 0-0
MOZ: Ricardo Jorge Francisco Maia de Campos, Daniel Almiro Lobo „Miró“, Edson André Sitoe „Mexer“, Zainadine Abdula Chavango Júnior, Gabriel Macuvele „Gabito“, Momed António Hagy, Eduardo Jumisse (81.Manuel Uetimane „Manuelito“), Stélio Marcelino Ernesto „Telinho“, Antonio Afonso Jongve (79.Mário Sebastião Sinamunda), Hélder Pelembe, Reginaldo Artur Faife (30.Clésio Bauque). Trainer: Gert Engels (Germany).
GUI: Abdul Aziz Keita, Kamil Zayatte, Ibrahima Diallo, Florentin Peilé Pogba, Lanfia Camara, Thierno Lamine Bah, Ismaël Traoré, Abdoul Razzagui Camara (90.Salim Cissé), Abdoulaye Sadio Diallo, Mohamed Lamine Yattara (60.Mathias Fassou Pogba), Alhassane Bangoura (61.Mohammed Diarra). Trainer: Michel Dussuyer (France).
Cautions: Thierno Lamine Bah, Florentin Peilé Pogba.

26.03.2013, Borg El Arab Stadium, Alexandria; Attendance: 10,000
Referee: Badara Diatta (Senegal)

EGYPT - ZIMBABWE **2-1(0-0)**

EGY: Abdel Wahed El-Sayed, Wael Mohamed Gomaa Kamel El Hooty, Ahmed Shadid Mahmoud Kenawi, Mohamed Nasser Nagieb El Ghareeb, Ahmed Eissa Elmohamady Abdel-Fattah (66.Ahmed Eid Abdel Malek), Mohamed Aboutrika, Mohamed Ibrahim (45+1.Ahmed Fathi Abdel Moneim Ahmed Ibrahim), Hosny Abd Rabo Abd El Motaleb Ibrahim, Mohamed Salah Ghaly, Mohamed Naser El Sayed El Nenny, Mohamed Nagy Ismail Afash „Geddo" (80.Ahmed Abdel Azim Fathy Gaafar). Trainer: Robert Bradley (United States).

ZIM: Washington Arubi, Augustine Mbara, Ocean Mushure, Lincoln Zvasiya, Patson Jaure, Archford Uche Gutu, Denver Nigel Mukamba, Silas Songani (59.Ovidy Obvious Karuru), Knowledge Musona, Khama Billiat (82.Tafadzwa Paul Rusike), Brian Abbas Amidu (58.Roderick Mutuma). Trainer: Klaus-Dieter Pangels (Germany).

Goals: 1-0 Hosny Abd Rabo Abd El Motaleb Ibrahim (64), 1-1 Knowledge Musona (74), 2-1 Mohamed Aboutrika (88 penalty).

Cautions: Patson Jaure, Washington Arubi, Augustine Mbara.

09.06.2013, National Sports Stadium, Harare; Attendance: 40,000
Referee: Bakary Papa Gassama (Gambia)

ZIMBABWE - EGYPT **2-4(1-2)**

ZIM: Washington Arubi, Ocean Mushure, Lincoln Zvasiya, Patson Jaure, Hardlife Zvirekwi, Devon Chafa, Felix Chindungwe (46.Khama Billiat), Archford Uche Gutu (60.Denver Nigel Mukamba), Tafadzwa Paul Rusike (69.Ovidy Obvious Karuru), Knowledge Musona, Cuthbert Malajila. Trainer: Klaus-Dieter Pangels (Germany).

EGY: Ahmed Sherif Ekramy, Ahmed Fathi Abdel Moneim Ahmed Ibrahim, Mahmoud Fathallah Abdo El Henawy, Wael Mohamed Gomaa Kamel El Hooty, Ahmed Shadid Mahmoud Kenawi (87.Ahmed Temsah), Ahmed El Sayed Hegazy, Hossam Mohamed Ashour Sanad Attia, Mohamed Aboutrika, Ahmed Eid Abdel Malek (62.Ahmed Eissa Elmohamady Abdel-Fattah), Mohamed Salah Ghaly, Mohamed Naser El Sayed El Nenny (67.Ibrahim Salah Abdel-Fattah). Trainer: Robert Bradley (United States).

Goals: 0-1 Mohamed Aboutrika (5), 1-1 Knowledge Musona (21), 1-2 Mohamed Salah Ghaly (40), 1-3 Mohamed Salah Ghaly (76), 2-3 Lincoln Zvasiya (81), 2-4 Mohamed Salah Ghaly (83).

Cautions: Hossam Mohamed Ashour Sanad Attia.

09.06.2013, Stade du 28 Septembre, Conakry; Attendance: 14,000
Referee: Kouamé N'Dri (Côte d'Ivoire)

GUINEA - MOZAMBIQUE **6-1(3-1)**

GUI: Abdul Aziz Keita, Oumar Kalabane, Kamil Zayatte, Florentin Peilé Pogba (66.Lanfia Camara), Issiaga Sylla, Thierno Lamine Bah, Ibrahima Traoré, Abdoulaye Sadio Diallo (71.Mohammed Diarra), Seydouba Guinéenne Soumah (85.Alhassane Bangoura), Ibrahima Sory Conté, Mohamed Lamine Yattara. Trainer: Michel Dussuyer (France).

MOZ: Ricardo Jorge Francisco Maia de Campos, Daniel Almiro Lobo „Miró", João Xavier Mazive, Milton Mhabombe „Mambucho", Francisco Mioche „Chico", Elias Gaspar Pelembe „Dominguês", Momed António Hagy (46.António Alberto Diogo), Eduardo Jumisse, Stélio Marcelino Ernesto „Telinho", Saddan Guambe „Kito" (90.Abelardo Gomes Socola „Belito"), Mário Sebastião Sinamunda (75.Hélder Pelembe). Trainer: Gert Engels (Germany).

Goals: 1-0 Mohamed Lamine Yattara (15), 2-0 Abdoulaye Sadio Diallo (33), 2-1 Elias Gaspar Pelembe „Dominguês" (44 penalty), 3-1 Abdoulaye Sadio Diallo (45 penalty), 4-1 Ismaël Traoré (76), 5-1 Mohammed Diarra (81), 6-1 Mohamed Lamine Yattara (90).

Cautions: Kamil Zayatte, Florentin Peilé Pogba / Momed António Hagy, João Xavier Mazive.

16.06.2013, Estádio da Machava, Maputo; Attendance: 25,000
Referee: Janny Sikazwe (Zambia)

MOZAMBIQUE - EGYPT **0-1(0-1)**

MOZ: Ricardo Jorge Francisco Maia de Campos, Daniel Almiro Lobo „Miró“, Dário Khan, João Xavier Mazive, Elias Gaspar Pelembe „Dominguês“, Eduardo Jumisse (82.Mário Sebastião Sinamunda), Stélio Marcelino Ernesto „Telinho“ (61.Manuel Uetimane „Manuelito“), Saddan Guambe „Kito“, Francisco Mioche „Chico“, Hélder Pelembe (52.António Alberto Diogo), Apson Sonito Manjate. Trainer: João Chissano.
EGY: Ahmed Sherif Ekramy, Ahmed Fathi Abdel Moneim Ahmed Ibrahim, Wael Mohamed Gomaa Kamel El Hooty, Ahmed Shadid Mahmoud Kenawi, Ahmed El Sayed Hegazy, Hossam Mohamed Ashour Sanad Attia, Mohamed Aboutrika (89.Abdalla Mahmoud Said Bekhit), Ahmed Eid Abdel Malek (67.Ahmed Temsah), Amr Al Sulaya, Mohamed Salah Ghaly, Ahmed Abdel Azim Fathy Gaafar (46.Ahmed Eissa Elmohamady Abdel-Fattah). Trainer: Robert Bradley (United States).
Goal: 0-1 Mohamed Salah Ghaly (40).
Cautions: Francisco Mioche „Chico“ / Wael Mohamed Gomaa Kamel El Hooty.

16.06.2013, Stade du 28 Septembre, Conakry; Attendance: 14,000
Referee: Hamada Nampiandraza (Madagascar)

GUINEA - ZIMBABWE **1-0(1-0)**

GUI: Abdul Aziz Keita, Oumar Kalabane, Kamil Zayatte, Lanfia Camara, Mohammed Diarra (46.Habib-Jean Baldé), Issiaga Sylla, Ibrahima Traoré, Abdoulaye Sadio Diallo (85.Guy Lucien Michel Landel), Seydouba Guinéenne Soumah (64.Alhassane Bangoura), Ibrahima Sory Conté, Mohamed Lamine Yattara. Trainer: Michel Dussuyer (France).
ZIM: Washington Arubi, Ocean Mushure, Lincoln Zvasiya, Devon Chafa, Felix Chindungwe, Archford Uche Gutu, Tafadzwa Paul Rusike, Masimba Mambare (60.Cuthbert Malajila), Denver Nigel Mukamba, Erick Chipeta, Roderick Mutuma (60.Silas Songani). Trainer: Klaus-Dieter Pangels (Germany).
Goal: 1-0 Mohamed Lamine Yattara (37).
Cautions: Habib-Jean Baldé / Devon Chafa.

08.09.2013, Rufaro Stadium, Harare; Attendance: 7,000
Referee: Mahamadou Keita (Mali)

ZIMBABWE - MOZAMBIQUE **1-1(1-0)**

ZIM: George Chigova, Peter Moyo (63.Hardlife Zvirekwi), Bruce Kangwa, Patson Jaure, Oscar Machapa, Willard Katsande, Masimba Mambare (63.Donald Ngoma), Kudakwashe Mahachi, Tawanda Muparati (81.Charles Sibanda), Erick Chipeta, Nelson Mazivisa. Trainer: Ian Kuziva Gorowa.
MOZ: Víctor Soares "Soarito", Daniel Almiro Lobo „Miró“, Dário Ivan Khan, João Xavier Mazive (58.Saddan Guambe „Kito“), Elias Gaspar Pelembe „Dominguês“, Josemar Tiago Machaisse, Stélio Marcelino Ernesto „Telinho“, Guilherme Lourenço Manhique "Alvarito", António Alberto Diogo (65.Ivan Esculuades „Maninho“), Francisco Mioche „Chico“, Apson Sonito Manjate (46.Mário Sebastião Sinamunda). Trainer: João Chissano.
Goals: 1-0 Masimba Mambare (42), 1-1 Ivan Esculuades „Maninho“ (69).

10.09.2013, El Gouna Stadium, El Gouna; Attendance: n/a
Referee: Tessema Bamlak (Ethiopia)
EGYPT - GUINEA 4-2(1-1)
EGY: Ahmed Sherif Ekramy, Ahmed Fathi Abdel Moneim Ahmed Ibrahim, Ahmed Shadid Mahmoud Kenawi, Adam Mohamed El-Abd, Mohamed Nasser Nagieb El Ghareeb, Hossam El Sayed El Metwaly Ghaly, Mahmoud Abdel Razek Fadlallah „Shikabala" (85.Ahmed Eissa Elmohamady Abdel-Fattah), Mohamed Aboutrika, Ahmed Eid Abdel Malek (46.Mahmoud Abdel-Moneim „Kahraba"), Amr Al Sulaya (78.Amr Hassan Zaki), Mohamed Salah Ghaly. Trainer: Robert Bradley (United States).
GUI: Naby-Moussa Yattara, Kamil Zayatte, Habib-Jean Baldé, Ibrahima Sory Bangoura (79.Mohamed Lamine Yattara), Mamoudou Mara, Issiaga Sylla, Mohamed Sacko, Kévin Constant, Seydouba Guinéenne Soumah, Ibrahima Sory Conté, Salim Cissé (72.Mohammed Diarra). Trainer: Michel Dussuyer (France).
Goals: 0-1 Adam Mohamad El-Abd (4 own goal), 1-1 Hossam El Sayed El Metwaly Ghaly (38), 2-1 Mohamed Aboutrika (51 penalty), 2-2 Seydouba Guinéenne Soumah (57), 3-2 Mohamed Salah Ghaly (83), 4-2 Amr Hassan Zaki (86).
Cautions: Seydouba Guinéenne Soumah.
Sent off: Kamil Zayatte (49).

GROUP H

02.06.2012	Blida	Algeria - Rwanda	4-0(2-0)
03.06.2012	Cotonou	Benin - Mali	1-0(1-0)
10.06.2012	Kigali	Rwanda - Benin	1-1(0-0)
10.06.2012	Ouagadougou(MLI)	Mali - Algeria	2-1(1-1)
24.03.2013	Kigali	Rwanda - Mali	1-2(1-0)
26.03.2013	Blida	Algeria - Benin	3-1(1-1)
09.06.2013	Porto-Novo	Benin - Algeria	1-3(1-2)
09.06.2013	Bamako	Mali - Rwanda	1-1(0-1)
16.06.2013	Kigali	Rwanda - Algeria	0-1(0-0)
16.06.2013	Bamako	Mali - Benin	2-2(1-2)
08.09.2013	Porto-Novo	Benin - Rwanda	2-0(1-0)
10.09.2013	Blida	Algeria - Mali	1-0(0-0)

Algeria qualified for the Third Round.

FINAL STANDINGS

1.	Algeria	6	5	0	1	13 - 4	15
2.	Mali	6	2	2	2	7 - 7	8
3.	Benin	6	2	2	2	8 - 9	8
4.	Rwanda	6	0	2	4	3 - 11	2

02.06.2012, Stade "Mustapha Tchaker", Blida; Attendance: 20,000
Referee: Bakary Papa Gassama (Gambia)

ALGERIA - RWANDA 4-0(2-0)

ALG: Adi Raïs Cobos Adrien M'Bolhi Ouhab, Ismaël Mickael Bouzid, Abderahmane Hachoud, Carl Medjani, Djamel Eddine Mesbah, Adlène Guedioura, Mehdi Gregory Giuseppe Lacen, Ryad Boudebouz (66.Khaled Lemmouchia), Sofiane Feghouli (78.Foued Kadir), Rafik Zoheir Djebbour (53.Islam Slimani), El Arbi Hillel Soudani. Trainer: Vahid Halilhodžić (Bosnia-Herzegovina).
RWA: Jean-Claude Ndoli, Mao Kalisa, Jonas Nahimana, Fabrice Twagizimana, Eric Gasana Mbuyu Twite, Jean-Baptiste Mugiraneza (46.Emery Bayisenge), Haruna Niyonzima, Tumaine Ntamuhanga, Jean-Claude Iranzi, Olivier Karekezi (65.Labama Kamana Bokota), Meddie Kagere (85.Frédéric Ndaka). Trainer: Milutin Sredojević (Serbia).
Goals: 1-0 Sofiane Feghouli (26), 2-0 El Arbi Hillel Soudani (31), 3-0 Islam Slimani (79), 4-0 El Arbi Hillel Soudani (82).
Cautions: Tumaine Ntamuhanga.

03.06.2012, Stade de l'Amitié, Cotonou; Attendance: 20,000
Referee: Janny Sikazwe (Zambia)

BENIN - MALI 1-0(1-0)

BEN: Fabien Farnolle, Abdoul Khaled Akiola Adénon, Arsène Menessou Gbougnon (85.Romuald Boco), Jordan Adéoti, Anicet Kayodé Adjamossi, Jean Louis Pascal Angan (74.Jocelyn Ahouéya), Djiman Koukou, Stéphane Sessegnon (87.Abou Gariga Maïga), Razak Omotoyossi, Mickaël Poté, Bello Issiaka Babatounde. Trainer: Manuel Amoros (France).
MLI: Soumbeïla Diakité, Abdoulaye Maïga (39.Mahamadou N'Diaye), Drissa Diakité, Ousmane Berthé, Adama Tamboura, Tongo Hamed Doumbia, Kalilou Traoré (78.Cheikh Fantamady Diarra), Seydou Keïta, Abdoulaye Traoré, Cheick Tidiane Diabaté, Modibo Maïga (86.Mamadou Samassa). Trainer: Alain Giresse (France).
Goal: 1-0 Razak Omotoyossi (18).
Cautions: Arsène Menessou Gbougnon, Jordan Adéoti / Adama Tamboura, Ousmane Berthé.

10.06.2012, Stade Amahoro, Kigali; Attendance: 15,000
Referee: Tessema Bamlak (Ethiopia)
RWANDA - BENIN **1-1(0-0)**
RWA: Jean-Claude Ndoli, Solomon Nirisarike, Fabrice Twagizimana, Eric Gasana Mbuyu Twite (79.Jean-Baptiste Mugiraneza), Steven Emmanuel Godfroid Kunduma, Haruna Niyonzima, Tumaine Ntamuhanga, Jean-Claude Iranzi, Olivier Karekezi (65.Labama Kamana Bokota), Meddie Kagere, Elias Uzamukunda (25.Daddy Birori). Trainer: Milutin Sredojević (Serbia).
BEN: Fabien Farnolle, Abdoul Khaled Akiola Adénon, Arsène Menessou Gbougnon, Jordan Adéoti, Anicet Kayodé Adjamossi, Jocelyn Ahouéya (81.Abou Gariga Maïga), Djiman Koukou, Stéphane Sessegnon, Romuald Boco (76.Nouhoum Kobénam), Razak Omotoyossi, Mickaël Poté. Trainer: Manuel Amoros (France).
Goals: 0-1 Razak Omotoyossi (74), 1-1 Labama Kamana Bokota (88).
Cautions: Fabien Farnolle, Anicet Kayodé Adjamossi
Sent off: Abdoul Khaled Akiola Adénon (85).

10.06.2012, Stade du 4-Août, Ouagadougou (Burkina Faso); Attendance: 5,847
Referee: Daniel Frazer Bennett (South Africa)
MALI - ALGERIA **2-1(1-1)**
MLI: Soumbeïla Diakité, Mahamadou N'Diaye, Drissa Diakité, Ousmane Berthé (64.Idrissa Coulibaly), Souleymane Keïta, Adama Tamboura, Samba Sow, Kalilou Traoré, Abdoulaye Traoré (68.Cheick Tidiane Diabaté), Modibo Maïga, Mamadou Samassa (80.Cheikh Fantamady Diarra). Trainer: Alain Giresse (France).
ALG: Adi Raïs Cobos Adrien M'Bolhi Ouhab, Madjid Bougherra, Ismaël Mickael Bouzid, Carl Medjani, Djamel Eddine Mesbah (80.El Arbi Hillel Soudani), Adlène Guedioura, Mehdi Gregory Giuseppe Lacen, Ryad Boudebouz (58.Hameur Bouazza), Sofiane Feghouli (88.Rafik Zoheir Djebbour), Foued Kadir, Islam Slimani. Trainer: Vahid Halilhodžić (Bosnia-Herzegovina).
Goals: 0-1 Islam Slimani (6), 1-1 Mahamadou N'Diaye (30), 2-1 Modibo Maïga (80).
Cautions: Drissa Diakité, Cheick Tidiane Diabaté / Ismaël Mickael Bouzid.

24.03.2013, Stade Amahoro, Kigali; Attendance: 10,000
Referee: Hamada Nampiandraza (Madagascar)
RWANDA - MALI **1-2(1-0)**
RWA: Jean-Claude Ndoli, Mao Kalisa, Solomon Nirisarike, Fabrice Twagizimana (71.Jessy Reindorf), Edwin Ouon, Daddy Birori, Eric Gasana Mbuyu Twite, Haruna Niyonzima, Jean-Claude Iranzi, Olivier Karekezi (52.Elias Uzamukunda), Meddie Kagere. Trainer: Milutin Sredojević (Serbia).
MLI: Soumbeïla Diakité, Adama Coulibaly, Adama Tamboura, Fousséni Diawara, Ousmane Coulibaly (70.Sigamary Diarra), Molla Wagué, Seydou Keïta, Mohamed Lamine Sissoko (80.Mana Dembélé), Abdoulaye Traoré, Samba Sow, Mamadou Samassa (85.Salif Coulibaly). Trainer: Patrice Carteron (France).
Goals: 1-0 Meddie Kagere (36), 1-1 Mamadou Samassa (49), 1-2 Abdoulaye Traoré (54).
Cautions: Meddie Kagere, Eric Gasana Mbuyu Twite.

26.03.2013, Stade "Mustapha Tchaker", Blida; Attendance: 32,000
Referee: Rajindraparsad Seechurn (Mauritius)

ALGERIA - BENIN **3-1(1-1)**

ALG: Adi Raïs Cobos Adrien M'Bolhi Ouhab, Essaïd Belkalem, Faouzi Ghoulam, Carl Medjani, Mehdi Mostefa Sbaa, Yacine Brahimi (71.Hamza Koudri), Sofiane Feghouli, Adlène Guedioura, Saphir Sliti Taïder, Rafik Zoheir Djebbour (76.Islam Slimani), El Arbi Hillel Soudani (90+1.Abdelmoumene Djabou). Trainer: Vahid Halilhodžić (Bosnia-Herzegovina).

BEN: Fabien Ceddy Farnolle, Arsène Menessou Gbougnon, Emmanuel Imorou, Jordan Adéoti, Salomon Junior, Mouritala Ogunbiyi, Djiman Koukou, Bello Issiaka Babatounde, Romuald Boco (87.Guillaume Bèmènou), Abou Gariga Maïga (70.Razak Omotoyossi), Rudy Gestede. Trainer: Manuel Amoros (France).

Goals: 1-0 Sofiane Feghouli (10), 1-1 Rudy Gestede (26), 2-1 Saphir Sliti Taïder (60), 3-1 Islam Slimani (90+2).

Cautions: Essaïd Belkalem, Islam Slimani / Salomon Junior, Rudy Gestede, Djiman Koukou, Romuald Boco.

Sent off: Fabien Ceddy Farnolle (85).

09.06.2013, Stade "Charles de Gaulle", Porto-Novo; Attendance: 8,000
Referee: Néant Alioum (Cameroon)

BENIN - ALGERIA **1-3(1-2)**

BEN: Guillaume Bèmènou, Jordan Adéoti, Lazadi Fousséni, Badarou Nana Nafiou, Anicet Kayodé Adjamossi, Stéphane Sessègnon, Djiman Koukou, Romuald Boco (72.Didier Sossa), Jean Louis Pascal Angan (84.Oscar Olou), Jodel Dossou (70.Razak Omotoyossi), Rudy Gestede. Trainer: Manuel Amoros (France).

ALG: Adi Raïs Cobos Adrien M'Bolhi Ouhab, Madjid Bougherra, Djamel Eddine Mesbah, Essaïd Belkalem, Carl Medjani, Mehdi Mostefa Sbaa, Sofiane Feghouli (86.Adlène Guedioura), Mehdi Gregory Giuseppe Lacen, Saphir Sliti Taïder, El Arbi Hillel Soudani (64.Faouzi Ghoulam), Islam Slimani (74.Nabil Ghilas). Trainer: Vahid Halilhodžić (Bosnia-Herzegovina).

Goals: 1-0 Rudy Gestede (31), 1-1 Islam Slimani (38), 1-2 Islam Slimani (42), 1-3 Nabil Ghilas (78).

Cautions: Jean Louis Pascal Angan, Badarou Nana Nafiou, Jodel Dossou.

Sent off: Badarou Nana Nafiou (67).

09.06.2013, Stade 26 mars, Bamako; Attendance: 30,000
Referee: Med Said Kordi (Tunisia)

MALI - RWANDA **1-1(0-1)**

MLI: Soumbeïla Diakité, Adama Coulibaly (60.Salif Coulibaly), Adama Tamboura, Fousséni Diawara, Mahamadou Bamba N'Diaye, Seydou Keïta, Abdoulaye Traoré, Sigamary Diarra, Tongo Hamed Doumbia (70.Boubacar Sylla), Samba Sow (70.Mana Dembélé), Mamadou Samassa. Trainer: Amadou Pathé Diallo.

RWA: Jean-Claude Ndoli, Michel Rusheshangoga, Faustin Usengimana, Solomon Nirisarike, Abouba Sibomana, Haruna Niyonzima, Andrew Buteera (85.Jean-Baptiste Mugiraneza), Fabrice Twagizimana, Jean-Claude Iranzi (64.Patrick Papy Sibomana), Meddie Kagere, Olivier Karekezi. Trainer: Eric Nshimiyimana.

Goals: 0-1 Meddie Kagere (33), 1-1 Mahamadou Bamba N'Diaye (78).

Cautions: Haruna Niyonzima, Jean-Claude Ndoli.

Sent off: Haruna Niyonzima (65).

16.06.2013, Stade Amahoro, Kigali; Attendance: 15,000
Referee: Yakhouba Keita (Guinea)
RWANDA - ALGERIA **0-1(0-0)**
RWA: Jean-Claude Ndoli, Michel Rusheshangoga, Faustin Usengimana, Solomon Nirisarike, Abouba Sibomana, Fabrice Twagizimana, Andrew Buteera (74.Michel Ndahinduka), Tumaine Ntamuhanga (54.Alfred Mugabo), Jean-Claude Iranzi (46.Patrick Papy Sibomana), Olivier Karekezi, Meddie Kagere. Trainer: Eric Nshimiyimana.
ALG: Adi Raïs Cobos Adrien M'Bolhi Ouhab, Madjid Bougherra, Djamel Eddine Mesbah, Essaïd Belkalem, Carl Medjani, Mehdi Mostefa Sbaa, Yacine Brahimi (70.Foued Kadir), Sofiane Feghouli (85.Mehdi Gregory Giuseppe Lacen), Adlène Guedioura, Saphir Sliti Taïder, Islam Slimani (81.Rafik Zoheir Djebbour). Trainer: Vahid Halilhodžić (Bosnia-Herzegovina).
Goal: 0-1 Saphir Sliti Taïder (51).
Cautions: Andrew Buteera, Patrick Papy Sibomana, Meddie Kagere, Jean-Claude Ndoli /), Sofiane Feghouli, Adlène Guedioura.

16.06.2013, Stade 26 mars, Bamako; Attendance: 30,000
Referee: Bouchaïb El Ahrach (Morocco)
MALI - BENIN **2-2(1-2)**
MLI: Mamadou Samassa, Adama Coulibaly, Adama Tamboura, Ousmane Coulibaly, Mahamadou Bamba N'Diaye, Seydou Keïta, Abdoulaye Traoré (26.Cheick Tidiane Diabaté), Tongo Hamed Doumbia (55.Cheikh Fantamady Diarra), Yacouba Sylla, Mamadou Samassa, Mana Dembélé (73.Sigamary Diarra). Trainer: Amadou Pathé Diallo.
BEN: Saturnin Allagbé, Emmanuel Imorou, Jordan Adéoti, Salomon Junior (90.Oscar Olou), Lazadi Fousséni, Stéphane Sessègnon, Séïdath Konabe Tchomogo, Djiman Koukou, Jodel Dossou (72.Jean Louis Pascal Angan), Razak Omotoyossi, Rudy Gestede (79.Mohamed Aoudou). Trainer: Oumar Tchomogo.
Goals: 0-1 Stéphane Sessègnon (7), 1-1 Mamadou Samassa (14 penalty), 1-2 Razak Omotoyossi (31), 2-2 Cheick Tidiane Diabaté (69).
Cautions: Mahamadou Bamba N'Diaye, Seydou Keïta / Lazadi Fousséni, Djiman Koukou, Salomon Junior, Saturnin Allagbé, Jordan Adéoti.

08.09.2013, Stade "Charles de Gaulle", Porto-Novo; Attendance: 16,872
Referee: Aboubacar Mario Bangoura (Guinea)
BENIN - RWANDA **2-0(1-0)**
BEN: Saturnin Allagbé, Réda Johnson, Lazadi Fousséni, Séidou Barazé, Anicet Kayodé Adjamossi, Séïdath Konabe Tchomogo, Mouritala Ogunbiyi, Bello Issiaka Babatounde, Mickaël Poté, Razak Omotoyossi (67.Jodel Dossou), Rudy Gestede. Trainer: Oumar Tchomogo.
RWA: Evariste Mutuyimana, Solomon Nirisarike, Abouba Sibomana, Faustin Usengimana, Hamdan Bayiranga, Jean-Baptiste Mugiraneza, Mohamed Mushimiyimana (85.Emmanuel Sebanani), Jamal Mwiseneza, Haruna Niyonzima, Meddie Kagere, Michel Ndahinduka. Trainer: Eric Nshimiyimana.
Goals: 1-0 Mickaël Poté (36), 2-0 Bello Issiaka Babatounde (53).
Cautions: Anicet Kayodé Adjamossi / Jean-Baptiste Mugiraneza, Faustin Usengimana.

10.09.2013, Stade "Mustapha Tchaker", Blida; Attendance: 23,500
Referee: Eric Otogo-Castane (Gabon)

ALGERIA - MALI **1-0(0-0)**

ALG: Adi Raïs Cobos Adrien M'Bolhi Ouhab, Madjid Bougherra, Djamel Eddine Mesbah, Carl Medjani, Hassan Yebda, Mehdi Mostefa Sbaa (64.Amir Karaoui), Abdelmoumene Djabou, Nacer Eddine Khoualed, Saphir Sliti Taïder (88.Hocine El Orfi), El Arbi Hillel Soudani (90.Ishak Belfodil), Nabil Ghilas. Trainer: Vahid Halilhodžić (Bosnia-Herzegovina).

MLI: Soumbeïla Diakité, Adama Tamboura, Idrissa Coulibaly, Mahamadou Bamba N'Diaye, Molla Wagué, Seydou Keïta, Abdoulaye Traoré (86.Mamadou Samassa), Tongo Hamed Doumbia (90+2.Alou Bagayoko), Sambou Yatabaré, Yacouba Sylla, Mana Dembélé (70.Cheibane Traoré). Trainer: Amadou Pathé Diallo.

Goal: 1-0 El Arbi Hillel Soudani (50).

Cautions: Madjid Bougherra, Hassan Yebda, Hocine El Orfi / Abdoulaye Traoré, Mahamadou Bamba N'Diaye.

GROUP I

02.06.2012	Yaoundé	Cameroon - Congo D.R.	1-0(0-0)
03.06.2012	Lomé	Togo - Libya	1-1(1-1)
10.06.2012	Kinshasa	Congo D.R. - Togo	2-0(1-0)
10.06.2012	Sfax (TUN)	Libya - Cameroon	2-1(1-1)
23.03.2013	Yaoundé	Cameroon - Togo	2-1(1-1)
24.03.2013	Kinshasa	Congo D.R. - Libya	0-0
07.06.2013	Tripoli	Libya - Congo D.R.	0-0
09.06.2013	Lomé	Togo - Cameroon	2-0(1-0): Awarded 0-3
14.06.2013	Tripoli	Libya - Togo	2-0(2-0)
16.06.2013	Kinshasa	Congo D.R. - Cameroon	0-0
08.09.2013	Yaoundé	Cameroon - Libya	1-0(1-0)
08.09.2013	Lomé	Togo - Congo D.R.	2-1(1-0)

Cameroon qualified for the Third Round.

FINAL STANDINGS

1.	Cameroon	6	4	1	1	8 - 3	13
2.	Libya	6	2	3	1	5 - 3	9
3.	Congo D.R.	6	1	3	2	3 - 3	6
4.	Togo	6	1	1	4	4 - 11	4

02.06.2012, Stade "Ahmadou Ahidjo", Yaoundé; Attendance: 10,000
Referee: Daniel Frazer Bennett (South Africa)

CAMEROON - CONGO D.R. 1-0(0-0)

CMR: Idriss Carlos Kameni, Dany Achille Nounkeu Tchounkeu, Henri Bedimo Nsamé, Aurélien Bayard Chedjou Fongang, Stéphane Mbia Etoundi, Georges Constant Mandjeck, Alexandre Dimitri Song Billong, Joël Landry Tsafack N'Guémo (80.Andongcho Mbuta), Jean-Eric Maxim Choupo-Moting, Leony Léonard Kweuke (61.Edgar Constant Nicaise Salli), Benjamin Moukandjo Bilé. Trainer: Denis Lavagne (France).

COD: Robert Muteba Kidiaba, Joël Kimwaki, Cédric Mongongu (70.Patrick Mampuya), Issama Mpeko, Bobo Ungenda Muselenge (16.Albert Milambo-Mutamba), Jean Kasusula Kiritsho, Landry Mulemo, Zola Matumona, Christian Fuanda Luzolo Kinkela (80.Déo Kanda A Mukok), Alain Dioko Kaluyituka, Trésor Mputu Mabi. Trainer: Claude Marie François Le Roy (France).

Goal: 1-0 Jean-Eric Maxim Choupo-Moting (54 penalty).

Cautions: Stéphane Mbia Etoundi, Alexandre Dimitri Song Billong / Bobo Ungenda Muselenge, Zola Matumona, Albert Milambo-Mutamba.

03.06.2012, Stade de Kegue, Lomé; Attendance: 15,000
Referee: Koman Coulibaly (Mali)

TOGO - LIBYA 1-1(1-1)

TOG: Baba Tchagouni, Niasidji Donou Kokou, Daré Nibombé, Serge Ognadon Akakpo, Abdoul-Gafar Mamah, Jacques Alaixys Romao, Kossi Prince Segbefia (56.Komlan Améwou), Sapol Mani (72.Moustapha Salifou), Abdoul-Razak Boukari, Serge Gakpé, Kalen Damessi (79.Lalawélé Atakora). Trainer: Didier Six (France).

LBY: Muhammad Nashnoush, Younes Hussain Al Shibani, Walid Jalal Al Sebai, Ali Salama, Rabea Aboubaker Al Laafi (83.Abdulaziz Belraysh), Muhammad Al Maghrabi, Abubakr Rajeb Al Abaidy (62.Marwan Mansour Mabrouk), Djamal Abdoulaye Mahamat Bindi, Ihaab Boussefi, Ahmed Saad Soleiman Osman, Ahmed Mahmoud Zuway (76.Abdullah Khalifa Grigma). Trainer: Abdulhafeedh Arbeesh.

Goals: 1-0 Kalen Damessi (8), 1-1 Ahmed Mahmoud Zuway (16).

Cautions: Niasidji Donou Kokou, Jacques Alaixys Romao / Rabea Aboubaker Al Laafi, Muhammad Nashnoush, Ahmed Saad Soleiman Osman, Walid Jalal Al Sebai.

10.06.2012, Stade des Martyrs, Kinshasa; Attendance: 50,000
Referee: Mohamed Farouk Abdel Meguid (Egypt)
CONGO D.R. - TOGO **2-0(1-0)**
COD: Robert Muteba Kidiaba, Joël Kimwaki, Cédric Mongongu, Issama Mpeko, Jean Kasusula Kiritsho, Albert Milambo-Mutamba, Zola Matumona (46.Landry Mulemo), Diego Kazadi Mutombo, Alain Dioko Kaluyituka, Dieumerci Mbokani Bezua (88.Yves Diba Ilunga), Trésor Mputu Mabi. Trainer: Claude Marie François Le Roy (France).
TOG: Baba Tchagouni, Vincent Bossou, Niasidji Donou Kokou, Serge Ognadon Akakpo, Abdoul-Gafar Mamah, Jacques Alaixys Romao, Kossi Prince Segbefia (77.Lalawélé Atakora), Komlan Améwou, Moustapha Salifou, Sename Dové Womé Dobe (53.Serge Gakpé), Abdoul-Razak Boukari (68.Kalen Damessi). Trainer: Didier Six (France).
Goals: 1-0 Trésor Mputu Mabi (23), 2-0 Dieumerci Mbokani Bezua (81 penalty).
Cautions: Alain Dioko Kaluyituka / Abdoul-Gafar Mamah.
Sent off: Albert Milambo-Mutamba (39).

10.06.2012, Stade "Taïeb Mhiri", Sfax (Tunisia); Attendance: 1,000
Referee: Mensur Maeruf (Eritrea)
LIBYA - CAMEROON **2-1(1-1)**
LBY: Muhammad Nashnoush, Younes Hussain Al Shibani, Walid Jalal Al Sebai, Ali Salama, Abdulaziz Belraysh (62.Mohammad Ali Jum'aa Esnaani), Muhammad Al Maghrabi, Marwan Mansour Mabrouk, Djamal Abdoulaye Mahamat Bindi, Ihaab Boussefi (78.Abdullah Khalifa Grigma; 85.Hamed Snousi Haneesh), Ahmed Saad Soleiman Osman, Ahmed Mahmoud Zuway. Trainer: Abdulhafeedh Arbeesh.
CMR: Idriss Carlos Kameni, Henri Bedimo Nsamé, Aurélien Bayard Chedjou Fongang, Stéphane Mbia Etoundi, Georges Constant Mandjeck, Nicolas Alexis Julio N'Koulou N'Doubena, Alexandre Dimitri Song Billong, Joël Landry Tsafack N'Guémo, Vincent Aboubakar (67.Edgar Constant Nicaise Salli), Jean-Eric Maxim Choupo-Moting, Benjamin Moukandjo Bilé (89.Hervé Yannick N'Djeng). Trainer: Denis Lavagne (France).
Goals: 1-0 Ahmed Mahmoud Zuway (6), 1-1 Jean-Eric Maxim Choupo-Moting (15), 2-1 Hamed Snousi Haneesh (90+3).
Cautions: Ahmed Saad Soleiman Osman, Abdulaziz Belraysh, Hamed Snousi Haneesh / Joël Landry Tsafack N'Guémo.

23.03.2013, Stade Omnisports „Ahmadou-Ahidjo" Yaoundé; Attendance: 30,000
Referee: Djamel Haimoudi (Algeria)
CAMEROON - TOGO **2-1(1-1)**
CMR: Charles-Hubert Itandje, Benoît Pierre David Assou-Ekotto, Benoît Christian Angbwa Ossoemeyang, Nicolas Alexis Julio N'Koulou N'Doubena, Joël Job Matip, Jean-Armel Kana-Biyik, Jean II Makoun, Achille Emaná Edzimbi (56.Stéphane Mbia Etoundi), Samuel Eto'o Fils (85.Alexandre Dimitri Song Billong), Leony Léonard Kweuke, Benjamin Moukandjo Bilé (68.Fabrice Olinga Essono). Trainer: Jean-Paul Akono.
TOG: Baba Tchagouni, Serge Ognadon Akakpo, Abdoul-Gafar Mamah, Vincent Bossou, Sadat Ouro-Akoriko, Dakonam Ortega Djené, Komlan Améwou, Jacques Alaixys Cigánek „Alaixys Romao", Sename Dové Womé Dobe, Serge Gakpé, Euloge Placca Fessou (67.Lalawélé Atakora). Trainer: Didier Six (France).
Goals: 1-0 Samuel Eto'o Fils (41 penalty), 1-1 Sename Dové Womé Dobe (45+1), 2-1 Samuel Eto'o Fils (82).
Cautions: Samuel Eto'o Fils, Fabrice Olinga Essono, Benoît Pierre David Assou-Ekotto / Jacques Alaixys Cigánek „Alaixys Romao".

24.03.2013, Stade des Martyrs, Kinshasa; Attendance: 53,500
Referee: William Agbovi (Ghana)
CONGO D.R. - LIBYA 0-0
COD: Robert Muteba Kidiaba, Gabriel Abdala Zakuani, Cédric Mongongu, Jean Kasusula Kilitsho, Issama Mpeko, Youssouf Mulumbu, Toko Nzuzi Bundebele (46.Distel Zola), Yannick Bolasie (83.Héritier Luvumbu Nzinga), Dieumerci Mbokani Bezua, Trésor Mputu Mabi, Yves Diba Ilunga (69.Alain Dioko Kaluyituka). Trainer: Claude Marie François Le Roy (France).
LBY: Muhammad Nashnoush, Muhammad Al Maghrabi, Mohamed Munir Abdussalam, Ahmed Al Alwany, Abdelrahman Fetori (68.Ahmed Benali), Ahmed Mohamed Al Sagheer, Salem Ablo (90+4.Motasem Sabbou), Abubakr Rajeb Al Abaidy, Ahmed Al Trbi, Faisal Saleh Al Badri, Ahmed Mahmoud Zuway (79.Mohammad Al Ghanodi). Trainer: Abdulhafeedh Arbeesh.
Cautions: Faisal Saleh Al Badri.

07.06.2013, Stade 11 Juin, Tripoli; Attendance: 35,000
Referee: Joshua Bondo (Botswana)
LIBYA - CONGO D.R. 0-0
LBY: Muhammad Nashnoush, Walid Jalal Al Sebai, Younes Hussain Al Shibani, Muhammad Al Maghrabi, Abubakr Rajeb Al Abaidy, Ahmed Al Trbi, Salem Ablo (74.Mohamed Elgadi), Mohammad Al Ghanodi (82.Mohamed Munir Abdussalam), Faisal Saleh Al Badri, Ahmed Saad Soleiman Osman, Éamon Zayed (63.Abdulsalam Omar). Trainer: Abdulhafeedh Arbeesh.
COD: Robert Muteba Kidiaba, Gabriel Abdala Zakuani, Cédric Mongongu (78.Chancel Mbemba Mangulu), Jean Kasusula Kilitsho, Patou Simbi Ebunga, Issama Mpeko, Youssouf Mulumbu, Distel Zola, Yannick Bolasie (58.Landry Mulemo), Trésor Mputu Mabi, Firmin Ndombe Mubele (88.Hervé Mianga Ndonga). Trainer: Claude Marie François Le Roy (France).
Cautions: Abdulsalam Omar.

09.06.2013, Stade de Kégué, Lomé; Attendance: 20,000
Referee: Rajindraparsad Seechurn (Mauritius)
TOGO - CAMEROON 2-0(1-0)*
TOG: Baba Tchagouni, Serge Ognadon Akakpo, Abdoul-Gafar Mamah, Vincent Bossou, Dakonam Ortega Djené, Moustapha Salifou (84.Sadat Ouro-Akoriko), Komlan Améwou, Jacques Alaixys Cigánek „Alaixys Romao", Sename Dové Womé Dobe, Serge Gakpé (67.Lalawélé Atakora), Jonathan Ayité (57.Backer Aloenouvo). Trainer: Didier Six (France).
CMR: Charles-Hubert Itandje, Aurélien Bayard Chedjou Fongang, Nicolas Alexis Julio N'Koulou N'Doubena, Henri Bédimo Nsamé, Dany Achille Nounkeu Tchounkeu, Joël Job Matip (46.Leony Léonard Kweuke), Jean II Makoun (66.Stéphane Mbia Etoundi), Alexandre Dimitri Song Billong, Eyong Tarkang Enoh, Hervé Yannick N'Djeng (46.Jacques Zoua Daogari), Vincent Aboubakar. Trainer: Volker Finke (Germany).
Goals: 1-0 Komlan Améwou (31), 2-0 Lalawélé Atakora (71).
Cautions: Vincent Bossou / Henri Bédimo Nsamé, Nicolas Alexis Julio N'Koulou N'Doubena.
**Please note: the match was awarded by FIFA 3-0 for Cameroon because Togo fielded an ineligible player (Alaixys Romao).*

14.06.2013, June 11 Stadium, Tripoli; Attendance: 40,000
Referee: Mohamed Benouza (Algeria)

LIBYA - TOGO 2-0(2-0)

LBY: Muhammad Nashnoush, Younes Hussain Al Shibani, Muhammad Al Maghrabi, Ali Salama, Mohamed Munir Abdussalam, Abubakr Rajeb Al Abaidy, Ahmed Al Trbi, Ahmed Mahmoud Zuway (58.Abdulsalam Omar), Faisal Saleh Al Badri, Salem Ablo (77.Abdelrahman Fetori), Ahmed Saad Soleiman Osman (86.Suhaib Sulaiman Shafshuf). Trainer: Abdulhafeedh Arbeesh.

TOG: Baba Tchagouni, Serge Ognadon Akakpo, Abdoul-Gafar Mamah, Vincent Bossou, Sadat Ouro-Akoriko, Dakonam Ortega Djené, Komlan Améwou, Sapol Mani (53.Lalawélé Atakora), Sename Dové Womé Dobe, Serge Gakpé (60.Backer Aloenouvo), Francis Koné (75.Moustapha Salifou). Trainer: Didier Six (France).

Goals: 1-0 Faisal Saleh Al Badri (7 penalty), 2-0 Komlan Amèwou (17 own goal).
Cautions: Ahmed Saad Soleiman Osman.

16.06.2013, Stade des Martyrs, Kinshasa; Attendance: 80,000
Referee: Badara Diatta (Senegal)

CONGO D.R. - CAMEROON 0-0

COD: Robert Muteba Kidiaba, Gabriel Abdala Zakuani (88.Eric Bokanga Musau), Cédric Mongongu, Jean Kasusula Kilitsho, Patou Simbi Ebunga (46.Firmin Ndombe Mubele), Issama Mpeko, Youssouf Mulumbu, Distel Zola, Dieumerci Mbokani Bezua, Trésor Mputu Mabi, Yves Diba Ilunga (46.Yannick Bolasie). Trainer: Claude Marie François Le Roy (France).

CMR: Charles-Hubert Itandje, Aurélien Bayard Chedjou Fongang, Nicolas Alexis Julio N'Koulou N'Doubena, Henri Bédimo Nsamé, Dany Achille Nounkeu Tchounkeu (46.Stéphane Mbia Etoundi), Joël Job Matip, Alexandre Dimitri Song Billong, Eyong Tarkang Enoh, Leony Léonard Kweuke, Benjamin Moukandjo Bilé (85.Jean II Makoun), Vincent Aboubakar (42.Hervé Yannick N'Djeng). Trainer: Volker Finke (Germany).

Cautions: Trésor Mputu Mabi / Henri Bédimo Nsamé.

08.09.2013, Stade Omnisports „Ahmadou-Ahidjo" Yaoundé; Attendance: 35,000
Referee: Noumandiez Doué (Côte d'Ivoire)

CAMEROON - LIBYA 1-0(1-0)

CMR: Charles-Hubert Itandje, Aurélien Bayard Chedjou Fongang, Gaëtan Bong Songo, Nicolas Alexis Julio N'Koulou N'Doubena, Dany Achille Nounkeu Tchounkeu, Joël Job Matip, Jean II Makoun (2.Stéphane Mbia Etoundi), Alexandre Dimitri Song Billong (87.Joël Landry Tsafack N'Guémo), Eyong Tarkang Enoh, Samuel Eto'o Fils (60.Jacques Zoua Daogari), Jean-Eric Maxim Choupo-Moting. Trainer: Volker Finke (Germany).

LBY: Muhammad Nashnoush, Younes Hussain Al Shibani, Muhammad Al Maghrabi, Ali Salama, Osama Abdusalam, Marwaan Mansour Mabrouk, Abubakr Rajeb Al Abaidy (60.Abdulsalam Omar), Ahmed Al Trbi, Éamon Zayed (73.Mohammad Al Ghanodi), Ahmed Saad Soleiman Osman, Faisal Saleh Al Badri (46.Gamal Mohamed). Trainer: Abdulhafeedh Arbeesh.

Goal: 1-0 Aurélien Bayard Chedjou Fongang (41).
Cautions: Eyong Tarkang Enoh / Ali Salama, Abubakr Rajeb Al Abaidy, Ahmed Saad Soleiman Osman.

08.09.2013, Stade de Kégué, Lomé; Attendance: 16,000
Referee: Bouchaïb El Ahrach (Morocco)

TOGO - CONGO D.R. **2-1(1-0)**

TOG: Baba Tchagouni, Serge Ognadon Akakpo, Abdoul-Gafar Mamah, Vincent Bossou, Sadat Ouro-Akoriko, Dakonam Ortega Djené, Komlan Améwou, Lalawélé Atakora, Sename Dové Womé Dobe, Serge Gakpé (66.Abdel-Farid Zato-Arouna), Francis Koné (78.Backer Aloenouvo). Trainer: Didier Six (France).

COD: Parfait Mandanda, Cédric Mongongu, Hervé Mianga Ndonga, Chancel Mbemba Mangulu, Patou Simbi Ebunga, Mapuata Cédric Makiadi (52.Mavuanga Cedrick Mbidi), Youssouf Mulumbu, Zola Matumona, Distel Zola, Eric Bokanga Musau, Blaise Lelo Mbele (46.Tychique Ntela Kalema). Trainer: Jean-Santos N'Diela Muntubila.

Goals: 1-0 Lalawélé Atakora (35), 1-1 Patou Simbi Ebunga (81), 2-1 Backer Aloenouvo (90+3).

Cautions: Sadat Ouro-Akoriko, Dakonam Ortega Djené / Distel Zola, Blaise Lelo Mbele, Youssouf Mulumbu.

GROUP J

02.06.2012	Dakar	Senegal - Liberia	3-1(1-1)
03.06.2012	Luanda	Angola - Uganda	1-1(1-0)
09.06.2012	Kampala	Uganda - Senegal	1-1(0-1)
10.06.2012	Monrovia	Liberia - Angola	0-0
23.03.2013	Conakry	Senegal - Angola	1-1(1-0)
24.03.2013	Paynesville	Liberia - Uganda	2-0(1-0)
08.06.2013	Kampala	Uganda - Liberia	1-0(1-0)
08.06.2013	Luanda	Angola - Senegal	1-1(0-1)
15.06.2013	Kampala	Uganda - Angola	2-1(0-0)
16.06.2013	Paynesville	Liberia - Senegal	0-2(0-1)
07.09.2013	Lubango	Angola - Liberia	4-1(1-0): Awarded 3-0
07.09.2013	Marrakech (MAR)	Senegal - Uganda	1-0(0-0)

Senegal qualified for the Third Round.

FINAL STANDINGS

1.	Senegal	6	3	3	0	9 - 4	12
2.	Uganda	6	2	2	2	5 - 6	8
3.	Angola	6	1	4	1	7 - 5	7
4.	Liberia	6	1	1	4	3 - 9	4

02.06.2012, Stade "Léopold Sédar Senghor", Dakar; Attendance: 15,000
Referee: Noumandiez Doué (Côte d'Ivoire)
SENEGAL - LIBERIA 3-1(1-1)
SEN: Ousmane Mané, Abdoulaye Ba, Papa Gueye, Cheikh M'Bengué, Ludovic Lamine Sané, Idrissa Gana Gueye, Mohamed Diamé (79.Cheikhou Kouyaté), Ibrahima Baldé (58.Ibrahima Touré), Papiss Demba Cissé, Pape Moussa Konaté (46.Dame N'Doye), Sadio Mané. Trainer: Amara Traoré.
LBR: Nathaniel Sherman, Jimmy Dixon, Patrick Nyema Gerhardt, Solomon Grimes, George Gebro, Alsény Këïta Kamolosilah, Theo Lewis Weeks, Anthony Snoti Laffor (65.Solomon Wesseh), Francis Doe Forkey, Dioh Williams (73.Marcus Macaulay), Patrick Wleh (41.Zah Rahan Krangar). Trainer: Kaetu Smith.
Goals: 0-1 Francis Doe Forkey (15), 1-1 Ibrahima Baldé (32), 2-1 Dame N'Doye (72), 3-1 Sadio Mané (83).
Cautions: Francis Doe Forkey.
Sent off: Solomon Grimes (62).

03.06.2012, Estádio 11 de Novembro, Luanda; Attendance: 48,000
Referee: Gehad Grisha (Egypt)
ANGOLA - UGANDA 1-1(1-0)
ANG: Adilson Cipriano da Cruz "Neblú", Bartolomeu Jacinto Quissanga "Bastos", Massunguna Alex Afonso "Dani Massunguna", António Luís dos Santos Serrado "Lunguinha", Regio Francisco Congo Zalata "Mingo Bile" (40.N'kembo Garcia "Kêmbua"), Amândio Felipe da Costa "Amaro", Calesso Ginga Luís "Mano", Djalma Braume Manuel Abel Campos (88.Adawá Mokanga), Mateus Galiano da Costa (75.Adriano Belmiro Duarte Nicolau "Yano"), Mateus Alberto Contreiras Gonçalves "Manucho", João Hernani Rosa Barros "Manucho Barros". Trainer: Romeu Filemon.
UGA: Denis Masinde Onyango, Henry Kalungi, Andrew Mwesigwa, Simeon Massa, Godfrey Walusimbi, Hassan Mawanda Wasswa, Johnson Bagoole (50.Moses Oloya), Patrick Ochan (67.Anthony Mawejje), Martin Kayongo-Mutumba, Emmanuel Okwi, Michael Sserumaga (58.Joseph Nestroy Kizito). Trainer: Robert Williamson (Scotland).
Goals: 1-0 Djalma Braume Manuel Abel Campos (7), 1-1 Emmanuel Okwi (88).
Cautions: Djalma Braume Manuel Abel Campos, Amândio Felipe da Costa "Amaro" / Johnson

Bagoole.

09.06.2012, "Nelson Mandela" National Stadium, Kampala; Attendance: 30,000
Referee: Mohamed Benouza (Algeria)
UGANDA - SENEGAL **1-1(0-1)**
UGA: Denis Masinde Onyango, Henry Kalungi, Simeon Massa, Andrew Mwesigwa (70.Hassan Mawanda Wasswa), Godfrey Walusimbi, Patrick Ochan, Martin Kayongo-Mutumba, Dan Wagaluka (56.Moses Oloya), Anthony Mawejje, Emmanuel Okwi, Brian Umony (56.Geoffrey Massa). Trainer: Robert Williamson (Scotland).
SEN: Ousmane Mané, Abdoulaye Ba, Papa Gueye, Cheikh M'Bengué, Ludovic Lamine Sané, Rémi Gomis (73.Stéphane Diarra Badji), Idrissa Gana Gueye, Souleymane Camara (80.Ibrahima Touré), Papiss Demba Cissé, Sadio Mané (90.Jacques Faty), Dame N'Doye. Trainer: Amara Traoré.
Goals: 0-1 Papiss Demba Cissé (37), 1-1 Godfrey Walusimbi (85 penalty).
Cautions: Andrew Mwesigwa, Godfrey Walusimbi / Papiss Demba Cissé.

10.06.2012, "Antoinette Tubman" Stadium, Monrovia; Attendance: 15,000
Referee: Ould Ali Lemghaifry (Mauritania)
LIBERIA - ANGOLA **0-0**
LBR: Nathaniel Sherman, Jimmy Dixon, Omega Alamadine Roberts, Dennis Teah, George Gebro, Alsény Këïta Kamolosilah, Zah Rahan Krangar (60.Anthony Snoti Laffor), Theo Lewis Weeks (70.Martin Karndu), James Zortiah (43.Sékou Jabateh Oliseh), Francis Doe Forkey, Dioh Williams. Trainer: Kaetu Smith.
ANG: Landú Mavanga, Bartolomeu Jacinto Quissanga "Bastos", Massunguna Alex Afonso "Dani Massunguna", António Luís dos Santos Serrado "Lunguinha", Regio Francisco Congo Zalata "Mingo Bile" (75.Manuel Gaspar Costa), Dominique Kisoka Jeadot Kivuvu, Adawá Mokanga, Miguel Geraldo Quiame, Djalma Braume Manuel Abel Campos (82.Calesso Ginga Luís "Mano"), Mateus Alberto Contreiras Gonçalves "Manucho", João Hernani Rosa Barros "Manucho Barros" (90+4.Amândio Felipe da Costa "Amaro"). Trainer: Romeu Filemon.
Cautions: Jimmy Dixon.

23.03.2013, Stade du 28 Septembre, Conakry (Guinea); Attendance: 13,500
Referee: Néant Alioum (Cameroon)
SENEGAL - ANGOLA **1-1(1-0)**
SEN: Bouna Coundoul, Moustapha Bayal Sall, Ludovic Lamine Sané, Cheikh M'Bengué, Papakouli Diop (89.Mame Biram Diouf), Zargo Touré, Mohamed Diamé, Idrissa Gana Gueye, Sadio Mané, Moussa Sow (68.Issiar Dia), Demba Ba (77.Papiss Demba Cissé). Trainer: Alain Giresse (France).
ANG: Landú Mavanga, Amândio Felipe da Costa „Amaro", Regio Francisco Congo Zalata „Mingo Bile", Fabrício Mafuta, Bartolomeu Jacinto Quissanga „Bastos", Mario Manuel de Oliveira „Ito", Manuel Gaspar Costa, Mateus Galiano da Costa, Guilherme Afonso, Hermenegildo da Costa Paulo Bartolomeu „Geraldo" (79.Dorivaldo António Dias „Vado Dias"), Adriano Belmiro Duarte Nicolau „Yano". Trainer: Gustavo Antonio Ferrín Rodríguez (Uruguay).
Goals: 1-0 Moussa Sow (40), 1-1 Amândio Felipe da Costa „Amaro" (75).
Cautions: Sadio Mané / Bartolomeu Jacinto Quissanga „Bastos",Adriano Belmiro Duarte Nicolau „Yano",Dorivaldo António Dias „Vado Dias",Landú Mavanga.

24.03.2013, "Samuel Kanyon Doe" Sports Complex, Paynesville; Attendance: 25,000
Referee: Mohamed Farouk Mahmoud (Egypt)

LIBERIA - UGANDA 2-0(1-0)

LBR: Nathaniel Sherman, Patrick Nyema Gerhardt, Solomon Grimes, Dennis Teah, Ansu Touré, Sékou Jabateh Oliseh, Tonia Tisdell (84.Zah Rahan Krangar), Alsény Këïta Kamolosilah, Anthony Snoti Laffor (77.Theo Lewis Weeks), Francis Doe Forkey, Patrick Wleh (63.Eddie Foday Boakay). Trainer: Frank Wontee Nagbe.

UGA: Denis Masinde Onyango, Andrew Mwesigwa, Henry Kalungi, Godfrey Walusimbi, Denis Iguma, Hassan Mawanda Wasswa, Michael Mutyaba, Moses Oloya (79.Saidi Kyeyune), Geoffrey Baba Kizito (72.Boban Ziruntusa), Geoffrey Massa, Emmanuel Arnold Okwi (70.Robert Ssentongo). Trainer: Robert Williamson (Scotland).

Goals: 1-0 Patrick Wleh (32), 2-0 Anthony Snoti Laffor (50).

Cautions: Nathaniel Sherman, Anthony Snoti Laffor, Patrick Wleh, Solomon Wesseh (on the bench) / Denis Iguma, Denis Masinde Onyango.

08.06.2013, „Nelson Mandela" National Stadium, Kampala; Attendance: 8,400
Referee: Adam Cordier (Chad)

UGANDA - LIBERIA 1-0(1-0)

UGA: Robert Odongkara, Andrew Mwesigwa, Godfrey Walusimbi, Isaac Isinde, Denis Iguma, Hassan Mawanda Wasswa, Geoffrey Baba Kizito (65.Saidi Kyeyune), Luwagga William Kizito (46.Martin Kayongo-Mutumba), Geoffrey Massa, Anthony Mawejje, Emmanuel Arnold Okwi (90+1.Dan Sserunkuma). Trainer: Milutin Sredojević (Serbia).

LBR: Nathaniel Sherman, Omega Alamadine Roberts, Solomon Wesseh, Francis Jalabah, Ansu Touré, Sékou Jabateh Oliseh (86.Herron Berrian), Zah Rahan Krangar, Theo Lewis Weeks, Eddie Foday Boakay (60.Tonia Tisdell), Anthony Snoti Laffor, Patrick Wleh. Trainer: Frank Wontee Nagbe.

Goal: 1-0 Anthony Mawejje (4).

Cautions: Martin Kayongo-Mutumba.

08.06.2013, Estádio 11 de Novembro, Luanda; Attendance: 40,000
Referee: Bernard Camille (Seychelles)

ANGOLA - SENEGAL 1-1(0-1)

ANG: Landú Mavanga, Amândio Felipe da Costa „Amaro", Massunguna Alex Afonso „Dani Massunguna" (83.Adawá Mokanga), Fabrício Mafuta, Bartolomeu Jacinto Quissanga „Bastos", Ilídio José Panzo „Pirolito", Mario Manuel de Oliveira „Ito", Mateus Galiano da Costa (46.Guilherme Afonso), Djalma Braume Manuel Abel Campos, Hermenegildo da Costa Paulo Bartolomeu „Geraldo" (46.Ricardo Job Estevão), Adriano Belmiro Duarte Nicolau „Yano". Trainer: Gustavo Antonio Ferrín Rodríguez (Uruguay).

SEN: Bouna Coundoul, Lamine Gassama, Ludovic Lamine Sané, Cheikh M'Bengué, Mohamed Diamé, Idrissa Gana Gueye, Serigne Modou Kara Mbodji, Sadio Mané, Stéphane Diarra Badji (87.Pape Amodou Sougou), Mame Biram Diouf (79.Moussa Sow), Papiss Demba Cissé (90+4.Salif Sané). Trainer: Alain Giresse (France).

Goals: 0-1 Papiss Demba Cissé (23), 1-1 Guilherme Afonso (51).

Cautions: Mario Manuel de Oliveira „Ito",Adriano Belmiro Duarte Nicolau „Yano" / Lamine Gassama, Mohamed Diamé, Idrissa Gana Gueye.

15.06.2013, „Nelson Mandela“ National Stadium, Kampala; Attendance: 40,000
Referee: Rédouane Jiyed (Morocco)
UGANDA - ANGOLA **2-1(0-0)**
UGA: Robert Odongkara, Andrew Mwesigwa, Godfrey Walusimbi, Isaac Isinde, Denis Iguma, Hassan Mawanda Wasswa, Moses Oloya (60.Hamis Kiiza), Geoffrey Baba Kizito (70.Martin Kayongo-Mutumba), Geoffrey Massa (60.Robert Ssentongo), Anthony Mawejje, Emmanuel Arnold Okwi. Trainer: Milutin Sredojević (Serbia).
ANG: Hugo Miguel Barreto Henriques Marques, Amândio Felipe da Costa „Amaro“, António Gonçalo Cassule „Gomito“ (46.Adawá Mokanga), Fabrício Mafuta, Bartolomeu Jacinto Quissanga „Bastos“, Ilídio José Panzo „Pirolito“, Mario Manuel de Oliveira „Ito“, Mateus Galiano da Costa, Djalma Braume Manuel Abel Campos (68.Hermenegildo da Costa Paulo Bartolomeu „Geraldo“), Guilherme Afonso, Ricardo Job Estevão (88.Manuel David Afonso "Ary Papel"). Trainer: Gustavo Antonio Ferrín Rodríguez (Uruguay).
Goals: 0-1 Ricardo Job Estevão (57), 1-1 Emmanuel Arnold Okwi (83), 2-1 Anthony Mawejje (89).
Cautions: Hassan Mawanda Wasswa, Isaac Isinde, Anthony Mawejje, Robert Ssentongo / Amândio Felipe da Costa „Amaro“,Mateus Galiano da Costa, Hermenegildo da Costa Paulo Bartolomeu „Geraldo“,Ilídio José Panzo „Pirolito“.
Sent off: Fabrício Mafuta (86).

16.06.2013, "Samuel Kanyon Doe" Sports Complex, Paynesville; Attendance: 35,000
Referee: Davies Omweno (Kenya)
LIBERIA - SENEGAL **0-2(0-1)**
LBR: Nathaniel Sherman, Alex Began Karmo (48.Francis Jalabah), Omega Alamadine Roberts, Solomon Wesseh, Ansu Touré, Zah Rahan Krangar, Theo Lewis Weeks, Tonia Tisdell (65.Sékou Jabateh Oliseh), Anthony Snoti Laffor, Francis Doe Forkey, Patrick Wleh (77.Herron Berrian). Trainer: Frank Wontee Nagbe.
SEN: Bouna Coundoul, Lamine Gassama, Ludovic Lamine Sané, Pape Ndiaye Souaré, Serigne Modou Kara Mbodji, Mohamed Diamé, Idrissa Gana Gueye, Sadio Mané (90.Pape Amodou Sougou), Stéphane Diarra Badji, Moussa Sow (74.Mame Biram Diouf), Papiss Demba Cissé (63.Salif Sané). Trainer: Alain Giresse (France).
Goals: 0-1 Papiss Demba Cissé (18 penalty), 0-2 Papiss Demba Cissé (53).
Cautions: Nathaniel Sherman, Alex Began Karmo, Omega Alamadine Roberts / Papiss Demba Cissé, Pape Ndiaye Souaré, Stéphane Diarra Badji.

07.09.2013, Tundavala National Stadium, Lubango; Attendance: 3,000
Referee: Slim Jedidi (Tunisia)
ANGOLA - LIBERIA **4-1(1-0)***
ANG: Hugo Miguel Barreto Henriques Marques, Pedro Victor Mingas "Kibeixa", António Nzayinawo „Abdul“, Filipe Malanda, Natael Paulo Nasuekama, Mario Manuel de Oliveira „Ito“, Ilídio José Panzo „Pirolito“ (88.Osvaldo de Jesús Kitenga „Vado“), Manuel David Afonso "Ary Papel" (78.Diógenes Capemba João), Guilherme Afonso, Cristóvao Paciencia „Mabululu“ (65.Adawá Mokanga), Guedes Lupapa. Trainer: Gustavo Antonio Ferrín Rodríguez (Uruguay).
LBR: Nathaniel Sherman, Myers Garlo, Solomon Wesseh, Trokon Zeon, Alpha James (46.Gideon Williams), Prince Saydee, Eddie Wulue, Marcus Macaulay, Samuel Thompson (70.Sylvanus Nimely), Mohammed Varney, Prince Boley (46.James Soto Roberts). Trainer: Frank Wontee Nagbe.
Goals: 1-0 Guedes Lupapa (2), 2-0 Cristóvao Paciencia „Mabululu“ (47), 3-0 Guilherme Afonso (60), 4-0 António Nzayinawo „Abdul“ (63), 4-1 Marcus Macaulay (79).
Cautions: Guilherme Afonso, Manuel David Afonso "Ary Papel" / Trokon Zeon.
Sent off: Gideon Williams (88).
**Please note: FIFA awarded Angola a 3–0 win as a result of Liberia fielding an ineligible player, Nathaniel Sherman.*

07.09.2013, Stade de Marrakech, Marrakech (Morocco); Attendance: 2,000
Referee: Daniel Frazer Bennett (South Africa)

SENEGAL - UGANDA **1-0(0-0)**

SEN: Bouna Coundoul, Lamine Gassama, Cheikhou Kouyaté (90+1.Salif Sané), Papiss Mison Djilobodji, Issa Cissokho, Mohamed Diamé, Idrissa Gana Gueye, Sadio Mané, Moussa Sow (90+3.Stéphane Diarra Badji), Henri Saivet, Mame Biram Diouf (75.Dame N'Doye). Trainer: Alain Giresse (France).

UGA: Robert Odongkara, Andrew Mwesigwa, Godfrey Walusimbi, Isaac Isinde, Denis Iguma, Hassan Mawanda Wasswa, Geoffrey Baba Kizito (59.Moses Oloya), Brian Majwega, Anthony Mawejje, Hamis Kiiza (81.Martin Kayongo-Mutumba), Emmanuel Arnold Okwi (84.Frank Kalanda). Trainer: Milutin Sredojević (Serbia).

Goal: 1-0 Sadio Mané (85).

Cautions: Isaac Isinde.

Sent off: Godfrey Walusimbi (36).

THIRD ROUND

In the third round, the 10 group winners from the second round were drawn into five home-and-away ties. The winners of each tie were qualified for the 2014 FIFA World Cup finals.

12.10.2013	Abidjan	Côte d'Ivoire – Senegal	3-1(2-0)
16.11.2013	Casablanca (MAR)	Senegal - Côte d'Ivoire	1-1(0-0)

(***Côte d'Ivoire*** *qualified for the 2014 World Cup Final Tournament*)

12.10.2013	Ouagadougou	Burkina Faso - Algeria	3-2(1-0)
19.11.2013	Blida	Algeria – Burkina Faso	1-0(0-0)

(***Algeria*** *qualified for the 2014 World Cup Final Tournament*)

13.10.2013	Addis Abeba	Ethiopia – Nigeria	1-2(0-0)
16.11.2013	Calabar	Nigeria – Ethiopia	2-0(1-0)

(***Nigeria*** *qualified for the 2014 World Cup Final Tournament*)

13.10.2013	Radès	Tunisia – Cameroon	0-0
17.11.2013	Yaoundé	Cameroon – Tunisia	4-1(2-0)

(***Cameroon*** *qualified for the 2014 World Cup Final Tournament*)

15.10.2013	Kumasi	Ghana – Egypt	6-1(3-1)
19.11.2013	Cairo	Egypt – Ghana	2-1(1-0)

(***Ghana*** *qualified for the 2014 World Cup Final Tournament*)

12.10.2013, Stade "Félix Houphouët-Boigny", Abidjan; Attendance: 30,000
Referee: Rajindraparsad Seechurn (Mauritius)

CÔTE D'IVOIRE – SENEGAL 3-1(2-0)

CIV: Boubacar Barry, Arthur Etienne Boka, Souleymane Bamba, Serge Aurier, Alain Didier Zokora Deguy, Gnégnéri Yaya Touré, Cheik Ismael Tioté, Sereso Geoffroy Gonzaroua Die „Serey Die", Didier Yves Drogba Tébily (77.Lacina Traoré), Salomon Armand Magloire Kalou (55.Giovanni-Guy Yann Sio), Gervais Yao Kouassi „Gervinho" (89.Max-Alain Gradel). Trainer: Sabri Lamouchi (France).
SEN: Bouna Coundoul, Lamine Gassama (51.Issa Cissokho), Cheikhou Kouyaté, Ludovic Lamine Sané, Pape Ndiaye Souaré, Alfred John Momar N'Diaye (46.Sadio Mané), Mohamed Diamé, Idrissa Gana Gueye, Moussa Sow (79.Henri Saivet), Dame N'Doye, Papiss Demba Cissé. Trainer: Alain Giresse (France).
Goals: 1-0 Didier Yves Drogba Tébily (3), 2-0 Ludovic Lamine Sané (14 own goal), 3-0 Salomon Armand Magloire Kalou (49), 3-1 Papiss Demba Cissé (90+4).
Cautions: Boubacar Barry, Cheik Ismael Tioté, Sereso Geoffroy Gonzaroua Die „Serey Die" / Cheikhou Kouyaté.

16.11.2013, Stade "Mohamed V", Casablanca (Morocco); Attendance: 15,000
Referee: Djamel Haimoudi (Algeria)

SENEGAL - CÔTE D'IVOIRE 1-1(0-0)

SEN: Bouna Coundoul, Ludovic Lamine Sané, Pape Ndiaye Souaré (90+2.Mame Biram Diouf), Papiss Mison Djilobodji, Serigne Modou Kara Mbodji, Salif Sané, Idrissa Gana Gueye, Sadio Mané, Stéphane Diarra Badji (82.Henri Saivet), Dame N'Doye (65.Moussa Sow) Papiss Demba Cissé. Trainer: Alain Giresse (France).
CIV: Boubacar Barry, Kolo Habib Touré, Souleymane Bamba, Serge Aurier, Christian Koffi Ndri „Romaric", Alain Didier Zokora Deguy, Gnégnéri Yaya Touré, Jean-Jacques Gosso Gosso, Didier Yves Drogba Tébily, Salomon Armand Magloire Kalou, Gervais Yao Kouassi „Gervinho" (80.Giovanni-Guy Yann Sio). Trainer: Sabri Lamouchi (France).
Goals: 1-0 Moussa Sow (72 penalty), 1-1 Salomon Armand Magloire Kalou (90+4).

Cautions: Gnégnéri Yaya Touré, Jean-Jacques Gosso Gosso, Gervais Yao Kouassi „Gervinho".
(***Côte d'Ivoire*** *qualified for the 2014 World Cup Final Tournament*)

12.10.2013, Stade du 4 Août, Ouagadougou; Attendance: 31,000
Referee: Janny Sikazwe (Zambia)
BURKINA FASO - ALGERIA 3-2(1-0)
BFA: Daouda Diakité, Bakary Koné (8.Steeve Yago), Paul Kéba Koulibaly, Jean-Noël Lingani (68.Mady Saïdou Panandétiguiri), Charles Kaboré, Mohamed Koffi (78.Bertrand Isidore Traoré), Djakaridja Koné, Jonathan Sundy Zongo, Beninwende Yann Jonathan Pitroipa, Aristide Bancé, Préjuce Niguimbe Nakoulma. Trainer: Paul Put (Belgium).
ALG: Adi Raïs Cobos Adrien M'Bolhi Ouhab, Madjid Bougherra, Djamel Eddine Mesbah, Essaïd Belkalem, Carl Medjani, Hassan Yebda (68.Adlène Guedioura), Mehdi Mostefa Sbaa, Sofiane Feghouli (90+2.Foued Kadir), Saphir Sliti Taïder (83.Mehdi Gregory Giuseppe Lacen), El Arbi Hillel Soudani, Islam Slimani. Trainer: Vahid Halilhodžić (Bosnia-Herzegovina).
Goals: 1-0 Beninwende Yann Jonathan Pitroipa (45+2), 1-1 Sofiane Feghouli (50), 2-1 Djakaridja Koné (65), 2-2 Carl Medjani (69), 3-2 Aristide Bancé (85 penalty).
Cautions: Mohamed Koffi / Djamel Eddine Mesbah, Essaïd Belkalem, Adlène Guedioura.

19.11.2013, Stade "Mustapha Tchaker", Blida; Attendance: 35,000
Referee: Badara Diatta (Senegal)
ALGERIA – BURKINA FASO 1-0(0-0)
ALG: Mohamed Lamine Zemmamouche, Madjid Bougherra, Faouzi Ghoulam, Carl Medjani, Mehdi Mostefa Sbaa (86.Saphir Sliti Taïder), Yacine Brahimi (68.Hassan Yebda), Sofiane Feghouli (90.Foued Kadir), Nacer Eddine Khoualed, Mehdi Gregory Giuseppe Lacen, El Arbi Hillel Soudani, Islam Slimani. Trainer: Vahid Halilhodžić (Bosnia-Herzegovina).
BFA: Daouda Diakité, Mady Saïdou Panandétiguiri, Bakary Koné, Steeve Yago (78.Alain Sibiri Traoré), Charles Kaboré, Wilfred Benjamin Balima, Florent Rouamba (65.Aristide Bancé), Djakaridja Koné, Beninwende Yann Jonathan Pitroipa, Jonathan Sundy Zongo (64.Bertrand Isidore Traoré), Préjuce Niguimbe Nakoulma. Trainer: Paul Put (Belgium).
Goal: 1-0 Madjid Bougherra (49).
Cautions: Madjid Bougherra / Charles Kaboré, Steeve Yago.
(***Algeria*** *qualified for the 2014 World Cup Final Tournament*)

13.10.2013, Addis Abeba Stadium, Addis Abeba; Attendance: 22,000
Referee: Néant Alioum (Cameroon)
ETHIOPIA – NIGERIA 1-2(0-0)
ETH: Jemal Tassew Bushra, Abebaw Butako, Aynalem Hailu Reda, Degu Debebe, Siyoum Tesfaye, Adane Girma Gebreyes (64.Oumed Oukri), Menyahel Teshome Beyene, Asrat Megersa Gobena, Behailu Assefa, Salaheldin Ahmed Said, Shimelis Bekele Godo (74.Addis Hintsa). Trainer: Sewnet Beshaw.
NGA: Vincent Enyeama, Uwa Elderson Echiéjilé, Efetobore Ambrose Emuobo, Godfrey Itama Oboabona, Azubuike Emanuel Egwuekwe, John Michael Nchekwube Obinna, Victor Moses (67.Aide Brown Ideye), Ogenyi Eddy Onazi, Emmanuel Chinenye Emenike, Ahmed Musa, Nnamdi Chidiebere Oduamadi (65.Emmanuel Nosakhare Igiebor). Trainer: Stephen Okechukwu Keshi.
Goals: 1-0 Behailu Assefa (57), 1-1 Emmanuel Chinenye Emenike (67), 1-2 Emmanuel Chinenye Emenike (90 penalty).
Cautions: Siyoum Tesfaye, Adane Girma Gebreyes, Addis Hintsa, Aynalem Hailu Reda.

16.11.2013, "U. J. Esuene" Stadium, Calabar; Attendance: 8,000
Referee: Bakary Papa Gassama (Gambia)

NIGERIA – ETHIOPIA **2-0(1-0)**

NGA: Vincent Enyeama, Uwa Elderson Echiéjilé, Efetobore Ambrose Emuobo, Kenneth Josiah Omeruo (68.Azubuike Emanuel Egwuekwe), Godfrey Itama Oboabona, John Michael Nchekwube Obinna, Victor Moses (79.Victor Nsofor Obinna), Ogenyi Eddy Onazi, Aide Brown Ideye (59.Sunday Mba), Emmanuel Chinenye Emenike, Ahmed Musa. Trainer: Stephen Okechukwu Keshi.

ETH: Sisay Bancha Basa, Alula Girma Mekonnen, Abebaw Butako, Aynalem Hailu Reda, Saladin Bargecho, Adane Girma Gebreyes, Menyahel Teshome Beyene (81.Dawit Fekadu), Asrat Megersa Gobena, Salaheldin Ahmed Said, Getaneh Kebede Gebeto (60.Behailu Assefa), Shimelis Bekele Godo (75.Addis Hintsa). Trainer: Sewnet Beshaw.

Goals: 1-0 Victor Moses (20 penalty), 2-0 Victor Nsofor Obinna (81).

Cautions: Victor Moses, Kenneth Josiah Omeruo, Godfrey Itama Oboabona / Adane Girma Gebreyes, Salaheldin Ahmed Said, Saladin Bargecho, Aynalem Hailu Reda.

(***Nigeria** qualified for the 2014 World Cup Final Tournament*)

13.10.2013, Stade Olympique de Radès, Radès; Attendance: 30,900
Referee: Koman Coulibaly (Mali)

TUNISIA – CAMEROON **0-0**

TUN: Moez Ben Chérifia, Alaeddine Yahia, Yassine Salim Mikari, Sameh Derbali, Syam Ben Youssef, Yassine Chikhaoui (83.Änis Ben-Hatira), Hocine Ragued, Wissem Ben Yahia, Samuel Allagui (46.Fakhreddine Ben Youssef), Mohamed Amine Chermiti (75.Issam Jemâa), Saber Khelifa. Trainer: Rudolf Jozef Krol (Holland).

CMR: Charles-Hubert Itandje, Aurélien Bayard Chedjou Fongang, Nicolas Alexis Julio N'Koulou N'Doubena, Allan-Roméo Nyom (69.Jean-Armel Kana-Biyik), Dany Achille Nounkeu Tchounkeu, Joël Job Matip, Jean II Makoun (77.Mohammadou Idrissou), Alexandre Dimitri Song Billong, Eyong Tarkang Enoh, Samuel Eto'o Fils (90.Jean-Eric Maxim Choupo-Moting), Pierre Achille Webó Kouamo. Trainer: Volker Finke (Germany).

Cautions: Hocine Ragued / Allan-Roméo Nyom, Joël Job Matip.

17.11.2013, Stade Omnisports „Ahmadou-Ahidjo" Yaoundé; Attendance: 35,570
Referee: Rajindraparsad Seechurn (Mauritius)

CAMEROON – TUNISIA **4-1(2-0)**

CMR: Charles-Hubert Itandje, Benoît Pierre David Assou-Ekotto, Aurélien Bayard Chedjou Fongang, Nicolas Alexis Julio N'Koulou N'Doubena, Stéphane Mbia Etoundi (67.Dany Achille Nounkeu Tchounkeu), Jean II Makoun, Alexandre Dimitri Song Billong, Eyong Tarkang Enoh, Samuel Eto'o Fils, Pierre Achille Webó Kouamo (61.Jean-Eric Maxim Choupo-Moting), Benjamin Moukandjo Bilé (83.Joël Landry Tsafack N'Guémo). Trainer: Volker Finke (Germany).

TUN: Moez Ben Chérifia, Karim Haggui, Yassine Salim Mikari, Sameh Derbali, Syam Ben Youssef, Yassine Chikhaoui (46.Ahmed Akaïchi), Hocine Ragued, Wissem Ben Yahia (73.Samuel Allagui), Mohamed Amine Chermiti (46.Fabien Camus), Saber Khelifa, Fakhreddine Ben Youssef. Trainer: Rudolf Jozef Krol (Holland).

Goals: 1-0 Pierre Achille Webó Kouamo (3), 2-0 Benjamin Moukandjo Bilé (29), 2-1 Ahmed Akaïchi (50), 3-1 Jean II Makoun (65), 4-1 Jean II Makoun (85).

Cautions: Benjamin Moukandjo Bilé.

(***Cameroon** qualified for the 2014 World Cup Final Tournament*)

15.10.2013, Baba Yara Stadium, Kumasi; Attendance: 38,000
Referee: Bouchaïb El Ahrach (Morocco)

GHANA – EGYPT 6-1(3-1)

GHA: Abdul Fatawu Dauda, Jerry Akaminko, Samuel Diadie Inkoom, Daniel Tawiah Opare, Rashid Sumaila, Michael Kojo Essien, Sulleyman Ali Muntari (83.Emmanuel Agyemang-Badu), Kwadwo Asamoah, Asamoah Gyan (79.Wakaso Mubarak), André Morgan Rami Ayew (83.Christian Atsu Twasam), Majeed Abdul Waris. Trainer: James Kwesi Appiah.
EGY: Ahmed Sherif Ekramy (57.Ahmed Nassr Abdel Razak El-Shenawy), Ahmed Fathi Abdel Moneim Ahmed Ibrahim, Wael Mohamed Gomaa Kamel El Hooty, Ahmed Shadid Mahmoud Kenawi (45+1.Mahmoud Abdel Razek Fadlallah „Shikabala"), Mohamed Nasser Nagieb El Ghareeb, Hossam El Sayed El Metwaly Ghaly, Hossam Mohamed Ashour Sanad Attia (40.Ahmed Eissa Elmohamady Abdel-Fattah), Walid Soliman Saed, Mohamed Aboutrika, Mohamed Salah Ghaly, Mohamed Naser El Sayed El Nenny. Trainer: Robert Bradley (United States).
Goals: 1-0 Asamoah Gyan (4), 2-0 Wael Mohamed Gomaa Kamel El Hooty (22 own goal), 2-1 Mohamed Aboutrika (41 penalty), 3-1 Majeed Abdul Waris (44), 4-1 Asamoah Gyan (54), 5-1 Sulleyman Ali Muntari (73 penalty), 6-1 Christian Atsu Twasam (89).
Cautions: Rashid Sumaila / Hossam El Sayed El Metwaly Ghaly, Ahmed Nassr Abdel Razak El-Shenawy, Mohamed Naser El Sayed El Nenny.

16.11.2013, 30 June Stadium, Cairo; Attendance: 25,000
Referee: Noumandiez Doué (Côte d'Ivoire)

EGYPT – GHANA 2-1(1-0)

EGY: Ahmed Sherif Ekramy, Ahmed Fathi Abdel Moneim Ahmed Ibrahim (56.Hosny Abd Rabo Abd El Motaleb Ibrahim), Mohamed Nasser Nagieb El Ghareeb, Mohamed Abdel Marhoum Shafy, Ramy Hisham Abdel Aziz Rabia, Hossam El Sayed El Metwaly Ghaly, Hazem Mohamed Abdel Hamid Emam, Mohamed Aboutrika, Mohamed Salah Ghaly, Mahmoud Abdel-Moneim „Kahraba" (40.Mohamed Nagy Ismail Afash „Geddo"), Amr Hassan Zaki (62.Mahmoud Abdel Razek Fadlallah „Shikabala"). Trainer: Robert Bradley (United States).
GHA: Abdul Fatawu Dauda, Harrison Afful, Jerry Akaminko, Daniel Tawiah Opare, Rashid Sumaila, Michael Kojo Essien, Sulleyman Ali Muntari (73.Emmanuel Agyemang-Badu), Kwadwo Asamoah, Asamoah Gyan, André Morgan Rami Ayew (58.Wakaso Mubarak), Majeed Abdul Waris (79.Kevin-Prince Boateng). Trainer: James Kwesi Appiah.
Goals: 1-0 Amr Hassan Zaki (25), 2-0 Mohamed Nagy Ismail Afash „Geddo" (83), 2-1 Kevin-Prince Boateng (89).
Cautions: Ramy Hisham Abdel Aziz Rabia, Mohamed Nagy Ismail Afash „Geddo" / Jerry Akaminko, Daniel Tawiah Opare, Sulleyman Ali Muntari, Wakaso Mubarak.
*(**Ghana** qualified for the 2014 World Cup Final Tournament)*

ASIA

Four or five Asian teams could reach the final tournament. Four teams will qualify directly, a fifth team will play against a national team belonging to CONMEBOL (South America).

From the 46 Asian Football Confederation (AFC) teams, 43 entered the qualification. The AFC released a ranking list before the qualifiers drawing to determine when each country will begin to play the qualifying rounds:

Places 1 to 5:
Japan, South Korea, Australia, North Korea, Bahrain - this national teams played in the 2010 FIFA World Cup finals and the intercontinental play-offs, so they do not compete in the qualification rounds, being automatically qualified for the first group stage.

Places 6 to 27:
Saudi Arabia, Iran, Qatar, Uzbekistan, United Arab Emirates, Syria, Oman, Jordan, Iraq, Singapore, China P.R., Kuwait, Thailand, Turkmenistan, Lebanon, Yemen, Tajikistan, Hong Kong, Indonesia, Kyrgyzstan, Maldives, India – this national teams received a bye to the second round of qualifiers.

Places 28-43:
Malaysia, Afghanistan, Cambodia, Nepal, Bangladesh, Sri Lanka, Vietnam, Mongolia, Pakistan, Palestine, Timor-Leste, Macau, Chinese Taipei, Myanmar, Philippines, Laos – this national teams played in the first qualifying round.

29.06.2011	Kathmandu	Nepal – Timor-Leste	2-1(1-0)
02.07.2011	Kathmandu	Timor-Leste - Nepal	0-5(0-1)

29.06.2011, Dasarath Rangasala Stadium, Kathmandu; Attendance: 9,000
Referee: Ali Sabbagh (Lebanon)

NEPAL – TIMOR-LESTE 2-1(1-0)

NEP: Kiran Chemzong, Rabin Shrestha (59.Bikash Singh Chhetri), Rohit Chand, Biraj Maharjan, Sagar Thapa, Nirajan Khadka (80.Bijay Gurung), Sandeep Rai, Shiva Shrestha (67.Bhola Nath Silwal), Anil Gurung, Bharat Khawas, Ju Manu Rai. Trainer: Graham Paul Roberts (England).
TLS: Diamantino Leong „Ady", Juvitu Correia Da Silva, Nazario Do Carmo, Raul Dias Monterio Isac, Salvador Carlos, Eusebio Hermenio de Almeida, Helder Mota Ricardo „Eric" (46.Bertolomeu Verdial Valadares), José João Pereira, Anggisu de Almeida Barbosa (46.Vicente Ramos Freitas), Emílio Jaime Luis da Silva Perosa „Ary", Chiquito Felipe Do Carmo (75.Zico Luzinho Ingles Casimiro). Trainer: Antonio Carlos Vieira (Brazil).
Goals: 1-0 Anil Gurung (15 penalty), 1-1 Juvitu Correia Da Silva (47), 2-1 Ju Manu Rai (71).
Cautions: Shiva Shrestha, Bharat Khawas, Bijay Gurung / Diamantino Leong „Ady",Anggisu de Almeida Barbosa, Salvador Carlos.
Sent off: Bharat Khawas (54).

02.07.2011, Dasarath Rangasala Stadium, Kathmandu; Attendance: 15,000
Referee: Lee Min-Hu (Korea Republic)

TIMOR-LESTE - NEPAL 0-5(0-1)

TLS: Diamantino Leong „Ady", Juvitu Correia Da Silva, Nazario Do Carmo (43.José João Pereira), Raul Dias Monterio Isac, Salvador Carlos (22.Afonso Carson), Vicente Ramos Freitas, Emílio Jaime Luis da Silva Perosa „Ary", Chiquito Felipe Do Carmo, Zico Luzinho Ingles Casimiro, Anggisu de Almeida Barbosa, Moises Natalino De Jesus (52.Helder Mota Ricardo „Eric"). Trainer: Antonio Carlos Vieira (Brazil).
NEP: Kiran Chemzong, Rohit Chand, Bikash Singh Chhetri, Biraj Maharjan, Sagar Thapa, Nirajan Khadka, Sandeep Rai (82.Shiva Shrestha), Jagjeet Shrestha, Bhola Nath Silwal (72.Anil Ojha), Anil Gurung, Ju Manu Rai (64.Sujal Shrestha). Trainer: Graham Paul Roberts (England).
Goals: 0-1 Anil Gurung (3 penalty), 0-2 Bhola Nath Silwal (56), 0-3 Ju Manu Rai (60), 0-4 Jagjeet Shrestha (89), 0-5 Sujal Shrestha (90).
Cautions: Emílio Jaime Luis da Silva Perosa „Ary",José João Pereira, Chiquito Felipe Do Carmo / Sagar Thapa.
(Nepal won 7-1 on aggregate and advanced to the 2nd Round)

29.06.2011	Kuala Lumpur	Malaysia – Chinese Taipei	2-1(1-0)
03.07.2011	Taipei	Chinese Taipei - Malaysia	3-2(2-2)

29.06.2011, Bukit Jalil National Stadium, Kuala Lumpur; Attendance: 45,000
Referee: Chaiya Mahapab (Thailand)

MALAYSIA – CHINESE TAIPEI 2-1(1-0)

MAS: Mohd Sharbinee Allawee Ramli, Mohd Aidil Zafuan Abdul Razak, Mohamad Fadhli Mohd Shas, Mohd Asraruddin Putra Omar, Mohd Amirul Hadi Zainal, Mohd Helmi Remeli, Baddrol Bakhtiar, Mohd Safiq Rahim (82.Mohd Shakir Shaari), Mohammad Amar Rohidan, Kunanlan Subramaniam, Mohammad Safee Mohd Sali. Trainer: Krishnasamy Rajagopal.
TPE: Lin Po-cheng, Chang Yung-hsien, Chen Yu-lin, Chen Yi-wei (76.Wu Pai-ho), Lin Cheng-yi, Chan Che-yuan (73.Wu Chun-ching), Chen Po-liang, Tsai Hsien-tang, Chang Han (90+5.Chen Po-hao), Lo Chih-an, Lo Chih-en. Trainer: Lo Chih-tsung.
Goals: 1-0 Mohd Safiq Rahim (28), 2-0 Mohd Aidil Zafuan Abdul Razak (55), 2-1 Chen Po-liang (77).
Cautions: Kunanlan Subramaniam, Baddrol Bakhtiar / Lin Po-cheng.

03.07.2011, Chungshan Soccer Stadium, Taipei; Attendance: 16,768
Referee: Võ Minh Trí (Vietnam)

CHINESE TAIPEI - MALAYSIA 3-2(2-2)

TPE: Lin Po-cheng (46.Wei Sheng-hsin), Chang Yung-hsien, Chen Yu-lin, Lin Cheng-yi, Xavier Chen, Chan Che-yuan, Chen Po-liang, Lo Chih-an (82.Wu Pai-ho), Tsai Hsien-tang, Chang Han, Lo Chih-en (65.Wu Chun-ching). Trainer: Lo Chih-tsung.

MAS: Mohd Sharbinee Allawee Ramli, Mohd Aidil Zafuan Abdul Razak, Mahalli Jasuli, Mohamad Fadhli Mohd Shas, Mohd Asraruddin Putra Omar, Mohd Amirul Hadi Zainal (65.Suppiah Chanturu), Mohd Safiq Rahim, Mohammad Amar Rohidan, Kunanlan Subramaniam, Norshahrul Idlan Talaha, Abdul Hadi Yahya (77.Ahmad Fakri Saarani). Trainer: Krishnasamy Rajagopal.

Goals: 0-1 Mohd Aidil Zafuan Abdul Razak (8), 1-1 Chang Han (31), 1-2 Mohd Safiq Rahim (40), 2-2 Chen Po-liang (44 penalty), 3-1 Xavier Chen (75 penalty).

Cautions: Chen Yu-lin / Mahalli Jasuli, Mohamad Fadhli Mohd Shas, Mohd Aidil Zafuan Abdul Razak, Mohd Sharbinee Allawee Ramli.

(Malaysia won on away goals rule (4-4 on aggregate) and advanced to the 2nd Round)

29.06.2011	Dhaka	Bangladesh - Pakistan	3-0(2-0)
03.07.2011	Lahore	Pakistan - Bangladesh	0-0

29.06.2011, Bangabandhu Stadium, Dhâkâ; Attendance: 5,326
Referee: Mohammad Abu Loum (Jordan)

BANGLADESH - PAKISTAN 3-0(2-0)

BAN: Biplop Bhattacharjee, Mohamed Ariful Islam Arif, Mohamed Linkon, Mohamed Razaul Karim, Atiqur Rahman Meshu, Mohamed Nasirul Islam Nasir (75.Mohamed Mamun Miah), Shakil Ahmed (84.Abdul Baten Mojumder Komol), Mohamed Zahid Hossain (51.Mithun Chowdhury), Mohamed Mamunul Islam, Mohamed Monaem Khan Raju, Mohamed Jahid Hassan Ameli. Trainer: Gjorgje Jovanovski (Macedonia).

PAK: Jaffar Khan, Zeshan Rehman, Manzoor Ahmad, Sammar Ishaq, Atif Bashir Qureshi, Hassnain Abbas, Adnan Farooq Ahmed, Syed Arif Hussain (83.Ahmad Akhbar Khan), Faisal Iqbal, Kalim Ullah Khan (46.Muhammad Ikram), Muhammad Rasool (67.Muhammad Qasim). Trainer: Umar Farooq Tariq Lufti.

Goals: 1-0 Mohamed Jahid Hassan Ameli (1), 2-0 Mohamed Zahid Hossain (22), 3-0 Mohamed Razaul Karim (56).

Cautions: Mohamed Monaem Khan Raju, Mohamed Linkon / Zeshan Rehman, Adnan Farooq Ahmed.

03.07.2011, Punjab Stadium, Lahore; Attendance: 3,500
Referee: Ali Hasan Ebrahim Abdulnabi (Bahrain)

PAKISTAN - BANGLADESH 0-0

PAK: Jaffar Khan, Manzoor Ahmad, Sammar Ishaq, Atif Bashir Qureshi, Muhammad Ahmad, Hassnain Abbas, Adnan Farooq Ahmed, Faisal Iqbal, Arif Mehmood (79.Ahmad Akhbar Khan), Muhammad Qasim (33.Kalim Ullah Khan), Muhammad Rasool (69.Muhammad Ikram). Trainer: Umar Farooq Tariq Lufti.

BAN: Biplop Bhattacharjee, Mohamed Ariful Islam Arif, Mohamed Linkon, Mohamed Razaul Karim, Mohamed Mamun Miah (62.Atiqur Rahman Meshu), Mohamed Nasirul Islam Nasir, Shakil Ahmed (62.Mohamed Zahid Hossain), Mohamed Mamunul Islam, Mohamed Monaem Khan Raju (57.Abdul Baten Mojumder Komol), Mithun Chowdhury, Mohamed Jahid Hassan Ameli. Trainer: Nikola Ilievski (Macedonia).

Cautions: Muhammad Ikram, Atif Bashir Qureshi / Mohamed Mamun Miah, Mohamed Jahid Hassan Ameli, Biplop Bhattacharjee.

(Bangladesh won 3-0 on aggregate and advanced to the 2nd Round)

29.06.2011	Phnom Penh	Cambodia - Laos	4-2(0-1)
03.07.2011	Vientiane	Laos – Cambodia	6-2(2-1,4-2)

29.06.2011, National Olympic Stadium, Phnom Penh; Attendance: 24,800
Referee: Yadollah Jahanbazi (Iran)
CAMBODIA - LAOS 4-2(0-1)
CAM: Ouk Mic, Pheak Rady, Sok Rithy, Tieng Tiny, Touch Pancharong (87.Lay Raksmey), Chhin Chhoeun (80.Pung Soksana), Tum Saray (32.Sam El Nasa), Sun Sopanha, Chhun Sothearath, Khoun Laboravy, Kouch Sokumpheak. Trainer: Lee Tae-Hoon (Korea Republic).
LAO: Chintana Souksavath, Saynakhonevieng Phommapanya, Ketsada Souksavanh, Moukda Souksavath, Kanya Kounvongsa, Souliya Syphasay (71.Phatthana Syvilay), Keoviengphet Liththideth, Manolom Phomsouvanh, Kanlaya Sysomvang (80.Pangnasith Phettikone), Soukaphone Vongchiengkham, Khampheng Sayavutthi (62.Lamnao Singto). Trainer: Hans-Peter Schaller (Austria).
Goals: 0-1 Manolom Phomsouvanh (9), 1-1 Khoun Laboravy (51), 2-1 Sam El Nasa (57), 2-2 Manolom Phomsouvanh (59), 3-2 Kouch Sokumpheak (67), 4-2 Sam El Nasa (88).
Cautions: Kanlaya Sysomvang.

03.07.2011, National Stadium, Vientiane; Attendance: 9,000
Referee: Ryuji Sato (Japan)
LAOS – CAMBODIA 6-2(2-1,4-2)
LAO: Chintana Souksavath, Saynakhonevieng Phommapanya, Ketsada Souksavanh, Moukda Souksavath, Souliya Syphasay (73.Kanlaya Sysomvang), Konekham Inthammavong, Keoviengphet Liththideth, Manolom Phomsouvanh, Soukaphone Vongchiengkham, Khampheng Sayavutthi, Lamnao Singto (89.Visay Phaphouvanin). Trainer: Hans-Peter Schaller (Austria).
CAM: Ouk Mic, Pheak Rady (49.Lay Raksmey), Sok Rithy, Tieng Tiny, Touch Pancharong, Chhin Chhoeun, Sun Sopanha, Chhun Sothearath, Sam El Nasa (54.Tith Dina), Khoun Laboravy, Kouch Sokumpheak. Trainer: Lee Tae-Hoon (Korea Republic).
Goals: 1-0 Lamnao Singto (19), 2-0 Khampheng Sayavutthi (31), 2-1 Chhin Chhoeun (45), 3-1 Souliya Syphasay (47), 4-1 Lamnao Singto (55), 4-2 Kouch Sokumpheak (75), 3-2 Visay Phaphouvanin (94), 4-2 Kanlaya Sysomvang (112).
Cautions: Konekham Inthammavong / Ouk Mic, Sok Rithy, Chhun Sothearath.
(Laos won 8-6 on aggregate and advanced to the 2nd Round)

29.06.2011	Colombo	Sri Lanka - Philippines	1-1(1-0)
03.07.2011	Manila	Philippines – Sri Lanka	4-0(2-0)

29.06.2011, Sugathadasa Stadium, Colombo; Attendance: 4,000
Referee: Tayeb Shamsuzzaman (Bangladesh)
SRI LANKA - PHILIPPINES 1-1(1-0)
SRI: Manannalage Manjula Sampath Kumara Fernando, Nawarathna Athapaththu Mudiyanselage Anurudda Bandara Warakagoda, Lahiru Tharaka Silva Sembukutti Kankanamge (62.Lankesara Kolitha Chathuranga Kumara), Well Don Rohana Dinesh Ruwan Thilaka, Sumeda Dilki Kumar Wewalage, Fazlur Rahman Abdul Aziz, Chathura Gunaratne Wellala Hettige, Sanka Danushka Wijesiri, Kaiz Mohammed Shafraz, Pasqual Handi Nadeeka Pushpakumara (83.Mohamed Izmath Mohamed Zain), Mohamed Naufer Mohamed Izzadeen (67.Nimal Fernando Dehiwalage). Trainer: Jang Jung (Korea Republic).
PHI: Neil Leonard Dula Etheridge, Alexander Charles Luis Borromeo, Anton Edward Quimson del Rosario, Robert James Dazo Gier, Stephan Markus Cabizares Schröck, Ángel Aldeguer Guirado, Paul Mulders, Manuel Gelito Ott, Emelio Asada Caligdong, James Joseph Placer Younghusband, Philip James Placer Younghusband (40.Nathaniel George Payos Burkey; 76.Ian Bayona Araneta). Trainer: Hans Michael Weiß (Germany).
Goals: 1-0 Chathura Gunaratne Wellala Hettige (43), 1-1 Nathaniel George Payos Burkey (50).
Cautions: Pasqual Handi Nadeeka Pushpakumara, Kaiz Mohammed Shafraz, Nimal Fernando

Dehiwalage / James Joseph Placer Younghusband, Stephan Markus Cabizares Schröck, Alexander Charles Luis Borromeo.

03.07.2011, Rizal Memorial Stadium, Manila; Attendance: 12,500
Referee: Kim Sang-Woo (Korea Republic)
PHILIPPINES – SRI LANKA **4-0(2-0)**
PHI: Neil Leonard Dula Etheridge, Alexander Charles Luis Borromeo, Anton Edward Quimson del Rosario, Robert James Dazo Gier, Stephan Markus Cabizares Schröck, Ángel Aldeguer Guirado, Paul Mulders, Manuel Gelito Ott, James Joseph Placer Younghusband, Emelio Asada Caligdong (77.Roel Jimena Gener), Philip James Placer Younghusband (65.Ian Bayona Araneta). Trainer: Hans Michael Weiß (Germany).
SRI: Manannalage Manjula Sampath Kumara Fernando, Nawarathna Athapaththu Mudiyanselage Anurudda Bandara Warakagoda, Lankesara Kolitha Chathuranga Kumara, Well Don Rohana Dinesh Ruwan Thilaka, Sumeda Dilki Kumar Wewalage, Fazlur Rahman Abdul Aziz (36.Lahiru Tharaka Silva Sembukutti Kankanamge), Chathura Gunaratne Wellala Hettige (75.Mohamed Izmath Mohamed Zain), Sanka Danushka Wijesiri, Nimal Fernando Dehiwalage, Kaiz Mohammed Shafraz (59.Mohamed Nizam Nagur Meera), Mohamed Naufer Mohamed Izzadeen. Trainer: Jang Jung (Korea Republic).
Goals: 1-0 Emelio Asada Caligdong (19), 2-0 Philip James Placer Younghusband (43), 3-0 Ángel Guirado Aldeguer (51), 4-0 Philip James Placer Younghusband (57 penalty).
Cautions: Anton Edward Quimson del Rosario, Stephan Markus Cabizares Schröck, Alexander Charles Luis Borromeo, Ian Bayona Araneta / Well Don Rohana Dinesh Ruwan Thilaka, Chathura Gunaratne Wellala Hettige, Lahiru Tharaka Silva Sembukutti Kankanamge, Well Don Rohana Dinesh Ruwan Thilaka.
Sent off: Well Don Rohana Dinesh Ruwan Thilaka (89).
(Philippines won 5-1 on aggregate and advanced to the 2nd Round)

29.06.2011	Tursunzoda (TJK)	Afghanistan - Palestine	0-2(0-1)
03.07.2011	Al-Ram	Palestine - Afghanistan	1-1(1-0)

29.06.2011, Metallurg Stadium, Tursunzoda (Tajikistan); Attendance: 5,000
Referee: Naser Al Ghafary (Jordan)
AFGHANISTAN - PALESTINE **0-2(0-1)**
AFG: Hamidullah Yousufzai, Muqadar Qazizadah (80.Waheed Nadeem), Djelaluddin Shrityar, Faisal Sakhi Zada, Zohib Islam Amiri, Harez Arian Habib, Israfeel Kohistani, Zubayr Amiri (46.Hashmatullah Barakzai), Mohammad Yusef Mashriqi, Mohammad Bilal Arzou, Mohammad Sediq Walizada (46.Masihullah Barakzai). Trainer: Mohammad Yousef Karger.
PLE: Mohammed Abdullah Shbair, Husam Abu Saleh, Omar Jarun, Khaled Mahdi, Roberto Bishara Adauy, Aatef Abu Bilal (90.Ashraf Nomaan Al Fawaghrah), Khader Youssef Abu Hammad (77.Murad Ismail Said), Sulaiman Al Obaid, Husam Wadi, Ahmed Keshkesh (66.Ismail Al Amour), Murad Alyan. Trainer: Moussa Bezaz (Algeria).
Goals: 0-1 Murad Alyan (28), 0-2 Ismail Al Amour (89).
Cautions: Faisal Sakhi Zada, Mohammad Yusef Mashriqi, Zohib Islam Amiri.

03.07.2011, „Faisal Al-Husseini" International Stadium, Al Ram; Attendance: 9,000
Referee: Banjar Mohammed Al Dosari (Qatar)
PALESTINE - AFGHANISTAN **1-1(1-0)**
PLE: Abdullah Al Sidawi, Husam Abu Saleh, Ismail Al Amour (87.Iyad Abu Gharqoud), Abdelatif Al Bahdari, Omar Jarun, Roberto Bishara Adauy, Khader Youssef Abu Hammad (68.Murad Ismail Said), Sulaiman Al Obaid, Husam Wadi, Atef Abu Bilal (60.Ashraf Nomaan Al Fawaghrah), Murad Alyan. Trainer: Moussa Bezaz (Algeria).
AFG: Hamidullah Yousufzai, Djelaluddin Shrityar, Zohib Islam Amiri, Faisal Sakhi Zada, Israfeel Kohistani, Harez Arian Habib, Masihullah Barakzai (61.Ghulam Hazraf Niyazi), Mustafa Hadid (85.Waheed Nadeem), Mohammad Yusef Mashriqi, Mohammad Bilal Arzou, Mohammad Sediq Walizada (46.Sayed Maqsood Hashemi). Trainer: Mohammad Yousef Karger.

Goals: 1-0 Husam Wadi (11), 1-1 Mohammad Bilal Arzou (63).
Cautions: Roberto Bishara Adauy, Husam Abu Saleh / Mohammad Sediq Walizada, Israfeel Kohistani, Harez Arian Habib.
(Palestine won 3-1 on aggregate and advanced to the 2nd Round)

29.06.2011	Hồ Chí Minh City	Vietnam - Macau	6-0(3-0)
03.07.2011	Macau	Macau - Vietnam	1-7(0-4)

29.06.2011, Thong Nhat Stadium, Hồ Chí Minh City; Attendance: 20,000
Referee: Dmitriy Mashentsev (Kyrgyzstan)
VIETNAM - MACAU 6-0(3-0)
VIE: Nguyễn Mạnh Dũng, Đoàn Việt Cường, Huỳnh Quang Thanh, Nguyễn Anh Tuấn, Nguyễn Thành Long Giang, Phạm Thành Lương (77.Hoàng Đình Tùng), Phan Thanh Hưng, Phan Văn Tài Em (46.Nguyễn Minh Châu), Nguyễn Văn Quyết, Nguyễn Quang Hải (63.Nguyễn Ngọc Thanh), Lê Công Vinh. Trainer: Falko Götz (Germany).
MAC: Leong Chon Kit, Kwok Siu Tin, Lao Pak Kin, Cheang Cheng Ieong, Kong Cheng Hou, Cheung Chit Un, Che Chi Man, Wong Wa Lon, Ho Man Hou (46.Leong Ka Hang), Herculano Monteiro Soares, Niki Torrão. Trainer: Leung Sui Wing (Hong Kong).
Goals: 1-0 Lê Công Vinh (19), 2-0 Lê Công Vinh (36), 3-0 Lê Công Vinh (39 penalty), 4-0 Phạm Thành Lương (62), 5-0 Nguyễn Ngọc Thanh (67), 6-0 Nguyễn Ngọc Thanh (87).
Cautions: Đoàn Việt Cường, Hoàng Đình Tùng / Wong Wa Lon, Leong Chon Kit.

03.07.2011, Estádio Campo Desportivo, Macau; Attendance: 500
Referee: Kadhum Auda (Iraq)
MACAU - VIETNAM 1-7(0-4)
MAC: Ho Man Fai, Lam Ka Pou, Lao Pak Kin (39.Kwok Siu Tin), Cheang Cheng Ieong, Cheung Chit Un, Che Chi Man (77.Chan Man Hei), Leong Chong In (50.Leong Ka Hang), Lam Ka Chon, Herculano Monteiro Soares, Ho Man Hou, Niki Torrão. Trainer: Leung Sui Wing (Hong Kong).
VIE: Nguyễn Mạnh Dũng, Đoàn Việt Cường (60.Nguyễn Ngọc Thanh), Huỳnh Quang Thanh, Nguyễn Thành Long Giang, Trương Đình Luật, Nguyễn Minh Châu, Phạm Thành Lương (46.Nguyễn Ngọc Duy), Võ Duy Nam (74.Nguyễn Trọng Hoàng), Nguyễn Văn Quyết, Nguyễn Quang Hải, Lê Công Vinh. Trainer: Falko Götz (Germany).
Goals: 0-1 Huỳnh Quang Thanh (3), 0-2 Nguyễn Quang Hải (24), 0-3 Lê Công Vinh (29), 0-4 Lê Công Vinh (43), 1-4 Leong Ka Hang (60), 1-5 Lê Công Vinh (75), 1-6 Lê Công Vinh (82), 1-7 Huỳnh Quang Thanh (86).
Cautions: Ho Man Hou / Đoàn Việt Cường, Nguyễn Thành Long Giang.
(Vietnam won 13-1 on aggregate and advanced to the 2nd Round)

29.06.2011	Ulanbaatar	Mongolia - Myanmar	1-0(0-0)
03.07.2011	Yangon	Myanmar - Mongolia	2-0(0-0)

29.06.2011, MFF Football Centre, Ulanbaatar; Attendance: 3,500
Referee: Kim Jong-Hyeok (Korea Republic)

MONGOLIA - MYANMAR **1-0(0-0)**

MGL: Tseveensuren Ganbayar, Olzvoi Ochbayar (66.Munkhbaatar Altankhuu), Baasangyn Erdenebayar, Tserenjav Enkhjargal, Bayasgalan Garidmagnai, Pagamsuren Altantulga (86.Tsedenbal Tumenjargal), Amgalan Chinzorig, Murun Altankhuyag, Norjmoo Tsedenbal, Tsend-Ayush Khurelbaatar, Ganbaatarin Tugsbayar (69.Tsagaantsooj Munkh-Erdene). Trainer: Erdenebat Sandagdorj.

MYA: Kyaw Zin Htet, Min Ko Ko, Min Min Thu (65.Kyi Lin), Zaw Zaw Oo, Zaw Min Tun, Shwe Hlaing Win, Yan Aung Win, David Htan, Yan Aung Kyaw, Pai Soe (84.Mai Aih Naing), Kyaw Ko Ko. Trainer: Milan Živadinović (Serbia).

Goal: 1-0 Tsend-Ayush Khurelbaatar (48).

Cautions: Min Ko Ko.

Sent off: Kyaw Ko Ko (90).

03.07.2011, Thuwunna Stadium, Yangon; Attendance: 18,000
Referee: Liu Kwok Man (Hong Kong)

MYANMAR - MONGOLIA **2-0(0-0)**

MYA: Kyaw Zin Htet, Khin Maung Lwin, Min Min Thu (58.Kyaw Zayar Win), Zaw Zaw Oo, Zaw Min Tun, Yan Aung Win, David Htan (79.Kyi Lin), Yan Aung Kyaw, Pai Soe, Mai Aih Naing, Yan Paing (90.Soe Min Oo). Trainer: Milan Živadinović (Serbia).

MGL: Tseveensuren Ganbayar, Olzvoi Ochbayar, Baasangyn Erdenebayar, Tserenjav Enkhjargal, Bayasgalan Garidmagnai, Pagamsuren Altantulga (78.Gongorjav Davaa-Ochir), Amgalan Chinzorig, Tsagaantsooj Munkh-Erdene, Norjmoo Tsedenbal (89.Munkh-Od Ochkhuu), Tsend-Ayush Khurelbaatar, Murun Altankhuyag. Trainer: Erdenebat Sandagdorj.

Goals: 1-0 Pai Soe (61), 2-0 Mai Aih Naing (85).

Cautions: Min Min Thu / Olzvoi Ochbayar, Baasangyn Erdenebayar, Pagamsuren Altantulga.

Sent off: Olzvoi Ochbayar (90+1).

(*Myanmar won 2-1 on aggregate and advanced to the 2nd Round*)

23.07.2011	Buriram	Thailand - Palestine	1-0(1-0)
28.07.2011	Al-Ram	Palestine - Thailand	2-2(1-1)

23.07.2011, new I-mobile Stadium, Buriram; Attendance: 17,000
Referee: Lee Min-Hu (Korea Republic)

THAILAND - PALESTINE **1-0(1-0)**

THA: Kawin Thammasatchanan, Nattaporn Phanrit, Suttinan Phukhom, Cholratit Jantakam, Pichithpong Choeichiu, Jakkraphan Kaewprom (84.Prat Samakrat), Adul Lahso, Suchao Nuchnum, Datsakorn Thonglao, Chakrit Buathong (49.Kirati Keawsombut; 77.Suree Sukha), Teerasil Dangda. Trainer: Winfried Schäfer (Germany).

PLE: Mohamed Abdullah Shbair, Majed Mostafa Abu Seidu, Abdelatif Al Bahdari, Omar Jarun, Ismail Al Amour (90.Ashraf Nomaan Al Fawaghrah), Khaled Mahdi, Khader Yousef Abu Hammad, Murad Ismail Said (46.Hussam Wadi), Mohammed Ahmed Mahmoud Samara (54.Ali Khatib), Atef Abu Bilal, Murad Alyan. Trainer: Moussa Bezaz (Algeria).

Goal: 1-0 Jakkraphan Kaewprom (19).

Cautions: Suchao Nuchnum, Teerasil Dangda / Murad Alyan, Mohamed Abdullah Shbair, Abdelatif Al Bahdari, Majed Mostafa Abu Seidu, Ismail Al Amour, Khaled Mahdi.

28.07.2011, "Faisal Al-Husseini" International Stadium, Al-Ram; Attendance: 11,500
Referee: Salah Mohamed Al Abbasi (Bahrain)

PALESTINE - THAILAND **2-2(1-1)**

PLE: Mohamed Abdullah Shbair, Abdelatif Al Bahdari, Ahmed Harbi, Omar Jarun, Khaled Mahdi, Ismail Al Amour (75.Nadim Sulaiman Al Obaid), Khader Yousef Abu Hammad, Ashraf Nomaan Al Fawaghrah (65.Iyad Abu Gharqoud), Fahed Attal (53.Ali Khatib), Hussam Wadi, Murad Alyan. Trainer: Moussa Bezaz (Algeria).

THA: Kawin Thammasatchanan, Nattaporn Phanrit, Suree Sukha (48.Rangsan Vivatchaichok), Suttinan Phukhom, Cholratit Jantakam, Pichithpong Choeichiu, Jakkraphan Kaewprom, Suchao Nuchnum, Adul Lahso, Datsakorn Thonglao, Teerasil Dangda. Trainer: Winfried Schäfer (Germany).

Goals: 1-0 Murad Alyan (5), 1-1 Datsakorn Thonglao (33), 2-1 Murad Alyan (90), 2-2 Datsakorn Thonglao (90+5)

Cautions: Murad Alyan, Ismail Al Amour / Rangsan Vivatchaichok.

(Thailand won 3-2 on aggregate and advanced to the 3rd Round)

23.07.2011	Beirut	Lebanon – Bangladesh	4-0(2-0)
28.07.2011	Dhâkâ	Bangladesh – Lebanon	2-0(0-0)

23.07.2011, „Camille Chamoun“ Sports City Stadium, Beirut; Attendance: 2,000
Referee: Kadhum Auda Lazim (Iraq)

LEBANON – BANGLADESH **4-0(2-0)**

LIB: Elias Freijeh, Ali Al Saadi, Ramez Dayoub, Walid Ismail, Hamza Aboud, Hamzah Salameh, Abbas Ahmed Atwi (51.Tarek El Ali), Zakaria Yehya Charara (59.Hussein Dakik), Mahmoud El Ali (80.Mohammed Baqir Younis), Akram Moghrabi, Hassan Maatouk. Trainer: Johannes Theodor Bücker (Germany).

BAN: Mamun Khan, Mohamed Nasirul Islam Nasir (46.Mithun Chowdhury), Mohamed Waly Faisal (61.Atiqur Rahman Meshu), Mohamed Razaul Karim, Mohammed Sujan, Mohamed Ariful Islam Arif, Mohamed Mamunul Islam Mamun, Shakil Ahmed, Mohammed Zahid Hossain (46.Mohammed Robin), Mohamed Monaem Khan Raju, Mohamed Jahid Hassan Ameli. Trainer: Nikola Ilievski (Macedonia).

Goals: 1-0 Hassan Maatouk (16), 2-0 Mahmoud El Ali (27), 3-0 Ali Al Saadi (55), 4-0 Mahmoud El Ali (64).

Cautions: Shakil Ahmed.

28.07.2011, Bangabandhu National Stadium, Dhâkâ; Attendance: 11,000
Referee: Apisit Aonrak (Thailand)

BANGLADESH – LEBANON 2-0(0-0)

BAN: Mamun Khan, Mohamed Razaul Karim (67.Mohamed Nasirul Islam Nasir), Atiqur Rahman Meshu, Mohammed Sujan, Mohamed Ariful Islam Arif, Mohamed Mamunul Islam Mamun, Mohammed Zahid Hossain (30.Shakil Ahmed), Pranotosh Kumar Das (58.Abdul Baten Mazumder Komol), Mohamed Monaem Khan Raju, Mohamed Jahid Hassan Ameli, Mithun Chowdhury. Trainer: Nikola Ilievski (Macedonia).

LIB: Elias Freijeh, Ali Al Saadi, Ramez Dayoub, Walid Ismail, Hamza Aboud, Hamzah Salameh, Khodor Salameh, Zakaria Yehya Charara (66.Mohamed Hassan Hammoud), Mahmoud El Ali, Akram Moghrabi (79.Zoheir Abdullah), Hassan Maatouk (90+1.Imad Al Miri). Trainer: Johannes Theodor Bücker (Germany).

Goals: 1-0 Mithun Chowdhury (52), 2-0 Mohamed Jahid Hassan Ameli (88).

Cautions: Mohamed Ariful Islam Arif, Mohamed Monaem Khan Raju, Mohamed Jahid Hassan Ameli.

(Lebanon won 4-2 on aggregate and advanced to the 3rd Round)

23.07.2011	Kunming	China P.R. – Laos	7-2(1-2)
28.07.2011	Vientiane	Laos - China P.R.	1-6(0-2)

23.07.2011, Tuodong Stadium, Kunming; Attendance: 13,500
Referee: Strebre Delovski (Australia)

CHINA P.R. – LAOS 7-2(1-2)

CHN: Yang Zhi, Du Wei, Rong Hao, Liu Jianye, Li Xuepeng, Yu Hai (70.Yu Hanchao), Zheng Zhi (46.Chen Tao), Yang Hao, Hao Junmin, Deng Zhuoxiang, Gao Lin (33.Yang Xu). Trainer: Gao Hongbo.

LAO: Sourasay Keosouvandaeng, Saynakhonevieng Phommapanya, Ketsada Souksavanh, Moukda Souksavath, Souliya Syphasay (78.Kanlaya Sysomvang), Konekham Inthammavong, Keoviengphet Liththideth, Manolom Phomsouvanh (40.Souksadakone Liapvisay), Soukaphone Vongchiengkham, Visay Phaphouvanin (75.Khamphoumy Hanvilay), Khampheng Sayavutthi. Trainer: Hans-Peter Schaller (Austria).

Goals: 0-1 Soukaphone Vongchiengkham (4), 0-2 Visay Phaphouvanin (31), 1-2 Yang Xu (45+2), 2-2 Chen Tao (52), 3-2 Yang Xu (54), 4-2 Yang Xu (73), 5-2 Hao Junmin (82), 6-2 Chen Tao (88), 7-2 Hao Junmin (90+1 penalty).

Cautions: Ketsada Souksavanh, Visay Phaphouvanin, Souliya Syphasay, Soukaphone Vongchiengkham, Saynakhonevieng Phommapanya.

28.07.2011, National Stadium, Vientiane; Attendance: 13,000
Referee: Tayeb Shamsuzzaman (Bangladesh)

LAOS - CHINA P.R. 1-6(0-2)

LAO: Chintana Souksavath, Saynakhonevieng Phommapanya, Ketsada Souksavanh, Moukda Souksavath, Souliya Syphasay (58.Kanlaya Sysomvang), Konekham Inthammavong (74.Phatthana Syvilay), Keoviengphet Liththideth, Manolom Phomsouvanh, Soukaphone Vongchiengkham, Visay Phaphouvanin (62.Lamnao Singto), Khampheng Sayavutthi. Trainer: Hans-Peter Schaller (Austria).

CHN: Yang Zhi (46.Zhang Lie), Du Wei (60.Feng Xiaoting), Zhao Peng, Wu Xi, Zhang Xinxin, Li Xuepeng, Zhao Xuri, Yu Hanchao, Deng Zhuoxiang, Qu Bo (46.Feng Renliang), Yang Xu. Trainer: Gao Hongbo.

Goals: 0-1 Qu Bo (23), 0-2 Yu Hanchao (35), 1-2 Visay Phaphouvanin (47), 1-3 Deng Zhuoxiang (67), 1-4 Deng Zhuoxiang (83), 1-5 Yu Hanchao (88), 1-6 Yang Xu (90+2).

Cautions: Saynakhonevieng Phommapanya, Souliya Syphasay, Visay Phaphouvanin, Konekham Inthammavong, Lamnao Singto.

(China P.R. won 13-3 on aggregate and advanced to the 3rd Round)

23.07.2011	Aşgabat	Turkmenistan – Indonesia	1-1(1-1)
28.07.2011	Jakarta	Indonesia - Turkmenistan	4-3(3-0)

23.07.2011, Olympic Stadium, Aşgabat; Attendance: 7,500
Referee: Mohsen Torky (Iran)
TURKMENISTAN – INDONESIA 1-1(1-1)
TKM: Maksatmyrat Şamyradow, Maksim Belyh, Goçguly Goçgulyýew, Dawid Sarkisow, Bahtiýar Hojaahmedow, Nazar Çöliýew (58.Ruslan Mingazow), Myrat Hamrayew, Vyacheslav Krendelev (73.Guwanç Abylow), Artur Geworkyan, Arslanmyrat Amanow (67.Gahrymanberdi Çoňkaýew), Mämmedaly Garadanow. Trainer: Yazguly Hojageldiyew.
IDN: Ferry Rotinsulu, Ricardo Salampessy, Muhammad Roby, Zulkifli Syukur (90+3.Oktovianus Maniani), Muhammad Ridwan, Muhammad Nasuha (86.Supardi Nasir), Firman Utina (90+1.Eka Ramdani), Muhammad Ilham, Ahmad Bustomi, Boaz Theofilius Erwin Solossa, Cristian Gérard Alvaro Gonzáles. Trainer: Wilhelmus Gerardus Rijsbergen (Holland).
Goals: 1-0 Vyacheslav Krendelev (11), 1-1 Muhammad Ilham (30).
Cautions: Dawid Sarkisow, Maksim Belyh, Myrat Hamrayew / Ricardo Salampessy, Firman Utina, Muhammad Nasuha, Zulkifli Syukur, Oktovianus Maniani.
Sent off: Artur Geworkyan (76).

28.07.2011, Gelora Bung Karno Stadium, Jakarta; Attendance: 88,000
Referee: Benjamin Jon Williams (Australia)
INDONESIA - TURKMENISTAN 4-3(3-0)
IDN: Ferry Rotinsulu, Ricardo Salampessy (85.Hamka Hamzah), Muhammad Roby, Zulkifli Syukur, Muhammad Ridwan, Muhammad Nasuha, Firman Utina (75.Tony Sucipto), Muhammad Ilham (85.Oktovianus Maniani), Ahmad Bustomi, Boaz Theofilius Erwin Solossa, Cristian Gérard Alvaro Gonzáles. Trainer: Wilhelmus Gerardus Rijsbergen (Holland).
TKM: Maksatmyrat Şamyradow, Guwanç Abylow, Begli Annageldiyew (46.Serdar Annaorazow), Maksim Belyh, Goçguly Goçgulyýew, Dawid Sarkisow, Guwanç Hangeldiyew (46.Arslanmyrat Amanow), Bahtiýar Hojaahmedow, Ruslan Mingazow (63.Aleksandr Boliyan), Gahrymanberdi Çoňkaýew, Berdimyrat Şamyradow. Trainer: Yazguly Hojageldiyew.
Goals: 1-0 Cristian Gérard Alvaro Gonzáles (10), 2-0 Cristian Gérard Alvaro Gonzáles (18), 3-0 Muhammad Nasuha (42), 3-1 Muhammad Nashua (70 own goal), 4-1 Muhammad Ridwan (76), 4-2 Berdimyrat Şamyradow (83), 4-3 Gahrymanberdi Çoňkaýew (86 penalty).
Cautions: Muhammad Nasuha, Muhammad Ilham, Muhammad Ridwan / Berdimyrat Şamyradow, Bahtiýar Hojaahmedow, Gahrymanberdi Çoňkaýew, Dawid Sarkisow.
Sent off: Bahtiýar Hojaahmedow (78).
(Indonesia won 5-4 on aggregate and advanced to the 3rd Round)

23.07.2011	Hawalli	Kuwait – Philippines	3-0(1-0)
28.07.2011	Manila	Phlippines - Kuwait	1-2(1-0)

23.07.2011, "Mohammed Al Hamad" Stadium, Hawalli; Attendance: 20,000
Referee: Mohammad Abu Loum (Jordan)
KUWAIT – PHILIPPINES 3-0(1-0)
KUW: Nawaf Khaled Al Khaldi, Hussain Ali Al Fadhel, Mesaed Neda Al Enazi, Fahad Awadh Shaheen Shehan, Amer Maatooq Al Fadhel, Talal Ahmad Al Amer (78.Jarah Mohammed Al Ataiqi), Fahad Ebrahim Al Ansari, Waleed Ali Hussein Jumah, Fahad Saleh Hussain Al Enezi (58.Abdulaziz Ashwan), Bader Ahmed Al Mutawa, Yousef Nasser Al Sulaiman (89.Ali Abdulrahman Abdulrahim Al Kandari). Trainer: Goran Tufegdžić (Serbia).
PHI: Neil Leonard Dula Etheridge, Anton Edward Quimson del Rosario, Jason Abbott Abantao Sabio, Robert James Dazo Gier, Jason Nicolas Maria Dantes de Jong, Ángel Aldeguer Guirado (90+2.Misagh Medina Bahadoran), Ray Anthony Pepito Jónsson, Manuel Gelito Ott, James Joseph Placer Younghusband, Emelio Asada Caligdong (90.Simon Clive Barbon Greatwich), Philip James Placer

Younghusband. Trainer: Hans Michael Weiß (Germany).
Goals: 1-0 Yousef Nasser Al Sulaiman (17), 2-0 Mesaed Neda Al Enazi (68), 3-0 Fahad Ebrahim Al Ansari (85).
Cautions: Hussain Ali Al Fadhel, Mesaed Neda Al Enazi / Jason Nicolas Maria Dantes de Jong, Simon Clive Barbon Greatwich.

28.07.2011, Rizal Memorial Stadium, Manila; Attendance: 13,000
Referee: Liu Kwok Man (Hong Kong)
PHLIPPINES - KUWAIT **1-2(1-0)**
PHI: Neil Leonard Dula Etheridge, Alexander Charles Luis Borromeo, Anton Edward Quimson del Rosario, Robert James Dazo Gier, Stephan Markus Cabizares Schröck, Ángel Aldeguer Guirado (80.Misagh Medina Bahadoran), Ray Anthony Pepito Jónsson, Manuel Gelito Ott, James Joseph Placer Younghusband, Emelio Asada Caligdong (88.Ian Bayona Araneta), Philip James Placer Younghusband. Trainer: Hans Michael Weiß (Germany).
KUW: Nawaf Khaled Al Khaldi, Ahmad Saad Al Rashidi, Mesaed Neda Al Enazi (75.Saleh Shaikh Al Hendi), Mohamed Sinad, Fahad Ebrahim Al Ansari, Jarah Mohammed Al Ataiqi (75.Saleh Al Sheikh Al Hendi), Khaled Ali Nasser Al Qahtani, Waleed Ali Hussein Jumah, Abdulaziz Ashwan, Bader Ahmed Al Mutawa, Yousef Nasser Al Sulaiman (63.Talal Ahmad Al Amer). Trainer: Goran Tufegdžić (Serbia).
Goals: 1-0 Stephan Markus Cabizares Schröck (45), 1-1 Yousef Nasser Al Sulaiman (63), 1-2 Waleed Ali Hussein Jumah (85).
Cautions: Ángel Aldeguer Guirado, Stephan Markus Cabizares Schröck, Anton Edward Quimson del Rosario / Fahad Ebrahim Al Ansari.
Sent off: Fahad Ebrahim Al Ansari (63).
(Kuwait won 5-1 on aggregate and advanced to the 3rd Round)

23.07.2011	Muscat	Oman – Myanmar	2-0(1-0) Awarded 3-0
28.07.2011	Yangon	Myanmar - Oman	0-2(0-2) Awarded 0-3

23.07.2011, Seeb Stadium, Muscat; Attendance: 6,300
Referee: Ali Sabbagh (Lebanon)
OMAN – MYANMAR **2-0(1-0)***
OMA: Ali Abdullah Harib Al Habsi, Abdulrahman Saleh Khalfan Al Alawi (49.Rashid Jumaa Mubarak Al Farsi), Mohammed Abdullah Mubarak Al Balushi, Saad Suhail Jumaa Al Mukhaini, Mohammed Saleh Al Maslami, Ahmed Hadid Thuwaini Al Mukhaini, Fawzi Bashir Rajab Bait Doorbeen, Qasim Said Sanjoor Hardan (72.Juma Darwish Al Mashri), Ahmed Mubarak Obaid Al Mahaijri, Ismail Sulaiman Ashoor Al Ajmi, Amad Ali Suleiman Al Hosni (46.Hassan Rabia Suwaidan Al Hosni). Trainer: Paul Le Guen (France).
MYA: Kyaw Zin Htet, Khin Maung Lwin, Min Min Thu, Zaw Min Tun, Yan Aung Win, Moe Win, Yan Aung Kyaw, Kyaw Zayar Win, Kyaw Ko Ko, Mai Aih Naing (59.Pai Soe), Yan Paing (90.Kyi Lin). Trainer: Sann Win.
Goals: 1-0 Amad Ali Suleiman Al Hosni (22), 2-0 Ismail Sulaiman Ashoor Al Ajmi (79).
**Please note: FIFA awarded the match 3-0 for Oman.*

28.07.2011, Thuwunna Youth Training Center Stadium, Yangon; Attendance: 30,000
Referee: Ryuji Sato (Japan)
MYANMAR - OMAN 0-2(0-2)
MYA: Kyaw Zin Htet, Khin Maung Lwin, Min Min Thu, Zaw Min Tun, Moe Win, Yan Aung Win, Yan Aung Kyaw, Pai Soe, Kyaw Ko Ko, Mai Aih Naing, Yan Paing. Trainer: Sann Win.
OMA: Ali Abdullah Harib Al Habsi, Mohammed Abdullah Mubarak Al Balushi, Rashid Jumaa Mubarak Al Farsi, Mohammed Saleh Al Maslami, Saad Suhail Jumaa Al Mukhaini, Ahmed Hadid Thuwaini Al Mukhaini, Juma Darwish Al Mashri, Fawzi Bashir Rajab Bait Doorbeen, Ahmed Mubarak Obaid Al Mahaijri, Ismail Sulaiman Ashoor Al Ajmi, Amad Ali Suleiman Al Hosni. Trainer: Paul Le Guen (France).
Goals: 0-1 Amad Ali Suleiman Al Hosni (23), 0-2 Ismail Sulaiman Ashoor Al Ajmi (39).
Cautions: Yan Paing, Zaw Min Tun.
**Please note: Due to a pitch invasion, the match was abandoned after 45+2 minutes with Oman leading 2–0; FIFA awarded the match 3-0 for the hosts.*
(Oman won 6-0 on aggregate and advanced to the 3rd Round)

23.07.2011	Dammam	Saudi Arabia – Hong Kong	3-0(2-0)
28.07.2011	Hong Kong	Hong Kong - Saudi Arabia	0-5(0-1)

23.07.2011, "Prince Mohamed bin Fahd" Stadium, Dammam; Attendance: 20,354
Referee: Vladislav Tseytlin (Uzbekistan)
SAUDI ARABIA – HONG KONG 3-0(2-0)
KSA: Hassan Bader Al Otaibi, Osama Mabrouk Awad Al Muwallad Al Harbi, Osama Abdul Razzaq Al Hawsawi, Abdullah Jaman Shuhail, Taisir Jaber Al Jassam, Hassan Muath Fallatah, Ahmed Ibrahim Otaif, Mohammed Noor Al Hawsawi (78.Khaled Asiri Al Zealaiy), Nassir Ali Al Shamrani, Nawaf Shaker Al Abed, Yousef Mansoor Al Salem (84.Saud Hamood Hasan). Trainer: Rogério Moraes Lourenço (Brazil).
HKG: Yapp Hung Fai, Sham Kwok Fai, Chak Ting Fung (52.Lee Hong Lim), Lo Kwan Yee, Lee Chi Ho, Chan Wai Ho, Chu Siu Kei (62.So Wai Chuen), Leung Chun Pong, Kwok Kin Pong, Chan Siu Ki, Lee Wai Lim (84.Ye Jia). Trainer: Liu Chun Fai.
Goals: 1-0 Nassir Ali Al Shamrani (45+1), 2-0 Osama Mabrouk Awad Al Muwallad Al Harbi (45+3), 3-0 Nassir Ali Al Shamrani (47).
Cautions: Hassan Muath Fallatah, Nawaf Shaker Al Abed / Lee Chi Ho, Chak Ting Fung, Chan Siu Ki, Kwok Kin Pong.

28.07.2011, Siu Sai Wan Sports Ground, Hong Kong; Attendance: 1,402
Referee: Võ Minh Trí (Vietnam)
HONG KONG - SAUDI ARABIA 0-5(0-1)
HKG: Yapp Hung Fai, So Wai Chuen, Lee Chi Ho (84.Sham Kwok Fai), Chan Wai Ho, Leung Chun Pong, Kwok Kin Pong, Wong Chin Hung, Lo Kwan Yee, Ye Jia (80.Chu Siu Kei), Chan Siu Ki, Lee Wai Lim (80.Lee Hong Lim). Trainer: Liu Chun Fai.
KSA: Hassan Bader Al Otaibi, Osama Mabrouk Awad Al Muwallad Al Harbi (72.Hamad Mohsen Al Montashari), Hassan Muath Fallatah, Osama Abdul Razzaq Al Hawsawi, Abdullah Jaman Shuhail, Taisir Jaber Al Jassam, Ahmed Ibrahim Otaif (74.Ibrahim Ghaleb), Mohammed Noor Al Hawsawi, Nassir Ali Al Shamrani, Nawaf Shaker Al Abed, Yousef Mansoor Al Salem (66.Mohammad Al Sahlawi). Trainer: Rogério Moraes Lourenço (Brazil).
Goals: 0-1 Hassan Muath Fallatah (34), 0-2 Mohammed Noor Al Hawsawi (71 penalty), 0-3 Nassir Ali Al Shamrani (73), 0-4 Mohammad Al Sahlawi (78), 0-5 Osama Abdul Razzaq Al Hawsawi (90+2).
Cautions: Chan Siu Ki, Chan Wai Ho, Kwok Kin Pong / Nassir Ali Al Shamrani, Nawaf Shaker Al Abed, Osama Mabrouk Awad Al Muwallad Al Harbi, Mohammad Al Sahlawi, Abdullah Jaman Shuhail.
Sent off: Leung Chun Pong (70).
(Saudi Arabia won 8-0 on aggregate and advanced to the 3rd Round)

23.07.2011	Tehran	Iran – Maldives	4-0(1-0)
28.07.2011	Malé	Maldives - Iran	0-1(0-1)

23.07.2011, Azadi Stadium, Tehran; Attendance: 20,195
Referee: Chaiya Alee Mahapab (Thailand)

IRAN – MALDIVES 4-0(1-0)

IRN: Seyed Mehdi Rahmati Osgouei, Seyed Hadi Aghily Anvar, Khosro Heydari, Seyed Jalal Hosseini Khoshkebejari, Mehrdad Pooladi (62.Ehsan Hajsafi), Ghasem Haddadifar, Maziar Zare Eshghdoust (60.Mohammad Ghazi Najafabadi), Mohammad Ali Karimi Pashaki, Hadi Norouzi (83.Saeid Daghighi Masouleh), Karim Ansarifard, Mohamad Reza Khalatbari. Trainer: Carlos Manuel Brito Leal Queiroz (Portugal).

MDV: Imran Mohamed, Assad Abdul Ghani (68.Ahmed Abdulla), Mohamed Ibrahim Sabah, Mohamed Jameel, Muhammad Umair, Akram Abdul Ghani, Mohamed Arif, Mukhthar Naseer (50.Shamweel Qasim), Ibrahim Fazeel, Ashad Ali (76.Ismail Faruhad), Ali Ashfaq. Trainer: Diego Andrés Cruciani (Argentina).

Goals: 1-0 Karim Ansarifard (4), 2-0 Karim Ansarifard 61), 3-0 Mohammad Ali Karimi Pashaki (68), 4-0 Saeid Daghighi Masouleh (86).

Cautions: Karim Ansarifard, Maziar Zare Eshghdoust, Mohammad Ali Karimi Pashaki / Mukhthar Naseer, Imran Mohamed, Ali Ashfaq, Mohamed Ibrahim Sabah.

28.07.2011, Rasmee Dhandu Stadium, Malé; Attendance: 9,000
Referee: Kim Sang-Woo (Korea Republic)

MALDIVES - IRAN 0-1(0-1)

MDV: Imran Mohamed, Mohamed Jameel, Ahmed Saeed, Muhammad Umair, Ahmed Shafiu, Akram Abdul Ghani, Mohamed Arif, Mukhthar Naseer (81.Shamweel Qasim), Ibrahim Fazeel, Ashad Ali (86.Ismail Mohamed), Ali Ashfaq. Trainer: Diego Andrés Cruciani (Argentina).

IRN: Seyed Mehdi Rahmati Osgouei, Seyed Hadi Aghily Anvar (69.Mohammad Nosrati), Khosro Heydari, Seyed Jalal Hosseini Khoshkebejari, Mehrdad Pooladi, Ghasem Haddadifar, Maziar Zare Eshghdoust (60.Sahand-Pejman Nouri Roudsari), Mohammad Ali Karimi Pashaki, Hadi Norouzi (77.Milad Zeneyedpour), Karim Ansarifard, Mohamad Reza Khalatbari. Trainer: Carlos Manuel Brito Leal Queiroz (Portugal).

Goal: 0-1 Mohamad Reza Khalatbari (45+1).

Cautions: Ahmed Saeed, Ahmed Shafiu, Mukhthar Naseer, Ashad Ali / Seyed Hadi Aghily Anvar, Maziar Zare Eshghdoust, Karim Ansarifard, Sahand-Pejman Nouri Roudsari.

(Iran won 5-0 on aggregate and advanced to the 3rd Round)

23.07.2011	Amman(JOR)	Syria – Tajikistan	2-1(1-0) Awarded 0-3
28.07.2011	Tursunzoda	Tajiistan - Syria	0-4(0-2) Awarded 3-0

23.07.2011, "King Abdullah" Stadium, Amman (Jordan); Attendance: 2,500
Referee: Nasser Darwish (Jordan)

SYRIA – TAJIKISTAN 2-1(1-0)*

SYR: Kawa Hesso, Belal Abduldaim (56.Burhan Sahyouni), Ali Dyab, Mohamad Estanbeli (70.Raja Rafe), Nadim Sabagh (81.Majed Homsi), Feras Fissal Esmaeel, Mahmoud Nezaa Al Amenah, Abdelrazaq Al Hussain, Jehad Al Hussain Fadel, Firas Mohamad Al Khatib, George Mourad. Trainer: Nizar Mahrous.

TJK: Alisher Tuychiev, Farrukh Choriev, Sokhib Savankulov, Nuriddin Davronov, Asatullo Nurulloev, Jamshed Ismailov, Ibrahim Rabimov, Dilshod Vasiev (90+1.Furug Qodirov), Yusuf Rabiev (83.Farkhod Tokhirov), Makhmadali Sadykov, Kamil Saidov (73.Fatkhullo Fatkhuloev). Trainer: Pulod Kodirov.

Goals: 1-0 George Mourad (45+1), 1-1 Kamil Saidov (47), 2-1 Raja Rafe (77).
**FIFA awarded Tajikistan a 3–0 win because Syria fielded an ineligible player (George Mourad).*

28.07.2011, Metallurg Stadium, Tursunzoda; Attendance: 9,000
Referee: Dmitriy Mashentsev (Kyrgyzstan)
TAJIISTAN - SYRIA **0-4(0-2)***
TJK: Alisher Tuychiev, Farrukh Choriev, Davronjon Ergashev, Sokhib Savankulov, Makhmadali Sadykov, Nuriddin Davronov (46.Dilshod Vasiev), Jamshed Ismailov, Khurshed Makhmudov (73.Davrondzhon Tukhtasunov), Yusuf Rabiev, Ibrahim Rabimov, Kamil Saidov (39.Fatkhullo Fatkhuloev). Trainer: Pulod Kodirov.
SYR: Kawa Hesso, Belal Abduldaim, Ali Dyab, Majed Homsi (62.Maher Al Sayed), Nadim Sabagh, Feras Fissal Esmaeel, Mahmoud Nezaa Al Amenah, Abdelrazaq Al Hussain, Jehad Al Hussain Fadel (71.George Mourad), Firas Mohamad Al Khatib, Raja Rafe (78.Samer Awadh). Trainer: Nizar Mahrous.
Goals: 0-1 Raja Rafe (6), 0-2 Raja Rafe (35), 0-3 Nadim Sabagh (53), 0-4 Farrukh Choriev (86 own goal).
**FIFA awarded Tajikistan a 3–0 win because Syria fielded an ineligible player (George Mourad).*
(Tajikistan won 6-0 on aggregate and advanced to the 3rd Round)

23.07.2011	Doha	Qatar – Vietnam	3-0(1-0)
28.07.2011	Hà Nội	Vietnam - Qatar	2-1(0-1)

23.07.2011, "Jassim bin Hamad" Stadium, Doha; Attendance: 6,786
Referee: Hamad Madhad Saif Al Badwawi (United Arab Emirates)
QATAR – VIETNAM **3-0(1-0)**
QAT: Qasem Abdulhamed Burhan, Bilal Mohammed Rajab, Ibrahim Majid Abdulmajid, Meshal Abdullah Mubarak Budawood, Mohammed Kasola, Lawrence Awuley Quaye, Wesam Abdulmajid Rizik, Ahmed Mohamed Al Sayed (83.Fábio César Montezine), Khalfan Ibrahim Al Khalfan (90+2.Hamid Ismail Khalifa), Mohammed Razak (59.Yusef Ahmed Ali), Andrés Sebastián Soria Quintana. Trainer: Milovan Rajevac (Serbia).
VIE: Nguyễn Mạnh Dũng, Huỳnh Quang Thanh, Nguyễn Thành Long Giang, Nguyễn Văn Biển, Trần Chí Công, Trần Đình Đồng (59.Nguyễn Quang Hải), Lê Tấn Tài, Nguyễn Văn Quyết (70.Pham Thành Lương), Phan Văn Tài Em, Lê Công Vinh (75.Nguyễn Ngọc Thanh), Nguyễn Trọng Hoàng. Trainer: Falko Götz (Germany).
Goals: 1-0 Mohammed Kasola (6), 2-0 Meshal Abdullah Mubarak Budawood (51), 3-0 Yusef Ahmed Ali (68).
Cautions: Wesam Abdulmajid Rizik, Nguyễn Quang Hải, Trần Chí Công.

28.07.2011, "Mỹ Đình" National Stadium, Hà Nội; Attendance: 20,000
Referee: Daniel Peter Green (Australia)
VIETNAM - QATAR **2-1(0-1)**
VIE: Nguyễn Mạnh Dũng, Đoàn Việt Cường, Huỳnh Quang Thanh, Nguyễn Thành Long Giang, Trần Chí Công, Lê Tấn Tài, Pham Thành Lương (62.Nguyễn Văn Quyết), Phan Văn Tài Em (34.Nguyễn Minh Châu), Lê Công Vinh, Nguyễn Trọng Hoàng, Nguyễn Ngọc Thanh (70.Nguyễn Quang Hải). Trainer: Falko Götz (Germany).
QAT: Qasem Abdulhamed Burhan, Mohamed Mousa Abbas Ali, Ibrahim Majid Abdulmajid, Meshal Abdullah Mubarak Budawood, Mohammed Kasola, Lawrence Awuley Quaye, Wesam Abdulmajid Rizik, Ahmed Mohamed Al Sayed (68.Mohammed Razak), Khalfan Ibrahim Al Khalfan, Yusef Ahmed Ali (46.Fábio César Montezine), Andrés Sebastián Soria Quintana (90.Hamid Ismail Khalifa). Trainer: Milovan Rajevac (Serbia).
Goals: 0-1 Yusef Ahmed Ali (16), 1-1 Nguyễn Trọng Hoàng (60), 2-1 Nguyễn Quang Hải (78).
Cautions: Đoàn Việt Cường, Pham Thành Lương, Trần Chí Công / Wesam Abdulmajid Rizik, Khalfan Ibrahim Al Khalfan, Meshal Abdullah Mubarak Budawood.
(Qatar won 4-2 on aggregate and advanced to the 3rd Round)

23.07.2011	Arbil	Iraq – Yemen	2-0(1-0)
28.07.2011	Al Ain (UAE)	Yemen - Iraq	0-0

23.07.2011, "Franso Hariri" Stadium, Arbil; Attendance: 20,000
Referee: Valentin Kovalenko (Uzbekistan)

IRAQ – YEMEN **2-0(1-0)**

IRQ: Mohammed Gassid Kadhim Al Jaberi, Ali Hussein Rehema Al Ka'abi Al Mutairi, Bassim Abbas Gatea Al Ogaili, Samal Saeed Mujbel, Salam Shakir Ali (46.Mahdi Karim Ajeel), Muthana Khalid Salih Al Masloukhi, Qusay Muneer Abboodi Al Hussein, Karrar Jassim Mohammed Al Mahmodi, Hawar Mulla Mohammed Taher Zibari, Alaa Abdul-Zahra Khashan Al Azzawi (83.Samer Saeed Mujbel), Younis Mahmoud Khalaf (90.Amjad Radhi Yousif Al Janabi). Trainer: Wolfgang Sidka (Germany).

YEM: Salem Abdullah Awad Saeed, Zaher Mohammed Farid Al Fadhli, Ahmed Sadeq Al Khamri, Nazar Riziq, Fuad Abdo Mohammed Al Ammari, Haitham Abdo Saeed Thabit Al Asbahi (69.Hussein Ahmed Al Ghazi), Ala'a Mohammed Abdullah Al Sassi, Hamada Ahmed Mohammed Al Zubairi, Munassar Awadh Abdullah Ba Haj, Khaled Hassan Hussein Baleid (78.Mohammed Alwah), Ayman Al Hajri (66.Awsam Omar Al Sayed). Trainer: Amine Al Sunaini.

Goals: 1-0 Hawar Mulla Mohammed Taher Zibari (9), 2-0 Alaa Abdul-Zahra Khashan Al Azzawi (63).

Cautions: Munassar Awadh Abdullah Ba Haj.

28.07.2011, "Sheikh Khalifa" International Stadium, Al Ain (United Arab Emirates); Attendance: 1,500
Referee: Muhsen Basma (Syria)

YEMEN - IRAQ **0-0**

YEM: Salem Abdullah Awad Saeed, Zaher Mohammed Farid Al Fadhli, Ahmed Sadeq Al Khamri, Nazar Riziq, Fuad Abdo Mohammed Al Ammari, Haitham Abdo Saeed Thabit Al Asbahi (58.Hussein Ahmed Al Ghazi), Ala'a Mohammed Abdullah Al Sassi, Hamada Ahmed Mohammed Al Zubairi, Munassar Awadh Abdullah Ba Haj, Khaled Hassan Hussein Baleid (64.Ahmed Ali Al Dhaheri), Ayman Al Hajri (79.Wahid Mohammad Al Khayat). Trainer: Amine Al Sunaini.

IRQ: Mohammed Gassid Kadhim Al Jaberi, Ali Hussein Rehema Al Ka'abi Al Mutairi, Bassim Abbas Gatea Al Ogaili, Samal Saeed Mujbel, Mahdi Karim Ajeel, Muthana Khalid Salih Al Masloukhi, Qusay Muneer Abboodi Al Hussein, Karrar Jassim Mohammed Al Mahmodi (86.Samer Saeed Mujbel), Hawar Mulla Mohammed Taher Zibari (61.Ahmad Ayad Anwar), Alaa Abdul-Zahra Khashan Al Azzawi, Younis Mahmoud Khalaf (90+4.Amjad Radhi Yousif Al Janabi). Trainer: Wolfgang Sidka (Germany).

Cautions: Ahmed Sadeq Al Khamri / Younis Mahmoud Khalaf, Bassim Abbas Gatea Al Ogaili, Muthana Khalid Salih Al Masloukhi.

(Iraq won 2-0 on aggregate and advanced to the 3rd Round)

23.07.2011	Singapore	Singapore – Malaysia	5-3(4-1)
28.07.2011	Luala Lumpur	Malaysia - Singapore	1-1(0-0)

23.07.2011, Jalan Besar Stadium, Singapore; Attendance: 6,000
Referee: Nawaf Abdullah Ghayyath Shukralla (Bahrain)

SINGAPORE – MALAYSIA 5-3(4-1)

SIN: Mohamad Izwan Mahbud, Daniel Mark Bennett, Muhammad Safuwan Baharudin, Juma'at Jantan (90+3.Mohamad Shaiful Esah Nain), Ismail Yunos, Fahrudin Mustafić, Hariss Harun, Mohammad Shahril Ishak (69.Shahdan Sulaiman), Shi Jiayi, Qiu Li (90.Fazrul Nawaz Shahul Hameed), Aleksandar Đurić. Trainer: Radojko Avramović (Serbia).
MAS: Mohd Sharbinee Allawee Ramli, Mahali Jasuli, Mohamad Fadhli Mohd Shas, Mohd Asraruddin Putra Omar, Ismail Faruqi Asha'ri (46.Mohd Amirul Hadi Zainal), Mohd Azmi Muslim, Mohd Safiq Rahim, Mohammad Amar Rohidan, Kunanlan Subramaniam, Ahmad Fakri Saarani (64.Mohd Amri Yahyah), Mohammad Safee Mohd Sali (83.Izzaq Faris Ramlan). Trainer: Datuk Krishnasamy Rajagopal.
Goals: 0-1 Mohammad Safee Mohd Sali (1), 1-1 Aleksandar Đurić (7), 2-1 Qiu Li (22), 3-1 Fahrudin Mustafić (44), 4-1 Shi Jiayi (45), 4-2 Mohd Amri Yahyah (70), 4-3 Mohammad Safee Mohd Sali (71), 5-3 Aleksandar Đurić (82).
Cautions: Ismail Yunos, Qiu Li / Ahmad Fakri Saarani.
Sent off: Mohd Safiq Rahim (51), Ismail Yunos (55).

28.07.2011, National Stadium, Bukit Jalil, Kuala Lumpur; Attendance: 90,000
Referee: Hiroyoshi Takayama (Japan)

MALAYSIA - SINGAPORE 1-1(0-0)

MAS: Khairul Fahmi Che Mat, Mahali Jasuli, Mohamad Fadhli Mohd Shas, Mohd Asraruddin Putra Omar, Mohd Aidil Zafuan Abdul Razak (22.Mohd Azmi Muslim), Mohd Amirul Hadi Zainal, Ismail Faruqi Asha'ri (63.Kandasamy Gurusamy), Mohammad Amar Rohidan, Kunanlan Subramaniam, Mohd Amri Yahyah (71.Ahmad Fakri Saarani), Mohammad Safee Mohd Sali. Trainer: Datuk Krishnasamy Rajagopal.
SIN: Mohamad Izwan Mahbud, Daniel Mark Bennett, Muhammad Safuwan Baharudin, Mohamad Shaiful Esah Nain (83.Mohamad Abdul), Juma'at Jantan, Fahrudin Mustafić, Hariss Harun, Mohammad Shahril Ishak (79.Fazrul Nawaz Shahul Hameed), Shi Jiayi, Qiu Li, Aleksandar Đurić. Trainer: Radojko Avramović (Serbia).
Goals: 1-0 Mohammad Safee Mohd Sali (58), 1-1 Shi Jiayi (73).
Cautions: Ahmad Fakri Saarani / Shi Jiayi, Daniel Mark Bennett, Shaiful Esah Nain, Mohamad Izwan Mahbud.
Sent off: Ahmad Fakri Saarani (71).
(*Singapore won 6-4 on aggregate and advanced to the 3rd Round*)

23.07.2011	Tashkent	Uzbekistan – Kyrgyzstan	4-0(1-0)
28.07.2011	Bishkek	Kyrgyzstan - Uzbekistan	0-3(0-0)

23.07.2011, Pakhtakor Markaziy Stadium, Tashkent; Attendance: 20,257
Referee: Abdullah Mohamed Balideh (Qatar)

UZBEKISTAN – KYRGYZSTAN 4-0(1-0)

UZB: Ignatiy Nesterov, Shavkat Mullajanov, Islom Tuhtahujaev, Vitaliy Denisov, Stanislav Andreyev, Viktor Karpenko (76.Javlon Ibragimov), Azizbek Haydarov, Timur Kapadze, Server Djeparov (66.Bakhodyr Nasymov), Marat Bikmaev (57.Ulugbek Bakaev), Aleksandr Geynrikh. Trainer: Vadim Abramov.
KGZ: Vladislav Volkov (74.Ruslan Amirov), Marat Adzhiniyazov, Davron Askarov, Azamat Baimatov, Valeriy Kichin (59.Shuhrat Rahmanov), Kursanbek Sheratov, Veniamin Shumeyko, Ruslan Sydykov, Anatoliy Vlasichev, Mirlan Murzaev (70.Vladimir Khoroshunov), Kayumzhan Sharipov. Trainer: Marat Dzhumakeev.

Goals: 1-0 Aleksandr Geynrikh (28), 2-0 Marat Bikmaev (49), 3-0 Server Djeparov (56), 4-0 Ulugbek Bakaev (90+2).
Cautions: Azamat Baimatov, Davron Askarov, Veniamin Shumeyko, Marat Adzhiniyazov.

28.07.2011, Spartak Stadium, Bishkek; Attendance: 14,700
Referee: Ali Hasan Ebrahim Abdulnabi (Bahrain)
KYRGYZSTAN - UZBEKISTAN 0-3(0-0)
KGZ: Ruslan Amirov, Marat Adzhiniyazov, Davron Askarov, Azamat Baimatov, Kursanbek Sheratov, Ruslan Sydykov, Ruslan Djamshidov (46.Kayumzhan Sharipov), Aybek Orozaliev, Shuhrat Rahmanov, Anatoliy Vlasichev, Mirlan Murzaev. Trainer: Marat Dzhumakeev.
UZB: Ignatiy Nesterov, Shavkat Mullajanov, Islom Tuhtahujaev, Salim Mustafayev, Stanislav Andreyev, Viktor Karpenko (68.Javlon Ibragimov), Timur Kapadze (74.Jasur Hasanov), Lutfulla Turayev, Server Djeparov, Ulugbek Bakaev (63.Bakhodyr Nasymov), Aleksandr Geynrikh. Trainer: Vadim Abramov.
Goals: 0-1 Viktor Karpenko (47), 0-2 Bakhodyr Nasymov (65), 0-3 Bakhodyr Nasymov (90).
Cautions: Shuhrat Rahmanov, Kursanbek Sheratov / Salim Mustafayev, Shavkat Mullajanov.
(Uzbekistan won 7-0 on aggregate and advanced to the 3rd Round)

23.07.2011	Al Ain	United Arab Emirates – India	3-0(2-0)
28.07.2011	New Delhi	India - United Arab Emirates	2-2(0-1)

23.07.2011, "Sheikh Khalifa" International Stadium, Al Ain; Attendance: 3,179
Referee: Banjari Mohammed Al Dosari (Qatar)
UNITED ARAB EMIRATES – INDIA 3-0(2-0)
UAE: Ali Khaseif Humad Khaseif Housani, Mohamed Ahmed Ali Gharib Juma, Hamdan Ismaeel Mohammed Al Kamali, Yousef Jaber Naser Al Hammadi, Waleed Abbas Murad Yousuf Al Balooshi, Amer Abdulrahman Abdullah Hussein Al Hammadi, Ali Ahmad Ali Mohammed Al Wehaibi (55.Theyab Awana Ahmed Hussein Al Musabi), Amir Mubarak Al Hammadi (88.Ahmed Khamis Ali Al Abri), Ismaeel Salem Ismaeel Saeed Al Hammadi, Mohamed Saeed Rashed Saiwed Al Shehhi (69.Ahmed Jumaa Anbar Mubarak Al Araimi Al Junaibi), Ahmed Khalil Sebait Mubarak Al Junaibi. Trainer: Srečko Katanec (Slovenia).
IND: Subrata Pal, Samir Subaj Naik, Moiranghtem Govin Singh, Syed Rahim Nabi, Debabrata Roy, Raju Eknath Gaikwad, Climax Lawrence, Steven Benedict Dias (28.Karanjit Singh), Mehtab Hossain (57.Jewel Raja Shaikh), Sunil Chhetri (84.Lalrindika Ralte), Jeje Lalpekhlua. Trainer: Armando Agnelo Colaço.
Goals: 1-0 Hamdan Ismaeel Mohammed Al Kamali (21), 2-0 Mohamed Saeed Rashed Saiwed Al Shehhi (29), 3-0 Ismaeel Salem Ismaeel Saeed Al Hammadi (82).
Cautions: Ismaeel Salem Ismaeel Saeed Al Hammadi / Syed Rahim Nabi, Mehtab Hossain.
Sent off: Debabrata Roy (20), Subrata Pal (23).

28.07.2011, Ambedkar Stadium, New Delhi; Attendance: 13,000
Referee: Malik Abdul Malik Abdul Bashir (Singapore)
INDIA - UNITED ARAB EMIRATES 2-2(0-1)
IND: Karanjit Singh, Samir Subaj Naik, Syed Rahim Nabi, Raju Eknath Gaikwad, Climax Lawrence, Steven Benedict Dias (62.Lalrindika Ralte), Clifford Rayes Miranda (84.Jewel Raja Shaikh), Gouramangi Moirangthem Singh, Mehtab Hossain, Sunil Chhetri, Jeje Lalpekhlua. Trainer: Armando Agnelo Colaço.
UAE: Ali Khaseif Humad Khaseif Housani, Hamdan Ismaeel Mohammed Al Kamali, Yousef Jaber Naser Al Hammadi, Khalid Sebil Ibrahim Ahmed Lashkari (90.Faris Jumaa Hassan Al Saadi), Waleed Abbas Murad Yousuf Al Balooshi, Amer Abdulrahman Abdullah Hussein Al Hammadi, Ali Ahmad Ali Mohammed Al Wehaibi, Amir Mubarak Al Hammadi (88.Mohammed Fawzi Jawhar Faraj Abdullah Al Jahwar), Ismaeel Salem Ismaeel Saeed Al Hammadi, Mohamed Saeed Rashed Saiwed Al Shehhi, Ahmed Khalil Sebait Mubarak Al Junaibi (77.Saeed Salem Saleh Salem Al Kathiri). Trainer: Srečko Katanec (Slovenia).

Goals: 0-1 Mohamed Saeed Rashed Saiwed Al Shehhi (39), 0-2 Ali Ahmad Ali Mohammed Al Wehaibi (71), 1-2 Jeje Lalpekhlua (73), 2-2 Gouramangi Moirangthem Singh (90+2).
Cautions: Sunil Chhetri.
(United Arab Emirates won 5-2 on aggregate and advanced to the 3rd Round)

23.07.2011	Amman	Jordan - Nepal	9-0(4-0)
28.07.2011	Kathmandu	Nepal - Jordan	1-1(0-0)

23.07.2011, Amman International Stadium, Amman; Attendance: 17,000
Referee: Yadollah Jahanbazi (Iran)
JORDAN - NEPAL **9-0(4-0)**
JOR: Amer Shafia Mahmoud Sabbah, Anas Walid Khaled Bani Yaseen, Bashar Mustafa Bani Yaseen, Suleiman Mawafaq Al Salman (71.Anas Jamal Mohammad Hijah), Fathi Omar Othman Basem, Baha'a Abdel-Rahman Mustafa Suleiman, Shadi Nadmi Abu Hashash (85.Saeed Hassan Al Murjan), Amer Deeb Mohammad Khalil, Hassan Mahmoud Abdel Fatah, Abdallah Khaled Deeb Salim (78.Hamza Ali Khaled Al Dardour), Ahmed Hayel Ibrahim. Trainer: Adnan Hamad Majeed Al Abbasi (Iraq).
NEP: Kiran Chemzong, Rohit Chand, Bikash Singh Chhetri, Biraj Maharjan, Sagar Thapa, Nirajan Khadka, Sandeep Rai (67.Rabin Shrestha), Shiva Shrestha, Bhola Nath Silwal, Anil Gurung (88.Santosh Sahukhala), Ju Manu Rai (35.Bharat Khawas). Trainer: Graham Paul Roberts (England).
Goals: 1-0 Hassan Mahmoud Abdel Fatah (10), 2-0 Amer Deeb Mohammad Khalil (23), 3-0 Ahmed Hayel Ibrahim (32), 4-0 Abdallah Khaled Deeb Salim (45+1), 5-0 Amer Deeb Mohammad Khalil (57), 6-0 Ahmed Hayel Ibrahim (68), 7-0 Hassan Mahmoud Abdel Fatah (74), 8-0 Hassan Mahmoud Abdel Fatah (84), 9-0 Hassan Mahmoud Abdel Fatah (90+3).
Cautions: Shadi Nadmi Abu Hashash / Anil Gurung.

28.07.2011, Dasarath Rangasala Stadium, Kathmandu; Attendance: 20,000
Referee: Fan Qi (China P.R.)
NEPAL - JORDAN **1-1(0-0)**
NEP: Kiran Chemzong, Rohit Chand, Biraj Maharjan (66.Bharat Khawas), Rabin Shrestha, Sagar Thapa, Bijay Gurung, Nirajan Khadka, Sandeep Rai, Jagjeet Shrestha (76.Sujal Shrestha), Bhola Nath Silwal (66.Ju Manu Rai), Santosh Sahukhala. Trainer: Graham Paul Roberts (England).
JOR: Lo'ai Salem Atallah Al Amaireh, Anas Walid Khaled Bani Yaseen, Mohamed Munir Ahmed Al Muattasim, Suleiman Mawafaq Al Salman (81.Mohammad Ali Mustafa), Fathi Omar Othman Basem, Baha'a Abdel-Rahman Mustafa Suleiman, Saeed Hassan Al Murjan, Amer Deeb Mohammad Khalil (67.Hamza Ali Khaled Al Dardour), Abdallah Khaled Deeb Salim, Ahmed Hayel Ibrahim, Anas Jamal Mohammad Hijah (46.Mohammad Abdulsaleh Al Dhemeri). Trainer: Adnan Hamad Majeed Al Abbasi (Iraq).
Goals: 0-1 Saeed Hassan Al Murjan (62), 1-1 Bharat Khawas (80).
Cautions: Nirajan Khadka / Amer Deeb Mohammad Khalil, Mohamed Munir Ahmed Al Muattasim.
(Jordan won 10-1 on aggregate and advanced to the 3rd Round)

AFC WORLD CUP QUALIFIERS – 3rd Round

The 20 teams - using the FIFA Ranking from July 2011 - were divided into four pots for the draw, each containing five teams.

Pot 1	*Pot 2*	*Pot 3*	*Pot 4*
Japan	Uzbekistan	Bahrain	Korea D.P.R.
Australia	Qatar	Syria	Thailand
Korea Republic	Jordan	Oman	Singapore
Iran	Saudi Arabia	Iraq	Indonesia
China P.R.	Kuwait	United Arab Emirates	Lebanon

Please note: Syria - after after being disqualified by FIFA on 19 August 2011, was replaced by Tajikistan.

GROUP A

02.09.2011	Kunming	China P.R. - Singapore	2-1(0-1)
02.09.2011	Arbil	Iraq - Jordan	0-2(0-1)
06.09.2011	Singapore	Singapore - Iraq	0-2(0-0)
06.09.2011	Amman	Jordan - China P.R.	2-1(0-0)
11.10.2011	Singapore	Singapore - Jordan	0-3(0-1)
11.10.2011	Shenzhen	China P.R. - Iraq	0-1(0-1)
11.11.2011	Doha (QAT)	Iraq - China P.R.	1-0(0-0)
11.11.2011	Amman	Jordan - Singapore	2-0(1-0)
15.11.2011	Singapore	Singapore - China P.R.	0-4(0-1)
15.11.2011	Amman	Jordan - Iraq	1-3(1-0)
29.02.2012	Guangzhou	China P.R. - Jordan	3-1(1-0)
29.02.2012	Doha (QAT)	Iraq - Singapore	7-1(4-1)

FINAL STANDINGS

1.	**Iraq**	6	5	0	1	14	-	4	15
2.	**Jordan**	6	4	0	2	11	-	7	12
3.	China P.R.	6	3	0	3	10	-	6	9
4.	Singapore	6	0	0	6	2	-	20	0

Iraq and Jordan advanced to the 4th Round.

02.09.2011, Tuodong Stadium, Kunming; Attendance: 17,000
Referee: Andre El Haddad (Lebanon)

CHINA P.R. - SINGAPORE 2-1(0-1)

CHN: Yang Zhi, Sun Xiang, Du Wei, Li Weifeng, Liu Jianye, Yu Hai (90+2.Hao Junmin), Zhao Xuri, Huang Bowen (67.Zheng Zhi), Chen Tao, Qu Bo (67.Yu Dabao), Yang Xu. Trainer: José Antonio Camacho Alfaro (Spain).

SIN: Mohamad Izwan Mahbud (55.Lionel Lewis), Daniel Mark Bennett, Muhammad Safuwan Baharudin, Mohamad Shaiful Esah Nain, Juma'at Jantan, Mohamed Isa Mohamed Halim (84.Shahdan Sulaiman), Fahrudin Mustafić, Mohammad Shahril Ishak, Shi Jiayi (62.Mohamed Hafiz Rahim), Qiu Li, Aleksandar Đurić. Trainer: Radojko Avramović (Serbia).

Goals: 0-1 Aleksandar Đurić (33), 1-1 Zheng Zhi (69 penalty), 2-1 Yu Hai (73).

Cautions: Yu Hai, Yang Xu / Fahrudin Mustafić, Lionel Lewis, Juma'at Jantan, Qiu Li.

02.09.2011, "Franso Harir" Stadium, Arbil; Attendance: 24,000
Referee: Nawaf Abdullah Ghayyath Shukralla (Bahrain)

IRAQ - JORDAN **0-2(0-1)**

IRQ: Mohammed Gassid Kadhim Al Jaberi, Ali Hussein Rehema Al Ka'abi Al Mutairi, Bassim Abbas Gatea Al Ogaili, Samal Saeed Mujbel, Salam Shakir Ali, Qusay Muneer Abboodi Al Hussein, Nashat Akram Abid Ali (60.Amjad Radhi Yousif Al Janabi), Karrar Jassim Mohammed Al Mahmodi (73.Saad Abdul Amir), Hawar Mulla Mohammed Taher Zibari (46.Emad Mohammed Ridha), Alaa Abdul-Zahra Khashan Al Azzawi, Younis Mahmoud Khalaf. Trainer: Arthur Antunes Coimbra "Zico" (Brazil).
JOR: Amer Shafia Mahmoud Sabbah, Bashar Mustafa Bani Yaseen, Anas Walid Khaled Bani Yaseen, Fathi Omar Othman Basem, Khalil Zayid Bani Attiah, Baha'a Abdel-Rahman Mustafa Suleiman, Shadi Nadmi Abu Hashash, Amer Deeb Mohammad Khalil (82.Mahmoud Omar Shelbaieh), Hassan Mahmoud Abdel Fatah, Abdallah Khaled Deeb Salim (90.Saeed Hassan Al Murjan), Ahmed Hayel Ibrahim (67.Odai Yousef Ismail Al Saify). Trainer: Adnan Hamad Majeed Al Abbasi (Iraq).
Goals: 0-1 Hassan Mahmoud Abdel Fatah (43), 0-2 Abdallah Khaled Deeb Salim (47).
Cautions: , Qusay Muneer Abboodi Al Hussein / Amer Deeb Mohammad Khalil, Anas Walid Khaled Bani Yaseen, Khalil Zayid Bani Attiah, Odai Yousef Ismail Al Saify, Mahmoud Omar Shelbaieh.

06.09.2011, Jalan Besar Stadium, Singapore; Attendance: 5,505
Referee: Minoru Tojo (Japan)

SINGAPORE - IRAQ **0-2(0-0)**

SIN: Lionel Lewis, Daniel Mark Bennett, Muhammad Safuwan Baharudin, Mohamad Shaiful Esah Nain, Juma'at Jantan, Mohamed Isa Mohamed Halim (81.Sevki Sha'ban), Fahrudin Mustafić, Mohammad Shahril Ishak, Qiu Li (46.Fazrul Nawaz Shahul Hameed), Aleksandar Đurić, Mohamed Hafiz Rahim (57.Shi Jiayi). Trainer: Radojko Avramović (Serbia).
IRQ: Mohammed Gassid Kadhim Al Jaberi, Ali Hussein Rehema Al Ka'abi Al Mutairi, Bassim Abbas Gatea Al Ogaili, Samal Saeed Mujbel, Salam Shakir Ali, Muthana Khalid Salih Al Masloukhi (88.Fareed Majeed Ghadban), Qusay Muneer Abboodi Al Hussein, Nashat Akram Abid Ali (68.Saad Abdul Amir), Alaa Abdul-Zahra Khashan Al Azzawi, Mustafa Karim Abdullah (65.Amir Sabah Hussein Al Hamadani), Younis Mahmoud Khalaf. Trainer: Arthur Antunes Coimbra "Zico" (Brazil).
Goals: 0-1 Alaa Abdul-Zahra Khashan Al Azzawi (49), 0-2 Younis Mahmoud Khalaf (86).
Cautions: Daniel Mark Bennett, Fahrudin Mustafić / Muthana Khalid Salih Al Masloukhi, Amir Sabah Hussein Al Hamadani, Alaa Abdul-Zahra Khashan Al Azzawi.

06.09.2011, Amman International Stadium, Amman; Attendance: 19,000
Referee: Ravshan Irmatov (Uzbekistan)

JORDAN - CHINA P.R. **2-1(0-0)**

JOR: Amer Shafia Mahmoud Sabbah, Anas Walid Khaled Bani Yaseen, Bashar Mustafa Bani Yaseen, Fathi Omar Othman Basem, Khalil Zayid Bani Attiah (65.Hatam Mohammed Yusuf Aqel), Baha'a Abdel-Rahman Mustafa Suleiman, Shadi Nadmi Abu Hashash, Amer Deeb Mohammad Khalil, Hassan Mahmoud Abdel Fatah, Abdallah Khaled Deeb Salim (66.Odai Yousef Ismail Al Saify), Ahmed Hayel Ibrahim. Trainer: Adnan Hamad Majeed Al Abbasi (Iraq).
CHN: Yang Zhi, Sun Xiang, Li Weifeng, Feng Xiaoting, Liu Jianye (80.Wu Xi), Yu Hai (78.Feng Renliang), Zheng Zhi, Zhao Xuri, Huang Bowen (59.Yu Dabao), Hao Junmin, Yang Xu. Trainer: José Antonio Camacho Alfaro (Spain).
Goals: 1-0 Baha'a Abdel-Rahman Mustafa Suleiman (49), 2-0 Amer Deeb Mohammad Khalil (55), 2-1 Hao Junmin (56)
Cautions: Hassan Mahmoud Abdel Fatah, Fathi Omar Othman Basem / Huang Bowen, Zheng Zhi, Liu Jianye.

11.10.2011, Jalan Besar Stadium, Singapore; Attendance: 3,799
Referee: Choi Myung-Yong (Korea Republic)
SINGAPORE - JORDAN **0-3(0-1)**
SIN: Mohamad Izwan Mahbud, Daniel Mark Bennett, Juma'at Jantan, Muhammad Safuwan Baharudin, Shi Jiayi (46.Fahrudin Mustafić), Mohamad Shaiful Esah Nain, Hariss Harun, Fazrul Nawaz Shahul Hameed (61.Muhammad Khairul Nizam Mohammad Kamal), Mohammad Shahril Ishak, Mohamed Hafiz Rahim (46.Muhammad Raihan), Aleksandar Đurić. Trainer: Radojko Avramović (Serbia).
JOR: Amer Shafia Mahmoud Sabbah, Khalil Zayid Bani Attiah, Bashar Mustafa Bani Yaseen, Anas Walid Khaled Bani Yaseen, Fathi Omar Othman Basem, Baha'a Abdel-Rahman Mustafa Suleiman, Shadi Nadmi Abu Hashash, Odai Yousef Ismail Al Saify (73.Amer Deeb Mohammad Khalil), Hassan Mahmoud Abdel Fatah (84.Anas Jamal Mohammad Hijah), Abdallah Khaled Deeb Salim, Ahmed Hayel Ibrahim (80.Mahmoud Omar Shelbaieh). Trainer: Adnan Hamad Majeed Al Abbasi (Iraq).
Goals: 0-1 Abdallah Khaled Deeb Salim (11), 0-2 Anas Walid Khaled Bani Yaseen (54), 0-3 Ahmed Hayel Ibrahim (63).
Cautions: Odai Yousef Ismail Al Saify, Anas Walid Khaled Bani Yaseen.

11.10.2011, Shenzhen Stadium, Shenzhen; Attendance: 25,021
Referee: Saeid Mozaffarizadeh Yazdi (Iran)
CHINA P.R. - IRAQ **0-1(0-1)**
CHN: Yang Zhi, Sun Xiang, Du Wei, Wu Xi, Li Weifeng, Zheng Zhi, Chen Tao (46.Zhang Chengdong), Huang Xiyang, Feng Renliang (83.Yu Hai), Yu Hanchao (63.Wu Pingfeng), Gao Lin. Trainer: José Antonio Camacho Alfaro (Spain).
IRQ: Mohammed Gassid Kadhim Al Jaberi, Samal Saeed Mujbel, Ali Hussein Rehema Al Ka'abi Al Mutairi, Salam Shakir Ali, Bassim Abbas Gatea Al Ogaili, Qusay Muneer Abboodi Al Hussein, Muthana Khalid Salih Al Masloukhi, Alaa Abdul-Zahra Khashan Al Azzawi (90+3.Samer Saeed Mujbel), Nashat Akram Abid Ali, Mustafa Karim Abdullah (68.Husam Kadhim Jabur Al Shuwaili), Younis Mahmoud Khalaf (90+2.Emad Mohammed Ridha). Trainer: Arthur Antunes Coimbra "Zico" (Brazil).
Goal: 0-1 Younis Mahmoud Khalaf (45).
Cautions: Bassim Abbas Gatea Al Ogaili, Salam Shakir Ali, Younis Mahmoud Khalaf.
Sent off: Bassim Abbas Gatea Al Ogaili (66).

11.11.2011, Grand Hamad Stadium, Doha (Qatar); Attendance: 5,000
Referee: Peter Daniel Green (Australia)
IRAQ - CHINA P.R. **1-0(0-0)**
IRQ: Mohammed Gassid Kadhim Al Jaberi, Ali Hussein Rehema Al Ka'abi Al Mutairi, Husam Kadhim Jabur Al Shuwaili, Samal Saeed Mujbel, Salam Shakir Ali, Muthana Khalid Salih Al Masloukhi, Qusay Muneer Abboodi Al Hussein, Nashat Akram Abid Ali, Alaa Abdul-Zahra Khashan Al Azzawi (76.Karrar Jassim Mohammed Al Mahmodi), Mustafa Karim Abdullah (67.Samer Saeed Mujbel), Younis Mahmoud Khalaf (90+4.Emad Mohammed Ridha). Trainer: Arthur Antunes Coimbra "Zico" (Brazil).
CHN: Yang Zhi, Sun Xiang, Li Weifeng, Liu Jianye, Zhang Linpeng, Zheng Zhi, Zhao Xuri Ausgewechselt, Yu Hanchao (47.Wu Pingfeng), Liu Jian (57.Han Peng), Hao Junmin, Gao Lin (80.Zhang Chengdong). Trainer: José Antonio Camacho Alfaro (Spain).
Goal: 1-0 Younis Mahmoud Khalaf (90+2).
Cautions: Husam Kadhim Jabur Al Shuwaili, Samal Saeed Mujbel / Li Weifeng, Sun Xiang.
Sent off: Zhang Linpeng (85).

11.11.2011, Amman International Stadium, Amman; Attendance: 19,000
Referee: Benjamin Jon Williams (Australia)
JORDAN - SINGAPORE **2-0(1-0)**
JOR: Amer Shafia Mahmoud Sabbah, Hatam Mohammed Yusuf Aqel, Bashar Mustafa Bani Yaseen, Fathi Omar Othman Basem, Khalil Zayid Bani Attiah, Baha'a Abdel-Rahman Mustafa Suleiman, Shadi Nadmi Abu Hashash, Amer Deeb Mohammad Khalil, Abdallah Khaled Deeb Salim (78.Anas Jamal Mohammad Hijah), Ahmed Hayel Ibrahim (87.Hamza Ali Khaled Al Dardour), Hassan Mahmoud Abdel Fatah. Trainer: Adnan Hamad Majeed Al Abbasi (Iraq).
SIN: Lionel Lewis, Daniel Mark Bennett, Mohamad Shaiful Esah Nain, Juma'at Jantan (73.Sevki Sha'ban), Mohamed Noh Rahman, Ismail Yunos, Fahrudin Mustafić (90.Mohamed Hafiz Rahim), Mohammad Shahril Ishak, Shi Jiayi, Aleksandar Đurić (71.Firdaus Idros), Fazrul Nawaz Shahul Hameed. Trainer: Radojko Avramović (Serbia).
Goals: 1-0 Ahmed Hayel Ibrahim (15), 2-0 Amer Deeb Mohammad Khalil (65).

15.11.2011, Jalan Besar Stadium, Singapore; Attendance: 5,474
Referee: Abdullah Mohamed Balideh (Qatar)
SINGAPORE - CHINA P.R. **0-4(0-1)**
SIN: Lionel Lewis, Daniel Mark Bennett, Mohamad Shaiful Esah Nain (33.Sevki Sha'ban), Mohamed Noh Rahman, Ismail Yunos, Fahrudin Mustafić, Firdaus Idros, Mohammad Shahril Ishak (72.Mohamed Hafiz Rahim), Shi Jiayi (46.Mohamad Abdul), Aleksandar Đurić, Fazrul Nawaz Shahul Hameed. Trainer: Radojko Avramović (Serbia).
CHN: Yang Zhi, Li Weifeng, Zhao Peng, Liu Jianye, Zheng Zheng, Yu Hai (87.Yu Dabao), Zhao Xuri, Huang Bowen, Hao Junmin, Chen Tao (84.Zheng Zhi), Gao Lin (84.Zhang Chengdong). Trainer: José Antonio Camacho Alfaro (Spain).
Goals: 0-1 Yu Hai (42), 0-2 Li Weifeng (57), 0-3 Zheng Zheng (73), 0-4 Zheng Zheng (82).
Cautions: Fahrudin Mustafić / Gao Lin.
Sent off: Huang Bowen (67).

15.11.2011, Amman International Stadium, Amman; Attendance: 13,000
Referee: Ali Hamad Madhad Saif Al Badwawi (United Arab Emirates)
JORDAN - IRAQ **1-3(1-0)**
JOR: Amer Shafia Mahmoud Sabbah, Khalil Zayid Bani Attiah, Anas Walid Khaled Bani Yaseen (83.Hatam Mohammed Yusuf Aqel), Bashar Mustafa Bani Yaseen, Fathi Omar Othman Basem, Baha'a Abdel-Rahman Mustafa Suleiman, Shadi Nadmi Abu Hashash, Amer Deeb Mohammad Khalil, Hassan Mahmoud Abdel Fatah, Ahmed Hayel Ibrahim, Abdallah Khaled Deeb Salim (58.Odai Yousef Ismail Al Saify). Trainer: Adnan Hamad Majeed Al Abbasi (Iraq).
IRQ: Mohammed Gassid Kadhim Al Jaberi, Samal Saeed Mujbel, Ali Hussein Rehema Al Ka'abi Al Mutairi, Salam Shakir Ali, Bassim Abbas Gatea Al Ogaili, Qusay Muneer Abboodi Al Hussein, Muthana Khalid Salih Al Masloukhi, Alaa Abdul-Zahra Khashan Al Azzawi (46.Karrar Jassim Mohammed Al Mahmodi), Nashat Akram Abid Ali, Mustafa Karim Abdullah (46.Hawar Mulla Mohammed Taher Zibari), Younis Mahmoud Khalaf. Trainer: Arthur Antunes Coimbra "Zico" (Brazil).
Goals: 1-0 Hassan Mahmoud Abdel Fatah (17), 1-1 Nashat Akram Abid Ali (55), 1-2 Qusay Muneer Abboodi Al Hussein (67), 1-3 Nashat Akram Abid Ali (81).
Cautions: Anas Walid Khaled Bani Yaseen / Alaa Abdul-Zahra Khashan Al Azzawi.

29.02.2012, Guangzhou University City Stadium, Guangzhou; Attendance: 6,104
Referee: Võ Minh Trí (Vietnam)

CHINA P.R. - JORDAN 3-1(1-0)

CHN: Zeng Cheng, Sun Xiang, Zhao Peng, Qin Sheng (86.Liu Jian), Liu Jianye, Zhang Linpeng, Lü Peng, Yu Hanchao (90.Yu Hai), Hao Junmin, Chen Tao (76.Yu Dabao), Gao Lin. Trainer: José Antonio Camacho Alfaro (Spain).

JOR: Amer Shafia Mahmoud Sabbah, Ibrahim Farhan Al Zawahreh, Mohamed Munir Ahmed Al Muattasim, Shareef Nassar Adnan, Fathi Omar Othman Basem, Khalil Zayid Bani Attiah, Baha'a Abdel-Rahman Mustafa Suleiman (85.Hamza Ali Khaled Al Dardour), Shadi Nadmi Abu Hashash (74.Saeed Hassan Al Murjan), Amer Deeb Mohammad Khalil (66.Suleiman Mawafaq Al Salman), Abdallah Khaled Deeb Salim, Raed Abdel-Reahman Fraeh Al Nawateer. Trainer: Adnan Hamad Majeed Al Abbasi (Iraq).

Goals: 1-0 Hao Junmin (43), 2-0 Hao Junmin (69), 2-1 Fathi Omar Othman Basem (85), 3-1 Yu Dabao (88).

Cautions: Chen Tao, Qin Sheng, Zhao Peng / Mohamed Munir Ahmed Al Muattasim, Shareef Nassar Adnan.

29.02.2012, Grand Hamad Stadium, Doha (Qatar); Attendance: 950
Referee: Abdullah Mohamed Al Hilali (Oman)

IRAQ - SINGAPORE 7-1(4-1)

IRQ: Mohammed Gassid Kadhim Al Jaberi, Ali Hussein Rehema Al Ka'abi Al Mutairi, Bassim Abbas Gatea Al Ogaili, Samal Saeed Mujbel, Salam Shakir Ali, Muthana Khalid Salih Al Masloukhi (89.Saad Abdul-Amir Al Zirjawi), Qusay Muneer Abboodi Al Hussein, Nashat Akram Abid Ali, Karrar Jassim Mohammed Al Mahmodi (30.Mustafa Karim Abdullah), Hawar Mulla Mohammed Taher Zibari (73.Luay Salah Hassan Al Khafaji), Karrar Jassim Mohammed Al Mahmodi. Trainer: Arthur Antunes Coimbra "Zico" (Brazil).

SIN: Hassan Abdullah Sunny, Daniel Mark Bennett, Baihakki Khaizan, Muhammad Irwan Shah Arismail, Mohamed Isa Mohamed Halim (46.Fazrul Nawaz Shahul Hameed), Fahrudin Mustafić (71.Agu Casmir), Mohammad Shahril Ishak, Shi Jiayi, Shahdan Sulaiman, Ruzaini Zainal (55.Delwinder Singh), Qiu Li. Trainer: Radojko Avramović (Serbia).

Goals: 1-0 Karrar Jassim Mohammed Al Mahmodi (4), 2-0 Karrar Jassim Mohammed Al Mahmodi (11), 3-0 Hawar Mulla Mohammed Taher Zibari (22 penalty), 3-1 Mohamed Isa Mohamed Halim (28), 4-1 Nashat Akram Abid Ali (36 penalty), 5-1 Mustafa Karim Abdullah (47), 6-1 Karrar Jassim Mohammed Al Mahmodi (61), 7-1 Karrar Jassim Mohammed Al Mahmodi (90+3).

Cautions: Hassan Abdullah Sunny, Baihakki Khaizan, Fahrudin Mustafić.

GROUP B

02.09.2011	Goyang	Korea Republic - Lebanon	6-0(2-0)
02.09.2011	Al Ain	United Arab Emirates - Kuwait	2-3(0-1)
06.09.2011	Beirut	Lebanon - United Arab Emirates	3-1(1-1)
06.09.2011	Kuwait City	Kuwait - Korea Republic	1-1(0-1)
11.10.2011	Suwon	Korea Republic - United Arab Emirates	2-1(0-0)
11.10.2011	Beirut	Lebanon - Kuwait	2-2(1-0)
11.11.2011	Kuwait City	Kuwait - Lebanon	0-1(0-0)
11.11.2011	Al Ain	United Arab Emirates - Korea Republic	0-2(0-0)
15.11.2011	Kuwait City	Kuwait - United Arab Emirates	2-1(0-1)
15.11.2011	Beirut	Lebanon - Korea Republic	2-1(2-1)
29.02.2012	Seoul	Korea Republic - Kuwait	2-0(0-0)
29.02.2012	Al Ain	United Arab Emirates - Lebanon	4-2(2-2)

FINAL STANDINGS

1.	**Korea Republic**	6	4	1	1	14 - 4	13
2.	**Lebanon**	6	3	1	2	10 - 14	10
3.	Kuwait	6	2	2	2	8 - 9	8
4.	United Arab Emirates	6	1	0	5	9 - 14	3

Korea Republic and Lebanon advanced to the 4th Round.

02.09.2011, Goyang Stadium, Goyang; Attendance: 37,655
Referee: Abdul Malik Bashir (Singapore)
KOREA REPUBLIC - LEBANON 6-0(2-0)
KOR: Jung Sung-Ryong, Cha Du-Ri, Hong Jeong-Ho, Lee Jung-Soo, Hong Chul, Ki Sung-Yueng, Lee Yong-Rae, Koo Ja-Cheol (75.Kim Jung-Woo), Nam Tae-Hee (86.Yoon Bit-Garam), Park Chu-Young (70.Lee Keun-Ho), Ji Dong-Won. Trainer: Cho Kwang-Rae.
LIB: Ziad Ali Al Samad, Ramez Dayoub, Walid Ismail (53.Ali Al Saadi), Youssef Wasef Mohamad (81.Abbas Kenaan), Mohammed Baqir Younis, Haytham Faour, Mohamĕd Shamas, Abbas Ali Atwi (68.Khodor Salameh), Mahmoud El Ali, Akram Moghrabi, Hassan Maatouk. Trainer: Johannes Theodor Bücker (Germany).
Goals: 1-0 Park Chu-Young (8), 2-0 Park Chu-Young 45), 3-0 Ji Dong-Won (66), 4-0 Park Chu-Young (67), 5-0 Kim Jung-Woo (82), 6-0 Ji Dong-Won (85).
Cautions: Ramez Dayoub, Walid Ismail.

02.09.2011, Al Qatara Stadium, Al Ain; Attendance: 8,715
Referee: Muhsen Basma (Syria)
UNITED ARAB EMIRATES - KUWAIT 2-3(0-1)
UAE: Majed Nasser Humaid Bakheit Al Maqdami, Hamdan Ismaeel Mohammed Al Kamali, Yousef Jaber Naser Al Hammadi, Khalid Sebil Ibrahim Ahmed Lashkari, Waleed Abbas Murad Yousuf Al Balooshi, Subait Khater Fayel Khamis Al Mukhaini, Amer Abdulrahman Abdullah Hussein Al Hammadi (67.Amir Mubarak Al Hammadi), Ali Ahmad Ali Mohammed Al Wehaibi (51.Saeed Salem Saleh Salem Al Kathiri), Ismaeel Salem Ismaeel Saeed Al Hammadi, Mohamed Saeed Rashed Saiwed Al Shehhi (57.Mahmoud Khamis Al Hammadi), Ahmed Khalil Sebait Mubarak Al Junaibi. Trainer: Srečko Katanec (Slovenia).
KUW: Nawaf Khaled Al Khaldi, Hussain Ali Al Fadhel (83.Khaled Ali Nasser Al Qahtani), Mohammed Rashid Sinad Al Fadhli, Fahad Awadh Shaheen Shehan, Amer Maatooq Al Fadhel, Talal Ahmad Al Amer, Jarah Mohammed Al Ataiqi (77.Saleh Al Sheikh Al Hendi), Fahad Saleh Hussain Al Enezi, Bader Ahmed Al Mutawa, Abdulaziz Ashwan (56.Waleed Ali Hussein Jumah), Yousef Nasser Al Sulaiman. Trainer: Goran Tufegdžić (Serbia).
Goals: 0-1 Yousef Nasser Al Sulaiman (7), 0-2 Bader Ahmed Al Mutawa (51), 0-3 Yousef Nasser Al Sulaiman (65), 1-3 Ismaeel Salem Ismaeel Saeed Al Hammadi (84), 2-3 Ahmed Khalil Sebait Mubarak

Al Junaibi (89).
Cautions: Fahad Saleh Hussain Al Enezi, Amer Maatooq Al Fadhel, Waleed Ali Hussein Jumah.

06.09.2011, "Camille Chamoun" Sports City Stadium, Beirut; Attendance: 4,000
Referee: Alireza Faghani (Iran)
LEBANON - UNITED ARAB EMIRATES 3-1(1-1)
LIB: Ziad Ali Al Samad, Abbas Kenaan, Ramez Dayoub, Ali Al Saadi, Walid Ismail, Haytham Faour, Roda Antar, Hassan Maatouk (86.Mohaméd Shamas), Abbas Ahmed Atwi, Akram Moghrabi (54.Mahmoud El Ali), Mohammed Mahmoud Ghaddar (69.Mohamad Haidar). Trainer: Johannes Theodor Bücker (Germany).
UAE: Majed Nasser Humaid Bakheit Al Maqdami, Khalid Sebil Ibrahim Ahmed Lashkari (76.Amir Mubarak Al Hammadi), Mohamed Ahmed Ali Gharib Juma, Waleed Abbas Murad Yousuf Al Balooshi, Yousef Jaber Naser Al Hammadi, Ismaeel Salem Ismaeel Saeed Al Hammadi, Amer Abdulrahman Abdullah Hussein Al Hammadi, Subait Khater Fayel Khamis Al Mukhaini, Mahmoud Khamis Al Hammadi (63.Saeed Salem Saleh Salem Al Kathiri), Mohamed Saeed Rashed Saiwed Al Shehhi (56.Ahmed Jumaa Anbar Mubarak Al Araimi Al Junaibi), Ahmed Khalil Sebait Mubarak Al Junaibi. Trainer: Srečko Katanec (Slovenia).
Goals: 0-1 Mahmoud Khamis Al Hammadi (16), 1-1 Mohammed Mahmoud Ghaddar (37), 2-1 Akram Moghrabi (53), 3-1 Roda Antar (83).
Cautions: Ali Al Saadi, Abbas Kenaan / Khalid Sebil Ibrahim Ahmed Lashkari, Waleed Abbas Murad Yousuf Al Balooshi, Ismaeel Salem Ismaeel Saeed Al Hammadi, Yousef Jaber Naser Al Hammadi.

06.09.2011, Kuwait Peace and Friendship Stadium, Kuwait City; Attendance: 20,000
Referee: Mohsen Torky (Iran)
KUWAIT - KOREA REPUBLIC 1-1(0-1)
KUW: Nawaf Khaled Al Khaldi, Hussain Ali Al Fadhel, Mohammed Rashid Sinad Al Fadhli, Fahad Awadh Shaheen Shehan, Amer Maatooq Al Fadhel (80.Ahmad Saad Al Rashidi), Talal Ahmad Al Amer (88.Jarah Mohammed Al Ataiqi), Fahad Ebrahim Al Ansari, Fahad Saleh Hussain Al Enezi, Waleed Ali Hussein Jumah (75.Abdulaziz Ashwan), Bader Ahmed Al Mutawa, Yousef Nasser Al Sulaiman. Trainer: Goran Tufegdžić (Serbia).
KOR: Jung Sung-Ryong, Cha Du-Ri (17.Kim Jae-Sung), Hong Jeong-Ho, Lee Jung-Soo, Hong Chul, Ki Sung-Yueng, Lee Yong-Rae, Koo Ja-Cheol (79.Kim Jung-Woo), Nam Tae-Hee (64.Yeom Ki-Hun), Park Chu-Young, Ji Dong-Won. Trainer: Cho Kwang-Rae.
Goals: 0-1 Park Chu-Young (8), 1-1 Hussain Ali Al Fadhel (53).
Cautions: Waleed Ali Hussein Jumah / Kim Jae-Sung.

11.10.2011, Suwon World Cup Stadium, Suwon; Attendance: 28,689
Referee: Tan Hai (China P.R.)
KOREA REPUBLIC - UNITED ARAB EMIRATES 2-1(0-0)
KOR: Jung Sung-Ryong, Choi Hyo-Jin, Hong Jeong-Ho, Lee Jung-Soo, Kim Young-Kwon, Ki Sung-Yueng, Lee Yong-Rae, Koo Ja-Cheol (61.Nam Tae-Hee), Seo Jung-Jin, Park Chu-Young (79.Lee Dong-Gook), Ji Dong-Won (72.Son Heung-Min). Trainer: Cho Kwang-Rae.
UAE: Majed Nasser Humaid Bakheit Al Maqdami, Mohamed Ahmed Ali Gharib Juma, Hamdan Ismaeel Mohammed Al Kamali, Abdullah Mousa Mohamed Ahmed Esmaeil Al Bloushi, Waleed Abbas Murad Yousuf Al Balooshi, Subait Khater Fayel Khamis Al Mukhaini (82.Ahmed Jumaa Anbar Mubarak Al Araimi Al Junaibi), Ali Ahmad Ali Mohammed Al Wehaibi (59.Mohamed Saeed Rashed Saiwed Al Shehhi), Ismaeel Salem Ismaeel Saeed Al Hammadi, Ismail Matar Ibrahim Khamis Al Mukhaini Al Junaibi, Saeed Hassan Salem Al Kas, Mohammed Fawzi Jawhar Faraj Abdullah Al Jahwar. Trainer: Abdullah Masfar.
Goals: 1-0 Park Chu-Young (50), 2-0 Hamdan Ismail Mohammed Al Kamali (63 own goal), 2-1 Ismail Matar Ibrahim Khamis Al Mukhaini Al Junaibi (90).
Cautions: Hong Jeong-Ho, Koo Ja-Cheol, Park Chu-Young / Hamdan Ismaeel Mohammed Al Kamali.

11.10.2011, "Camille Chamoun" Sports City Stadium, Beirut; Attendance: 32,000
Referee: Masaaki Toma (Japan)

LEBANON - KUWAIT **2-2(1-0)**

LIB: Ziad Ali Al Samad, Mohammed Baqir Younis, Bilal Shiekh El Najarin, Youssef Wasef Mohamad, Ramez Dayoub, Haytham Faour, Roda Antar, Mahmoud El Ali (68.Ahmad Zreik), Abbas Ahmed Atwi, Hassan Maatouk, Mohammed Mahmoud Ghaddar (55.Akram Moghrabi; 95.Mohamad Haidar). Trainer: Johannes Theodor Bücker (Germany).

KUW: Nawaf Khaled Al Khaldi, Amer Maatooq Al Fadhel (84.Mohamed Rashed Al Fadhli), Hussain Ali Al Fadhel, Mesaed Neda Al Enazi, Fahad Awadh Shaheen Shehan, Talal Ahmad Al Amer, Fahad Ebrahim Al Ansari (87.Fahad Mohammad Aaidh Al Rashidi), Fahad Saleh Hussain Al Enezi, Bader Ahmed Al Mutawa, Hussain Mohsen Al Moussawi (46.Abdulaziz Ahmad Al Misha'an Al Enezi), Yousef Nasser Al Sulaiman. Trainer: Goran Tufegdžić (Serbia).

Goals: 1-0 Hassan Maatouk (15), 1-1 Mesaed Neda Al Enazi (50), 2-1 Hassan Maatouk (86), 2-2 Mahmoud Baquir Younes (89 own goal).

Cautions: Hassan Maatouk / Fahad Saleh Hussain Al Enezi, Hussain Ali Al Fadhel, Mesaed Neda Al Enazi.

11.11.2011, Peace and Friendship Stadium, Kuwait City; Attendance: 17,500
Referee: Valentin Kovalenko (Uzbekistan)

KUWAIT - LEBANON **0-1(0-0)**

KUW: Nawaf Khaled Al Khaldi, Amer Maatooq Al Fadhel (75.Yaqoub Abdullah Al Taher), Mohammed Rashid Sinad Al Fadhli, Mesaed Neda Al Enazi, Fahad Awadh Shaheen Shehan (84.Hussain Mohsen Al Moussawi), Waleed Ali Hussein Jumah, Fahad Ebrahim Al Ansari (59.Fahad Mohammad Aaidh Al Rashidi), Talal Ahmad Al Amer, Abdulaziz Ahmad Al Misha'an Al Enezi, Bader Ahmed Al Mutawa, Yousef Nasser Al Sulaiman. Trainer: Goran Tufegdžić (Serbia).

LIB: Ziad Ali Al Samad, Abbas Kenaan (10.Walid Ismail), Bilal Shiekh El Najarin, Youssef Wasef Mohamad (12.Ali Al Saadi), Ramez Dayoub, Haytham Faour, Roda Antar, Ahmad Zreik, Abbas Ahmed Atwi, Hassan Maatouk (83.Mohammed Mahmoud Ghaddar), Mahmoud El Ali. Trainer: Johannes Theodor Bücker (Germany).

Goal: 0-1 Mahmoud El Ali (57).

Cautions: Abdulaziz Ahmad Al Misha'an Al Enezi, Yousef Nasser Al Sulaiman / Roda Antar, Hassan Maatouk.

11.11.2011, Al-Rashid Stadium, Dubai; Attendance: 8,272
Referee: Ravshan Irmatov (Uzbekistan)

UNITED ARAB EMIRATES - KOREA REPUBLIC **0-2(0-0)**

UAE: Majed Nasser Humaid Bakheit Al Maqdami, Ali Abbas Yasin Al Hosany, Mohamed Ahmed Ali Gharib Juma, Faris Jumaa Hassan Al Saadi, Basheer Saeed Basheer Sanqour Al Hammadi, Abdullah Mousa Mohamed Ahmed Esmaeil Al Bloushi, Ali Ahmad Ali Mohammed Al Wehaibi (57.Ahmed Khalil Sebait Mubarak Al Junaibi), Subait Khater Fayel Khamis Al Mukhaini (74.Essa Obeid Hassan Hirok), Mohammed Fawzi Jawhar Faraj Abdullah Al Jahwar, Ismaeel Salem Ismaeel Saeed Al Hammadi (90.Abdullah Qasem Abdullah Hassan Mansoor), Ismail Matar Ibrahim Khamis Al Mukhaini Al Junaibi. Trainer: Abdullah Masfar.

KOR: Jung Sung-Ryong, Cha Du-Ri, Lee Jung-Soo, Kwak Tae-Hwi, Hong Cheol (64.Lee Seung-Ki), Hong Jeong-Ho, Lee Yong-Rae, Koo Ja-Cheol, Seo Jung-Jin (79.Lee Keun-Ho), Park Chu-Young, Ji Dong-Won (46.Son Heung-Min). Trainer: Cho Kwang-Rae.

Goals: 0-1 Lee Keun-Ho (88), 0-2 Park Chu-Young (90+3).

Cautions: Ali Abbas Yasin Al Hosany, Faris Jumaa Hassan Al Saadi, Majed Nasser Humaid Bakheit Al Maqdami / Cha Du-Ri, Park Chu-Young.

15.11.2011, Peace and Friendship Stadium, Kuwait City; Attendance: 10,000
Referee: Abdullah Mohamed Al Hilali (Oman)
KUWAIT - UNITED ARAB EMIRATES 2-1(0-1)
KUW: Nawaf Khaled Al Khaldi, Amer Maatooq Al Fadhel, Hussain Ali Al Fadhel, Mohammed Rashid Sinad Al Fadhli, Fahad Awadh Shaheen Shehan, Fahad Ebrahim Al Ansari, Waleed Ali Hussein Jumah, Jarah Mohammed Al Ataiqi (78.Talal Naif Abdullah Asheq Al Enazi), Fahad Saleh Hussain Al Enezi (73.Abdulaziz Ahmad Al Misha'an Al Enezi), Bader Ahmed Al Mutawa, Yousef Nasser Al Sulaiman (84.Talal Ahmad Al Amer). Trainer: Goran Tufegdžić (Serbia).
UAE: Majed Nasser Humaid Bakheit Al Maqdami, Issa Ahmed Abdulaziz Ahmed Al Marzouqi, Faris Jumaa Hassan Al Saadi, Basheer Saeed Basheer Sanqour Al Hammadi, Abdullah Mousa Mohamed Ahmed Esmaeil Al Bloushi (80.Saeed Salem Saleh Salem Al Kathiri), Ali Ahmad Ali Mohammed Al Wehaibi (88.Essa Obeid Hassan Hirok), Ali Abbas Yasin Al Hosany, Subait Khater Fayel Khamis Al Mukhaini (65.Waleed Abbas Murad Yousuf Al Balooshi), Amir Mubarak Al Hammadi, Ismaeel Salem Ismaeel Saeed Al Hammadi, Ismail Matar Ibrahim Khamis Al Mukhaini Al Junaibi. Trainer: Abdullah Masfar.
Goals: 0-1 Ismail Matar Ibrahim Khamis Al Mukhaini Al Junaibi (18), 1-1 Fahad Saleh Hussain Al Enezi (49), 2-1 Walid Abbas Al Bloushi (66 own goal).
Cautions: Bader Ahmed Al Mutawa, Amer Maatooq Al Fadhel / Abdullah Mousa Mohamed Ahmed Esmaeil Al Bloushi, Majed Nasser Humaid Bakheit Al Maqdami, Ali Abbas Yasin Al Hosany, Ismaeel Salem Ismaeel Saeed Al Hammadi.

15.11.2011, "Camille Chamoun" Sports City Stadium, Beirut; Attendance: 35,000
Referee: Khalil Ibrahim Al Ghamdi (Saudi Arabia)
LEBANON - KOREA REPUBLIC 2-1(2-1)
LIB: Ziad Ali Al Samad, Ramez Dayoub, Bilal Shiekh El Najarin, Ali Al Saadi, Walid Ismail, Haytham Faour, Roda Antar, Ahmad Zreik, Hassan Chaito (84.Akram Moghrabi), Abbas Ahmed Atwi (82.Mohaméd Shamas), Mahmoud El Ali (90.Mohamad Haidar). Trainer: Johannes Theodor Bücker (Germany).
KOR: Jung Sung-Ryong, Cha Du-Ri, Lee Jung-Soo, Kwak Tae-Hwi, Lee Yong-Rae, Hong Jeong-Ho (71.Yoon Bit-Garam), Koo Ja-Cheol, Seo Jung-Jin (53.Nam Tae-Hee), Lee Seung-Ki, Son Heung-Min (46.Ji Dong-Won), Lee Keun-Ho. Trainer: Cho Kwang-Rae.
Goals: 1-0 Ali Al Saadi (5), 1-1 Koo Ja-Cheol (20 penalty), 2-1 Abbas Ahmed Atwi (32).
Cautions: Roda Antar, Ahmad Zreik / Koo Ja-Cheol.

29.02.2012, Seoul World Cup Stadium, Seoul; Attendance: 46,551
Referee: Yuichi Nishimura (Japan)
KOREA REPUBLIC - KUWAIT 2-0(0-0)
KOR: Jung Sung-Ryong, Choi Hyo-Jin, Kwak Tae-Hwi, Lee Jung-Soo, Park Won-Jae, Kim Sang-Sik (78.Kim Jae-Sung), Kim Do-Heon (52.Ki Sung-Yueng), Han Sang-Woon (64.Kim Shin-Wook), Park Chu-Young, Lee Keun-Ho, Lee Dong-Gook. Trainer: Choi Kang-Hee.
KUW: Nawaf Khaled Al Khaldi, Mohammad Frieh Al Rashidi (77.Abdulaziz Ahmad Al Misha'an Al Enezi), Mesaed Neda Al Enazi, Yaqoub Abdullah Al Taher, Fahad Awadh Shaheen Shehan, Fahad Ebrahim Al Ansari, Talal Naif Abdullah Asheq Al Enazi (67.Hamad Naif Al Enezi), Fahad Saleh Hussain Al Enezi, Waleed Ali Hussein Jumah, Bader Ahmed Al Mutawa, Yousef Nasser Al Sulaiman. Trainer: Goran Tufegdžić (Serbia).
Goals: 1-0 Lee Dong-Gook (65), 2-0 Lee Keun-Ho (71).
Cautions: Kim Shin-Wook, Ki Sung-Yueng / Bader Ahmed Al Mutawa, Talal Naif Abdullah Asheq Al Enazi, Mesaed Neda Al Enazi, Fahad Ebrahim Al Ansari.

29.02.2012, Al-Nahyan Stadium, Abu Dhabi; Attendance: 10,000
Referee: Peter Daniel Green (Australia)
UNITED ARAB EMIRATES - LEBANON 4-2(2-2)
UAE: Ali Khaseif Humad Khaseif Housani, Issa Ahmed Abdulaziz Ahmed Al Marzouqi, Basheer Saeed Basheer Sanqour Al Hammadi, Faris Jumaa Hassan Al Saadi, Yousef Jaber Naser Al Hammadi, Adel Abdullah Abbas Abdullah, Yaqoub Yousif Al Hosani, Ali Ahmad Ali Mohammed Al Wehaibi (90+3.Khalid Sebil Ibrahim Ahmed Lashkari), Ismail Matar Ibrahim Khamis Al Mukhaini Al Junaibi, Abdullah Qasem Abdullah Hassan Mansoor (74.Abdul Aziz Fayez Subait Khalifa Al Alawi), Essa Obeid Hassan Hirok (88.Adnan Hussain Al Balooshi). Trainer: Abdullah Masfar.
LIB: Abbas Hassan, Ramez Dayoub, Bilal Shiekh El Najarin, Youssef Wasef Mohamad, Walid Ismail, Haytham Faour, Mohaméd Shamas (60.Ali Al Saadi), Ahmad Zreik, Abbas Ahmed Atwi, Hassan Maatouk (81.Hassan Chaito), Mahmoud El Ali (31.Akram Moghrabi). Trainer: Johannes Theodor Bücker (Germany).
Goals: 0-1 Basheer Saeed Basheer Sanqour Al Hammadi (20), 1-1 Mahmoud El Ali (23), 2-1 Ali Ahmad Ali Mohammed Al Wehaibi (38), 2-2 Hassan Maatouk (45), 3-2 Ismail Matar Ibrahim Khamis Al Mukhaini Al Junaibi (68), 4-2 Basheer Saeed Basheer Sanqour Al Hammadi (78).
Cautions: Abdul Aziz Fayez Subait Khalifa Al Alawi / Bilal Shiekh El Najarin.

GROUP C

02.09.2011	Saitama	Japan - Korea D.P.R.	1-0(0-0)
02.09.2011	Tursunzoda	Tajikistan - Uzbekistan	0-1(0-0)
06.09.2011	P'yōngyang	Korea D.P.R. - Tajikistan	1-0(1-0)
06.09.2011	Tashkent	Uzbekistan - Japan	1-1(1-0)
11.10.2011	Osaka	Japan - Tajikistan	8-0(4-0)
11.10.2011	P'yōngyang	Korea D.P.R. - Uzbekistan	0-1(0-1)
11.11.2011	Tashkent	Uzbekistan - Korea D.P.R.	1-0(0-0)
11.11.2011	Dushanbe	Tajikistan - Japan	0-4(0-1)
15.11.2011	Tashkent	Uzbekistan - Tajikistan	3-0(1-0)
15.11.2011	P'yōngyang	Korea D.P.R. - Japan	1-0(0-0)
29.02.2012	Toyota	Japan - Uzbekistan	0-1(0-0)
29.02.2012	Khujand	Tajikistan - Korea D.P.R.	1-1(0-0)

FINAL STANDINGS

1.	**Uzbekistan**	6	5	1	0	8	-	1	16
2.	**Japan**	6	3	1	2	14	-	3	10
3.	Korea D.P.R.	6	2	1	3	3	-	4	7
4.	Tajikistan	6	0	1	5	1	-	18	1

Uzbekistan and Japan advanced to the 4th Round.

02.09.2011, Saitama Stadium 2002, Saitama; Attendance: 54,624
Referee: Ali Hamad Madhad Saif Al Badwawi (United Arab Emirates)
JAPAN - KOREA D.P.R. 1-0(0-0)
JPN: Eiji Kawashima, Yasuyuki Konno, Yūichi Komano, Atsuto Uchida, Maya Yoshida, Yasuhito Endō, Makoto Hasebe, Yosuke Kashiwagi (60.Hiroshi Kiyotake), Shinji Kagawa, Tadanari Lee (70.Mike Havenaar), Shinji Okazaki. Trainer: Alberto Zaccheroni (Italy).
PRK: Ri Myong-Guk, Jon Kwang-Ik, Pak Nam-Chol II, Ri Kwang-Chon, Cha Jong-Hyok, Ahn Yong-Hak, Pak Nam-Chol I (56.Pak Kwang-Ryong), Ri Chol-Myong (78.Pak Song-Chol I), Ryang Yong-Gi, Jong Tae-Se (90.An Chol-Hyok), Jong Il-Gwan. Trainer: Yun Jong-Su.
Goal: 1-0 Maya Yoshida (90+4).
Cautions: Ri Kwang-Chon, Ri Myong-Guk, Ahn Yong-Hak.
Sent off: Pak Kwang-Ryong (84).

02.09.2011, Metallurg Stadium, Tursunzoda; Attendance: 15,000
Referee: Tan Hai (China P.R.)
TAJIKISTAN - UZBEKISTAN 0-1(0-0)
TJK: Alisher Tuychiev, Davronjon Ergashev, Eraj Rajabov, Sokhib Savankulov, Farkhod Vasiev, Nuriddin Davronov, Fatkhullo Fatkhuloev (68.Ilhomzhon Ortikov), Yusuf Rabiev, Jahongir Jalilov, Makhmadali Sadykov (59.Ibrahim Rabimov), Numondzhon Khakimov (51.Dilshod Vasiev). Trainer: Alimzhon Rafikov.
UZB: Ignatiy Nesterov, Shavkat Mullajanov, Islom Tuhtahujaev, Vitaliy Denisov, Stanislav Andreyev (46.Timur Kapadze), Odil Ahmedov, Viktor Karpenko (46.Sanzhar Tursunov), Azizbek Haydarov, Server Djeparov (65.Ulugbek Bakaev), Aleksandr Geynrikh, Maksim Shatskikh. Trainer: Vadim Abramov.
Goal: 0-1 Maksim Shatskikh (72).
Cautions: Aleksandr Geynrikh, Islom Tuhtahujaev.

06.09.2011, Yanggakdo Stadium, P'yōngyang; Attendance: 28,000
Referee: Võ Minh Trí (Vietnam)
KOREA D.P.R. - TAJIKISTAN 1-0(1-0)
PRK: Kim Myong-Gil, Jon Kwang-Ik, Pak Nam-Chol II, Ri Kwang-Chon, Cha Jong-Hyok (83.Ri Kwang-Hyok), Ahn Yong-Hak, Pak Nam-Chol I, Ri Chol-Myong (87.Pak Song-Chol I), Ryang Yong-Gi, Jong Tae-Se (60.An Chol-Hyok), Jong Il-Gwan. Trainer: Yun Jong-Su.
TJK: Alisher Tuychiev, Davronjon Ergashev, Umed Khabibulloev, Eraj Rajabov, Sokhib Savankulov, Nuriddin Davronov, Fatkhullo Fatkhuloev (65.Dilshod Vasiev), Ibrahim Rabimov (65.Makhmadali Sadykov), Jahongir Jalilov, Khurshed Makhmudov, Yusuf Rabiev (87.Farkhod Tokhirov). Trainer: Alimzhon Rafikov.
Goal: 1-0 Pak Nam-Chol I (14).
Cautions: Cha Jong-Hyok / Sokhib Savankulov, Nuriddin Davronov.

06.09.2011, Pakhtakor Markaziy Stadium, Tashkent; Attendance: 32,000
Referee: Khalil Ibrahim Al Ghamdi (Saudi Arabia)
UZBEKISTAN - JAPAN 1-1(1-0)
UZB: Ignatiy Nesterov, Shavkat Mullajanov, Islom Tuhtahujaev, Vitaliy Denisov, Odil Ahmedov, Viktor Karpenko (76.Anzur Ismailov), Azizbek Haydarov, Timur Kapadze, Server Djeparov, Ulugbek Bakaev (53.Sanzhar Tursunov), Aleksandr Geynrikh (79.Maksim Shatskikh). Trainer: Vadim Abramov.
JPN: Eiji Kawashima, Yasuyuki Konno, Yūichi Komano (81.Tomoaki Makino), Atsuto Uchida, Yuki Abe (46.Hiroshi Kiyotake), Maya Yoshida, Yasuhito Endō, Makoto Hasebe, Shinji Kagawa, Tadanari Lee (66.Mike Havenaar), Shinji Okazaki. Trainer: Alberto Zaccheroni (Italy).
Goals: 1-0 Server Djeparov (8), 1-1 Shinji Okazaki (68).

11.10.2011, Nagai Stadium, Osaka; Attendance: 44,688
Referee: Benjamin Jon Williams (Australia)
JAPAN - TAJIKISTAN 8-0(4-0)
JPN: Eiji Kawashima, Yasuyuki Konno, Yūichi Komano, Yuto Nagatomo, Maya Yoshida, Yasuhito Endō, Makoto Hasebe (62.Hajime Hosogai), Kengo Nakamura, Shinji Kagawa, Mike Havenaar (49.Tadanari Lee), Shinji Okazaki (77.Jungo Fujimoto). Trainer: Alberto Zaccheroni (Italy).
TJK: Alisher Tuychiev, Davronjon Ergashev, Eraj Rajabov, Sokhib Savankulov, Akmal Saburov, Nuriddin Davronov, Fatkhullo Fatkhuloev (39.Dilshod Vasiev), Khurshed Makhmudov (67.Ibrahim Rabimov), Jahongir Jalilov, Makhmadali Sadykov, Kamil Saidov (80.Farrukh Choriev). Trainer: Alimzhon Rafikov.
Goals: 1-0 Mike Havenaar (11), 2-0 Shinji Okazaki (19), 3-0 Yūichi Komano (35), 4-0 Shinji Kagawa (41), 5-0 Mike Havenaar (47), 6-0 Kengo Nakamura (56), 7-0 Shinji Kagawa (68), 8-0 Shinji Okazaki (74).
Cautions: Yasuyuki Konno.

11.10.2011, Yanggakdo Stadium, P'yōngyang; Attendance: 29,000
Referee: Alireza Faghani (Iran)
KOREA D.P.R. - UZBEKISTAN 0-1(0-1)
PRK: Ri Myong-Guk, Jon Kwang-Ik, Pak Nam-Chol II, Ri Kwang-Hyok, Cha Jong-Hyok, Ahn Yong-Hak (85.Pak Nam-Chol I), Kim Yong-Jun (56.Pak Song-Chol I), Ryang Yong-Gi, Jong Tae-Se, Jong Il-Gwan (33.Ri Chol-Myong), Pak Kwang-Ryong. Trainer: Yun Jong-Su.
UZB: Ignatiy Nesterov, Islom Tuhtahujaev, Vitaliy Denisov, Odil Ahmedov, Viktor Karpenko (55.Shavkat Mullajanov), Jasur O. Hasanov II (32.Vagiz Galiulin), Azizbek Haydarov, Timur Kapadze, Sanzhar Tursunov, Server Djeparov, Aleksandr Geynrikh (64.Marat Bikmaev). Trainer: Vadim Abramov.
Goal: 0-1 Aleksandr Geynrikh (15).
Cautions: Shavkat Mullajanov, Server Djeparov, Sanzhar Tursunov.

11.11.2011, Pakhtakor Markaziy Stadium, Tashkent; Attendance: 27,525
Referee: Andre El Haddad (Lebanon)

UZBEKISTAN - KOREA D.P.R. 1-0(0-0)

UZB: Ignatiy Nesterov, Islom Tuhtahujaev, Vitaliy Denisov, Odil Ahmedov, Viktor Karpenko (55.Shavkat Mullajanov), Azizbek Haydarov, Timur Kapadze (88.Lutfulla Turayev), Vagiz Galiulin, Server Djeparov, Aleksandr Geynrikh, Maksim Shatskikh (75.Sanzhar Tursunov). Trainer: Vadim Abramov.

PRK: Ri Myong-Guk, Jang Song-Hyok, Jon Kwang-Ik, Pak Nam-Chol II, Ri Kwang-Chon, Cha Jong-Hyok (42.Ri Kwang-Hyok), Ahn Yong-Hak (65.Pak Song-Chol I), Pak Nam-Chol I, Ri Chol-Myong, Ryang Yong-Gi (54.Jong Il-Gwan), Jong Tae-Se. Trainer: Yun Jong-Su.

Goal: 1-0 Timur Kapadze (49).

Cautions: Vagiz Galiulin / Cha Jong-Hyok, Pak Nam-Chol II, Ahn Yong-Hak.

11.11.2011, Central Stadium, Dushanbe; Attendance: 18,000
Referee: Kim Dong-Jin (Korea Republic)

TAJIKISTAN - JAPAN 0-4(0-1)

TJK: Alisher Tuychiev, Davronjon Ergashev, Eraj Rajabov, Sokhib Savankulov, Farkhod Vasiev, Nuriddin Davronov, Khurshed Makhmudov, Ibrahim Rabimov (69.Makhmadali Sadykov), Dilshod Vasiev, Jahongir Jalilov (57.Fatkhullo Fatkhuloev), Kamil Saidov (67.Akhtam Khamrakulov). Trainer: Alimzhon Rafikov.

JPN: Eiji Kawashima, Yasuyuki Konno, Yūichi Komano, Atsuto Uchida (88.Masahiko Inoha), Maya Yoshida, Yasuhito Endō, Makoto Hasebe, Kengo Nakamura (86.Hiroshi Kiyotake), Shinji Kagawa, Mike Havenaar (56.Ryoichi Maeda), Shinji Okazaki. Trainer: Alberto Zaccheroni (Italy).

Goals: 0-1 Yasuyuki Konno (36), 0-2 Shinji Okazaki (61), 0-3 Ryoichi Maeda (82), 0-4 Shinji Okazaki (90+2).

Cautions: Kamil Saidov.

15.11.2011, Pakhtakor Markaziy Stadium, Tashkent; Attendance: 5,325
Referee: Mohamed Abdelkarim Ismail Al Zarouni (United Arab Emirates)

UZBEKISTAN - TAJIKISTAN 3-0(1-0)

UZB: Ignatiy Nesterov, Shavkat Mullajanov, Islom Tuhtahujaev, Vitaliy Denisov, Odil Ahmedov, Azizbek Haydarov (81.Anzur Ismailov), Timur Kapadze (72.Server Djeparov), Vagiz Galiulin, Sanzhar Tursunov, Aleksandr Geynrikh, Bakhodyr Nasymov (56.Ulugbek Bakaev). Trainer: Vadim Abramov.

TJK: Alisher Tuychiev, Davronjon Ergashev, Eraj Rajabov, Sokhib Savankulov, Farkhod Vasiev, Nuriddin Davronov, Jamshed Ismailov (46.Akmal Saburov), Khurshed Makhmudov, Dilshod Vasiev, Akhtam Khamrakulov, Kamil Saidov. Trainer: Alimzhon Rafikov.

Goals: 1-0 Sanzhar Tursunov (34), 2-0 Odil Ahmedov (60), 3-0 Aleksandr Geynrikh (72).

Cautions: Odil Ahmedov, Aleksandr Geynrikh, Shavkat Mullajanov, Sanzhar Tursunov, Islom Tuhtahujaev, Server Djeparov, Vagiz Galiulin / Davronjon Ergashev, Dilshod Vasiev.

Sent off: Eraj Rajabov (86).

15.11.2011, "Kim Il-Sung" Stadium, P'yōngyang; Attendance: 50,000
Referee: Nawaf Abdullah Ghayyath Shukralla (Bahrain)

KOREA D.P.R. - JAPAN 1-0(0-0)

PRK: Ri Myong-Guk, Jang Song-Hyok, Jon Kwang-Ik (90+5.Ri Pae-Hun), Pak Nam-Chol II, Ri Kwang-Chon, Ri Kwang-Hyok, Pak Nam-Chol I, Pak Song-Chol I, Jong Tae-Se (35.Pak Song-Chol II; 87.Ri Chol-Myong), Jong Il-Gwan, Pak Kwang-Ryong. Trainer: Yun Jong-Su.

JPN: Shusaku Nishikawa, Yasuyuki Konno, Yuzo Kurihara, Yūichi Komano, Hajime Hosogai, Masahiko Inoha, Makoto Hasebe, Kengo Nakamura (62.Atsuto Uchida), Hiroshi Kiyotake (85.Tadanari Lee), Ryoichi Maeda (77.Mike Havenaar), Shinji Okazaki. Trainer: Alberto Zaccheroni (Italy).

Goal: 1-0 Pak Nam-Chol II (50).

Cautions: Jong Il-Gwan, Jang Song-Hyok, Pak Nam-Chol I, Pak Song-Chol II, Ri Kwang-Chon, Ri Kwang-Hyok / Ryoichi Maeda.

Sent off: Jong Il-Gwan (77).

29.02.2012, Toyota Stadium, Aichi; Attendance: 42,720
Referee: Abdullah Mohamed Balideh (Qatar)
JAPAN - UZBEKISTAN **0-1(0-0)**
JPN: Eiji Kawashima, Yasuyuki Konno, Yuto Nagatomo (84.Yūichi Komano), Atsuto Uchida, Maya Yoshida, Yasuhito Endō, Makoto Hasebe, Shinji Kagawa, Jungo Fujimoto (46.Takashi Inui), Mike Havenaar (66.Tadanari Lee), Shinji Okazaki. Trainer: Alberto Zaccheroni (Italy).
UZB: Ignatiy Nesterov, Artyom Filiposyan, Anzur Ismailov, Stanislav Andreyev (58.Dilshod Rakhmatullayev), Islom Inomov, Azizbek Haydarov, Timur Kapadze, Ildar Magdeev (38.Oybek Kilichev), Jasur Hasanov, Bakhodyr Nasymov, Aleksandr Shadrin (65.Shavkat Salomov). Trainer: Vadim Abramov.
Goal: 0-1 Aleksandr Shadrin (54).
Cautions: Aleksandr Shadrin, Shavkat Salomov.

29.02.2012, 20-Letie Nezavisimosti Stadium, Khujand; Attendance: 35,000
Referee: Banjari Mohammed Al Dosari (Qatar)
TAJIKISTAN - KOREA D.P.R. **1-1(0-0)**
TJK: Alisher Tuychiev, Davronjon Ergashev, Aleksey Negmatov, Sokhib Savankulov, Fatkhullo Fatkhuloev, Farkhod Vasiev, Nuriddin Davronov, Jahongir Jalilov (66.Ilhomzhon Ortikov), Akhtam Khamrakulov (76.Kamil Saidov), Makhmadali Sadykov, Farkhod Tokhirov (90.Dilshod Vasiev). Trainer: Kemal Alispahić (Bosnia-Herzegovina).
PRK: Ri Myong-Guk, Jang Song-Hyok, Jon Kwang-Ik, Jang Myong-Il, Pak Nam-Chol II, Ri Kwang-Chon, Ri Hyong-Mu, Pak Song-Chol I, Ri Chol-Myong (78.Kim Ju-Song), Jang Kuk-Chol, Pak Song-Chol II. Trainer: Yun Jong-Su.
Goals: 0-1 Jang Song-Hyok (53 penalty), 1-1 Akhtam Khamrakulov (61).
Cautions: Makhmadali Sadykov.

GROUP D

02.09.2011	Brisbane	Australia - Thailand	2-1(0-1)
02.09.2011	Muscat	Oman - Saudi Arabia	0-0
06.09.2011	Riyadh	Saudi Arabia - Australia	1-3(0-1)
06.09.2011	Bangkok	Thailand - Oman	3-0(2-0)
11.10.2011	Sydney	Australia - Oman	3-0(1-0)
11.10.2011	Bangkok	Thailand - Saudi Arabia	0-0
11.11.2011	Riyadh	Saudi Arabia - Thailand	3-0(0-0)
11.11.2011	Muscat	Oman - Australia	1-0(1-0)
15.11.2011	Riyadh	Saudi Arabia - Oman	0-0
15.11.2011	Bangkok	Thailand - Australia	0-1(0-0)
29.02.2012	Melbourne	Australia - Saudi Arabia	4-2(1-2)
29.02.2012	Muscat	Oman - Thailand	2-0(1-0)

FINAL STANDINGS

1.	**Australia**	6	5	0	1	13 - 5	15
2.	**Oman**	6	2	2	2	3 - 6	8
3.	Saudi Arabia	6	1	3	2	6 - 7	6
4.	Thailand	6	1	1	4	4 - 8	4

Australia and Oman advanced to the 4th Round.

02.09.2011, Suncorp Stadium, Brisbane; Attendance: 24,540
Referee: Abdullah Mohamed Balideh (Qatar)
AUSTRALIA - THAILAND 2-1(0-1)
AUS: Mark Schwarzer, Lucas Edward Neill, Matthew Thomas Špiranović, Brett Michael Emerton (79.Alex Brosque), Luke Wilksire, Brett Trevor Holman (90.James Troisi), Timothy Filiga Cahill (71.Robbie Thomas Kruse), Carl Valeri, Matthew Graham McKay, Neil Martin Kilkenny, Joshua Blake Kennedy. Trainer: Holger Osieck (Germany).
THA: Sinthaweechai Hathairattanakool, Niweat Siriwong, Suree Sukha (74.Arthit Sunthornpit), Supachai Komsilp, Cholratit Jantakam, Jakkraphan Kaewprom, Adul Lahso, Datsakorn Thonglao, Rangsan Vivatchaichok, Sompong Soleb (56.Suttinan Phukhom), Teerasil Dangda. Trainer: Winfried Schäfer (Germany).
Goals: 0-1 Teerasil Dangda (15), 1-1 Joshua Blake Kennedy (58), 2-1 Alex Brosque (86).
Cautions: Carl Valeri, Matthew Graham McKay / Rangsan Vivatchaichok, Supachai Komsilp.

02.09.2011, Al-Seeb Stadium, Muscat; Attendance: 14,000
Referee: Abdulrahman Abdou (Qatar)
OMAN - SAUDI ARABIA 0-0
OMA: Ali Abdullah Harib Al Habsi, Rashid Jumaa Mubarak Al Farsi, Mohammed Abdullah Mubarak Al Balushi, Ahmed Mubarak Obaid Al Mahaijri, Hassan Yousuf Mudhafar Al Gheilani, Saad Suhail Jumaa Al Mukhaini, Ahmed Hadid Thuwaini Al Mukhaini, Juma Darwish Al Mashri, Fawzi Bashir Rajab Bait Doorbeen (88.Mohammed Saleh Al Maslami), Ismail Sulaiman Ashoor Al Ajmi (71.Hassan Rabia Suwaidan Al Hosni), Amad Ali Suleiman Al Hosni (44.Hussein Ali Farah Al Hadhri). Trainer: Paul Le Guen (France).
KSA: Hassan Bader Al Otaibi, Abdullah Al Dossary, Hamad Mohsen Al Montashari, Abdullah Mohammed Al Zori Al Dosari, Osama Abdul Razzaq Al Hawsawi, Taisir Jaber Al Jassam, Saud Hamood Hasan, Saud Ali Khariri, Moataz Siddiq Al Mousa (69.Ahmed Ibrahim Otaif), Nassir Ali Al Shamrani (81.Yahya Sulaiman Al Shehri), Yasser Saeed Al Qahtani (68.Naif Ahmad Taib Hazazi). Trainer: Franklin Edmundo Rijkaard (Holland).
Cautions: Ahmed Mubarak Obaid Al Mahaijri / Hamad Mohsen Al Montashari, Abdullah Al Dossary.

06.09.2011, „Prince Mohamed bin Fahd" Stadium, Dammam; Attendance: 15,000
Referee: Yuichi Nishimura (Japan)

SAUDI ARABIA - AUSTRALIA 1-3(0-1)

KSA: Hassan Bader Al Otaibi, Hamad Mohsen Al Montashari, Rashed Al Raheeb, Abdullah Mohammed Al Zori Al Dosari, Hassan Muath Fallatah (46.Yahya Sulaiman Al Shehri), Osama Abdul Razzaq Al Hawsawi, Taisir Jaber Al Jassam, Ahmed Ibrahim Otaif (60.Nassir Ali Al Shamrani), Saud Ali Khariri, Nawaf Shaker Al Abed (79.Mohammad Al Sahlawi), Naif Ahmad Taib Hazazi. Trainer: Franklin Edmundo Rijkaard (Holland).

AUS: Mark Schwarzer, Lucas Edward Neill, Saša Ognenovski, Luke Wilkshire, Michael Anthony Zullo (79.Robbie Thomas Kruse), Brett Michael Emerton, Brett Trevor Holman (87.Timothy Filiga Cahill), Michael John Jedinak, Carl Valeri, Joshua Blake Kennedy (89.Mark Daniel Milligan), Matthew Graham McKay. Trainer: Holger Osieck (Germany).

Goals: 0-1 Joshua Blake Kennedy (40), 0-2 Joshua Blake Kennedy (56), 1-2 Nassir Ali Al Shamrani (65), 1-3 Luke Wilksire (77 penalty).

Cautions: Hamad Mohsen Al Montashari, Mohammad Al Sahlawi / Michael Anthony Zullo.

06.09.2011, Rajamangala Stadium, Bangkok; Attendance: 19,000
Referee: Kim Dong-Jin (Korea Republic)

THAILAND - OMAN 3-0(2-0)

THA: Sinthaweechai Hathairattanakool, Niweat Siriwong, Supachai Komsilp, Cholratit Jantakam, Surat Sukha, Jakkraphan Kaewprom, Adul Lahso (46.Suchao Nuchnum), Datsakorn Thonglao, Rangsan Vivatchaichok, Teerasil Dangda (70.Chatree Chimtalay), Sompong Soleb (61.Suree Sukha). Trainer: Winfried Schäfer (Germany).

OMA: Ali Abdullah Harib Al Habsi, Mohammed Abdullah Mubarak Al Balushi, Rashid Jumaa Mubarak Al Farsi, Ahmed Mubarak Obaid Al Mahaijri, Hassan Yousuf Mudhafar Al Gheilani (46.Ismail Sulaiman Ashoor Al Ajmi), Ahmed Hadid Thuwaini Al Mukhaini, Qasim Said Sanjoor Hardan (46.Hussein Ali Farah Al Hadhri), Saad Suhail Jumaa Al Mukhaini, Juma Darwish Al Mashri (46.Ismail Sulaiman Ashoor Al Ajmi), Fawzi Bashir Rajab Bait Doorbeen, Amad Ali Suleiman Al Hosni. Trainer: Paul Le Guen (France).

Goals: 1-0 Sompong Soleb (35), 2-0 Teerasil Dangda (41), 3-0 Rashid Juma Mubarak Al Farsi (90 own goal).

Cautions: Juma Darwish Al Mashri, Mohammed Abdullah Mubarak Al Balushi, Fawzi Bashir Rajab Bait Doorbeen.

11.10.2011, ANZ Stadium, Sydney; Attendance: 24,732
Referee: Valentin Kovalenko (Uzbekistan)

AUSTRALIA - OMAN 3-0(1-0)

AUS: Adam Jay Federici, Lucas Edward Neill, Matthew Thomas Špiranović, Rhys Williams (71.Robbie Thomas Kruse), Luke Wilkshire, Michael Anthony Zullo (86.Alex Brosque), Brett Trevor Holman, Michael John Jedinak, Carl Valeri, Matthew Graham McKay, Joshua Blake Kennedy (90.Neil Martin Kilkenny). Trainer: Holger Osieck (Germany).

OMA: Ali Abdullah Harib Al Habsi, Abdulrahman Saleh Al Alaoui, Mohammed Abdullah Mubarak Al Balushi, Rashid Jumaa Mubarak Al Farsi, Saad Suhail Jumaa Al Mukhaini, Ahmed Mubarak Obaid Al Mahaijri, Ahmed Hadid Thuwaini Al Mukhaini (66.Eid Mohamed Eid Al Farsi), Juma Darwish Al Mashri, Abdul Aziz Humaid Mubarak Al Muqbali, Amad Ali Suleiman Al Hosni (Hassan Rabia Suwaidan Al Hosni), Ismail Sulaiman Ashoor Al Ajmi (84.Hamood Saleh Said Al Saadi). Trainer: Paul Le Guen (France).

Goals: 1-0 Brett Trevor Holman (8), 2-0 Joshua Blake Kennedy (65), 3-0 Michael John Jedinak (85).

Cautions: Joshua Blake Kennedy, Luke Wilkshire.

11.10.2011, Rajamangala Stadium, Bangkok; Attendance: 42,000
Referee: Ravshan Irmatov (Uzbekistan)
THAILAND - SAUDI ARABIA 0-0
THA: Sinthaweechai Hathairattanakool, Niweat Siriwong, Suree Sukha (58.Suchao Nuchnum), Supachai Komsilp, Cholratit Jantakam, Surat Sukha (79.Sompong Soleb), Jakkraphan Kaewprom, Adul Lahso, Rangsan Vivatchaichok, Datsakorn Thonglao, Teerasil Dangda (90+2.Chatree Chimtalay). Trainer: Winfried Schäfer (Germany).
KSA: Walid Abdullah Ali, Abdullah Al Dossary, Osama Mabrouk Awad Al Muwallad Al Harbi, Hassan Muath Fallatah, Osama Abdul Razzaq Al Hawsawi, Abdulaziz Saeed Al Dosari (57.Nassir Ali Al Shamrani), Ahmed Mohammed Al Fraidi (89.Ahmed Ibrahim Otaif), Taisir Jaber Al Jassam, Saud Ali Khariri, Mohammed Noor Al Hawsawi, Yasser Saeed Al Qahtani (81.Naif Ahmad Taib Hazazi). Trainer: Franklin Edmundo Rijkaard (Holland).
Cautions: Nassir Ali Al Shamrani.

11.11.2011, "King Fahd" International Stadium, Riyadh; Attendance: 32,500
Referee: Liu Kwok Man (Hong Kong)
SAUDI ARABIA - THAILAND 3-0(0-0)
KSA: Walid Abdullah Ali, Abdullah Al Dossary, Osama Mabrouk Awad Al Muwallad Al Harbi, Hassan Muath Fallatah, Osama Abdul Razzaq Al Hawsawi, Ahmed Mohammed Al Fraidi (84.Ahmed Ibrahim Otaif), Taisir Jaber Al Jassam (56.Nassir Ali Al Shamrani), Saud Ali Khariri, Mohammed Noor Al Hawsawi, Mohammad Bander Al Shalhoub (75.Nawaf Shaker Al Abed), Naif Ahmad Taib Hazazi. Trainer: Franklin Edmundo Rijkaard (Holland).
THA: Sinthaweechai Hathairattanakool, Theeratorn Boonmatan, Niweat Siriwong, Suree Sukha, Cholratit Jantakam, Jakkraphan Kaewprom, Adul Lahso, Apipoo Suntornpanavej (35.Pichithpong Choeichiu; 67.Surachart Sareepim), Suchao Nuchnum, Datsakorn Thonglao, Kirati Keawsombut (67.Pipob On-Mo). Trainer: Winfried Schäfer (Germany).
Goals: 1-0 Ahmed Mohammed Al Fraidi (59), 2-0 Naif Ahmad Taib Hazazi (80), 3-0 Mohammed Noor Al Hawsawi (89).
Cautions: Osama Mabrouk Awad Al Muwallad Al Harbi, Nawaf Shaker Al Abed / Pichithpong Choeichiu, Cholratit Jantakam, Surachart Sareepim, Teeratep Winothai (on the bench).
Sent off: Theeratorn Boonmatan (90+3).

11.11.2011, „Sultan Qaboos“ Sports Complex, Muscat; Attendance: 4,500
Referee: Ali Hasan Ebrahim Abdulnabi (Bahrain)
OMAN - AUSTRALIA 1-0(1-0)
OMA: Ali Abdullah Harib Al Habsi, Hassan Yousuf Mudhafar Al Gheilani, Mohammed Abdullah Mubarak Al Balushi, Abdulrahman Saleh Khalfan Al Alawi, Abdul Sallam Amur Juma Al Mukhaini, Saad Suhail Jumaa Al Mukhaini, Hussein Ali Farah Al Hadhri (70.Ismail Sulaiman Ashoor Al Ajmi), Eid Mohamed Eid Al Farsi, Mohamed Hamed Hidaib Al Mukhaini (60.Fawzi Bashir Rajab Bait Doorbeen), Amad Ali Suleiman Al Hosni (79.Qasim Said Sanjoor Hardan), Abdul Aziz Humaid Mubarak Al Muqbali. Trainer: Paul Le Gucn (France).
AUS: Mark Schwarzer, Lucas Edward Neill, Rhys Williams (72.Brett Michael Emerton), Matthew Thomas Špiranović, Luke Wilkshire, Brett Trevor Holman, Michael John Jedinak, Carl Valeri, Matthew Graham McKay, Harold Kewell (53.Robbie Thomas Kruse), Joshua Blake Kennedy. Trainer: Holger Osieck (Germany).
Goal: 1-0 Amad Ali Suleiman Al Hosni (18).
Cautions: Mohammed Abdullah Mubarak Al Balushi, Abdul Aziz Humaid Mubarak Al Muqbali, Ismail Sulaiman Ashoor Al Ajmi / Lucas Edward Neill.

15.11.2011, "King Fahd" International Stadium, Riyadh; Attendance: 62,740
Referee: Mohsen Torky (Iran)
SAUDI ARABIA - OMAN 0-0
KSA: Walid Abdullah Ali, Hassan Muath Fallatah, Osama Mabrouk Awad Al Muwallad Al Harbi, Osama Abdul Razzaq Al Hawsawi, Abdullah Al Dossary, Saud Ali Khariri, Ahmed Ibrahim Otaif (53.Nassir Ali Al Shamrani), Mohammed Noor Al Hawsawi, Ahmed Mohammed Al Fraidi, Mohammad Bander Al Shalhoub (63.Nawaf Shaker Al Abed), Naif Ahmad Taib Hazazi (83.Yasser Saeed Al Qahtani). Trainer: Franklin Edmundo Rijkaard (Holland).
OMA: Ali Abdullah Harib Al Habsi, Hassan Yousuf Mudhafar Al Gheilani, Mohammed Abdullah Mubarak Al Balushi, Abdul Sallam Amur Juma Al Mukhaini, Saad Suhail Jumaa Al Mukhaini, Hussein Ali Farah Al Hadhri (75.Juma Darwish Al Mashri), Fawzi Bashir Rajab Bait Doorbeen, Ali Hilal Saud Al Jabri, Eid Mohamed Eid Al Farsi, Abdul Aziz Humaid Mubarak Al Muqbali, Amad Ali Suleiman Al Hosni (67.Ismail Sulaiman Ashoor Al Ajmi). Trainer: Paul Le Guen (France).
Cautions: Saud Ali Khariri, Osama Mabrouk Awad Al Muwallad Al Harbi, Ahmed Mohammed Al Fraidi / Eid Mohamed Eid Al Farsi.

15.11.2011, Suphachalasai Stadium, Bangkok; Attendance: 19,400
Referee: Saeid Mozaffarizadeh (Iran)
THAILAND - AUSTRALIA 0-1(0-0)
THA: Sinthaweechai Hathairattanakool, Nattaporn Phanrit, Niweat Siriwong, Suree Sukha, Supachai Komsilp, Cholratit Jantakam, Pichithpong Choeichiu (80.Sarawut Masuk), Jakkraphan Kaewprom, Rangsan Vivatchaichok (62.Teerathep Winothai), Datsakorn Thonglao, Kirati Keawsombut (73.Pipob On-Mo). Trainer: Winfried Schäfer (Germany).
AUS: Mark Schwarzer, Lucas Edward Neill, Luke Wilkshire, Matthew Thomas Špiranović, Michael Anthony Zullo, Brett Michael Emerton, Brett Trevor Holman (83.Robbie Thomas Kruse), Michael John Jedinak (90.Neil Martin Kilkenny), Carl Valeri, Matthew Graham McKay, Joshua Blake Kennedy (86.Alex Brosque). Trainer: Holger Osieck (Germany).
Goal: 0-1 Brett Trevor Holman (77).
Cautions: Rangsan Vivatchaichok, Cholratit Jantakam / Matthew Graham McKay, Michael John Jedinak, Luke Wilkshire, Brett Michael Emerton.

29.02.2012, AAMI Park, Melbourne; Attendance: 24,240
Referee: Kim Dong-Jin (Korea Republic)
AUSTRALIA - SAUDI ARABIA 4-2(1-2)
AUS: Mark Schwarzer, Lucas Edward Neill, Matthew Thomas Špiranović (82.David Raymond Carney), Jade Bronson North, Saša Ognenovski, Brett Michael Emerton, Mark Daniel Milligan, Harold Kewell, James Troisi (62.Archibald Gerald Thompson), Alex Brosque (87.Nicholas Alberto Carle), Mark Bresciano. Trainer: Holger Osieck (Germany).
KSA: Walid Abdullah Ali, Hassan Muath Fallatah, Osama Abdul Razzaq Al Hawsawi, Kamel Al Mousa Fallatah, Abdullah Al Dossary, Saud Ali Khariri, Taisir Jaber Al Jassam, Salem Al Dosari, Ahmed Mohammed Al Fraidi (66.Ahmed Ibrahim Otaif), Mohammad Bander Al Shalhoub (79.Naif Ahmad Taib Hazazi), Nassir Ali Al Shamrani (73.Yasser Saeed Al Qahtani). Trainer: Franklin Edmundo Rijkaard (Holland).
Goals: 0-1 Salem Al Dosari (19), 1-1 Alex Brosque (43), 1-2 Nassir Ali Al Shamrani (45), 2-2 Harold Kewell (73), 3-2 Alex Brosque (75), 4-2 Brett Michael Emerton (77).
Cautions: Saud Ali Khariri, Nassir Ali Al Shamrani.

29.02.2012, "Sultan Qaboos" Sports Complex, Muscat; Attendance: 22,000
Referee: Masaaki Toma (Japan)

OMAN - THAILAND 2-0(1-0)

OMA: Ali Abdullah Harib Al Habsi, Hassan Yousuf Mudhafar Al Gheilani, Mohammed Abdullah Mubarak Al Balushi, Abdul Sallam Amur Juma Al Mukhaini (90+2.Eid Mohamed Eid Al Farsi), Saad Suhail Jumaa Al Mukhaini, Hussein Ali Farah Al Hadhri (72.Juma Darwish Al Mashri), Ahmed Mubarak Obaid Al Mahaijri, Ahmed Hadid Thuwaini Al Mukhaini, Fawzi Bashir Rajab Bait Doorbeen, Amad Ali Suleiman Al Hosni (69.Nasser Sulaiman Abdullah Al Ali), Abdul Aziz Humaid Mubarak Al Muqbali. Trainer: Paul Le Guen (France).

THA: Kawin Thammasatchanan, Jetsada Jitsawad, Niweat Siriwong, Suree Sukha, Anucha Kitpongsri, Pichithpong Choeichiu, Jakkraphan Kaewprom (65.Teerathep Winothai), Jirawat Makarom, Suchao Nuchnum (38.Sumanya Purisai), Sutee Suksomkit, Teerasil Dangda. Trainer: Winfried Schäfer (Germany).

Goals: 1-0 Hussein Ali Farah Al Hadhri (8), 2-0 Abdul Aziz Humaid Mubarak Al Muqbali (90+2).

Cautions: Abdul Sallam Amur Juma Al Mukhaini, Juma Darwish Al Mashri / Pichithpong Choeichiu, Sumanya Purisai, Jetsada Jitsawad.

Sent off: Teerathep Winothai (85).

GROUP E

02.09.2011	Tehran	Iran - Indonesia	3-0(0-0)
02.09.2011	Riffa	Bahrain - Qatar	0-0
06.09.2011	Doha	Qatar - Iran	1-1(0-0)
06.09.2011	Jakarta	Indonesia - Bahrain	0-2(0-1)
11.10.2011	Tehran	Iran - Bahrain	6-0(3-0)
11.10.2011	Jakarta	Indonesia - Qatar	2-3(2-2)
11.11.2011	Doha	Qatar - Indonesia	4-0(2-0)
11.11.2011	Riffa	Bahrain - Iran	1-1(1-0)
15.11.2011	Doha	Qatar - Bahrain	0-0
15.11.2011	Jakarta	Indonesia - Iran	1-4(1-3)
29.02.2012	Tehran	Iran - Qatar	2-2(1-1)
29.02.2012	Riffa	Bahrain - Indonesia	10-0(4-0)

FINAL STANDINGS

1.	**Iran**	6	3	3	0	17 - 5	12
2.	**Qatar**	6	2	4	0	10 - 5	10
3.	Bahrain	6	2	3	1	13 - 7	9
4.	Indonesia	6	0	0	6	3 - 26	0

Iran and Qatar advanced to the 4th Round.

02.09.2011, Azadi Stadium, Tehran; Attendance: 75,800
Referee: Masaaki Toma (Japan)
IRAN - INDONESIA 3-0(0-0)
IRN: Seyed Mehdi Rahmati Osgouei, Seyed Hadi Aghily Anvar, Khosro Heydari, Seyed Jalal Hosseini Khoshkebejari, Mehrdad Pooladi, Javad Nekounam, Ghasem Haddadifar (70.Andranik Teymourian), Gholamreza Rezaei (64.Hossein Mahini), Mohammad Ali Karimi Pashaki, Farhad Majidi Ghadikolaei, Mohamad Reza Khalatbari (65.Ehsan Hajsafi). Trainer: Carlos Manuel Brito Leal Queiroz (Portugal).
IDN: Markus Haris Maulana, Hamka Hamzah, Muhammad Roby, Zulkifli Syukur, Muhammad Ridwan, Firman Utina (81.Oktovianus Maniani), Hariono (70.Tony Sucipto), Benny Wahyudi, Muhammad Ilham (61.Irfan Haarys Bachdim), Bambang Pamungkas, Cristian Gérard Alvaro Gonzáles. Trainer: Wilhelmus Gerardus Rijsbergen (Holland).
Goals: 1-0 Javad Nekounam (53), 2-0 Javad Nekounam (74), 3-0 Andranik Teymourian (87).
Cautions: Muhammad Roby, Muhammad Ilham, Zulkifli Syukur.

02.09.2011, Bahrain National Stadium, Riffa; Attendance: 5,000
Referee: Mohamed Abdelkarim Ismail Al Zarouni (United Arab Emirates)
BAHRAIN - QATAR 0-0
BHR: Sayed Mohammed Jaffer Sabet, Mohamed Husain Bahzad, Abdulla Rahman Al Marzooqi, Saleh Abdulhameed Mahmeedi, Rashid Khalil Ali Al Houti, Hussain Ali Baba Mohammed (70.Mohammed Tayeb Al Alawi), Hamad Rakea Humood Al Anezi (85.Fahad Yusuf Abdulla Ahmed Hassan Al Hardan), Salman Isa (77.Mahmood Abdulrahman Mohammed Noor), Faouzi Mubarak Aaish, Abdullah Omar Ismail, Ismaeel Abdullatif Hassan. Trainer: Peter John Taylor (England).
QAT: Qasem Abdulhamed Burhan, Marcone Amaral Costa Júnior, Bilal Mohammed Rajab, Ibrahim Majid Abdulmajid, Hamid Ismail Khalifa (65.Mohamed Mousa Abbas Ali), Mohammed Kasola, Lawrence Awuley Quaye, Ahmed Mohamed Al Sayed (79.Hussain Ali Shehab), Mohamed Omar Hashim Ali Saeed (79.Jaralla Ali Jamal Ameer Al Marri), Fábio César Montezine, Andrés Sebastián Soria Quintana. Trainer: Sebastião Barroso Lazaroni (Brazil).
Cautions: Abdulla Rahman Al Marzooqi / Hamid Ismail Khalifa, Bilal Mohammed Rajab, Fábio César Montezine.

06.09.2011, "Jassim Bin Hamad" Stadium, Doha; Attendance: 8,125
Referee: Choi Myung-Yong (Korea Republic)

QATAR - IRAN **1-1(0-0)**

QAT: Qasem Abdulhamed Burhan, Marcone Amaral Costa Júnior, Bilal Mohammed Rajab, Ibrahim Majid Abdulmajid, Hamid Ismail Khalifa, Hussain Ali Shehab (64.Fahad Satam Al Shammari; 90.Mohammed Razak), Lawrence Awuley Quaye, Wesam Abdulmajid Rizik, Ahmed Mohamed Al Sayed, Fábio César Montezine (65.Khalfan Ibrahim Al Khalfan), Andrés Sebastián Soria Quintana. Trainer: Sebastião Barroso Lazaroni (Brazil).

IRN: Seyed Mehdi Rahmati Osgouei, Seyed Hadi Aghily Anvar, Khosro Heydari, Seyed Jalal Hosseini Khoshkebejari, Mehrdad Pooladi, Javad Nekounam (37.Maziar Zare Eshghdoust), Andranik Teymourian, Karim Ansarifard, Gholamreza Rezaei, Mohammad Ali Karimi Pashaki (70.Farhad Majidi Ghadikolaei), Mohamad Reza Khalatbari (63.Mojtaba Jabbari Kordgeshlagi). Trainer: Carlos Manuel Brito Leal Queiroz (Portugal).

Goals: Seyed Hadi Aghily Anvar (47)

Cautions: Hussain Ali Shehab, Hamid Ismail Khalifa, Wesam Abdulmajid Rizik, Ibrahim Majid Abdulmajid / Khosro Heydari, Maziar Zare Eshghdoust.

06.09.2011, Gelora Bung Karno Stadium, Jakarta; Attendance: 85,000
Referee: Lee Min-Hu (Korea Republic)

INDONESIA - BAHRAIN **0-2(0-1)**

IDN: Markus Haris Maulana, Hamka Hamzah, Muhammad Roby, Muhammad Ridwan, Muhammad Nasuha (61.Supardi Nasir), Firman Utina (46.Hariono), Benny Wahyudi, Ahmad Bustomi (90+3.Ferdinand Alfred Sinaga), Boaz Theofilius Erwin Solossa, Bambang Pamungkas, Cristian Gérard Alvaro Gonzáles. Trainer: Wilhelmus Gerardus Rijsbergen (Holland).

BHR: Sayed Mohammed Jaffer Sabet, Mohamed Husain Bahzad, Abdulla Rahman Al Marzooqi, Rashid Khalil Ali Al Houti, Hussain Ali Baba Mohammed, Hamad Rakea Humood Al Anezi, Faouzi Mubarak Aaish (90+15.Mahmood Abdulrahman Mohammed Noor), Sayed Dhiya Saaed, Abdullah Omar Ismail, Ismaeel Abdullatif Hassan (90+8.Ahmed Mubarak Al Khattal), Mohammed Tayeb Al Alawi (68.Mohamed Dawood Saad Salman). Trainer: Peter John Taylor (England).

Goals: 0-1 Sayed Dhiya Saaed (45+1), 0-2 Ismaeel Abdullatif Hassan (70).

Cautions: Hariono, Cristian Gérard Alvaro Gonzáles / Hussain Ali Baba Mohammed.

11.10.2011, Azadi Stadium, Tehran; Attendance: 82,000
Referee: Peter Daniel Green (Australia)

IRAN - BAHRAIN **6-0(3-0)**

IRN: Seyed Mehdi Rahmati Osgouei, Seyed Hadi Aghily Anvar, Khosro Heydari, Seyed Jalal Hosseini Khoshkebejari, Mehrdad Pooladi, Javad Nekounam, Andranik Teymourian, Mojtaba Jabbari Kordgeshlagi (66.Karim Ansarifard), Mohammad Ghazi Najafabadi (73.Gholamreza Rezaei), Milad Meydavoudi (46.Hossein Mahini), Mohamad Reza Khalatbari. Trainer: Carlos Manuel Brito Leal Queiroz (Portugal).

BHR: Sayed Mohammed Jaffer Sabet, Mohamed Husain Bahzad, Abdulla Rahman Al Marzooqi, Mohamed Dawood Saad Salman, Rashid Khalil Ali Al Houti, Hussain Ali Baba Mohammed, Hamad Rakea Humood Al Anezi, Faouzi Mubarak Aaish (73.Mahmood Abdulrahman Mohammed Noor), Sayed Dhiya Saaed (46.Saleh Abdulhameed Mahmeedi), Abdullah Omar Ismail, Ismaeel Abdullatif Hassan (88.Fahad Yusuf Abdulla Ahmed Hassan Al Hardan). Trainer: Peter John Taylor (England).

Goals: 1-0 Seyed Jalal Hosseini Khoshkebejari (22), 2-0 Mojtaba Jabbari Kordgeshlagi (34), 3-0 Seyed Hadi Aghily Anvar (42), 4-0 Andranik Teymourian (52), 5-0 Karim Ansarifard (75), 6-0 Gholamreza Rezaei (83).

Cautions: Milad Meydavoudi, Andranik Teymourian.

Sent off: Rashid Khalil Ali Al Houti (1).

11.10.2011, Gelora Bung Karno Stadium, Jakarta; Attendance: 28,000
Referee: Malik Abdul Malik Abdul Bashir (Singapore)

INDONESIA - QATAR 2-3(2-2)

IDN: Ferry Rotinsulu, Hamka Hamzah (88.Yongki Aribowo), Muhammad Roby, Zulkifli Syukur, Muhammad Ridwan, Purwaka Yudhi Pratomo (75.Ahmad Bustomi), Supardi Nasir, Firman Utina (81.Hariono), Muhammad Ilham, Bambang Pamungkas, Cristian Gérard Alvaro Gonzáles. Trainer: Wilhelmus Gerardus Rijsbergen (Holland).

QAT: Baba Malick N'Diaye, Marcone Amaral Costa Júnior, Mohamed Mousa Abbas Ali (82.Mesaad Ali Al Hamad), Bilal Mohammed Rajab, Ibrahim Majid Abdulmajid, Wesam Abdulmajid Rizik, Abdulaziz Abdullah Mubarak Al Sulaiti (74.Hussain Ali Shehab), Mohamed Omar Hashim Ali Saeed, Khalfan Ibrahim Al Khalfan, Mohammed Abdul Mottalib Al Sayed, Mohammed Razak (84.Andrés Sebastián Soria Quintana). Trainer: Sebastião Barroso Lazaroni (Brazil).

Goals: 0-1 Abdulaziz Abdullah Mubarak Al Sulaiti (14), 1-1 Cristian Gérard Alvaro Gonzáles (26), 1-2 Khalfan Ibrahim Al Khalfan (32), 2-2 Cristian Gérard Alvaro Gonzáles (35), 3-2 Mohammed Razak (59).

Cautions: Firman Utina, Hamka Hamzah, Bambang Pamungkas / Mohamed Omar Hashim Ali Saeed, Mohamed Mousa Abbas Ali, Ibrahim Majid Abdulmajid.

11.11.2011, "Jassim bin Hamad" Stadium, Doha; Attendance: 6,500
Referee: Muhsen Basma (Syria)

QATAR - INDONESIA 4-0(2-0)

QAT: Qasem Abdulhamed Burhan, Marcone Amaral Costa Júnior, Bilal Mohammed Rajab, Meshal Abdullah Mubarak Budawood, Hamid Ismail Khalifa, Hussain Ali Shehab, Abdulaziz Abdullah Mubarak Al Sulaiti, Mohamed Omar Hashim Ali Saeed (65.Mohammed Kasola), Younes Ali Rahmati, Khalfan Ibrahim Al Khalfan (67.Hassan Khalid Al Haydous), Mohammed Razak (46.Andrés Sebastián Soria Quintana). Trainer: Sebastião Barroso Lazaroni (Brazil).

IDN: Hendro Kartiko, Hamka Hamzah, Muhammad Roby, Zulkifli Syukur, Muhammad Ridwan, Purwaka Yudhi Pratomo, Supardi Nasir (46.Mahyadi Panggabean), Firman Utina (72.Muhammad Ilham), Tony Sucipto (61.Cristian Gérard Alvaro Gonzáles), Boaz Theofilius Erwin Solossa, Bambang Pamungkas. Trainer: Wilhelmus Gerardus Rijsbergen (Holland).

Goals: 1-0 Mohammed Razak (30), 2-0 Khalfan Ibrahim Al Khalfan (34), 3-0 Khalfan Ibrahim Al Khalfan (64), 4-0 Andrés Sebastián Soria Quintana (90+2).

Cautions: Hendro Kartiko.

11.11.2011, Bahrain National Stadium, Riffa; Attendance: 18,000
Referee: Malik Abdul Bashir (Singapore)

BAHRAIN - IRAN 1-1(1-0)

BHR: Sayed Mohammed Jaffer Sabet, Mohamed Husain Bahzad, Mohamed Dawood Saad Salman, Saleh Abdulhameed Mahmeedi, Hamad Rakea Humood Al Anezi, Mahmood Merza Mahdi Ahmed Al Ajmi, Faouzi Mubarak Aaish (76.Fahad Yusuf Abdulla Ahmed Hassan Al Hardan), Sayed Dhiya Saaed (26.Mahmood Abdulrahman Mohammed Noor), Abdulwahab Al Malood, Ismaeel Abdullatif Hassan, Ali Muneer Mohamed Redha Abdulhusain. Trainer: Peter John Taylor (England).

IRN: Seyed Mehdi Rahmati Osgouei, Seyed Hadi Aghily Anvar, Seyed Jalal Hosseini Khoshkebejari, Hossein Mahini, Mehrdad Pooladi, Javad Nekounam, Andranik Teymourian, Mojtaba Jabbari Kordgeshlagi, Karim Ansarifard (61.Mohammad Ghazi Najafabadi), Gholamreza Rezaei (78.Milad Meydavoudi), Mohamad Reza Khalatbari (61.Javad Kazemian). Trainer: Carlos Manuel Brito Leal Queiroz (Portugal).

Goals: 1-0 Mahmood Merza Mahdi Ahmed Al Ajmi (45+1), 1-1 Mojtaba Jabbari Kordgeshlagi (90+2).

Cautions: Hamad Rakea Humood Al Anezi, Mohamed Dawood Saad Salman / Hossein Mahini.

15.11.2011, „Jassim Bin Hamad" Stadium, Doha; Attendance: 10,509
Referee: Yuichi Nishimura (Japan)

QATAR - BAHRAIN 0-0

QAT: Qasem Abdulhamed Burhan, Marcone Amaral Costa Júnior, Bilal Mohammed Rajab, Ibrahim Majid Abdulmajid, Mohammed Kasola, Hamid Ismail Khalifa (86.Hassan Khalid Al Haydous), Hussain Ali Shehab (63.Mohamed Mousa Abbas Ali), Abdulaziz Abdullah Mubarak Al Sulaiti, Younes Ali Rahmati, Khalfan Ibrahim Al Khalfan, Mohammed Razak (82.Andrés Sebastián Soria Quintana). Trainer: Sebastião Barroso Lazaroni (Brazil).

BHR: Sayed Mohammed Jaffer Sabet, Mohamed Husain Bahzad (80.Mahmood Abdulrahman Mohammed Noor), Mohamed Dawood Saad Salman (60.Abdulla Baba Fatadi), Saleh Abdulhameed Mahmeedi, Hamad Rakea Humood Al Anezi, Mahmood Merza Mahdi Ahmed Al Ajmi (59.Sami Mohamed Saeed Al Husaini), Faouzi Mubarak Aaish, Abdulwahab Al Malood, Abdullah Omar Ismail, Ismaeel Abdullatif Hassan, Ali Muneer Mohamed Redha Abdulhusain. Trainer: Peter John Taylor (England).

Cautions: Younes Ali Rahmati / Mohamed Husain Bahzad, Ali Muneer Mohamed Redha Abdulhusain, Ismaeel Abdullatif Hassan.

15.11.2011, Gelora Bung Karno Stadium, Jakarta; Attendance: 6,000
Referee: Tan Hai (China P.R.)

INDONESIA - IRAN 1-4(1-3)

IDN: Hendro Kartiko, Hamka Hamzah, Muhammad Ridwan, Supardi Nasir, Wahyu Wijiastanto, Mahyadi Panggabean (46.Benny Wahyudi), Hariono, Fandy Mochtar (46.Firman Utina), Bambang Pamungkas, Cristian Gérard Alvaro Gonzáles, Samsul Arif Munip (68.Muhammad Ilham). Trainer: Wilhelmus Gerardus Rijsbergen (Holland).

IRN: Seyed Mehdi Rahmati Osgouei, Seyed Hadi Aghily Anvar, Seyed Jalal Hosseini Khoshkebejari, Hossein Mahini, Javad Nekounam, Andranik Teymourian (63.Maziar Zare Eshghdoust), Ehsan Hajsafi, Mojtaba Jabbari Kordgeshlagi, Gholamreza Rezaei (46.Javad Kazemian), Mohammad Ghazi Najafabadi, Milad Meydavoudi (66.Mohamad Reza Khalatbari). Trainer: Carlos Manuel Brito Leal Queiroz (Portugal).

Goals: 0-1 Milad Meydavoudi (7), 0-2 Mojtaba Jabbari Kordgeshlagi (19), 0-3 Gholamreza Rezaei (24), 1-3 Bambang Pamungkas (44), 1-4 Javad Nekounam (72 penalty).

Cautions: Wahyu Wijiastanto, Cristian Gérard Alvaro Gonzáles / Gholamreza Rezaei, Javad Kazemian.

29.02.2012, Azadi Stadium, Tehran; Attendance: 51,300
Referee: Ravshan Irmatov (Uzbekistan)

IRAN - QATAR 2-2(1-1)

IRN: Seyed Seyed Mehdi Rahmati Osgouei Osgouei, Seyed Hadi Aghily Anvar, Khosro Heydari (85.Hossein Mahini), Seyed Seyed Jalal Hosseini Khoshkebejari, Mehrdad Pooladi, Javad Nekounam, Sahand-Pejman Nouri Roudsari, Mohammad Ali Karimi Pashaki, Ashkan Dejagah, Mohammad Ghazi Najafabadi (72.Karim Ansarifard), Mohamad Reza Khalatbari (66.Milad Nouri). Trainer: Carlos Manuel Brito Leal Queiroz (Portugal).

QAT: Qasem Abdulhamed Burhan, Ibrahim Abdullah Al Ghanim, Mesaad Ali Al Hamad, Meshal Abdullah Mubarak Budawood, Talal Hassan Ali Al Bloushi (78.Fábio César Montezine), Mohammed Kasola, Lawrence Awuley Quaye, Wesam Abdulmajid Rizik, Khalfan Ibrahim Al Khalfan (75.Mohammed Razak), Yusef Ahmed Ali (62.Hassan Khalid Al Haydous), Andrés Sebastián Soria Quintana. Trainer: Paulo Autuori de Mello (Brazil).

Goals: 1-0 Ashkan Dejagah (5), 1-1 Khalfan Ibrahim Al Khalfan (9), 2-1 Ashkan Dejagah (50), 2-2 Mohammed Kasola (85).

Cautions: Seyed Seyed Jalal Hosseini Khoshkebejari / Fábio César Montezine.

29.02.2012, Bahrain National Stadium, Riffa; Attendance: 3,000
Referee: Andre El Haddad (Lebanon)
BAHRAIN - INDONESIA **10-0(4-0)**
BHR: Sayed Mohammed Jaffer Sabet, Abdulla Rahman Al Marzooqi, Saleh Abdulhameed Mahmeedi, Waleed Mohammed Abdulla Ali Al Hayam, Mahmood Abdulrahman Mohammed Noor (90+2.Fahad Yusuf Abdulla Ahmed Hassan Al Hardan), Salman Isa Ali Ghuloom, Sayed Dhiya Saaed, Abdulwahab Al Malood, Abdullah Omar Ismail, Ismaeel Abdullatif Hassan, Mohammed Tayeb Al Alawi. Trainer: Peter John Taylor (England).
IDN: Syamsidar, Gunawan Dwi Cahyo (67.Benny Wahyudi), Diego Muhammad Robbie Michiels, Abdul Rahman Sulaeman, Hengky Ardiles, Aditya Putra Dewa (60.Ricky Akbar Ohorella), Muhammad Taufiq, Slamet Nurcahyo (5.Andi Muhammad Guntur), Rendy Irawan Saputra, Ferdinand Alfred Sinaga, Irfan Haarys Bachdim. Trainer: Wilhelmus Gerardus Rijsbergen (Holland).
Goals: 1-0 Ismaeel Abdullatif Hassan (4 penalty), 2-0 Mohammed Tayeb Al Alawi (16), 3-0 Mahmood Abdulrahman Mohammed Noor (34 penalty), 4-0 Mahmood Abdulrahman Mohammed Noor (41), 5-0 Mohammed Tayeb Al Alawi (60), 6-0 Sayed Dhiya Saaed (62), 7-0 Mohammed Tayeb Al Alawi (65), 8-0 Ismaeel Abdullatif Hassan (71), 9-0 Sayed Dhiya Saaed (82), 10-0 Sayed Dhiya Saaed (90+4).
Cautions: Diego Muhammad Robbie Michiels, Abdul Rahman Sulaeman.
Sent off: Syamsidar (5).

AFC WORLD CUP QUALIFIERS – 4th Round

In the fourth round, the 10 teams were divided into two groups of five teams. The top two teams from each group will advance to the 2014 FIFA World Cup finals in Brazil, while the two third-placed teams advance to the fifth round.

The draw for Round Four was held on 9 March 2012 in Kuala Lumpur (Malaysia), with the teams seeded according to their March 7, 2012 FIFA Ranking. The ten teams were split into five pots, with each group containing a team from each pot.

Pot 1	*Pot 2*	*Pot 3*	*Pot 4*	*Pot 5*
Australia Korea Republic	Japan Iran	Uzbekistan Iraq	Jordan Qatar	Oman Lebanon

GROUP A

03.06.2012	Tashkent	Uzbekistan - Iran	0-1(0-0)
03.06.2012	Beirut	Lebanon - Qatar	0-1(0-0)
08.06.2012	Beirut	Lebanon - Uzbekistan	1-1(1-1)
08.06.2012	Doha	Qatar - Korea Republic	1-4(1-1)
12.06.2012	Goyang	Korea Republic - Lebanon	3-0(1-0)
12.06.2012	Tehran	Iran - Qatar	0-0
11.09.2012	Tashkent	Uzbekistan - Korea Republic	2-2(1-1)
11.09.2012	Beirut	Lebanon - Iran	1-0(1-0)
16.10.2012	Doha	Qatar - Uzbekistan	0-1(0-1)
16.10.2012	Tehran	Iran - Korea Republic	1-0(0-0)
14.11.2012	Doha	Qatar - Lebanon	1-0(0-0)
14.11.2012	Tehran	Iran - Uzbekistan	0-1(0-0)
26.03.2013	Seoul	Korea Republic - Qatar	2-1(0-0)
26.03.2013	Tashkent	Uzbekistan - Lebanon	1-0(0-0)
04.06.2013	Doha	Qatar - Iran	0-1(0-0)
04.06.2013	Beirut	Lebanon - Korea Republic	1-1(1-0)
11.06.2013	Seoul	Korea Republic - Uzbekistan	1-0(1-0)
11.06.2013	Tehran	Iran - Lebanon	4-0(2-0)
18.06.2013	Ulsan	Korea Republic - Iran	0-1(0-0)
18.06.2013	Tashkent	Uzbekistan - Qatar	5-1(0-1)

FINAL STANDINGS

1.	**IRAN**	8	5	1	2	8	-	2	16
2.	**KOREA REPUBLIC**	8	4	2	2	13	-	7	14
3.	**Uzbekistan**	8	4	2	2	11	-	6	14
4.	Qatar	8	2	1	5	5	-	13	7
5.	Lebanon	8	1	2	5	3	-	12	5

Iran and Korea Republic qualified for the Final Tournament.
Uzbekistan qualified for the 5th Round.

03.06.2012, JAR Stadium, Tashkent; Attendance: 9,000
Referee: Yuichi Nishimura (Japan)
UZBEKISTAN - IRAN 0-1(0-0)
UZB: Ignatiy Nesterov, Anzur Ismailov, Jasur K. Hasanov II (68.Lutfulla Turayev), Stanislav Andreyev, Odil Ahmedov, Islom Inomov, Viktor Karpenko (52.Marat Bikmaev), Azizbek Haydarov, Timur Kapadze, Jasur Hasanov (87.Ulugbek Bakaev), Aleksandr Geynrikh. Trainer: Vadim Abramov.
IRN: Seyed Mehdi Rahmati Osgouei, Seyed Jalal Hosseini Khoshkebejari, Hossein Mahini, Pejman Montazeri, Javad Nekounam, Andranik Teymourian, Omid Ebrahimi (46.Khosro Heydari), Ehsan Hajsafi (61.Mohamad Reza Khalatbari), Mojtaba Jabbari Kordgeshlagi (75.Karim Ansarifard), Sahand-Pejman Nouri Roudsari, Mohammad Ali Karimi Pashaki. Trainer: Carlos Manuel Brito Leal Queiroz (Portugal).
Goal: 0-1 Mohamad Reza Khalatbari (90+4).

03.06.2012, "Camille Chamoun" Sports City Stadium, Beirut; Attendance: 40,000
Referee: Nawaf Abdullah Ghayyath Shukralla (Bahrain)
LEBANON - QATAR 0-1(0-0)
LIB: Ziad Ali Al Samad, Ramez Dayoub (79.Nader Matar), Walid Ismail, Youssef Wasef Mohamad, Bilal Shiekh El Najarin, Hussein Dakik (86.Hassan Jamam Mohammad), Haytham Faour, Abbas Ahmed Atwi, Ahmad Zreik, Mohammed Mahmoud Ghaddar (86.Hassan Chaito), Hassan Maatouk. Trainer: Johannes Theodor Bücker (Germany).
QAT: Qasem Abdulhamed Burhan, Ibrahim Majid Abdulmajid, Mesaad Ali Al Hamad, Khalid Muftah Mayouf, Mohammed Kasola, Lawrence Awuley Quaye, Wesam Abdulmajid Rizik, Khalfan Ibrahim Al Khalfan (90+3.Marcone Amaral Costa Júnior), Yusef Ahmed Ali (83.Talal Hassan Ali Al Bloushi), Adel Lami Khalid Mohamed (77.Younes Ali Rahmati), Andrés Sebastián Soria Quintana. Trainer: Paulo Autuori de Mello (Brazil).
Goal: 0-1 Andrés Sebastián Soria Quintana (64).
Cautions: Haytham Faour, Ramez Dayoub, Hassan Chaito / Andrés Sebastián Soria Quintana, Ibrahim Majid Abdulmajid, Khalfan Ibrahim Al Khalfan.

08.06.2012, "Camille Chamoun" Sports City Stadium, Beirut; Attendance: 13,000
Referee: Abdullah Mohamed Al Hilali (Oman)
LEBANON - UZBEKISTAN 1-1(1-1)
LIB: Ziad Ali Al Samad, Ali Al Saadi, Walid Ismail, Youssef Wasef Mohamad, Bilal Shiekh El Najarin, Hussein Dakik, Haytham Faour (65.Mohaméd Shamas), Hassan Jamam Mohammad (80.Nader Matar), Abbas Ahmed Atwi (66.Hassan Chaito), Ahmad Zreik, Hassan Maatouk. Trainer: Johannes Theodor Bücker (Germany).
UZB: Ignatiy Nesterov, Anzur Ismailov, Jasur K. Hasanov II (90.Marat Bikmaev), Islom Tuhtahujaev, Vitaliy Denisov, Odil Ahmedov, Viktor Karpenko, Timur Kapadze, Sanzhar Tursunov (88.Jasur Hasanov), Server Djeparov, Aleksandr Geynrikh (75.Ulugbek Bakaev). Trainer: Mirjalol Qosimov.
Goals: 0-1 Jasur K. Hasanov II (12), 1-1 Ali Al Saadi (36).
Cautions: Islom Tuhtahujaev, Aleksandr Geynrikh, Jasur K. Hasanov II.

08.06.2012, "Jassim Bin Hamad" Stadium, Doha; Attendance: 10,730
Referee: Hamad Madhad Saif Al Badwawi (United Arab Emirates)
QATAR - KOREA REPUBLIC 1-4(1-1)
QAT: Qasem Abdulhamed Burhan, Ibrahim Majid Abdulmajid (62.Hamid Ismail Khalifa), Mesaad Ali Al Hamad (70.Mohammed Razak), Khalid Muftah Mayouf, Talal Hassan Ali Al Bloushi, Mohammed Kasola, Lawrence Awuley Quaye (73.Fábio César Montezine), Wesam Abdulmajid Rizik, Khalfan Ibrahim Al Khalfan, Yusef Ahmed Ali, Andrés Sebastián Soria Quintana. Trainer: Paulo Autuori de Mello (Brazil).
KOR: Jung Sung-Ryong, Choi Hyo-Jin, Kwak Tae-Hwi, Lee Jung-Soo, Park Joo-Ho, Koo Ja-Cheol (55.Kim Shin-Wook), Ki Sung-Yueng, Kim Bo-Kyung, Lee Keun-Ho, Kim Do-Heon (80.Ji Dong-Won), Lee Dong-Gook (75.Nam Tae-Hee). Trainer: Choi Kang-Hee.
Goals: 1-0 Yusef Ahmed Ali (22), 1-1 Lee Keun-Ho (26), 1-2 Kwak Tae-Hwi (55), 1-3 Kim Shin-

Wook (64), 1-4 Lee Keun-Ho (80).
Cautions: Wesam Abdulmajid Rizik, Yusef Ahmed Ali, Mohammed Kasola / Kim Shin-Wook.

12.06.2012, Goyang Stadium, Goyang; Attendance: 36,756
Referee: Masaaki Toma (Japan)
KOREA REPUBLIC - LEBANON **3-0(1-0)**
KOR: Jung Sung-Ryong, Oh Beom-Seok, Kwak Tae-Hwi, Lee Jung-Soo, Park Joo-Ho, Kim Bo-Kyung, Kim Jung-Woo (78.Ji Dong-Won), Ki Sung-Yueng (20.Koo Ja-Cheol), Yeom Ki-Hun (63.Son Heung-Min), Lee Keun-Ho, Lee Dong-Gook. Trainer: Choi Kang-Hee.
LIB: Ziad Ali Al Samad, Ramez Dayoub, Walid Ismail, Youssef Wasef Mohamad, Bilal Shiekh El Najarin, Hussein Dakik, Mohaméd Shamas (86.Mohamad Haidar), Hassan Jamam Mohammad (63.Akram Moghrabi), Abbas Ahmed Atwi, Ahmad Zreik, Hassan Maatouk (54.Zakaria Yehya Charara). Trainer: Johannes Theodor Bücker (Germany).
Goals: 1-0 Kim Bo-Kyung (30), 2-0 Kim Bo-Kyung (48), 3-0 Koo Ja-Cheol (90).
Cautions: Park Joo-Ho / Zakaria Yehya Charara, Ahmad Zreik.

12.06.2012, Azadi Stadium, Tehran; Attendance: 100,000
Referee: Peter Daniel Green (Australia)
IRAN - QATAR **0-0**
IRN: Seyed Mehdi Rahmati Osgouei, Seyed Hadi Aghily Anvar, Khosro Heydari, Seyed Jalal Hosseini Khoshkebejari, Hossein Mahini (54.Ashkan Dejagah), Mehrdad Pooladi, Javad Nekounam, Andranik Teymourian, Karim Ansarifard (90+1.Maziar Zare Eshghdoust), Ehsan Hajsafi (46.Mohamad Reza Khalatbari), Mohammad Ali Karimi Pashaki. Trainer: Carlos Manuel Brito Leal Queiroz (Portugal).
QAT: Qasem Abdulhamed Burhan, Ibrahim Abdullah Al Ghanim, Marcone Amaral Costa Júnior, Ibrahim Majid Abdulmajid, Talal Hassan Ali Al Bloushi, Mohammed Kasola, Younes Ali Rahmati, Khalfan Ibrahim Al Khalfan, Fábio César Montezine (90+3.Yusef Ahmed Ali), Adel Lami Khalid Mohamed (46.Majdi Abdulla Siddiq), Andrés Sebastián Soria Quintana. Trainer: Paulo Autuori de Mello (Brazil).
Cautions: Andranik Teymourian, Mohammad Ali Karimi Pashaki / Ibrahim Majid Abdulmajid, Qasem Abdulhamed Burhan, Fábio César Montezine.

11.09.2012, Pakhtakor Markaziy Stadium, Tashkent; Attendance: 33,000
Referee: Benjamin Jon Williams (Australia)
UZBEKISTAN - KOREA REPUBLIC **2-2(1-1)**
UZB: Ignatiy Nesterov, Anzur Ismailov, Artyom Filiposyan, Server Djeparov, Timur Kapadze, Jasur O. Hasanov I (83.Vagiz Galiulin), Sanzhar Tursunov, Fozil Musaev, Akmal Shorahmedov, Shohruh Gadoev, Ulugbek Bakaev (66.Aleksandr Geynrikh). Trainer: Mirjalol Qosimov.
KOR: Jung Sung-Ryong, Ko Yo-Han, Kwak Tae-Hwi, Lee Jung-Soo, Park Joo-Ho, Ha Dae-Sung (83.Yoon Bit-Garam), Ki Sung-Yueng, Lee Chung-Yong (55.Kim Shin-Wook), Kim Bo-Kyung, Lee Keun-Ho (74.Park Chu-Young), Lee Dong-Gook. Trainer: Choi Kang-Hee.
Goals: 1-0 Ki Sung-Yong (13 own goal), 1-1 Artyom Filiposyan (44 own goal), 1-2 Lee Dong-Gook (57), 2-2 Sanzhar Tursunov (59).
Cautions: Anzur Ismailov, Artyom Filiposyan.

11.09.2012, "Camille Chamoun" Sports City Stadium, Beirut; Attendance: 14,000
Referee: Tan Hai (China P.R.)

LEBANON - IRAN 1-0(1-0)

LIB: Abbas Hassan, Youssef Wasef Mohamad, Ali Hamam, Bilal Shiekh El Najarin, Walid Ismail, Roda Antar (70.Mohamad Shamas), Abbas Ahmad Atwi (89.Amer Khan), Haytham Faour, Hassan Chaito (72.Mahmoud El Ali), Hassan Maatouk, Mohamad Haidar. Trainer: Johannes Theodor Bücker (Germany).

IRN: Seyed Mehdi Rahmati Osgouei, Seyed Hadi Aghily Anvar, Hossein Mahini, Pejman Montazeri, Mohammad Ali Karimi Pashaki, Javad Nekounam, Masoud Soleimani Shojaei, Mohammad Noori, Pejman Nouri Roudsari (46.Ehsan Hajsafi), Karim Ansarifard (47.Mohammad Ghazi Najafabadi), Mohammed Reza Khalatbari (68.Mohammad Gholami Khalil Mahaleh). Trainer: Carlos Manuel Brito Leal Queiroz (Portugal).

Goal: 1-0 Roda Antar (28).

Cautions: Mohamad Haidar, Abbas Hassan, Mohaméd Shamas / Pejman Nouri Roudsari, Mohammad Noori.

16.10.2012, „Jassim bin Hamad" Stadium, Doha; Attendance: 11,260
Referee: Tan Hai (China P.R.)

QATAR - UZBEKISTAN 0-1(0-1)

QAT: Qasem Abdulhamed Burhan, Ibrahim Abdullah Al Ghanim (46.Hamid Ismail Hassan Khalifa Hamid), Marcone Amaral Costa Júnior, Khalid Muftah Mayouf, Mohammed Kasola, Talal Hassan Ali Al Bloushi, Wesam Abdulmajid Rizik, Khalfan Ibrahim Khalfan Al Khalfan, Lawrence Awuley Quaye (46.Hassan Khalid Al Haydous), Andrés Sebastián Soria Quintana, Mohammed Razak (76.Magid Mohammed Hassan). Trainer: Paulo Autuori de Mello (Brazil).

UZB: Ignatiy Nesterov, Anzur Ismailov, Islom Tuhtahujaev, Akmal Shorahmedov, Azizbek Haydarov, Shohruh Gadoev (75.Vitaliy Denisov), Timur Kapadze, Sanzhar Tursunov (90+2.Oleg Zoteev), Server Djeparov, Jasur O. Hasanov I, Ulugbek Bakaev (87.Aleksandr Geynrikh). Trainer: Mirjalol Qosimov.

Goal: 0-1 Sanzhar Tursunov (13).

Cautions: Lawrence Awuley Quaye, Talal Hassan Ali Al Bloushi / Jasur O. Hasanov I, Anzur Ismailov, Vitaliy Denisov.

16.10.2012, Azadi Stadium, Tehran; Attendance: 99,885
Referee: Abdul Malik Abdul Malik Abdul Bashir (Singapore)

IRAN - KOREA REPUBLIC 1-0(0-0)

IRN: Seyed Mehdi Rahmati Osgouei, Seyed Jalal Hosseini Khoshkebejari, Pejman Montazeri, Khosro Heydari, Mehrdad Pooladi, Javad Nekounam, Masoud Soleimani Shojaei, Seyed Ashkan Dejagah, Andranik Teymourian (89.Maziar Zare Eshghdoust), Mohammad Noori (65.Hossein Mahini), Reza Ghoochannejhad Nournia (73.Mohammed Reza Khalatbari). Trainer: Carlos Manuel Brito Leal Queiroz (Portugal).

KOR: Jung Sung-Ryong, Oh Beom-Seok, Kwak Tae-Hwi, Jung In-Hwan, Yoon Suk-Young, Park Jong-Woo (77.Ha Dae-Sung), Ki Sung-Yueng, Kim Bo-Kyung (53.Son Heung-Min), Kim Shin-Wook, Lee Keun-Ho (69.Lee Chung-Yong), Park Chu-Young. Trainer: Choi Kang-Hee.

Goal: 1-0 Javad Nekounam (76).

Cautions: Masoud Soleimani Shojaei, Mehrdad Pooladi / Park Jong-Woo, Oh Beom-Seok, Park Chu-Young.

Sent off: Masoud Soleimani Shojaei (55).

14.11.2012, „Jassim Bin Hamad“ Stadium, Doha; Attendance: 12,870
Referee: Khalil Ibrahim Al Ghamdi (Saudi Arabia)
QATAR - LEBANON **1-0(0-0)**
QAT: Qasem Abdulhamed Burhan, Ibrahim Majid Abdulmajid, Mesaad Ali Al Hamad (64.Yousef Ahmed Ali), Khalid Muftah Mayouf (70.Adel Lami Khalid Mohamed), Mohammed Kasola, Talal Hassan Ali Al Bloushi, Wesam Abdulmajid Rizik, Fábio César Montezine (78.Lawrence Awuley Quaye), Khalfan Ibrahim Khalfan Al Khalfan, Hassan Khalid Al Haydous, Andrés Sebastián Soria Quintana. Trainer: Paulo Autuori de Mello (Brazil).
LIB: Abbas Hassan, Youssef Wasef Mohamad, Bilal Shiekh El Najarin, Walid Ismail, Roda Antar, Abbas Ahmad Atwi (81.Fayez Shamsin), Hassan Maatouk (76.Hassan Chaito), Ahmad Zreik, Haytham Faour (86.Hassan El Mohamad), Mahmoud El Ali, Mohamad Haidar. Trainer: Johannes Theodor Bücker (Germany).
Goal: 1-0 Andrés Sebastián Soria Quintana (75).
Cautions: Mohammed Kasola, Lawrence Awuley Quaye / Youssef Wasef Mohamad.

14.11.2012, Azadi Stadium, Tehran; Attendance: 43,700
Referee: Ali Hamad Madhad Saif Al Badwawi (United Arab Emirates)
IRAN - UZBEKISTAN **0-1(0-0)**
IRN: Seyed Mehdi Rahmati Osgouei, Seyed Jalal Hosseini Khoshkebejari, Pejman Montazeri, Khosro Heydari, Javad Nekounam, Seyed Ashkan Dejagah, Andranik Teymourian (80.Alireza Abbasfard), Mohammad Noori (67.Pejman Nouri Roudsari), Mehrdad Pooladi, Reza Ghoochannejhad Nournia, Mohammed Reza Khalatbari (46.Karim Ansarifard). Trainer: Carlos Manuel Brito Leal Queiroz (Portugal).
UZB: Ignatiy Nesterov, Artyom Filiposyan, Islom Tuhtahujaev, Vitaliy Denisov, Akmal Shorahmedov, Azizbek Haydarov, Shohruh Gadoev (65.Oleg Zoteev), Fozil Musaev, Sanzhar Tursunov (90+2.Islom Inomov), Server Djeparov, Ulugbek Bakaev (82.Aleksandr Geynrikh). Trainer: Mirjalol Qosimov.
Goal: 0-1 Ulugbek Bakaev (71).
Cautions: Seyed Ashkan Dejagah, Mohammad Noori / Azizbek Haydarov, Server Djeparov, Akmal Shorahmedov, Sanzhar Tursunov, Islom Tuhtahujaev.

26.03.2013, Seoul World Cup Stadium, Seoul; Attendance: 37,222
Referee: Yuichi Nishimura (Japan)
KOREA REPUBLIC - QATAR **2-1(0-0)**
KOR: Jung Sung-Ryong, Oh Beom-Seok, Jung In-Hwan, Kwak Tae-Hwi, Park Won-Jae, Koo Ja-Cheol, Ki Sung-Yueng, Ji Dong-Won (53.Lee Dong-Gook), Lee Keun-Ho (81.Son Heung-Min), Lee Chung-Yong, Kim Shin-Wook. Trainer: Choi Kang-Hee.
QAT: Qasem Abdulhamed Burhan, Bilal Mohammed Rajab, Ibrahim Abdullah Al Ghanim, Ibrahim Majid Abdulmajid, Mosaab Mahmoud Mohamed Al Hassan, Hamid Ismail Hassan Khalifa Hamid (90+3.Abdulaziz Abdullah Mubarak Al Sulaiti), Abdelkarim Hassan Fadlalla (75.Mahir Yousef Bakr), Talal Hassan Ali Al Bloushi, Wesam Abdulmajid Rizik, Khalfan Ibrahim Khalfan Al Khalfan, Andrés Sebastián Soria Quintana (90+5.Ahmed Yasser Mohammedi). Trainer: Fahad Abdullah Al Thani Alzraa.
Goals: 1-0 Lee Keun-Ho (60), 1-1 Khalfan Ibrahim Khalfan Al Khalfan (64), 2-1 Son Heung-Min (90+6).
Cautions: Kwak Tae-Hwi, Ki Sung-Yueng / Andrés Sebastián Soria Quintana, Wesam Abdulmajid Rizik, Mosaab Mahmoud Mohamed Al Hassan.

26.03.2013, Bunyodkor Stadium, Tashkent; Attendance: 31,197
Referee: Abdul Malik Abdul Bashir (Singapore)
UZBEKISTAN - LEBANON 1-0(0-0)
UZB: Ignatiy Nesterov, Artyom Filiposyan (55.Farhod Tadjiyev), Anzur Ismailov, Jasur O. Hasanov I (46.Oleg Zoteev), Akmal Shorahmedov, Odil Ahmedov, Azizbek Haydarov, Shohruh Gadoev, Sanzhar Tursunov, Server Djeparov (90.Fozil Musaev), Ulugbek Bakaev. Trainer: Mirjalol Qosimov.
LIB: Abbas Hassan, Youssef Wasef Mohamad, Ali Hamam, Mootaz Jounaidi, Walid Ismail, Adnan Haidar, Mohamad Shamas, Haytham Faour (71.Hassan Maatouk), Hassan Chaito, Abbas Ali Atwi (83.Alexis Khazzaka), Mohamad Haidar (82.Abbas Ahmad Atwi). Trainer: Johannes Theodor Bücker (Germany).
Goal: 1-0 Server Djeparov (63).
Cautions: Farhod Tadjiyev.

04.06.2013, „Jassim Bin Hamad" Stadium, Doha; Attendance: 11,872
Referee: Abdul Malik Abdul Malik Abdul Bashir (Singapore)
QATAR - IRAN 0-1(0-0)
QAT: Qasem Abdulhamed Burhan, Bilal Mohammed Rajab, Ibrahim Abdullah Al Ghanim, Ibrahim Majid Abdulmajid, Mosaab Mahmoud Mohamed Al Hassan, Abdelkarim Hassan Fadlalla (67.Magid Mohammed Hassan), Talal Hassan Ali Al Bloushi, Wesam Abdulmajid Rizik, Khalfan Ibrahim Khalfan Al Khalfan, Yousef Ahmed Ali (81.Abdulqadir Ilyas Bakr), Hassan Khalid Al Haydous (69.Hamid Ismail Hassan Khalifa Hamid). Trainer: Fahad Abdullah Al Thani Alzraa.
IRN: Rahman Ahmadi, Seyed Jalal Hosseini Khoshkebejari, Pejman Montazeri, Mohammad-Hashem Beikzadeh, Amir Hossein Sadeghi, Khosro Heydari (90+3.Gholamreza Rezaei), Javad Nekounam, Masoud Soleimani Shojaei, Andranik Teymourian, Mojtaba Jabbari Kordgeshlagi (85.Mohammed Reza Khalatbari), Reza Ghoochannejhad Nournia (88.Omid Ebrahimi). Trainer: Carlos Manuel Brito Leal Queiroz (Portugal).
Goal: 0-1 Reza Ghoochannejhad Nournia (66).
Cautions: Bilal Mohammed Rajab, Qasem Abdulhamed Burhan / Reza Ghoochannejhad Nournia.

04.06.2013, "Camille Chamoun" Sports City Stadium, Beirut; Attendance: 8,430
Referee: Benjamin Jon Williams (Australia)
LEBANON - KOREA REPUBLIC 1-1(1-0)
LIB: Abbas Hassan, Youssef Wasef Mohamad (88.Amer Khan), Mootaz Jounaidi, Walid Ismail, Mohamed Zein Tahan, Abbas Ahmad Atwi, Mohamad Shamas (90+1.Nour Mansour), Haytham Faour, Hassan Maatouk, Hassan Chaito (84.Abbas Ali Atwi), Mohamad Haidar. Trainer: Johannes Theodor Bücker (Germany).
KOR: Jung Sung-Ryong, Shin Kwang-Hoon, Kwak Tae-Hwi, Kim Chi-Woo, Kim Nam-Il, Kim Bo-Kyung (86.Ji Dong-Won), Han Kook-Young (50.Kim Shin-Wook), Kim Kee-Hee, Lee Chung-Yong, Lee Dong-Gook, Lee Keun-Ho (70.Son Heung-Min). Trainer: Choi Kang-Hee.
Goals: 1-0 Hassan Maatouk (12), 1-1 Kim Chi-Woo (90+7).
Cautions: Walid Ismail, Haytham Faour, Mohamad Haidar / Lee Chung-Yong.
Sent off: Walid Ismail (90+8).

11.06.2013, Seoul World Cup Stadium, Seoul; Attendance: 50,699
Referee: Minoru Tōjō (Japan)
KOREA REPUBLIC - UZBEKISTAN 1-0(1-0)
KOR: Jung Sung-Ryong, Kim Chang-Soo, Kwak Tae-Hwi (81.Kim Kee-Hee), Kim Young-Gwon, Kim Chi-Woo, Park Jong-Woo, Lee Myung-Joo, Lee Keun-Ho (64.Lee Dong-Gook), Lee Chung-Yong (90+3.Ji Dong-Won), Kim Shin-Wook, Son Heung-Min. Trainer: Choi Kang-Hee.
UZB: Ignatiy Nesterov, Anzur Ismailov, Islom Tuhtahujaev, Vitaliy Denisov, Akmal Shorahmedov (76.Sanzhar Tursunov), Odil Ahmedov, Azizbek Haydarov, Shohruh Gadoev, Timur Kapadze (84.Farhod Tadjiyev), Server Djeparov, Ulugbek Bakaev (75.Aleksandr Geynrikh). Trainer: Mirjalol Qosimov.
Goal: 1-0 Akmal Shorahmedov (42 own goal).

Cautions: Park Jong-Woo, Kim Shin-Wook / Ulugbek Bakaev, Shohruh Gadoev.

11.06.2013, Azadi Stadium, Tehran; Attendance: 91,300
Referee: Masaaki Toma (Japan)
IRAN - LEBANON 4-0(2-0)
IRN: Rahman Ahmadi, Seyed Jalal Hosseini Khoshkebejari, Pejman Montazeri, Mohammad-Hashem Beikzadeh (80.Ehsan Hajsafi), Khosro Heydari, Javad Nekounam, Masoud Soleimani Shojaei (69.Mohsen Mosalman), Andranik Teymourian, Mojtaba Jabbari Kordgeshlagi (71.Gholamreza Rezaei), Reza Ghoochannejhad Nournia, Mohammed Reza Khalatbari. Trainer: Carlos Manuel Brito Leal Queiroz (Portugal).
LIB: Abbas Hassan, Mootaz Jounaidi, Hassan Daher, Mohamed Zein Tahan, Abbas Ahmad Atwi, Hassan Maatouk, Mohamad Shamas, Hamzah Salameh (76.Nour Mansour), Hassan Chaito (45+1.Nader Matar), Mahmoud Kojok (67.Mohamad Ahmed Atwi), Fayez Shamsin. Trainer: Johannes Theodor Bücker (Germany).
Goals: 1-0 Mohammed Reza Khalatbari (39), 2-0 Javad Nekounam (45+1), 3-0 Reza Ghoochannejhad Nournia (46), 4-0 Javad Nekounam (86).
Cautions: Abbas Ahmad Atwi, Fayez Shamsin, Abbas Hassan.

18.06.2013, Ulsan Munsu Football Stadium, Ulsan; Attendance: 42,243
Referee: Tan Hai (China P.R.)
KOREA REPUBLIC - IRAN 0-1(0-0)
KOR: Jung Sung-Ryong, Kim Chang-Soo, Kim Young-Gwon, Jang Hyun-Soo, Kim Chi-Woo, Kim Kee-Hee, Lee Myung-Joo, Lee Dong-Gook, Kim Shin-Wook, Son Heung-Min (74.Kim Bo-Kyung), Ji Dong-Won (65.Lee Keun-Ho). Trainer: Choi Kang-Hee.
IRN: Rahman Ahmadi, Seyed Jalal Hosseini Khoshkebejari, Pejman Montazeri, Mohammad-Hashem Beikzadeh, Amir Hossein Sadeghi, Khosro Heydari (68.Gholamreza Rezaei), Javad Nekounam, Masoud Soleimani Shojaei (83.Ehsan Hajsafi), Andranik Teymourian, Mojtaba Jabbari Kordgeshlagi, Reza Ghoochannejhad Nournia (90+1.Farzad Jalal Hatemi). Trainer: Carlos Manuel Brito Leal Queiroz (Portugal).
Goal: 0-1 Reza Ghoochannejhad Nournia (60).
Cautions: Andranik Teymourian, Masoud Soleimani Shojaei, Mojtaba Jabbari Kordgeshlagi.

18.06.2013, Bunyodkor Stadium, Tashkent; Attendance: 34,000
Referee: Peter Daniel Green (Australia)
UZBEKISTAN - QATAR 5-1(0-1)
UZB: Ignatiy Nesterov, Anzur Ismailov, Vitaliy Denisov, Akmal Shorahmedov, Odil Ahmedov, Timur Kapadze, Sanzhar Tursunov, Server Djeparov, Jasur O. Hasanov I (68.Oleg Zoteev), Aleksandr Geynrikh (60.Bakhodyr Nasymov), Farhod Tadjiyev (46.Ulugbek Bakaev). Trainer: Mirjalol Qosimov.
QAT: Ahamed Sufeyan Ahmed Al Abunora, Ibrahim Abdullah Al Ghanim, Ibrahim Majid Abdulmajid, Mosaab Mahmoud Mohamed Al Hassan (57.Hamid Ismail Hassan Khalifa Hamid), Abdelkarim Hassan Fadlalla, Talal Hassan Ali Al Bloushi, Hussain Ali Shehab (31.Khalfan Ibrahim Khalfan Al Khalfan), Hamad Mohammed Al Obaidi (42.Mohammed Kasola), Yousef Ahmed Ali, Hassan Khalid Al Haydous, Abdulqadir Ilyas Bakr. Trainer: Fahad Abdullah Al Thani Alzraa.
Goals: 0-1 Abdulqadir Ilyas Bakr (37), 1-1 Bakhodyr Nasymov (61), 2-1 Oleg Zoteev (72), 3-1 Bakhodyr Nasymov (74), 4-1 Odil Ahmedov (87), 5-1 Ulugbek Bakaev (90+1).
Cautions: Timur Kapadze / Yousef Ahmed Ali, Talal Hassan Ali Al Bloushi, Ahamed Sufeyan Ahmed Al Abunora.

GROUP B

03.06.2012	Saitama	Japan - Oman	3-0(1-0)
03.06.2012	Amman	Jordan - Iraq	1-1(1-1)
08.06.2012	Saitama	Japan - Jordan	6-0(4-0)
08.06.2012	Muscat	Oman - Australia	0-0
12.06.2012	Brisbane	Australia - Japan	1-1(0-0)
12.06.2012	Doha (QAT)	Iraq - Oman	1-1(1-1)
11.09.2012	Saitama	Japan - Iraq	1-0(1-0)
11.09.2012	Amman	Jordan - Australia	2-1(0-0)
16.10.2012	Muscat	Oman - Jordan	2-1(0-0)
16.10.2012	Doha (QAT)	Iraq - Australia	1-2(0-0)
14.11.2012	Muscat	Oman - Japan	1-2(0-1)
14.11.2012	Doha (QAT)	Iraq - Jordan	1-0(0-0)
26.03.2013	Sydney	Australia - Oman	2-2(0-1)
26.03.2013	Amman	Jordan - Japan	2-1(1-0)
04.06.2013	Saitama	Japan - Australia	1-1(0-0)
04.06.2013	Muscat	Oman - Iraq	1-0(1-0)
11.06.2013	Melbourne	Australia - Jordan	4-0(1-0)
11.06.2013	Doha (QAT)	Iraq - Japan	0-1(0-0)
18.06.2013	Sydney	Australia - Iraq	1-0(0-0)
18.06.2013	Amman	Jordan - Oman	1-0(0-0)

FINAL STANDINGS

1.	**JAPAN**	8	5	2	1	16 - 5	17
2.	**AUSTRALIA**	8	3	4	1	12 - 7	13
3.	**Jordan**	8	3	1	4	7 - 16	10
4.	Oman	8	2	3	3	7 - 10	9
5.	Iraq	8	1	2	5	4 - 8	5

Japan and Australia qualified for the Final Tournament.
Jordan qualified for the 5th Round.

03.06.2012, Saitama Stadium 2002, Saitama; Attendance: 63,551
Referee: Ravshan Irmatov (Uzbekistan)

JAPAN - OMAN 3-0(1-0)

JPN: Eiji Kawashima, Yasuyuki Konno, Yuto Nagatomo, Atsuto Uchida (58.Hiroki Sakai), Maya Yoshida, Yasuhito Endō (86.Hajime Hosogai), Makoto Hasebe, Keisuke Honda, Shinji Kagawa, Ryoichi Maeda, Shinji Okazaki (74.Hiroshi Kiyotake). Trainer: Alberto Zaccheroni (Italy).
OMA: Ali Abdullah Harib Al Habsi, Jaber Mohammed Saghayar Al Owaisi, Abdul Sallam Amur Juma Al Mukhaini, Saad Suhail Jumaa Al Mukhaini, Hussein Ali Farah Al Hadhri (67.Ismail Sulaiman Ashoor Al Ajmi), Ahmed Mubarak Obaid Al Mahaijri, Ahmed Hadid Thuwaini Al Mukhaini (65.Ali Hilal Saud Al Jabri), Fawzi Bashir Rajab Bait Doorbeen, Mohammed Saleh Al Maslami, Raed Ibrahim Saleh, Amad Ali Suleiman Al Hosni (66.Abdul Aziz Humaid Mubarak Al Muqbali). Trainer: Paul Le Guen (France).
Goals: 1-0 Keisuke Honda (11), 2-0 Ryoichi Maeda (51), 3-0 Shinji Okazaki (54).
Cautions: Atsuto Uchida / Fawzi Bashir Rajab Bait Doorbeen.

03.06.2012, Amman International Stadium, Amman; Attendance: 13,000
Referee: Valentin Kovalenko (Uzbekistan)

JORDAN - IRAQ 1-1(1-1)

JOR: Amer Shafia Mahmoud Sabbah, Anas Walid Khaled Bani Yaseen, Bashar Mustafa Bani Yaseen, Fathi Omar Othman Basem, Khalil Zayid Bani Attiah, Baha'a Abdel-Rahman Mustafa Suleiman, Shadi Nadmi Abu Hashash, Amer Deeb Mohammad Khalil (75.Anas Jamal Mohammad Hijah), Hamza Ali Khaled Al Dardour (46.Abdallah Khaled Deeb Salim), Ahmed Hayel Ibrahim, Odai Yousef Ismail Al Saify (63.Thayer Fayed Al Bawab). Trainer: Adnan Hamad Majeed Al Abbasi (Iraq).

IRQ: Mohammed Gassid Kadhim Al Jaberi, Ali Hussein Rehema Al Ka'abi Al Mutairi, Bassim Abbas Gatea Al Ogaili, Samal Saeed Mujbel, Salam Shakir Ali, Muthana Khalid Salih Al Masloukhi, Qusay Muneer Abboodi Al Hussein, Nashat Akram Abid Ali, Karrar Jassim Mohammed Al Mahmodi (88.Alaa Abdul-Zahra Khashan Al Azzawi), Hawar Mulla Mohammed Taher Zibari (88.Mustafa Karim Abdullah), Younis Mahmoud Khalaf. Trainer: Arthur Antunes Coimbra "Zico" (Brazil).

Goals: 0-1 Nashat Akram Abid Ali (14), 1-1 Ahmed Hayel Ibrahim (43).

Cautions: Odai Yousef Ismail Al Saify / Bassim Abbas Gatea Al Ogaili, Ali Hussein Rehema Al Ka'abi Al Mutairi.

08.06.2012, Saitama Stadium 2002, Saitama; Attendance: 60,874
Referee: Kim Dong-Jin (Korea Republic)

JAPAN - JORDAN 6-0(4-0)

JPN: Eiji Kawashima, Yasuyuki Konno (72.Masahiko Inoha), Yuto Nagatomo, Atsuto Uchida, Maya Yoshida (44.Yuzo Kurihara), Yasuhito Endō, Makoto Hasebe, Keisuke Honda (57.Kengo Nakamura), Shinji Kagawa, Ryoichi Maeda, Shinji Okazaki. Trainer: Alberto Zaccheroni (Italy).

JOR: Amer Shafia Mahmoud Sabbah, Bashar Mustafa Bani Yaseen, Mohamed Munir Ahmed Al Muattasim, Fathi Omar Othman Basem (44.Mohammad Abdulsaleh Al Dhemeri), Khalil Zayid Bani Attiah, Baha'a Abdel-Rahman Mustafa Suleiman, Saeed Hassan Al Murjan, Abdallah Khaled Deeb Salim, Thayer Fayed Al Bawab (59.Anas Jamal Mohammad Hijah), Ahmed Hayel Ibrahim (77.Shadi Nadmi Abu Hashash), Odai Yousef Ismail Al Saify. Trainer: Adnan Hamad Majeed Al Abbasi (Iraq).

Goals: 1-0 Ryoichi Maeda (18), 2-0 Keisuke Honda (22), 3-0 Keisuke Honda (31), 4-0 Shinji Kagawa (35), 5-0 Keisuke Honda (53 penalty), 6-0 Yuzo Kurihara (89).

Cautions: Makoto Hasebe / Abdallah Khaled Deeb Salim, Khalil Zayid Bani Attiah, Amer Shafia Mahmoud Sabbah.

Sent off: Abdallah Khaled Deeb Salim (27).

08.06.2012, „Sultan Qaboos" Sports Complex, Muscat; Attendance: 11,000
Referee: Alireza Faghani (Iran)

OMAN - AUSTRALIA 0-0

OMA: Ali Abdullah Harib Al Habsi, Mohammed Abdullah Mubarak Al Balushi, Saad Suhail Jumaa Al Mukhaini, Ahmed Mubarak Obaid Al Mahaijri, Juma Darwish Al Mashri (67.Hussein Ali Farah Al Hadhri), Mohammed Saleh Al Maslami, Eid Mohamed Eid Al Farsi (72.Ali Hilal Saud Al Jabri), Mohamed Hamed Hidaib Al Mukhaini, Raed Ibrahim Saleh, Amad Ali Suleiman Al Hosni (85.Waleed Abdallah Ameir Al Saadi), Ismail Sulaiman Ashoor Al Ajmi. Trainer: Paul Le Guen (France).

AUS: Mark Schwarzer, Lucas Edward Neill, Saša Ognenovski, Luke Wilkshire (82.Robbie Thomas Kruse), Harold Kewell (58.Archibald Gerald Thompson), David Raymond Carney, Jade Bronson North, Carl Valeri, Matthew Graham McKay, Alex Brosque, Mark Bresciano. Trainer: Holger Osieck (Germany).

Cautions: Saša Ognenovski.

12.06.2012, Suncorp Stadium, Brisbane; Attendance: 40,189
Referee: Khalil Ibrahim Al Ghamdi (Saudi Arabia)
AUSTRALIA - JAPAN 1-1(0-0)
AUS: Mark Schwarzer, Lucas Edward Neill, Saša Ognenovski, Luke Wilksire (90.Robbie Thomas Kruse), Jade Bronson North, Carl Valeri, Timothy Filiga Cahill, David Raymond Carney, Mark Bresciano (13.Mark Daniel Milligan), Matthew Graham McKay (64.Nikita Rukavytsya), Alex Brosque. Trainer: Holger Osieck (Germany).
JPN: Eiji Kawashima, Yasuyuki Konno, Yuzo Kurihara, Yuto Nagatomo, Atsuto Uchida (73.Hiroki Sakai), Yasuhito Endō, Makoto Hasebe, Keisuke Honda, Shinji Kagawa (90+2.Masahiko Inoha), Ryoichi Maeda, Shinji Okazaki (87.Hiroshi Kiyotake). Trainer: Alberto Zaccheroni (Italy).
Goals: 0-1 Yuzo Kurihara (64), 1-1 Luke Wilksire (70 penalty).
Cautions: Mark Daniel Milligan / Yuzo Kurihara, Yasuyuki Konno, Atsuto Uchida, Keisuke Honda.
Sent off: Mark Daniel Milligan (56), Yuzo Kurihara (89).

12.06.2012, Grand Hamad Stadium, Doha (Qatar); Attendance: 1,650
Referee: Abdulrahman Abdou (Qatar)
IRAQ - OMAN 1-1(1-1)
IRQ: Mohammed Gassid Kadhim Al Jaberi, Ali Hussein Rehema Al Ka'abi Al Mutairi, Bassim Abbas Gatea Al Ogaili, Samal Saeed Mujbel, Salam Shakir Ali, Muthana Khalid Salih Al Masloukhi, Qusay Muneer Abboodi Al Hussein, Nashat Akram Abid Ali (66.Alaa Abdul-Zahra Khashan Al Azzawi), Karrar Jassim Mohammed Al Mahmodi (84.Mustafa Karim Abdullah), Hawar Mulla Mohammed Taher Zibari (69.Hammadi Ahmed), Younis Mahmoud Khalaf. Trainer: Arthur Antunes Coimbra "Zico" (Brazil).
OMA: Ali Abdullah Harib Al Habsi, Mohammed Abdullah Mubarak Al Balushi, Abdul Sallam Amur Juma Al Mukhaini, Saad Suhail Jumaa Al Mukhaini, Hussein Ali Farah Al Hadhri (65.Fawzi Bashir Rajab Bait Doorbeen), Ahmed Mubarak Obaid Al Mahaijri, Mohammed Saleh Al Maslami, Eid Mohamed Eid Al Farsi (84.Ali Hilal Saud Al Jabri), Raed Ibrahim Saleh, Amad Ali Suleiman Al Hosni, Abdul Aziz Humaid Mubarak Al Muqbali (46.Ismail Sulaiman Ashoor Al Ajmi). Trainer: Paul Le Guen (France).
Goals: 0-1 Mohammed Abdullah Mubarak Al Balushi (8), 1-1 Younis Mahmoud Khalaf (37 penalty).
Cautions: Samal Saeed Mujbel / Saad Suhail Jumaa Al Mukhaini, Abdul Sallam Amur Juma Al Mukhaini, Amad Ali Suleiman Al Hosni.

11.09.2012, Saitama Stadium 2002, Saitama; Attendance: 60,593
Referee: Abdul Malik Abdul Bashir (Singapore)
JAPAN - IRAQ 1-0(1-0)
JPN: Eiji Kawashima, Yūichi Komano, Masahiko Inoha, Maya Yoshida, Yuto Nagatomo, Yasuhito Endō, Makoto Hasebe, Shinji Okazaki, Keisuke Honda, Hiroshi Kiyotake (89.Hajime Hosogai), Ryoichi Maeda (90.Mike Havenaar). Trainer: Alberto Zaccheroni (Italy).
IRQ: Noor Sabri Abbas Al Bairawi, Ahmad Ibrahim Khalaf, Hussam Kadhim Jabur Al Shuwaili, Ali Bahjat Fadhil, Khaldoun Ibrahim Mohammed Al Bu Mohammed, Muthana Khalid Salih Al Masloukhi, Waleed Salem Edwairej Al Lami, Ahmed Yasin Ghani (78.Karrar Jassim Mohammed Al Mahmodi), Hammadi Ahmad Abdullah Al Daiya, Alaa Abdul-Zahra Khashan Al Azzawi (75.Nashat Akram Abid Ali), Amjad Radhi Yousif Al Janabi (65.Younis Mahmoud Khalaf). Trainer: Arthur Antunes Coimbra "Zico" (Brazil).
Goal: 1-0 Ryoichi Maeda (25).

11.09.2012, „King Abdullah" International Stadium, Amman; Attendance: 16,000
Referee: Abdullah Dor Mohammad Balideh Baloushi (Qatar)

JORDAN - AUSTRALIA 2-1(0-0)

JOR: Amer Shafia Mahmoud Sabbah, Anas Walid Khaled Bani Yaseen, Abdel-Ilah Yusef Abed Al Hanahneh, Fathi Omar Othman Basem, Mohammad Ali Mustafa, Mohammad Abdulsaleh Al Dhemeri (46.Saeed Hassan Al Murjan), Amer Deeb Mohammad Khalil, Hassan Mahmoud Abdel Fattah (83.Hamza Ali Khaled Al Dardour), Odai Yousef Ismail Al Saify (75.Anas Jamal Mohammad Hijah), Shadi Nadmi Abu Hashhash, Ahmad Hayel Ibrahim. Trainer: Adnan Hamad Majid Al Abbassi (Iraq).
AUS: Mark Schwarzer, Lucas Edward Neill, Luke Wilkshire, David Raymond Carney, Saša Ognenovski (14.Matthew Thomas Špiranović), Mark Bresciano (46.Michael John Jedinak), Timothy Filiga Cahill, Brett Trevor Holman (75.Archibald Gerald Thompson), Matthew Graham McKay, Robbie Thomas Kruse, Alex Brosque. Trainer: Holger Osieck (Germany).
Goals: 1-0 Hassan Mahmoud Abdel Fattah (48 penalty), 2-0 Amer Deeb Mohammad Khalil (73), 2-1 Archibald Gerald Thompson (86).
Cautions: Amer Shafia Mahmoud Sabbah, Fathi Omar Othman Basem / Luke Wilkshire.

16.10.2012, "Sultan Qaboos" Sports Complex, Muscat; Attendance: 26,000
Referee: Nawaf Abdullah Ghayyath Shukralla (Bahrain)

OMAN - JORDAN 2-1(0-0)

OMA: Ali Abdullah Harib Al Habsi, Hassan Yousuf Mudhafar Al Gheilani, Mohammed Abdullah Mubarak Al Balushi (9.Jaber Mohammed Saghayar Al Owaisi), Saad Suhail Jumaa Al Mukhaini, Ahmed Mubarak Obaid Al Mahaijri, Fawzi Bashir Rajab Bait Doorbeen (55.Eid Mohamed Eid Al Farsi), Juma Darwish Al Mashri, Mohammed Saleh Al Maslami, Raed Ibrahim Saleh, Amad Ali Suleiman Al Hosni (82.Abdul Aziz Humaid Mubarak Al Muqbali), Ismail Sulaiman Ashoor Al Ajmi. Trainer: Paul Le Guen (France).
JOR: Lo'ai Salem Atallah Al Amaireh, Anas Walid Khaled Bani Yaseen, Sulaiman Mawafaq Al Salman, Mohammad Ali Mustafa, Mohammad Abdulsaleh Al Dhemeri, Amer Deeb Mohammad Khalil, Saeed Hassan Al Murjan, Hassan Mahmoud Abdel Fattah (85.Hamza Ali Khaled Al Dardour), Odai Yousef Ismail Al Saify (66.Abdallah Khaled Deeb Salim), Shadi Nadmi Abu Hashhash, Ahmad Hayel Ibrahim (58.Thayer Fayed Al Bawab). Trainer: Adnan Hamad Majid Al Abbassi (Iraq).
Goals: 1-0 Ahmed Mubarak Obaid Al Mahaijri (62), 2-0 Juma Darwish Al Mashri (87), 2-1 Thayer Fayed Al Bawab (90).
Cautions: Hassan Yousuf Mudhafar Al Gheilani, Ali Abdullah Harib Al Habsi, Saad Suhail Jumaa Al Mukhaini / Anas Walid Khaled Bani Yaseen, Mohammad Abdulsaleh Al Dhemeri, Sulaiman Mawafaq Al Salman, Saeed Hassan Al Murjan.

16.10.2012, Grand Hamad Stadium, Doha (Qatar); Attendance: 2,183
Referee: Lee Min-Hu (Korea Republic)

IRAQ - AUSTRALIA 1-2(0-0)

IRQ: Noor Sabri Abbas Al Bairawi, Samal Saeed Mujbel, Salam Shaker Ali Dad, Ahmad Ibrahim Khalaf, Hussam Kadhim Jabur Al Shuwaili, Khaldoun Ibrahim Mohammed Al Bu Mohammed, Muthana Khalid Salih Al Masloukhi (64.Alaa Abdul-Zahra Khashan Al Azzawi), Ahmed Yasin Ghani, Nashat Akram Abid Ali (83.Osama Jabar Shafia Rashid), Younis Mahmoud Khalaf, Hammadi Ahmad Abdullah Al Daiya (60.Mustafa Karim Abdullah). Trainer: Arthur Antunes Coimbra "Zico" (Brazil).
AUS: Mark Schwarzer, Lucas Edward Neill, Luke Wilkshire, Matthew Thomas Špiranović, Timothy Filiga Cahill (90.James Robert Holland), Brett Trevor Holman, Carl Valeri, Michael John Jedinak, Matthew Graham McKay Robbie Thomas Kruse (79.Thomas Michael Oar), Alex Brosque (75.Archibald Gerald Thompson). Trainer: Holger Osieck (Germany).
Goals: 1-0 Alaa Abdul-Zahra Khashan Al Azzawi (72), 1-1 Timothy Filiga Cahill (80), 1-2 Archibald Gerald Thompson (84).
Cautions: Salam Shaker Ali Dad, Khaldoun Ibrahim Mohammed Al Bu Mohammed / Carl Valeri, Lucas Edward Neill, Timothy Filiga Cahill.

14.11.2012, "Sultan Qaboos" Sports Complex, Muscat; Attendance: 28,360
Referee: Abdullah Dor Mohammad Balideh Baloushi (Qatar)
OMAN - JAPAN 1-2(0-1)
OMA: Ali Abdullah Harib Al Habsi, Hassan Yousuf Mudhafar Al Gheilani, Abdul Sallam Amur Juma Al Mukhaini, Rashid Juma Mubarak Al Farsi (73.Eid Mohamed Eid Al Farsi), Ahmed Mubarak Obaid Al Mahaijri, Fawzi Bashir Rajab Bait Doorbeen, Juma Darwish Al Mashri, Mohammed Saleh Al Maslami, Raed Ibrahim Saleh, Amad Ali Suleiman Al Hosni (46.Abdullah Saleh Abdul Hadi), Ismail Sulaiman Ashoor Al Ajmi (40.Abdul Aziz Humaid Mubarak Al Muqbali). Trainer: Paul Le Guen (France).
JPN: Eiji Kawashima, Yasuyuki Konno, Maya Yoshida, Yuto Nagatomo, Hiroki Sakai, Yasuhito Endō (90+4.Hideto Takahashi), Makoto Hasebe, Shinji Okazaki, Keisuke Honda, Hiroshi Kiyotake (85.Hajime Hosogai), Ryoichi Maeda (64.Gōtoku Sakai). Trainer: Alberto Zaccheroni (Italy).
Goals: 0-1 Hiroshi Kiyotake (20), 1-1 Ahmed Mubarak Obaid Al Mahaijri (77), 1-2 Shinji Okazaki (90).
Cautions: Ahmed Mubarak Obaid Al Mahaijri.

14.11.2012, Grand Hamad Stadium, Doha (Qatar); Attendance: 1,755
Referee: Tan Hai (China P.R.)
IRAQ - JORDAN 1-0(0-0)
IRQ: Noor Sabri Abbas Al Bairawi, Ali Hussein Rehema Al Ka'abi Al Mutairi, Ahmad Ibrahim Khalaf, Ali Bahjat Fadhil, Khaldoun Ibrahim Mohammed Al Bu Mohammed, Waleed Salem Edwairej Al Lami, Ahmed Yasin Ghani, Saad Abdul-Amir Al Zirjawi, Osama Jabar Shafia Rashid (77.Nabeel Sabah Zghaiyer Al Helechi), Hammadi Ahmad Abdullah Al Daiya (90+2.Samal Saeed Mujbel), Hussam Ibrahim Ali Al Sarray (82.Amjad Radhi Yousif Al Janabi). Trainer: Arthur Antunes Coimbra "Zico" (Brazil).
JOR: Amer Shafia Mahmoud Sabbah, Fathi Omar Othman Basem, Mohammad Ali Mustafa, Mohammad Abdulsaleh Al Dhemeri, Amer Deeb Mohammad Khalil, Saeed Hassan Al Murjan (89.Hamza Ali Khaled Al Dardour), Hassan Mahmoud Abdel Fattah, Khalil Zayid Bani Attiah, Shadi Nadmi Abu Hashhash, Abdallah Khaled Deeb Salim (62.Odai Yousef Ismail Al Saify), Thayer Fayed Al Bawab (62.Ahmad Hayel Ibrahim). Trainer: Adnan Hamad Majid Al Abbassi (Iraq).
Goal: 1-0 Hammadi Ahmad Abdullah Al Daiya (86).
Cautions: Ali Bahjat Fadhil, Saad Abdul-Amir Al Zirjawi, Hammadi Ahmad Abdullah Al Daiya.

26.03.2013, Stadium Australia, Sydney; Attendance: 34,603
Referee: Ravshan Irmatov (Uzbekistan)
AUSTRALIA - OMAN 2-2(0-1)
AUS: Mark Schwarzer, Luke Wilkshire, Robert Richard Cornthwaite, Michael Errol Thwaite, Timothy Filiga Cahill, Brett Trevor Holman, Michael John Jedinak, Matthew Graham McKay, Robbie Thomas Kruse (68.Archibald Gerald Thompson), James Robert Holland (53.Mark Bresciano; 77.Thomas Michael Oar), Alex Brosque. Trainer: Holger Osieck (Germany).
OMA: Ali Abdullah Harib Al Habsi, Hassan Yousuf Mudhafar Al Gheilani, Abdul Sallam Amur Juma Al Mukhaini, Saad Suhail Jumaa Al Mukhaini, Ahmed Mubarak Obaid Al Mahaijri, Qasim Said Sanjoor Hardan (90+2.Ali Hilal Saud Al Jabri), Mohammed Saleh Al Maslami, Eid Mohamed Eid Al Farsi (84.Jaber Mohammed Saghayar Al Owaisi), Abdul Aziz Humaid Mubarak Al Muqbali, Raed Ibrahim Saleh, Amad Ali Suleiman Al Hosni (69.Ismail Sulaiman Ashoor Al Ajmi). Trainer: Paul Le Guen (France).
Goals: 0-1 Abdul Aziz Humaid Mubarak Al Muqbali (6), 0-2 Michael John Jedinak (49 own goal), 1-2 Timothy Filiga Cahill (52), 2-2 Brett Trevor Holman (85).
Cautions: Robert Richard Cornthwaite / Saad Suhail Jumaa Al Mukhaini, Amad Ali Suleiman Al Hosni, Raed Ibrahim Saleh.

26.03.2013, "King Abdullah" International Stadium, Amman; Attendance: 18,000
Referee: Alireza Faghani (Iran)

JORDAN - JAPAN 2-1(1-0)

JOR: Amer Shafia Mahmoud Sabbah, Anas Walid Khaled Bani Yaseen, Fathi Omar Othman Basem, Oday Samir Zahran (39.Adnan Suleiman Hassan Adous), Mohammad Ali Mustafa, Amer Deeb Mohammad Khalil (84.Hamza Ali Khaled Al Dardour), Saeed Hassan Al Murjan, Khalil Zayid Bani Attiah, Shadi Nadmi Abu Hashhash, Odai Yousef Ismail Al Saify (64.Abdallah Khaled Deeb Salim), Ahmad Hayel Ibrahim. Trainer: Adnan Hamad Majid Al Abbassi (Iraq).

JPN: Eiji Kawashima, Yasuyuki Konno, Atsuto Uchida, Maya Yoshida, Gōtoku Sakai (79.Yūichi Komano), Yasuhito Endō, Makoto Hasebe, Shinji Okazaki, Hiroshi Kiyotake (86.Takashi Inui), Ryoichi Maeda (63.Mike Havenaar), Shinji Kagawa. Trainer: Alberto Zaccheroni (Italy).

Goals: 1-0 Khalil Zayid Bani Attiah (45+1), 2-0 Ahmad Hayel Ibrahim (60), 2-1 Shinji Kagawa (69).

Cautions: Shadi Nadmi Abu Hashhash, Amer Shafia Mahmoud Sabbah, Mohammad Ali Mustafa, Fathi Omar Othman Basem.

04.06.2013, Saitama 2002 Stadium, Saitama; Attendance: 62,172
Referee: Nawaf Abdullah Ghayyath Shukralla (Bahrain)

JAPAN - AUSTRALIA 1-1(0-0)

JPN: Eiji Kawashima, Yasuyuki Konno, Atsuto Uchida (86.Mike Havenaar), Maya Yoshida, Yuto Nagatomo, Yasuhito Endō, Makoto Hasebe, Shinji Okazaki (88.Hiroshi Kiyotake), Keisuke Honda, Ryoichi Maeda (80.Yuzo Kurihara), Shinji Kagawa. Trainer: Alberto Zaccheroni (Italy).

AUS: Mark Schwarzer, Lucas Edward Neill, Luke Wilkshire, Mark Daniel Milligan, Saša Ognenovski, Mark Bresciano, Timothy Filiga Cahill, Brett Trevor Holman (72.Dario Vidošić), Matthew Graham McKay, Robbie Thomas Kruse (90+3.Archibald Gerald Thompson), Thomas Michael Oar. Trainer: Holger Osieck (Germany).

Goals: 0-1 Thomas Michael Oar (81), 1-1 Keisuke Honda (90+1 penalty).

Cautions: Makoto Hasebe / Mark Bresciano, Matthew Graham McKay.

04.06.2013, "Sultan Qaboos" Sports Complex, Muscat; Attendance: 18,300
Referee: Kim Dong-Jin (Korea Republic)

OMAN - IRAQ 1-0(1-0)

OMA: Faiz Al Rashidi, Hassan Yousuf Mudhafar Al Gheilani, Abdul Sallam Amur Juma Al Mukhaini, Saad Suhail Jumaa Al Mukhaini, Ahmed Mubarak Obaid Al Mahaijri, Qasim Said Sanjoor Hardan (71.Ali Hilal Saud Al Jabri), Mohammed Saleh Al Maslami, Eid Mohamed Eid Al Farsi (90+4.Ali Salim Obaid Bait Al Nahar), Abdul Aziz Humaid Mubarak Al Muqbali, Raed Ibrahim Saleh, Ismail Sulaiman Ashoor Al Ajmi (89.Hassan Rabia Suwaidan Al Hosni). Trainer: Paul Le Guen (France).

IRQ: Noor Sabri Abbas Al Bairawi, Salam Shaker Ali Dad, Ali Hussein Rehema Al Ka'abi Al Mutairi, Ahmad Ibrahim Khalaf, Ali Adnan Kadhim Nassir Al Tameemi, Muthana Khalid Salih Al Masloukhi (87.Amjad Radhi Yousif Al Janabi), Nashat Akram Abid Ali, Humam Tariq Faraj Na'oush (55.Saad Abdul-Amir Al Zirjawi), Saif Salman Hashim Al Mohammadawi (58.Mustafa Karim Abdullah), Younis Mahmoud Khalaf, Alaa Abdul-Zahra Khashan Al Azzawi. Trainer: Vladimir Petrović (Serbia).

Goal: 1-0 Ismail Sulaiman Ashoor Al Ajmi (45+3).

Cautions: Abdul Sallam Amur Juma Al Mukhaini, Faiz Al Rashidi, Hassan Yousuf Mudhafar Al Gheilani / Nashat Akram Abid Ali.

11.06.2013, Docklands Stadium, Melbourne; Attendance: 43,785
Referee: Abdul Malik Abdul Bashir (Singapore)
AUSTRALIA - JORDAN 4-0(1-0)
AUS: Mark Schwarzer, Lucas Edward Neill, Luke Wilkshire, Mark Daniel Milligan, Saša Ognenovski, Mark Bresciano, Timothy Filiga Cahill, Brett Trevor Holman (71.Tomas Petar Rogić), Matthew Graham McKay, Robbie Thomas Kruse (87.Dario Vidošić), Thomas Michael Oar (60.Archibald Gerald Thompson). Trainer: Holger Osieck (Germany).
JOR: Amer Shafia Mahmoud Sabbah (88.Ahmed Abdel-Sattar Nawwas), Anas Walid Khaled Bani Yaseen, Fathi Omar Othman Basem, Mohammad Ali Mustafa, Amer Deeb Mohammad Khalil (67.Yaseen Anas Al Bakhit), Saeed Hassan Al Murjan, Khalil Zayid Bani Attiah, Adnan Suleiman Hassan Adous, Odai Yousef Ismail Al Saify (67.Hamza Ali Khaled Al Dardour), Shadi Nadmi Abu Hashhash, Ahmad Hayel Ibrahim. Trainer: Adnan Hamad Majid Al Abbassi (Iraq).
Goals: 1-0 Mark Bresciano (15), 2-0 Timothy Filiga Cahill (61), 3-0 Robbie Thomas Kruse (76), 4-0 Lucas Edward Neill (84).
Cautions: Khalil Zayid Bani Attiah, Anas Walid Khaled Bani Yaseen, Fathi Omar Othman Basem.

11.06.2013, Grand Hamad Stadium, Doha (Qatar); Attendance: 1,100
Referee: Valentin Kovalenko (Uzbekistan)
IRAQ - JAPAN 0-1(0-0)
IRQ: Noor Sabri Abbas Al Bairawi, Ali Hussein Rehema Al Ka'abi Al Mutairi, Ahmad Ibrahim Khalaf, Dhurgham Ismail Dawood Al Quraishi, Ali Adnan Kadhim Nassir Al Tameemi, Saad Abdul-Amir Al Zirjawi (85.Karrar Jassim Mohammed Al Mahmodi), Waleed Salem Edwairej Al Lami, Saif Salman Hashim Al Mohammadawi, Younis Mahmoud Khalaf, Alaa Abdul-Zahra Khashan Al Azzawi, Hammadi Ahmad Abdullah Al Daiya (79.Ali Bahjat Fadhil). Trainer: Vladimir Petrović (Serbia).
JPN: Eiji Kawashima, Yasuyuki Konno, Masahiko Inoha (90+4.Hideto Takahashi), Yuto Nagatomo, Hiroki Sakai, Yasuhito Endō, Hajime Hosogai, Shinji Okazaki, Hiroshi Kiyotake (67.Kengo Nakamura), Mike Havenaar (70.Ryoichi Maeda), Shinji Kagawa. Trainer: Alberto Zaccheroni (Italy).
Goal: 0-1 Shinji Okazaki (89).
Cautions: Alaa Abdul-Zahra Khashan Al Azzawi, Ali Hussein Rehema Al Ka'abi Al Mutairi.
Sent off: Alaa Abdul-Zahra Khashan Al Azzawi (82).

18.06.2013, Stadium Australia, Sydney; Attendance: 80,523
Referee: Alireza Faghani (Iran)
AUSTRALIA - IRAQ 1-0(0-0)
AUS: Mark Schwarzer, Lucas Edward Neill, Luke Wilkshire, Mark Daniel Milligan, Saša Ognenovski, Mark Bresciano, Timothy Filiga Cahill (78.Joshua Blake Kennedy), Brett Trevor Holman (61.Tomas Petar Rogić), Matthew Graham McKay, Robbie Thomas Kruse (79.Archibald Gerald Thompson), Thomas Michael Oar. Trainer: Holger Osieck (Germany).
IRQ: Noor Sabri Abbas Al Bairawi, Ahmad Ibrahim Khalaf, Ali Bahjat Fadhil, Dhurgham Ismail Dawood Al Quraishi (66.Hawar Mulla Mohammed Taher Zibari), Ali Adnan Kadhim Nassir Al Tameemi, Khaldoun Ibrahim Mohammed Al Bu Mohammed, Waleed Salem Edwairej Al Lami, Karrar Jassim Mohammed Al Mahmodi, Saad Abdul-Amir Al Zirjawi, Humam Tariq Faraj Na'oush (74.Hammadi Ahmad Abdullah Al Daiya), Saif Salman Hashim Al Mohammadawi (79.Osama Ali Mohammed). Trainer: Vladimir Petrović (Serbia).
Goal: 1-0 Joshua Blake Kennedy (83).
Cautions: Saša Ognenovski / Waleed Salem Edwairej Al Lami, Humam Tariq Faraj Na'oush, Saif Salman Hashim Al Mohammadawi, Ali Adnan Kadhim Nassir Al Tameemi.

18.06.2013, „King Abdullah" International Stadium, Amman; Attendance: 14,000
Referee: Valentin Kovalenko (Uzbekistan)

JORDAN - OMAN **1-0(0-0)**

JOR: Amer Shafia Mahmoud Sabbah, Anas Walid Khaled Bani Yaseen, Mohammad Ali Mustafa, Mohammad Abdulsaleh Al Dhemeri, Amer Deeb Mohammad Khalil (69.Baha' Abdel-Rahman Mustafa Suleiman), Saeed Hassan Al Murjan, Khalil Zayid Bani Attiah, Shadi Nadmi Abu Hashhash, Abdallah Khaled Deeb Salim (79.Hamza Ali Khaled Al Dardour), Odai Yousef Ismail Al Saify (54.Adnan Suleiman Hassan Adous), Ahmad Hayel Ibrahim. Trainer: Adnan Hamad Majid Al Abbassi (Iraq).

OMA: Faiz Al Rashidi, Jaber Mohammed Saghayar Al Owaisi, Abdul Sallam Amur Juma Al Mukhaini, Saad Suhail Jumaa Al Mukhaini, Ahmed Mubarak Obaid Al Mahaijri, Qasim Said Sanjoor Hardan (74.Hussain Ali Farah Al Hadhri), Mohammed Saleh Al Maslami, Eid Mohamed Eid Al Farsi, Abdul Aziz Humaid Mubarak Al Muqbali, Raed Ibrahim Saleh (59.Amad Ali Suleiman Al Hosni), Ismail Sulaiman Ashoor Al Ajmi (68.Fahad Khamis Al Jalabubi). Trainer: Paul Le Guen (France).

Goal: 1-0 Ahmad Hayel Ibrahim (58).

Cautions: Ahmad Hayel Ibrahim, Adnan Suleiman Hassan Adous.

AFC WORLD CUP QUALIFIERS – 5th Round

06.09.2013	Amman	Jordan - Uzbekistan	1-1(1-1)
10.09.2013	Tashkent	Uzbekistan- Jordan	1-1; 7-8 pen

06.09.2013, "King Abdullah" Stadium, Amman; Attendance: 16,819
Referee: Yuichi Nishimura (Japan)
JORDAN - UZBEKISTAN 1-1(1-1)
JOR: Amer Shafia Mahmoud Sabbah, Anas Walid Khaled Bani Yaseen, Oday Samir Zahran, Mohammad Ali Mustafa, Mohammad Abdulsaleh Al Dhemeri, Saeed Hassan Al Murjan (79.Amer Deeb Mohammad Khalil), Hassan Mahmoud Abdel Fattah (60.Abdallah Khaled Deeb Salim), Mossab Al Laham, Khalil Zayid Bani Attiah, Shadi Nadmi Abu Hashhash (46.Odai Yousef Ismail Al Saify), Ahmad Hayel Ibrahim. Trainer: Hossam Hassan Hussein (Egypt).
UZB: Murotjon Zukhurov, Anzur Ismailov, Vitaliy Denisov, Yegor Krimets (40.Islom Tuhtahujaev), Islom Inomov, Server Djeparov, Timur Kapadze, Odil Ahmedov, Jasur O. Hasanov I, Sanzhar Tursunov (88.Djamshid Iskandarov), Bakhodyr Nasymov (65.Ulugbek Bakaev).Trainer: Mirjalol Qosimov.
Goals: 1-0 Mossab Al Laham (30), 1-1 Server Djeparov (35).
Cautions: Anzur Ismailov.

10.09.2013, Pakhtakor Markaziy Stadium, Tashkent; Attendance: 25,621
Referee: Benjamin Jon Williams (Australia)
UZBEKISTAN- JORDAN 1-1(1-1,1-1,1-1); 8-9 on penalties
UZB: Murotjon Zukhurov, Anzur Ismailov, Vitaliy Denisov, Islom Tuhtahujaev, Jasur K. Hasanov II (59.Igor Sergeev), Server Djeparov, Timur Kapadze, Odil Ahmedov, Akmal Shorahmedov, Oleg Zoteev (46.Sanzhar Tursunov), Bakhodyr Nasymov (82.Ivan Nagaev).Trainer: Mirjalol Qosimov.
JOR: Amer Shafia Mahmoud Sabbah, Anas Walid Khaled Bani Yaseen, Oday Samir Zahran, Mohammad Ali Mustafa, Mohammad Abdulsaleh Al Dhemeri, Amer Deeb Mohammad Khalil, Mossab Al Laham (90+1.Odai Yousef Ismail Al Saify), Saeed Hassan Al Murjan, Khalil Zayid Bani Attiah (56.Abdallah Khaled Deeb Salim), Ahmed Saleh Samir (83.Adnan Suleiman Hassan Adous), Ahmad Hayel Ibrahim. Trainer: Hossam Hassan Hussein (Egypt).
Goals: 1-0 Anzur Ismailov (5), 1-1 Saeed Hassan Al Murjan (43).
Penalties: Odil Ahmedov (missed); Anas Walid Khaled Bani Yaseen 0-1; Server Djeparov 1-1; Odai Yousef Ismail Al Saify 1-2; Timur Kapadze 2-2; Abdallah Khaled Deeb Salim 2-3; Islom Tuhtahujaev 3-3; Saeed Hassan Al Murjan 3-4; Igor Sergeev 4-4; Ahmad Hayel Ibrahim (missed); Akmal Shorahmedov 5-4; Adnan Suleiman Hassan Adous 5-5; Vitaliy Denisov 6-5; Mohammad Ali Mustafa 6-6; Ivan Nagaev 7-6; Amer Deeb Mohammad Khalil 7-7; Sanzhar Tursunov 8-7; Oday Samir Zahran 8-8; Anzur Ismailov (missed); Mohammad Abdulsaleh Al Dhemeri 8-9.
Cautions: Ivan Nagaev / Amer Deeb Mohammad Khalil, Abdallah Khaled Deeb Salim, Amer Shafia Mahmoud Sabbah, Mohammad Abdulsaleh Al Dhemeri.

Jordan qualified for the Intercontinental Play-offs.

OCEANIA

The four lowest-ranked nations (American Samoa, Cook Islands, Samoa, and Tonga) competed in the first round of qualifying: a single round-robin tournament in Apia (Samoa), from 22–26 November 2011. Samoa, as winners of the frist round, joined the remaining seven OFC teams in the 2012 OFC Nations Cup, which also doubled as the second qualifying round. The four semi-finalists of the OFC Nations Cup advanced to the third round, which consisted of a double round-robin held on a home-and-away basis between 7 September 2012 and 26 March 2013.

New Zealand, as the winners of the third round, were qualified to the Intercontinental play-offs against Mexico, the fourth-placed team from CONCACAF.

FIRST ROUND

GROUP A

22.11.2011	Apia	American Samoa - Tonga	2-1(1-0)
22.11.2011	Apia	Cook Islands - Samoa	2-3(1-2)
24.11.2011	Apia	American Samoa - Cook Islands	1-1(1-0)
24.11.2011	Apia	Samoa - Tonga	1-1(1-0)
26.11.2011	Apia	Samoa - Samoa American	1-0(0-0)
26.11.2011	Apia	Tonga - Cook Islands	2-1(1-1)

FINAL STANDINGS

1.	**Samoa**	3	2	1	0	5 - 3	7
2.	Tonga	3	1	1	1	4 - 4	4
3.	American Samoa	3	1	1	1	3 - 3	4
4.	Cook Islands	3	0	1	2	4 - 6	1

Samoa qualified for the second round.

22.11.2011, National Soccer Stadium, Apia; Attendance: 150
Referee: Andrew Achari (Fiji)
AMERICAN SAMOA - TONGA 2-1(1-0)
ASA: Nicky Salapu, Daru Taumua, Liatama Amisone Jr. (84.Suani Uelese), Uasila'a Heleta, Justin Mana'o, Rawlston Ray Masania'i, Ramin Shahin Ott (68.Tala Rafe Luvu), Johnny Saelua, Shalom Luani, Charlie Uhrle, Faimalo Tapui (87.Diamond Ott). Trainer: Thomas Rongen (Holland).
TGA: Kaneti Felela, Sione Tovo (58.Kinitoni Falatau), Samisoni Mafi, Folio Moeaki, Ilalio Leakona, Unaloto Ki-Atenoa Feao, Fineasi Palei (79.Siosifa Moimoi), Pio Palu (65.Timote Maamaaloa), Lafaele Moala, Sione Teu, Malakai Savieti. Trainer: Christopher Williams (Australia).
Goals: 1-0 Ramin Shahin Ott (43), 2-0 Shalom Luani (74), 2-1 Unaloto Ki-Atenoa Feao (88).
Cautions: Uasila'a Heleta, Tala Rafe Luvu / Unaloto Ki-Atenoa Feao, Fineasi Palei.

22.11.2011, National Soccer Stadium, Apia; Attendance: 600
Referee: Peter O'Leary (New Zealand)
COOK ISLANDS - SAMOA 2-3(1-2)
COK: Iona Lupena, Joseph Miitamariki, Nikorima Te Miha, Tahiri Elikana, Nathan Tisam, Grover Harmon, Gichin Fuhiniu (48.Roger Manuel), Taylor Saghabi (57.John Michael Quijano), Campbell Best, Emiel Burrows (51.Paul Luiz van Eijk), Paavo Mustonen. Trainer: Shane Arthur Rufer (New Zealand).
SAM: Kilisimasi Toetu, Charles Bell, Vaalii Faalogo, Silao Malo (61.Shaun Easthope), Jarrell Sale, Andrew Setefano, Max Tom Hoeflich, Lionel Taylor (78.Albert Bell), Jared Curtis, Desmond Richmond Fa'aiuaso, Luki Gosche (56.Fereti Gosche). Trainer: Tunoa Lui (American Samoa).
Goals: 0-1 Luki Gosche (19), 1-1 Campbell Best (35), 1-2 Luki Gosche (36), 2-2 Campbell Best (84),

2-3 Albert Bell (90+1).
Cautions: Iona Lupena / Luki Gosche, Max Tom Hoeflich.

24.11.2011, National Soccer Stadium, Apia; Attendance: 300
Referee: Bruce George (Vanuatu)
AMERICAN SAMOA - COOK ISLANDS 1-1(1-0)
ASA: Nicky Salapu, Daru Taumua, Liatama Amisone Jr., Uasila'a Heleta (81.Diamond Ott), Justin Mana'o, Rawlston Ray Masania'i, Tala Rafe Luvu (90.Suani Uelese), Ramin Shahin Ott, Charlie Uhrle (73.Faimalo Tapui), Shalom Luani, Johnny Saelua. Trainer: Thomas Rongen (Holland).
COK: Tony Lloyd Jamieson, Joseph Miitamariki, Nikorima Te Miha, Tahiri Elikana, Nathan Tisam, Paul Luiz van Eijk (57.Joseph Ngauora), Grover Harmon, Gichin Fuhiniu (70.Tuka Tisam), Paul Branden Turepu (88.Taylor Saghabi), Campbell Best, Paavo Mustonen. Trainer: Shane Arthur Rufer (New Zealand).
Goals: 1-0 Shalom Luani (24), 1-1 Tala Rafe Luvu (62 own goal).
Cautions: Johnny Saelua / Paul Luiz van Eijk.

24.11.2011, National Soccer Stadium, Apia; Attendance: 180
Referee: Averii Jacques (Tahiti)
SAMOA - TONGA 1-1(1-0)
SAM: Kilisimasi Toetu, Charles Bell (61.Albert Bell), Vaalii Faalogo, Silao Malo, Jarrell Sale, Andrew Setefano, Max Tom Hoeflich (80.Mike Saofaiga Foai), Lionel Taylor, Jared Curtis, Shaun Easthope, Desmond Richmond Fa'aiuaso. Trainer: Tunoa Lui (American Samoa).
TGA: Kaneti Felela, Sione Tovo (57.Timote Maamaaloa), Samisoni Mafi, Folio Moeaki, Ilalio Leakona, Unaloto Ki-Atenoa Feao, Fineasi Palei, Lafaele Moala, Sione Teu (81.Lokoua Taufahema), Kinitoni Falatau (74.Siosifa Moimoi), Malakai Savieti. Trainer: Christopher Williams (Australia).
Goals: 1-0 Shaun Easthope (43 penalty), 1-1 Lokoua Taufahema (81).
Cautions: Jared Curtis, Desmond Richmond Fa'aiuaso, Shaun Easthope / Ilalio Leakona, Unaloto Ki-Atenoa Feao.

26.11.2011, National Soccer Stadium, Apia; Attendance: 800
Referee: Peter O'Leary (New Zealand)
SAMOA - SAMOA AMERICAN 1-0(0-0)
SAM: Kilisimasi Toetu, Charles Bell, Vaalii Faalogo, Silao Malo (90.Mike Saofaiga Foai), Jarrell Sale, Andrew Setefano, Lionel Taylor, Jared Curtis (90.Penetito Tumua), Shaun Easthope, Desmond Richmond Fa'aiuaso, Luki Gosche (84.Joseph Hoeflich). Trainer: Tunoa Lui (American Samoa).
ASA: Nicky Salapu, Daru Taumua, Liatama Amisone Jr., Uasila'a Heleta (32.Suani Uelese), Justin Mana'o, Rawlston Ray Masania'i, Tala Rafe Luvu (73.Charlie Uhrle), Ramin Shahin Ott, Johnny Saelua, Shalom Luani, Faimalo Tapui (55.Diamond Ott). Trainer: Thomas Rongen (Holland).
Goal: 1-0 Silao Malo (89).
Cautions: Shaun Easthope / Daru Taumua, Liatama Amisone Jr.

26.11.2011, National Soccer Stadium, Apia; Attendance: 200
Referee: Isidore Assiene-Ambassa (New Caledonia)
TONGA - COOK ISLANDS 2-1(1-1)
TGA: Kaneti Felela, Samisoni Mafi, Folio Moeaki, Ilalio Leakona, Siosifa Moimoi (87.Lokoua Taufahema), Fineasi Palei, Lafaele Moala (89.Viliami Vaitaki), Sione Teu, Timote Maamaaloa (72.Pio Palu), Kinitoni Falatau, Malakai Savieti. Trainer: Christopher Williams (Australia).
COK: Tony Lloyd Jamieson, Joseph Miitamariki, Nikorima Te Miha, Tahiri Elikana, Teriiahoroa Framhein (69.Nathan Tisam), Grover Harmon, Paul Branden Turepu (58.Taylor Saghabi), Tuka Tisam (81.Junior Puroku), Campbell Best, Paavo Mustonen, Joseph Ngauora. Trainer: Shane Arthur Rufer (New Zealand).
Goals: 1-0 Timote Maamaaloa (26), 1-1 Grover Harmon (35), 2-1 Kinitoni Falatau (90).
Cautions: Samisoni Mafi / Paavo Mustonen.

SECOND ROUND
(2012 OFC Nations Cup)

GROUP A

01.06.2012	Honiara	Samoa - Tahiti	1-10(0-4)
01.06.2012	Honiara	Vanuatu - New Caledonia	2-5(0-1)
03.06.2012	Honiara	Vanuatu - Samoa	5-0(2-0)
03.06.2012	Honiara	Tahiti - New Caledonia	4-3(3-0)
05.06.2012	Honiara	New Caledonia - Samoa	9-0(6-0)
05.06.2012	Honiara	Tahiti - Vanuatu	4-1(2-0)

FINAL STANDINGS

1.	**Tahiti**	3	3	0	0	18 - 5	9
2.	**New Caledonia**	3	2	0	1	17 - 6	6
3.	Vanuatu	3	1	0	2	8 - 9	3
4.	Samoa	3	0	0	3	1 - 24	0

01.06.2012, Lawson Tama Stadium, Honiara; Attendance: 3,000
Referee: Gerald Oiaka (Solomon Islands)
SAMOA - TAHITI **1-10(0-4)**
SAM: Motu Hafoka, Vaalii Faalogo, Silao Malo, Jarrell Sale, Sapati Umutaua (88.Peni Kitiona), Andrew Setefano, Joseph Hoeflich (68.Masei Amosa), Sopo FaKaua, Luki Gosche (64.Amilale Esaroma), Mike Saofaiga Foai, Spencer Keli. Trainer: Malo Vaga.
TAH: Mickaël Roche, Angelo Tchen, Jonathan Tehau, Tamatoa Wagemann, Nicolas Vallar, Vincent Simon Lo-Shing, Heimano Bourebare (57.Pierre Kohumoetini), Lorenzo Tehau, Alvin Tehau (53.Teaonui Tehau), Hiroana Poroiae, Steevy Chong Hue (73.Manaraii Porlier). Trainer: Eddy Etaeta.
Goals: 0-1 Lorenzo Tehau (8), 0-2 Jonathan Tehau (17), 0-3 Alvin Tehau (19), 0-4 Alvin Tehau (38), 0-5 Teaonui Tehau (54), 0-6 Steevy Chong Hue (60), 1-6 Silao Malo (70), 1-7 Jonathan Tehau (78), 1-8 Lorenzo Tehau (83), 1-9 Lorenzo Tehau (84), 1-10 Lorenzo Tehau (85).
Cautions: Mike Saofaiga Foai, Andrew Setefano / Hiroana Poroiae.

01.06.2012, Lawson Tama Stadium, Honiara; Attendance: 7,000
Referee: Peter O'Leary (New Zealand)
VANUATU - NEW CALEDONIA **2-5(0-1)**
VAN: Ernest Bong, Derek Malas, Selwyn Sese Ala, Alphonse Bongnaim, Brian Kaltack, Robert Tom, Jean Nako Naprapol, Jean Robert Yelou (70.Dominique Fred), François Sakama (40.Robert Tasso), Roddy Lenga, Joseph Namariau. Trainer: Percy Avock.
NCL: Rocky Nyikeine, Jean-Patrick Wakanumuné, Judikael Ixoéé, Dick Kauma, Joël Wakanumuné, Noël Kaudré (60.Roy Kayara), Marius Bako (74.Miguel Kayara), Olivier Dokunengo, Dominique Wacalie, Bertrand Kaï, Georges Gope-Fenepej (90+3.Jacques Haeko). Trainer: Alain Moizan (France).
Goals: 0-1 Bertrand Kaï (32), 1-1 Robert Tasso (52), 1-2 Bertrand Kaï (58), 2-2 Jean Nako Naprapol (61), 2-3 Georges Gope-Fenepej (66), 2-4 Bertrand Kaï (76), 2-5 Roy Kayara (87).

03.06.2012, Lawson Tama Stadium, Honiara; Attendance: 2,200
Referee: John Saohu (Solomon Islands)

VANUATU - SAMOA 5-0(2-0)

VAN: Seiloni Iaruel, Derek Malas (56.Silas Namatak), Paul Young, Dominique Fred, Brian Kaltack, Lucien Hinge, Kevin Shem, Freddy Vava, Jean Nako Naprapol (79.Kensi Tangis), Michel Kaltack, Jean Kaltack (71.Robert Tasso). Trainer: Percy Avock.
SAM: Ethan Elisaia Hanns, Vaalii Faalogo, Silao Malo, Jarrell Sale, Sapati Umutaua (69.Patrick Asiata), Masei Amosa (52.Mike Saofaiga Foai), Andrew Setefano, Sopo FaKaua, Suivai Ataga (77.Joseph Hoeflich), Amilale Esaroma, Spencer Keli. Trainer: Malo Vaga.
Goals: 1-0 Jean Nako Naprapol (26), 2-0 Brian Kaltack (45+1), 3-0 Derek Malas (46), 4-0 Robert Tasso (74), 5-0 Freddy Vava (90+3).
Cautions: Seiloni Iaruel, Lucien Hinge / Sapati Umutaua, Silao Malo.

03.06.2012, Lawson Tama Stadium, Honiara; Attendance: 3,500
Referee: Christopher Simon Kerr (New Zealand)

TAHITI - NEW CALEDONIA 4-3(3-0)

TAH: Mickaël Roche, Teheivarii Ludivion, Angelo Tchen, Jonathan Tehau, Nicolas Vallar (66.Tamatoa Wagemann), Vincent Simon Lo-Shing, Heimano Bourebare, Lorenzo Tehau (88.Teaonui Tehau), Alvin Tehau (75.Roihau Degage), Henri Caroine, Steevy Chong Hue. Trainer: Eddy Etaeta.
NCL: Rocky Nyikeine, Jean-Patrick Wakanumuné, Judikael Ixoéé (46.Emile Béaruné), Dick Kauma, Joël Wakanumuné, Marius Bako, Roy Kayara, Olivier Dokunengo (71.Miguel Kayara), Dominique Wacalie, Bertrand Kaï (46.Jacques Haeko), Georges Gope-Fenepej. Trainer: Alain Moizan (France).
Goals: 1-0 Alvin Tehau (19), 2-0 Nicolas Vallar (29 penalty), 3-0 Lorenzo Tehau (32), 3-1 Marius Bako (74), 3-2 Jacques Haeko (80), 4-2 Steevy Chong Hue (84), 4-3 Dick Kauma (86).
Cautions: Alvin Tehau / Judikael Ixoéé, Marius Bako.
Sent off: Georges Gope-Fenepej (28), Jean-Patrick Wakanumuné (54).

05.06.2012, Lawson Tama Stadium, Honiara; Attendance: 1,000
Referee: Gerald Oiaka (Solomon Islands)

NEW CALEDONIA - SAMOA 9-0(6-0)

NCL: Jean-Marc Ounemoa, Judikael Ixoéé, Emile Béaruné, Georges Béaruné, Jonathan Kakou, Noël Kaudré, Roy Kayara (57.Joël Wakanumuné), Miguel Kayara (57.Bertrand Kaï), Iamel Kabeu, Kalaje Gnipate, Jacques Haeko. Trainer: Alain Moizan (France).
SAM: Aukusitino Aitupe (46.Motu Hafoka), Vaalii Faalogo, Silao Malo, Jarrell Sale, Sapati Umutaua, Masei Amosa, Andrew Setefano, Sopo FaKaua, Mike Saofaiga Foai, Amilale Esaroma (83.Tamoto Fenika), Spencer Keli (46.Patrick Asiata). Trainer: Malo Vaga.
Goals: 1-0 Roy Kayara (10), 2-0 Jacques Haeko (11), 3-0 Iamel Kabeu (22), 4-0 Judikael Ixoéé (25 penalty), 5-0 Kalaje Gnipate (45), 6-0 Jacques Haeko (45+1), 7-0 Jacques Haeko (72), 8-0 Jacques Haeko (90), 9-0 Jacques Haeko (90+1).

05.06.2012, Lawson Tama Stadium, Honiara; Attendance: 1,000
Referee: Peter O'Leary (New Zealand)

TAHITI - VANUATU 4-1(2-0)

TAH: Xavier Samin, Teheivarii Ludivion, Angelo Tchen, Jonathan Tehau (78.Pierre Kohumoetini), Nicolas Vallar, Edson Lemaire, Heimano Bourebare (89.Tamatoa Wagemann), Lorenzo Tehau, Alvin Tehau (65.Roihau Degage), Henri Caroine, Teaonui Tehau. Trainer: Eddy Etaeta.
VAN: Ernest Bong, Derek Malas, Paul Young, Alphonse Bongnaim, Brian Kaltack (67.Kensi Tangis), Kevin Shem, Jean Robert Yelou (19.Freddy Vava), Roddy Lenga (54.Michel Kaltack), Silas Namatak, Robert Tasso, Joseph Namariau. Trainer: Percy Avock.
Goals: 1-0 Nicolas Vallar (15 penalty), 2-0 Jonathan Tehau (38), 3-0 Alvin Tehau (57), 4-0 Teaonui Tehau (87), 4-1 Robert Tasso (90+5).
Cautions: Edson Lemaire, Tamatoa Wagemann / Ernest Bong.

GROUP B

02.06.2012	Honiara	Fiji - New Zealand	0-1(0-1)
02.06.2012	Honiara	Solomon Islands - Papua New Guinea	1-0(1-0)
04.06.2012	Honiara	Papua New Guinea - New Zealand	1-2(0-1)
04.06.2012	Honiara	Fiji - Solomon Islands	0-0
06.06.2012	Honiara	Papua New Guinea - Fiji	1-1(0-1)
06.06.2012	Honiara	New Zealand - Solomon Islands	1-1(1-0)

FINAL STANDINGS

1.	**New Zealand**	3	2	1	0	4 - 2	7
2.	**Solomon Islands**	3	1	2	0	2 - 1	5
3.	Fiji	3	0	2	1	1 - 2	2
4.	Papua New Guinea	3	0	1	2	2 - 4	1

02.06.2012, Lawson Tama Stadium, Honiara; Attendance: 15,000
Referee: Isidore Assiene-Ambassa (New Caledonia)
FIJI - NEW ZEALAND 0-1(0-1)
FIJ: Simione Moci Tamanisau, Taniela Evo Waqa, Samuela Ibo Kautoga, Remueru Tekiate, Samuela Vuluma Vula, Alvin Singh (61.Ilisoni Tuinawaivuvu), Pita Bolatoga Senibiaukula, Alvin Avinesh, Avinesh Waran Swamy, Roy Krishna, Osea Vakatalesau. Trainer: Juan Carlos Buzzetti (Uruguay).
NZL: Mark Nelson Paston (54.Jacob Christopher Gleeson), Ivan Robert Vicelich, Tony James Lochhead, Benjamin Robert Sigmund, Thomas Jefferson Smith, Michael Ryan McGlinchey, Marco Rodrigo Rojas (54.Christopher Grant Wood), Christopher John Killen, Leonidas Christos Bertos, Konstantinos Barbarouses (81.Rory Michael Fallon), Shane Edward Smeltz. Trainer: Ricki Lloyd Herbert.
Goal: 0-1 Thomas Jefferson Smith (9).
Cautions: Alvin Singh, Osea Vakatalesau / Leonidas Christos Bertos, Rory Michael Fallon, Ivan Robert Vicelich.

02.06.2012, Lawson Tama Stadium, Honiara; Attendance: 15,000
Referee: Norbert Hauata (Tahiti)
SOLOMON ISLANDS - PAPUA NEW GUINEA 1-0(1-0)
SOL: Felix Ray, Nelson Sale Kilifa, Freddie Kini, Hadisi Aengari Gagame, Henry Samuel Luito'o Fa'arodo, Jeffery Bule, Joses Nawo (64.Mostyn Beui), Tome Faisi, James Naka (52.Jack Maeli Wetney), Leslie Nate, Benjamin Totori. Trainer: Jacob Moli.
PNG: Leslie Kalai, Koriak Upaiga, Daniel Joe, Valentine Nelson, Kelly Jampu, David Muta, Samuel Kini, Michael Foster (73.Jeremy Yasasa), Niel Hans (46.Eric Komeng), Kema Jack, Reginald Davani (46.Raymond Gunemba). Trainer: Frank Farina (Australia).
Goal: 1-0 Benjamin Totori (5).
Cautions: Kelly Jampu.

04.06.2012, Lawson Tama Stadium, Honiara; Attendance: 3,000
Referee: Bruce George (Vanuatu)
PAPUA NEW GUINEA - NEW ZEALAND 1-2(0-1)
PNG: Koriak Upaiga, Kila Iaravai Polena, Daniel Joe, Valentine Nelson, David Muta, Samuel Kini (62.Niel Hans), Eric Komeng (84.Jeremy Yasasa), Michael Foster, Kema Jack, Raymond Gunemba (62.Jamal Seeto). Trainer: Frank Farina (Australia).
NZL: Jacob Christopher Gleeson, Ivan Robert Vicelich, Tony James Lochhead, Benjamin Robert Sigmund (85.Tim Myers), Thomas Jefferson Smith, Michael Ryan McGlinchey, Christopher John Killen (58.Aaron Daniel Clapham), Konstantinos Barbarouses, Shane Edward Smeltz (68.Timothy John Payne), Jeremy Russell Brockie, Christopher Grant Wood. Trainer: Ricki Lloyd Herbert.
Goals: 0-1 Shane Edward Smeltz (2), 0-2 Christopher Grant Wood (53), 1-2 Niel Hans (88 penalty).

Cautions: Kema Jack / Tony James Lochhead, Aaron Daniel Clapham.
Sent off: Tony James Lochhead (88).

04.06.2012, Lawson Tama Stadium, Honiara; Attendance: 12,000
Referee: Kader Zitouni (Tahiti)
FIJI - SOLOMON ISLANDS 0-0
FIJ: Simione Moci Tamanisau, Taniela Evo Waqa, Samuela Ibo Kautoga (33.Alvin Singh), Remueru Tekiate, Samuela Vuluma Vula (80.Paulo Posiano), Pita Bolatoga Senibiaukula, Ilisoni Tuinawaivuvu, Alvin Avinesh, Avinesh Waran Swamy, Roy Krishna (66.Maciu Dunadamu), Osea Vakatalesau. Trainer: Juan Carlos Buzzetti (Uruguay).
SOL: Felix Ray, Nelson Sale Kilifa, Loni Qaraba, Henry Samuel Luito'o Fa'arodo, Abraham Iniga (78.Nicholas Muri), Mostyn Beui (26.Jeffery Bule), Tome Faisi, James Naka, Leslie Nate (50.Jack Maeli Wetney), Joe Luwi, Seni Fonua Ngava. Trainer: Jacob Moli.
Cautions: Pita Bolatoga Senibiaukula, Samuela Vuluma Vula, Ilisoni Tuinawaivuvu, Paulo Posiano.

06.06.2012, Lawson Tama Stadium, Honiara; Attendance: 3,000
Referee: Kader Zitouni (Tahiti)
PAPUA NEW GUINEA - FIJI 1-1(0-1)
PNG: Leslie Kalai, Koriak Upaiga, Kila Iaravai Polena, Daniel Joe, Valentine Nelson, David Muta, Samuel Kini (79.Reginald Davani), Eric Komeng (64.Jeremy Yasasa), Michael Foster, Kema Jack, Raymond Gunemba (65.Jamal Seeto). Trainer: Frank Farina (Australia).
FIJ: Simione Moci Tamanisau, Taniela Evo Waqa, Remueru Tekiate, Samuela Vuluma Vula, Alvin Singh, Pita Bolatoga Senibiaukula, Alvin Avinesh, Avinesh Waran Swamy, Roy Krishna (83.Misaele Draunibaka), Maciu Dunadamu, Osea Vakatalesau (58.Apisai Smith). Trainer: Juan Carlos Buzzetti (Uruguay).
Goals: 0-1 Maciu Dunadamu (14), 1-1 Kema Jack (85).
Cautions: Koriak Upaiga, Reginald Davani / Simione Moci Tamanisau, Alvin Singh, Remueru Tekiate.

06.06.2012, Lawson Tama Stadium, Honiara; Attendance: 18,000
Referee: Norbert Hauata (Tahiti)
NEW ZEALAND - SOLOMON ISLANDS 1-1(1-0)
NZL: Jacob Christopher Gleeson, Michael Joseph Boxall, Ian Hogg, Thomas Jefferson Smith, Tim Myers, Marco Rodrigo Rojas (59.Konstantinos Barbarouses), Aaron Daniel Clapham, Timothy John Payne, Rory Michael Fallon (64.Adam McGeorge), Leonidas Christos Bertos (59.Jeremy Russell Brockie), Christopher Grant Wood. Trainer: Ricki Lloyd Herbert.
SOL: Felix Ray, Nelson Sale Kilifa, Freddie Kini (40.Joshua Tuasulia), Hadisi Aengari Gagame, Henry Samuel Luito'o Fa'arodo, Jack Maeli Wetney, Jeffery Bule, Joses Nawo (85.James Naka), Tome Faisi (49.Aleck Wickham), Leslie Nate, Benjamin Totori. Trainer: Jacob Moli.
Goals: 1-0 Christopher Grant Wood (14), 1-1 Benjamin Totori (57).
Cautions: Thomas Jefferson Smith / Joses Nawo.

SEMI-FINALS

08.06.2012	Honiara	Tahiti - Solomon Islands	1-0(1-0)
08.06.2012	Honiara	New Zealand - New Caledonia	0-2(0-0)

08.06.2012, Lawson Tama Stadium, Honiara; Attendance: 15,000
Referee: Peter O'Leary (New Zealand)
TAHITI - SOLOMON ISLANDS 1-0(1-0)
TAH: Xavier Samin, Teheivarii Ludivion, Angelo Tchen, Jonathan Tehau, Nicolas Vallar, Vincent Simon Lo-Shing, Heimano Bourebare, Lorenzo Tehau, Alvin Tehau, Henri Caroine, Steevy Chong Hue (76.Teaonui Tehau). Trainer: Eddy Etaeta.
SOL: Felix Ray (27.Shadrack Ramoni), Nelson Sale Kilifa, Hadisi Aengari Gagame, Loni Qaraba, Henry Samuel Luito'o Fa'arodo, Jack Maeli Wetney (78.Joe Luwi), Jeffery Bule, Tome Faisi, James Naka (45+1.Joses Nawo), Leslie Nate, Benjamin Totori. Trainer: Jacob Moli.
Goal: 1-0 Jonathan Tehau (16).
Cautions: Angelo Tchen, Henri Caroine, Lorenzo Tehau / Jeffery Bule, Nelson Sale Kilifa.

08.06.2012, Lawson Tama Stadium, Honiara; Attendance: 10,000
Referee: Norbert Hauata (Tahiti)
NEW ZEALAND - NEW CALEDONIA 0-2(0-0)
NZL: Jacob Christopher Gleeson, Ivan Robert Vicelich, Tony James Lochhead (86.Rory Michael Fallon), Benjamin Robert Sigmund, Thomas Jefferson Smith, Michael Ryan McGlinchey, Christopher John Killen, Leonidas Christos Bertos (63.Jeremy Russell Brockie), Konstantinos Barbarouses, Shane Edward Smeltz, Christopher Grant Wood (63.Marco Rodrigo Rojas). Trainer: Ricki Lloyd Herbert.
NCL: Rocky Nyikeine, Judikael Ixoéé, Emile Béaruné, Joël Wakanumuné, Marius Bako, Olivier Dokunengo, Dominique Wacalie, Bertrand Kaï (88.Noël Kaudré), Georges Gope-Fenepej, Iamel Kabeu, Jacques Haeko (74.Roy Kayara). Trainer: Alain Moizan (France).
Goals: 0-1 Bertrand Kaï (60), 0-2 Georges Gope-Fenepej (90+2).
Cautions: Leonidas Christos Bertos, Benjamin Robert Sigmund / Rocky Nyikeine.

THIRD PLACE PLAY-OFF

10.06.2012, Lawson Tama Stadium, Honiara; Attendance: 15,000
Referee: Kader Zitouni (Tahiti)
SOLOMON ISLANDS - NEW ZEALAND 3-4(0-3)
SOL: Nelson Sale Kilifa, Aleck Wickham, Joshua Tuasulia (38.Hadisi Aengari Gagame), Henry Samuel Luito'o Fa'arodo, Abraham Iniga, Jeffery Bule, Himson Teleda, Tome Faisi, Seni Fonua Ngava (46.Leslie Nate), Nicholas Muri (32.Benjamin Totori). Trainer: Jacob Moli.
NZL: Jacob Christopher Gleeson, Michael Joseph Boxall, Ian Hogg, Thomas Jefferson Smith (53.Ivan Robert Vicelich), Tim Myers, Marco Rodrigo Rojas (77.Shane Edward Smeltz), Aaron Daniel Clapham, Timothy John Payne, Konstantinos Barbarouses, Jeremy Russell Brockie, Christopher Grant Wood (64.Cameron Drew Neru Howieson). Trainer: Ricki Lloyd Herbert.
Goals: 0-1 Christopher Grant Wood (11), 0-2 Christopher Grant Wood (25), 0-3 Christopher Grant Wood (31), 1-3 Himson Teleda (48), 2-3 Benjamin Totori (54), 3-3 Benjamin Totori (88), 3-4 Shane Edward Smeltz (90).
Cautions: Tome Faisi / Ian Hogg, Tim Myers, Jeremy Russell Brockie, Timothy John Payne.

FINAL

10.06.2012, Lawson Tama Stadium, Honiara; Attendance: 10,000
Referee: Peter O'Leary (New Zealand)
TAHITI - NEW CALEDONIA **1-0(1-0)**
TAH: Xavier Samin, Teheivarii Ludivion, Angelo Tchen, Jonathan Tehau, Nicolas Vallar, Vincent Simon Lo-Shing, Heimano Bourebare (90+2.Roihau Degage), Lorenzo Tehau (89.Manaraii Porlier), Alvin Tehau, Henri Caroine, Steevy Chong Hue. Trainer: Eddy Etaeta.
NCL: Rocky Nyikeine, Judikael Ixoéé, Emile Béaruné, Joël Wakanumuné, Marius Bako, Olivier Dokunengo (67.Roy Kayara), Dominique Wacalie, Bertrand Kaï, Georges Gope-Fenepej, Iamel Kabeu, Jacques Haeko. Trainer: Alain Moizan (France).
Goal: 1-0 Steevy Chong Hue (11).
Cautions: Lorenzo Tehau, Angelo Tchen / Judikael Ixoéé, Marius Bako, Olivier Dokunengo, Emile Béaruné.

THIRD ROUND
(2008 OFC Nations Cup)

07.09.2012	Nouméa	New Caledonia - New Zealand	0-2(0-1)
07.09.2012	Honiara	Solomon Islands - Tahiti	2-0(1-0)
11.09.2012	Auckland	New Zealand - Solomon Islands	6-1(2-0)
11.09.2012	Papeete	Tahiti - New Caledonia	0-4(0-0)
12.10.2012	Honiara	Solomon Islands - New Caledonia	2-6(1-2)
12.10.2012	Papeete	Tahiti - New Zealand	0-2(0-1)
16.10.2012	Nouméa	New Caledonia - Solomon Islands	5-0(4-0)
16.10.2012	Christchurch	New Zealand - Tahiti	3-0(1-0)
22.03.2013	Dunedin	New Zealand - New Caledonia	2-1(1-0)
22.03.2013	Papeete	Tahiti - Solomon Islands	2-0(1-0)
26.03.2013	Honiara	Solomon Islands - New Zealand	0-2(0-1)
26.03.2013	Nouméa	New Caledonia - Tahiti	1-0(0-0)

FINAL STANDINGS

1.	**New Zealand**	6	6	0	0	17	-	2	18
2.	New Caledonia	6	4	0	2	17	-	6	12
3.	Tahiti	6	1	0	5	2	-	12	3
4.	Solomon Islands	6	1	0	5	5	-	21	3

New Zealand qualified for the Intercontinental Play-offs.

07.09.2012, Stade Numa-Daly Magenta, Nouméa; Attendance: 6,000
Referee: Norbert Hauata (Tahiti)
NEW CALEDONIA - NEW ZEALAND **0-2(0-1)**
NCL: Rocky Nyikeine, Jérémie Kouriane Dokunengo (81.Miguel Kayara), Emile Béaruné, Joël Wakanumuné, Noël Kaudré (55.Jacques Haeko), Olivier Dokunengo, Dominique Wacalie, Bertrand Kaï, Georges Gope-Fenepej, César Lolohéa Ngalo-Manuotalaha, Iamel Kabeu (55.Roy Kayara). Trainer: Alain Moizan (France).
NZL: Mark Nelson Paston, Ivan Robert Vicelich, Tony James Lochhead, Winston Wiremu Reid, Thomas Jefferson Smith, Ryan William Nelsen, Michael Ryan McGlinchey (74.Timothy John Payne), Leonidas Christos Bertos, Shane Edward Smeltz, Jeremy Russell Brockie (81.Konstantinos Barbarouses), Christopher Grant Wood (90+2.Marco Rodrigo Rojas). Trainer: Ricki Lloyd Herbert.
Goals: 0-1 Shane Edward Smeltz (12), 0-2 Christopher Grant Wood (40).
Cautions: Iamel Kabeu, Dominique Wacalie / Michael Ryan McGlinchey, Shane Edward Smeltz, Winston Wiremu Reid.

07.09.2012, Lawson Tama Stadium, Honiara; Attendance: 22,000
Referee: Jamie Cross (New Zealand)

SOLOMON ISLANDS - TAHITI 2-0(1-0)

SOL: Samson Koti, Nelson Sale Kilifa, Hadisi Aengari Gagame, Emmanuel Poila, Henry Samuel Luito'o Fa'arodo (86.Jack Maeli Wetney), Mostyn Beui, Joses Nawo, Himson Teleda, Tome Faisi, Leslie Nate, Benjamin Totori (62.Ian Paia). Trainer: Jacob Moli.
TAH: Xavier Samin, Teheivarii Ludivion, Jonathan Tehau, Nicolas Vallar, Vincent Simon Lo-Shing, Yannick Vero (60.Tauraa Marmouyet), Alvin Tehau, Sébastien Labayen, Henri Caroine (14.Efrain Arañeda Estay; 75.Teaonui Tehau), Stanley Atani, Steevy Chong Hue. Trainer: Eddy Etaeta.
Goal: 1-0 Henry Samuel Luito'o Fa'arodo (17), 2-0 Himson Teleda (60).
Cautions: Leslie Nate, Mostyn Beui, Himson Teleda / Steevy Chong Hue, Sébastien Labayen.
Sent off: Nicolas Vallar (45).

11.09.2012, North Harbour Stadium, Auckland; Attendance: 7,931
Referee: Bertrand Billon (New Caledonia)

NEW ZEALAND - SOLOMON ISLANDS 6-1(2-0)

NZL: Mark Nelson Paston, Ivan Robert Vicelich (82.Marco Rodrigo Rojas), Tony James Lochhead, Winston Wiremu Reid, Thomas Jefferson Smith, Ryan William Nelsen (73.Benjamin Robert Sigmund), Michael Ryan McGlinchey, Christopher John Killen, Leonidas Christos Bertos, Konstantinos Barbarouses, Shane Edward Smeltz (73.Christopher Grant Wood). Trainer: Ricki Lloyd Herbert.
SOL: Samson Koti (43.Paul Huia), Nelson Sale Kilifa, Freddie Kini, Hadisi Aengari Gagame, Henry Samuel Luito'o Fa'arodo, Jeffery Bule, Joses Nawo, Tome Faisi, Leslie Nate, Benjamin Totori, Gagame Feni (55.Himson Teleda). Trainer: Jacob Moli.
Goals: 1-0 Shane Edward Smeltz (12), 2-0 Konstantinos Barbarouses (25), 2-1 Henry Samuel Luito'o Fa'arodo (51), 3-1 Christopher John Killen (53), 4-1 Tony James Lochhead (69), 5-1 Christopher Grant Wood (80), 6-1 Marco Rodrigo Rojas (83).
Cautions: Christopher Grant Wood.

11.09.2012, Stade Pater Te Hono Nui, Pirae; Attendance: 574
Referee: Andrew Achari (Fiji)

TAHITI - NEW CALEDONIA 0-4(0-0)

TAH: Xavier Samin, Teheivarii Ludivion, Tauraa Marmouyet, Angelo Tchen, Jonathan Tehau, Vincent Simon Lo-Shing, Lorenzo Tehau (85.Roihau Degage), Alvin Tehau, Hiroana Poroiae (54.Axel Williams), Stanley Atani (66.Teaonui Tehau), Steevy Chong Hue. Trainer: Eddy Etaeta.
NCL: Rocky Nyikeine, Emile Béaruné, Yohann Mercier, Joël Wakanumuné (46.Pierre Nyikeine), Noël Kaudré (73.Miguel Kayara), Roy Kayara, Dominique Wacalie, Bertrand Kaï, Georges Gope-Fenepej, César Lolohéa Ngalo-Manuotalaha, Iamel Kabeu. Trainer: Alain Moizan (France).
Goals: 0-1 César Lolohéa Ngalo-Manuotalaha (55), 0-2 Bertrand Kaï (56), 0-3 Bertrand Kaï (63), 0-4 Georges Gope-Fenepej (89).
Cautions: Stanley Atani, Tauraa Marmouyet / Emile Béaruné.

12.10.2012, Lawson Tama Stadium, Honiara; Attendance: 8,000
Referee: Peter O'Leary (New Zealand)

SOLOMON ISLANDS - NEW CALEDONIA 2-6(1-2)

SOL: Samson Koti, Hadisi Aengari Gagame (45+2.Loni Qaraba), Emmanuel Poila, Henry Samuel Luito'o Fa'arodo, Mostyn Beui (68.Joe Luwi), Joses Nawo (68.Paul Hiri), Tome Faisi, Leslie Nate, Benjamin Totori, Tutizama Tanito, Seni Fonua Ngava. Trainer: Jacob Moli.
NCL: Rocky Nyikeine, Jean-Patrick Wakanumuné, Pierre Nyikeine, Yohann Mercier, Joël Wakanumuné, Noël Kaudré, Roy Kayara (79.Jacques Haeko), Dominique Wacalie, Bertrand Kaï, Georges Gope-Fenepej, César Lolohéa Ngalo-Manuotalaha. Trainer: Alain Moizan (France).
Goals: 0-1 Roy Kayara (8), 1-1 Tutizama Tanito (34), 1-2 Georges Gope-Fenepej (45), 2-2 Joses Nawo (63), 2-3 Emmanuel Poila (78 own goal), 2-4 Georges Gope-Fenepej (82), 2-5 Jacques Haeko (90), 2-6 Georges Gope-Fenepej (90+1).
Cautions: Noël Kaudré, Dominique Wacalie, Pierre Nyikeine.

12.10.2012, Stade Pater Te Hono Nui, Pirae; Attendance: 600
Referee: Bruce George (Vanuatu)
TAHITI - NEW ZEALAND 0-2(0-1)
TAH: Xavier Samin, Pierre Kugogne, Tauraa Marmouyet (61.Vincent Simon Lo-Shing), Angelo Tchen, Jonathan Tehau, Nicolas Vallar, Yannick Vero, Lorenzo Tehau (81.Axel Williams), Alvin Tehau, Stanley Atani (73.Efrain Arañeda Estay), Steevy Chong Hue. Trainer: Eddy Etaeta.
NZL: Glen Robert Moss, Ivan Robert Vicelich, Tony James Lochhead, Benjamin Robert Sigmund, Thomas Jefferson Smith, Michael Ryan McGlinchey, Timothy John Payne (73.Konstantinos Barbarouses), Christopher John Killen, Leonidas Christos Bertos, Shane Edward Smeltz (89.Daniel Phillip Keat), Christopher Grant Wood (61.Jeremy Russell Brockie). Trainer: Ricki Lloyd Herbert.
Goals: 0-1 Shane Edward Smeltz (24), 0-2 Benjamin Robert Sigmund (82).
Cautions: Angelo Tchen / Timothy John Payne, Tony James Lochhead.

16.10.2012, Stade Numa-Daly Magenta, Nouméa; Attendance: 4,000
Referee: Kader Zitouni (Tahiti)
NEW CALEDONIA - SOLOMON ISLANDS 5-0(4-0)
NCL: Rocky Nyikeine, Jean-Patrick Wakanumuné, Emile Béaruné, Pierre Nyikeine, Yohann Mercier, Roy Kayara (80.Jacques Haeko), Olivier Dokunengo (60.Noël Kaudré), Bertrand Kaï, Georges Gope-Fenepej, César Lolohéa Ngalo-Manuotalaha, Iamel Kabeu (86.Georges Béaruné). Trainer: Alain Moizan (France).
SOL: Samson Koti, Willie Lamani (72.Joachim Waroi), Loni Qaraba, Emmanuel Poila, Henry Samuel Luito'o Fa'arodo, Mostyn Beui, Joses Nawo, Tome Faisi, Leslie Nate, Benjamin Totori, Tutizama Tanito (86.Paul Hiri). Trainer: Jacob Moli.
Goals: 1-0 Georges Gope-Fenepej (5), 2-0 Roy Kayara (12), 3-0 Iamel Kabeu (31), 4-0 César Lolohéa Ngalo-Manuotalaha (45), 5-0 César Lolohéa Ngalo-Manuotalaha (90).
Cautions: Joses Nawo.

16.10.2012, AMI Stadium, Christchurch; Attendance: 10,751
Referee: Gerald Oiaka (Solomon Islands)
NEW ZEALAND - TAHITI 3-0(1-0)
NZL: Glen Robert Moss, Ivan Robert Vicelich (66.Daniel Phillip Keat), Tony James Lochhead, Benjamin Robert Sigmund, Thomas Jefferson Smith, Ryan William Nelsen (86.Leonidas Christos Bertos), Michael Ryan McGlinchey, Marco Rodrigo Rojas (69.Shane Edward Smeltz), Christopher John Killen, Konstantinos Barbarouses, Jeremy Russell Brockie. Trainer: Ricki Lloyd Herbert.
TAH: Mickaël Roche, Teheivarii Ludivion, Pierre Kugogne, Tauraa Marmouyet, Jonathan Tehau, Nicolas Vallar, Yannick Vero, Lorenzo Tehau (66.Teaonui Tehau), Alvin Tehau (71.Axel Williams), Stanley Atani, Steevy Chong Hue. Trainer: Eddy Etaeta.
Goals: 1-0 Michael Ryan McGlinchey (3), 2-0 Christopher John Killen (90), 3-0 Michael Ryan McGlinchey (90+3).
Cautions: Christopher John Killen, Benjamin Robert Sigmund / Nicolas Vallar.

22.03.2013, Forsyth Barr Stadium, Dunedin; Attendance: 9,000
Referee: Strebre Delovski (Australia)
NEW ZEALAND - NEW CALEDONIA 2-1(1-0)
NZL: Mark Nelson Paston, Ivan Robert Vicelich, Winston Wiremu Reid, Thomas Jefferson Smith, Michael Ryan McGlinchey, Marco Rodrigo Rojas, Christopher John Killen (75.Timothy John Payne), Leonidas Christos Bertos, Shane Edward Smeltz (90.Ian Hogg), Jeremy Russell Brockie (80.Konstantinos Barbarouses), Christopher Grant Wood. Trainer: Ricki Lloyd Herbert.
NCL: Rocky Nyikeine, Judikael Ixoéé, Emile Béaruné, Joël Wakanumuné, Noël Kaudré (77.Iamel Kabeu), Roy Kayara (87.Kalaje Gnipate), Olivier Dokunengo, Dominique Wacalie, Bertrand Kaï, Georges Gope-Fenepej, César Lolohéa Ngalo-Manuotalaha. Trainer: Alain Moizan (France).
Goals: 1-0 Christopher John Killen (10), 1-1 César Lolohéa Ngalo-Manuotalaha (56), 2-1 Thomas Jefferson Smith (90+4).
Cautions: Leonidas Christos Bertos / César Lolohéa Ngalo-Manuotalaha, Emile Béaruné, Joël Wakanumuné.

22.03.2013, Stade Pater Te Hono Nui, Pirae; Attendance: 550
Referee: Andrew Achari (Fiji)
TAHITI - SOLOMON ISLANDS 2-0(1-0)
TAH: Mickaël Roche, Teheivarii Ludivion, Angelo Tchen, Jonathan Tehau, Nicolas Vallar, Vincent Simon Lo-Shing (71.Edson Lemaire), Heimano Bourebare, Yannick Vero (75.Stephane Faatiarau), Stanley Atani, Teaonui Tehau (71.Samuel Hnanyine), Steevy Chong Hue. Trainer: Eddy Etaeta.
SOL: Sammy Oso, Stewart Quan, Andrew Maeribu (25.Calvin Erick), George Lagoda, Michael Fifi'i, Henry Samuel Luito'o Fa'arodo, Benjamin Totori, Andrew Abba (74.Tony Havea), Joachim Rande, Alex Waimora, Wesley Keni Olea. Trainer: Jacob Moli.
Goals: 1-0 Steevy Chong Hue (28), 2-0 Nicolas Vallar (82).
Cautions: Heimano Bourebare, Yannick Vero / Joachim Rande.

26.03.2013, Lawson Tama Stadium, Honiara; Attendance: 5,600
Referee: Averii Jacques (Tahiti)
SOLOMON ISLANDS - NEW ZEALAND 0-2(0-1)
SOL: Samson Koti, Freddie Kini, Arnold Keni, Henry Samuel Luito'o Fa'arodo, Leonard Rokoto, Himson Teleda (83.Clifford Wate), Paul Hiri (62.Joe Luwi), George Wagena, David Naitoro (63.Edika Maetaa), Benjamin Totori, Tutizama Tanito. Trainer: Jacob Moli.
NZL: Jacob Spoonley, Andrew Durante, Benjamin Robert Sigmund, Ian Hogg, Aaron James Scott (83.Leonidas Christos Bertos), Cameron Lindsay, Aaron Daniel Clapham, Daniel Phillip Keat, Timothy John Payne, Konstantinos Barbarouses, Luke Rowe. Trainer: Ricki Lloyd Herbert.
Goals: 0-1 Timothy John Payne (3), 0-2 Timothy John Payne (88).
Cautions: Leonard Rokoto / Ian Hogg.

26.03.2013, Stade Numa-Daly Magenta, Nouméa; Attendance: 1,000
Referee: Rakesh Varman (Fiji)
NEW CALEDONIA - TAHITI 1-0(0-0)
NCL: Steeve Ixoéé, Jean-Patrick Wakanumuné, Judikael Ixoéé, Joël Wakanumuné, Noël Kaudré, Roy Kayara, Olivier Dokunengo (53.Georges Béaruné), Dominique Wacalie, Bertrand Kaï (71.Miguel Kayara), Georges Gope-Fenepej (63.Kalaje Gnipate), César Lolohéa Ngalo-Manuotalaha. Trainer: Alain Moizan (France).
TAH: Xavier Samin, Stephane Faatiarau (59.Rainui Aroita), Angelo Tchen, Tamatoa Wagemann, Edson Lemaire, Efrain Arañeda Estay, Hiroana Poroiae, Henri Caroine, Garry Rochette (63.Ricky Aitamai), Stanley Atani, Yohann Tihoni (82.Teaonui Tehau). Trainer: Eddy Etaeta.
Goal: 1-0 César Lolohéa Ngalo-Manuotalaha (86).
Cautions: Bertrand Kaï / Efrain Arañeda Estay.

INTERCONTINENTAL PLAY-OFFS

13.11.2013	Ciudad de México	Mexico – New Zealand	5-1(2-0)
20.11.2013	Wellington	New Zealand - Mexico	2-4(0-3)

02.06.2012, Estadio Azteca, Ciudad de México; Attendance: 99,832
Referee: Viktor Kassai (Hungary)
MEXICO – NEW ZEALAND **5-1(2-0)**
MEX: Moisés Alberto Muñoz Rodríguez, Rafael Márquez Álvarez, Francisco Javier Rodríguez Pinedo, Paul Nicolás Aguilar Rojas, Juan Carlos Valenzuela Hernández, Miguel Arturo Layún Prado, Luis Arturo Montes Jiménez (59.Antônio Naelson Matías „Sinha"), Juan Carlos Medina Alonso, Carlos Alberto Peña Rodríguez (64.Jesús Alonso Escoboza Lugo), Oribe Peralta Morones (81.Jesús Antonio Molina Granados), Raúl Alonso Jiménez Rodríguez. Trainer: Miguel Ernesto Herrera Aguirre.
NZL: Glen Robert Moss, Ivan Robert Vicelich, Tony James Lochhead, Andrew Durante, Thomas Jefferson Smith, Michael Ryan McGlinchey, Jeremy John Christie (53.Christopher Paul James), Leonidas Christos Bertos, Konstantinos Barbarouses, Jeremy Russell Brockie (59.Marco Rodrigo Rojas), Christopher Grant Wood (67.Rory Michael Fallon). Trainer: Ricki Lloyd Herbert.
Goals: 1-0 Paul Nicolás Aguilar Rojas (32), 2-0 Raúl Alonso Jiménez Rodríguez (40), 3-0 Oribe Peralta Morones (48), 4-0 Oribe Peralta Morones (80), 5-0 Rafael Márquez Álvarez (84), 5-1 Christopher Paul James (88).
Cautions: Christopher Grant Wood, Ivan Robert Vicelich, Andrew Durante, Leonidas Christos Bertos, Christopher Paul James.

02.06.2012, Westpac Stadium, Wellington; Attendance: 35,206
Referee: Dr. Felix Brych (Germany)
NEW ZEALAND - MEXICO **2-4(0-3)**
NZL: Glen Robert Moss, Andrew Durante, Thomas Jefferson Smith, Bill Poni Tuiloma (50.Louis Fenton), Storm James Roux, Michael Ryan McGlinchey, Christopher Paul James, Marco Rodrigo Rojas (73.Craig Charles Glendinning Henderson), Konstantinos Barbarouses, Shane Edward Smeltz (54.Rory Michael Fallon), Jeremy Russell Brockie. Trainer: Ricki Lloyd Herbert.
MEX: Moisés Alberto Muñoz Rodríguez, Rafael Márquez Álvarez, Francisco Javier Rodríguez Pinedo, Paul Nicolás Aguilar Rojas, Juan Carlos Valenzuela Hernández, Miguel Arturo Layún Prado, Luis Arturo Montes Jiménez (58.Jesús Alonso Escoboza Lugo), Juan Carlos Medina Alonso, Carlos Alberto Peña Rodríguez, Oribe Peralta Morones (76.Antônio Naelson Matías „Sinha"), Raúl Alonso Jiménez Rodríguez (68.Jesús Aldo de Nigris Guajardo). Trainer: Miguel Ernesto Herrera Aguirre.
Goals: 0-1 Oribe Peralta Morones (14), 0-2 Oribe Peralta Morones (29), 0-3 Oribe Peralta Morones (33), 1-3 Christopher Paul James (80 penalty), 2-3 Rory Michael Fallon (83), 2-4 Carlos Alberto Peña Rodríguez (86).
Cautions: Shane Edward Smeltz, Konstantinos Barbarouses, Christopher Paul James / Luis Arturo Montes Jiménez, Moisés Alberto Muñoz Rodríguez, Juan Carlos Medina Alonso.

MEXICO qualified for the Final Tournament.

13.11.2013	Amman	Jordan – Uruguay	0-5(0-2)
20.11.2013	Montevideo	Uruguay - Jordan	0-0

13.11.2013, Amman International Stadium, Amman; ; Attendance: 17,370
Referee: Svein Oddvar Moen (Norway)
JORDAN – URUGUAY **0-5(0-2)**
JOR: Mohammad Shatnawi, Hatem Mohammad Yusuf Aqel, Oday Samir Zahran (53.Thayer Fayed Al Bawab), Shareef Adnan Nassar, Tareq Ziad Jabr Khattab, Saeed Hassan Al Murjan, Alaa' Walid Bashir Maflah Al Shaqran, Khalil Zayid Bani Attiah (65.Rakan Bani Khaled Al Khalidi), Adnan Suleiman Hassan Adous, Odai Yousef Ismail Al Saify (59.Mossab Al Laham), Ahmad Hayel Ibrahim. Trainer: Hossam Hassan Hussein (Egypt).
URU: Martín Andrés Silva Leites, Diego Alfredo Lugano Morena, Victorio Maximiliano Pereira Páez, José Martín Cáceres Silva, Diego Roberto Godín Leal, Cristian Gabriel Rodríguez Barotti, Egidio Raúl Arévalo Ríos, Marcelo Nicolás Lodeiro Benítez (70.Álvaro Daniel Pereira Barragán), Luis Alberto Suárez Díaz (81.Diego Martín Forlán Corazzo), Edinson Roberto Cavani Gómez, Christian Ricardo Stuani Curbelo (70.Gastón Ezequiel Ramírez Pereyra). Trainer: Óscar Wáshington Tabárez Silva.
Goals: 0-1 Victorio Maximiliano Pereira Páez (22), 0-2 Christian Ricardo Stuani Curbelo (42), 0-3 Marcelo Nicolás Lodeiro Benítez (69), 0-4 Cristian Gabriel Rodríguez Barotti (78), 0-5 Edinson Roberto Cavani Gómez (90+2).
Cautions: Odai Yousef Ismail Al Saify, Saeed Hassan Al Murjan, Mossab Al Laham.

20.11.2013, Estadio Centenario, Montevideo; ; Attendance: 62,000
Referee: Jonas Eriksson (Sweden)
URUGUAY - JORDAN **0-0**
URU: Martín Andrés Silva Leites, Diego Alfredo Lugano Morena, Victorio Maximiliano Pereira Páez, José Martín Cáceres Silva, Diego Roberto Godín Leal, Cristian Gabriel Rodríguez Barotti, Egidio Raúl Arévalo Ríos, Marcelo Nicolás Lodeiro Benítez (61.Gastón Ezequiel Ramírez Pereyra), Luis Alberto Suárez Díaz, Edinson Roberto Cavani Gómez (82.Abel Mathías Hernández Platero), Christian Ricardo Stuani Curbelo (61.Diego Martín Forlán Corazzo). Trainer: Óscar Wáshington Tabárez Silva.
JOR: Mohammad Shatnawi, Hatem Mohammad Yusuf Aqel, Oday Samir Zahran, Mohammad Abdulsaleh Al Dhemeri, Tareq Ziad Jabr Khattab, Shareef Adnan Nassar, Mohammad Khair Al Jamal (60. Khalil Zayid Bani Attiah), Adnan Suleiman Hassan Adous, Shadi Nadmi Abu Hashhash, Abdallah Khaled Deeb Salim (87.Yousef Ahmad Al Rawashdeh), Ahmad Hayel Ibrahim (90+1.Thayer Fayed Al Bawab). Trainer: Hossam Hassan Hussein (Egypt).
Cautions: Diego Roberto Godín Leal / Mohammad Abdulsaleh Al Dhemeri, Adnan Suleiman Hassan Adous, Oday Samir Zahran.

URUGUAY qualified for the Final Tournament.

WORLD CUP
THE FINAL TOURNAMENT

The 20th FIFA World Cup Final Tournament took place in Brazil from 12 June to 13 July 2014. The Final Tournament group draw was staged in Mata de São João on 6 December 2013. The 32 teams have been divided in advance by FIFA into four pots based on seedings and geographic regions. The seeding was based on the November 2013 FIFA World Ranking No two teams from the same confederation were drawn in the same group, except allowing a maximum of two European teams in a group.

Pot 1 (Seeds: host & top 7):
Brazil, Argentina, Colombia, Uruguay, Belgium, Germany, Spain, Switzerland.

Pot 2 (Africa & South America):
Algeria, Cameroon, Ghana, Côte d'Ivoire, Nigeria, Chile, Ecuador (+ 1 team from Europe).

Pot 3 (Asia, North/Central America and Caribbean):
Australia, Iran, Japan, Korea Republic, Costa Rica, Honduras, Mexico, United States.

Pot 4 (Europe):
Bosnia-Herzegovina, Croatia, England, France, Greece, Italy (drawn into Pot 2), Holland, Portugal, Russia..

The 32 teams were drawn as follows:

GROUP A	GROUP B
Brazil	Spain
Croatia	Holland
Mexico	Chile
Cameroon	Australia

GROUP C	GROUP D
Colombia	Uruguay
Greece	Costa Rica
Côte d'Ivoire	England
Japan	Italy

GROUP E	GROUP F
Switzerland	Argentina
Ecuador	Bosnia-Herzegovina
France	Iran
Honduras	Nigeria

GROUP G	GROUP H
Germany	Belgium
Portugal	Algeria
Ghana	Russia
United States	Korea Republic

List of venues:

City	Stadium	Capacity
Belo Horizonte	Estádio Mineirão	58,259
Brasília	Estádio Nacional "Mané Garrincha"	69,432
Cuiabá	Arena Pantanal	41,112
Curitiba	Arena da Baixada	39,631
Fortaleza	Estádio Castelão	60,348
Manaus	Arena do Amazônia	40,549
Natal	Arena das Dunas	39,971
Porto Alegre	Estádio Beira-Rio	43,394
Recife	Arena Pernambuco	42,583
Rio de Janeiro	Estádio "Jornalista Mário Filho" (Maracanã)	74,738
Salvador	Arena Fonte Nova	51,708
São Paulo	Arena São Paulo	62,601

GROUP A

12.06.2014	São Paulo	Brazil - Croatia	3-1(1-1)
13.06.2014	Natal	Mexico - Cameroon	1-0(0-0)
17.06.2014	Fortaleza	Brazil - Mexico	0-0
18.06.2014	Manaus	Cameroon - Croatia	0-4(0-1)
23.06.2014	Brasília	Cameroon - Brazil	1-4(1-2)
23.06.2014	Recife	Croatia - Mexico	1-3(0-0)

FINAL STANDINGS

1.	**Brazil**	3	2	1	0	7 - 2	7
2.	**Mexico**	3	2	1	0	4 - 1	7
3.	Croatia	3	1	0	2	6 - 6	3
4.	Cameroon	3	0	0	3	1 - 9	0

12.06.2014, Arena de São Paulo, São Paulo; Attendance: 62,103
Referee: Yuichi Nishimura (Japan)

BRAZIL - CROATIA **3-1(1-1)**

BRA: Júlio César Soares de Espíndola, Daniel Alves da Silva, Thiago Emiliano da Silva, David Luiz Moreira Marinho, Marcelo Vieira da Silva Júnior, José Paulo Bezerra Maciel Júnior „Paulinho III" (63.Anderson Hernanes de Carvalho Andrade Lima), Luiz Gustavo Dias, Givanildo Vieira de Souza „Hulk" (68.Bernard Anício Caldeira Duarte), Oscar dos Santos Emboaba Júnior, Neymar da Silva Santos Júnior (88.Ramires Santos do Nascimento), Frederico Chaves Guedes "Fred". Trainer: Luíz Felipe Scolari.

CRO: Stipe Pletikosa, Darijo Srna, Vedran Ćorluka, Dejan Lovren, Šime Vrsaljko, Luka Modrić, Ivan Rakitić, Ivan Perišić, Mateo Kovačić (61.Marcelo Brozović), Ivica Olić, Nikica Jelavić (78.Ante Rebić). Trainer: Niko Kovač.

Goals: 0-1 Marcelo Vieira da Silva Júnior (11 own goal), 1-1 Neymar da Silva Santos Júnior (29), 2-1 Neymar da Silva Santos Júnior (71 penalty), 3-1 Oscar dos Santos Emboaba Júnior (90+1).

Cautions: Neymar da Silva Santos Júnior, Luiz Gustavo Dias / Vedran Ćorluka, Dejan Lovren.

13.06.2014, Arena das Dunas, Natal; Attendance: 39,216
Referee: Wilmar Alexander Roldán Pérez (Colombia)
MEXICO - CAMEROON 1-0(0-0)
MEX: Francisco Guillermo Ochoa Magaña, Rafael Márquez Álvarez, Francisco Javier Rodríguez Pinedo, José Andrés Guardado Hernández (69.Marco Jhonfai Fabián de la Mora), Paul Nicolás Aguilar Rojas, Héctor Alfredo Moreno Herrera, Miguel Arturo Layún Prado, Héctor Miguel Herrera López (90+2.Carlos Arnoldo Salcido Flores), José Juan Vázquez Gómez, Oribe Peralta Morones (74.Javier Hernández Balcázar), Giovani dos Santos Ramírez. Trainer: Miguel Ernesto Herrera Aguirre.
CMR: Charles-Hubert Itandje, Benoît Pierre David Assou-Ekotto, Aurélien Bayard Chedjou Fongang, Nicolas Alexis Julio N'Koulou N'Doubena, Cédric Djeugoué (46.Dany Achille Nounkeu Tchounkeu), Stéphane Mbia Etoundi, Alexandre Dimitri Song Billong (79.Pierre Achille Webó Kouamo), Eyong Tarkang Enoh, Samuel Eto'o Fils, Jean-Eric Maxim Choupo-Moting, Benjamin Moukandjo Bilé. Trainer: Volker Finke (Germany).
Goal: 1-0 Oribe Peralta Morones (61).
Cautions: Héctor Alfredo Moreno Herrera / Dany Achille Nounkeu Tchounkeu.

17.06.2014, Estádio Castelão, Fortaleza
Attendance: 60,342
Referee: Cüneyt Çakır (Turkey)
BRAZIL - MEXICO 0-0
BRA: Júlio César Soares de Espíndola, Daniel Alves da Silva, Thiago Emiliano da Silva, David Luiz Moreira Marinho, Marcelo Vieira da Silva Júnior, José Paulo Bezerra Maciel Júnior „Paulinho III", Luiz Gustavo Dias, Oscar dos Santos Emboaba Júnior (Willian Borges da Silva), Ramires Santos do Nascimento (Bernard Anício Caldeira Duarte), Frederico Chaves Guedes "Fred" (João Alves de Assis Silva "Jô"), Neymar da Silva Santos Júnior. Trainer: Luíz Felipe Scolari.
MEX: Francisco Guillermo Ochoa Magaña, Rafael Márquez Álvarez, Francisco Javier Rodríguez Pinedo, José Andrés Guardado Hernández, Paul Nicolás Aguilar Rojas, Héctor Alfredo Moreno Herrera, Miguel Arturo Layún Prado, Héctor Miguel Herrera López (76.Marco Jhonfai Fabián de la Mora), José Juan Vázquez Gómez, Oribe Peralta Morones (74.Javier Hernández Balcázar), Giovani dos Santos Ramírez (84.Raúl Alonso Jiménez Rodríguez). Trainer: Miguel Ernesto Herrera Aguirre.
Cautions: Ramires Santos do Nascimento, Thiago Emiliano da Silva / Paul Nicolás Aguilar Rojas, José Juan Vázquez Gómez.

18.06.2014, Arena da Amazônia, Manaus; Attendance: 39,982
Referee: Pedro Proença Oliveira Alves Garcia (Portugal)
CAMEROON - CROATIA 0-4(0-1)
CMR: Charles-Hubert Itandje, Benoît Pierre David Assou-Ekotto, Aurélien Bayard Chedjou Fongang (46.Dany Achille Nounkeu Tchounkeu), Nicolas Alexis Julio N'Koulou N'Doubena, Joël Job Matip, Stéphane Mbia Etoundi, Alexandre Dimitri Song Billong, Eyong Tarkang Enoh, Jean-Eric Maxim Choupo-Moting (75.Edgar Nicaise Constant Salli), Benjamin Moukandjo Bilé, Vincent Aboubakar (70.Pierre Achille Webó Kouamo). Trainer: Volker Finke (Germany).
CRO: Stipe Pletikosa, Darijo Srna, Vedran Ćorluka, Dejan Lovren, Danijel Pranjić, Luka Modrić, Ivan Rakitić, Ivan Perišić (78.Ante Rebić), Jorge Sammir Cruz Campos (72.Mateo Kovačić), Ivica Olić (69.Eduardo Alves da Silva), Mario Mandžukić. Trainer: Niko Kovač.
Goals: 0-1 Ivica Olić (11), 0-2 Ivan Perišić (48), 0-3 Mario Mandžukić (61), 0-4 Mario Mandžukić (73).
Cautions: Eduardo Alves da Silva.
Sent off: Alexandre Dimitri Song Billong (40).

23.06.2014, Estádio Nacional „Mané Garrincha", Brasília; Attendance: 69,112
Referee: Jonas Eriksson (Sweden)
CAMEROON - BRAZIL 1-4(1-2)
CMR: Charles-Hubert Itandje, Nicolas Alexis Julio N'Koulou N'Doubena, Allan-Roméo Nyom, Henri Bedimo Nsamé, Joël Job Matip, Joël Landry Tsafack N'Guémo, Stéphane Mbia Etoundi, Eyong Tarkang Enoh, Jean-Eric Maxim Choupo-Moting (81.Jean II Makoun), Benjamin Moukandjo Bilé (58.Edgar Nicaise Constant Salli), Vincent Aboubakar (72.Pierre Achille Webó Kouamo). Trainer: Volker Finke (Germany).
BRA: Júlio César Soares de Espíndola, Daniel Alves da Silva, Thiago Emiliano da Silva, David Luiz Moreira Marinho, Marcelo Vieira da Silva Júnior, Luiz Gustavo Dias, José Paulo Bezerra Maciel Júnior „Paulinho III" (46.Fernando Luiz Rosa „Fernandinho"), Oscar dos Santos Emboaba Júnior, Givanildo Vieira de Souza „Hulk" (63.Ramires Santos do Nascimento), Frederico Chaves Guedes "Fred", Neymar da Silva Santos Júnior (71.Willian Borges da Silva). Trainer: Luíz Felipe Scolari.
Goals: 0-1 Neymar da Silva Santos Júnior (17), 1-1 Joël Job Matip (26), 1-2 Neymar da Silva Santos Júnior (34), 1-3 Frederico Chaves Guedes "Fred" (49), 1-4 Fernando Luiz Rosa „Fernandinho" (84).
Cautions: Eyong Tarkang Enoh, Edgar Nicaise Constant Salli, Stéphane Mbia Etoundi.

23.06.2014, Arena Pernambuco, Recife; Attendance: 41,212
Referee: Ravshan Irmatov (Uzbekistan)
CROATIA - MEXICO 1-3(0-0)
CRO: Stipe Pletikosa, Darijo Srna, Vedran Ćorluka, Dejan Lovren, Šime Vrsaljko (58.Mateo Kovačić), Luka Modrić, Danijel Pranjić (74.Nikica Jelavić), Ivan Perišić, Ivan Rakitić, Ivica Olić (69.Ante Rebić), Mario Mandžukić. Trainer: Niko Kovač.
MEX: Francisco Guillermo Ochoa Magaña, Rafael Márquez Álvarez, Francisco Javier Rodríguez Pinedo, José Andrés Guardado Hernández (84.Marco Jhonfai Fabián de la Mora), Paul Nicolás Aguilar Rojas, Héctor Alfredo Moreno Herrera, Miguel Arturo Layún Prado, Héctor Miguel Herrera López, José Juan Vázquez Gómez, Oribe Peralta Morones (79.Carlos Alberto Peña Rodríguez), Giovani dos Santos Ramírez (62.Javier Hernández Balcázar). Trainer: Miguel Ernesto Herrera Aguirre.
Goals: 0-1 Rafael Márquez Álvarez (72), 0-2 José Andrés Guardado Hernández (75), 0-3 Javier Hernández Balcázar (82), 1-3 Ivan Perišić (87).
Cautions: Ivan Rakitić / Rafael Márquez Álvarez, José Juan Vázquez Gómez.
Sent off: Ante Rebić (89).

GROUP B

13.06.2014	Salvador	Spain - Holland	1-5(1-1)
13.06.2014	Cuiabá	Chile - Australia	3-1(2-1)
18.06.2014	Porto Alegre	Australia - Holland	2-3(1-1)
18.06.2014	Rio de Janeiro	Spain - Chile	0-2(0-2)
23.06.2014	Curitiba	Australia - Spain	0-3(0-1)
23.06.2014	São Paulo	Holland - Chile	2-0(0-0)

FINAL STANDINGS

1.	**Holland**	3	3	0	0	10 - 3	9
2.	**Chile**	3	2	0	1	5 - 3	6
3.	Spain	3	1	0	2	4 - 7	3
4.	Australia	3	0	0	3	3 - 9	0

13.06.2014, Arena Fonte Nova, Salvador; Attendance: 48,173
Referee: Nicola Rizzoli (Italy)
SPAIN - HOLLAND 1-5(1-1)
ESP: Iker Casillas Fernández, Sergio Ramos García, Gerard Piqué i Bernabeu, César Azpilicueta Tanco, Jordi Alba Ramos, Andrés Iniesta Luján, Xabier Alonso Olano „Xabi Alonso" (63.Pedro Eliezer Rodríguez Ledesma), Xavier Hernández i Creus „Xavi", David Josué Jiménez Silva (78.Francesc Fàbregas Soler „Cesc Fàbregas"), Sergio Busquets Burgos, Diego da Silva Costa (63.Fernando José Torres Sanz). Trainer: Vicente del Bosque González.
NED: Jasper Cillessen, Ron Peter Vlaar, Daryl Janmaat, Stefan de Vrij (77.Joël Ivo Veltman), Rolando Maximiliano Martins Indi, Wesley Sneijder, Nigel de Jong, Jonathan Alexander de Guzmán (62.Georginio Gregion Emile Wijnaldum), Daley Blind, Arjen Robben, Robin van Persie (79.Jeremain Marciano Lens). Trainer: Aloysius Paulus Maria van Gaal.
Goals: 1-0 Xabier Alonso Olano „Xabi Alonso" (27 penalty), 1-1 Robin van Persie (44), 1-2 Arjen Robben (53), 1-3 Stefan de Vrij (64), 1-4 Robin van Persie (72), 1-5 Arjen Robben (80).
Cautions: Iker Casillas Fernández / Jonathan Alexander de Guzmán, Stefan de Vrij, Arjen Robben.

13.06.2014, Arena Pantanal, Cuiabá; Attendance: 40,275
Referee: Noumandiez Doué (Côte d'Ivoire)
CHILE - AUSTRALIA 3-1(2-1)
CHI: Claudio Andrés Bravo Muñoz, Gonzalo Alejandro Jara Reyes, Eugenio Esteban Mena Reveco, Jorge Luis Valdivia Toro (68.Jean André Emanuel Beausejour Coliqueo), Arturo Erasmo Vidal Pardo (60.Felipe Alejandro Gutiérrez Leiva), Mauricio Aníbal Isla Isla, Marcelo Alfonso Díaz Rojas, Gary Alexis Medel Soto, Charles Mariano Aránguiz Sandoval, Alexis Alejandro Sánchez Sánchez, Eduardo Jesús Vargas Rojas (88.Mauricio Ricardo Pinilla Ferrera). Trainer: Jorge Luis Sampaoli Moya (Argentina).
AUS: Mathew David Ryan, Matthew Thomas Špiranović, Alexander William Wilkinson, Ivan Frankie Franjić (49.Ryan James McGowan), Jason Alan Davidson, Mark Bresciano (78.James Troisi), Timothy Filiga Cahill, Mark Daniel Milligan, Michael John Jedinak, Mathew Allan Leckie, Thomas Michael Oar (69.Benjamin Halloran). Trainer: Angelos Postecoglou.
Goals: 1-0 Alexis Alejandro Sánchez Sánchez (12), 2-0 Jorge Luis Valdivia Toro (14), 2-1 Timothy Filiga Cahill (35), 3-1 Jean André Emanuel Beausejour Coliqueo (90+2).
Cautions: Charles Mariano Aránguiz Sandoval / Timothy Filiga Cahill, Michael John Jedinak, Mark Daniel Milligan.

18.06.2014, Estádio Beira-Rio, Porto Alegre; Attendance: 42,877
Referee: Djamel Haimoudi (Algeria)
AUSTRALIA - HOLLAND 2-3(1-1)
AUS: Mathew David Ryan, Matthew Thomas Špiranović, Ryan James McGowan, Alexander William Wilkinson, Jason Alan Davidson, Mark Bresciano (51.Oliver John Bozanić), Timothy Filiga Cahill (69.Benjamin Halloran), Michael John Jedinak, Matthew Graham McKay, Mathew Allan Leckie, Thomas Michael Oar (77.Adam Jake Taggart). Trainer: Angelos Postecoglou.
NED: Jasper Cillessen, Ron Peter Vlaar, Daryl Janmaat, Stefan de Vrij, Rolando Maximiliano Martins Indi (45+3.Memphis Depay), Wesley Sneijder, Nigel de Jong, Jonathan Alexander de Guzmán (78.Georginio Gregion Emile Wijnaldum), Daley Blind, Arjen Robben, Robin van Persie (87.Jeremain Marciano Lens). Trainer: Aloysius Paulus Maria van Gaal.
Goals: 0-1 Arjen Robben (20), 1-1 Timothy Filiga Cahill (21), 2-1 Michael John Jedinak (54 penalty), 2-2 Robin van Persie (58), 2-3 Memphis Depay (68).
Cautions: Timothy Filiga Cahill / Robin van Persie.

18.06.2014, Estádio „Jornalista Mário Filho" (Maracanã), Rio de Janeiro; Attendance: 74,101
Referee: Mark Geiger (United States)
SPAIN - CHILE 0-2(0-2)
ESP: Iker Casillas Fernández, Sergio Ramos García, César Azpilicueta Tanco, Jordi Alba Ramos, Andrés Iniesta Luján, Xabier Alonso Olano „Xabi Alonso" (46.Jorge Resurrección Merodio „Koke"), David Josué Jiménez Silva, Javier Martínez Aginaga, Sergio Busquets Burgos, Diego da Silva Costa (64.Fernando José Torres Sanz), Pedro Eliezer Rodríguez Ledesma (76.Santiago Cazorla González). Trainer: Vicente del Bosque González.
CHI: Claudio Andrés Bravo Muñoz, Gonzalo Alejandro Jara Reyes, Eugenio Esteban Mena Reveco, Arturo Erasmo Vidal Pardo (88.Carlos Emilio Carmona Tello), Mauricio Aníbal Isla Isla, Marcelo Alfonso Díaz Rojas, Gary Alexis Medel Soto, Francisco Andrés Silva Gajardo, Charles Mariano Aránguiz Sandoval (64.Felipe Alejandro Gutiérrez Leiva), Alexis Alejandro Sánchez Sánchez, Eduardo Jesús Vargas Rojas (85.Jorge Luis Valdivia Toro). Trainer: Jorge Luis Sampaoli Moya (Argentina).
Goals: 0-1 Eduardo Jesús Vargas Rojas (20), 0-2 Charles Mariano Aránguiz Sandoval (43).
Cautions: Xabier Alonso Olano „Xabi Alonso" / Arturo Erasmo Vidal Pardo, Eugenio Esteban Mena Reveco.

23.06.2014, Arena da Baixada, Curitiba; Attendance: 39,375
Referee: Nawaf Abdullah Ghayyath Shukralla (Bahrain)
AUSTRALIA - SPAIN 0-3(0-1)
AUS: Mathew David Ryan, Matthew Thomas Špiranović, Ryan James McGowan, Alexander William Wilkinson, Jason Alan Davidson, Oliver John Bozanić (72.Mark Bresciano), Michael John Jedinak, Matthew Graham McKay, Mathew Allan Leckie, Thomas Michael Oar (61.James Troisi), Adam Jake Taggart (46.Benjamin Halloran). Trainer: Angelos Postecoglou.
ESP: José Manuel Reina Páez, Sergio Ramos García, Juan Francisco Torres Belén „Juanfran", Raúl Albiol Tortajada, Jordi Alba Ramos, Andrés Iniesta Luján, Xabier Alonso Olano „Xabi Alonso" (84.David Josué Jiménez Silva), Santiago Cazorla González (68.Francesc Fàbregas Soler „Cesc Fàbregas"), Jorge Resurrección Merodio „Koke", Fernando José Torres Sanz, David Villa Sánchez (57.Juan Manuel Mata García „Juan Mata"). Trainer: Vicente del Bosque González.
Goals: 0-1 David Villa Sánchez (36), 0-2 Fernando José Torres Sanz (69), 0-3 Juan Manuel Mata García „Juan Mata" (82).
Cautions: Matthew Thomas Špiranović, Michael John Jedinak / Sergio Ramos García.

23.06.2014, Arena de São Paulo, São Paulo; Attendance: 62,996
Referee: Bakary Papa Gassama (Gambia)

HOLLAND - CHILE **2-0(0-0)**

NED: Jasper Cillessen, Ron Peter Vlaar, Daryl Janmaat, Stefan de Vrij, Wesley Sneijder (75.Leroy Johan Fer), Nigel de Jong, Georginio Gregion Emile Wijnaldum, Daley Blind, Dirk Kuijt (89.Terence Kongolo), Arjen Robben, Jeremain Marciano Lens (69.Memphis Depay). Trainer: Aloysius Paulus Maria van Gaal.
CHI: Claudio Andrés Bravo Muñoz, Gonzalo Alejandro Jara Reyes, Eugenio Esteban Mena Reveco, Mauricio Aníbal Isla Isla, Marcelo Alfonso Díaz Rojas, Gary Alexis Medel Soto, Francisco Andrés Silva Gajardo (70.Jorge Luis Valdivia Toro), Charles Mariano Aránguiz Sandoval, Felipe Alejandro Gutiérrez Leiva (46.Jean André Emanuel Beausejour Coliqueo), Alexis Alejandro Sánchez Sánchez, Eduardo Jesús Vargas Rojas (81.Mauricio Ricardo Pinilla Ferrera). Trainer: Jorge Luis Sampaoli Moya (Argentina).
Goals: 1-0 Leroy Johan Fer (77), 2-0 Memphis Depay (90+2).
Cautions: Daley Blind / Francisco Andrés Silva Gajardo.

GROUP C

14.06.2014	Belo Horizonte	Colombia - Greece	3-0(1-0)
14.06.2014	Recife	Côte d'Ivoire - Japan	2-1(0-1)
19.06.2014	Brasília	Colombia - Côte d'Ivoire	2-1(0-0)
19.06.2014	Natal	Japan - Greece	0-0
24.06.2014	Cuiabá	Japan - Colombia	1-4(1-1)
24.06.2014	Fortaleza	Greece - Côte d'Ivoire	2-1(1-0)

FINAL STANDINGS

1.	**Colombia**	3	3	0	0	9 - 2	9
2.	**Greece**	3	1	1	1	2 - 4	4
3.	Côte d'Ivoire	3	1	0	2	4 - 5	3
4.	Japan	3	0	1	2	2 - 6	1

14.06.2014, Estádio Mineirão, Belo Horizonte; Attendance: 57,174
Referee: Mark Geiger (United States)

COLOMBIA - GREECE **3-0(1-0)**

COL: David Ospina Ramírez, Mario Alberto Yepes Díaz, Cristián Eduardo Zapata Valencia, Pablo Estifer Armero (74.Santiago Arias Naranjo), Abel Enrique Aguilar Tapias (69.Alexander Mejía Sabalza), Juan Camilo Zúñiga Mosquera, Carlos Alberto Sánchez Moreno, Juan Guillermo Cuadrado Bello, James David Rodríguez Rubio, Teófilo Antonio Gutiérrez Roncancio (76.Jackson Arley Martínez Valencia), Segundo Víctor Ibarbo Guerrero. Trainer: José Néstor Pékerman (Argentina).
GRE: Orestis-Spyridon Karnezis, José LIoyd Holebas, Vasileios Torosidis, Sokratis Papastathopoulos, Konstantinos Manolas, Konstantinos Katsouranis, Panagiotis Giórgos Kone (78.Giórgos Karagounis), Giánnis Maniatis, Giórgos Samaras, Theofanis Gekas (64.Konstantinos Mitroglou), Dimitrios Salpingidis (57.Giánnis Fetfatzidis). Trainer: Fernando Manuel Costa Santos (Portugal).
Goals: 1-0 Pablo Estifer Armero (5), 2-0 Teófilo Antonio Gutiérrez Roncancio (58), 3-0 James David Rodríguez Rubio (90+3).
Cautions: Carlos Alberto Sánchez Moreno / Sokratis Papastathopoulos, Dimitrios Salpingidis.

14.06.2014, Arena Pernambuco, Recife; Attendance: 40,267
Referee: Enrique Roberto Osses Zencovich (Chile)

CÔTE D'IVOIRE - JAPAN 2-1(0-1)

CIV: Boubacar Barry, Arthur Etienne Boka (75.Tohouri Zahoui Constant Djakpa), Souleymane Bamba, Serge Aurier, Alain Didier Zokora Deguy, Gnégnéri Yaya Touré, Cheik Ismael Tioté, Sereso Geoffroy Gonzaroua Die (62.Didier Yves Drogba Tébily), Salomon Armand Magloire Kalou, Gervais Yao Kouassi „Gervinho", Wilfried Guemiand Bony (78.Didier Ya Konan). Trainer: Sabri Lamouchi (France).
JPN: Eiji Kawashima, Atsuto Uchida, Masato Morishige, Maya Yoshida, Yuto Nagatomo, Makoto Hasebe (54.Yasuhito Endō), Keisuke Honda, Hotaru Yamaguchi, Shinji Okazaki, Shinji Kagawa (86.Yojiro Takahagi), Yuya Osako (68.Yoshito Ōkubo). Trainer: Alberto Zaccheroni (Italy).
Goals: 0-1 Keisuke Honda (16), 1-1 Wilfried Guemiand Bony (64), 2-1 Gervais Yao Kouassi „Gervinho" (66).
Cautions: Souleymane Bamba, Alain Didier Zokora Deguy / Maya Yoshida, Masato Morishige.

19.06.2014, Estádio Nacional „Mané Garrincha", Brasília; Attendance: 68,748
Referee: Howard Melton Webb (England)

COLOMBIA - CÔTE D'IVOIRE 2-1(0-0)

COL: David Ospina Ramírez, Mario Alberto Yepes Díaz, Cristián Eduardo Zapata Valencia, Pablo Estifer Armero (72.Santiago Arias Naranjo), Abel Enrique Aguilar Tapias (79.Alexander Mejía Sabalza), Juan Camilo Zúñiga Mosquera, Carlos Alberto Sánchez Moreno, Juan Guillermo Cuadrado Bello, James David Rodríguez Rubio, Teófilo Antonio Gutiérrez Roncancio, Segundo Víctor Ibarbo Guerrero (53.Juan Fernando Quintero Paniagua). Trainer: José Néstor Pékerman (Argentina).
CIV: Boubacar Barry, Arthur Etienne Boka, Souleymane Bamba, Serge Aurier, Alain Didier Zokora Deguy, Gnégnéri Yaya Touré, Cheik Ismael Tioté, Sereso Geoffroy Gonzaroua Die (73.Mathis Gazoa Kippersund Bolly), Gervais Yao Kouassi „Gervinho", Max-Alain Gradel (67.Salomon Armand Magloire Kalou), Wilfried Guemiand Bony (60.Didier Yves Drogba Tébily). Trainer: Sabri Lamouchi (France).
Goals: 1-0 James David Rodríguez Rubio (64), 2-0 Juan Fernando Quintero Paniagua (70), 2-1 Gervais Yao Kouassi „Gervinho" (73).
Cautions: Alain Didier Zokora Deguy, Cheik Ismael Tioté.

19.06.2014, Arena das Dunas, Natal; Attendance: 39,485
Referee: Joel Antonio Aguilar Chicas (El Salvador)

JAPAN - GREECE 0-0

JPN: Eiji Kawashima, Yasuyuki Konno, Atsuto Uchida, Maya Yoshida, Yuto Nagatomo, Makoto Hasebe (46.Yasuhito Endō), Keisuke Honda, Hotaru Yamaguchi, Shinji Okazaki, Yoshito Ōkubo, Yuya Osako (57.Shinji Kagawa). Trainer: Alberto Zaccheroni (Italy).
GRE: Orestis-Spyridon Karnezis, José LIoyd Holebas, Vasileios Torosidis, Sokratis Papastathopoulos, Konstantinos Manolas, Konstantinos Katsouranis, Panagiotis Giórgos Kone (81.Dimitrios Salpingidis), Giánnis Maniatis, Giánnis Fetfatzidis (41.Giórgos Karagounis), Giórgos Samaras, Konstantinos Mitroglou (35.Theofanis Gekas). Trainer: Fernando Manuel Costa Santos (Portugal).
Cautions: Makoto Hasebe / Konstantinos Katsouranis, Giórgos Samaras, Vasileios Torosidis.
Sent off: Konstantinos Katsouranis (38).

24.06.2014, Arena Pantanal, Cuiabá; Attendance: 40,340
Referee: Pedro Proença Oliveira Alves Garcia (Portugal)

JAPAN - COLOMBIA 1-4(1-1)

JPN: Eiji Kawashima, Yasuyuki Konno, Atsuto Uchida, Maya Yoshida, Yuto Nagatomo, Makoto Hasebe, Toshihiro Aoyama (62.Hotaru Yamaguchi), Keisuke Honda, Shinji Okazaki (69.Yojiro Takahagi), Shinji Kagawa (85.Hiroshi Kiyotake), Yoshito Ōkubo. Trainer: Alberto Zaccheroni (Italy).
COL: David Ospina Ramírez (85.Faryd Camilo Mondragón Alí), Pablo Estifer Armero, Carlos Enrique Valdés Parra, Santiago Arias Naranjo, Éder Fabián Álvarez Balanta, Alexander Mejía Sabalza, Fredy Alejandro Guarín Vásquez, Juan Guillermo Cuadrado Bello (46.Carlos Mario Carbonero Mancilla), Gustavo Adrián Ramos Vásquez, Jackson Arley Martínez Valencia, Juan Fernando Quintero Paniagua (46.James David Rodríguez Rubio). Trainer: José Néstor Pékerman (Argentina).
Goals: 0-1 Juan Guillermo Cuadrado Bello (17 penalty), 1-1 Shinji Okazaki (45+1), 1-2 Jackson Arley Martínez Valencia (55), 1-3 Jackson Arley Martínez Valencia (82), 1-4 James David Rodríguez Rubio (89).
Cautions: Yasuyuki Konno / Fredy Alejandro Guarín Vásquez.

24.06.2014, Estádio Castelão, FortalezaAttendance: 59,095
Referee: Carlos Alfredo Vera Rodríguez (Ecuador)

GREECE - CÔTE D'IVOIRE 2-1(1-0)

GRE: Orestis-Spyridon Karnezis (24.Panagiotis Georgios Glykos), José Lloyd Holebas, Vasileios Torosidis, Sokratis Papastathopoulos, Konstantinos Manolas, Giórgos Karagounis (78.Theofanis Gekas), Lazaros Christodoulopoulos, Panagiotis Giórgos Kone (12.Andreas Samaris), Giánnis Maniatis, Giórgos Samaras, Dimitrios Salpingidis. Trainer: Fernando Manuel Costa Santos (Portugal).
CIV: Boubacar Barry, Kolo Habib Touré, Arthur Etienne Boka, Souleymane Bamba, Serge Aurier, Gnégnéri Yaya Touré, Cheik Ismael Tioté (61.Wilfried Guemiand Bony), Sereso Geoffroy Gonzaroua Die, Salomon Armand Magloire Kalou, Didier Yves Drogba Tébily (78.Ismaël Tiémoko Diomandé), Gervais Yao Kouassi „Gervinho" (83.Giovanni-Guy Yann Sio). Trainer: Sabri Lamouchi (France).
Goals: 1-0 Andreas Samaris (42), 1-1 Wilfried Guemiand Bony (74), 2-1 Giórgos Samaras (90+3 penalty).
Cautions: Didier Yves Drogba Tébily, Salomon Armand Magloire Kalou, Sereso Geoffroy Gonzaroua Die.

GROUP D

14.06.2014	Fortaleza	Uruguay – Costa Rica	1-3(1-0)
14.06.2014	Manaus	England - Italy	1-2(1-1)
19.06.2014	São Paulo	Uruguay - England	2-1(1-0)
20.06.2014	Recife	Italy - Costa Rica	0-1(0-1)
24.06.2014	Natal	Italy - Uruguay	0-1(0-0)
24.06.2014	Belo Horizonte	Costa Rica - England	0-0

FINAL STANDINGS

1.	**Costa Rica**	3	2	1	0	4 - 1	7
2.	**Uruguay**	3	2	0	1	4 - 4	6
3.	Italy	3	1	0	2	2 - 3	3
4.	England	3	0	1	2	2 - 4	1

14.06.2014, Estádio Castelão, Fortaleza; Attendance: 58,679
Referee: Dr. Felix Brych (Germany)
URUGUAY – COSTA RICA **1-3(1-0)**
URU: Néstor Fernando Muslera Micol, Diego Alfredo Lugano Morena, Victorio Maximiliano Pereira Páez, José Martín Cáceres Silva, Diego Roberto Godín Leal, Cristian Gabriel Rodríguez Barotti (76.Abel Mathías Hernández Platero), Walter Alejandro Gargano Guevara (60.Álvaro Rafael González Luengo), Egidio Raúl Arévalo Ríos, Diego Martín Forlán Corazzo (60.Marcelo Nicolás Lodeiro Benítez), Edinson Roberto Cavani Gómez, Christian Ricardo Stuani Curbelo. Trainer: Óscar Wáshington Tabárez Silva.
CRC: Keylor Antonio Navas Gamboa, Míchael Umaña Corrales, Júnior Enrique Díaz Campbell, Óscar Esau Duarte Gaitan, Cristian Esteban Gamboa Luna, Geancarlo González Castro, Celso Borges Mora, Cristian Bolaños Navarro (89.Michael Barrantes Rojas), Yeltsin Ignacio Tejeda Valverde (74.José Miguel Cubero Loria), Bryan Jafet Ruíz González (83.Marcos Danilo Ureña Porras), Joël Nathaniel Campbell Samuels. Trainer: Jorge Luis Pinto Afanador (Colombia).
Goals: 1-0 Edinson Roberto Cavani Gómez (24 penalty), 1-1 Joël Nathaniel Campbell Samuels (54), 1-2 Óscar Esau Duarte Gaitan (57), 1-3 Marcos Danilo Ureña Porras (84).
Cautions: Diego Alfredo Lugano Morena, Walter Alejandro Gargano Guevara, José Martín Cáceres Silva.
Sent off: Victorio Maximiliano Pereira Páez (90+4).

14.06.2014, Arena da Amazônia, Manaus; Attendance: 39,800
Referee: Björn Kuipers (Holland)
ENGLAND - ITALY **1-2(1-1)**
ENG: Charles Joseph John Hart, Philip Nikodem Jagielka, Glen McLeod Cooper Johnson, Leighton John Baines, Gary James Cahill, Steven George Gerrard, Jordan Brian Henderson (73.Jack Andrew Garry Wilshere), Raheem Shaquille Sterling, Wayne Mark Rooney, Daniel Andre Sturridge (80.Adam David Lallana), Daniel Nii Tackie Mensah Welbeck (61.Ross Barkley). Trainer: Roy Hodgson.
ITA: Salvatore Sirigu, Andrea Barzagli, Gabriel Paletta, Giorgio Chiellini, Matteo Darmian, Daniele De Rossi, Andrea Pirlo, Claudio Marchisio, Antonio Candreva (79.Marco Parolo), Marco Verratti (57.Thiago Motta), Mario Balotelli (73.Ciro Immobile). Trainer: Cesare Claudio Prandelli.
Goals: 0-1 Claudio Marchisio (35), 1-1 Daniel Andre Sturridge (37), 1-2 Mario Balotelli (50).
Cautions: Raheem Shaquille Sterling.

19.06.2014, Arena de São Paulo, São Paulo; Attendance: 62,575
Referee: Carlos Velasco Carballo (Spain)
URUGUAY - ENGLAND **2-1(1-0)**
URU: Néstor Fernando Muslera Micol, José Martín Cáceres Silva, Diego Roberto Godín Leal, Álvaro Daniel Pereira Barragán, José María Giménez de Vargas, Cristian Gabriel Rodríguez Barotti, Álvaro Rafael González Luengo (79.Jorge Ciro Fucile Perdomo), Egidio Raúl Arévalo Ríos, Marcelo Nicolás Lodeiro Benítez (67.Christian Ricardo Stuani Curbelo), Luis Alberto Suárez Díaz (88.Sebastián Coates Nión), Edinson Roberto Cavani Gómez. Trainer: Óscar Wáshington Tabárez Silva.
ENG: Charles Joseph John Hart, Philip Nikodem Jagielka, Glen McLeod Cooper Johnson, Leighton John Baines, Gary James Cahill, Steven George Gerrard, Jordan Brian Henderson (87.Rickie Lee Lambert), Raheem Shaquille Sterling (64.Ross Barkley), Wayne Mark Rooney, Daniel Andre Sturridge, Daniel Nii Tackie Mensah Welbeck (71.Adam David Lallana). Trainer: Roy Hodgson.
Goals: 1-0 Luis Alberto Suárez Díaz (39), 1-1 Wayne Mark Rooney (75), 2-1 Luis Alberto Suárez Díaz (85).
Cautions: Diego Roberto Godín Leal / Steven George Gerrard.

20.06.2014, Arena Pernambuco, Recife; Attendance: 40,285
Referee: Enrique Roberto Osses Zencovich (Chile)
ITALY - COSTA RICA **0-1(0-1)**
ITA: Gianluigi Buffon, Andrea Barzagli, Giorgio Chiellini, Matteo Darmian, Ignazio Abate, Daniele De Rossi, Andrea Pirlo, Thiago Motta (46.Antonio Cassano), Claudio Marchisio (69.Alessio Cerci), Antonio Candreva (57.Lorenzo Insigne), Mario Balotelli. Trainer: Cesare Claudio Prandelli.
CRC: Keylor Antonio Navas Gamboa, Míchael Umaña Corrales, Júnior Enrique Díaz Campbell, Óscar Esau Duarte Gaitan, Cristian Esteban Gamboa Luna, Geancarlo González Castro, Celso Borges Mora, Cristian Bolaños Navarro, Yeltsin Ignacio Tejeda Valverde (68.José Miguel Cubero Loria), Bryan Jafet Ruíz González (81.Randall Brenes Moya), Joël Nathaniel Campbell Samuels (74.Marcos Danilo Ureña Porras). Trainer: Jorge Luis Pinto Afanador (Colombia).
Goal: 0-1 Bryan Jafet Ruíz González (44).
Cautions: Mario Balotelli / José Miguel Cubero Loria.

24.06.2014, Arena das Dunas, Natal; Attendance: 39,706
Referee: Marco Antonio Rodríguez Moreno (Mexico)
ITALY - URUGUAY **0-1(0-0)**
ITA: Gianluigi Buffon, Andrea Barzagli, Leonardo Bonucci, Giorgio Chiellini, Matteo Darmian, Mattia De Sciglio, Andrea Pirlo, Claudio Marchisio, Marco Verratti (75.Thiago Motta), Mario Balotelli (46.Marco Parolo), Ciro Immobile (71.Antonio Cassano). Trainer: Cesare Claudio Prandelli.
URU: Néstor Fernando Muslera Micol, José Martín Cáceres Silva, Diego Roberto Godín Leal, Álvaro Daniel Pereira Barragán (63.Christian Ricardo Stuani Curbelo), José María Giménez de Vargas, Cristian Gabriel Rodríguez Barotti (78.Gastón Ezequiel Ramírez Pereyra), Álvaro Rafael González Luengo, Egidio Raúl Arévalo Ríos, Marcelo Nicolás Lodeiro Benítez (46.Victorio Maximiliano Pereira Páez), Luis Alberto Suárez Díaz, Edinson Roberto Cavani Gómez. Trainer: Óscar Wáshington Tabárez Silva.
Goal: 0-1 Diego Roberto Godín Leal (81).
Cautions: Mario Balotelli, Mattia De Sciglio / Egidio Raúl Arévalo Ríos, Néstor Fernando Muslera Micol.
Sent off: Claudio Marchisio (59).

24.06.2014, Estádio Mineirão, Belo Horizonte; Attendance: 57,823
Referee: Djamel Haimoudi (Algeria)

COSTA RICA - ENGLAND 0-0

CRC: Keylor Antonio Navas Gamboa, Roy Miller Hernández, Júnior Enrique Díaz Campbell, Óscar Esau Duarte Gaitan, Cristian Esteban Gamboa Luna, Geancarlo González Castro, Celso Borges Mora (78.Michael Barrantes Rojas), Yeltsin Ignacio Tejeda Valverde, Bryan Jafet Ruíz González, Randall Brenes Moya (59.Cristian Bolaños Navarro), Joël Nathaniel Campbell Samuels (65.Marcos Danilo Ureña Porras). Trainer: Jorge Luis Pinto Afanador (Colombia).

ENG: Ben Anthony Foster, Gary James Cahill, Christopher Lloyd Smalling, Philip Anthony Jones, Luke Paul Hoare Shaw, Frank James Lampard, James Philip Milner (76.Wayne Mark Rooney), Adam David Lallana (62.Raheem Shaquille Sterling), Jack Andrew Garry Wilshere (73.Steven George Gerrard), Ross Barkley, Daniel Andre Sturridge. Trainer: Roy Hodgson.

Cautions: Geancarlo González Castro / Ross Barkley, Adam David Lallana.

GROUP E

15.06.2014	Brasília	Switzerland - Ecuador	2-1(0-1)
15.06.2014	Porto Alegre	France - Honduras	3-0(1-0)
20.06.2014	Salvador	Switzerland – France	2-5(0-3)
20.06.2014	Curitiba	Honduras - Ecuador	1-2(1-1)
25.06.2014	Manaus	Honduras - Switzerland	0-3(0-2)
25.06.2014	Rio de Janeiro	Ecuador - France	0-0

FINAL STANDINGS

1.	**France**	3	2	1	0	8 - 2	7
2.	**Switzerland**	3	2	0	1	7 - 6	6
3.	Ecuador	3	1	1	1	3 - 3	4
4.	Honduras	3	0	0	3	1 - 8	0

15.06.2014, Estádio Nacional „Mané Garrincha", Brasília; Attendance: 68,351
Referee: Ravshan Irmatov (Uzbekistan)

SWITZERLAND - ECUADOR 2-1(0-1)

SUI: Diego Orlando Benaglio, Stephan Lichtsteiner, Johan Danon Djourou-Gbadjere, Steve von Bergen, Ricardo Iván Rodríguez Araya, Valon Behrami, Gökhan Inler, Valentin Stocker (46.Admir Mehmedi), Xherdan Shaqiri, Granit Xhaka, Josip Drmić (75.Haris Seferović). Trainer: Ottmar Hitzfeld (Germany).

ECU: Alexander Domínguez Carabalí, Jorge Daniel Guagua Tamayo, Walter Orlando Ayoví Corozo, Juan Carlos Paredes Reasco, Frickson Rafael Erazo Vivero, Luis Antonio Valencia Mosquera, Christian Fernando Noboa Tello, Carlos Armando Gruezo Arboleda, Felipe Salvador Caicedo Corozo (70.Michael Antonio Arroyo Mina), Jefferson Antonio Montero Vite (77.Joao Robin Rojas Mendoza), Enner Remberto Valencia Lastra. Trainer: Reinaldo Rueda Rivera (Colombia).

Goals: 0-1 Enner Remberto Valencia Lastra (22), 1-1 Admir Mehmedi (48), 2-1 Haris Seferović (90+3).

Cautions: Johan Danon Djourou-Gbadjere / Juan Carlos Paredes Reasco.

15.06.2014, Estádio Beira-Rio, Porto Alegre; Attendance: 43,012
Referee: Sandro Meira Ricci (Brazil)
FRANCE - HONDURAS **3-0(1-0)**
FRA: Hugo Lloris, Mathieu Debuchy, Patrice Latyr Evra, Mamadou Sakho, Raphaël Varane, Blaise Matuidi, Mathieu Valbuena (78.Olivier Giroud), Yohan Cabaye (65.Rio Antonio Zoba Mavuba), Paul Labile Pogba (57.Moussa Sissoko), Karim Mostafa Benzema, Antoine Griezmann. Trainer: Didier Claude Deschamps.
HON: Noel Eduardo Valladares Bonilla, Maynor Alexis Figueroa Róchez, Emilio Arturo Izaguirre Girón, Víctor Salvador Bernárdez Blanco (46.Osman Danilo Chávez Guity), Brayan Antonio Beckeles, Wilson Roberto Palacios Suazo, Roger Aníbal Espinoza Ramírez, Luis Fernando Garrido, Andy Najar Rodríguez (58.Jorge Aarón Claros Juárez), Carlos Yaír Costly Molina, Jerry Ricardo Bengtson Bodden (46.Oscar Boniek García Ramírez). Trainer: Luis Fernando Suárez (Colombia).
Goals: 1-0 Karim Mostafa Benzema (45 penalty), 2-0 Noel Eduardo Valladares Bonilla (48 own goal), 3-0 Karim Mostafa Benzema (72).
Cautions: Patrice Latyr Evra, Paul Labile Pogba, Yohan Cabaye / Wilson Roberto Palacios Suazo, Oscar Boniek García Ramírez, Luis Fernando Garrido.
Sent off: Wilson Roberto Palacios Suazo (43).

20.06.2014, Arena Fonte Nova, Salvador; Attendance: 51,003
Referee: Björn Kuipers (Holland)
SWITZERLAND – FRANCE **2-5(0-3)**
SUI: Diego Orlando Benaglio, Stephan Lichtsteiner, Johan Danon Djourou-Gbadjere, Steve von Bergen (9.Philippe Sylvain Senderos), Ricardo Iván Rodríguez Araya, Valon Behrami (46.Blerim Džemaili), Gökhan Inler, Xherdan Shaqiri, Granit Xhaka, Admir Mehmedi, Haris Seferović (69.Josip Drmić). Trainer: Ottmar Hitzfeld (Germany).
FRA: Hugo Lloris, Mathieu Debuchy, Patrice Latyr Evra, Mamadou Sakho (66.Laurent Koscielny), Raphaël Varane, Blaise Matuidi, Mathieu Valbuena (82.Antoine Griezmann), Yohan Cabaye, Moussa Sissoko, Karim Mostafa Benzema, Olivier Giroud (63.Paul Labile Pogba). Trainer: Didier Claude Deschamps.
Goals: 0-1 Olivier Giroud (17), 0-2 Blaise Matuidi (18), 0-3 Mathieu Valbuena (40), 0-4 Karim Mostafa Benzema (67), 0-5 Moussa Sissoko (73), 1-5 Blerim Džemaili (81), 2-5 Granit Xhaka (87).
Cautions: Yohan Cabaye.

20.06.2014, Arena da Baixada, Curitiba; Attendance: 39,224
Referee: Benjamin Jon Williams (Australia)
HONDURAS - ECUADOR **1-2(1-1)**
HON: Noel Eduardo Valladares Bonilla, Maynor Alexis Figueroa Róchez, Emilio Arturo Izaguirre Girón (46.Juan Carlos García Álvarez), Víctor Salvador Bernárdez Blanco, Brayan Antonio Beckeles, Oscar Boniek García Ramírez (82.Marvin Antonio Chávez), Jorge Aarón Claros Juárez, Roger Aníbal Espinoza Ramírez, Luis Fernando Garrido (71.Mario Roberto Martínez Hernández), Carlos Yaír Costly Molina, Jerry Ricardo Bengtson Bodden. Trainer: Luis Fernando Suárez (Colombia).
ECU: Alexander Domínguez Carabalí, Jorge Daniel Guagua Tamayo, Walter Orlando Ayoví Corozo, Juan Carlos Paredes Reasco, Frickson Rafael Erazo Vivero, Luis Antonio Valencia Mosquera, Christian Fernando Noboa Tello, Tilson Oswaldo Minda Suscal (83.Carlos Armando Gruezo Arboleda), Felipe Salvador Caicedo Corozo (82.Édison Vicente Méndez Méndez), Jefferson Antonio Montero Vite (90+2.Gabriel Eduardo Achilier Zurita), Enner Remberto Valencia Lastra. Trainer: Reinaldo Rueda Rivera (Colombia).
Goals: 1-0 Carlos Yaír Costly Molina (31), 1-1 Enner Remberto Valencia Lastra (34), 1-2 Enner Remberto Valencia Lastra (65).
Cautions: Víctor Salvador Bernárdez Blanco, Jerry Ricardo Bengtson Bodden / Luis Antonio Valencia Mosquera, Enner Remberto Valencia Lastra, Jefferson Antonio Montero Vite.

25.06.2014, Arena da Amazônia, Manaus; Attendance: 40,322
Referee: Néstor Fabián Pitana (Argentina)
HONDURAS - SWITZERLAND 0-3(0-2)
HON: Noel Eduardo Valladares Bonilla, Maynor Alexis Figueroa Róchez, Juan Carlos García Álvarez, Víctor Salvador Bernárdez Blanco, Brayan Antonio Beckeles, Oscar Boniek García Ramírez (77.Andy Najar Rodríguez), Jorge Aarón Claros Juárez, Wilson Roberto Palacios Suazo, Roger Aníbal Espinoza Ramírez (46.Marvin Antonio Chávez), Carlos Yaír Costly Molina (40.Jerry Nelson Palacios Suazo), Jerry Ricardo Bengtson Bodden. Trainer: Luis Fernando Suárez (Colombia).
SUI: Diego Orlando Benaglio, Johan Danon Djourou-Gbadjere, Stephan Lichtsteiner, Ricardo Iván Rodríguez Araya, Fabian Lukas Schär, Valon Behrami, Gökhan Inler, Xherdan Shaqiri (87.Blerim Džemaili), Granit Xhaka (77.Michael Rico Lang), Admir Mehmedi, Josip Drmić (73.Haris Seferović). Trainer: Ottmar Hitzfeld (Germany).
Goals: 0-1 Xherdan Shaqiri (6), 0-2 Xherdan Shaqiri (31), 0-3 Xherdan Shaqiri (71).
Cautions: Jerry Nelson Palacios Suazo.

25.06.2014, Estádio „Jornalista Mário Filho" (Maracanã), Rio de Janeiro; Attendance: 73,749
Referee: Noumandiez Doué (Côte d'Ivoire)
ECUADOR - FRANCE 0-0
ECU: Alexander Domínguez Carabalí, Jorge Daniel Guagua Tamayo, Walter Orlando Ayoví Corozo, Juan Carlos Paredes Reasco, Frickson Rafael Erazo Vivero, Luis Antonio Valencia Mosquera, Christian Fernando Noboa Tello (90.Felipe Salvador Caicedo Corozo), Tilson Oswaldo Minda Suscal, Michael Antonio Arroyo Mina (82.Gabriel Eduardo Achilier Zurita), Jefferson Antonio Montero Vite (63.Alex Renato Ibarra Mina), Enner Remberto Valencia Lastra. Trainer: Reinaldo Rueda Rivera (Colombia).
FRA: Hugo Lloris, Bacary Sagna, Mamadou Sakho (61.Raphaël Varane), Laurent Koscielny, Lucas Digne, Blaise Matuidi (67.Olivier Giroud), Moussa Sissoko, Morgan Schneiderlin, Paul Labile Pogba, Karim Mostafa Benzema, Antoine Griezmann (79.Loïc Rémy). Trainer: Didier Claude Deschamps.
Cautions: Frickson Rafael Erazo Vivero.
Sent off: Luis Antonio Valencia Mosquera (50).

GROUP F

15.06.2014	Rio de Janeiro	Argentina - Bosnia-Herzegovina	2-1(1-0)
16.06.2014	Curitiba	Iran - Nigeria	0-0
21.06.2014	Belo Horizonte	Argentina - Iran	1-0(0-0)
21.06.2014	Cuiabá	Nigeria - Bosnia-Herzegovina	1-0(1-0)
25.06.2014	Porto Alegre	Nigeria - Argentina	2-3(1-2)
25.06.2014	Salvador	Bosnia-Herzegovina - Iran	3-1(1-0)

FINAL STANDINGS

1.	**Argentina**	3	3	0	0	6 - 3	9
2.	**Nigeria**	3	1	1	1	3 - 3	4
3.	Bosnia-Herzegovina	3	1	0	2	4 - 4	3
4.	Iran	3	0	1	2	1 - 4	1

15.06.2014, Estádio „Jornalista Mário Filho" (Maracanã), Rio de Janeiro; Attendance: 74,738
Referee: Joel Antonio Aguilar Chicas (El Salvador)

ARGENTINA - BOSNIA-HERZEGOVINA 2-1(1-0)

ARG: Sergio Germán Romero, Pablo Javier Zabaleta Girod, Ezequiel Marcelo Garay González, Hugo Armando Campagnaro (46.Fernando Rubén Gago), Federico Fernández, Faustino Marcos Alberto Rojo, Javier Alejandro Mascherano, Maximiliano Rubén Rodríguez (46.Gonzalo Gerardo Higuaín), Ángel Fabián di María Hernández, Lionel Andrés Messi, Sergio Leonel Agüero del Castillo (87.Lucas Rodrigo Biglia). Trainer: Alejandro Sabella.
BIH: Asmir Begović, Emir Spahić, Mensur Mujdža (69.Vedad Ibišević), Ermin Bičakčić, Muhamed Bešić, Sead Kolašinac, Zvjezdan Misimović (74.Haris Medunjanin), Miralem Pjanić, Senad Lulić, Izet Hajrović (71.Edin Višća), Edin Džeko. Trainer: Safet Sušić.
Goals: 1-0 Sead Kolašinac (3 own goal), 2-0 Lionel Andrés Messi (65), 2-1 Vedad Ibišević (84).
Cautions: Faustino Marcos Alberto Rojo / Emir Spahić.

16.06.2014, Arena da Baixada, Curitiba; Attendance: 39,081
Referee: Carlos Alfredo Vera Rodríguez (Ecuador)

IRAN - NIGERIA 0-0

IRN: Alireza Haghighi, Seyed Jalal Hosseini Khoshkebejari, Pejman Montazeri, Amir Hossein Sadeghi, Khosro Heydari (89.Masoud Soleimani Shojaei), Javad Nekounam, Seyed Ashkan Dejagah (78.Alireza Jahanbakhsh Jirandeh), Andranik Teymourian, Ehsan Hajsafi, Mehrdad Pooladi, Reza Ghoochannejhad Nournia. Trainer: Carlos Manuel Brito Leal Queiroz (Portugal).
NGA: Vincent Enyeama, Efetobore Ambrose Emuobo, Kenneth Josiah Omeruo, Godfrey Itama Oboabona (29.Joseph Ikpo Yobo), Juwon Oshaniwa, John Michael Nchekwube Obinna, Victor Moses (52.Foluwashola Ameobi), Ogenyi Eddy Onazi, Ramon Olamilekan Azeez (69.Peter Osaze Odemwingie), Emmanuel Chinenye Emenike, Ahmed Musa. Trainer: Stephen Okechukwu Keshi.
Cautions: Andranik Teymourian.

21.06.2014, Estádio Mineirão, Belo Horizonte; Attendance: 57,698
Referee: Milorad Mažić (Serbia)

ARGENTINA - IRAN 1-0(0-0)

ARG: Sergio Germán Romero, Pablo Javier Zabaleta Girod, Ezequiel Marcelo Garay González, Federico Fernández, Faustino Marcos Alberto Rojo, Javier Alejandro Mascherano, Fernando Rubén Gago, Ángel Fabián di María Hernández (90+4.Lucas Rodrigo Biglia), Lionel Andrés Messi, Sergio Leonel Agüero del Castillo (77.Ezequiel Iván Lavezzi), Gonzalo Gerardo Higuaín (77.Rodrigo Sebastián Palacio). Trainer: Alejandro Sabella.

IRN: Alireza Haghighi, Seyed Jalal Hosseini Khoshkebejari, Pejman Montazeri, Amir Hossein Sadeghi, Javad Nekounam, Masoud Soleimani Shojaei (77.Khosro Heydari), Seyed Ashkan Dejagah (85.Alireza Jahanbakhsh Jirandeh), Andranik Teymourian, Ehsan Hajsafi (88.Reza Haghighi Shandiz), Mehrdad Pooladi, Reza Ghoochannejhad Nournia. Trainer: Carlos Manuel Brito Leal Queiroz (Portugal).

Goal: 1-0 Lionel Andrés Messi (90+1).

Cautions: Javad Nekounam, Masoud Soleimani Shojaei.

21.06.2014, Arena Pantanal, Cuiabá; Attendance: 40,499
Referee: Peter O'Leary (New Zealand)

NIGERIA - BOSNIA-HERZEGOVINA 1-0(1-0)

NGA: Vincent Enyeama, Joseph Ikpo Yobo, Efetobore Ambrose Emuobo, Kenneth Josiah Omeruo, Juwon Oshaniwa, John Michael Nchekwube Obinna, Ogenyi Eddy Onazi, Michel Babatunde (75.Christantus Ejike Uzoenyi), Peter Osaze Odemwingie, Emmanuel Chinenye Emenike, Ahmed Musa (65.Foluwashola Ameobi). Trainer: Stephen Okechukwu Keshi.

BIH: Asmir Begović, Emir Spahić, Mensur Mujdža, Toni Šunjić, Muhamed Bešić, Zvjezdan Misimović, Haris Medunjanin (64.Tino-Sven Sušić), Miralem Pjanić, Senad Lulić (58.Sejad Salihović), Izet Hajrović (57.Vedad Ibišević), Edin Džeko. Trainer: Safet Sušić.

Goal: 1-0 Peter Osaze Odemwingie (29).

Cautions: John Michael Nchekwube Obinna / Haris Medunjanin.

25.06.2014, Estádio Beira-Rio, Porto Alegre; Attendance: 43,285
Referee: Nicola Rizzoli (Italy)

NIGERIA - ARGENTINA 2-3(1-2)

NGA: Vincent Enyeama, Joseph Ikpo Yobo, Efetobore Ambrose Emuobo, Kenneth Josiah Omeruo, Juwon Oshaniwa, John Michael Nchekwube Obinna, Ogenyi Eddy Onazi, Michel Babatunde (66.Michael Okechukwu Uchebo), Peter Osaze Odemwingie (80.Uche Innocent Nwofor), Emmanuel Chinenye Emenike, Ahmed Musa. Trainer: Stephen Okechukwu Keshi.

ARG: Sergio Germán Romero, Pablo Javier Zabaleta Girod, Ezequiel Marcelo Garay González, Federico Fernández, Faustino Marcos Alberto Rojo, Javier Alejandro Mascherano, Fernando Rubén Gago, Ángel Fabián di María Hernández, Lionel Andrés Messi (63.Ricardo Gabriel Álvarez), Sergio Leonel Agüero del Castillo (38.Ezequiel Iván Lavezzi), Gonzalo Gerardo Higuaín (90+1.Lucas Rodrigo Biglia). Trainer: Alejandro Sabella.

Goals: 0-1 Lionel Andrés Messi (3), 1-1 Ahmed Musa (4), 1-2 Lionel Andrés Messi (45+1), 2-2 Ahmed Musa (47), 2-3 Faustino Marcos Alberto Rojo (50).

Cautions: Juwon Oshaniwa, Kenneth Josiah Omeruo.

25.06.2014, Arena Fonte Nova, Salvador; Attendance: 48,011
Referee: Carlos Velasco Carballo (Spain)
BOSNIA-HERZEGOVINA - IRAN **3-1(1-0)**
BIH: Asmir Begović, Emir Spahić, Avdija Vršajević, Toni Šunjić, Muhamed Bešić, Sead Kolašinac, Anel Hadžić (61.Ognjen Vranješ), Miralem Pjanić, Tino-Sven Sušić (79.Sejad Salihović), Vedad Ibišević, Edin Džeko (84.Edin Višća). Trainer: Safet Sušić.
IRN: Alireza Haghighi, Seyed Jalal Hosseini Khoshkebejari, Pejman Montazeri, Amir Hossein Sadeghi, Javad Nekounam, Masoud Soleimani Shojaei (46.Khosro Heydari), Seyed Ashkan Dejagah (68.Karim Ansarifard), Andranik Teymourian, Ehsan Hajsafi (63.Alireza Jahanbakhsh Jirandeh), Mehrdad Pooladi, Reza Ghoochannejhad Nournia. Trainer: Carlos Manuel Brito Leal Queiroz (Portugal).
Goals: 1-0 Edin Džeko (23), 2-0 Miralem Pjanić (59), 2-1 Reza Ghoochannejhad Nournia (82), 3-1 Avdija Vršajević (83).
Cautions: Muhamed Bešić / Karim Ansarifard.

GROUP G

16.06.2014	Salvador	Germany - Portugal	4-0(3-0)
16.06.2014	Natal	Ghana - United States	1-2(0-1)
21.06.2014	Fortaleza	Germany - Ghana	2-2(0-0)
22.06.2014	Manaus	United States – Portugal	2-2(0-1)
26.06.2014	Recife	United States - Germany	0-1(0-0)
26.06.2014	Brasília	Portugal - Ghana	2-1(1-0)

FINAL STANDINGS

1.	**Germany**	3	2	1	0	7 - 2	7
2.	**United States**	3	1	1	1	4 - 4	4
3.	Portugal	3	1	1	1	4 - 7	4
4.	Ghana	3	0	1	2	4 - 6	1

16.06.2014, Arena Fonte Nova, Salvador; Attendance: 51,081
Referee: Milorad Mažić (Serbia)
GERMANY - PORTUGAL **4-0(3-0)**
GER: Manuel Peter Neuer, Philipp Lahm, Per Mertesacker, Jérôme Agyenim Boateng, Benedikt Höwedes, Mats Julian Hummels (73.Shkodran Mustafi), Mesut Özil (63.André Horst Schürrle), Sami Khedira, Toni Kroos, Mario Götze, Thomas Müller (82.Lukas Josef Podolski). Trainer: Joachim Löw.
POR: Rui Pedro dos Santos Patrício, Képler Laveran Lima Ferreira „Pepe“, Bruno Eduardo Regufe Alves, Fábio Alexandre da Silva Coentrão (65.André Gomes Magalhães de Almeida), João Pedro da Silva Pereira, Raul José Trindade Meireles, Luís Carlos Almeida da Cunha „Nani“, Miguel Luís Pinto Veloso (46.Ricardo Miguel Moreira da Costa), João Filipe Iria Santos Moutinho, Cristiano Ronaldo dos Santos Aveiro, Hugo Miguel Pereira de Almeida (28.Éderzito António Macedo Lopes „Éder“). Trainer: Paulo Jorge Gomes Bento.
Goals: 1-0 Thomas Müller (12 penalty), 2-0 Mats Julian Hummels (32), 3-0 Thomas Müller (45+1), 4-0 Thomas Müller (78).
Cautions: João Pedro da Silva Pereira.
Sent off: Képler Laveran Lima Ferreira „Pepe“ (37).

16.06.2014, Arena das Dunas, Natal; Attendance: 39,760
Referee: Jonas Eriksson (Sweden)

GHANA - UNITED STATES 1-2(0-1)

GHA: Adambathia Larsen Kwarasey, John Boye, Jonathan Mensah, Daniel Tawiah Opare, Sulleyman Ali Muntari, Kwadwo Asamoah, Mohammed Rabiu Alhassan (71.Michael Kojo Essien), André Morgan Rami Ayew, Jordan Pierre Ayew (59.Kevin-Prince Boateng), Asamoah Gyan, Christian Atsu Twasam (78.Albert Danquah Adomah). Trainer: James Kwesi Appiah.

USA: Timothy Matthew Howard, DaMarcus Lamont Beasley, Fabian Marco Johnson, Geoffrey Scott Cameron, Matt Besler (46.John Anthony Brooks), Jermaine Jones, Michael Sheehan Bradley, Kyle Robert Beckerman, Alejandro Bedoya (77.Graham Jonathan Zusi), Clinton Drew Dempsey, Josmer Volmy Altidore (23.Aron Jóhannsson). Trainer: Jürgen Klinsmann (Germany).

Goals: 0-1 Clinton Drew Dempsey (1), 1-1 André Morgan Rami Ayew (82), 1-2 John Anthony Brooks (86).

Cautions: Mohammed Rabiu Alhassan, Sulleyman Ali Muntari.

21.06.2014, Estádio Castelão, Fortaleza; Attendance: 59,621
Referee: Sandro Meira Ricci (Brazil)

GERMANY - GHANA 2-2(0-0)

GER: Manuel Peter Neuer, Philipp Lahm, Per Mertesacker, Jérôme Agyenim Boateng (46.Shkodran Mustafi), Benedikt Höwedes, Mats Julian Hummels, Mesut Özil, Sami Khedira (70.Bastian Schweinsteiger), Toni Kroos, Mario Götze (69.Miroslav Josef Klose), Thomas Müller. Trainer: Joachim Löw.

GHA: Abdul Fatawu Dauda, Harrison Afful, John Boye, Jonathan Mensah, Sulleyman Ali Muntari, Kevin-Prince Boateng (52.Jordan Pierre Ayew), Kwadwo Asamoah, Mohammed Rabiu Alhassan (78.Emmanuel Agyemang-Badu), André Morgan Rami Ayew, Asamoah Gyan, Christian Atsu Twasam (72.Wakaso Mubarak). Trainer: James Kwesi Appiah.

Goals: 1-0 Mario Götze (51), 1-1 André Morgan Rami Ayew (54), 1-2 Asamoah Gyan (63), 2-2 Miroslav Josef Klose (71).

Cautions: Sulleyman Ali Muntari.

21.06.2014, Arena da Amazônia, Manaus; Attendance: 40,123
Referee: Néstor Fabián Pitana (Argentina)

UNITED STATES – PORTUGAL 2-2(0-1)

USA: Timothy Matthew Howard, DaMarcus Lamont Beasley, Fabian Marco Johnson, Geoffrey Scott Cameron, Matt Besler, Jermaine Jones, Michael Sheehan Bradley, Kyle Robert Beckerman, Graham Jonathan Zusi (90+1.Omar González), Alejandro Bedoya (72.DeAndre Yedlin), Clinton Drew Dempsey (87.Christopher Elliott Wondolowski). Trainer: Jürgen Klinsmann (Germany).

POR: António Alberto Bastos Pimparel "Beto", Ricardo Miguel Moreira da Costa, Bruno Eduardo Regufe Alves, João Pedro da Silva Pereira, Raul José Trindade Meireles (69.Silvestre Manuel Gonçalves Varela), Luís Carlos Almeida da Cunha „Nani", Miguel Luís Pinto Veloso, João Filipe Iria Santos Moutinho, André Gomes Magalhães de Almeida (46.William Silva de Carvalho), Cristiano Ronaldo dos Santos Aveiro, Hélder Manuel Marques Postiga (16.Éderzito António Macedo Lopes „Éder"). Trainer: Paulo Jorge Gomes Bento.

Goals: 0-1 Luís Carlos Almeida da Cunha „Nani" (5), 1-1 Jermaine Jones (64), 2-1 Clinton Drew Dempsey (81), 2-2 Silvestre Manuel Gonçalves Varela (90+5).

Cautions: Jermaine Jones.

26.06.2014, Arena Pernambuco, Recife; Attendance: 41,876
Referee: Ravshan Irmatov (Uzbekistan)

UNITED STATES - GERMANY **0-1(0-0)**

USA: Timothy Matthew Howard, DaMarcus Lamont Beasley, Fabia Robe Johnson, Matt Besler, Omar González, Jermaine Jones, Michael Sheehan Bradley, Kyle Robe Johnson, Matt Besler, Davis (59.Alejandro Bedoya), Graham Jonathan Zusi (84.DeAndre Yedlinan, Bradley Joseph Trainer: Jürgen Klinsmann (Germany). on Drew Dempsey.

GER: Manuel Peter Neuer, Philipp Lahm, Per Mertesacker, Jérôme Agye Höwedes, Mats Julian Hummels, Bastian Schweinsteiger (76.Mario Götze), ateng, Benedikt Horst Schürrle), Toni Kroos, Lukas Josef Podolski (46.Miroslav Josef Klose), ThoÖzil (89.André Joachim Löw. iller. Trainer:

Goal: 0-1 Thomas Müller (55).
Cautions: Omar González, Kyle Robert Beckerman / Benedikt Höwedes.

26.06.2014, Estádio Nacional „Mané Garrincha“, Brasília; Attendance: 67,540
Referee: Nawaf Abdullah Ghayyath Shukralla (Bahrain)

PORTUGAL - GHANA **2-1(1-0)**

POR: António Alberto Bastos Pimparel “Beto” (89.Eduardo dos Reis Carvalho), Képler Laveran Lima Ferreira „Pepe“, Bruno Eduardo Regufe Alves, João Pedro da Silva Pereira (61.Silvestre Manuel Gonçalves Varela), Luís Carlos Almeida da Cunha „Nani“, Miguel Luís Pinto Veloso, João Filipe Iria Santos Moutinho, Rúben Filipe Marques Amorim, William, Cristiano Ronaldo dos Santos Aveiro, Éderzito António Macedo Lopes „Éder“ (69.Adelino André Vieira de Freitas „Vieirinha“). Trainer: Paulo Jorge Gomes Bento.

GHA: Abdul Fatawu Dauda, Harrison Afful, John Boye, Jonathan Mensah, Kwadwo Asamoah, Mohammed Rabiu Alhassan (76.Ebenezer Afriyie Acquah), Emmanuel Agyemang-Badu, André Morgan Rami Ayew (82.Wakaso Mubarak), Majeed Abdul Waris (71.Jordan Pierre Ayew), Asamoah Gyan, Christian Atsu Twasam. Trainer: James Kwesi Appiah.

Goals: 1-0 John Boye (30 own goal), 1-1 Asamoah Gyan (57), 2-1 Cristiano Ronaldo dos Santos Aveiro (80).
Cautions: João Filipe Iria Santos Moutinho / Harrison Afful, Majeed Abdul Waris, Jordan Pierre Ayew.

GROUP H

Date	Venue	Match	Result
17.06.2014	Belo H	Belgium - Algeria	2-1(0-1)
17.06.2014	Cuiab	Russia - Korea Republic	1-1(0-0)
22.06.2014	Rio e	Belgium - Russia	1-0(0-0)
22.06.2014	Por	Korea Republic - Algeria	2-4(0-3)
26.06.2014	S	Korea Republic - Belgium	0-1(0-0)
26.06.2014	C	Algeria - Russia	1-1(0-1)

FINAL STANDINGS

1.	**ium**	3	3	0	0	4	-	1	9
2.	**geria**	3	1	1	1	6	-	5	4
3.	ussia	3	0	2	1	2	-	3	2
	Korea Republic	3	0	1	2	3	-	6	1

17.0 2014, Estádio Mineirão, Belo Horizonte; Attendance: 56,800
Re ree: Marco Antonio Rodríguez Moreno (Mexico)
B LGIUM - ALGERIA **2-1(0-1)**
BEL: Thibaut Nicolas Marc Courtois, Vincent Jean Mpoy Kompany, Daniel Van Buyten, Jan Bert Lieve Vertonghen, Tobias Albertine Maurits Alderweireld, Mousa Sidi Yaya Dembélé (65.Marouane Abdellatif Fellaini-Bakkioui), Axel Laurent Angel Lambert Witsel, Eden Michael Hazard, Nacer Chadli (46.Dries Mertens), Kevin De Bruyne, Romelu Menama Lukaku (58.Divock Okoth Origi). Trainer: Marc Robert Wilmots.
ALG: Adi Raïs Cobos Adrien M'Bolhi Ouhab, Madjid Bougherra, Rafik Halliche, Faouzi Ghoulam, Carl Medjani (84.Nabil Ghilas), Mehdi Mostefa Sbaa, Sofiane Feghouli, Saphir Sliti Taïder, Nabil Bentaleb, El Arbi Hillel Soudani (66.Islam Slimani), Riyad Mahrez (71.Mehdi Gregory Giuseppe Lacen). Trainer: Vahid Halilhodžić (Bosnia-Herzegovina).
Goals: 0-1 Sofiane Feghouli (25 penalty), 1-1 Marouane Abdellatif Fellaini-Bakkioui (70), 2-1 Dries Mertens (80).
Cautions: Jan Bert Lieve Vertonghen / Nabil Bentaleb.

17.06.2014, Arena Pantanal, Cuiabá; Attendance: 37,603
Referee: Néstor Fabián Pitana (Argentina)
RUSSIA - KOREA REPUBLIC **1-1(0-0)**
RUS: Igor Akinfeev, Vasili Berezutski, Sergei Ignashevich, Andrey Yeshchenko, Yuri Zhirkov (71.Aleksandr Kerzhakov), Dmitri Kombarov, Aleksandr Samedov, Viktor Fayzulin, Denis Glushakov (72.Igor Denisov), Oleg Shatov (59.Alan Dzagoev), Aleksandr Kokorin. Trainer: Fabio Capello (Italy).
KOR: Jung Sung-Ryong, Yoon Suk-Young, Kim Young-Gwon, Hong Jeong-Ho (72.Hwang Seok-Ho), Lee Yong, Ki Sung-Yueng, Lee Chung-Yong, Koo Ja-Cheol, Han Kook-Young, Park Chu-Young (56.Lee Keun-Ho), Son Heung-Min (84.Kim Bo-Kyung). Trainer: Hong Myung-Bo.
Goals: 0-1 Lee Keun-Ho (68), 1-1 Aleksandr Kerzhakov (74).
Cautions: Oleg Shatov / Son Heung-Min, Ki Sung-Yueng, Koo Ja-Cheol.

22.06.2014, Estádio „Jornalista Mário Filho" (Maracanã), Rio de Janeiro; Attendance: 73,819
Referee: Dr. Felix Brych (Germany)

BELGIUM - RUSSIA **1-0(0-0)**

BEL: Thibaut Nicolas Marc Courtois, Vincent Jean Mpoy Kompany, Daniel Van Buyten, Thomas Vermaelen (31.Jan Bert Lieve Vertonghen), Tobias Albertine Maurits Alderweireld, Marouane Abdellatif Fellaini-Bakkioui, Axel Laurent Angel Lambert Witsel, Eden Michael Hazard, Kevin De Bruyne, Dries Mertens (75.Kevin Antonio Joel Gislain Mirallas y Castillo), Romelu Menama Lukaku (57.Divock Okoth Origi). Trainer: Marc Robert Wilmots.
RUS: Igor Akinfeev, Vasili Berezutski, Sergei Ignashevich, Aleksei Kozlov (62.Andrey Yeshchenko), Dmitri Kombarov, Aleksandr Samedov (90.Aleksandr Kerzhakov), Viktor Fayzulin, Denis Glushakov, Oleg Shatov (83.Alan Dzagoev), Aleksandr Kokorin, Maksim Kanunnikov. Trainer: Fabio Capello (Italy).
Goal: 1-0 Divock Okoth Origi (88).
Cautions: Tobias Albertine Maurits Alderweireld, Axel Laurent Angel Lambert Witsel / Denis Glushakov.

22.06.2014, Estádio Beira-Rio, Porto Alegre; Attendance: 42,732
Referee: Wilmar Alexander Roldán Pérez (Colombia)

KOREA REPUBLIC - ALGERIA **2-4(0-3)**

KOR: Jung Sung-Ryong, Yoon Suk-Young, Kim Young-Gwon, Hong Jeong-Ho, Lee Yong, Ki Sung-Yueng, Lee Chung-Yong (64.Lee Keun-Ho), Koo Ja-Cheol, Han Kook-Young (78.Ji Dong-Won), Park Chu-Young (57.Kim Shin-Wook), Son Heung-Min. Trainer: Hong Myung-Bo.
ALG: Adi Raïs Cobos Adrien M'Bolhi Ouhab, Madjid Bougherra (89.Essaïd Belkalem), Djamel Eddine Mesbah, Rafik Halliche, Aïssa Mandi, Carl Medjani, Yacine Brahimi (77.Mehdi Gregory Giuseppe Lacen), Sofiane Feghouli, Abdelmoumene Djabou (73.Nabil Ghilas), Nabil Bentaleb Islam Slimani. Trainer: Vahid Halilhodžić (Bosnia-Herzegovina).
Goals: 0-1 Islam Slimani (26), 0-2 Rafik Halliche (28), 0-3 Abdelmoumene Djabou (38), 1-3 Son Heung-Min (50), 1-4 Yacine Brahimi (62), 2-4 Koo Ja-Cheol (72).
Cautions: Lee Yong, Han Kook-Young / Madjid Bougherra.

26.06.2014, Arena de São Paulo, São Paulo; Attendance: 61,397
Referee: Benjamin Jon Williams (Australia)

KOREA REPUBLIC - BELGIUM **0-1(0-0)**

KOR: Kim Seung-Gyu, Yoon Suk-Young, Kim Young-Gwon, Hong Jeong-Ho, Lee Yong, Ki Sung-Yueng, Lee Chung-Yong, Koo Ja-Cheol, Han Kook-Young (46.Lee Keun-Ho), Kim Shin-Wook (66.Kim Bo-Kyung), Son Heung-Min (73.Ji Dong-Won). Trainer: Hong Myung-Bo.
BEL: Thibaut Nicolas Marc Courtois, Daniel Van Buyten, Jan Bert Lieve Vertonghen, Anthony Henri Vanden Borre, Nicolas Robert Christian Lombaerts, Mousa Sidi Yaya Dembélé, Marouane Abdellatif Fellaini-Bakkioui, Steven Arnold Defour, Adnan Januzaj (60.Nacer Chadli), Kevin Antonio Joel Gislain Mirallas y Castillo (88.Eden Michael Hazard), Dries Mertens (60.Divock Okoth Origi). Trainer: Marc Robert Wilmots.
Goal: 0-1 Jan Bert Lieve Vertonghen (77).
Cautions: Hong Jeong-Ho / Mousa Sidi Yaya Dembélé.
Sent off: Steven Arnold Defour (44).

26.06.2014, Arena da Baixada, Curitiba; Attendance: 39,311
Referee: Cüneyt Çakır (Turkey)

ALGERIA - RUSSIA **1-1(0-1)**

ALG: Adi Raïs Cobos Adrien M'Bolhi Ouhab, Djamel Eddine Mesbah, Rafik Halliche, Essaïd Belkalem, Aïssa Mandi, Carl Medjani, Yacine Brahimi (71.Hassan Yebda), Sofiane Feghouli, Abdelmoumene Djabou (77.Nabil Ghilas), Nabil Bentaleb, Islam Slimani (90+1.El Arbi Hillel Soudani). Trainer: Vahid Halilhodžić (Bosnia-Herzegovina).

RUS: Igor Akinfeev, Vasili Berezutski, Sergei Ignashevich, Aleksei Kozlov, Dmitri Kombarov, Aleksandr Samedov, Viktor Fayzulin, Denis Glushakov (46.Igor Denisov), Oleg Shatov (67.Alan Dzagoev), Aleksandr Kerzhakov (81.Maksim Kanunnikov), Aleksandr Kokorin. Trainer: Fabio Capello (Italy).

Goals: 0-1 Aleksandr Kokorin (6), 1-1 Islam Slimani (60).

Cautions: Djamel Eddine Mesbah, Nabil Ghilas, Liassine Cadamuro-Bentaïba (on the bench) / Dmitri Kombarov, Aleksei Kozlov.

SECOND ROUND OF 16

28.06.2014	Belo Horizonte	Brazil - Chile	1-1(1-1,1-1,1-1); 3-2 pen
28.06.2014	Rio de Janeiro	Colombia - Uruguay	2-0(1-0)
29.06.2014	Fortaleza	Holland - Mexico	2-1(0-0)
29.06.2014	Recife	Costa Rica - Greece	1-1(0-0,1-1,1-1); 5-3 pen
30.06.2014	Brasília	France - Nigeria	2-0(0-0)
30.06.2014	Porto Alegre	Germany - Algeria	2-1(0-0,0-0)
01.07.2014	São Paulo	Argentina - Switzerland	1-0(0-0,0-0)
01.07.2014	Salvador	Belgium – United States	2-1(0-0,0-0)

28.06.2014, Estádio Mineirão, Belo Horizonte; Attendance: 57,714
Referee: Howard Melton Webb (England)
BRAZIL - CHILE **1-1(1-1,1-1,1-1); 3-2 on penalties**

BRA: Júlio César Soares de Espíndola, Daniel Alves da Silva, Thiago Emiliano da Silva, David Luiz Moreira Marinho, Marcelo Vieira da Silva Júnior, Fernando Luiz Rosa „Fernandinho“ (72.Ramires Santos do Nascimento), Luiz Gustavo Dias, Oscar dos Santos Emboaba Júnior (106.Willian Borges da Silva), Givanildo Vieira de Souza „Hulk“, Frederico Chaves Guedes "Fred" (64.João Alves de Assis Silva "Jô"), Neymar da Silva Santos Júnior. Trainer: Luíz Felipe Scolari.
CHI: Claudio Andrés Bravo Muñoz, Gonzalo Alejandro Jara Reyes, Eugenio Esteban Mena Reveco, Arturo Erasmo Vidal Pardo (87.Mauricio Ricardo Pinilla Ferrera), Mauricio Aníbal Isla Isla, Marcelo Alfonso Díaz Rojas, Gary Alexis Medel Soto (108.José Manuel Rojas Bahamondes), Francisco Andrés Silva Gajardo, Charles Mariano Aránguiz Sandoval, Alexis Alejandro Sánchez Sánchez, Eduardo Jesús Vargas Rojas (57.Felipe Alejandro Gutiérrez Leiva). Trainer: Jorge Luis Sampaoli Moya (Argentina).
Goals: 1-0 David Luiz Moreira Marinho (18), 1-1 Alexis Alejandro Sánchez Sánchez (32).
Penalties: David Luiz Moreira Marinho 1-0; Mauricio Ricardo Pinilla Ferrera (saved); Willian Borges da Silva (missed); Alexis Alejandro Sánchez Sánchez (saved); Marcelo Vieira da Silva Júnior 2-0; Charles Mariano Aránguiz Sandoval 2-1; Givanildo Vieira de Souza „Hulk“ (saved); Marcelo Alfonso Díaz Rojas 2-2; Neymar da Silva Santos Júnior 3-2; Gonzalo Alejandro Jara Reyes (missed)
Cautions: Givanildo Vieira de Souza „Hulk“, Luiz Gustavo Dias, João Alves de Assis Silva "Jô", Daniel Alves da Silva / Eugenio Esteban Mena Reveco, Francisco Andrés Silva Gajardo, Mauricio Ricardo Pinilla Ferrera.

28.06.2014, Estádio „Jornalista Mário Filho“ (Maracanã), Rio de Janeiro; Attendance: 73,804
Referee: Björn Kuipers (Holland)
COLOMBIA - URUGUAY **2-0(1-0)**
COL: David Ospina Ramírez, Mario Alberto Yepes Díaz, Cristián Eduardo Zapata Valencia, Pablo Estifer Armero, Abel Enrique Aguilar Tapias, Juan Camilo Zúñiga Mosquera, Carlos Alberto Sánchez Moreno, Juan Guillermo Cuadrado Bello (81.Fredy Alejandro Guarín Vásquez), James David Rodríguez Rubio (85.Gustavo Adrián Ramos Vásquez), Teófilo Antonio Gutiérrez Roncancio (68.Alexander Mejía Sabalza), Jackson Arley Martínez Valencia. Trainer: José Néstor Pékerman (Argentina).
URU: Néstor Fernando Muslera Micol, Victorio Maximiliano Pereira Páez, José Martín Cáceres Silva, Diego Roberto Godín Leal, Álvaro Daniel Pereira Barragán (53.Gastón Ezequiel Ramírez Pereyra), José María Giménez de Vargas, Cristian Gabriel Rodríguez Barotti, Álvaro Rafael González Luengo (67.Abel Mathías Hernández Platero), Egidio Raúl Arévalo Ríos, Diego Martín Forlán Corazzo (53.Christian Ricardo Stuani Curbelo), Edinson Roberto Cavani Gómez.Trainer: Óscar Wáshington Tabárez Silva.
Goals: 1-0 James David Rodríguez Rubio (28), 2-0 James David Rodríguez Rubio (50).
Cautions: Pablo Estifer Armero / José María Giménez de Vargas, Diego Alfredo Lugano Morena (on the bench).

29.06.2014, Estádio Castelão, Fortaleza; Attendance: 58,817
Referee: Pedro Proença Oliveira Alves Garcia (Portugal)

HOLLAND - MEXICO 2-1(0-0)

NED: Jasper Cillessen, Paul Johannes Gerardus Verhaegh (56.Memphis Depay), Ron Peter Vlaar, Stefan de Vrij, Wesley Sneijder, Nigel de Jong (9.Rolando Maximiliano Martins Indi), Georginio Gregion Emile Wijnaldum, Daley Blind, Dirk Kuijt, Arjen Robben, Robin van Persie (76.Dirk Jan Klaas Huntelaar). Trainer: Aloysius Paulus Maria van Gaal.

MEX: Francisco Guillermo Ochoa Magaña, Rafael Márquez Álvarez, Francisco Javier Rodríguez Pinedo, José Andrés Guardado Hernández, Carlos Arnoldo Salcido Flores, Paul Nicolás Aguilar Rojas, Héctor Alfredo Moreno Herrera (46.Diego Antonio Reyes Rosales), Miguel Arturo Layún Prado, Héctor Miguel Herrera López, Oribe Peralta Morones (75.Javier Hernández Balcázar), Giovani dos Santos Ramírez (61.Javier Ignacio Aquino Carmona). Trainer: Miguel Ernesto Herrera Aguirre.

Goals: 0-1 Giovani dos Santos Ramírez (48), 1-1 Wesley Sneijder (88), 2-1 Dirk Jan Klaas Huntelaar (90+4 penalty).

Cautions: Paul Nicolás Aguilar Rojas, Rafael Márquez Álvarez, José Andrés Guardado Hernández.

29.06.2014, Arena Pernambuco, Recife; Attendance: 41,242
Referee: Benjamin Jon Williams (Australia)

COSTA RICA - GREECE 1-1(0-0,1-1,1-1); 5-3 on penalties

CRC: Keylor Antonio Navas Gamboa, Míchael Umaña Corrales, Júnior Enrique Díaz Campbell, Óscar Esau Duarte Gaitan, Cristian Esteban Gamboa Luna (77.Jhonny Acosta Zamora), Geancarlo González Castro, Celso Borges Mora, Cristian Bolaños Navarro (83.Randall Brenes Moya), Yeltsin Ignacio Tejeda Valverde (66.José Miguel Cubero Loria), Bryan Jafet Ruíz González, Joël Nathaniel Campbell Samuels. Trainer: Jorge Luis Pinto Afanador (Colombia).

GRE: Orestis-Spyridon Karnezis, José Lloyd Holebas, Vasileios Torosidis, Sokratis Papastathopoulos, Konstantinos Manolas, Giórgos Karagounis, Lazaros Christodoulopoulos, Giánnis Maniatis (78.Konstantinos Katsouranis), Andreas Samaris (58.Konstantinos Mitroglou), Giórgos Samaras, Dimitrios Salpingidis (69.Theofanis Gekas). Trainer: Fernando Manuel Costa Santos (Portugal).

Goals: 1-0 Bryan Jafet Ruíz González (52), 1-1 Sokratis Papastathopoulos (90+1).

Penalties: Celso Borges Mora 1-0; Konstantinos Mitroglou 1-1; Bryan Jafet Ruíz González 2-1; Lazaros Christodoulopoulos 2-2; Geancarlo González Castro 3-2; José Lloyd Holebas 3-3; Joël Nathaniel Campbell Samuels 4-3; Theofanis Gekas (saved); Míchael Umaña Corrales 5-3.

Cautions: Óscar Esau Duarte Gaitan, Yeltsin Ignacio Tejeda Valverde, Óscar Esteban Granados Maroto (on the bench), Bryan Jafet Ruíz González, Keylor Antonio Navas Gamboa / Andreas Samaris, Konstantinos Manolas.

Sent off: Óscar Esau Duarte Gaitan (66).

30.06.2014, Estádio Nacional „Mané Garrincha“, Brasília; Attendance: 67,882
Referee: Mark Geiger (United States)

FRANCE - NIGERIA 2-0(0-0)

FRA: Hugo Lloris, Mathieu Debuchy, Patrice Latyr Evra, Laurent Koscielny, Raphaël Varane, Blaise Matuidi, Mathieu Valbuena (90+4.Moussa Sissoko), Yohan Cabaye, Paul Labile Pogba, Karim Mostafa Benzema, Olivier Giroud (62.Antoine Griezmann). Trainer: Didier Claude Deschamps.

NGA: Vincent Enyeama, Joseph Ikpo Yobo, Efetobore Ambrose Emuobo, Kenneth Josiah Omeruo, Juwon Oshaniwa, John Michael Nchekwube Obinna, Victor Moses (89.Uche Innocent Nwofor), Ogenyi Eddy Onazi (59.Reuben Shalu Gabriel), Peter Osaze Odemwingie, Emmanuel Chinenye Emenike, Ahmed Musa. Trainer: Stephen Okechukwu Keshi.

Goals: 1-0 Paul Labile Pogba (79), 2-0 Joseph Ikpo Yobo (90+1 own goal).

Cautions: Blaise Matuidi.

30.06.2014, Estádio Beira-Rio, Porto Alegre; Attendance: 43,063
Referee: Sandro Meira Ricci (Brazil)

GERMANY - ALGERIA **2-1(0-0,0-0)**

GER: Manuel Peter Neuer, Philipp Lahm, Per Mertesacker, Jérôme Agyenim Boateng, Benedikt Höwedes, Shkodran Mustafi (70.Sami Khedira), Bastian Schweinsteiger (109.Christoph Kramer), Mesut Özil, Toni Kroos, Mario Götze (46.André Horst Schürrle), Thomas Müller. Trainer: Joachim Löw.

ALG: Adi Raïs Cobos Adrien M'Bolhi Ouhab, Rafik Halliche (97.Madjid Bougherra), Essaïd Belkalem, Aïssa Mandi, Faouzi Ghoulam, Mehdi Mostefa Sbaa, Sofiane Feghouli, Mehdi Gregory Giuseppe Lacen, Saphir Sliti Taïder (78.Yacine Brahimi), El Arbi Hillel Soudani (100.Abdelmoumene Djabou), Islam Slimani. Trainer: Vahid Halilhodžić (Bosnia-Herzegovina).

Goals: 1-0 André Horst Schürrle (92), 2-0 Mesut Özil (119), 2-1 Abdelmoumene Djabou (120+1).

Cautions: Philipp Lahm / Rafik Halliche.

01.07.2014, Arena de São Paulo, São Paulo; Attendance: 63,255
Referee: Jonas Eriksson (Sweden)

ARGENTINA - SWITZERLAND **1-0(0-0,0-0)**

ARG: Sergio Germán Romero, Pablo Javier Zabaleta Girod, Ezequiel Marcelo Garay González, Federico Fernández, Faustino Marcos Alberto Rojo (105+1.José María Basanta Pavone), Javier Alejandro Mascherano, Fernando Rubén Gago (106.Lucas Rodrigo Biglia), Ángel Fabián di María Hernández, Lionel Andrés Messi, Gonzalo Gerardo Higuaín, Ezequiel Iván Lavezzi (74.Rodrigo Sebastián Palacio). Trainer: Alejandro Sabella.

SUI: Diego Orlando Benaglio, Stephan Lichtsteiner, Johan Danon Djourou-Gbadjere, Ricardo Iván Rodríguez Araya, Fabian Lukas Schär, Valon Behrami, Gökhan Inler, Xherdan Shaqiri, Granit Xhaka (66.Gelson da Conceição Tavares Fernandes), Admir Mehmedi (113.Blerim Džemaili), Josip Drmić (82.Haris Seferović). Trainer: Ottmar Hitzfeld (Germany).

Goal: 1-0 Ángel Fabián di María Hernández (118).

Cautions: Faustino Marcos Alberto Rojo, Ángel Fabián di María Hernández, Ezequiel Marcelo Garay González / Granit Xhaka, Gelson da Conceição Tavares Fernandes.

01.07.2014, Arena Fonte Nova, Salvador; Attendance: 51,227
Referee: Djamel Haimoudi (Algeria)

BELGIUM – UNITED STATES **2-1(0-0,0-0)**

BEL: Thibaut Nicolas Marc Courtois, Vincent Jean Mpoy Kompany, Daniel Van Buyten, Jan Bert Lieve Vertonghen, Tobias Albertine Maurits Alderweireld, Marouane Abdellatif Fellaini-Bakkioui, Axel Laurent Angel Lambert Witsel, Eden Michael Hazard (111.Nacer Chadli), Kevin De Bruyne, Dries Mertens (60.Kevin Antonio Joel Gislain Mirallas y Castillo), Divock Okoth Origi (91.Romelu Menama Lukaku). Trainer: Marc Robert Wilmots.

USA: Timothy Matthew Howard, DaMarcus Lamont Beasley, Fabian Marco Johnson (32.DeAndre Yedlin), Geoffrey Scott Cameron, Matt Besler, Omar González, Jermaine Jones, Michael Sheehan Bradley, Graham Jonathan Zusi (72.Christopher Elliott Wondolowski), Alejandro Bedoya (105+2.Julian Wesley Green), Clinton Drew Dempsey. Trainer: Jürgen Klinsmann (Germany).

Goals: 1-0 Kevin De Bruyne (93), 2-0 Romelu Menama Lukaku (105), 2-1 Julian Wesley Green (107).

Cautions: Vincent Jean Mpoy Kompany / Geoffrey Scott Cameron.

QUARTER-FINALS

04.07.2014	Rio de Janeiro	France - Germany	0-1(0-1)
04.07.2014	Fortaleza	Brazil - Colombia	2-1(1-0)
05.07.2014	Brasília	Argentina - Belgium	1-0(1-0)
05.07.2014	Salvador	Holland – Costa Rica	0-0; 4-3 pen

04.07.2014, Estádio „Jornalista Mário Filho" (Maracanã), Rio de Janeiro; Attendance: 74,240
Referee: Néstor Fabián Pitana (Argentina)

FRANCE - GERMANY **0-1(0-1)**

FRA: Hugo Lloris, Mathieu Debuchy, Patrice Latyr Evra, Mamadou Sakho (72.Laurent Koscielny), Raphaël Varane, Blaise Matuidi, Mathieu Valbuena (85.Olivier Giroud), Yohan Cabaye (73.Loïc Rémy), Paul Labile Pogba, Karim Mostafa Benzema, Antoine Griezmann. Trainer: Didier Claude Deschamps.

GER: Manuel Peter Neuer, Philipp Lahm, Jérôme Agyenim Boateng, Benedikt Höwedes, Mats Julian Hummels, Bastian Schweinsteiger, Mesut Özil (83.Mario Götze), Sami Khedira, Toni Kroos (90+2.Christoph Kramer), Miroslav Josef Klose (69.André Horst Schürrle), Thomas Müller. Trainer: Joachim Löw.

Goal: 0-1 Mats Julian Hummels (12).

Cautions: Sami Khedira, Bastian Schweinsteiger.

04.07.2014, Estádio Castelão, Fortaleza; Attendance: 60,342
Referee: Carlos Velasco Carballo (Spain)

BRAZIL - COLOMBIA **2-1(1-0)**

BRA: Júlio César Soares de Espíndola, Maicon Douglas Sisenando, Thiago Emiliano da Silva, David Luiz Moreira Marinho, Marcelo Vieira da Silva Júnior, Fernando Luiz Rosa „Fernandinho", José Paulo Bezerra Maciel Júnior „Paulinho III" (86.Anderson Hernanes de Carvalho Andrade Lima), Givanildo Vieira de Souza „Hulk" (83.Ramires Santos do Nascimento), Oscar dos Santos Emboaba Júnior, Frederico Chaves Guedes "Fred", Neymar da Silva Santos Júnior (88.Henrique Adriano Buss „Henrique III"). Trainer: Luíz Felipe Scolari.

COL: David Ospina Ramírez, Mario Alberto Yepes Díaz, Cristián Eduardo Zapata Valencia, Pablo Estifer Armero, Juan Camilo Zúñiga Mosquera, Carlos Alberto Sánchez Moreno, Fredy Alejandro Guarín Vásquez, Juan Guillermo Cuadrado Bello (80.Juan Fernando Quintero Paniagua), James David Rodríguez Rubio, Teófilo Antonio Gutiérrez Roncancio (70.Carlos Arturo Bacca Ahumada), Segundo Víctor Ibarbo Guerrero (46.Gustavo Adrián Ramos Vásquez). Trainer: José Néstor Pékerman (Argentina).

Goals: 1-0 Thiago Emiliano da Silva (7), 2-0 David Luiz Moreira Marinho (69), 2-1 James David Rodríguez Rubio (80 penalty).

Cautions: Thiago Emiliano da Silva, Júlio César Soares de Espíndola / James David Rodríguez Rubio, Mario Alberto Yepes Díaz.

05.07.2014, Estádio Nacional „Mané Garrincha", Brasília; Attendance: 68,551
Referee: Nicola Rizzoli (Italy)

ARGENTINA - BELGIUM **1-0(1-0)**

ARG: Sergio Germán Romero, Martín Gastón Demichelis, Pablo Javier Zabaleta Girod, Ezequiel Marcelo Garay González, José María Basanta Pavone, Javier Alejandro Mascherano, Lucas Rodrigo Biglia, Ángel Fabián di María Hernández (33.Enzo Nicolás Pérez), Lionel Andrés Messi, Gonzalo Gerardo Higuaín (81.Fernando Rubén Gago), Ezequiel Iván Lavezzi (71.Rodrigo Sebastián Palacio). Trainer: Alejandro Sabella.

BEL: Thibaut Nicolas Marc Courtois, Vincent Jean Mpoy Kompany, Daniel Van Buyten, Jan Bert Lieve Vertonghen, Tobias Albertine Maurits Alderweireld, Marouane Abdellatif Fellaini-Bakkioui, Axel Laurent Angel Lambert Witsel, Eden Michael Hazard (75.Nacer Chadli), Kevin De Bruyne, Kevin Antonio Joel Gislain Mirallas y Castillo (60.Dries Mertens), Divock Okoth Origi (59.Romelu Menama Lukaku). Trainer: Marc Robert Wilmots.

Goal: 1-0 Gonzalo Gerardo Higuaín (8).

Cautions: Lucas Rodrigo Biglia / Eden Michael Hazard, Tobias Albertine Maurits Alderweireld.

05.07.2014, Arena Fonte Nova, Salvador; Attendance: 51,179
Referee: Ravshan Irmatov (Uzbekistan)

HOLLAND - COSTA RICA **0-0; 4-3 on penalties**

NED: Jasper Cillessen (120+1.Timothy Michael Krul), Ron Peter Vlaar, Stefan de Vrij, Rolando Maximiliano Martins Indi (106.Dirk Jan Klaas Huntelaar), Wesley Sneijder, Georginio Gregion Emile Wijnaldum, Daley Blind, Dirk Kuijt, Arjen Robben, Robin van Persie, Memphis Depay (76.Jeremain Marciano Lens). Trainer: Aloysius Paulus Maria van Gaal.
CRC: Keylor Antonio Navas Gamboa, Míchael Umaña Corrales, Júnior Enrique Díaz Campbell, Cristian Esteban Gamboa Luna (79.David Myrie Medrano), Geancarlo González Castro, Jhonny Acosta Zamora, Celso Borges Mora, Cristian Bolaños Navarro, Yeltsin Ignacio Tejeda Valverde (97.José Miguel Cubero Loria), Bryan Jafet Ruíz González, Joël Nathaniel Campbell Samuels (66.Marcos Danilo Ureña Porras). Trainer: Jorge Luis Pinto Afanador (Colombia).
Penalties: Celso Borges Mora 0-1; Robin van Persie 1-1; Bryan Jafet Ruíz González (saved); Arjen Robben 2-1; Geancarlo González Castro 2-2; Wesley Sneijder 3-2 ; Cristian Bolaños Navarro 3-3; Dirk Kuijt 4-3; Míchael Umaña Corrales (saved).
Cautions: Rolando Maximiliano Martins Indi, Dirk Jan Klaas Huntelaar / Júnior Enrique Díaz Campbell, Míchael Umaña Corrales, Geancarlo González Castro, Jhonny Acosta Zamora.

SEMI-FINALS

08.07.2014	Belo Horizonte	Brazil – Germany	1-7(0-5)
09.07.2014	São Paulo	Holland - Argentina	0-0; 2-4 pen

08.07.2014, Estádio Mineirão, Belo Horizonte; Attendance: 58,141
Referee: Marco Antonio Rodríguez Moreno (Mexico)

BRAZIL - GERMANY **1-7(0-5)**

BRA: Júlio César Soares de Espíndola, Maicon Douglas Sisenando, David Luiz Moreira Marinho, Dante Bonfim Costa Santos, Marcelo Vieira da Silva Júnior, Luiz Gustavo Dias, Fernando Luiz Rosa „Fernandinho“ (46.José Paulo Bezerra Maciel Júnior „Paulinho III“), Oscar dos Santos Emboaba Júnior, Givanildo Vieira de Souza „Hulk“ (46.Ramires Santos do Nascimento), Frederico Chaves Guedes “Fred” (69.Willian Borges da Silva), Bernard Anício Caldeira Duarte. Trainer: Luíz Felipe Scolari.
GER: Manuel Peter Neuer, Philipp Lahm, Jérôme Agyenim Boateng, Benedikt Höwedes, Mats Julian Hummels (46.Per Mertesacker), Bastian Schweinsteiger, Mesut Özil, Sami Khedira (76.Julian Draxler), Toni Kroos, Miroslav Josef Klose (58.André Horst Schürrle), Thomas Müller. Trainer: Joachim Löw.
Goals: 0-1 Thomas Müller (11), 0-2 Miroslav Josef Klose (23), 0-3 Toni Kroos (24), 0-4 Toni Kroos (26), 0-5 Sami Khedira (29), 0-6 André Horst Schürrle (69), 0-7 André Horst Schürrle (79), 1-7 Oscar dos Santos Emboaba Júnior (90).
Cautions: Dante Bonfim Costa Santos.

09.07.2014, Arena de São Paulo, São Paulo; Attendance: 63,267
Referee: Cüneyt Çakır (Turkey)

HOLLAND - ARGENTINA **0-0; 2-4 on penalties**

NED: Jasper Cillessen, Ron Peter Vlaar, Stefan de Vrij, Rolando Maximiliano Martins Indi (46.Daryl Janmaat), Wesley Sneijder, Nigel de Jong (62.Jordy Clasie), Georginio Gregion Emile Wijnaldum, Daley Blind, Dirk Kuijt, Arjen Robben, Robin van Persie (96.Dirk Jan Klaas Huntelaar). Trainer: Aloysius Paulus Maria van Gaal.

ARG: Sergio Germán Romero, Martín Gastón Demichelis, Pablo Javier Zabaleta Girod, Ezequiel Marcelo Garay González, Faustino Marcos Alberto Rojo, Javier Alejandro Mascherano, Lucas Rodrigo Biglia, Enzo Nicolás Pérez (81.Rodrigo Sebastián Palacio), Lionel Andrés Messi, Gonzalo Gerardo Higuaín (82.Sergio Leonel Agüero del Castillo), Ezequiel Iván Lavezzi (101.Maximiliano Rubén Rodríguez). Trainer: Alejandro Sabella.

Penalties: Ron Peter Vlaar (saved); Lionel Andrés Messi 0-1 ; Arjen Robben 1-1; Ezequiel Marcelo Garay González 1-2; Wesley Sneijder (saved); Sergio Leonel Agüero del Castillo 1-3; Dirk Kuijt 2-3; Maximiliano Rubén Rodríguez 2-4.

Cautions: Rolando Maximiliano Martins Indi, Dirk Jan Klaas Huntelaar / Martín Gastón Demichelis.

3rd PLACE PLAY-OFF

12.07.2014, Estádio Nacional „Mané Garrincha", Brasília; Attendance: 68,034
Referee: Djamel Haimoudi (Algeria)

BRAZIL - HOLLAND **0-3(0-2)**

BRA: Júlio César Soares de Espíndola, Maicon Douglas Sisenando, Thiago Emiliano da Silva, David Luiz Moreira Marinho, Maxwell Scherrer Cabelino Andrade, José Paulo Bezerra Maciel Júnior „Paulinho III" (57.Anderson Hernanes de Carvalho Andrade Lima), Luiz Gustavo Dias (46.Fernando Luiz Rosa „Fernandinho"), Oscar dos Santos Emboaba Júnior, Ramires Santos do Nascimento (73.Givanildo Vieira de Souza „Hulk"), João Alves de Assis Silva "Jô", Willian Borges da Silva. Trainer: Luíz Felipe Scolari.

NED: Jasper Cillessen (90+3.Michel Armand Vorm), Ron Peter Vlaar, Stefan de Vrij, Rolando Maximiliano Martins Indi, Jonathan Alexander de Guzmán, Georginio Gregion Emile Wijnaldum, Daley Blind (70.Daryl Janmaat), Jordy Clasie (90.Joël Ivo Veltman), Dirk Kuijt, Arjen Robben, Robin van Persie. Trainer: Aloysius Paulus Maria van Gaal.

Goals: 0-1 Robin van Persie (3 penalty), 0-2 Daley Blind (16), 0-3 Georginio Gregion Emile Wijnaldum (90+1).

Cautions: Thiago Emiliano da Silva, Fernando Luiz Rosa „Fernandinho",Oscar dos Santos Emboaba Júnior / Arjen Robben, Jonathan Alexander de Guzmán.

FINAL

13.07.2014, Estádio „Jornalista Mário Filho" (Maracanã), Rio de Janeiro; Attendance: 74,738
Referee: Nicola Rizzoli (Italy)

GERMANY - ARGENTINA **1-0(0-0,0-0)**

GER: Manuel Peter Neuer, Philipp Lahm, Jérôme Agyenim Boateng, Benedikt Höwedes, Mats Julian Hummels, Bastian Schweinsteiger, Mesut Özil (120.Per Mertesacker), Toni Kroos, Christoph Kramer (32.André Horst Schürrle), Miroslav Josef Klose (88.Mario Götze), Thomas Müller. Trainer: Joachim Löw.

ARG: Sergio Germán Romero, Pablo Javier Zabaleta Girod, Martín Gastón Demichelis, Ezequiel Marcelo Garay González, Faustino Marcos Alberto Rojo, Javier Alejandro Mascherano, Lucas Rodrigo Biglia, Enzo Nicolás Pérez (86.Fernando Rubén Gago), Lionel Andrés Messi, Gonzalo Gerardo Higuaín (78.Rodrigo Sebastián Palacio), Ezequiel Iván Lavezzi (46.Sergio Leonel Agüero del Castillo). Trainer: Alejandro Sabella.

Goal: 1-0 Mario Götze (113).

Cautions: Bastian Schweinsteiger, Benedikt Höwedes / Javier Alejandro Mascherano, Sergio Leonel Agüero del Castillo.

WORLD CUP 2014 FINAL RANKING

1.	Germany	7	6	1	0	18	-	4	19
2.	Argentina	7	5	1	1	8	-	4	16
3.	Holland	7	5	2	0	15	-	4	17
4.	Brazil	7	3	2	2	11	-	14	11
5.	Colombia	5	4	0	1	12	-	4	12
6.	Belgium	5	4	0	1	6	-	3	12
7.	France	5	3	1	1	10	-	3	10
8.	Costa Rica	5	2	3	0	5	-	2	9
9.	Chile	4	2	1	1	6	-	4	7
10.	Mexico	4	2	1	1	5	-	3	7
11.	Switzerland	4	2	0	2	7	-	7	6
12.	Uruguay	4	2	0	2	4	-	6	6
13.	Greece	4	1	2	1	3	-	5	5
14.	Algeria	4	1	1	2	7	-	7	4
15.	United States	4	1	1	2	5	-	6	4
16.	Nigeria	4	1	1	2	3	-	5	4
17.	Ecuador	3	1	1	1	3	-	3	4
18.	Portugal	3	1	1	1	4	-	7	4
19.	Croatia	3	1	0	2	6	-	6	3
20.	Bosnia-Herzegovina	3	1	0	2	4	-	4	3
21.	Côte d'Ivoire	3	1	0	2	4	-	5	3
22.	Italy	3	1	0	2	2	-	3	3
23.	Spain	3	1	0	2	4	-	7	3
24.	Russia	3	0	2	1	2	-	3	2
25.	Ghana	3	0	1	2	4	-	6	1
26.	England	3	0	1	2	2	-	4	1
27.	Korea Republic	3	0	1	2	3	-	6	1
28.	Iran	3	0	1	2	1	-	4	1
29.	Japan	3	0	1	2	2	-	6	1
30.	Australia	3	0	0	3	3	-	9	0
31.	Honduras	3	0	0	3	1	-	8	0
32.	Cameroon	3	0	0	3	1	-	9	0

WORLD CUP AWARDS

GOLDEN BALL (best player of the World Cup final tournament)
Lionel Andrés Messi (Argentina)

GOLDEN BOOT (best goalscorer)
James David Rodríguez Rubio (Colombia)

GOLDEN GLOVE (best goalkeeper of the tournament)
Manuel Peter Neuer (Germany)

BEST YOUNG PLAYER
Paul Labile Pogba (France)

FIFA FAIR-PLAY TROPHY
Colombia

GOALSCORERS

6 goals: **James David Rodríguez Rubio** (Colombia)
5 goals: Thomas Müller (Germany)
4 goals: Lionel Andrés Messi (Argentina)
Neymar da Silva Santos Júnior (Brazil)
Robin van Persie (Holland)
3 goals: Enner Remberto Valencia Lastra (Ecuador)
Karim Mostafa Benzema (France)
André Horst Schürrle (Germany)
Arjen Robben (Holland)
Xherdan Shaqiri (Switzerland)
2 goals: Abdelmoumene Djabou, Islam Slimani (Algeria)
Timothy Filiga Cahill (Australia)
David Luiz Moreira Marinho, Oscar dos Santos Emboaba Júnior (Brazil)
Alexis Alejandro Sánchez Sánchez (Chile)
Jackson Arley Martínez Valencia (Colombia)
Bryan Jafet Ruíz González (Costa Rica)
Wilfried Guemiand Bony, Gervais Yao Kouassi „Gervinho" (Côte d'Ivoire)
Mario Mandžukić, Ivan Perišić (Croatia)
Mario Götze, Mats Julian Hummels, Miroslav Josef Klose, Toni Kroos (Germany)
André Morgan Rami Ayew, Asamoah Gyan (Ghana)
Memphis Depay (Holland)
Ahmed Musa (Nigeria)
Clinton Drew Dempsey (United States)
Luis Alberto Suárez Díaz (Uruguay)
1 goal: Yacine Brahimi, Sofiane Feghouli, Rafik Halliche (Algeria), Ángel Fabián di María Hernández, Gonzalo Gerardo Higuaín, Faustino Marcos Alberto Rojo (Argentina), Michael John Jedinak (Australia), Kevin De Bruyne, Marouane Abdellatif Fellaini-Bakkioui, Romelu Menama Lukaku, Dries Mertens, Divock Okoth Origi, Jan Bert Lieve Vertonghen (Belgium), Edin Džeko, Vedad Ibišević, Miralem Pjanić, Avdija Vršajević (Bosnia-Herzegovina), Fernando Luiz Rosa „Fernandinho", Frederico Chaves Guedes "Fred", Thiago Emiliano da Silva (Brazil), Joël Job Matip (Cameroon), Charles Mariano Aránguiz Sandoval, Jean André Emanuel Beausejour Coliqueo, Jorge Luis Valdivia Toro, Eduardo Jesús Vargas Rojas (Chile), Pablo Estifer Armero, Juan Guillermo Cuadrado Bello, Teófilo Antonio Gutiérrez Roncancio, Juan Fernando Quintero Paniagua (Colombia), Joël Nathaniel Campbell Samuels, Óscar Esau Duarte Gaitan, Marcos Danilo Ureña Porras (Costa Rica), Ivica Olić (Croatia), Wayne Mark Rooney, Daniel Andre Sturridge (England), Olivier Giroud, Blaise Matuidi, Paul Labile Pogba, Moussa Sissoko, Mathieu Valbuena (France), Sami Khedira, Mesut Özil (Germany), Sokratis Papastathopoulos, Giórgos Samaras, Andreas Samaris (Greece), Daley Blind, Stefan de Vrij, Leroy Johan Fer, Dirk Jan Klaas Huntelaar, Wesley Sneijder, Georginio Gregion Emile Wijnaldum (Holland), Carlos Yaír Costly Molina (Honduras), Reza Ghoochannejhad Nournia (Iran), Mario Balotelli, Claudio Marchisio (Italy), Keisuke Honda, Shinji Okazaki (Japan), Koo Ja-Cheol, Lee Keun-Ho, Son Heung-Min (Korea Republic), Giovani dos Santos Ramírez, José Andrés Guardado Hernández, Javier Hernández Balcázar, Rafael Márquez Álvarez, Oribe Peralta Morones (Mexico), Peter Osaze Odemwingie (Nigeria), Cristiano Ronaldo dos Santos Aveiro, Luís Carlos Almeida da Cunha „Nani", Silvestre Manuel Gonçalves Varela (Portugal), Aleksandr Kerzhakov, Aleksandr Kokorin (Russia), Juan Manuel Mata García „Juan Mata", Fernando José Torres Sanz, David Villa Sánchez, Xabier Alonso Olano „Xabi Alonso" (Spain), Blerim Džemaili, Admir Mehmedi, Haris Seferović, Granit Xhaka (Switzerland), John Anthony Brooks, Julian Wesley Green, Jermaine Jones (United States), Edinson Roberto Cavani Gómez, Diego Roberto Godín Leal (Uruguay)

Own goals:

5 Sead Kolašinac (Bosnia-Herzegovina), against Argentina
Marcelo Vieira da Silva Júnior (Brazil), against Croatia
John Boye (Ghana), against Portugal
Noel Eduardo Valladares Bonilla (Honduras), against France
Joseph Phillip Yobo (Nigeria), against France

Total number og goals scored: **171**
Average goals per match: **2.67**

LIST OF REFEREES

Name	DOB	Country	M
Djamel Haimoudi	10.12.1970	Algeria	4
Assistants: Rédouane Achik (Morocco), Abdelhalk Etchiali (Algeria)			
Ravshan Irmatov	09.08.1977	Uzbekistan	4
Assistants: Abduhamidullo Rasulov (Uzbekistan), Bahadyr Kochkarov (Kyrgyzstan)			
Néstor Fabián Pitana	17.06.1975	Argentina	4
Assistants: Hernán Maidana (Argentina), Juan Pablo Belatti (Argentina)			
Nicola Rizzoli	05.10.1971	Italy	4
Assistants: Renato Faverani (Italy), Andrea Stefani (Italy)			
Cüneyt Çakır	23.11.1976	Turkey	3
Assistants: Bahattin Duran (Turkey), Tarık Ongun (Turkey)			
Jonas Eriksson	28.03.1974	Sweden	3
Assistants: Mathias Klasenius (Sweden), Daniel Wärnmark (Sweden)			
Mark Geiger	25.08.1974	United States	3
Assistants: Mark Hurd (United States), Joe Fletcher (Canada)			
Björn Kuipers	28.03.1973	Holland	3
Assistants: Sander van Roekel (Holland), Erwin Zeinstra (Holland)			
Pedro Proença Oliveira Alves Garcia	03.11.1970	Portugal	3
Assistants: Bertino Miranda (Portugal), Tiago Trigo (Portugal)			
Sandro Meira Ricci	19.11.1974	Brazil	3
Assistants: Emerson De Carvalho (Brazil), Marcelo Van Gasse (Brazil)			
Marco Antonio Rodríguez Moreno	10.11.1973	Mexico	3
Assistants: Marvin Torrentera (Mexico), Marcos Quintero (Mexico)			
Carlos Velasco Carballo	16.03.1971	Spain	3
Assistants: Roberto Alonso Fernández (Spain), Juan Carlos Yuste Jiménez (Spain)			
Benjamin Jon Williams	14.04.1977	Australia	3
Assistants: Matthew Cream (Australia), Hakan Anaz (Australia)			
Joel Antonio Aguilar Chicas	02.07.1975	El Salvador	2
Assistants: William Torres (El Salvador), Juan Zumba (El Salvador)			
Dr. Felix Brych	03.08.1975	Germany	2
Assistants: Stefan Lupp (Germany), Mark Borsch (Germany)			
Noumandiez Doué	29.09.1970	Côte d'Ivoire	2
Assistants: Songuifolo Yeo (Côte d'Ivoire), Jean-Claude Birumushahu (Burundi)			
Nawaf Abdullah Ghayyath Shukralla	13.10.1976	Bahrain	2
Assistants: Yaser Tulefat (Bahrain), Ebrahim Saleh (Bahrain)			
Milorad Mažić	23.03.1973	Serbia	2
Assistants: Milovan Ristić (Serbia), Dalibor Đurđević (Serbia)			
Enrique Roberto Osses Zencovich	26.05.1974	Chile	2
Assistants: Carlos Astroza (Chile), Sergio Román (Chile)			

Wilmar Alexander Roldán Pérez 24.01.1980 Colombia 2
Assistants: Humberto Clavijo (Colombia), Eduardo Díaz (Colombia)
Carlos Alfredo Vera Rodríguez 25.06.1976 Ecuador 2
Assistants: Christian Lescano (Ecuador), Byron Romero (Ecuador)
Howard Melton Webb 14.07.1971 England 2
Assistants: Michael Mullarkey (England), Darren Cann (England)
Bakary Papa Gassama 10.02.1979 Gambia 1
Assistants: Evarist Menkouande (Cameroon), Félicien Kabanda (Rwanda)
Yuichi Nishimura 17.04.1972 Japan 1
Assistants: Toru Sagara (Japan), Toshiyuki Nagi (Japan)
Peter O'Leary 03.03.1972 New Zealand 1
Assistants: Jan-Hendrik Hintz (New Zealand), Mark Rule (New Zealand)

WORLD CUP SQUADS

ALGERIA

	Name	DOB	Club	M	G
		Goalkeepers			
1	Cédric Si Mohamed	09.01.1985	Club Sportif Constantinois	0	0
16	Mohamed Lamine Zemmamouche	19.03.1985	Union Sportive de la Médina d'Alger	0	0
23	Adi Raïs Cobos Adrien M'Bolhi Ouhab	25.04.1986	PFC CSKA Sofia (BUL)	4	0
		Defenders			
2	Madjid Bougherra	07.10.1982	Lekhwiya SC Doha (QAT)	3	0
3	Faouzi Ghoulam	01.02.1991	SSC Napoli (ITA)	2	0
4	Essaïd Belkalem	01.01.1989	Watford FC (ENG)	3	0
5	Rafik Halliche	02.09.1986	Associação Académica de Coimbra (POR)	4	1
6	Djamel Eddine Mesbah	09.10.1984	AS Livorno Calcio (ITA)	2	0
12	Carl Medjani	15.05.1985	Valenciennes FC	3	0
17	Liassine Cadamuro-Bentaïba	05.03.1988	RCD Mallorca (ESP)	0	0
20	Aïssa Mandi	22.10.1991	Stade de Reims (FRA)	3	0
		Midfielders			
7	Hassan Yebda	14.05.1984	Udinese Calcio (ITA)	1	0
8	Mehdi Gregory Giuseppe Lacen	15.05.1984	Getafe CF (ESP)	3	0
10	Sofiane Feghouli	26.12.1989	Valencia CF (ESP)	4	1
11	Yacine Brahimi	08.02.1990	Granada CF (ESP)	3	1
14	Nabil Bentaleb	24.11.1994	Tottenham Hotspur FC London (ENG)	3	0
18	Abdelmoumene Djabou	31.01.1987	Club Africain Tunis (TUN)	3	2
19	Saphir Sliti Taïder	29.02.1992	FC Internazionale Milano (ITA)	2	0
21	Riyad Mahrez	21.02.1991	Leicester City FC(ENG)	1	0
22	Mehdi Mostefa Sbaa	30.08.1983	AC Ajaccio (FRA)	2	0
		Forwards			
9	Nabil Ghilas	20.04.1990	FC do Porto (POR)	3	0
13	Islam Slimani	18.06.1988	Sporting Clube de Portugal Lisboa (POR)	4	2
15	El Arbi Hillel Soudani	25.11.1987	NK Dinamo Zagreb (CRO)	3	0
		Trainer			
	Vahid Halilhodžić (Bosnia-Herzegovina)	15.10.1952			

ARGENTINA

	Name	DOB	Club	M	G
		Goalkeepers			
1	Sergio Germán Romero	22.02.1987	AS Monaco (FRA)	7	0
12	Agustín Ignacio Orión	26.01.1981	CA Boca Juniors Buenos Aires	0	0
21	Mariano Gonzalo Andújar	30.07.1983	Calcio Catania (ITA)	0	0
		Defenders			
2	Ezequiel Marcelo Garay González	10.10.1986	Sport Lisboa e Benfica (POR)	7	0
3	Hugo Armando Campagnaro	27.06.1980	FC Internazionale Milano (ITA)	1	0
4	Pablo Javier Zabaleta Girod	16.01.1985	Manchester City FC (ENG)	7	0
15	Martín Gastón Demichelis	20.12.1980	Manchester City FC (ENG)	3	0
16	Faustino Marcos Alberto Rojo	20.03.1990	Sporting Clube de Portugal Lisboa (POR)	6	1
17	Federico Fernández	21.02.1989	SSC Napoli (ITA)	4	0
23	José María Basanta Pavone	03.04.1984	CF Monterrey (MEX)	2	0
		Midfielders			
5	Fernando Rubén Gago	10.04.1986	CA Boca Juniors Buenos Aires	6	0
6	Lucas Rodrigo Biglia	30.01.1986	SS Lazio Roma (ITA)	7	0
7	Ángel Fabián di María Hernández	14.02.1988	Real Madrid CF (ESP)	5	1
8	Enzo Nicolás Pérez	22.06.1986	Sport Lisboa e Benfica (POR)	3	0
11	Maximiliano Rubén Rodríguez	02.01.1981	CA Newell's Old Boys	2	0
13	Augusto Matías Fernández	10.04.1986	Real Club Celta de Vigo (ESP)	0	0
14	Javier Alejandro Mascherano	08.06.1984	FC Barcelona (ESP)	7	0
19	Ricardo Gabriel Álvarez	12.04.1988	Internazionale FC Milano (ITA)	1	0
		Forwards			
9	Gonzalo Gerardo Higuaín	10.12.1987	SSC Napoli (ITA)	7	1
10	Lionel Andrés Messi	24.06.1987	FC Barcelona (ESP)	7	4
18	Rodrigo Sebastián Palacio	05.02.1982	FC Internazionale Milano (ITA)	5	0
20	Sergio Leonel Agüero del Castillo	02.06.1988	Manchester City FC (ENG)	5	0
22	Ezequiel Iván Lavezzi	03.05.1985	Paris Saint-Germain FC (FRA)	6	0
		Trainer			
	Alejandro Javier Sabella	05.11.1954			

AUSTRALIA

FOOTBALL
FEDERATION
AUSTRALIA

	Name	DOB	Club	M	G
			Goalkeepers		
1	Mathew David Ryan	08.04.1992	Club Brügge KV (BEL)	3	0
12	Mitchell James Langerak	22.08.1988	BV Borussia Dortmund (GER)	0	0
18	Eugen-Josip Galeković	12.06.1981	Adelaide United FC	0	0
			Defenders		
2	Ivan Frankie Franjić	10.09.1987	Brisbane Roar FC	1	0
3	Jason Alan Davidson	29.06.1991	Heracles Almelo (NED)	3	0
6	Matthew Thomas Špiranović	27.06.1988	Western Sydney Wanderers FC	3	0
8	Bailey Colin Wright	28.07.1992	Preston North End FC (ENG)	0	0
13	Oliver John Bozanić	08.01.1989	FC Luzern (SUI)	2	0
19	Ryan James McGowan	15.08.1989	Shandong Luneng Taishan FC (CHN)	3	0
22	Alexander William Wilkinson	13.08.1984	Jeonbuk Hyundai Motors FC (KOR)	3	0
			Midfielders		
5	Mark Daniel Milligan	04.08.1985	Melbourne Victory FC	1	0
10	Benjamin Halloran	14.06.1992	TSV Fortuna Düsseldorf II (GER)	3	0
11	Thomas Michael Oar	10.12.1991	FC Utrecht (NED)	3	0
14	James Troisi	03.07.1988	Melbourne Victory FC	2	0
15	Michael John Jedinak	03.08.1984	Crystal Palace FC London (ENG)	3	1
16	James Robert Holland	15.05.1989	FK Austria Wien (AUT)	0	0
17	Matthew Graham McKay	11.01.1983	Brisbane Roar FC	2	0
20	Dario Vidošić	08.04.1987	FC Sion (SUI)	0	0
21	Massimo Corey Luongo	25.09.1992	Swindon Town FC (ENG)	0	0
23	Mark Bresciano	11.02.1980	Al-Gharafa Sports Club Al-Rayyan (QAT)	3	0
			Forwards		
4	Timothy Filiga Cahill	06.12.1979	New York Red Bulls (USA)	2	2
7	Mathew Allan Leckie	04.02.1991	FSV Frankfurt (GER)	3	0
9	Adam Jake Taggart	02.06.1993	Newcastle United Jets FC	2	0
			Trainer		
	Angelos "Ange" Postecoglou	27.08.1965			

BELGIUM

	Name	DOB	Club	M	G
		Goalkeepers			
1	Thibaut Nicolas Marc Courtois	11.05.1992	Club Atlético de Madrid (ESP)	5	0
12	Simon Luc Hildebert Mignolet	06.08.1988	Liverpool FC (ENG)	0	0
13	Sammy Andre Bossut	11.08.1985	SV Zulte Waregem	0	0
		Defenders			
2	Tobias Albertine Maurits Alderweireld	02.03.1989	Club Atlético de Madrid (ESP)	4	0
3	Thomas Vermaelen	14.11.1985	Arsenal FC London (ENG)	1	0
4	Vincent Jean Mpoy Kompany	10.04.1986	Manchester City FC (ENG)	4	0
5	Jan Bert Lieve Vertonghen	24.04.1987	Tottenham Hotspur FC London (ENG)	5	1
15	Daniel Van Buyten	7.02.1978	FC Bayern München (GER)	5	0
18	Nicolas Robert Christian Lombaerts	20.03.1985	FK Zenit St. Petersburg (RUS)	1	0
21	Anthony Henri Vanden Borre	24.10.1987	RSC Anderlecht Bruxelles	1	0
23	Laurent Franco Ciman	05.08.1985	R Standard Liège	0	0
		Midfielders			
6	Axel Laurent Angel Lambert Witsel	12.01.1989	FK Zenit St. Petersburg (RUS)	4	0
7	Kevin De Bruyne	28.06.1991	VfL Wolfsburg (GER)	4	1
8	Marouane Abdellatif Fellaini-Bakkioui	22.11.1987	Manchester United FC (ENG)	5	1
10	Eden Michael Hazard	07.01.1991	Chelsea FC London (ENG)	5	0
11	Kevin Antonio Joel Gislain Mirallas y Castillo	05.10.1987	Everton FC Liverpool (ENG)	4	0
16	Steven Arnold Defour	15.04.1988	FC do Porto (POR)	1	0
19	Mousa Sidi Yaya Dembélé	16.07.1987	Tottenham Hotspur FC London (ENG)	2	0
20	Adnan Januzaj	05.02.1995	Manchester United FC (ENG)	1	0
22	Nacer Chadli	02.10.1989	Tottenham Hotspur FC London (ENG)	4	0
		Forwards			
9	Romelu Menama Lukaku	13.05.1993	Everton FC Liverpool (ENG)	4	1
14	Dries Mertens	06.05.1987	SSC Napoli (ITA)	5	1
17	Divock Okoth Origi	18.04.1995	Lille OSC (FRA)	5	1
		Trainer			
	Marc Robert Wilmots	22.02.1969			

BOSNIA-HERZEGOVINA

	Name	DOB	Club	M	G
		Goalkeepers			
1	Asmir Begović	20.06.1987	Stoke City FC (ENG)	3	0
12	Jasmin Fejzić	15.05.1986	VfR Aalen (GER)	0	0
22	Asmir Avdukić	13.05.1981	FK Borac Banja Luka	0	0
		Defenders			
2	Avdija Vršajević	06.03.1986	HNK Hajduk Split (CRO)	1	1
3	Ermin Bičakčić	24.01.1990	TSV Eintracht Braunschweig (GER)	1	0
4	Emir Spahić	18.08.1980	TSV Bayer Leverkusen (GER)	3	0
5	Sead Kolašinac	20.06.1993	FC Schalke 04 Gelsenkirchen (GER)	2	0
6	Ognjen Vranješ	24.10.1989	Elazığspor Kulubü (TUR)	1	0
7	Muhamed Bešić	10.09.1992	Ferencvárosi TC (HUN)	3	0
13	Mensur Mujdža	28.03.1984	SC Freiburg (GER)	2	0
15	Toni Šunjić	15.12.1988	FC Zorya Luhansk (UKR)	2	0
		Midfielders			
8	Miralem Pjanić	02.04.1990	AS Roma (ITA)	3	1
10	Zvjezdan Misimović	05.06.1982	Guizhou Renhe FC (CHN)	2	0
14	Tino-Sven Sušić	13.02.1992	HNK Hajduk Split (CRO)	2	0
16	Senad Lulić	18.01.1986	SS Lazio Roma (ITA)	2	0
17	Senijad Ibričić	26.09.1985	Kayseri Erciyesspor (TUR)	0	0
18	Haris Medunjanin	08.03.1985	Gaziantepspor (TUR)	2	0
20	Izet Hajrović	04.08.1991	Galatasaray SK Istanbul (TUR)	2	0
21	Anel Hadžić	16.08.1989	SK Sturm Graz (AUT)	1	0
23	Sejad Salihović	08.10.1984	TSG 1899 Hoffenheim (GER)	2	0
		Forwards			
9	Vedad Ibišević	06.08.1984	VfB Stuttgart (GER)	3	1
11	Edin Džeko	17.03.1986	Manchester City FC (ENG)	3	1
19	Edin Višća	17.02.1990	İstanbul Başakşehir FK (TUR)	2	0
		Trainer			
	Safet Sušić	13.04.1955			

BRAZIL

	Name	DOB	Club	M	G
		Goalkeepers			
1	Jefferson de Oliveira Galvão	02.01.1983	Botafogo de FR Rio de Janeiro	0	0
12	Júlio César Soares de Espíndola	03.09.1979	Toronto FC (CAN)	7	0
22	Victor Leandro Bagy	21.01.1983	Atlético Mineiro Belo Horizonte	0	0
		Defenders			
2	Daniel Alves da Silva	06.05.1983	FC Barcelona (ESP)	4	0
3	Thiago Emiliano da Silva	22.09.1984	Paris Saint-Germain FC (FRA)	6	1
4	David Luiz Moreira Marinho	22.04.1987	Chelsea FC London (ENG)	7	2
6	Marcelo Vieira da Silva Júnior	12.05.1988	Real Madrid CF (ESP)	6	0
13	Dante Bonfim Costa Santos	18.10.1983	FC Bayern München (GER)	1	0
14	Maxwell Scherrer Cabelino Andrade	27.08.1981	Paris Saint-Germain FC (FRA)	1	0
15	Henrique Adriano Buss "Henrique III"	14.10.1986	SSC Napoli (ITA)	1	0
23	Maicon Douglas Sisenando	26.07.1981	AS Roma (ITA)	3	0
		Midfielders			
5	Fernando Luiz Rosa „Fernandinho“	04.05.1985	Manchester City FC (ENG)	5	1
8	José Paulo Bezerra Maciel Júnior „Paulinho III“	25.07.1988	Tottenham Hotspur FC London (ENG)	6	0
11	Oscar dos Santos Emboaba Júnior	09.09.1991	Chelsea FC London (ENG)	7	2
16	Ramires Santos do Nascimento	24.03.1987	Chelsea FC London (ENG)	7	0
17	Luiz Gustavo Dias	23.07.1987	VfL Wolfsburg (GER)	6	0
18	Anderson Hernanes de Carvalho Andrade Lima	29.05.1985	FC Internazionale Milano (ITA)	3	0
19	Willian Borges da Silva	09.08.1988	Chelsea FC London (ENG)	5	0
20	Bernard Anício Caldeira Duarte	08.09.1992	FK Shakhtar Donetsk (UKR)	3	0
		Forwards			
7	Givanildo Vieira de Souza „Hulk“	25.07.1986	FK Zenit St. Petersburg (RUS)	6	0
9	Frederico Chaves Guedes "Fred"	03.10.1983	Fluminense FC Rio de Janeiro	6	1
10	Neymar da Silva Santos Júnior	05.02.1992	FC Barcelona (ESP)	5	4
21	João Alves de Assis Silva "Jô"	20.03.1987	Atlético Mineiro Belo Horizonte	3	0
		Trainer			
	Luiz Felipe Scolari	09.11.1948			

CAMEROON

	Name	DOB	Club	M	G
		Goalkeepers			
1	Maxime Loïc Feudjou Nguegang	14.04.1992	Coton Sport FC de Garoua	0	0
16	Charles-Hubert Itandje	02.11.1982	Konyaspor Kulübü (TUR)	3	0
23	Sammy N'Djock	25.02.1990	Fethiyespor Kulübü (TUR)	0	0
		Defenders			
2	Benoît Pierre David Assou-Ekotto	24.03.1984	Queen's Park Rangers FC London (ENG)	2	0
3	Nicolas Alexis Julio N'Koulou N'Doubena	27.03.1990	Olympique de Marseille (FRA)	3	0
4	Cédric Djeugoué	28.08.1992	Coton Sport FC de Garoua	1	0
5	Dany Achille Nounkeu Tchounkeu	11.04.1986	Beşiktaş JK Istanbul (TUR)	2	0
12	Henri Bedimo Nsamé	04.06.1984	Olympique Lyonnais (FRA)	1	0
14	Aurélien Bayard Chedjou Fongang	20.06.1985	Galatasaray SK Istanbul (TUR)	2	0
21	Joël Job Matip	08.08.1991	FC Schalke 04 Gelsenkirchen (GER)	2	1
22	Allan-Roméo Nyom	10.05.1988	Granada CF (ESP)	1	0
		Midfielders			
6	Alexandre Dimitri Song Billong	09.09.1987	FC Barcelona (ESP)	2	0
7	Joël Landry Tsafack N'Guémo	28.11.1985	Girondins de Bordeaux (FRA)	1	0
11	Jean II Makoun	29.05.1983	Stade Rennais FC (FRA)	1	0
17	Stéphane Mbia Etoundi	20.05.1986	Sevilla FC (ESP)	3	0
18	Eyong Tarkang Enoh	23.03.1986	Antalyaspor Kulübü (TUR)	3	0
20	Edgar Nicaise Constant Salli	17.08.1992	Racing Club Lens (FRA)	2	0
		Forwards			
8	Benjamin Moukandjo Bilé	12.11.1988	AS Nancy-Lorraine (FRA)	3	0
9	Samuel Eto'o Fils	10.03.1981	Chelsea FC London (ENG)	1	0
10	Vincent Aboubakar	22.01.1992	FC Lorient (FRA)	2	0
13	Jean-Eric Maxim Choupo-Moting	23.03.1989	1.FSV Mainz 05 (GER)	3	0
15	Pierre Achille Webó Kouamo	20.01.1982	Fenerbahçe SK Istanbul (TUR)	3	0
19	Fabrice Olinga Essono	12.05.1996	SV Zulte Waregem (BEL)	0	0
		Trainer			
	Volker Finke (Germany)	24.03.1948			

CHILE

	Name	DOB	Club	M	G
		Goalkeepers			
1	Claudio Andrés Bravo Muñoz	13.04.1983	Real Sociedad de Fútbol San Sebastián (ESP)	4	0
12	Cristopher Benjamín Toselli Ríos	15.06.1988	CD Universidad Católica Santiago	0	0
23	Johnny Cristián Herrera Muñoz	09.05.1981	CF de la Universidad de Chile Santiago	0	0
		Defenders			
2	Eugenio Esteban Mena Reveco	18.07.1988	Santos FC (BRA)	4	0
3	Miiko Martín Albornoz Inola	30.11.1990	Malmö FF (SWE)	0	0
4	Mauricio Aníbal Isla Isla	12.06.1988	Juventus FC Torino (ITA)	4	0
13	José Manuel Rojas Bahamondes	23.06.1983	CF de la Universidad de Chile Santiago	1	0
17	Gary Alexis Medel Soto	03.08.1987	Cardiff City FC (WAL)	4	0
18	Gonzalo Alejandro Jara Reyes	29.08.1985	Nottingham Forest FC (ENG)	4	0
		Midfielders			
5	Francisco Andrés Silva Gajardo	11.02.1986	CA Osasuna Pamplona (ESP)	3	0
6	Carlos Emilio Carmona Tello	21.02.1987	Atalanta Bergamasca Calcio (ITA)	1	0
8	Arturo Erasmo Vidal Pardo	22.05.1987	Juventus FC Torino (ITA)	3	0
10	Jorge Luis Valdivia Toro	19.01.1983	SE Palmeiras São Paulo (BRA)	3	1
15	Jean André Emanuel Beausejour Coliqueo	01.06.1984	Wigan Athletic FC (ENG)	2	1
16	Felipe Alejandro Gutiérrez Leiva	08.10.1990	FC Twente Enschede (NED)	4	0
19	José Pedro Fuenzalida Gana	22.02.1985	CSD Colo-Colo Santiago	0	0
20	Charles Mariano Aránguiz Sandoval	17.04.1989	Udinese Calcio (ITA)	4	1
21	Marcelo Alfonso Díaz Rojas	30.12.1986	FC Basel (SUI)	4	0
		Forwards			
7	Alexis Alejandro Sánchez Sánchez	19.12.1988	FC Barcelona (ESP)	4	2
9	Mauricio Ricardo Pinilla Ferrera	04.02.1984	Cagliari Calcio (ITA)	3	0
11	Eduardo Jesús Vargas Rojas	20.11.1989	Valencia CF (ESP)	4	1
14	Fabián Ariel Orellana Valenzuela	27.01.1986	RC Celta de Vigo (ESP)	0	0
22	Esteban Efraín Paredes Quintanilla	01.08.1980	CSD Colo-Colo Santiago	0	0
		Trainer			
	Jorge Luis Sampaoli Moya (Argentina)	13.03.1960			

COLOMBIA

	Name	DOB	Club	M	G
		Goalkeepers			
1	David Ospina Ramírez	31.08.1988	OGC Nice (FRA)	5	0
12	Camilo Andrés Vargas Gil	01.09.1989	Santa Fé CD Bogotá	0	0
22	Faryd Camilo Mondragón Alí	21.06.1971	Asociación Deportivo Cali	1	0
		Defenders			
2	Cristián Eduardo Zapata Valencia	30.09.1986	Milan AC (ITA)	4	0
3	Mario Alberto Yepes Díaz	13.01.1976	Atalanta Bergamasca Calcio (ITA)	4	0
4	Santiago Arias Naranjo	13.01.1992	PSV Eindhoven (NED)	3	0
7	Pablo Estifer Armero	02.11.1986	West Ham United FC London (ENG)	5	1
16	Éder Fabián Álvarez Balanta	26.02.1993	CA River Plate Buenos Aires (ARG)	1	0
18	Juan Camilo Zúñiga Mosquera	14.12.1986	SSC Napoli (ITA)	4	0
23	Carlos Enrique Valdés Parra	22.05.1985	CA San Lorenzo de Almagro (ARG)	1	0
		Midfielders			
5	Carlos Mario Carbonero Mancilla	25.07.1990	CA River Plate Buenos Aires (ARG)	1	0
6	Carlos Alberto Sánchez Moreno	06.02.1986	Elche CF (ESP)	4	0
8	Abel Enrique Aguilar Tapias	06.01.1985	FC Toulouse (FRA)	3	0
10	James David Rodríguez Rubio	12.07.1991	AS Monaco (FRA)	5	6
11	Juan Guillermo Cuadrado Bello	26.05.1988	AC Fiorentina Firenze (ITA)	5	1
13	Fredy Alejandro Guarín Vásquez	30.06.1986	FC Internazionale Milano (ITA)	3	0
14	Segundo Víctor Ibarbo Guerrero	19.05.1990	Cagliari Calcio (ITA)	3	0
15	Alexander Mejía Sabalza	07.09.1988	CD Atlético Nacional Medellín	4	0
20	Juan Fernando Quintero Paniagua	18.01.1993	FC do Porto (POR)	3	1
		Forwards			
9	Teófilo Antonio Gutiérrez Roncancio	17.05.1985	CA River Plate Buenos Aires (ARG)	4	1
17	Carlos Arturo Bacca Ahumada	31.12.1984	Sevilla FC (ESP)	1	0
19	Gustavo Adrián Ramos Vásquez	22.01.1986	Hertha BSC Berlin (GER)	3	0
21	Jackson Arley Martínez Valencia	03.10.1986	FC do Porto (POR)	3	2
		Trainer			
	José Néstor Pékerman (Argentina)	03.09.1949			

COSTA RICA

	Name	DOB	Club	M	G
		Goalkeepers			
1	Keylor Antonio Navas Gamboa	15.12.1986	Levante UD Valencia (ESP)	5	0
18	Patrick Alberto Pemberton Bernard	24.04.1982	Liga Deportiva Alajuelense	0	0
23	Daniel Arturo Cambronero Solano	08.01.1986	CS Herediano Heredia	0	0
		Defenders			
2	Jhonny Acosta Zamora	21.07.1983	Liga Deportiva Alajuelense	2	0
3	Geancarlo González Castro	08.02.1988	Columbus Crew (USA)	5	0
4	Míchael Umaña Corrales	16.07.1982	CD Saprissa San José	4	0
6	Óscar Esau Duarte Gaitan	03.06.1989	Club Brügge KV (BEL)	4	1
8	David Myrie Medrano	01.06.1988	CS Herediano Heredia	1	0
12	Waylon Dwayne Francis Box	20.09.1990	Columbus Crew (USA)	0	0
15	Júnior Enrique Díaz Campbell	12.09.1983	1. FSV Mainz 05 (GER)	5	0
16	Cristian Esteban Gamboa Luna	24.10.1989	Rosenborg BK Trondheim (NOR)	5	0
19	Roy Miller Hernández	24.11.1984	New York Red Bulls (USA)	1	0
		Midfielders			
5	Celso Borges Mora	27.08.1988	AIK Stockholm (SWE)	5	0
7	Cristian Bolaños Navarro	17.05.1984	FC København (DEN)	5	0
11	Michael Barrantes Rojas	04.10.1983	Ålesunds FK (NOR)	2	0
13	Óscar Esteban Granados Maroto	25.10.1985	CS Herediano Heredia	0	0
17	Yeltsin Ignacio Tejeda Valverde	17.03.1992	CD Saprissa San José	5	0
20	Diego Gerardo Calvo Fonseca	25.03.1991	Vålerenga Fotball Oslo (NOR)	0	0
22	José Miguel Cubero Loria	14.02.1987	CS Herediano Heredia	4	0
		Forwards			
9	Joël Nathaniel Campbell Samuels	10.02.1992	PAE Olympiacos Peiraiás (GRE)	5	1
10	Bryan Jafet Ruíz González	18.08.1985	PSV Eindhoven (NED)	5	2
14	Randall Brenes Moya	12.08.1983	CS Cartaginés Deportiva SA	3	0
21	Marcos Danilo Ureña Porras	05.03.1990	FK Kuban Krasnodar (RUS)	4	1
		Trainer			
	Jorge Luis Pinto Afanador (Colombia)	16.12.1952			

CÔTE D'IVOIRE

	Name	DOB	Club	M	G
		Goalkeepers			
1	Boubacar Barry	30.12.1979	KSC Lokeren Oost-Vlaanderen (BEL)	3	0
16	Guelassiognon Sylvain Gbohouo	29.10.1988	Séwé Sport de San-Pédro	0	0
23	Sayouba Mandé	15.06.1993	Stabæk Fotball (NOR)	0	0
		Defenders			
2	Ousmane Viera Diarrassouba	21.12.1986	Çaykur Rizespor (TUR)	0	0
3	Arthur Etienne Boka	02.04.1983	VfB Stuttgart (GER)	3	0
4	Kolo Habib Touré	19.03.1981	Liverpool FC (ENG)	1	0
5	Alain Didier Zokora Deguy	14.12.1980	Trabzonspor AŞ (TUR)	2	0
7	Jean-Daniel Akpa Akpro	11.10.1992	Toulouse FC (FRA)	0	0
17	Serge Aurier	24.12.1992	Toulouse FC (FRA)	3	0
18	Tohouri Zahoui Constant Djakpa	17.10.1986	SG Eintracht Frankfurt (FRA)	1	0
22	Souleymane Bamba	13.01.1985	Trabzonspor AŞ (TUR)	3	0
		Midfielders			
6	Mathis Gazoa Kippersund Bolly	14.11.1990	TSV Fortuna Düsseldorf (GER)	1	0
8	Salomon Armand Magloire Kalou	05.08.1985	Lille OSC (FRA)	3	0
9	Cheik Ismael Tioté	21.06.1986	Newcastle United FC (ENG)	3	0
14	Ismaël Tiémoko Diomandé	28.08.1992	AS Saint-Étienne (FRA)	1	0
19	Gnégnéri Yaya Touré	13.05.1983	Manchester City FC (ENG)	3	0
20	Sereso Geoffroy Gonzaroua Die „Serey Die"	07.11.1984	FC Basel (SUI)	3	0
		Forwards			
10	Gervais Yao Kouassi „Gervinho"	27.05.1987	AS Roma (ITA)	3	2
11	Didier Yves Drogba Tébily	11.03.1978	Galatasaray SK Istanbul (TUR)	3	0
12	Wilfried Guemiand Bony	10.12.1988	Swansea City AFC (WAL)	3	2
13	Didier Ya Konan	22.05.1984	Hannover'96 (GER)	1	0
15	Max-Alain Gradel	30.11.1987	AS Saint-Étienne (FRA)	1	0
21	Giovanni-Guy Yann Sio	31.03.1989	FC Basel (SUI)	1	0
		Trainer			
	Sabri Lamouchi (France)	09.11.1971			

CROATIA

	Name	DOB	Club	M	G
		Goalkeepers			
1	Stipe Pletikosa	08.01.1979	FK Rostov (RUS)	3	0
12	Oliver Zelenika	14.05.1993	NK Lokomotiva Zagreb	0	0
23	Danijel Subašić	27.10.1984	AS Monaco (FRA)	0	0
		Defenders			
2	Šime Vrsaljko	10.01.1992	Genoa CFC (ITA)	2	0
3	Danijel Pranjić	02.12.1981	Panathinaikos AO Athína (GRE)	2	0
5	Vedran Ćorluka	05.02.1986	FK Lokomotiv Moskva (RUS)	3	0
6	Dejan Lovren	05.07.1989	Southampton FC (ENG)	3	0
11	Darijo Srna	01.05.1982	FC Shakhtar Donetsk (UKR)	3	0
13	Gordon Schildenfeld	18.03.1985	Panathinaikos AO Athína (GRE)	0	0
21	Domagoj Vida	29.04.1989	FC Dynamo Kyiv (UKR)	0	0
		Midfielders			
4	Ivan Perišić	02.02.1989	VfL Wolfsburg (GER)	3	2
7	Ivan Rakitić	10.03.1988	Sevilla FC (ESP)	3	0
8	Ognjen Vukojević	20.12.1983	FC Dynamo Kyiv (UKR)	0	0
10	Luka Modrić	09.09.1985	Real Madrid CF (ESP)	3	0
14	Marcelo Brozović	16.10.1992	NK Dinamo Zagreb	1	0
15	Milan Badelj	25.02.1989	Hamburger SV (GER)	0	0
19	Jorge Sammir Cruz Campos	23.04.1987	Getafe CF	1	0
20	Mateo Kovačić	06.05.1994	FC Internazionale Milano (ITA)	3	0
		Forwards			
9	Nikica Jelavić	27.08.1985	Hull City AFC (ENG)	2	0
16	Ante Rebić	21.09.1993	AC Fiorentina (ITA)	3	0
17	Mario Mandžukić	21.05.1986	FC Bayern München (GER)	2	2
18	Ivica Olić	14.09.1979	VfL Wolfsburg (GER)	3	1
22	Eduardo Alves da Silva	25.02.1983	FC Shakhtar Donetsk (UKR)	1	0
		Trainer			
	Niko Kovač	15.10.1971			

ECUADOR

	Name	DOB	Club	M	G
		Goalkeepers			
1	Máximo Orlando Banguera Valdivieso	16.12.1985	Barcelona SC Guayaquil	0	0
12	Adrián Javier Bone Sánchez	08.09.1988	CD El Nacional Quito	0	0
22	Alexander Domínguez Carabalí	05.06.1987	LDU de Quito	3	0
		Defenders			
2	Jorge Daniel Guagua Tamayo	28.09.1981	CS Emelec Guayaquil	3	0
3	Frickson Rafael Erazo Vivero	05.05.1988	CR Flamengo Rio de Janeiro (BRA)	3	0
4	Juan Carlos Paredes Reasco	08.07.1987	Barcelona SC Guayaquil	3	0
10	Walter Orlando Ayoví Corozo	11.08.1979	CF Pachuca (MEX).	3	0
18	Óscar Dalmiro Bagüí Angulo	10.12.1982	CS Emelec Guayaquil	0	0
21	Gabriel Eduardo Achilier Zurita	24.03.1985	CS Emelec Guayaquil	2	0
		Midfielders			
5	Alex Renato Ibarra Mina	20.01.1991	SBV Vitesse Arnhem (NED).	1	0
6	Christian Fernando Noboa Tello	09.04.1985	FK Dinamo Moskva (RUS)	3	0
7	Jefferson Antonio Montero Vite	01.09.1989	CA Monarcas Morelia (MEX).	3	0
8	Édison Vicente Méndez Méndez	16.03.1979	Independiente Santa Fe Bogotá (COL)	1	0
9	Joao Robin Rojas Mendoza	14.07.1989	Cruz Azul FC C. de México (MEX)	1	0
14	Tilson Oswaldo Minda Suscal	26.07.1983	CD Chivas Carson (USA)	2	0
15	Michael Antonio Arroyo Mina	23.04.1987	CF Atlante Cancún (MEX)	2	0
16	Luis Antonio Valencia Mosquera	04.08.1985	Manchester United FC (ENG)	3	0
19	Luis Fernando Saritama Padilla	20.10.1983	Barcelona SC Guayaquil	0	0
20	Fidel Francisco Martínez Tenorio	15.02.1990	Club Tijuana (MEX)	0	0
23	Carlos Armando Gruezo Arboleda	19.04.1995	VfB Stuttgart (GER)	2	0
		Forwards			
11	Felipe Salvador Caicedo Corozo	05.09.1988	Al-Jazira SCC Abu Dhabi (UAE)	3	0
13	Enner Remberto Valencia Lastra	11.04.1989	CF Pachuca (MEX)	3	3
17	Jaime Javier Ayoví Corozo	21.02.1988	Club Tijuana (MEX)	0	0
		Trainer			
	Reinaldo Rueda Rivera (Colombia)	16.04.1957			

ENGLAND

	Name	DOB	Club	M	G
		Goalkeepers			
1	Charles Joseph John Hart	19.04.1987	Manchester City FC	2	0
13	Ben Anthony Foster	03.05.1983	West Bromwich Albion FC	1	0
22	Fraser Gerard Forster	17.03.1988	Celtic Glasgow FC (SCO)	0	0
		Defenders			
2	Glen McLeod Cooper Johnson	23.08.1984	Liverpool FC	2	0
3	Leighton John Baines	11.12.1984	Everton FC Liverpool	2	0
5	Gary James Cahill	19.12.1985	Chelsea FC London	3	0
6	Philip Nikodem Jagielka	17.08.1982	Everton FC Liverpool	2	0
12	Christopher Lloyd Smalling	22.11.1989	Manchester United FC	1	0
16	Philip Anthony Jones	21.02.1992	Manchester United FC	1	0
23	Luke Paul Hoare Shaw	12.07.1995	Southampton FC	1	0
		Midfielders			
4	Steven George Gerrard	30.05.1980	Liverpool FC	3	0
7	Jack Andrew Garry Wilshere	1.01.1992	Arsenal FC London	2	0
8	Frank James Lampard	20.06.1978	Chelsea FC London	1	0
14	Jordan Brian Henderson	17.06.1990	Liverpool FC	2	0
15	Alexander Mark David Oxlade-Chamberlain	15.08.1993	Arsenal FC London	0	0
17	James Philip Milner	04.01.1986	Manchester City FC	1	0
19	Raheem Shaquille Sterling	08.12.1994	Liverpool FC	3	0
20	Adam David Lallana	10.05.1988	Southampton FC	3	0
21	Ross Barkley	05.12.1993	Everton FC Liverpool	3	0
		Forwards			
9	Daniel Andre Sturridge	01.09.1989	Liverpool FC	3	1
10	Wayne Mark Rooney	24.10.1985	Manchester United FC	3	1
11	Daniel Nii Tackie Mensah Welbeck	26.11.1990	Manchester United FC	2	0
18	Rickie Lee Lambert	16.02.1982	Southampton FC	1	0
		Trainer			
	Roy Hodgson	09.08.1947			

FRANCE

	Name	DOB	Club	M	G
		Goalkeepers			
1	Hugo Lloris	26.12.1986	Tottenham Hotspur FC London (ENG)	5	0
16	Stéphane Ruffier	27.09.1986	AS Saint-Étienne	0	0
23	Mickaël Vincent André-Marie Landreau	14.05.1979	Sporting Club de Bastia	0	0
		Defenders			
2	Mathieu Debuchy	28.07.1985	Newcastle United FC London (ENG)	4	0
3	Patrice Latyr Evra	15.05.1981	Manchester United FC (ENG)	4	0
4	Raphaël Varane	25.04.1993	Real Madrid CF (ESP)	5	0
5	Mamadou Sakho	13.02.1990	Liverpool FC (ENG)	4	0
13	Eliaquim Mangala	13.02.1991	FC do Porto (POR)	0	0
15	Bacary Sagna	14.02.1983	Arsenal FC London (ENG)	1	0
17	Lucas Digne	20.07.1993	Paris Saint-Germain FC	1	0
21	Laurent Koscielny	10.09.1985	Arsenal FC London (ENG)	4	0
		Midfielders			
6	Yohan Cabaye	14.01.1986	Paris Saint-Germain FC	4	0
7	Rémy Cabella	08.03.1990	Montpellier Hérault SC	0	0
8	Mathieu Valbuena	28.09.1984	Olympique de Marseille	4	1
11	Antoine Griezmann	21.03.1991	Real Sociedad de Fútbol San Sebastián (ESP)	5	0
12	Rio Antonio Zoba Mavuba	08.03.1984	Lille OSC	1	0
14	Blaise Matuidi	09.04.1987	Paris Saint-Germain FC	5	1
18	Moussa Sissoko	16.08.1989	Newcastle United FC (ENG)	4	1
19	Paul Labile Pogba	15.03.1993	Juventus FC Torino (ITA)	5	1
22	Morgan Schneiderlin	08.11.1989	Southampton FC (ENG)	1	0
		Forwards			
9	Olivier Giroud	30.09.1986	Arsenal FC London (ENG)	5	1
10	Karim Mostafa Benzema	19.12.1987	Real Madrid CF (ESP)	5	3
20	Loïc Rémy	02.01.1987	Newcastle United FC (ENG)	2	0
		Trainer			
	Didier Claude Deschamps	15.10.1968			

GERMANY

★★★★

	Name	DOB	Club	M	G
		Goalkeepers			
1	Manuel Peter Neuer	27.03.1986	FC Bayern München	7	0
12	Ron-Robert Zieler	12.02.1989	Hannover'96	0	0
22	Roman Weidenfeller	06.08.1980	BV Borussia Dortmund	0	0
		Defenders			
2	Kevin Großkreutz	19.07.1988	BV Borussia Dortmund	0	0
3	Matthias Lukas Ginter	19.01.1994	SC Freiburg	0	0
4	Benedikt Höwedes	29.02.1988	FC Schalke 04 Gelsenkirchen	7	0
5	Mats Julian Hummels	16.12.1988	BV Borussia Dortmund	6	2
15	Erik Durm	12.05.1992	BV Borussia Dortmund	0	0
16	Philipp Lahm	11.11.1983	FC Bayern München	7	0
17	Per Mertesacker	29.09.1984	Arsenal FC London (ENG)	6	0
20	Jérôme Agyenim Boateng	03.09.1988	FC Bayern München	7	0
21	Shkodran Mustafi	17.04.1992	UC Sampdoria Genova (ITA)	3	0
		Midfielders			
6	Sami Khedira	04.04.1987	Real Madrid CF (ESP)	5	1
7	Bastian Schweinsteiger	01.08.1984	FC Bayern München	6	0
8	Mesut Özil	15.10.1988	Arsenal FC London (ENG)	7	1
9	André Horst Schürrle	06.11.1990	Chelsea FC London (ENG)	6	3
10	Lukas Josef Podolski	04.06.1985	Arsenal FC London (ENG)	2	0
13	Thomas Müller	13.09.1989	FC Bayern München	7	5
14	Julian Draxler	20.09.1993	FC Schalke 04 Gelsenkirchen	1	0
18	Toni Kroos	04.01.1990	FC Bayern München	7	2
19	Mario Götze	03.06.1992	FC Bayern München	6	2
23	Christoph Kramer	19.02.1991	VfL Borussia Mönchengladbach	3	0
		Forwards			
11	Miroslav Josef Klose	09.06.1978	SS Lazio Roma (ITA)	5	2
		Trainer			
	Joachim Löw	03.02.1960			

GHANA

	Name	DOB	Club	M	G
		Goalkeepers			
1	Stephen Adams	28.09.1989	Aduana Stars FC Dormaa Ahenkro	0	0
12	Adambathia Larsen Kwarasey	12.12.1987	Strømsgodset IF Drammen (NOR)	1	0
16	Abdul Fatawu Dauda	06.04.1985	Orlando Pirates FC Johannesburg (RSA)	2	0
		Defenders			
2	Samuel Diadie Inkoom	01.06.1989	AO Platania Chanion (GRE)	0	0
4	Daniel Tawiah Opare	18.10.1990	R Standard Liège (BEL)	1	0
15	Rashid Sumaila	18.12.1992	Mamelodi Sundowns FC (RSA)	0	0
19	Jonathan Mensah	13.07.1990	Evian Thonon Gaillard FC (FRA)	3	0
21	John Boye	23.04.1987	Stade Rennais FC (FRA)	3	0
23	Harrison Afful	24.06.1986	Espérance Sportive de Tunis (TUN)	2	0
		Midfielders			
5	Michael Kojo Essien	03.12.1982	Milan AC (ITA)	1	0
6	Ebenezer Afriyie Acquah	05.01.1992	Parma FC (ITA)	1	0
7	Christian Atsu Twasam	10.01.1992	SBV Vitesse Arnhem (NED)	3	0
8	Emmanuel Agyemang-Badu	02.12.1990	Udinese Calcio (ITA)	2	0
9	Kevin-Prince Boateng	6.03.1987	FC Schalke 04 Gelsenkirchen (GER)	2	0
10	André Morgan Rami Ayew	17.12.1989	Olympique de Marseille (FRA)	3	2
11	Sulleyman Ali Muntari	27.08.1984	Milan AC (ITA)	2	0
14	Albert Danquah Adomah	13.12.1987	Middlesbrough FC (ENG)	1	0
17	Mohammed Rabiu Alhassan	31.12.1989	FK Kuban Krasnodar (RUS)	3	0
20	Kwadwo Asamoah	09.12.1988	Juventus FC Torino (ITA)	3	0
22	Wakaso Mubarak	25.07.1990	FK Rubin Kazan (RUS)	2	0
		Forwards			
3	Asamoah Gyan	22.11.1985	Al-Ain Sports and Cultural Club (UAE)	3	2
13	Jordan Pierre Ayew	11.09.1991	FC Sochaux-Montbéliard (FRA)	3	0
18	Majeed Abdul Waris	19.09.1991	Valenciennes FC (FRA)	1	0
		Trainer			
	James Kwesi Appiah	30.06.1960			

GREECE

	Name	DOB	Club	M	G
		Goalkeepers			
1	Orestis-Spyridon Karnezis	11.07.1985	Granada CF (ESP)	4	0
12	Panagiotis Georgios Glykos	03.06.1986	PAOK Thessaloníki	1	0
13	Stefanos Kapino	18.03.1994	Panathinaïkos AO Athína	0	0
		Defenders			
3	Giorgos Tzavellas	26.11.1987	PAOK Thessaloníki	0	0
4	Konstantinos Manolas	14.06.1991	PAE Olympiacos Athína	4	0
5	Vangelis Moras	26.08.1981	Hellas Verona FC (ITA)	0	0
11	Loukas Vyntra	05.02.1981	Levante UD Valencia (ESP)	0	0
15	Vasileios Torosidis	10.06.1985	AS Roma (ITA)	4	0
19	Sokratis Papastathopoulos	09.06.1988	BV Borussia Dortmund (GER)	4	1
20	José LIoyd Holebas	27.06.1984	PAE Olympiacos Athína	4	0
		Midfielders			
2	Giánnis Maniatis	12.10.1986	PAE Olympiacos Athína	4	0
6	Alexandros Tziolis	13.02.1985	Kayserispor (TUR)	0	0
8	Panagiotis Giórgos Kone	26.07.1987	Bologna FC (ITA)	3	0
10	Giórgos Karagounis	06.03.1977	Fulham FC London (ENG)	4	0
16	Lazaros Christodoulopoulos	19.12.1986	Bologna FC (ITA)	2	0
18	Giánnis Fetfatzidis	21.12.1990	Genoa CFC (ITA)	2	0
21	Konstantinos Katsouranis	21.06.1979	PAOK Thessaloníki	3	0
22	Andreas Samaris	13.06.1989	PAE Olympiacos Athína	2	1
23	Panagiotis Tachtsidis	15.02.1991	Torino FC (ITA)	0	0
		Forwards			
7	Giórgos Samaras	21.02.1985	Celtic Glasgow FC (SCO)	4	1
9	Konstantinos Mitroglou	12.03.1988	Fulham FC London (ENG)	3	0
14	Dimitrios Salpingidis	18.08.1981	PAOK Thessaloníki	4	0
17	Theofanis Gekas	23.05.1980	Konyaspor Kulübü (TUR)	4	0
		Trainer			
	Fernando Manuel Costa Santos (Portugal)	10.10.1954			

HOLLAND

	Name	DOB	Club	M	G
		Goalkeepers			
1	Jasper Cillessen	22.04.1989	AFC Ajax Amsterdam	7	0
22	Michel Armand Vorm	03.10.1983	Swansea City AFC (WAL)	1	0
23	Timothy Michael Krul	03.04.1988	Newcastle United FC (ENG)	1	0
		Defenders			
2	Ron Peter Vlaar	16.02.1985	Aston Villa FC Birmingham (ENG)	7	0
3	Stefan de Vrij	05.02.1992	Feyenoord Rotterdam	7	1
4	Rolando Maximiliano Martins Indi	08.02.1992	Feyenoord Rotterdam	6	0
5	Daley Blind	09.03.1990	AFC Ajax Amsterdam	7	1
7	Daryl Janmaat	22.07.1989	Feyenoord Rotterdam	5	0
12	Paul Johannes Gerardus Verhaegh	01.09.1983	FC Augsburg (GER)	1	0
13	Joël Ivo Veltman	15.01.1992	AFC Ajax Amsterdam	2	0
14	Terence Kongolo	14.02.1994	Feyenoord Rotterdam	1	0
		Midfielders			
6	Nigel de Jong	13.11.1984	Milan AC (ITA)	5	0
8	Jonathan Alexander de Guzmán	13.09.1987	Swansea City AFC (WAL)	3	0
10	Wesley Sneijder	09.06.1984	Galatasaray SK İstanbul (TUR)	6	1
16	Jordy Clasie	27.06.1991	Feyenoord Rotterdam	2	0
18	Leroy Johan Fer	05.01.1990	Norwich City FC (ENG)	1	1
20	Georginio Gregion Emile Wijnaldum	11.11.1990	PSV Eindhoven	7	1
		Forwards			
9	Robin van Persie	06.08.1983	Manchester United FC (ENG)	6	4
11	Arjen Robben	23.01.1984	FC Bayern München (GER)	7	3
15	Dirk Kuijt	22.07.1980	Fenerbahçe SK İstanbul (TUR)	5	0
17	Jeremain Marciano Lens	24.11.1987	FC Dynamo Kyiv (UKR)	4	0
19	Dirk Jan Klaas Huntelaar	12.08.1983	FC Schalke 04 Gelsenkirchen (GER)	3	1
21	Memphis Depay	13.02.1994	PSV Eindhoven	4	2
		Trainer			
	Aloysius "Louis" Paulus Maria van Gaal	08.08.1951			

HONDURAS

	Name	DOB	Club	M	G
		Goalkeepers			
1	Luis Aurelio López Fernández	13.09.1993	Real CD España San Pedro Sula	0	0
18	Noel Eduardo Valladares Bonilla	03.05.1977	CD Olimpia Tegucigalpa	3	0
22	Donis Salatiel Escober Izaguirre	03.02.1980	CD Olimpia Tegucigalpa	0	0
		Defenders			
2	Osman Danilo Chávez Guity	29.07.1984	Qingdao Jonoon FC (CHN)	1	0
3	Maynor Alexis Figueroa Róchez	02.05.1983	Hull City AFC (ENG)	3	0
4	Juan Pablo Montes Montes	26.10.1985	CD Motagua Tegucigalpa	0	0
5	Víctor Salvador Bernárdez Blanco	24.05.1982	San José Earthquakes (USA)	3	0
6	Juan Carlos García Álvarez	08.03.1988	Wigan Athletic FC (ENG)	2	0
7	Emilio Arturo Izaguirre Girón	10.05.1986	Celtic Glasgow FC (SCO)	2	0
21	Brayan Antonio Beckeles	28.11.1985	CD Olimpia Tegucigalpa	3	0
		Midfielders			
8	Wilson Roberto Palacios Suazo	29.07.1984	Stoke City FC (ENG)	2	0
10	Mario Roberto Martínez Hernández	30.07.1989	Real CD España San Pedro Sula	1	0
12	Edder Gerardo Delgado Zerón	20.11.1986	Real CD España San Pedro Sula	0	0
14	Oscar Boniek García Ramírez	04.09.1984	Houston Dynamo (USA)	3	0
15	Roger Aníbal Espinoza Ramírez	25.10.1986	Wigan Athletic FC (ENG)	3	0
17	Andy Najar Rodríguez	16.03.1993	RSC Anderlecht Bruxelles (BEL)	2	0
19	Luis Fernando Garrido	05.11.1990	CD Olimpia Tegucigalpa	2	0
20	Jorge Aarón Claros Juárez	08.01.1986	CD Motagua Tegucigalpa	3	0
23	Marvin Antonio Chávez	03.11.1983	CD Chivas Carson (USA)	2	0
		Forwards			
9	Jerry Nelson Palacios Suazo	13.05.1982	LD Alajuelense (CRC)	1	0
11	Jerry Ricardo Bengtson Bodden	08.04.1987	New England Revolution (USA)	3	0
13	Carlos Yaír Costly Molina	18.07.1982	Real CD España San Pedro Sula	3	1
16	Rony Darío Martínez Alméndarez	16.10.1988	CD Real Sociedad Tocoa	0	0
		Trainer			
	Luis Fernando Suárez (Colombia)	23.12.1959			

IRAN

	Name	DOB	Club	M	G
		Goalkeepers			
1	Rahman Ahmadi	30.07.1980	Sepahan Esfahan FC	0	0
12	Alireza Haghighi	02.05.1988	Sporting Clube da Covilhã (POR)	3	0
22	Daniel Davari	06.01.1988	TSV Eintracht Braunschweig (GER)	0	0
		Defenders			
4	Seyed Jalal Hosseini Khoshkebejari	03.02.1982	Persepolis Tehran FC	3	0
5	Amir Hossein Sadeghi	06.09.1981	Esteghlal Tehran FC	3	0
13	Hossein Mahini	16.09.1986	Persepolis Tehran FC	0	0
15	Pejman Montazeri	06.09.1983	Umm Salal SC (QAT)	3	0
17	Seyed Ahmad Alenemeh	20.10.1982	Naft Tehran FC	0	0
19	Mohammad-Hashem Beikzadeh	22.01.1984	Esteghlal Tehran FC	0	0
20	Steven Mehrdad Beitashour	01.02.1987	Vancouver Whitecaps FC (CAN)	0	0
23	Mehrdad Pooladi	26.02.1987	Persepolis Tehran FC	3	0
		Midfielders			
2	Khosro Heydari	14.09.1983	Esteghlal Tehran FC	3	0
3	Ehsan Hajsafi	25.02.1990	Sepahan Esfahan FC	3	0
6	Javad Nekounam	07.09.1980	Kuwait SC Kaifan (KUW)	3	0
7	Masoud Soleimani Shojaei	09.06.1984	UD Las Palmas (ESP)	3	0
8	Reza Haghighi Shandiz	31.01.1989	Persepolis Tehran FC	1	0
9	Alireza Jahanbakhsh Jirandeh	11.08.1993	NEC Nijmegen (NED)	3	0
11	Ghasem Haddadifar	12.07.1983	Zob Ahan FC Eshafan	0	0
14	Andranik Teymourian	06.03.1983	Esteghlal Tehran FC	3	0
18	Bakhtiar Rahmani	22.11.1991	Foolad Khuzestan FC Ahvaz	0	0
21	Seyed Ashkan Dejagah	05.06.1986	Fulham FC London (ENG)	3	0
		Forwards			
10	Karim Ansarifard	03.04.1990	Tractor Sazi FC Tabriz	1	0
16	Reza Ghoochannejhad Nournia	20.09.1987	Charlton Athletic FC London (ENG)	3	1

	Trainer	
Carlos Manuel Brito Leal Queiroz (Portugal)	01.03.1953	

ITALY

	Name	DOB	Club	M	G
		Goalkeepers			
1	Gianluigi Buffon	28.01.1978	Juventus FC Torino	2	0
12	Salvatore Sirigu	12.01.1987	Paris Saint-Germain FC (FRA)	1	0
13	Mattia Perin	10.11.1992	Genoa CFC	0	0
		Defenders			
2	Mattia De Sciglio	20.10.1992	Milan AC	1	0
3	Giorgio Chiellini	14.08.1984	Juventus FC Torino	3	0
4	Matteo Darmian	02.12.1989	Torino FC	3	0
7	Ignazio Abate	12.11.1986	Milan AC	1	0
15	Andrea Barzagli	08.05.1981	Juventus FC Torino	3	0
19	Leonardo Bonucci	01.05.1987	Juventus FC Torino	1	0
20	Gabriel Paletta	15.02.1986	Parma FC	1	0
		Midfielders			
5	Thiago Motta	28.08.1982	Paris Saint-Germain FC (FRA)	3	0
6	Antonio Candreva	28.02.1987	SS Lazio Roma	2	0
8	Claudio Marchisio	19.01.1986	Juventus FC Torino	3	1
14	Alberto Aquilani	07.07.1984	AC Fiorentina	0	0
16	Daniele De Rossi	24.07.1983	AS Roma	2	0
18	Marco Parolo	25.01.1985	Parma FC	2	0
21	Andrea Pirlo	19.05.1979	Juventus FC Torino	3	0
23	Marco Verratti	05.11.1992	Paris Saint-Germain FC (FRA)	2	0
		Forwards			
9	Mario Balotelli	12.08.1990	Milan AC	3	1
10	Antonio Cassano	12.07.1982	Parma FC	2	0
11	Alessio Cerci	23.07.1987	Torino FC	1	0
17	Ciro Immobile	20.02.1990	Torino FC	2	0
22	Lorenzo Insigne	04.06.1991	SSC Napoli	1	0
		Trainer			
	Cesare Claudio Prandelli	19.08.1957			

JAPAN

	Name	DOB	Club	M	G
		Goalkeepers			
1	Eiji Kawashima	20.03.1983	R Standard Liège (BEL)	3	0
12	Shūsaku Nishikawa	18.06.1986	Urawa Red Diamonds	0	0
23	Shūichi Gonda	03.03.1989	Tokyo FC	0	0
		Defenders			
2	Atsuto Uchida	27.03.1988	FC Schalke 04 Gelsenkirchen (GER)	3	0
3	Gōtoku Sakai	14.03.1991	VfB Stuttgart (GER)	0	0
5	Yuto Nagatomo	12.09.1986	Internazionale FC Milano (ITA)	3	0
6	Masato Morishige	21.05.1987	FC Tokyo	1	0
15	Yasuyuki Konno	25.01.1983	Gamba Osaka	2	0
19	Masahiko Inoha	28.08.1985	Júbilo Iwata	0	0
21	Hiroki Sakai	12.04.1990	Hannover'96 (GER)	0	0
22	Maya Yoshida	24.08.1988	Southampton FC (ENG)	3	0
		Midfielders			
4	Keisuke Honda	13.06.1986	Milan AC (ITA)	3	1
7	Yasuhito Endō	28.01.1980	Gamba Osaka	2	0
8	Hiroshi Kiyotake	12.11.1989	1.FC Nürnberg (GER)	1	0
10	Shinji Kagawa	17.03.1989	Manchester United FC (ENG)	3	0
11	Yojiro Takahagi	03.01.1990	Sanfrecce Hiroshima FC	2	0
14	Toshihiro Aoyama	22.02.1986	Sanfrecce Hiroshima FC	1	0
16	Hotaru Yamaguchi	06.10.1990	Cerezo Osaka	3	0
17	Makoto Hasebe	18.01.1984	1.FC Nürnberg (GER)	3	0
20	M. Saitō	04.04.1990	Yokohama F. Marinos	0	0
		Forwards			
9	Shinji Okazaki	16.04.1986	1.FSV Mainz 05 (GER)	3	1
13	Yoshito Ōkubo	09.06.1982	Kawasaki Frontale	3	0
18	Yuya Osako	18.05.1990	TSV 1860 München (GER)	2	0
		Trainer			
	Alberto Zaccheroni (Italy)	01.04.1953			

KOREA REPUBLIC

	Name	DOB	Club	M	G
		Goalkeepers			
1	Jung Sung-Ryong	04.01.1985	Suwon Samsung Bluewings FC	2	0
21	Kim Seung-Gyu	30.09.1990	Ulsan Hyundai Horang-i	1	0
23	Lee Bum-Young	02.04.1989	Busan I'Park	0	0
		Defenders			
2	Kim Chang-Soo	12.09.1985	Kashiwa Reysol (JPN)	0	0
3	Yoon Suk-Young	13.02.1990	Queen's Park Rangers FC London (ENG)	3	0
4	Kwak Tae-Hwi	08.07.1981	Al Hilal FC Riyadh (KSA)	0	0
5	Kim Young-Gwon	27.02.1990	Guangzhou Evergrande FC (CHN)	3	0
6	Hwang Seok-Ho	27.06.1989	Sanfrecce Hiroshima (JPN)	1	0
12	Lee Yong	24.12.1986	Ulsan Hyundai FC	3	0
20	Hong Jeong-Ho	12.08.1989	FC Augsburg (GER)	3	0
22	Park Joo-Ho	16.01.1987	1.FSV Mainz 05 (GER)	0	0
		Midfielders			
7	Kim Bo-Kyung	06.10.1989	Cardiff City FC (WAL)	2	0
8	Ha Dae-Sung	02.03.1985	Beijing Guoan FC (CHN)	0	0
13	Koo Ja-Cheol	27.02.1989	1.FSV Mainz 05 (GER)	3	1
14	Han Kook-Young	19.04.1990	Kashiwa Reysol (JPN)	3	0
15	Park Jong-Woo	10.03.1989	Busan I'Park	0	0
16	Ki Sung-Yueng	24.01.1989	Sunderland AFC (ENG)	3	0
17	Lee Chung-Yong	02.07.1988	Bolton Wanderers FC (ENG)	3	0
		Forwards			
9	Son Heung-Min	08.07.1992	TSV Bayer 04 Leverkusen (GER)	3	1
10	Park Chu-Young	10.07.1985	Watford FC (ENG)	2	0
11	Lee Keun-Ho	11.04.1985	Sangju Sangmu Phoenix FC	3	1
18	Kim Shin-Wook	14.04.1988	Ulsan Hyundai Horang-i	2	0
19	Ji Dong-Won	28.05.1991	FC Augsburg (GER)	2	0
		Trainer			
Hong Myung-Bo		12.02.1969			

MEXICO

	Name	DOB	Club	M	G
		Goalkeepers			
1	José de Jesús Corona Rodríguez	26.01.1981	Cruz Azul FC Ciudad de México	0	0
12	Alfredo Talavera Díaz	18.09.1982	Deportivo Toluca FC	0	0
13	Francisco Guillermo Ochoa Magaña	13.07.1985	AC Ajaccio (FRA)	4	0
		Defenders			
2	Francisco Javier Rodríguez Pinedo	20.10.1981	CF América Ciudad de México	4	0
3	Carlos Arnoldo Salcido Flores	02.04.1980	CF Tigres de la UA de Nuevo León	2	0
4	Rafael Márquez Álvarez	13.02.1979	Club León FC	4	1
7	Miguel Arturo Layún Prado	25.06.1988	CF América Ciudad de México	4	0
15	Héctor Alfredo Moreno Herrera	17.01.1988	RCD Espanyol Barcelona (ESP)	4	0
16	Miguel Ángel Ponce Briseño	12.04.1989	Deportivo Toluca FC	0	0
22	Paul Nicolás Aguilar Rojas	06.03.1986	CF América Ciudad de México	4	0
		Midfielders			
5	Diego Antonio Reyes Rosales	19.09.1992	FC do Porto (POR)	1	0
6	Héctor Miguel Herrera López	19.04.1990	FC do Porto (POR)	4	0
8	Marco Jhonfai Fabián de la Mora	21.07.1989	Cruz Azul FC Ciudad de México	3	0
18	José Andrés Guardado Hernández	28.09.1986	TSV Bayer 04 Leverkusen (GER)	4	1
20	Javier Ignacio Aquino Carmona	11.02.1990	Villarreal CF (ESP)	1	0
21	Carlos Alberto Peña Rodríguez	29.03.1990	Club León FC	1	0
23	José Juan Vázquez Gómez	14.03.1988	Club León FC	3	0
		Forwards			
9	Raúl Alonso Jiménez Rodríguez	05.05.1991	CF América Ciudad de México	1	0
10	Giovani dos Santos Ramírez	11.05.1989	Villarreal CF (ESP)	4	1
11	Alan Pulido Izaguirre	08.03.1991	CF Tigres de la UA de Nuevo León	0	0
14	Javier Hernández Balcázar	01.06.1988	Manchester United FC (ENG)	4	1
17	Isaác Brizuela Muñoz	28.08.1990	Deportivo Toluca FC	0	0
19	Oribe Peralta Morones	12.01.1984	Club Santos Laguna Torreón	4	1
		Trainer			
	Miguel Ernesto Herrera Aguirre	18.03.1968			

NIGERIA

	Name	DOB	Club	M	G
		Goalkeepers			
1	Vincent Enyeama	29.08.1982	Lille OSC (FRA)	4	0
16	Augustine Amamchukwu Ejide	08.04.1984	Hapoel Be'er Sheva FC (ISR)	0	0
21	Chigozie Agbim	28.11.1984	Gombe United FC	0	0
		Defenders			
2	Joseph Ikpo Yobo	06.09.1980	Norwich City FC (ENG)	4	0
5	Efetobore Ambrose Emuobo	18.10.1988	Celtic Glasgow FC (SCO)	4	0
6	Azubuike Emanuel Egwuekwe	16.07.1989	Warri Wolves FC	0	0
12	Odunlami Kunle	30.04.1991	Sunshine Stars FC Akure	0	0
13	Juwon Oshaniwa	14.09.1990	MS Ashdod (ISR)	4	0
14	Godfrey Itama Oboabona	16.08.1990	Çaykur Rizespor (TUR)	1	0
22	Kenneth Josiah Omeruo	17.10.1993	Middlesbrough FC (ENG)	4	0
		Midfielders			
3	Christantus Ejike Uzoenyi	23.03.1988	Enugu Rangers International FC	1	0
4	Reuben Shalu Gabriel	25.09.1990	KV Red Star Waasland-Beveren (BEL)	1	0
10	John Michael Nchekwube Obinna	22.04.1987	Chelsea FC London (ENG)	4	0
11	Victor Moses	12.12.1990	Liverpool FC (ENG)	2	0
15	Ramon Olamilekan Azeez	12.12.1992	UD Almería (ESP)	1	0
17	Ogenyi Eddy Onazi	25.12.1992	SS Lazio Roma (ITA)	4	0
18	Michel Babatunde	24.12.1992	FK Volyn Lutsk (UKR)	2	0
		Forwards			
7	Ahmed Musa	14.10.1992	FK CSKA Moskva (RUS)	4	2
8	Peter Osaze Odemwingie	15.07.1981	Stoke City FC (ENG)	4	1
9	Emmanuel Chinenye Emenike	10.05.1987	Fenerbahçe SK Istanbul (TUR)	4	0
19	Uche Innocent Nwofor	17.09.1991	SC Heerenveen (NED)	2	0
20	Michael Okechukwu Uchebo	02.02.1990	Cercle Brugge KSV (BEL)	1	0
23	Foluwashola Ameobi	12.10.1981	Newcastle United FC (ENG)	2	0
		Trainer			
Stephen Okechukwu Keshi		23.01.1962			

PORTUGAL

	Name	DOB	Club	M	G
		Goalkeepers			
1	Eduardo dos Reis Carvalho	19.09.1982	Sporting Clube de Braga	1	0
12	Rui Pedro dos Santos Patrício	15.02.1988	Sporting Clube de Portugal Lisboa	1	0
22	António Alberto Bastos Pimparel "Beto"	01.05.1982	Sevilla FC (ESP)	2	0
		Defenders			
2	Bruno Eduardo Regufe Alves	27.11.1981	Fenerbahçe SK Istanbul (TUR)	3	0
3	Képler Laveran Lima Ferreira „Pepe"	26.02.1983	Real Madrid CF (ESP)	2	0
5	Fábio Alexandre da Silva Coentrão	11.03.1988	Real Madrid CF (ESP)	1	0
13	Ricardo Miguel Moreira da Costa	16.05.1981	Valencia CF (ESP)	2	0
14	Luís Carlos Novo Neto	26.05.1988	FC Zenit Saint Petersburg (RUS)	0	0
19	André Gomes Magalhães de Almeida	10.09.1990	Sport Lisboa e Benfica	2	0
21	João Pedro da Silva Pereira	25.02.1984	Valencia CF (ESP)	3	0
		Midfielders			
4	Miguel Luís Pinto Veloso	11.05.1986	FC Dynamo Kyiv (UKR)	3	0
6	William Silva de Carvalho	07.04.1992	Portugal Sporting CP	2	0
8	João Filipe Iria Santos Moutinho	08.09.1986	AS Monaco (FRA)	3	0
10	Adelino André Vieira de Freitas „Vieirinha"	24.01.1986	VfL Wolfsburg (GER)	1	0
15	Rafa Silva	17.05.1993	Sporting Clube de Braga	0	0
16	Raul José Trindade Meireles	17.03.1983	Fenerbahçe SK Istanbul (TUR)	2	0
17	Luís Carlos Almeida da Cunha „Nani"	17.11.1986	Manchester United FC (ENG)	3	1
18	Silvestre Manuel Gonçalves Varela	02.02.1985	FC do Porto	2	1
20	Rúben Amorim	27.01.1985	Sport Lisboa e Benfica	1	0
		Forwards			
7	Cristiano Ronaldo dos Santos Aveiro	05.02.1985	Real Madrid CF (ESP)	3	1
9	Hugo Miguel Pereira de Almeida	23.05.1984	Beşiktaş JK Istanbul (TUR)	1	0
11	Éderzito António Macedo Lopes „Éder"	22.12.1987	Sporting Clube de Braga	3	0
23	Hélder Manuel Marques Postiga	02.08.1982	SS Lazio Roma (ITA)	1	0
		Trainer			
	Paulo Jorge Gomes Bento	20.06.1969			

RUSSIA

	Name	DOB	Club	M	G
		Goalkeepers			
1	Igor Akinfeev	08.04.1986	FK CSKA Moskva	3	0
12	Yuri Lodygin	26.05.1990	FK Zenit Saint Petersburg	0	0
16	Sergei Ryzhikov	19.09.1980	FK Rubin Kazan	0	0
		Defenders			
2	Aleksei Kozlov	16.11.1986	FK Dynamo Moskva	2	0
3	Georgi Shchennikov	27.04.1991	FK CSKA Moskva	0	0
4	Sergei Ignashevich	14.07.1979	FK CSKA Moskva	3	0
5	Andrei Semyonov	24.03.1989	FK Terek Grozny	0	0
13	Vladimir Granat	22.05.1987	FK Dynamo Moskva	0	0
14	Vasili Berezutski	20.06.1982	FK CSKA Moskva	3	0
22	Andrey Yeshchenko	09.02.1984	FK Anzhi Makhachkala	2	0
		Midfielders			
7	Igor Denisov	17.05.1984	FK Dynamo Moskva	2	0
8	Denis Glushakov	27.01.1987	FK Spartak Moskva	3	0
10	Alan Dzagoev	17.06.1990	FK CSKA Moskva	3	0
15	Pavel Mogilevets	25.01.1993	FK Rubin Kazan	0	0
17	Oleg Shatov	29.07.1990	FK Zenit Saint Petersburg	3	0
18	Yuri Zhirkov	20.08.1983	FK Dynamo Moskva	1	0
20	Viktor Fayzulin	22.04.1986	FK Zenit Saint Petersburg	3	0
21	Aleksei Ionov	18.02.1989	FK Dynamo Moskva	0	0
23	Dmitri Kombarov	22.01.1987	FK Spartak Moskva	3	0
		Forwards			
6	Maksim Kanunnikov	14.07.1991	FK Amkar Perm	2	0
9	Aleksandr Kokorin	19.03.1991	FK Dynamo Moskva	3	1
11	Aleksandr Kerzhakov	27.11.1982	FK Zenit Saint Petersburg	3	1
19	Aleksandr Samedov	19.07.1984	FK Lokomotiv Moskva	3	0
		Trainer			
	Fabio Capello (Italy)	18.06.1946			

SPAIN

	Name	DOB	Club	M	G
		Goalkeepers			
1	Iker Casillas Fernández	20.05.1981	Real Madrid CF	2	0
12	David de Gea Quintana	07.11.1990	Manchester United FC (ENG)	0	0
23	José Manuel Reina Páez	31.08.1982	SSC Napoli (ITA)	1	0
		Defenders			
2	Raúl Albiol Tortajada	04.09.1985	SSC Napoli (ITA)	1	0
3	Gerard Piqué i Bernabeu	02.02.1987	FC Barcelona	1	0
5	Juan Francisco Torres Belén „Juanfran"	09.01.1985	Club Atlético de Madrid	1	0
15	Sergio Ramos García	30.03.1986	Real Madrid CF	3	0
18	Jordi Alba Ramos	21.03.1989	FC Barcelona	3	0
22	César Azpilicueta Tanco	28.08.1989	Chelsea FC London (ENG)	2	0
		Midfielders			
4	Javier Martínez Aginaga	02.09.1988	FC Bayern München (GER)	1	0
6	Andrés Iniesta Luján	11.05.1984	FC Barcelona	3	0
8	Xavier Hernández i Creus „Xavi"	25.01.1980	FC Barcelona	1	0
10	Francesc Fàbregas Soler „Cesc Fàbregas"	04.05.1987	FC Barcelona	2	0
13	Juan Manuel Mata García „Juan Mata"	28.04.1988	Manchester United FC (ENG)	1	1
14	Xabier Alonso Olano „Xabi Alonso"	25.11.1981	Real Madrid CF	3	1
16	Sergio Busquets Burgos	16.07.1988	FC Barcelona	2	0
17	Jorge Resurrección Merodio „Koke"	08.01.1992	Club Atlético de Madrid	2	0
20	Santiago Cazorla González	13.12.1984	Arsenal FC London (ENG)	2	0
21	David Josué Jiménez Silva	08.01.1986	Manchester City FC (ENG)	3	0
		Forwards			
7	David Villa Sánchez	03.12.1981	Club Atlético de Madrid	1	1
9	Fernando José Torres Sanz	20.03.1984	Chelsea FC London (ENG)	3	1
11	Pedro Eliezer Rodríguez Ledesma	28.07.1987	FC Barcelona	2	0
19	Diego da Silva Costa	07.10.1988	Club Atlético de Madrid	2	0
		Trainer			
	Vicente Del Bosque González	23.12.1950			

SWITZERLAND

	Name	DOB	Club	M	G
		Goalkeepers			
1	Diego Orlando Benaglio	08.09.1983	VfL Wolfsburg (GER)	4	0
12	Yann Sommer	17.12.1988	FC Basel	0	0
21	Roman Bürki	14.11.1990	Grasshopper Club Zürich	0	0
		Defenders			
2	Stephan Lichtsteiner	16.01.1984	Juventus FC Torino	4	0
3	Reto Pirmin Ziegler	16.01.1986	US Sassuolo Calcio (ITA)	0	0
4	Philippe Sylvain Senderos	14.02.1985	Valencia CF	1	0
5	Steve von Bergen	10.06.1983	BSC Young Boys Bern	2	0
6	Michael Rico Lang	08.02.1991	Grasshopper Club Zürich	1	0
13	Ricardo Iván Rodríguez Araya	25.08.1992	VfL Wolfsburg (GER)	4	0
20	Johan Danon Djourou-Gbadjere	18.01.1987	Hamburger SV (GER)	4	0
22	Fabian Lukas Schär	20.12.1991	FC Basel	2	0
		Midfielders			
7	Tranquillo Barnetta	22.05.1985	SG Eintracht Frankfurt (GER)	0	0
8	Gökhan Inler	27.06.1984	SSC Napoli (ITA)	4	0
10	Granit Xhaka	27.09.1992	VfL Borussia Mönchengladbach (GER)	4	1
11	Valon Behrami	19.04.1985	SSC Napoli (ITA)	4	0
14	Valentin Stocker	12.04.1989	FC Basel	1	0
15	Blerim Džemaili	12.04.1986	SSC Napoli (ITA)	3	1
16	Gelson da Conceição Tavares Fernandes	02.09.1986	SC Freiburg (GER)	1	0
23	Xherdan Shaqiri	10.10.1991	FC Bayern München (GER)	4	3
		Forwards			
9	Haris Seferović	22.02.1992	Real Sociedad de Fútbol San Sebastián (ESP)	4	1
17	Mario Gavranović	24.11.1989	FC Zürich	0	0
18	Admir Mehmedi	16.03.1991	SC Freiburg (GER)	4	1
19	Josip Drmić	08.08.1992	1. FC Nürnberg (GER)	4	0
		Trainer			
	Ottmar Hitzfeld (Germany)	12.01.1949			

UNITED STATES

	Name	DOB	Club	M	G
		Goalkeepers			
1	Timothy Matthew Howard	06.03.1979	Everton FC Liverpool (ENG)	4	0
12	Bradley „Brad" Edwin Guzan	09.09.1984	Aston Villa FC Birmingham (ENG)	0	0
22	Nicholas Paul "Nick" Rimando	17.06.1979	Real Salt Lake	0	0
		Defenders			
2	DeAndre Yedlin	09.07.1993	Seattle Sounders FC	3	0
3	Omar González	11.10.1988	Los Angeles Galaxy	3	0
5	Matt Besler	11.02.1987	Sporting Kansas City	4	0
6	John Anthony Brooks	28.01.1993	Hertha BSC Berlin (GER)	1	1
7	DaMarcus Lamont Beasley	24.05.1982	CF Puebla (MEX)	4	0
20	Geoffrey Scott Cameron	11.07.1985	Stoke City FC (ENG)	3	0
21	Timothy Chandler	29.03.1990	1.FC Nürnberg (GER)	0	0
23	Fabian Marco Johnson	11.12.1987	TSG 1899 Hoffenheim (GER)	4	0
		Midfielders			
4	Michael Sheehan Bradley	31.07.1987	Toronto FC (CAN)	4	0
10	Mikkel Morgenstar Pålssønn Diskerud	02.10.1990	Rosenborg BK Trondheim (NOR)	0	0
11	Alejandro Bedoya	29.04.1987	FC Nantes (FRA)	4	0
13	Jermaine Jones	03.11.1981	Beşiktaş JK Istanbul (TUR)	4	1
14	Bradley Joseph Davis	08.11.1981	Houston Dynamo	1	0
15	Kyle Robert Beckerman	23.04.1982	Real Salt Lake	3	0
16	Julian Wesley Green	06.06.1995	FC Bayern München (GER)	1	1
19	Graham Jonathan Zusi	18.08.1986	Sporting Kansas City	4	0
		Forwards			
8	Clinton „Clint" Drew Dempsey	09.03.1983	Seattle Sounders FC	4	2
9	Aron Jóhannsson	10.11.1990	AZ'67 Alkmaar (NED)	1	0
17	Josmer „Jozy" Volmy Altidore	06.11.1989	Sunderland AFC (ENG)	1	0
18	Christopher Elliott Wondolowski	28.01.1983	San José Earthquakes	2	0
		Trainer			
	Jürgen Klinsmann (Germany)	30.07.1964			

URUGUAY

	Name	DOB	Club	M	G
		Goalkeepers			
1	Néstor Fernando Muslera Micol	16.06.1986	SK Galatasaray Istanbul (TUR)	4	0
12	Rodrigo Martín Muñoz Salomón	22.01.1982	Club Libertad Asunción	0	0
23	Martín Andrés Silva Leites	25.03.1983	CR Vasco da Gama Rio de Janeiro (BRA)	0	0
		Defenders			
2	Diego Alfredo Lugano Morena	02.11.1980	West Bromwich Albion FC (ENG)	1	0
3	Diego Roberto Godín Leal	16.02.1986	Club Atlético de Madrid (ESP)	4	1
4	Jorge Ciro Fucile Perdomo	19.11.1984	FC do Porto (POR)	1	0
13	José María Giménez de Vargas	20.01.1995	Club Atlético de Madrid (ESP)	3	0
16	Victorio Maximiliano Pereira Páez	08.06.1984	Sport Lisboa e Benfica (POR)	3	0
19	Sebastián Coates Nión	07.10.1990	Club Nacional de Football Montevideo	1	0
22	José Martín Cáceres Silva	07.04.1987	Juventus FC Torino (ITA)	4	0
		Midfielders			
5	Walter Alejandro Gargano Guevara	27.07.1984	Parma FC (ITA)	1	0
6	Álvaro Daniel Pereira Barragán	28.01.1985	São Paulo FC (BRA)	3	0
7	Cristian Gabriel Rodríguez Barotti	30.09.1985	Club Atlético de Madrid (ESP)	4	0
14	Marcelo Nicolás Lodeiro Benítez	21.03.1989	Botafogo de FR Rio de Janeiro (BRA)	3	0
15	Diego Fernando Pérez Aguado	18.05.1980	Bologna FC (ITA)	0	0
17	Egidio Raúl Arévalo Ríos	01.01.1982	CA Monarcas Morelia (MEX)	4	0
18	Gastón Ezequiel Ramírez Pereyra	02.12.1990	Southampton FC (ENG)	2	0
20	Álvaro Rafael González Luengo	29.10.1984	SS Lazio Roma (ITA)	4	0
		Forwards			
8	Abel Mathías Hernández Platero	08.08.1990	US Città de Palermo (ITA)	2	0
9	Luis Alberto Suárez Díaz	24.01.1987	Liverpool FC (ENG)	2	2
10	Diego Martín Forlán Corazzo	19.05.1979	Cerezo Osaka (JPN)	2	0
11	Christian Ricardo Stuani Curbelo	12.10.1986	RCD Espanyol Barcelona (ESP)	4	0
21	Edinson Roberto Cavani Gómez	14.02.1987	Paris Saint-Germain FC (FRA)	4	1
		Trainer			
	Óscar Wáshington Tabárez Sclavo	03.03.1947			